THE
WEAVING, SPINNING, AND DYEING BOOK

Rachel Brown

THE
WEAVING,

SPINNING, AND DYEING BOOK

Illustrated by Rachel Brown and Cheryl McGowen

ALFRED A. KNOPF, NEW YORK   1978

THIS IS A BORZOI BOOK
PUBLISHED BY ALFRED A. KNOPF, INC.

Copyright © 1978 by Rachel Brown
All rights reserved under International and Pan-American
Copyright Conventions. Published in the United States by
Alfred A. Knopf, Inc., New York, and simultaneously in
Canada by Random House of Canada Limited, Toronto.
Distributed by Random House, Inc., New York.

Library of Congress Cataloging in Publication Data
Brown, Rachel.
Weaving, spinning, and dyeing.
Bibliography: p.
Includes index.
1.   Hand weaving. 2. Hand spinning. 3. Dyes and dyeing—
Textile fibers. I. Title.
TT848.B75   746.1   77–1653
ISBN: 0–394–49801–1
ISBN: 0-394-73383-5 pbk.

Manufactured in the United States of America

First Edition

This book is dedicated with love to the people who shared with me the work and play
at the Craft House in Arroyo Seco, New Mexico.

Barbara	Elsa	Judi	Reggie G.
Brooke	Gail	Lori	Rhoda
Candy	Hedy	Noel	Sophie
Cheryl	Jackie	Penny	Trippy
Debbie	Jane B.	Phoebe	Valerie
Delores	Jane G.	Reggie C.	Viola

CONTENTS

Chapter VI   THE NAVAJO LOOM   89

Chapter VII   THE TREADLE LOOM   117

Chapter VIII   FINISHING TECHNIQUES   193

Chapter IX   SPINNING   211

Chapter X   DYEING   245

Chapter XI   DESIGN AND COLOR   273

Color photographs follow pages 144 and 240.

ACKNOWLEDGMENTS

Special thanks go to:

Ellen McNeilly, for encouraging me to write the book and promising to help see that it got published; Cheryl McGowen, for getting totally involved, reading the manuscript, making excellent suggestions, and especially for her dedication and drawing talent which made it possible for us to meet the deadlines; Noël Ferris, for her work in collecting addresses and samples from suppliers; Lorelei Brown, for posing for the spinning illustrations and carding photograph; Brooke Tuthill, for bringing back from Bolivia the instructions for the Indian method of weaving the double weave; Shel Herschorn, for loaning me his typewriter (which burned up); Rockwell Driver, for introducing me to the Hopi belt loom and the San Sebastián weavers; Philbert Cruz, for showing me his Hopi weaving techniques; Marian Lujan, for being my guide on the Hopi and Navajo reservations; Barbara Marigold, for "selling" me on natural dyeing; Kristina Wilson (my weaving "commadre"), for sharing her ideas and helping me with the weavings to be photographed; Erik Brown, who is my consultant on the electric spinner; Cynthia Patterson, for the detailed plans of my favorite loom (which we had planned to use in the book, but didn't); Malcolm Brown (with whom I share much), for the many thoughts and discussions over the years on the subject of art; Wolcott Ely, for the loan of his books on color; Judi Graham, for reading parts of the manuscript, general encouragement, and helpful suggestions; Seth and Kinlock Brown, for loans that kept me going the last few months of writing; Sumiko Miller, for her help with the glossary; Jim and Fusako Miller, for taking good care of me for a few months so that I could devote all my time to editing; my father, John Miller, for all his help; Joan Loveless, for helping me with the weavings to be photographed; the people who loaned back my weavings to be photographed; Nancy Waight, Sandy Wright, Victoria Rabinowe, and Annie Kaufman of The Weaving Center in Santa Fe, for their contribution of fibers and tools; Christine Di Lisio, for letting us use her house for the cover photograph; Richard Enzer, for sharing with me the ups and downs of the five years it took to write the book; Lesley Brown, for her help and encouragement in the last few months of drawing; Louise Gelenter and Madelyn Johannes of La Lana Wools for their incredible generosity in helping me produce the spun and dyed yarns for the color photos; all the individuals and shops who contributed dyes, fibers, yarns, and equipment for the color photos (their names are listed in the keys to the photographs); and finally, the wonderfully helpful and patient three at Alfred A. Knopf who guided me in writing and illustrating my first book.

PREFACE

In many primitive cultures weaving, spinning, and dyeing constitute one of the major occupations, possibly second only to farming. In our technical society, because we are free from the *need* to pursue these crafts, the majority of us are not acquainted with the pleasure they give. Undeniably it is in man's nature to be creative, and although few of us would trade our lives for the hardships of primitive man, we do find satisfaction in creating objects for our own use, or just things of beauty to have or to give to a friend.

This book is as much for the experienced weaver as for the beginner. If you are just becoming interested in these crafts, there are many things you will be wanting to know: you'll have literally hundreds of questions. In this book I attempt to answer those questions. If you are already involved in weaving, spinning, and dyeing, I hope there will be many new ideas and ways of doing things that will interest you.

When I started writing this book, I thought I knew a great deal about weaving, spinning, and dyeing, since I had been actively involved with them for fifteen years. But working in a medium and writing about it are quite different. When you write something down that is going to be printed for thousands of people to read, you've got to make sure you know what you're talking about. So I started doing a lot of research, and I think I've gone through just about every book ever written on these subjects (well, that's obviously an exaggeration . . . but that's how I feel about it). The more I read the more humble I grew, and I soon came to the conclusion that my book would certainly not be the "last word" on these subjects, but rather what I hope is a well-organized presentation of most of the aspects of these three crafts, including instructions for several exciting projects ranging from the very simple to the very complex.

I noticed that most other authors on these subjects mention that there is no one correct way of doing things, and as I read on I became absolutely convinced of this. For example, early in my researching, I encountered the statement that the four-harness counterbalanced loom can only be used for balanced treadling (where there are always two harnesses down balanced by two harnesses up). This came as quite a shock, since I had been using this very loom for all kinds of weaves (double weave, double width, and double-face)—and quite successfully for years. Well, you can imagine how that made me wonder if I was qualified at all to be writing a book telling people how to weave! Later, I was relieved to read another authority who went only so far as to say that the counterbalanced loom "works inefficiently" for these weaves.

Then there was the problem of whether you are supposed to spin off to the left or to the right on the flyer wheel; I find that some authorities say "left," other authorities say "right," and still others say "both." And one well-known contemporary weaver recommends holding the selvedge with one hand while pulling the weft through to make a nice tight edge—a method I had always thought was absolutely to be avoided. In San Sebastián, outside Oaxaca, Mexico, I discovered an expert weaver who would grab the warp threads in one hand while beating down the weft with a spike in the other hand to make a very tight weave—certainly forbidden in all weaving books.

Which all goes to show that whatever works for you is right. What is important is to understand the real purpose of the methods and techniques and always to be open to new ideas or ways of doing the same thing better or more efficiently.

The approach of this book is to give you basic information that will make it possible for you to understand the processes of weaving, spinning, and dyeing—so that, no matter what tools or methods you are using, you will know what you are doing. Thus, instead of telling you the specific yarn and the exact number of threads, and describing in detail the movement of each hand and each thread, I try to explain the equipment and weaving instructions for projects in such a way that you can comprehend what is happening and will be able to create your own weavings, even if you don't have exactly the right materials and equipment on hand. I've taken for granted a certain amount of intelligence (my observation is that most people interested in weaving have brains that work very well), assuming that you would prefer to understand what you are doing rather than just to follow detailed step-by-step instructions.

One last note: the astute reader may get the idea that I have done very little natural dyeing . . . and that assumption is correct. I have done a great deal of synthetic dyeing, but have little practical experience with the natural dyes. So I have tried to gather together the important facts about natural dyeing—things that *I* wanted to know—and to set them down in a way that would be most useful. There are many excellent books on natural dyeing for those who want more thorough information.

And so, with great hopes that you will find in these pages (almost) everything you want to know about weaving, spinning, and dyeing, I present this book to you.

RACHEL BROWN

THE
WEAVING, SPINNING, AND DYEING BOOK

INTRODUCTION

It is very difficult to decide how to organize and present the varied and complicated information that has to be conveyed to you so that you can become a weaver, or so that you can improve your skill and learn new techniques if you are already a weaver. I have to talk about structures of weaves, equipment, and yarns. You have to become aware of all the things that professional and amateur weavers have found out through their experience. There have to be detailed instructions for making specific items—from belts to wall hangings.

I will start with the general and proceed to the specific. In Chapter I, I will present the general information about weaving you need. Following this, there will be chapters titled according to different loom types, and in each of these chapters will be instructions for the use of that loom and step-by-step instructions for projects that can be woven on it. You will see at a glance that the loom types range from the very simple or primitive to more sophisticated treadle looms. Three of these looms consist of not much more than a few sticks of wood (old broom handles will do), and yet they are by no means amateur tools. They have been used by professional weavers for thousands of years, and are probably more common throughout the world today than is our familiar floor loom—which, of course, deserves and receives a long chapter of its own.

There are many simple frame looms made for sale today, as well as the familiar table loom, but I find most of them inadequate tools for serious weaving because they are too light-weight and flimsy; they have no provisions for a rigid, immovable setup essential for ease in weaving. No matter how simple the loom of primitive weavers (whose livelihood or comfort depends on their craft), it is always extremely sturdy, made of parts that are securely set in the ground or attached to an immovable object. And, operated as it is by the human body, a primitive loom is completely adaptable to minute adjustments of tension and position. It is of no importance how the structure is finished or how it looks (the members are often the crudest pieces of wood), but the structure is functional. The primitive man or woman certainly does not put off his weaving until he has a few hundred dollars (or even a few dollars) to amass his equipment. With the objects that nature provides him—sticks, trees, rocks, plant and animal fibers, plant juices—he creates the fabrics, ropes, and sashes for his daily needs.

And *his* tools are a pleasure to work with. They work quietly and smoothly. There are very few parts to break; and if one breaks, he simply finds another piece of wood the right size and shapes it himself. There is none of the bother of noisy equipment or rickety construction that can make the craft a harassment instead of a pleasure. The weaver of the high Andes would certainly never trade his stick loom for one of the nicer-looking frame or table looms used by some weavers.

Contemporary craftsmen are taking a greater interest in these primitive looms now, and I feel it is very appropriate to describe their use. They will be of particular interest to those of you who are impatient to start weaving, but who can't afford hundreds of dollars' worth of equipment, and to you who are living a rather nomadic life and can't be hampered with extensive gear.

In the chapters titled according to the different loom types, the projects described are generally the ones that are traditionally woven on that type of loom. But since most primitive weaving techniques and designs are quite time-consuming, and most of us are trained to be concerned with time, I have also included some shortcut methods for weaving on the primitive looms, as well as a few simple, less time-consuming designs.

Projects range from simple items, such as belts, stoles, and rugs, to more difficult weavings, such as double-width and double-face fabrics, tapestries, and three-dimensional weavings. Certain projects can be just as easily woven on a different loom from the one for which they are described; in this case I have indicated the other loom or looms on which they can be woven. Also I have listed Suggestions for Other Projects in each chapter, so you will know other things that can be woven on a particular loom. In all, I have included many of the important techniques you will want to know, and these will give you a stepping-off point for original creations of your own.

You will discover that the emphasis in this book is on weaves that achieve design and interest through choice of fiber, color, texture, and hand control of the threads (such as tapestry and pickup) rather than the so-called structural weaves that require multi-harness looms and complicated drafts to indicate how the many harnesses are threaded. This latter type of weaving, so predominant in American colonial days, and very well done on factory looms today, has been the basic subject of many books on weaving. However, I find young weavers today turning to the weaves of more primitive cultures, such as American Indian, African, Middle Eastern, Mexican, and South American; these weaves do not require expensive looms with many harnesses.

Chapter VIII, "Finishing Techniques," will give you instructions on the many ways of making your woven piece into a beautifully finished, professional-looking product—no matter what loom it was woven on. Since much of the interest and success of the weaving depends on how it is finished, do not neglect this chapter.

After these chapters on weaving we will delve into spinning, dyeing (both natural and synthetic), design and color, how to sell your crafts, and, finally, where to get your equipment and supplies.

CHAPTER 1

THE BASICS OF WEAVING

A Definition of Weaving

First, let's talk about what weaving is. It is a method of interlacing threads to make a fabric. Knitting and crocheting (which use a single thread) and plaiting, sprang (a form of plaiting), and macramé (which uses multi-threads) also do this. What differentiates weaving from these other fabric-making techniques is that in weaving, there are always two distinct sets of threads involved: (1) the *warp,* a set of threads all spread out parallel to each other and held in tension, and (2) the *weft* (or woof), an independent thread. The weft winds its way under and over (and sometimes around) the warp threads in certain ways so as to join the two sets of threads together in some kind of fixed relationship, thus forming a fabric.

You can already see that within this definition there are many possibilities. The threads themselves can vary in size, texture, and color. The spacing between the threads can vary. Warp threads can be twisted. Both warp and weft can show, or only warp or only weft can form the surface of the fabric. And, most important of all, the weft can be intertwined in innumerable ways—even knotted, or cut after it is laid in place. By using these possibilities we have invented such marvelous weaves as tapestry, damask, brocade, corduroy, pile carpets, gauze, twill, satin, plain old hopsacking, and many, many others.

Figure 1 shows some of the ways that warp and weft threads can relate—ways used especially by the handweaver.

FIGURE 1. Some useful weave structures.

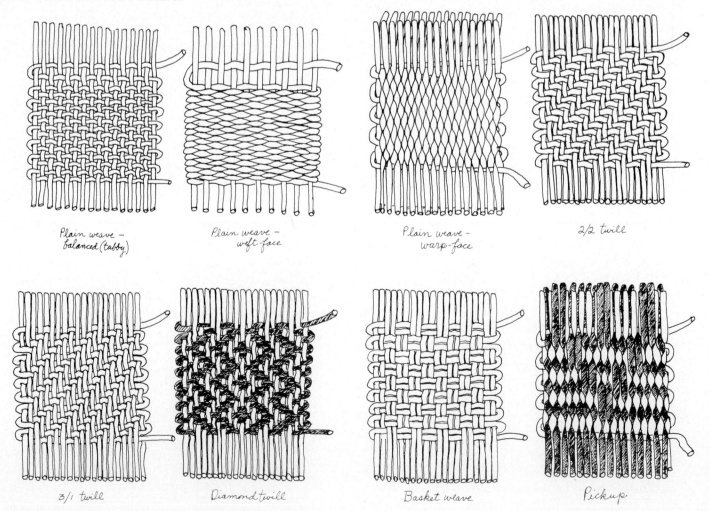

Plain weave – balanced (tabby)   Plain weave – weft-face   Plain weave – warp-face   2/2 twill

3/1 twill   Diamond twill   Basket weave   Pickup

FIGURE 1. continued

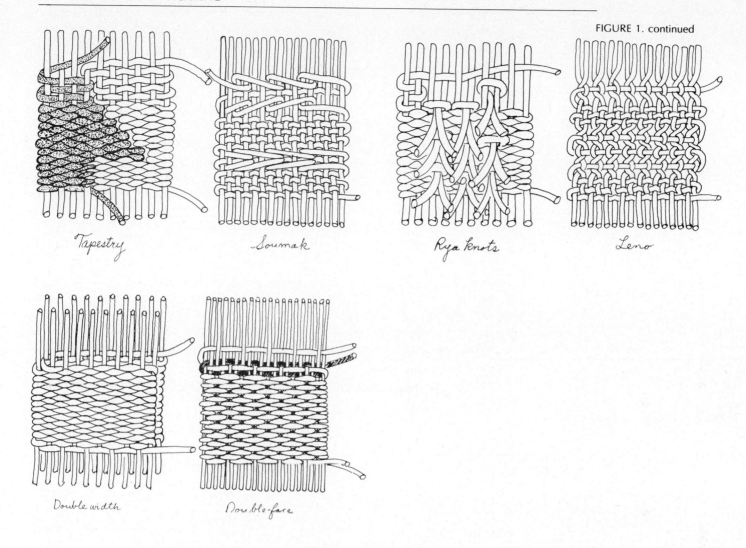

Tapestry   Soumak   Rya knots   Leno

Double width   Double-face

An Explanation of Weaving Methods and Equipment

A good way to learn what weaving methods and weaving equipment are all about is to pretend we're attacking the problem of weaving from scratch. After examining the structures in Figure 1, we can imagine that it would be possible to make small samples of these weaves by interlacing the threads with our fingers. Then, when we contemplate the hopeless tangle of threads and the days of work that would be involved in re-creating these weaves in the form of several yards of fabric, we can appreciate the devices that have been invented for weaving.

In the formation of fabric—the intertwining of the weft thread with the warp threads—the basic weaving process is similar whether one uses the most primitive loom or the most sophisticated multi-harness treadle loom. The process consists of:

1. *Organizing the threads:* packaging the thread in convenient form for unwinding.

2. *Winding the warp:* measuring out in sequence all the warp threads (the "ends").

3. *Spacing the warp:* spreading the warp ends so that there are the correct number per inch (the warp "sett").

4. *Tensioning the warp:* stretching the warp in tension in such a way that excess warp can be stored and advanced to a level convenient for weaving.

5. *Making the sheds:* lifting alternate warp threads, or groups of threads, to form a space (the "shed") through which the weft can pass.

6. *Placing the shot:* inserting the weft in the shed.

7. *Beating:* packing down the weft so that it lies beside the previous shot.

8. *Regulating the width:* keeping the width of the weaving consistent.

We have invented many different tools and devices to accomplish each of these steps with a maximum of efficiency and a minimum of confusion. Following is a brief description of these steps and the more common tools and devices (both primitive and sophisticated) used by the handweaver. Each process and piece of equipment will be discussed in more detail in its proper place in the chapters on loom types.

1. Organizing the threads

A ball of yarn is a useful package when you are dealing with small amounts. But, if you are manufacturing your own yarn, it has to be wound into skeins for washing or dyeing. To form skeins you could wind the yarn around your hand and elbow, your foot and knee, or the legs of a chair. But a *niddy-noddy* or a *skein winder* or *reel* comes in very handy. Commercial or homemade skeins of yarn are best unwound on a *swift,* which is adjustable and designed specifically for *un*winding skeins of different sizes.

For weaving on the more sophisticated treadle looms, where you are dealing with literally miles of thread for the warp, it is almost essential to have large *spools* or *cones* onto which your yarn can be wound (or buy the warp yarn in this form when possible). You need a *bobbin* or *spool winder* to wind the spools, and a *spool rack* (or *creel*) to hold the spools after they are wound.

FIGURE 2. Devices for organizing the threads.

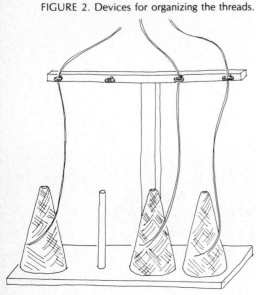

Cone rack

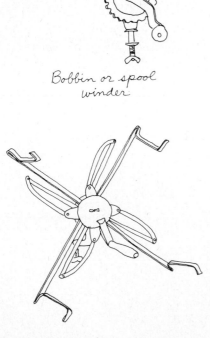

Bobbin or spool winder

Metal skein winder (adjustable)

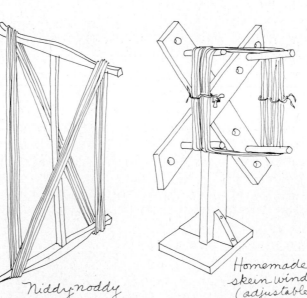

Niddy noddy

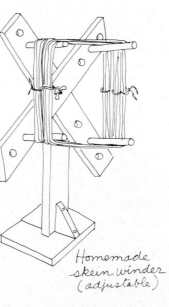

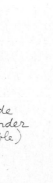

Homemade skein winder (adjustable)

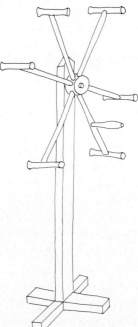

Skein winder

FIGURE 2. continued

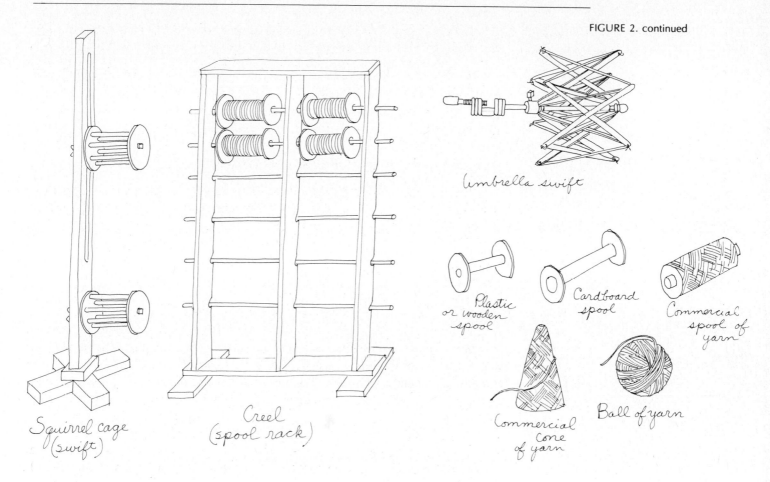

Umbrella swift

Plastic
or wooden
spool

Cardboard
spool

Commercial
spool of
yarn

Squirrel cage
(swift)

Creel
(spool rack)

Commercial
cone
of yarn

Ball of yarn

2. Winding the warp

One of the most exacting processes in weaving is measuring out and keeping in order the many, many threads for the warp—the warp "ends."

On the primitive stick looms this is accomplished quite simply by taking a single ball of thread and winding it back and forth in the form of a figure eight between two bars that are held apart at a distance that will be the finished length of the fabric. (Or it can be wound in a circle when the warp length needs to be consolidated into half the space for practical reasons.) When the warp is wound in a figure eight, the *cross* (or *lease*) that is formed keeps the threads in sequence. This warp is then transferred and attached to another set of bars, which are the loom bars. A very simple procedure, but this is only enough warp for one project. And here is one of the radical differences between the primitive loom and the modern treadle loom, which can store great lengths of warp that will serve for many weavings.

To prepare one of these long warps of, say, 600 threads, each 25 yards long (not an unusual warp for a treadle loom), is more complicated. You could put stakes in the ground 75 feet apart and simply walk back and forth with your ball of yarn 600 times. (Hm . . . let's see . . . that's 45,000 feet or close to 9 miles.) There must be an easier way! So we use a frame of wood, usually a yard wide, that has pegs down each side. By using 4 spools of thread and winding all 4 at the same time, back and forth from side to side of the frame, around the pegs (26 altogether) and back up again 75 times, you end up with 600 threads, each 25 yards long. This frame is called a *warping frame* or *warping board*.

An even more advanced tool for measuring out the warp threads for the treadle loom is the *vertical warping mill* or *reel,* which is a framework drum around which the warp is wound by turning the mill. Mills are often 4 yards around.

At the top and bottom of the warping board or mill there are three pegs in a line. In the course of winding, the warp threads are led around these pegs each time in a figure eight (the same cross or lease described in winding the warp on a primitive loom) to preserve the sequence of threads at both ends of this long warp. (There are shortcut methods that can be used for most warps that require only one cross.) A *warping paddle* (a wooden paddle with several holes in it) is sometimes used to run the warp threads through to keep them in order while winding with many spools at a time.

To remove the warp ends from the warping board or mill without letting them tangle, *ties* (or *chokes*) are made at various points, and a *chain* (like a giant crochet stitch) is made of the entire group of ends, so that they form a compact bundle that can be released bit by bit as the warp is wound onto the loom itself in a process called *beaming. Lease rods,* a pair of two flat sticks the width of the loom, are used to preserve the cross during the beaming.

In another warping method a *horizontal warping mill* is used to measure out the warp ends. In this case the warp may be beamed directly from the mill without the intermediate process of chaining.

In still another method, *sectional warping,* winding the warp (to measure the ends) and beaming the warp are one and the same process, thus eliminating the need for a warping board or mill. The warp ends are measured out by winding them from the spools directly onto the warp beam of the loom in two-inch sections at a time. A *sectional beam,* which has dividers, is required for this process, and a *tension box* (to provide the correct tension for the threads as they are wound on), and a *counter* (to count the yards as they are wound on) are usually used.

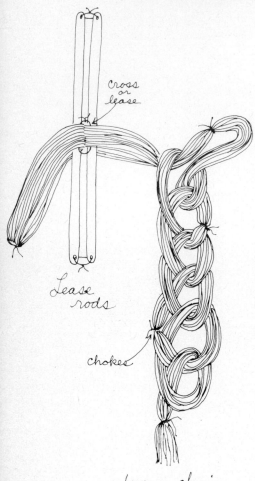

FIGURE 3. Warp winding devices.

cross or lease

Lease rods

chokes

Warp chain

Warping board

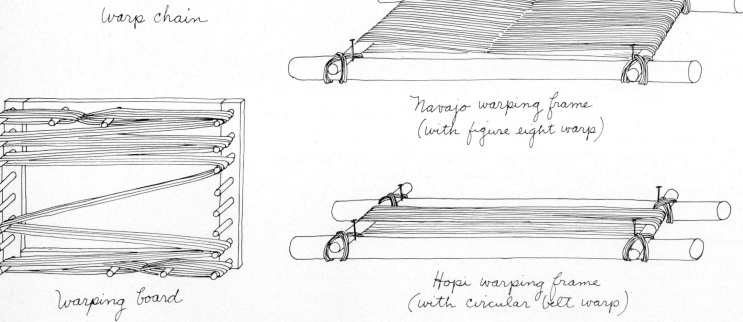

Navajo warping frame (with figure eight warp)

Hopi warping frame (with circular belt warp)

FIGURE 3. continued

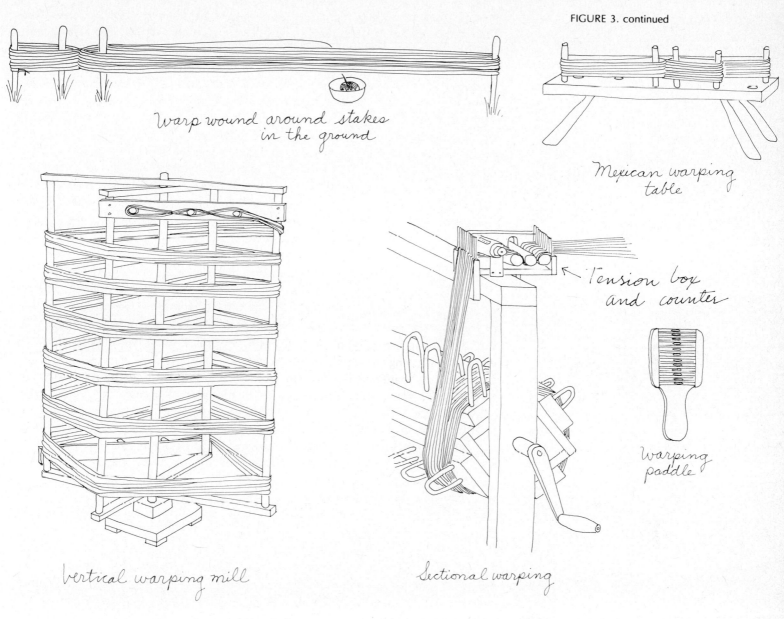

Warp wound around stakes in the ground

Mexican warping table

Vertical warping mill

Sectional warping

Tension box and counter

Warping paddle

FIGURE 4. Warp spacing devices.

3. Spacing the warp

On the primitive looms, after the warp is transferred to the loom bars, it is spread out so that there are the right number of ends per inch (the warp *sett*) and then held in this position by being bound in place by a thread. On most looms that are designed for belt weaving there is no need for spacing devices since the warp threads are simply placed as close together as possible so as to form a warp-face weave (see Figure 1).

On the treadle loom, the warp must be spread to its full width as it is beamed, and the tool that is used for this is called a *spreader* or *raddle.* It looks like a giant wooden comb, with dowels for teeth, and groups of threads pass in between these dowels as they are wound onto the loom. When you are using a horizontal warping mill or the sectional method of warping, the threads are automatically spaced properly on the beam.

During the weaving process, another comb with fine metal teeth serves to keep the warp thread perfectly spread to the correct sett. This is called a *reed* (because

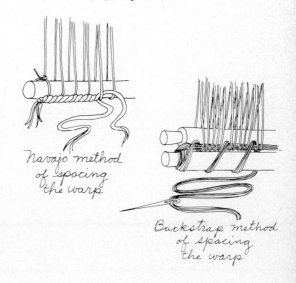

Navajo method of spacing the warp

Backstrap method of spacing the warp

FIGURE 4. continued

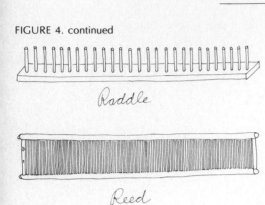

Raddle

Reed

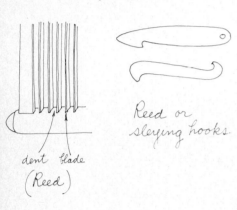

Reed or sleying hooks.

dent blade (Reed)

FIGURE 5. Warp tensioning, storage, and advancement devices.

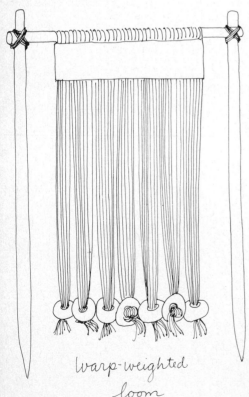

warp-weighted loom

originally it was made of reeds). The teeth are called *blades* and the spaces between the blades are called *dents*. The warp is set up so that the threads pass through the dents of the reed in a process called *sleying*. Sometimes the warp threads are "sleyed" in every dent, sometimes in every other dent, and sometimes two or more threads are sleyed through the same dent (*double* or *triple sleyed,* it's called). A *sleying hook* or *reed hook* is used to facilitate drawing the threads through the dents.

4. Tensioning the warp

The *loom* itself is the tool that provides the tension for the warp. One of the earliest means of providing tension was to hang the individual warp threads from a bar and tie big stones to the bottom ends of the threads. (Thank goodness we've worked our way past that stage! However, the *warp-weighted loom* is still used by the Laplanders, so it can't be too bad.) The weaver stands while weaving the beginning (at the top) and eventually sits as the fabric level gets lower.

Another primitive method for keeping the tension is to place the warp on two bars and stretch these in a vertical frame by means of ropes, levers, toggles, etc. The *Navajo loom,* the *Hopi belt loom,* and the *tapestry frame* are examples of these vertical looms. On the Navajo loom, the weaving begins at the bottom, and when the weaving level gets too high, the loom is lowered and the fabric is rolled up on the bottom bar. The warp of the Hopi belt loom is simply rotated around the bars to keep the weaving level at a convenient height.

Some primitive looms hold the warp out horizontally between strong stakes in the ground. The *ground loom* is common in South America and Middle Eastern countries (the *Middle Eastern rug loom*). As the weaving progresses the fabric can be rolled up on the front loom bar, or the weaver can simply sit on the part that is already woven, a practice that one sees in some Middle Eastern rug-weaving countries.

Probably the most common of the primitive methods of providing tension for the warp is to secure one end to a tree (or other fixed object) and attach the other end to a bar, which in turn is attached to a strap that goes around the weaver's back. This is called a *backstrap loom.* The weaver sits on the ground so that the warp is stretched in tension, and adjustments of the tension are accomplished by leaning forward or backward. As the cloth is woven it is rolled up on the front loom bar. Sometimes excess warp is simply wound around a rock. One never tries to weave much wider than 30 inches on a loom of this type, and the normal weaving width is much narrower. This is why you see many primitive fabrics that are made up of many narrow pieces sewn together.

The *inkle loom* is a compact framework with horizontal pegs; the warp is wound around these pegs and thus held in tension. As the weaving builds up, the warp is rotated on the pegs.

On the modern *floor* (or *treadle*) *loom* the warp tension is achieved by attaching one end of the warp to the *warp roller* or *beam* (on which a great length of warp may be "beamed") at the back of the loom, and the other end to the *cloth roller* or *beam* (which provides for cloth storage) at the front of the loom. Between these two beams the warp runs up and over two more horizontal beams called the *back beam* and the *breast beam,* placed at a convenient height for weaving. The rollers are cranked up so that the warp is pulled in opposite directions and held in position by a *ratchet and pawl* or *brake* system. The warp may be advanced to the proper position for weaving by means of these ratchets. Treadle looms can be equipped with two warp rollers (one for chained warps and one for sectional warps). The weaver can use whichever beam is appropriate or, in multi-layered weaving, the tension of two warps can be adjusted for each layer. This *double warp beam* is necessary only in very advanced techniques; two layered fabrics do not require a double warp beam.

FIGURE 5. continued

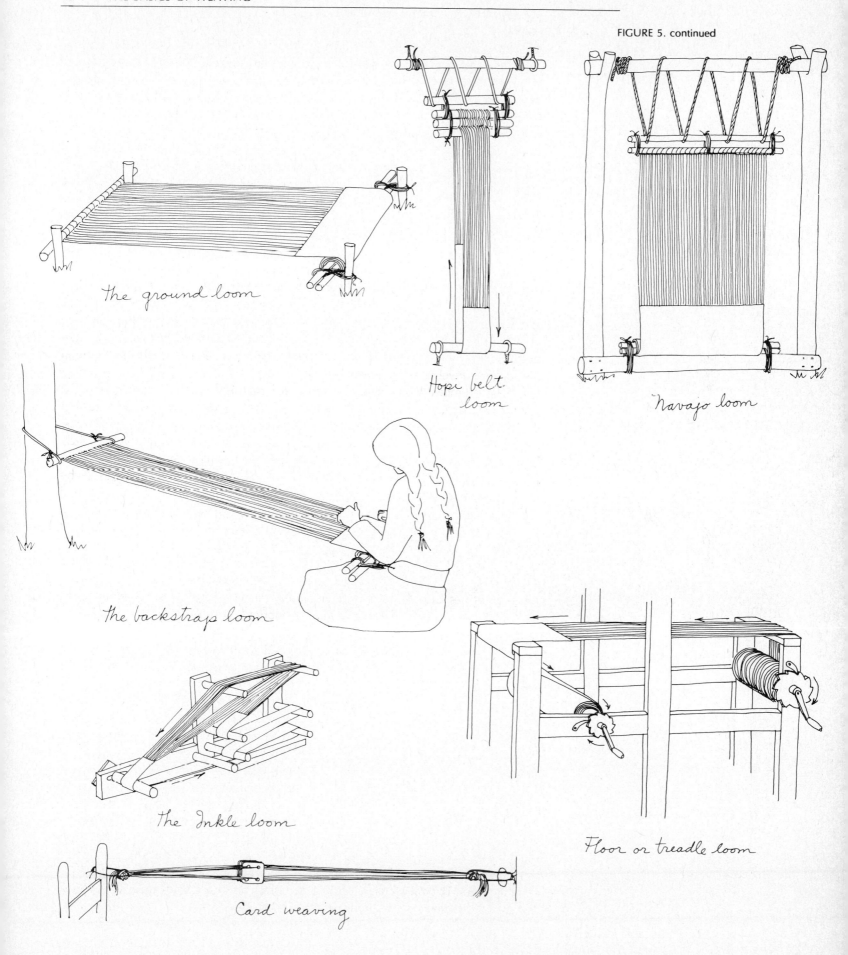

the ground loom

Hopi belt loom

Navajo loom

the backstrap loom

the Inkle loom

Floor or treadle loom

Card weaving

FIGURE 6. Shedding devices.

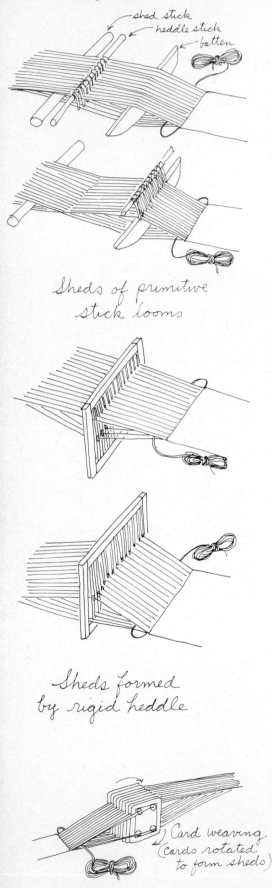

Sheds of primitive stick looms

Sheds formed by rigid heddle

Card weaving (cards rotated to form sheds)

5. Making the sheds

After the warp is stretched out in tension (either in some primitive fashion or on the treadle loom), we are ready to insert the weft thread—the actual weaving process. Now you could take a little ball of yarn and just start winding it under and over the warp threads—somewhat like darning. But very early in the history of weaving a quicker way was devised. On the primitive looms, by permanently fixing one set of alternating threads of the warp in an "up" position and the others in a "down" position, a space is made through which the weft can be passed. The space is called the *shed,* and the stick used to keep this group separated is a *shed stick* or *shed rod.*

For the next passage of the weft thread the two groups of warp threads (the upper and lower) have to switch positions. To accomplish this we attach permanent string loops (*heddles*) around all the lower warp threads, and with a stick (*heddle stick* or *heddle rod*) attached to these strings we are able to lift all the lower threads to the top position, thus forming an alternate shed through which the weft is passed. A flat stick called a *batten* or *sword* is inserted into each shed and turned on its edge to hold the threads well apart and leave the hands free to insert the weft. To pick up an occasional different group of threads, a sharp-pointed stick called a *pick* may be used.

Another method of raising and lowering alternate warp threads is to use a *rigid heddle* (also called *hole and slot*). This is a device, usually made of wood, that looks much like a reed, but with a hole in the center of each blade. Alternate warp ends are threaded through these holes, and the remaining threads are threaded in the spaces between the blades. When the rigid heddle is pushed down, it forces half the threads (the ones threaded through the holes) down; the remaining threads stay in the original position. When the heddle is held up, the opposite situation occurs; thus the two sheds are formed. An advantage to the rigid heddle is that it acts as a warp spacer also.

A unique method of raising and lowering warp threads is found in *card weaving.* Here warp threads are threaded through the holes in cardboard cards. The cards are turned so that different warp threads are brought to the top.

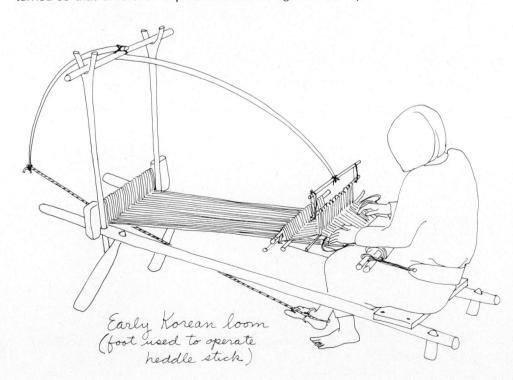

Early Korean loom (foot used to operate heddle stick.)

FIGURE 6. continued

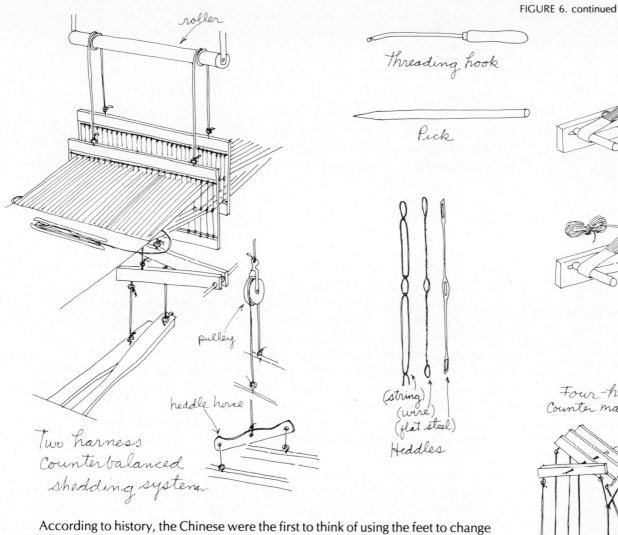

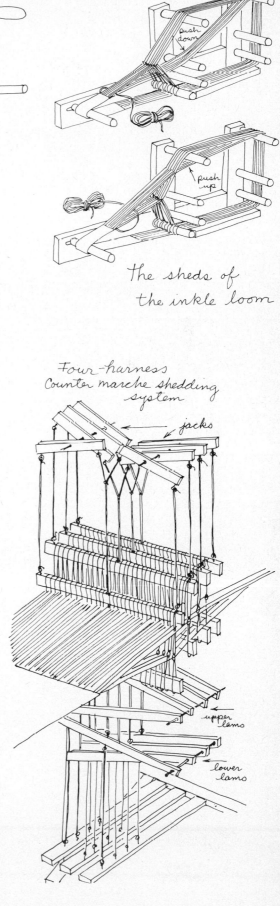

According to history, the Chinese were the first to think of using the feet to change the sheds. This method, still used today on some primitive looms (even of the back-strap type), has been perfected on the more advanced *treadle looms*. Permanent heddles made of *string, wire,* or *flat steel* are supported in a frame called a *shaft* or *harness* (the word used in the United States, and the word we will use in this book; in other countries "harness" refers to a set of shafts) and this is connected to a foot *treadle.*

On the simplest type of treadle loom there are two heddle shafts or harnesses. They are hung from *pulleys, rollers,* or *heddle horses* (kind of seesaw devices) so that when one shaft is pulled down by a treadle, the other shaft is raised, thus separating the alternate warp threads and forming a shed (called a *sinking shed,* because the treadle that is pressed lowers the corresponding harness). This type of loom is called a *counterbalanced loom.* When more than two shafts or harnesses are needed for raising and lowering a more complicated sequence of warp threads, each pair is counterbalanced with the other pair by a similar pulley system. A loom with two shafts or harnesses is called a *two-harness loom;* one with four, *four-harness,* and so forth.

When more than two harnesses and two treadles are used on any treadle loom, it is necessary to have intermediate horizontal bars (called *lams*) between the harnesses and the treadles, so that the many treadles (positioned off to the right or left, since they can't all be right in the center position) will still pull the harnesses down from their centers.

A more sophisticated treadle loom is the *counter marche loom,* so named for

FIGURE 6. continued

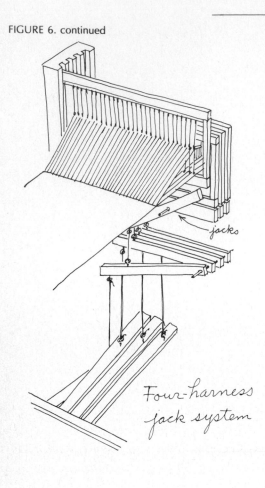

jacks

Four-harness jack system

its double set of marches (the old-world word for "lams") that work counter to each other. One set is tied directly to the harnesses for the purpose of pulling them down. The other set is tied to levers (or *jacks*) positioned above the harnesses for the purpose of pulling them up. Treadles are tied to some lams of one set and some of the other set, so that when a single treadle is pressed some harnesses are lowered and all the remaining harnesses are raised.

Of most recent design is the *jack loom,* which is a multi-harness loom that has jacks to raise each harness independently of the others. When a treadle is pressed the corresponding jack pushes (or sometimes pulls) the harness up. This is called a *rising shed* and the warp threads not raised by this action remain static.

To thread the heddles of a multi-harness loom so that a complex group of warp threads will be raised or lowered to make a certain weave structure, the weaver needs a code, or pattern, to go by. This is called a *draft,* and shows which heddles on which shafts are to be threaded with warp threads. A *threading hook* will be useful in passing the wrap threads through the heddles.

6. Placing the shot (called "throw" in England)

Raising the alternate warp threads and forming a shed mean that the weft can be "shot" through with greater speed than if the weft had to wind under and over each consecutive warp thread. One very convenient way to package the weft for its passage through the shed is to wind it in a figure eight around two fingers. This is called a *finger hank* or *butterfly.* It is wound in such a way that it will not unwind unless the weaver pulls the end out. It is most convenient for tapestry and belt weaving, where the weft passes only a short distance and where the weft has to be released so the hands will be free to make the next shed; the butterfly will just hang from the shed without unwinding. For wider weavings we invented tools called *shuttles* to shoot the weft through the shed.

The simplest form of shuttle, used by most primitive weavers when the butterfly is not appropriate, is a round stick several inches long. The yarn is wound back and forth the length of the stick, secured at each end by several turns around the point; this is called a *stick shuttle.* The next simplest form is a flat stick with notches at each end; this stick shuttle is sometimes called a *rug shuttle.* A small stick shuttle is often referred to as a *belt shuttle* because it is used for weaving narrow bands or belts; it has the added feature of one sharpened edge to beat each shot into place. *Rag shuttles* are made with two flat pieces of wood pointed at both ends and connected by two

FIGURE 7. Shuttle devices.

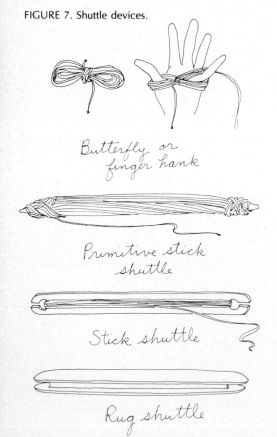

Butterfly or finger hank

Primitive stick shuttle

Stick shuttle

Rug shuttle

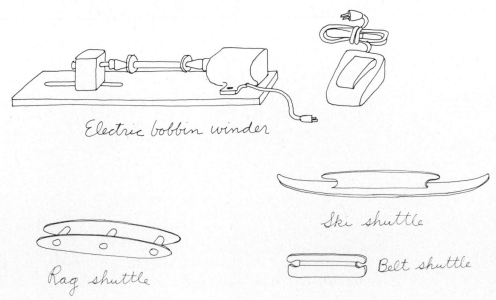

Electric bobbin winder

Rag shuttle

Ski shuttle

Belt shuttle

crossbars; the rags (for rag rugs) or heavy yarn are wound around the two crossbars. The *ski shuttle* is another stick shuttle, with each end curved like a ski, and the yarn is wound around a cleat centered on the ski.

A desire to throw the shuttle through the shed even faster on the horizontal warps of the treadle looms (on which very rapid changing of sheds is possible) led to the design of the *boat shuttle*. Inside a carved wooden boat is a spindle on which rests a *bobbin* or *quill*. The yarn is wound on this bobbin or quill, and as the boat shoots across the open shed, the yarn unwinds from the bobbin and trails out through a little hole on the side of the boat.

To wind the bobbins or quills you need a *bobbin winder* (mentioned previously). This can be hand-operated or electric. (Some spinning wheels can also be rigged to serve this purpose.) A *quill wheel,* a tool similar to a spinning wheel but designed specifically for winding bobbins or quills, may be used.

7. Beating

Finally, after you have placed a shot, you need something to pack it down against the previous one. For this you can use your fingers on very narrow weavings, but normally you will need a *comb, fork,* or *beater* when working on a primitive loom or when doing tapestry or rug weaving. The sword or batten used to hold the sheds open on a primitive loom is also used as a beater. On certain very tight weavings a *pick,* a very sturdy pointed tool, may be used to press the weft down between each individual warp thread. The *beater* or *batten* on the treadle loom is a frame of wood that holds the reed (which, you remember, is the metal comb used to keep the warp threads spaced properly). The beater pivots from a center at the base of the loom or sometimes hangs overhead, and can be manually swung forward to pack in the weft.

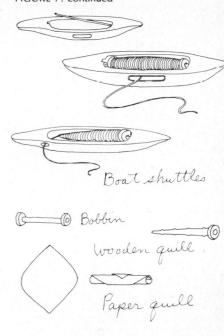

FIGURE 7. continued

Boat shuttles

Bobbin

Wooden quill

Paper quill

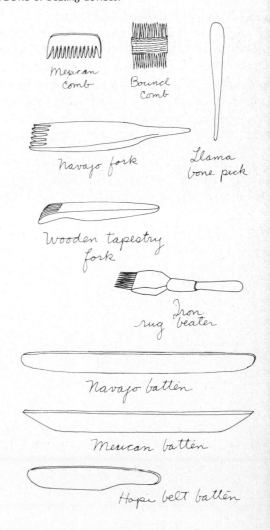

FIGURE 8. Beating devices.

Mexican comb

Bound comb

Navajo fork

Llama bone pick

Wooden tapestry fork

Iron rug beater

Navajo batten

Mexican batten

Hopi belt batten

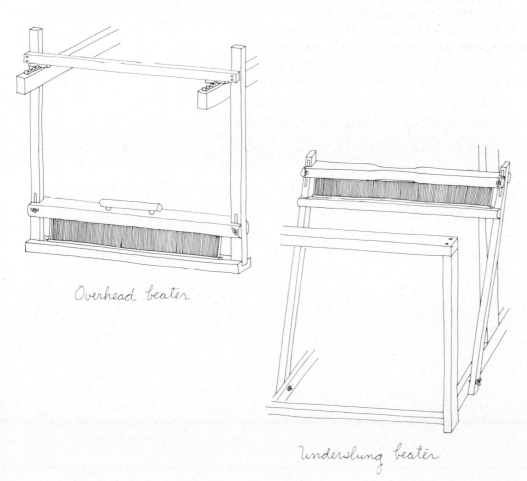

Overhead beater

Underslung beater

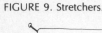

FIGURE 9. Stretchers.

Mexican stretcher

Hopi stretcher

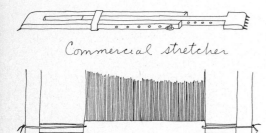

Commercial stretcher

Navajo "stretcher"

8. Regulating the width

Although inserting the weft with proper tension is the most important method for regulating the width of the weaving, tools called *stretchers* (or *temples* or *tenter hooks*) are sometimes used. They are rigid sticks, usually adjustable, with prongs or some such device so that they can be fastened into the edge of the fabric.

Getting Yourself Equipped

Just a few years ago the loom business in this country was quite limited. A small number of companies and individuals produced counterbalanced and jack looms and table looms (similar to a treadle loom but designed to sit on a table). They and the well-known Canadian company whose equipment (probably the most complete line anywhere) is distributed by many shops across the country were the major suppliers of weaving equipment for the American handweaver. Often we had to wait months or years for the "loom of our dreams."

Now the gap between supply and demand has been closed by two major sources. The first source developed as a natural solution to the problem—young men began making looms for their wives or girl friends. Some of these wood craftsmen have developed beautifully designed looms, which they are producing in quantity, and they are certainly making heavy competition for the older companies. Besides the looms, they are making beautiful hardwood accessories—with loving care.

The second new source comes from abroad. The Scandinavian countries are producing weaving equipment for importation into this country, and as many shops now carry Scandinavian equipment as American and Canadian. Their counter marche loom, which has always been their favorite type of loom, is just now becoming very popular with the American and British handweavers. You can even order direct from the manufacturer, which is sometimes cheaper (but not necessarily so). This equipment must definitely be looked into by the craftsman planning on buying a new loom or accessories. England also has some fine loom manufacturers that make their equipment available in the United States.

The duty on this foreign equipment is a minor expense, as it is only a very small percentage of the value of the equipment. The shipping cost is not very much more than shipping within this country.

Loom companies vary in their ability to deliver in a reasonable amount of time. *Be sure to get a definite delivery time agreed upon,* so you won't order and pay for a loom and then find out you're going to have a ten-month wait.

I'm certainly not going to promote any one company; you may find my views on loom types a bit slanted. You will have to talk with other weavers and find out as much as you can about the loom that interests you. And don't take it too seriously. If you make the wrong choice, you're still going to have a good working piece of equipment that will be very quickly bought by someone else when you have decided on the right loom or looms for you. This can be only after you have had considerable experience and know the type of weaving you will be doing.

I will pass on what I thought was a good piece of advice a Maytag repairman gave me years ago when I was going to buy an automatic washer: buy the model with the least gadgets possible. A complicated loom that does everything can take over—you and your craft.

Some pieces of equipment are easily made; in fact, occasionally you can make a better one than you can buy. In each of the following six chapters, the loom, its parts, and the accessories that are used with that loom are discussed in detail, with recommendations for features to look for and often a note about whether it is best to buy or make that piece of equipment. If you want to buy a treadle loom, for example, you need to read Chapter VII, "The Treadle Loom: Choosing the Right Treadle Loom for You."

Here are three possible ways of equipping yourself. I have included spinning equipment in the lists; I hope after you read this book you will be spinning at least some of your yarns.

Suggested equipment for the nomadic weaver

If you are moving often and can't have heavy equipment, or if your money is limited, or if you appreciate simplicity, here is a list of equipment that can be made by you for under $25, or purchased for under $100 from one of the suppliers listed in Chapter XIII. This equipment consists mainly of various-shaped sticks (which can be old broom handles, dowels, or sticks from the forest) and they will all roll up into a neat bundle. Except for raw wool, time, and yourself, this bundle will be everything you need to create your weavings, from minute to gigantic, from simple to complex. Refer to the chapters on each loom type for details.

Cards for card weaving.
Hopi belt loom and accessories.
Backstrap loom and accessories.
Navajo loom and accessories.
Hand spindles.
Hand cards or carders.

Recommended minimum studio equipment

If you intend to weave a great deal, and certainly if you are planning to make a living weaving, you will probably want to have a treadle loom. There is no doubt about it, you can produce more with a treadle loom than with a primitive loom in the same amount of time. To work efficiently with a treadle loom you will need these minimum accessories. The loom and the accessories will cost, at least, a few hundred dollars. Get an experienced weaver to examine any second-hand loom you are considering buying, and be sure to read Chapter VII, "The Treadle Loom: Choosing the Right Treadle Loom for You," before you make any purchases.

45-inch, 4-harness treadle loom (a counter marche that can be converted to counterbalanced).
Reed, 8 dents per inch.
1,000 heddles (string or wire, *not* flat steel).
Pair of lease rods or cross sticks.
12 warping spools.
Creel.
Large warping board or vertical mill.
Threading hook.
2 boat shuttles (largest size you can get).
2 dozen bobbins (for above).
4 stick shuttles (2 long and 2 medium length).
Bobbin winder (unless you have a spinning wheel that can be used).
Skein winder (adjustable); or swift, if you do not spin.
Stretcher.
Tapestry fork.

Cards for card weaving.
Inkle loom (or Hopi belt loom).
Spinning wheel.
Hand cards or carders.

The fully equipped studio

When you've been weaving a few years you are probably going to want a great deal more equipment than our recommended minimum studio equipment. By that time you'll have a pretty good idea of what looms and other pieces of equipment you want, and they will no doubt be different from my ideas. But, meanwhile, let's dream! This studio will accommodate more than one weaver, and the cost will run into a few thousand dollars.

Jack loom, 10-harness, 45-inch.
Counter marche loom, 4-harness, 45-inch (convertible to counterbalanced, if possible).
Counterbalanced rug loom, 4-harness, 60-inch (convertible to counter marche, if possible).
Reeds (3 different sizes for each loom).
Heddles (1,500 for each loom).
Lease rods or cross sticks (1 pair for each loom).
Navajo loom with large built-in frame.
Backstrap loom.
Hopi belt loom.
Inkle loom.
Cards for card weaving.
Vertical warping mill (large).
Small warping board (for backstrap loom and belts).
24 spools or cones for warping.
Large creel.
Cone holder.
Umbrella swift.
Squirrel cage.
Raddle.
Tension box and counter.
Threading hooks.
12 stick shuttles (of various types and lengths).
6 boat shuttles of various sizes.
6 dozen bobbins (for above).
Hand bobbin winder.
Electric bobbin winder.
Stretchers (3 different sizes).
Tapestry fork.
Iron rug beater.
Electric spinner (only as recommended in Chapter IX, "Spinning").
Spinning wheel (flyer type).
Large skein winder.
Navajo and various hand spindles (for teaching and spinning away from home).
Hand cards or carders (one pair with coarse teeth and one with fine).
Carding machine.
Indoor burners and outdoor fireplace for dyeing.
Sink with drain and running water (preferably hot and cold).

Automatic washer (for washing and rinsing wool and yarns).
Sewing machine.
Pressing table (see Chapter VIII, "Finishing Techniques: Pressing").
Iron.
Scissors.
Measuring tapes.

FIGURE 10. Your "dream studio."

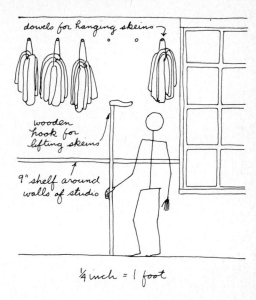

¼ inch = 1 foot

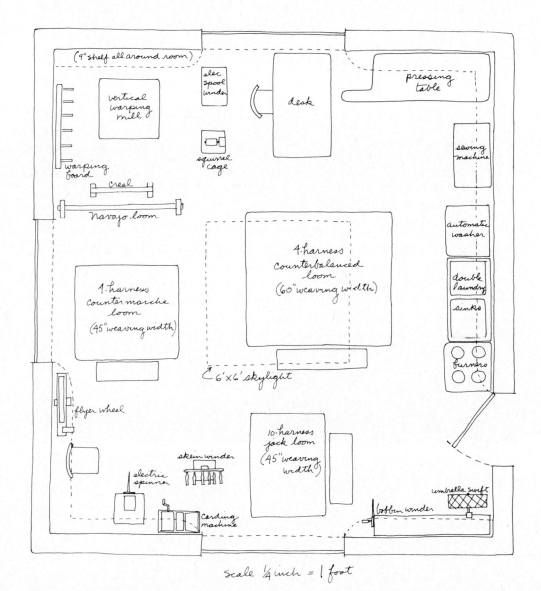

scale ¼ inch = 1 foot

Your Yarns

Choosing your yarns

Choosing the best yarn for a specific project can be quite a problem. You have to consider some conflicting aspects—aesthetics, function, cost, and your own taste. When I first started weaving I had a weakness for soft-textured yarns, while now I seem to have a passion for tightly twisted, rather hard and hairy yarns. What yarns appeal to you will be one of the factors that will make your weaving unique and personal.

One thing I discovered to my great amazement, when I was beginning this exciting craft, was that it is very difficult to make a fabric that is as beautiful as the yarn itself. A skein of yarn, the threads all lying loosely parallel and looping together, forming lights and shadows, is a very beautiful object in itself. To take these threads and interlace them and pack them together in such a way as to take full advantage of their beauty is a very challenging job indeed.

In the following pages I will discuss the different fibers yarns are made of, yarn sizes and numbering, specifications for warp and weft yarns, amounts needed for certain projects, cost, and finally suggestions for actually buying a basic supply of yarns. I will be talking only about the structure of the yarns; for color and other aesthetic aspects, please refer to Chapter XI, "Design and Color."

One important piece of advice: don't waste your time weaving with yarns that don't appeal to you just by themselves. You may think you are being economical by using some synthetics or mediocre yarns and colors because you can get them cheaply. Forget that frugal thought. Whatever you weave with them—after you have put in many dedicated hours at the loom—will also be so mediocre that it may turn you away from weaving altogether. There is absolutely no reason not to weave something very beautiful on your first try. With good materials to work with you've got half the battle won. Now, this does not mean that you have to start weaving with a very expensive yarn. There are many straightforward, simple, good-fibered, good-colored yarns on the market for reasonable prices. *Steer away from novelty yarns, synthetics, and garish colors.*

Please read Chapter IX, "Spinning," and Chapter X, "Dyeing," for ideas for spinning and dyeing your own yarn.

Different fibers and their functions

Cotton is one of the cheapest fibers to weave with and easy to use, but I find most commercial cotton yarns uninspiring. The yarns are usually mercerized (shiny) and the colors are limited. I don't recommend it for beginners because it is so fine and requires many warp threads per inch. And the weaving is slow with not very exciting results. For certain items of clothing and tablecloths, or anything that can be washed often, it is suitable. It is not good for bags, pillows, or rugs because it shows dirt so easily, and these items are difficult to wash.

Linen is used for its strength, sheen, and absorbency, so it also is good for household linens (as we refer to them whether of linen or not) and summer clothing. It is difficult to dye linen brilliant colors, so it is most often found either in pastels or in its natural state. Linen becomes more beautiful the more it is washed. Like cotton it shows dirt easily and should be used for items that can be easily and often washed. Plied linen makes excellent strong warp for rugs, although it is more difficult to use than wool because it is non-elastic. Heavy linen yarns make handsome wall hangings.

Jute and ramie are also vegetable fibers—jute being coarser than linen, and ramie being finer and shinier. Jute is not suitable for clothing because of its coarseness, but is excellent for wall hangings where a coarse, wiry texture is desirable. Ramie has the unusual property of being rot and heat resistant.

Silk is noted for its beautiful luster and its exceptional strength. It is most often used in clothing or tapestries because of its texture and its great affinity to dyes. But it is expensive.

Wool is probably the most useful fiber and used almost universally by hand-weavers for clothing, belts, bags, pillows, rugs, and wall hangings—and its price is modest. (For more explicit information on wool and hair refer to Chapter IX, "Spinning.") It sheds dirt better than other fibers, and because of its excellent ability to absorb dyes, and its matt surface, color is much more effective. Wool comes in a variety of textures, from very fine and soft such as Merino (excellent for clothing—even people allergic to wool can usually wear Merino) to extremely coarse and hairy like karakul (good for rugs and wall hangings). Spelsau is a breed of Norwegian sheep with wool that is medium coarse, long, and lustrous and is popular with handweavers in Europe.

Wool is spun into either woolen or worsted yarn. Woolen yarn is made up of both the long and short fibers of the fleece, which are carded together and then spun into an airy, rather fuzzy yarn with the fibers lying in every direction. Worsted yarn is made up of all long fibers, which are combed together to lie parallel with each other. When spun it makes a very smooth, dense, and strong yarn. English worsteds are the longest and glossiest fibers, while French worsteds are made of the longest and finest.

Other fibers that are similar to sheep's wool, but actually classified as "hair," are cashmere (from the Cashmere goat), a very, very soft fiber and very expensive; camel's hair or wool (the hair is the long fibers and the wool is the soft down underneath the hair)—excellent insulating fibers; alpaca (long, silky hair from the alpaca of South America)—great for clothing; and mohair (the very long and silky hair of the Angora goat, common in the southwestern United States). These hair yarns adapt themselves best to worsted spinning. Yak hair, cowhair, goat hair, and horsehair are also spun into yarn, usually of the worsted type, and make rather stiff, prickly yarns that are most often used for rugs, bags, pillows, or wall hangings. Their wiry texture makes them very interesting to the handweaver.

Yarn size

I will mention yarn count, or size, just briefly, so you will understand the numbers when you come across them. These are numbers by which yarn size and ply are described. It does not seem to be essential for weavers today to know yarn count, because now we are getting our yarns from all over the world, where the methods of describing size and ply are different. The handspun, ethnic yarns that are being imported today are not described by any system anyway. Because of this, I have described yarns by their approximate diameter rather than by official count.

Cotton, linen, woolen, and worsted yarns all can be described by count. No. 1 describes the size of the yarn that will be produced when spinning a certain base yardage from 1 pound of fiber. The base yardage for the different fibers varies.

For cotton, no. 1 is the size thread that results from spinning 840 yards from 1 pound of cotton fiber. No. 2 would be the size thread if twice this yardage (1,680 yards) was spun from 1 pound of cotton. And so on up. No. 10 would be a thread 8,400 yards long weighing 1 pound. So the higher the number, the finer the thread. This is single-ply thread, called "singles." When the thread is plied (2 or more threads twisted together), the number of plies is given along with the thread size, as 10/2 (2 plies of no. 10 thread) or 6/3 (3 plies of no. 6 thread). The first number is the size of the thread and the second number tells how many threads of this size there are in the final plied yarn.

FIGURE 11. Full-scale drawings of different sizes of yarn.

giant   heavy   med. heavy

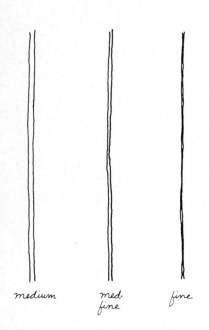

medium   med. fine   fine

You can figure out the yardage in 1 pound of numerically sized yarn. For example, 1 pound of 10/2 cotton would have half as much yardage (4,200) as no. 10 (8,400) because it is 2-plied.

No. 1 linen is the size thread that results from spinning 300 yards of thread from 1 pound of linen fiber. The size thread and the number of plies are abbreviated in the same way as with cotton.

Woolen yarns (usually spun with the oil in them and washed after woven) are numbered according to a 300- (or occasionally 1,600-) yard standard—just as linen is. *But* the number designating ply comes *first.* For instance 2/8 woolen is a yarn made of 2 strands of no. 8 thread.

Worsted yarns use a 560-yard base. Thus, a no. 1 worsted is the size thread that results from spinning 560 yards from 1 pound of combed wool or hair fibers. If the yarn is plied, the first number (as with woolen yarns) denotes the number of plies.

By knowing the size of the yarn and the number of plies you can figure how many yards are in a pound. For example, a 2-ply yarn of a certain size will have half as many yards in it as the single-ply yarn of that same size; a 3-ply yarn would have one-third as much.

In this book I simply refer to the size of the yarns as "fine," "medium fine," "medium," or whatever. I think this will be more useful to the majority of weavers who will be reading this book. In the chart in Figure 11, I have drawn the actual size of the yarn with my definition of its size. You can simply hold up a sample of yarn (*stretched out*) to determine if it fits within this definition.

Specifications for warp yarns

For your warp you must choose a strong yarn, as it takes quite a beating. It is under tension, lifted by the heddles every time a weft shot is placed, and rubbed mercilessly with the beater. Nothing will discourage you more quickly than a warp that is constantly breaking. Fine—even weak—yarns can be handled on the treadle loom by expert weavers who have perfect control over shuttle throwing and weft tension, but beginners should always make sure they have a good strong warp thread.

The other thing to keep in mind is the fuzziness of the yarn. Since it is being rubbed so much, a fuzzy yarn will start collecting in little balls on the heddles, or it will actually fuzz so much that closely set warp threads get stuck to each other, making it difficult, if not downright impossible, to separate the threads to form a shed. Loop mohair, although it might be considered a fuzzy yarn, actually works for a warp because it is strong, and the very long fibers are held in the loops and don't tend to fuzz up. It should not be set too close together, however. If a fine or fuzzy yarn is essential for the warp, it may be sized to give it strength and body during the weaving process (see Chapter VII, "The Treadle Loom: Making a Chained Warp").

For *weft-face weaves* (fabrics in which the weft forms the outer surface of the fabric), your warp yarn should be slightly finer or the same as the weft yarn. It is not a good idea to have a great disparity between the sizes. A fine warp with a heavy weft makes an imbalance that weakens the fabric. In any weft-face fabric, a warp that is larger than the weft will make a "rep" texture (which is a vertical ribbed surface). In some cases this may be desirable. For light-weight fabrics a fine two-ply yarn of a neutral color is perfect. It may be a stiff yarn, as it is the weft that bends around the warp in this type of fabric. For rugs (which are nearly always weft-face fabrics) I suggest a strong plied wool warp (two-ply to four-ply) of a natural color—a yarn that really hurts your fingers to break. Plied linen makes a strong warp for rugs and is excellent to use, but your warping methods must be very good to assure even tension; any unevenness will show up in the weaving—more so than with wool. On the Navajo loom, where the warp is in extreme tension, it is very difficult to work with linen because it has no resilience.

If the weft is the dominant element, but the warp will show slightly—a *modified weft-face weave*—choose a two-ply yarn of a color that will enhance the weft. Sometimes a deep, rich color similar to the weft is better than a neutral one, since the neutral color simply has the effect of graying the whole fabric. Most important to realize is that a white warp in this case (unless it is used with a white weft) can be very disturbing and make the whole weaving look a bit like cheap denim. In general, a single dark, rich color will be most likely to enhance the weft. Multi-colored warps are also disturbing in modified weft-face weaves.

For *balanced weaves* (fabrics in which warp and weft are equally predominant) your warp will probably be identical to the weft. When possible, use a plied yarn. If you want to make a fine fabric using single-ply yarn, sometimes you can buy wool yarns similar in size and color for both warp and weft; one yarn, labeled the warp, is spun stronger, and the other spun softer for the weft. The sizing method, mentioned above, can be used for single-ply yarns.

For *warp-face weaves* (fabrics in which the warp forms the outer surface of the fabric) you will want strong yarn as usual, but interest in color and structure also. In a warp-face weaving the warp threads have to be very close together, and for this reason fuzzy or overly textured yarns should be absolutely avoided. On the other hand, do not choose a very stiff yarn because it will not "bend" around the weft threads well enough to make a good, tight weave. The ideal warp yarn in this case is a soft but smooth and tightly spun two-ply or multi-ply yarn, such as worsted. For belt weaving, which is nearly always warp-face, a worsted yarn that you respin yourself (see Chapter IX, "Spinning: Respinning Commercial Yarn") is the very best.

Unless you plan to dye your warp yarns, it is most convenient to order them on cones, tubes, or spools ready for the warping process. Unfortunately, some of the nicest yarns come only in skein form, and you will have to wind them onto spools or cones yourself.

Further specifications for warp yarns will be found for each loom type, and for each project.

Specifications for weft yarns

Weft yarns can be just about anything you like. They don't take much wear during the process of weaving, but of course you will consider their durability in the final fabric.

For *weft-face weaves* some weavers prefer a single-ply weft, as it makes a smoother-textured fabric. In one of the most outstanding types of weft-face fabrics, the Navajo rug, the weft is nearly always a single-ply handspun wool yarn, the same weight or slightly heavier than the warp.

A plied yarn is also often used for weft-face fabrics. Most traditional tapestry yarns are lustrous two-ply wool yarns. Almost any yarn slightly heavier than the warp is suitable as long as it is pliable; a stiff yarn will not bend around the warp and pack down properly. Wefts of several different sizes and textures used together in the same weft-face fabric can be very interesting.

For *balanced weaves* the weft will be identical to the warp and the only limiting factor will be that it is a suitable yarn for warp also.

For *warp-face weaves* the most important single factor in choosing the weft yarn is its size, since it is not seen in the final fabric. The ideal weft yarn in this case is usually identical to the warp. A weft larger than the warp will make a "rep" texture—in this instance a horizontal ribbed texture. Finer weft will make a smoother, more flexible fabric. Many weavers like to use a smooth cotton weft that is lighter weight than the warp in their wool warp-face weavings. It is easier to handle during the weaving process because it slides smoothly through the shed, and it is easier to adjust its tension, but for this very reason it does not hold the warp in place in the final fabric as well as does a wool weft.

Weft yarns usually come in the form of skeins, and should definitely be in this form if you plan to dye them.

Amounts of yarn needed

Following is a *very* approximate and brief listing of amounts of yarn needed for some common projects, just to give you an idea of how much yarn you will need for your weavings. Please refer to specific projects for more exact information.

Belts—approximately 1/4 to 1/2 pound.
Bags—approximately 3/4 pound.
Pillows—approximately 1 pound.
Yardage—approximately 1 pound per square yard for medium-weight fabric.
Ponchos—1 to 4 pounds, depending on weight of fabric and size of poncho.
Rugs—1/4 to 1/2 pound per square foot, depending on weight of yarns used and type of weave. (Pile rugs can use up to 1 pound per square foot.)
Throws—2 to 3 pounds.
Blankets—4 to 5 pounds.

These amounts do not include any warp waste from tying onto the loom, or the foot or so that can't be woven at the end (on treadle-loom projects).

The cost of yarns

Besides aesthetics and function you have one more major consideration in choosing your yarns: cost. For small items such as belts and sashes the cost per pound is not a big problem, since you will be using only 1/4 to 1/2 pound anyway. But when you are choosing yarns for a 45-by-72-inch rug, for instance, you could pay as much as $100 just for the yarn, and you certainly don't want to do that. You will probably hope to keep the cost of the yarn down to $25 or under—and this *is* possible.

I believe in spinning and dyeing your own. Using the right equipment and the right methods, you can save money and not spend very much time at it. (See Chapters IX, "Spinning," and X; "Dyeing.") And you can certainly make yarns as beautiful as you can buy at any price—designed exactly for your needs. For large items such as rugs, which require heavy-weight yarns, it really makes sense to spin your own. But many of you may not be prepared to do this.

Here is a list of the possible ways to supply yourself with yarns, more or less in order of cost:

1. Buy raw fleece and card, spin, and dye it.

2. Buy combed fiber or roving from textile mills in large quantity and spin and dye it.

3. Buy natural (undyed) wool yarn from an inexpensive source in large quantities and dye it.

4. Buy bargain wool yarns and respin and/or redye them.

5. Become a retailer of yarns and get all your yarns at wholesale prices.

6. Always buy yarns in quantity lots so that you get a discount.

7. Seek out bargains and do comparative mail-order shopping.

8. Go directly to the supplier nearest you (or order from a mail-order supply house) and buy what you need. (In general, this is the most expensive way to do it, and not recommended if you're doing very much weaving. *But* . . . often these places have real bargains or closeouts that will enable you to get certain types of yarn as cheaply as anywhere.)

Suggestions for ordering a basic supply of yarns

If you are working on a treadle loom and are planning to do a great deal of weaving (but aren't going to spin most of your yarns), you can't keep ordering yarns for each project as you plan it. You have to have a basic supply of yarns on hand to choose from. This will mean an initial investment of well over $100 for the most basic stock, but you will have both warp and weft yarns for many different projects. Beyond these you will perhaps need more specific and unusual weft or rug yarns (though maybe you will spin your own). You're going to have to face the fact that you need to invest some money. If this scares you, just figure on making two of everything; you can *surely* sell the second item for enough to cover the yarn cost for both.

The first thing to do is refer to Chapter XIII, "Suppliers: Yarns." Pick out about 10 or 15 names and send for samples. Send a self-addressed stamped envelope for fast service. Foreign airmail takes only a few days. Most yarn companies charge for their samples, so there will undoubtedly have to be two exchanges of letters before you get your samples. But you will have an exciting experience in store just seeing the samples.

In our country many textile mills are making their yarns available to the craftsman; some produce yarns especially for him. And there are some beautiful yarns to be had. Besides this there are quite a few handspinners who are making their beautiful yarns (sometimes even vegetable dyed) available for purchase.

Canadian yarns have always been of good quality—usually simple single-ply, or plied yarns in nice natural sheep colors and a few dyed colors.

The Scandinavian countries excel in yarn production. They produce superior yarns in high-quality wool fibers—most notably spelsau, the long, lustrous fiber of the Norwegian sheep by that name. They also spin cowhair fibers into nice medium-weight single-ply yarn. Their yarns are usually single or double plied in very fine to quite heavy weights. These yarns are distinguished by a great variety of very beautiful natural and subtle dyed colors.

And, of course, the British Isles have long been producers of superior wools. There are many interesting sources there that make their yarns available. These are typically fine to medium fine in very nice naturals, heathers, and tweeds—usually single ply.

Although Australia and New Zealand are probably the most important producers of fine wool, they have not gotten into yarn production to the extent that they make yarns available for export. For the handweaver, their most important contribution is raw fiber.

And then there are all those beautiful ethnic yarns—from Greece (handspun goat hairs, and coarse wools in many different natural colors), Iran (also all handspun naturals), Colombia and Peru (handspuns in naturals and colors), Mexico (very heavy crude handspuns, and medium-weight single-ply yarns—these latter are sometimes too weak and loosely spun and should not be used), Afghanistan (coarse, hairy homespuns—karakul and goat hairs). Some of the suppliers specialize in these yarns —and usually at fairly good prices. The one direct source I know of (Greek) is probably the least expensive source for yarn in the list of suppliers.

Unless you order less than $10 worth of yarn from a foreign country, you will usually have to pay duty. I usually figure on duty and postage being about one-third to one-half the amount of the cost of the yarn itself.

Unless you order great quantities of yarns in many colors (which also means having great quantities of money) or unless you plan on dyeing your colors, you will be limited in your color combinations. My advice is to order mostly naturals and only a few of the most basic, rather muted colors. A deep blood red, a dark pine-needle green, a deep soft blue, and perhaps a rich golden yellow are probably the most useful colors. These will all go nicely together in twos or groups and all will be beautiful with any of the natural colors. Don't order a lot of brilliant colors that you'll have a hard time putting together. Save the brilliant or unusual color combinations for when you are dyeing your own, or can order enough quantity to have at *least* twenty colors.

I'm going to list some different yarns that I think you will find most useful. Five pounds of each is an absolute minimum; preferably you should order 10 pounds of each (except for no. 4 rug warp, 5 pounds of which may be enough to start with). Please refer to Figure 11 for drawings that indicate the actual size of the yarn.

1. Two- or 3-ply medium-fine wool or hair yarn as tightly spun as possible. At least 2 pounds of this should be in a very rich medium-yellowish-brown color if possible, so you can do one or two projects on Warp E. (See Chapter VII, "The Treadle Loom: Six Versatile Warps.") This yarn will be good for all belt projects (for these you may wish to respin it, if you want it to be the perfect yarn; unfortunately you can't buy really tightly spun yarn). This will also be good weft yarn for ponchos, pillows, handbags, as well as for many weft-face projects, especially fine tapestry. The Scandinavian medium-fine 2-ply yarns fit these specifications perfectly.

2. Single-ply medium-weight wool or hair yarn as tightly spun as you can find it. This will be useful as weft for pillows, handbags, light-weight rugs, and tapestries —also ponchos (if not too scratchy). Don't use it for warp unless you are quite experienced in handling problem warps. The most interesting single-ply yarns of this type would, of course, be handspun; but there are many mills, both domestic and foreign, that produce very nice yarn of this description.

3. Two-, 3-, or 4-ply medium-weight woolen or worsted yarn that is tightly spun (if possible) but *not scratchy* and not stiff. This will be used for both warp and weft of many projects—shawls, throws, blankets, ponchos, and any clothing. Some weavers make the mistake of weaving items designed for wearing with wools that may be aesthetically beautiful but that are terribly scratchy—sometimes even lining won't help. One has to be a living example of the old axiom "Pride suffers pain" to wear one of these garments, and it usually ends up just being looked at rather than worn.

Most yarns suitable for knitting can be used for weaving clothing, and since knitting yarns are usually plied, they can function as warp as well as weft. Unfortunately they are often quite loosely spun. Try to locate more tightly spun yarns because they will wear longer and "pill" (fuzz up) less. Alpaca and cashmere are very nice also. Probably your least expensive source for this type of yarn will be the Canadian manufacturers.

4. Three- or 4-ply medium-weight wool or hair yarn as tightly spun as you can find. It doesn't matter if it's scratchy or stiff, but it must be very strong—so strong that it is difficult to break with your bare hands. This will be used mainly for rug warp. It may have to be respun if it is to be used on the Navajo loom. If you prefer to use linen for strength, be forewarned that an imperfectly made (unevenly

tensioned) warp of linen will show up in the finished weaving. If you do use linen, choose a 4- or 5-ply linen approximately 1/16 inch in diameter.

A medium natural or creamy white is most commonly used for rug warps; it will show only at the fringed ends. Five pounds of this may be enough to get started with, but if it is a nice wool or hair yarn it may also be useful as weft in rugs or wall hangings, in which case you may want to order more, and in other natural colors. In the list of suppliers (Chapter XIII) I indicate some good rug warps.

5. Miscellaneous mill ends.* These are very inexpensive yarns that come in handy for belts, bags, tapestries, etc. They are usually rather hard, 2-ply yarns that come in insipid, uninspiring colors. So order only the neutral colors (unless you will be dyeing them) and make sure they are 100 percent wool; reprocessed is okay.

6. Medium- to heavy-weight handspun yarn—hairy and textured. This will be used for accents in weft-faced striped blankets, capes, etc. If you are not going to spin your own, there are cheap sources of this type of yarn—most notably Mexico, Greece, South America, and the Middle East.

7. Besides these basic yarns you will be needing yarns for specific projects, such as mohair yarns for stoles or throws; or specific additional colors; *and* rug wools, either commercial or foreign handspun. These rug wools you had better order with a specific rug design and colors in mind, since it will amount to quite a bit of money. Your most economical rug weft will, of course, be your own handspun yarn.

8. If you are a spinner, a supply of exotic fibers, such as camel's hair, yak, alpaca, silk, and karakul, to spin for specific projects will round out your supply of raw materials nicely.

Well, this is something to start with. As you weave you will find out what yarns you are most interested in and can stock and restock accordingly. I feel sure, however, that none of the above-mentioned yarns will sit on the shelf and collect dust for very long.

*Mill ends are called "thrums" in England.

CHAPTER II

CARD WEAVING

A Description

Card weaving (also called "tablet weaving") is a unique and very ancient technique of weaving. Evidence of its use thousands of years ago in Africa, Europe, Asia, and Iceland has been found in the form of both woven bands and the wooden tablets themselves. It seems not to have been practiced in the Americas, which is odd, because the ancient Peruvians made use of nearly every other weave structure known today. This fact, and the fact that it is so unusual a technique, make me think that it may have been conceived by one person and spread over the Eastern Hemisphere by roaming people, rather than invented in several areas independently, which appears to be the case with other weaving techniques. But enough amateur speculation!

The weaving apparatus consists in its entirety of several squares of cardboard (in the old days, wood) measuring about three or four inches on a side. The cards each have four holes placed near the corners. The warp threads are put through these holes and stretched in tension with the ends of the warp tied to two different stationary objects. One end can be tied to the weaver's waist or to the chair in which the weaver sits. The cards are turned as a group (or sometimes individually for variations in the design) to form the different sheds. The warp ends that pass through the two holes at the top of the card become the upper threads of the shed, and the warp ends that pass through the holes at the bottom of the cards are the lower threads of the shed. With each turn of the cards a different group of warp threads is at the top and bottom. The weft thread is placed in the shed after each turn, and packed down. The weft is wound in the form of a butterfly, or onto a belt shuttle.

Besides the standard square cards, there are triangular cards and hexagonal cards; and some cards are made with an extra hole in the center. The triangular cards with three holes make a lighter-weight fabric, and the hexagonal cards with six holes make a very heavy fabric. The cards with the extra hole in the center give extra strength to the fabric because of the extra thread. The square card remains the most popular and the most useful. Some cards are made of plastic, but ordinary cardboard is quite satisfactory and weighs less, which is advantageous.

A set of one hundred cards can be purchased from several different suppliers—and the cost is next to nothing. Fifty cards are plenty for most projects you will want to do.

Its Uses

Card weaving is a very popular weaving method, and the unusual technique makes it possible to weave intricate designs. Normally the cards are used to weave narrow fabrics such as bands, sashes, or belts because handling more than fifty cards at a time gets to be awkward. However, some weavers do use them to produce wide fabrics by setting up the warp on a regular treadle loom; in this case the loom serves only to hold the threads in a spread-out position and in tension; the warp threads are threaded through the cards instead of the heddles, and the weaving is done by turning the cards rather than by treadling.

The woven fabric produced in card weaving is heavy and twined and is particularly useful for narrow bands where strength is important—such as cinches or other horse tack and bag handles. It can also be used as edging on rugs—in which case the warp is strung up on the cards in the usual way, and the unfinished warp ends of the woven rug are used as weft.

The cards can also be used in quite a different way to weave two layers of fabric

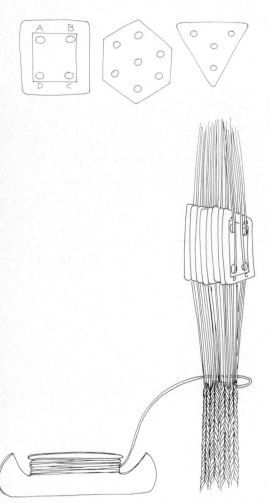

FIGURE 12. Card weaving.

—true double weave. In this technique the four warp threads of each card are not twined (as they are in normal card weaving), but form the warp for two separate fabrics.

An Analysis of the Technique

If we analyze the technique to find out exactly what is happening to the threads when the cards are turned (it seems to be such a mystifying transformation of threads into a woven pattern), we find that each individual card is actually twisting its four warp threads into a four-ply rope (or three-ply rope in the case of triangular cards, and six-ply rope in the case of hexagonal cards, and a rope with an invisible central core in the case of cards with the extra hole in the middle). The ropes make an S twist or a Z twist, depending upon which direction the card is turned, or whether the threads enter the holes of the card from the back or from the front. Figure 13 shows an S twist made by both of these two ways, and Figure 14 a Z twist made by both ways also.

During the weaving the cards can turn forward or backward or even can be flipped so that the threads enter the holes from the opposite side—thus making the ropes twist first in one direction and then the other, as desired. The reason for switching the twist is to make changes in the pattern.

With many cards threaded and turned together, what is produced is a whole set of four-ply ropes adjacent to each other. The weft thread holds these ropes together invisibly.

To understand how the patterns are formed, imagine that one rope has two red threads in the top holes of the card and two white threads in the bottom holes. As the card is turned and these four threads are twisted, the two colors twist around like the red and white of a barber's pole. At one turn of the card the two red threads are on top; at the next turn one red and one white thread; the next turn surfaces the two white threads; and the last turn, one white and one red; the fifth turn returns the card to its beginning position.

By threading different-colored threads in the holes of the cards and by turning the cards so as to "surface" the colors you desire, you can make each row of weaving different. In the simplest type of card weaving you turn all the cards as a group in the same direction. There are four different possible arrangements of the surface colors: (1) when A threads are surfaced, (2) when B threads are surfaced, (3) when C threads are surfaced, and (4) when D threads are surfaced. By repeating these rows of weaving, turning the cards four turns in one direction and four turns in reverse, you get a symmetrical repeating pattern. The pattern formed by the first four rows is repeated in mirror image in the next four rows. The pattern can be different depending on which shed is used to start with and to return to. In Figure 17 it is the A/D shed.

To get a greater variety of patterns the cards can be turned individually to "surface" the colors you desire.

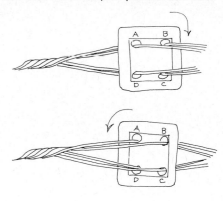

FIGURE 13. Two ways to produce an S twist.

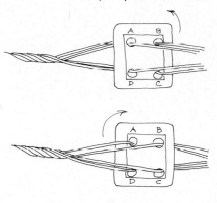

FIGURE 14. Two ways to produce a Z twist.

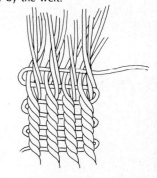

FIGURE 15. The ropes of the twisted warp are held together invisibly by the weft.

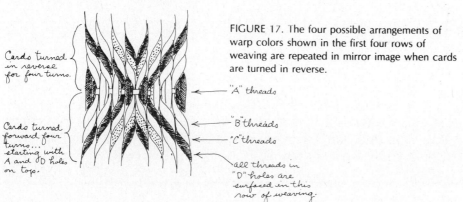

Cards turned in reverse for four turns.

Cards turned forward four turns... starting with A and D holes on top.

FIGURE 17. The four possible arrangements of warp colors shown in the first four rows of weaving are repeated in mirror image when cards are turned in reverse.

"A" threads

"B" threads

"C" threads

all threads in "D" holes are surfaced in this row of weaving.

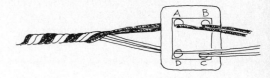

FIGURE 16. Barber-pole pattern formed by red threads in the top two holes of the card and white threads in the bottom two holes.

What You Will Need to Do Card Weaving

Cards (50 will be plenty; get the square ones made of cardboard).
Yarn (see Yarn Specifications).
A warping board (optional).
A belt shuttle (optional).
A ball winder, or spools and creel (optional).
A swift (optional).

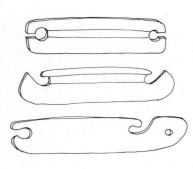

FIGURE 18. Three different models of belt shuttles.

The Butterfly vs. the Belt Shuttle

See Chapter I, "The Basics of Weaving: An Explanation of Weaving Methods and Equipment," for a description of the butterfly. I much prefer winding my weft in this form and packing each shot in with my fingers to using a belt shuttle. But some weavers prefer the shuttle. It is a simple gadget designed not only to hold the weft but to pack it in. And it is used for weaving belts on the inkle loom also.

A belt shuttle has some kind of notch at each end, through which the weft yarn is wound; usually enough yarn to complete one belt can be wound on. It should be made of hardwood, with one edge sharpened for beating in the weft. The proportions can be anywhere around 8 inches long and 2 inches wide. The type with the hole prevents accidental unwinding.

This tool would be easy to make, but is so easily procured and for so little money that it would hardly be worthwhile, unless you would enjoy the making of it.

Yarn Specifications

The warp yarn on any belt loom takes a tremendous beating. Since most belts are woven in the warp-face technique, the warp yarns are very close together and tend to stick and fuzz up. For that reason the warp yarn you choose for any belt should be *very strong* and as *smooth* as possible.

A linen or cotton warp would fill these specifications very well, but I find that colored patterns do not show up nearly as well with these fibers as they do with wool; and so I recommend a very tightly twisted wool yarn for any belt weaving. Unfortunately textile mills do not yet spin very tightly twisted yarns, and so the very best yarn you could possibly use for any belt weaving would be yarn that you respin yourself (see Chapter IX, "Spinning: Respinning Commercial Yarns").

If you don't want to go through all this, find a good strong plied yarn that is actually difficult to break with your bare hands. Definitely *do not* use handspun yarn unless it fits this description. The yarn should be a medium-fine yarn (see Chapter I, "The Basics of Weaving: Your Yarns"). Heavier yarns may be used when it is desirable to produce a thick fabric. The weft yarn should be the same as the warp, the same color as the edge warp thread.

FIGURE 19. A pattern draft for card weaving.

Drafting the Pattern

Figure 19 shows the way pattern drafts for card weaving work: the vertical lines represent the cards (and are numbered), and the horizontal lines represent the holes in the cards (and are lettered). Each space is marked with a symbol that indicates which color thread goes through that hole. From the draft you can see what the design in the final weaving will look like. By the same token you can make a design in the squares and follow this design when threading the cards.

Four turns of the cards in one direction will make the pattern as shown in the draft; four turns in reverse will make a mirror image of that pattern. Hold a small mirror up to the top edge of the draft to see what the design will look like in its entirety.

The arrows indicate from which direction the cards are threaded, front or back. Arrows pointing down to the right mean the card is threaded down (or from front to back); arrows pointing up mean the card is threaded up (or from back to front). The cards have printing on one side, which is considered the front side. Directions of the arrows (which means direction in which the rope will twist) should change whenever the lines in the design change direction. An easy way to decide which way the arrows point is to have them go in the same direction as the lines in the design.

In drafting your own designs avoid making too many changes in color from one square to the next; large bold areas and diagonals are the most effective. The design in your draft should look *very* simple. Don't forget it will be repeated in mirror image, and then this symmetrical design will be repeated throughout the weaving.

The pattern drafts for diagonal weave (Project II), double-face (Project III), and double weave (Project IV) are identical—one color is threaded in all A and B holes and another color in C and D.

Winding the Warp

When figuring the length of your warp you must allow for "takeup": after being twisted many times during the weaving process the threads will not be as long as they were when you started weaving; they will be about one-fourth to one-third less than their original length. Besides this, allow another 12 to 18 inches at each end of the warp that can't be woven; these ends will eventually be fringed. An 8-foot warp is a good length, and will make a belt about 5 feet in length, including fringe. To wind your warp the yarns must be in the form of balls, spools, or cones. Set the spools or cones on

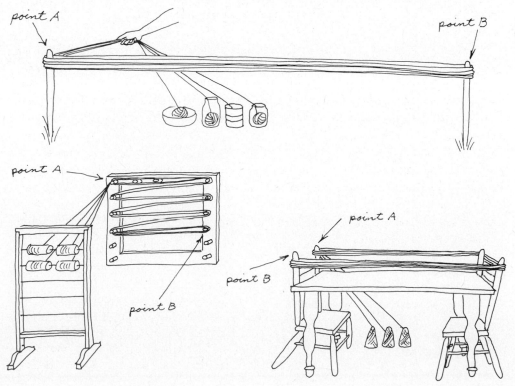

FIGURE 20. Three ways of measuring out warp threads for card weaving.

FIGURE 21. Making a chain loop around each group of four warp threads.

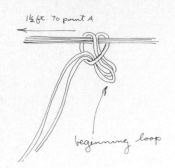

1½ ft. to point A

beginning loop

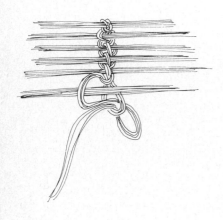

a spool rack, or the balls in jars or bowls to prevent them from rolling around and getting tangled.

Use a warping board, chairs on either side of a table, stakes in the ground, or two door knobs (if they happen to be located at the right distance apart) to wind the warp threads all the same length.

Starting with the last card (in the pattern draft the last card is represented by the four vertical spaces on the *left*), tie an end of each color yarn that is called for in *that* card to the first peg of the warping board (or to one stake in the ground, or one door knob, or one chair spoke). We will call this point A. Lead these threads to the proper peg on the warping board or to the other stake, or around the chairs to point B. The distance from point A to point B will be the length of your warp.

Loop the threads around point B to secure them in tension until you need these same colors again. If a certain color appears more than once in one card, lead this color back to point A (if it appears twice); then to point B again (if it appears three times); then to point A again (if it appears four times). Temporarily secure it to the last point. This will give you four threads of the proper colors for that card.

To keep these four threads separate from the following threads you will be winding on, take a piece of string or yarn about 3 yards long, double it and make a chain around these four threads about eighteen inches from point A. You will loop each group of four threads with this chain, to keep them separated and in sequence.

Proceed to measure out lengths of the proper-colored threads for each of the following cards, which means working from left to right on the pattern draft. Cut the warp off even at points A and B; if the warp is tied at various points before cutting off it will be easier to handle.

Another way to prepare the warp is to wind *all* the threads of one color that are called for in the entire belt, and then all the threads of the second color, and so forth. This would make measuring out the warp threads an easy procedure, *but* then the threads are all mixed up when you thread them through the holes in the cards. If there are very many threads called for, the resulting tangle can take a long time to comb out. By winding the four threads for each card at a time, and keeping them separate by making the chain, you will have warp threads for the entire belt all in order and need to pay very little attention after they are threaded in the cards.

Numbering the Cards

To prevent the cards from accidentally getting out of order during the weaving, the cards should be numbered (in pencil), and stacked face up with the last number on top.

Threading the Cards

Lay the warp out on the floor or table with the ends that have been separated into groups of four by string ties pointing toward you. Set the stack of numbered cards to the right of this. Starting with the card on top (with the highest number), and the group of four warp threads on the left (the first ones that were wound), thread the colors in the proper holes from back to front or front to back as the arrow in the pattern draft indicates. Set this card down to the left of the warp, face up. Proceed in this manner, threading all the cards in order (making sure they are threaded in the direction indicated by the arrows), and laying them down in a stack, face up. Finally the no. 1 card will be on top.

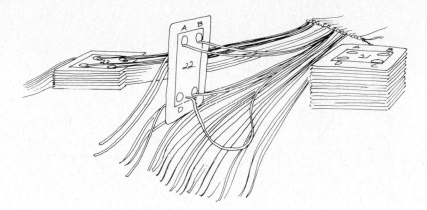

FIGURE 22. Threading the cards.

Tensioning the Warp

When the threading is completed, tie a knot in the other end of the warp, put a cord through this knot and tie it to some stationary object, such as a door knob, post, or leg of a heavy table. Untie any ties made before removing the warp from the warping board, and pull out the chain that separated each group of four warp threads. Comb out the loose ends in front of the cards, making sure there are no slack threads behind the cards. Slide each card back as far as is necessary to tie a knot in this end of the warp. Put a cord through this knot and tie it to a chair on which you will sit (or to a belt around your waist if you prefer to sit on the floor). If the warp is too long, and you don't want it stretched across the room, you can make a chain to shorten the warp as shown in Figure 3, in Chapter I. Start at the end farthest from the cards and tie the last loop made in the chain to the stationary object.

The cards should be facing right with the no. I card on the far right. Sit in the chair to the right of the warp, or on the floor in such a place as will provide moderate tension to the warp. There should be enough tension so that the warp threads separate easily, but not so much that the weft can't be packed down tightly in the shed.

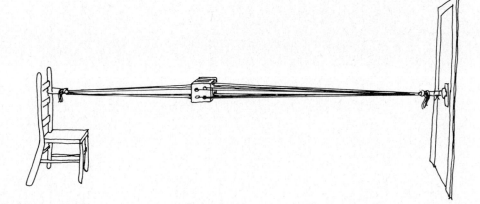

FIGURE 23. Warp tensioned and ready for weaving.

Preparing the Weft Yarn

Wind your weft in the form of a butterfly or onto a belt shuttle. You should be able to wind enough to complete the belt, but do not make the butterfly so large, or wind so much onto the belt shuttle, that it will be difficult to pass it through the shed. Splices in the weft are easily made.

The Weaving

Here we will describe the basic card-weaving technique used in Project I. Special techniques such as those in the other three projects will be described under those projects. Do not attempt any of those until you have mastered this basic weave.

Make sure the cards are in order, with the A and D holes on top. Slide cards, as a group, toward you and then back to separate the warp threads perfectly. There should be a nice triangular space (the shed) between the top and bottom threads.

Pass the weft through the open shed between the cards and you. Leave a twelve-inch tail hanging out. (This will be incorporated in the fringe later on.)

1. Turn cards one quarter turn forward (clockwise). C/D holes will be on top now. Slide cards toward you and then back to separate the shed. Pass the weft back through this shed, and pull until the weft just barely pulls up against the edge warp thread. (See below, "Keeping the Edges Even.")

2. Turn cards one quarter turn forward again. Slide cards back and forth to separate the shed. Beat previous weft tightly in place with fingers or sharp edge of belt shuttle. Pass weft back through this shed, pulling so it is up against the edge warp thread, and the warp threads all hide the weft.

3. Turn cards one quarter turn forward again. Slide cards back and forth to separate the shed. Beat previous weft into place. Pass weft back through this shed, pulling to adjust width of weaving. Pull weft just enough so that warp threads cover weft, but no more.

4. Turn cards one quarter turn forward again. (This turn brings you back to the A/D shed.) Beat previous weft into place. Pass weft through this shed.

Repeat these four turns, beating, placing weft, but this time turn the cards in *reverse*. The entire belt can be woven by repeating these four turns—first forward and

FIGURE 24.
a. Weft passed through the first shed.
b. Starting position of cards (A and D holes on top) and position of cards after each of four turns forward. The weft is passed through the shed in *each* of these positions.
c. Position of cards after each of four turns in reverse. The weft is passed through the shed in *each* of these positions.

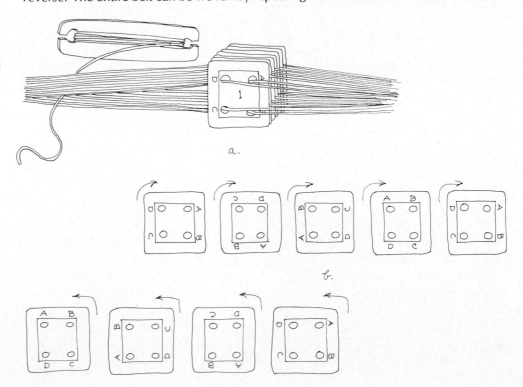

then in reverse. Always return to the A/D shed. The reverse turns, you will notice, *un*do the twist that developed in the warp threads behind the cards during the first four turns.

For variation in the pattern turn the cards eight or twelve times in one direction and the same in reverse. Or use the B/C shed (or C/D, or A/B) as the starting and return shed instead of A/D.

Keeping the Edges Even

As you insert the weft each time, hold out the weft thread from the previous row with fingers of one hand while the other hand pulls the weft through until it is right up against the edge warp thread. (This prevents the warp threads from bunching up on each other.) How tightly and consistently the weft is pulled each time determines the width and evenness of the edges.

Right at the beginning, after you have woven a couple of inches and established your weaving width, measure, and then keep checking every so often during the weaving. As a beginning weaver, you will find it easy to start weaving wider and wider —or narrower and narrower. But there is no reason not to weave a perfect belt on your very first try.

Turning the cards first forward and then backward reverses the twist of the "ropes." This makes a rather messy condition at the edges, which is disturbing only when you are using heavy yarns, or weaving a very narrow band. In these instances, if you are a perfectionist, remember that the nicest edges are made by turning the edge cards always in the same direction. If you do this you will need to comb out the warp occasionally to undo the twist and remedy uneven tension.

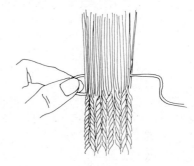

FIGURE 25. Holding the weft loop out until weft is completely pulled through the shed, which promotes even edges.

Keeping the Cards in Order

Every once in a while—or if a mistake occurs in the weaving—check the order of the cards and make sure the letters that appear by each hole are the same on each card. When you leave your weaving, slip a rubber band around the cards to hold them in order.

Splicing the Weft

If you run out of weft, simply splice a new weft by laying the two ends alongside each other in the same shed. The ends can be trimmed off later.

FIGURE 26. Splicing the weft.

Broken Warp Threads

If you use the proper yarn you won't have any broken warp threads, but if one does break, simply attach a new warp thread of the proper color to the upper knot of the warp, and bring the end down to meet the weaving (threading it through the proper hole in the card). Cut it about a foot beyond that point and tie it to the original broken warp end right at the weaving line, making sure the tension is the same as in the other threads. Later, this knot can be untied and the two ends woven into place with a needle. (I find this a much more convenient method than the standard practice of wrapping the new end around a pin set in the fabric.)

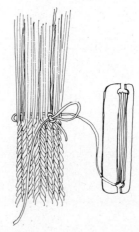

FIGURE 27. Mending a broken warp thread.

Combing Out Twisted Warp Threads

Unless you turn the cards exactly as many turns in reverse as you do forward, the warp threads behind the cards will get twisted and require combing out. To do this, untie the knot at the far end of the warp, and using a coarse comb proceed to comb out the threads directly above the cards. Move the cards up the warp as you have combed it. Do this until the twist is removed from the entire warp. Retie the knot and proceed as before.

Cutting Off

When the cards are too close to the upper knot of the warp to weave any more, break off your weft, leaving a foot extra. Untie the knot and slide the cards off the warp ends.

Finishing

Trim any weft splicing and sew in any broken warp threads.

The warp ends should be secured so that the weft won't unravel. I think the most attractive endings for these belts is either twisted fringe or four-strand braided fringe. The warp ends can be grouped together in such a way as to make some of the fringes solid colored if desired. Incorporate the leftover weft in the fringe.

Steam pressing gives the weaving a really "finished" look.

See Chapter VIII, "Finishing Techniques," for directions on how to do all this.

Project I. Belt (Basic Weave)*

FIGURE 28. A belt in basic card weaving.

This is the simplest form of card weaving, using 4 turns forward and 4 in reverse, as described in the general instructions. After you have practiced this you can vary the turns (12 forward and 12 reverse, or use a different shed as starting and returning points). The setup of the warp threads in the cards is the all-important design factor in this type of card weaving. You can use this pattern draft (Figure 29), the one in Figure 19, or make up your own. For your first projects do not use too many cards—not over 30 certainly. Thirty cards will make a width of over 2 inches with medium-fine yarn.

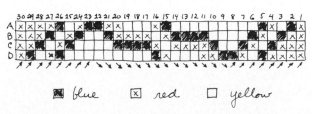

FIGURE 29. Three-color pattern for your first project.

Materials

Warp—Medium-fine 2-, 3-, or 4-ply wool or hair yarn, tightly spun and smooth. (Cotton or linen yarn may be used.)

Amount: Approximately 6 ounces.

Suggested colors: Red, yellow, and blue; or natural black, gray, and white.

*A good project for beginners.

Weft—Same as warp yarn.
Amount: Approximately 30 yards.
Color: Same as edge-warp threads.

Directions
Follow general instructions.

Project II. Belt (Diagonal Weave)

(Do not attempt this weave until you are completely familiar with the basic weave as in Project I.)

This technique has very handsome design possibilities. It is simply diagonal lines of two different colors; the diagonals can go in either direction according to your fancy. The diagonal lines in one direction are made by turning the cards forward, and the opposite diagonals are made by turning the cards in reverse. To make a combination of the diagonals in each row of weaving, some of the cards are turned forward and some of the cards are turned in reverse.

Materials
Warp—Medium-fine 2-, 3-, or 4-ply wool or hair yarn, tightly spun and smooth. (Cotton or linen yarn may be used.)
Amount: Approximately 6 ounces.
Suggested colors: Natural black and white for the diagonals; red for border.
Weft—Same as warp.
Amount: Approximately 30 yards.
Color: Red (or same as edge warp threads).

Directions
(If desired, plan on a warp length that will make two or three belts, because the next two projects can be made with exactly the same setup of warp threads.)
Set up warp as in the draft in Figure 31.

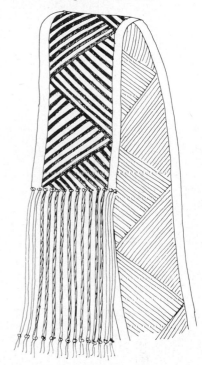

FIGURE 30. Diagonal weave belt.

FIGURE 31. Draft for diagonal weave. (Same draft can be used for double-face and double-weave projects.)

☒ red   ▨ black   ☐ white

Before starting to weave rearrange the cards so that instead of all the A holes being at the same corner, the cards will read A, B, C, and D, consecutively. (Border cards do not have to be rearranged, but can be to avoid confusion.)

Weave for an inch or so, turning all the cards forward one-quarter turn each time. This will make diagonal lines all in one direction. Now weave for the same distance turning all the cards in reverse one-quarter turn each time; the diagonals will now be going in the opposite direction.

To weave diagonals in two directions: Starting at one side of the warp, take the border cards and *2* of the black and white cards and move them forward on the warp. (This is simply to separate them from the rest.) Turn these 2 cards forward and the

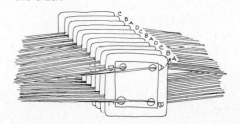

FIGURE 32. For diagonal weave rearrange cards in this order.

FIGURE 33. Turning some cards forward and some in reverse to make the diagonals go in opposite directions.

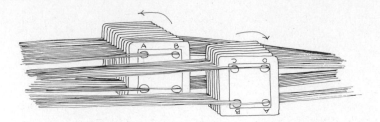

remaining cards in reverse; beat; insert weft. *Repeat.* Then take the *next 2* black and white cards and move them forward. Turn these and the previous cards forward and the remaining cards in reverse; beat; insert weft. *Repeat.* Continue this all the way across, until all the diagonals are going in the reverse direction. *Important:* You must always make *2* turns, inserting the weft after each turn, before moving the next 2 cards forward.

Variations of this meeting of the diagonals can be made. The diagonals may meet in the center: turn half the pack in one direction and half the pack in the other. And then on *both* sides of the center you can divide the pattern again. Or make a snake of diagonals all in one direction on a background of opposite diagonals. (If you are going to do a belt with the center symmetry, you should thread half the cards from the front and half from the back; then all the cards can be turned as a group and the diagonals will still go in opposite directions on either side of center.)

Project III. Belt (Double-Face)

(Do not attempt this weave until you are completely familiar with the basic weave as in Project I.)

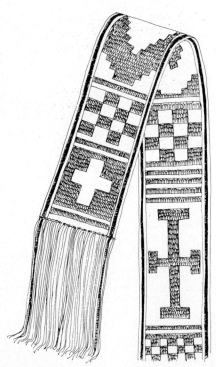

FIGURE 34. Double-face belt.

Using this double-face technique you can weave figures and letters in two colors, and they come out in reverse on the underneath side of the belt. At first you had better stick to simple checkerboards and bands, or you may get hopelessly confused. In fact it may take weaving a whole belt before you are completely sure of what you are doing. However, once you are at ease with this technique it is a wonderfully easy and quick way to make free-form designs.

Materials

Warp—Medium-fine 2-, 3-, or 4-ply wool or hair yarn, tightly spun and smooth. (Cotton or linen yarn may be used.)

   Amount: Approximately 6 ounces.

   Suggested colors: Red and green of same value and intensity (see Chapter XI, "Design and Color: Properties of Color"); natural black and white for the borders. (Or use same setup as in Project II.)

Weft—Same as the warp.

   Amount: Approximately 30 yards.

   Color: Same as edge warp threads.

Directions

(If desired, set up enough warp for two or three belts because Projects II and IV can be woven with the same setup.)

Set up warp as in draft for Project II: use red and green in place of the black and white—red in the A and B holes; black and white for the borders.

Start weaving by turning the cards all in one direction. This will make narrow horizontal bands: red when the A and B holes are on top and green when the C and D holes are on top.

To weave an area of solid red on top: When you come to the A and B shed (A and B holes at the top), weave this shed (insert weft) *and* the next one forward. Then reverse to the A/B shed again and weave it *and* the next shed in reverse.

Continue weaving these 3 sheds; the top side of the belt will be red and the underneath side green. (See Figure 35.)

To change to solid green on top: When you are either in position 1 or position 3 weave that shed and continue turning in the *same* direction one more turn. This will bring the C and D holes to position 1 or 3. Weave. Continue turning (and weaving) in this direction to bring C and D to top position (position 2 in Figure 36). Continue one more turn in same direction to bring C and D to the other side. From then on turn cards back and forth in these 3 positions to weave solid green on top (and red underneath). (Be sure you always weave after making a turn.)

To make half red and half green on top (reverse underneath): When you are in either position 1 or 3, turn half of the cards forward and half the cards in reverse, and weave this shed. This brings A and B to the top on half of the belt, and C and D to the top on the other half. Now continue weaving the 3 positions forward and reverse. (You can turn the whole group together.)

To return to solid color again: Starting from position 1 or 3 (never 2; this guarantees no long skips in warp threads), turn half the cards in reverse and half forward to bring either all A and B holes to the top (if you want red) or all C and D holes to the top (if you want green).

To make patterns: More intricate patterns can be made by the same method, but of course there will be more complicated groupings of cards. *Always make your switches of colors from top to bottom from position 1 or 3.* Once you've set up some of the cards with A and B on top and some with C and D on top, if you turn the cards *continuously* in one direction, the pattern will automatically reverse itself every second turn. You can make small checkerboard patterns this way.

Other uses: This double-face technique can be used in combination with the basic weave (as described in Project I) to elongate patterns.

Note: If some warp threads make very long skips (are not woven in), this means you have turned the cards in the wrong direction. If a long skip *has* occurred and you notice it only after you have woven past it, BEWARE of trying to take out the weaving to get back to that point. You will no doubt get into a hopeless mess. It will probably be better just to leave it. The best way is prevention. This you can accomplish by looking at the way the warp separates at the sides each time. If there is an extra-large separation, then you have probably turned the cards the wrong direction, and before you weave that shed check to make sure.

Project IV. Belt (Double Weave)

(Do not attempt this weave until you are completely familiar with the basic weave as in Project I.)

This technique makes reversible patterns just as the double-face weave in Project III does, but the weave structure and the method of turning the cards are quite different. In this weave the cards are not turned so as to ply the warp. Rather, the four threads that go through each hole of the cards are used as upper and lower warps for *two separate fabrics* (double cloth) whose structure is warp-face plain weave. The cards are turned so that two sheds are formed as illustrated in Figure 38.

Materials
Warp—Medium-fine 2-, 3-, or 4-ply wool or hair yarn, tightly spun and smooth. (Cotton or linen yarn may be used.)

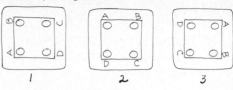

FIGURE 35. The three positions of cards to weave red on top and green underneath.

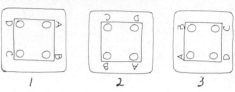

FIGURE 36. The three positions of cards to weave green on top and red underneath.

FIGURE 37. Double-weave belt.

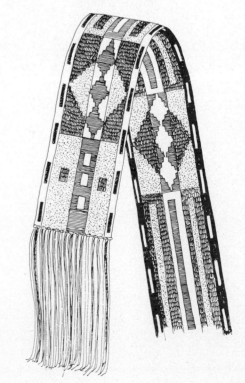

FIGURE 38. Positions of cards in double weave; two sheds are formed—an upper and a lower.

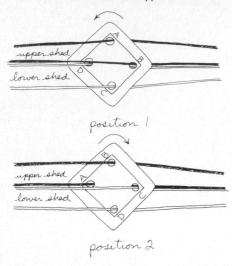

Amount: Approximately 6 ounces.

Suggested colors: Red, yellow, green, and blue (all rather muted); natural black and white for borders.

Weft—Same as warp.

Amount: 50 or 60 yards.

Color: Same as edge warp threads.

Directions

Set up warp as in draft below. (This setup can actually be considered identical with the setup for Projects II and III, but instead of using just two colors in the pattern area, I have inserted a band of 2 other colors down the center.)

FIGURE 39. Six-color draft for project in double weave.

■ black   ☐ red   ☒ green

☐ white   ⧄ blue   ⊡ yellow

Start with cards in position 1 (see Figure 38). Insert weft in upper shed from right to left, and then back through lower shed from left to right. (Pull weft so that warp threads cover the weft.)

With cards in position 2, insert weft in upper shed from right to left, and then back through lower shed from left to right.

By repeating these 2 sheds and inserting the weft, you form 2 separate fabrics, joined only at the sides where the weft turns. The top of the fabric will be in the colors that were threaded through the A and B holes, and the underneath side will be in the colors of the threads in C and D holes.

To reverse the colors so that the upper colors come out on the under side, switch the position of the cards so that A and B are on the bottom and C and D are on top. Make patterns by having some A and B threads on top as well as some C and D threads. Switch positions of cards at any point as dictated by the pattern. (It's up to you to make up the pattern.)

FIGURE 40. Pattern weaving: some cards with A and B holes used as upper shed; some cards with C and D holes used as upper shed.

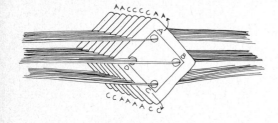

Suggestions for Other Projects

Weave fringes to add onto ponchos, using half-inch width of card weaving as the heading. (See Chapter VIII, "Finishing Techniques: Woven Fringe.")

At any point in the weaving of a card-woven belt you can divide the warp into three sections and weave each section with a separate weft. This will make three separate bands woven alongside each other. The bands themselves may then be braided by switching groups of cards to the opposite sides. Then continue with the weaving as usual, using one weft.

Weave small wall hangings using the different techniques (see Project III under the heading *Other uses*) to achieve unusual designs and shapes.

Leave some warp threads unwoven and then wrap them later. (See Chapter VIII, "Finishing Techniques: Wrapping.")

Weave handles for bags, guitar straps, cinches.

Make card-woven edges on rugs. (See Chapter VIII, "Finishing Techniques: Card-Woven Edge.")

CHAPTER III

THE INKLE LOOM

A Description of the Loom

The inkle loom is a small portable loom that consists of a simple framework on which are mounted horizontal pegs at certain intervals. The warp is wound around these pegs in a continuous circle, the pegs themselves providing the tension. String heddles looped around one of the pegs and every other warp thread hold this group of threads in a fixed position. The alternate group of warp threads can be grasped by the hand, behind these heddles, and raised or lowered to form the two different sheds. The weft can be wound in the form of a butterfly and pressed into place with the fingers; or it can be wound onto a belt shuttle that has a sharpened edge for beating down the weft.

The most common type of inkle loom has approximately eight pegs. The warp length is determined by how many pegs the warp is wound around, and eight feet is usually the maximum length possible. Normally fabric widths in excess of four and a half inches are not practical or possible because the warp tension puts too much strain on the pegs. To combat this very problem, some inkle looms are made with two framework sides supporting the pegs, and warps up to twelve inches wide can be woven. However, it is a very awkward procedure to warp a two-sided loom, and in my opinion a sturdy model of the open-sided type is the best.

Still another type of inkle loom, called the "English inkle," stands on the floor and resembles a warping board—in fact, they are usually designed to double as just that. The framework has several holes and removable pegs (for adjusting warp length), and bands of weaving many yards long can be woven.

Inkle looms usually have one removable or adjustable peg, so that warp tension can be changed during the weaving. This, however, is not an essential feature if you are going to use the loom only for warp-face weaving in wool (all of the following projects are of this type). The pulling and stretching of the wool warp during the weaving process are automatically compensated for by the fact that the weaving or fabric itself "takes up" a certain amount of warp length. For any other fiber, or for weft-face weaving, a tension adjustment will be necessary.

Although someone with a little experience in woodworking could easily make an inkle loom (especially the type with no tension adjustment), the effort is hardly worthwhile because there are so many good inkle looms available for very little.

Its Uses

The inkle looms are designed specifically for weaving narrow bands, sashes, or belts, usually of warp-face structure, and often with pickup patterns. Although other structures are possible on the inkle loom—such as tabby or weft face—the inkle loom does not lend itself well to this type of weaving because it has no provision whatsoever for spacing the warp threads. It's easiest simply to pull the weft tightly through the shed, thus pulling the warp threads right up against each other, to form a warp-face fabric.

Weaving on the inkle loom can be nearly as free an activity as knitting or crocheting. The loom is so light that it can be easily carried from room to room, or with you when traveling.

What You Will Need to Weave on an Inkle Loom

An inkle loom (preferably the open-sided type).
Yarn (see Yarn Specifications).

FIGURE 41. Inkle looms and accessories.

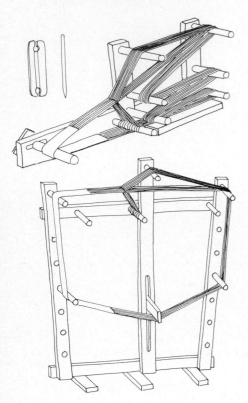

A belt shuttle (optional).
A pick (optional).
A ball winder or spools and creel (optional).
A swift (optional).

The Butterfly vs. the Belt Shuttle

See this heading in Chapter II, "Card Weaving."

The Pick

A sharp-pointed stick about the length of a pencil can be used to pick up warp threads when making pickup patterns. A dowel sharpened down to a point will be satisfactory. Lacking this tool you can simply do the pick-ups with your fingers, and for many weavers this method is preferable.

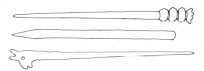

FIGURE 42. Various picks.

Making the Heddles

Heddles are not provided with most inkle looms, so you will have to make them. There are several possible ways. I will describe the ways I consider best for making two different types of heddles. The first type is a permanent heddle that remains attached to the loom; the warp is threaded through it as the warp is wound on the loom. The second type is a detachable heddle that is looped over the warp thread and heddle bar *after* the loom is warped. It is up to you which type of heddle and warping method you use. The first is easier for the beginner to understand and the second is faster. Both types of heddle should be made of fine, strong cotton or linen cord. Cotton rug warp makes good heddles.

Both types of heddle are attached to the heddle bar (or peg) and the length of the heddle should be such that when tied to the peg it just meets a piece of yarn stretched from the front loom peg to the top back peg. (See Figure 43.) Thirty heddles will suffice for the following projects.

Permanent heddles: Cut a piece of the cord (about 15 inches); tie it and attach it to the heddle bar as shown. Adjust to correct length and trim knot. Untie this heddle and use its length to measure and cut 29 more heddles. Tie and attach them all to the heddle bar.

Detachable heddles: Cut a piece of the cord (about 24 inches), tie it, and attach it to the heddle bar as shown. Adjust to correct length and trim knot. Untie this heddle and use its length to measure and cut 29 more. Tie them. These heddles will be put on *after* the warp is on the loom.

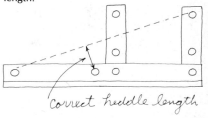

FIGURE 43. How to measure correct heddle length.

correct heddle length

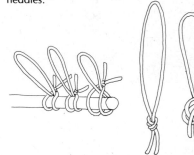

FIGURE 44. How to tie and attach permanent heddles.

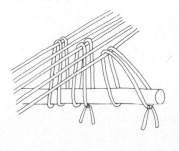

FIGURE 45. How to tie and attach detachable heddles.

Yarn Specifications

Specifications for the warp and weft yarns used on the inkle loom are exactly the same as those for card weaving. Refer to Chapter II, "Card Weaving: Yarn Specifications."

Warping the Loom

Winding the warp (measuring out the warp threads) and warping the loom (putting the warp onto the loom) are one and the same process on the inkle loom.

Decide on the finished length of your belt, allowing for a 9-inch fringe at each end and 4 or 5 inches for warp takeup and waste. A 6-foot finished length (including fringe) is good for a belt that is 2 or 2 1/2 inches wide (which is the approximate width of the belts in the following projects); a wider belt is best if it is slightly longer. Wind your warp around the appropriate pegs on the loom to make your warp the right length.

Since belts woven on the inkle loom are usually of warp-face structure (that is, the colored warp threads form the surface of the fabric), you will probably want at least two different colors for the warp. Refer to specific projects for color and pattern suggestions.

If the yarn is in skeins, make a ball of each color and place the balls each in a wide-mouth jar or bowl to keep them from rolling around as you wind their ends onto the loom. Or, if you have a spool rack and spools, use them.

There are two approaches to warp winding on the inkle loom. One approach (easier for the beginner to understand) is to thread the alternate warp threads through permanent heddles as the warp is wound. The second approach (much faster) is to wind the entire warp and then attach the detachable type of heddles.

In either case the warp threads follow the same paths: every other thread follows path A in Figure 46, and the alternate threads follow path B.

If your loom has an adjustable peg for tension, see next heading (The Warp Tension) for correct position of this peg *before* starting to wind the warp.

Method 1 (using permanent heddles)

a. Referring to a pattern draft in the following projects (or a design of your own), start with the first color of the group A threads (the upper-left-hand square of the draft). Take the free end of the ball or spool and pass it around the pegs, starting with the front peg and following path A, returning to the front peg. When you get back to this peg, cut the yarn, leaving enough to tie a knot so as to make this warp thread a continuous piece of yarn. Pull the two ends of the yarn *moderately* tight as you tie the knot. *Do not wrap the yarn around the peg*—the warp has to be free to rotate around the pegs.

b. Your next color to wind will be the first color in the group B threads in the draft. Take the free end of this ball or spool and pass it over the pegs, starting with the front peg and following path B *through* the first heddle on the left. Cut this piece and tie. (Your spacing is not important, because all the threads are pushed up against each other when you start weaving.)

c. Continue threading the warp ends, choosing the next color in group A (which *does not* go through the heddles), alternately with the next color in group B (which *does* go through the heddles), until all the warp threads in the design are wound on the loom, ending with an A thread.

Note: The tendency is to increase the tension as you proceed with the winding, so be conscious of keeping it consistent.

Method 2 (using detachable heddles)

a. Referring to the pattern drafts in the following projects (or a design of your own), start with the first color of the group A threads. Take the free end of the ball or spool and tie it temporarily to the front peg. Pass it around the pegs, following path A, returning to the front peg.

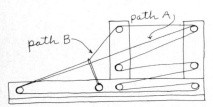

FIGURE 46. Every other warp thread follows path A; alternate threads follow path B.

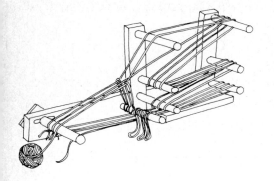

FIGURE 47. Warping the loom using permanent heddles. Each warp thread is tied at the front bar.

b. The next time around, pass the thread around the pegs following path B. Each time around the thread alternates from path A to path B until the entire warp is wound.

c. When changes of color occur (according to the pattern draft), break off the first color about two inches beyond the front peg and tie on the new color so that the two meet exactly at the peg. When two colors alternate for some distance, instead of changing colors and tying each time around, you can wind all of one color on the same path, and then wind the second color right over it following the opposite path. (In order to have this second thread in the correct position on all the pegs, you will have to slip the second color under the first on some of the pegs—you'll see what I mean when you do it.)

d. The final thread is broken off two inches beyond the front bar and tied to the original temporary knot of the first thread. You now have a continuous circular warp wound on the pegs, with every other thread following path A and alternate threads following path B.

Note: Watch the tension to see that you are not increasing it as you wind on.

e. Attach the heddles, as shown in Figure 45, on all the B warp threads. Be sure the A and B threads alternate perfectly as you are attaching the heddles. Loop each heddle over the warp thread first, pull it down through the other warp threads, and then slide it onto the heddle peg.

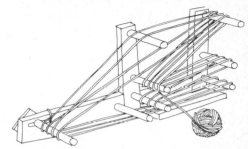

FIGURE 48. Warping the loom by winding continuous warp threads (heddles attached later).

The Warp Tension

For weaving warp-face fabrics the tension should be moderate. Before starting to wind the warp, the adjustable tension peg (if your loom has one) should be set at the middle point (except when using linen; see below). As you weave, depending on what fiber you are using, the tension may have to be adjusted. If you are using wool or cotton yarn, the takeup will probably be compensated for by the stretching-out of the yarn, and the tension will remain the same throughout. For nonelastic fibers such as linen, the tension will probably have to be adjusted regularly throughout the weaving. The adjustment peg will be moved to allow for the decrease in the circumference of the warp to allow for takeup; and it should be set at the beginning (before you ever wind a single warp thread) to the largest circumference.

If you want to weave a weft-face belt—a tapestry design, for example—the warp tension must be great. This means that you will start out, before you wind the warp threads on the loom, with the pegs set at the smallest circumference. Then as you weave and the warp threads get stretched you can make the circumference larger and larger as need be.

Rotating the Warp

Rotate the warp in a counterclockwise direction on the pegs, until the knots are about six inches beyond the front peg on the underneath side. The warp must be rotated to this position before starting to weave in order to allow for a nice long fringe, which is one of the main attractions of these belts. If you are weaving decorative bands for edging and do not want fringe, start weaving right above the knots.

As the weaving progresses and gets too close to the heddles, rotate the warp in the same manner.

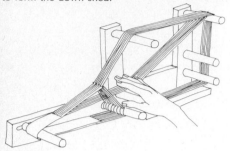

FIGURE 49. Hand pushing down on the A threads to form the down shed.

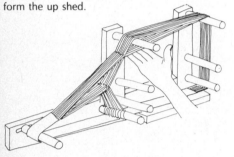

FIGURE 50. Hand pushing up on the A threads to form the up shed.

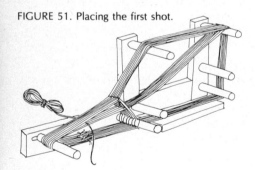

FIGURE 51. Placing the first shot.

How to Operate the Sheds

Place your right hand on the A group of warp threads behind the heddles and push these threads *down*. You will notice that this separates the A threads from the B threads in front of the heddles also. Place the fingers of your left hand in this space and separate the two groups from each other completely. This is your first shed, called the "down shed."

The second shed is formed by placing your right hand underneath the A group of threads behind the heddles and lifting these threads *up*. Again, this separates the A threads from the B threads, but this time the A threads are on top. Place the fingers of your left hand in this space in front of the heddles (called the "up shed") and separate the two groups from each other completely.

Preparing the Weft

See Chapter II, "Card Weaving: Preparing the Weft Yarn."

The Weaving

The warp is now rotated to the right position; you know how to operate the sheds; and you have your weft prepared. You are now ready to start the weaving.

1. Make the down shed. While holding this shed open with your left hand pass the butterfly or shuttle through from right to left. This first weft shot should be at a point about 9 inches in front of the warp knots. The direction of the weft is not an absolute rule, but it is most convenient when doing pickup patterns, as in Project II, so you might as well get in the habit of always passing weft from right to left on the down shed and left to right on the up shed.

Leave a 9-inch tail of weft hanging out at the right side of the warp; this will be incorporated in the fringe later on. Or, if there is to be no fringe, this tail should be woven back into the next shed.

2. Make the up shed. While holding this shed open with your right hand, pass the weft from left to right. Where the weft turns back to enter the second shed, hold it taut with your left hand until it is pulled all the way through. It is necessary to do this each time a shot is placed to prevent the warp threads from bunching up at the edges. Pull the weft tight enough so that all warp threads are neatly packed up against each other and no weft is showing. (Now place the original tail left hanging out of the first shed back in this shed along with the weft shot, if you don't want to leave it for fringe.) This will lock the end in place.

3. Make the down shed again. Now is the time to beat the previous shot into place with your fingers or the sharp edge of the belt shuttle. Place shot from right to left, controlling the loop of weft at the edge as described above, and again pulling the weft tight enough so that all warp threads are neatly packed up against each other. This controls the width of the weaving and should be consistent throughout.

4. Make the up shed again. Beat previous shot into place. Place shot from left to right.

Continue repeating these two sheds and beat each time immediately after changing the shed; then place the shot.

Keeping the Edges Even

How tightly the weft is pulled each time determines the width of your belt. It must be pulled just the same amount each time or you will get lumpy edges. Right at the beginning, when you have determined the width, measure the weaving and check it every 4 inches or so, because it is easy to start gradually weaving narrower or wider.

Holding the loop of weft at the edge until your other hand has pulled the weft all the way through the shed is very important for good edges. Warp tension also has to be moderately tight.

Cleaning the Heddles

You may have the problem of fuzz building up on the heddles, making them and the warp yarn stick together. This affects the ease with which your sheds are separated. You should carefully cut off the fuzz from the heddles every once in a while. Use scissors, but make sure you don't cut through the heddle!

Splicing the Weft

See Chapter II, "Card Weaving: Splicing the Weft."

Broken Warp Threads

Your warp threads should never break if you are using the proper yarn, but if the occasion arises, add a whole new length of the right-color warp thread by tying onto the knots in the warp and running the thread back to meet the weaving, threading it through a heddle if necessary. Tie the new and old ends together right at the weaving level. These ends are then woven in with a needle after the belt is removed from the loom. See Chapter II, "Card Weaving: Broken Warp Threads," for an illustration.

Cutting Off

When the weaving has been completed, the original knots in the warp will have traveled around to the top of the loom, since you have been rotating the warp in this direction as you weave. Weave until you are the same distance from the knots as you were when you started, so both fringes will be the same length. Break off the weft so that there is an end about as long as the fringe.

With scissors, cut right through the warp threads on either side of the knots (as close to the knots as possible) and remove the weaving from the loom.*

Finishing

See Chapter II, "Card Weaving: Finishing."

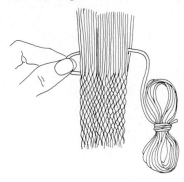

FIGURE 52. Holding the weft loop out until the weft is completely pulled through the shed, which promotes even edges.

---

*Or untie the knots if you want a long fringe.

FIGURE 53. A warp-face belt.

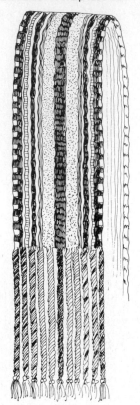

Project I. Warp-Face Belt *

(This project can also be woven on the Hopi belt loom.)

This is the simplest and most common type of belt to weave on the inkle loom. The structure is a warp-face plain weave (see Figure 1). The design is formed by varying the colors of the warp threads. The succession of colors you choose as you are winding the warp on the loom determines the design of the finished weaving; you will be amazed at the intricate designs that can be made by this simple method. Figure 55 illustrates how the drafted pattern shows up in the weaving.

One row of weaving exposes all A threads, and the next row exposes all B threads. These two rows simply alternate to form the pattern. Following is a list of some of the pattern possibilities when threading different sequences of warp threads.

1. When A and B threads are the same color for a certain distance, a solid band occurs in the weaving.

2. When a single thread of one color is wound, and is surrounded by threads all of another color, a line of dashes occurs in the weaving.

3. When a color is wound twice around, first on A path and then on B path, a wavy line is produced.

4. When the A threads are all one color, and the B threads all another color, horizontal bars occur.

5. When you thread as in no. 4, but switch positions of A and B colors at regular intervals, you get a checkerboard effect.

Materials

Warp—Strong 2-, 3-, or 4-ply medium-fine or medium-weight wool or hair yarn, tightly spun and smooth. (Cotton or linen may be used.)
Amount: Approximately 1/4 pound.
Suggested colors: 4 brilliant colors of the same value (see Chapter XI, "Design and Color: Properties of Color"); or 4 different naturals from white to black.
Weft—Same as warp.
Amount: About 30 yards.
Color: Same as edge warp threads.

Directions

Follow all the general directions given earlier in this chapter. Use the pattern draft (Figure 54) for this project or make up your own.

FIGURE 55. How the pattern shows up in the weaving.

the draft

⊠ black ☐ white

threads in row A follow path A
when warping the loom.
threads in row B follow path B
(through the heddles).

The weaving.

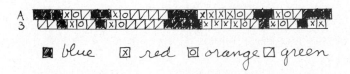

■ blue   ⊠ red   ◫ orange   ◨ green

FIGURE 54. Draft for warp-face belt.

* A good project for beginners.

Project II. Warp-Face Belt with Pickup Pattern

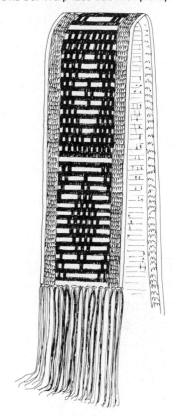

FIGURE 56. Warp-face belt with pickup pattern.

(This project can also be woven on the Hopi belt loom.)

Do not attempt this belt until you have first tried a plain woven one as in Project I.

Warp-face belts are often decorated with various designs that are achieved by picking up extra threads from the group of warp threads at the bottom of the shed, and adding them to the top group before inserting the weft. This means that the weft thread shows on the back side of the belt where the warps have been picked up to appear on the front. The warp for this type of belt is normally set up with a plain or striped border that will be woven in the regular manner. Then the center section (where the pickup pattern will occur) is threaded with the A threads one color and the B threads another. This makes a horizontal striped pattern when woven plain. The pickup occurs only on every other row of weaving, and the alternate rows are woven plain. The pickup is most easily made if the color to be picked up is threaded on the A path.

Materials

Warp—Strong 2-, 3-, or 4-ply medium-fine or medium-weight wool or hair yarn, tightly spun and smooth. (Cotton or linen may be used.)

Amount: Approximately 1/4 pound.

Suggested colors: Red and blue for the border; natural black and natural white for the center pickup section.

Weft—Same as warp.

Amount: About 30 yards.

Color: Same as edge warp threads.

Directions

Wind the warp as described in general instructions. Follow the draft in Figure 57.

FIGURE 57. Draft for belt with pickup pattern.

Weave an inch or so in plain weave, starting from right to left on the down shed, and ending with the up shed.

Directions for the pickup: Open the down shed and beat. Now hold this shed open with the left hand and pick up *every other* thread from the A threads below (do this only with the black and white threads in the center section—not the border threads). This means you will hold the upper border threads in your right hand and, as you pick up the alternate black threads, transfer them to your right hand also, then transfer the left-hand border threads (upper ones) onto your right hand also. While holding this new shed open pass the weft through from right to left.

Open the up shed, beat, and place shot from left to right.

Open the down shed, beat. This time pick up every other A thread from below. (the ones that were not picked up in the previous pickup row). Beat, and place shot in this new shed.

Open the up shed, beat, and place shot.

These four rows of weaving are repeated to make the pickup pattern. Always beat

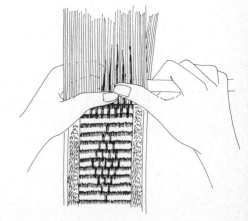

FIGURE 58. Picking up *every other* black thread from below.

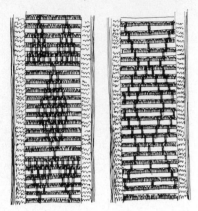

FIGURE 59. Solid shapes and outlined shapes.

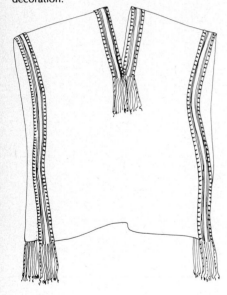

FIGURE 60. Woven inkle bands for poncho decoration.

immediately after opening the shed—before placing the shot. Do this for 8 rows. The entire center section will be filled with the pickup pattern.

To make diamonds and other shapes against the plain weave (striped) background, pick up the threads from the lower group *only* where the design actually should occur in that row of weaving. You can weave solid designs in the pickup pattern or just outline the shapes.

Suggestions for Other Projects

Make belts with other pickup patterns. For one shape pick up the dark threads, and then for the next shape pick up the light threads. Or pick up *two* threads at a time. Or warp the loom so that the pickup threads are all twice as heavy as the other threads. In this case make the background by weaving one shed plain with the finer threads up, and when the coarse threads are up weave under only every other one —dropping the alternates below. For the pattern areas, weave the shed with the coarse threads up plain, and weave the next shed with the fine threads up, picking up alternate coarse threads from below. (This makes a very attractive "pebbly" texture.) Still another pickup technique is described in Chapter IV, "The Hopi Belt Loom"; this is a pick *and* drop technique that makes the design come out in reverse colors on the back side of the belt.

Weave a belt in tapestry technique, using only 12 or so heddles, so that the warp is spaced far apart. Guatemalan fiesta headbands are woven in this technique, using silk threads.

Weave neck and side borders for a plain poncho; they can be sewn on by hand.

Weave narrow headbands or hatbands.

Weave straps for handbags.

See Chapter VIII, "Finishing Techniques: Woven Fringe," for directions on how to weave a decorative fringe.

Weave binding for ponchos or capes. (See Chapter VIII, "Finishing Techniques: Gimp.")

CHAPTER IV

THE HOPI BELT LOOM

A Description of the Loom

The Hopi belt loom is a beautifully simple weaving device that happens to be my favorite belt loom, mainly because the warp is stretched in a vertical position (as it is on the Navajo loom)—the most convenient position, in my opinion, for weaving with primitive tools.

The loom consists of two loom bars around which the warp is wound in a continuous circle (rather than in a figure eight, as it is on the Navajo loom). Winding the warp in a continuous circle means that warps of a certain length can be stretched vertically in tension in *half* the space (a rather essential factor when weaving 8-foot lengths and over), and the warp is rotated around the loom bars so that the weaving level is always directly in front of the weaver. These two loom bars, when warped, are held apart in tension vertically by being attached to a pole frame, or attached in any manner to the floor and ceiling.

The sheds are made in the upper warp threads of the circle by having a shed stick permanently placed under every other warp thread; and the alternate threads are strung with string heddles and pulled forward with a stick, called the heddle stick. A batten, a smooth flat stick sometimes shaped with a handle, is inserted in the sheds and turned on its side to hold the shed open while the weft is passed through. The batten doubles as a beater to pack in the weft. The weft is usually wound onto a stick or may be wound in a butterfly.

Two extra sticks or dowels are inserted into the warp next to the top loom bar, forming a figure eight of groups of threads. These stabilize the warp threads, keep them in order, and prevent the circle from slipping around the loom bars when the weft is beaten down.

This is not a loom you can buy; you will simply set it up when you are ready to weave, using dowels or old broom handles.

Its Uses

The loom is used by the Hopi men mainly to weave warp-face belts and ceremonial sashes, often quite wide, and usually with a picked design. The loom is also used by the Navajos and other Indian belt weavers in the Southwest. Any of the belts described in this book can be woven on this loom, except, of course, those described under card weaving. It is the perfect belt loom for any of you who travel a lot and like to take some weaving equipment along. It can be rolled up into a little bundle (with the weaving in progress), and can be set up by securing the top loom bar to some overhead fixed object and the bottom bar to the floor or ground. Or it can be set up as a backstrap loom. If you are using it regularly in your home you may want to build a permanent frame for it.

What You Will Need to Set Up and Weave on a Hopi Belt Loom

a. One 12-foot 2-by-4 or log about 3 inches in diameter. (This is for the temporary warping frame.)

b. Four nails at least 2 inches long. (Also for the warping frame.)

c. One 14-foot 2-by-4 or log about 3 inches in diameter with 8 very large nails for making joints, *or* (if you have a floor and ceiling that can be screwed into)

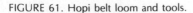

FIGURE 61. Hopi belt loom and tools.

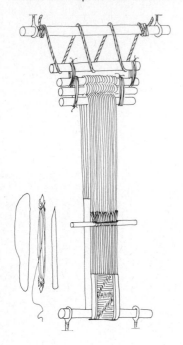

4 very large screw eyes (large enough so that 3/4-inch dowels will fit into them). (These are for the loom frame.)

d. Light-weight rope or nylon cord, about 6 yards. (This is to lash your warping frame together and later to lash the loom to the frame.)

e. Six smooth round sticks or dowels (old broom handles will do) about 3/4 inch in diameter. (Three of these should be 18 inches long and will be your loom bars and intermediate tension bar; three should be 10 inches long and will be the warp stabilizers and shed stick.)

f. One stick or dowel about 1/4 inch in diameter and 10 inches long. (This is the heddle stick.)

g. Medium-fine cotton cord, smooth and tightly twisted (for the string heddles).

h. A batten.

i. A shuttle (optional).

j. A pick (optional).

k. The yarn.

The Loom Frame and Alternatives

A portable frame can be made out of 2-by-4s as pictured in Figure 62. This is a convenient setup for your home if you do not want to nail or screw into the floor and ceiling. Unless it has a base, you will have to attach the frame to a door frame or some structure so that it will be rigidly held in a vertical position. Screw eyes large enough to accommodate the loom bars can also be used by simply screwing them into floor and ceiling. For weaving small headbands or anything that isn't too long, the bars may be lashed to a frame made of the forked branch of a tree. The Navajo loom frame makes an excellent place to set up the belt loom. (See Chapter VI, "The Navajo Loom: The Loom Frame.")

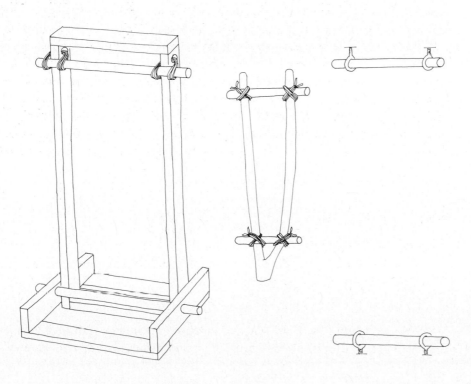

FIGURE 62. Loom frame and alternatives.

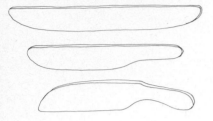

FIGURE 63. Battens for Hopi belt loom.

FIGURE 64. The stick shuttle.

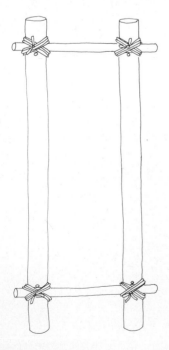

FIGURE 65. The warping frame.

The Batten

The authentic Hopi batten for the belt loom is a hardwood stick about 12 to 18 inches long and 2 1/2 inches wide, shaped somewhat like a club. One edge is sharpened for beating in the weft. The batten is inserted in the sheds with the sharp edge down, and is held with both hands to beat the previous weft into place. It is then turned on edge to hold that shed open while the weft is passed through.

This tool is manufactured by some of the suppliers of hardwood accessories, and most likely is carried by shops that specialize in Indian weaving tools. Any sword or batten of these approximate dimensions will serve the purpose.

The Butterfly vs. the Shuttle

As with other types of belt weaving, I find the most convenient method of packaging the weft is the butterfly described in Chapter I, "The Basics of Weaving: An Explanation of Weaving Methods and Equipment." But many weavers use the primitive stick shown in Figure 64. It is simply a smooth round stick several inches long with the ends shaped down to a point. The yarn is wound back and forth the length of the stick. Each turn is secured by winding the yarn around the end four or five times.

The Pick

See this heading in Chapter III, "The Inkle Loom."

Yarn Specifications

See Chapter II, "Card Weaving: Yarn Specifications," for specifications for your warp yarn. The Hopis often take dime-store 4-ply worsted yarn and respin it into a very tight, fine yarn that looks single ply. (See Chapter IX, "Spinning: Respinning Commercial Yarn.") This makes an excellent warp. The traditional Hopi colors are red and black, with some green at the borders.

The Hopis usually use a cotton weft that is slightly finer than the warp yarn. I prefer to use the same wool yarn as the edge warp threads because the fabric is more stable (with a cotton weft the warp threads can slide apart, exposing the weft). In any case the weft should be of the same color as the edge warp threads, because it will show very slightly as a little dot at the edges where it comes out of one shed and enters the next. This little dot can be distracting if it is in a different color.

Preparing the Warping Frame

Cut the rope or cord (d) into four pieces about 1 1/2 yards long. With these, lash the two loom bars (e) to the 12-foot log or 2-by-4 (a) (which has been cut in half) at a distance apart that is about 3 inches more than half the length of the finished belt. (A 6-foot belt is a good length.) Hammer the nails (b) halfway into the logs inside the lashings to prevent any slippage of the loom bars from their position when they are strung with the warp threads.

Winding the Warp

Refer to the draft (Figure 78) showing the sequence of colors that will be used in the warp of Project I. Traditional Hopi Belt (or any other draft, such as those in Chapter III, "The Inkle Loom"). In this circular warp that you are about to wind, every other thread in sequence will eventually be positioned on top of the shed stick; the alternate threads will be looped with string heddles and attached to the heddle stick. The top line of the draft represents the first set of threads, and the bottom line represents the second. Starting from the left side of the draft you will wind first the color indicated by the first square on top; the next thread you wind will be the color indicated by the first square in the bottom line; and so forth, alternating back and forth from top to bottom line of the draft.

To start, tie the end of the first thread to one of the loom bars about 3 inches from the center. This is a temporary knot. You will wind the warp spread out on the loom bars so that the threads are about 1/8 inch apart. This spacing does not have to be accurate because in this type of weaving the weft thread pulls the warp threads all up against each other in each row of weaving. You are spacing them apart now simply so you can see what you are doing.

Wind as many *complete* turns (around the other bar and back again) as there are threads called for in the draft. Each complete turn represents one square of the draft. The thread should always go *over* the top of the second loom bar and back *under* the first, so that you are making an elongated circle. (Sight through the threads from the side every once in a while to make sure you are winding them right.)

Make changes of color as indicated in the draft by breaking off the first color at the first loom bar and tying the end of the first color to the end of the new color *at* that loom bar (not around it). When you are alternating colors (as in the pickup pattern area), instead of breaking off and tying each time around, wind all one color and make a temporary tie. Then tie on the second color with a temporary tie and wind it in between each thread of the first color. When you have finished with this second color, tie the end to its beginning. (This will mean that the thread has to cross over to meet the last end, but this does not matter.) Continue winding by tying the next color onto the temporary tie left. When you have finished winding, tie the final end to the original temporary tie. Now the warp should be one continuous circle free to rotate around the bars.

The warp should be wound with moderate tension. How much or how little tension is not important at this point; what *is* important is that it be consistent throughout. The tendency usually is to wind tighter and tighter.

Inserting the Shed Stick

Working with the top warp threads only, pick up every other one all across the width of the warp and insert the stick or dowel (e), which will now be called the shed stick, underneath these threads. To prevent the shed stick from accidentally falling out, pass a cord or string over the top warp threads and tie both ends securely to the stick. Push the shed stick up out of the way.

Making the Heddles

Now pick up the alternate threads (the ones you didn't pick up for the shed stick). You will have to pick them up in between the other threads (make sure they alternate perfectly). Insert one of the extra dowels (e) under them.

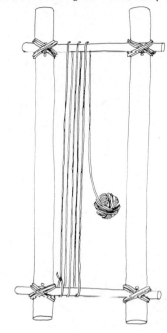

FIGURE 66. Winding the circular warp.

FIGURE 67. Tying colors together at the front bar.

FIGURE 68. Shed stick inserted under every other *top* thread and tied with string to prevent it from falling out.

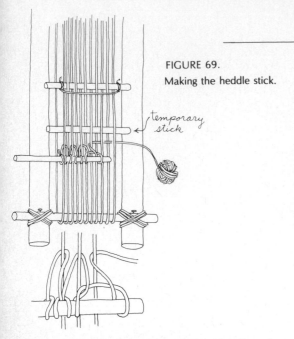

FIGURE 69.
Making the heddle stick.

temporary stick

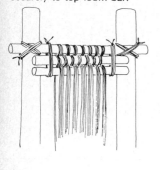

FIGURE 70. The completed heddle stick.

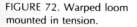

FIGURE 71. Warp stabilizers inserted and tied securely to top loom bar.

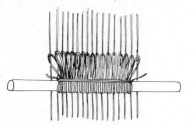

FIGURE 72. Warped loom mounted in tension.

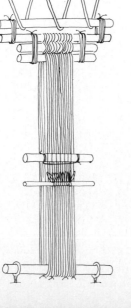

To make the string heddles, place the ball of string (g) to the right of the warp and pull the end through the top shed (where you inserted the last dowel). Tie the end of the string loosely to the heddle stick (f). Take this stick and hold it in the left hand so that it is poised parallel with the other sticks, and with its right end just over the left-hand warp threads. With your right hand pull the heddle string out from between the first and second warp threads on the left, and make a clockwise twist and slip the loop onto the right end of the stick. Adjust the length (slightly less than your batten is wide) and make another loop in a *counter*clockwise direction and slip it onto the heddle stick. This makes one complete heddle, which won't change in length during the weaving as do the heddles described for the Navajo loom. (Although I've never tried these heddles on the Navajo loom it seems as if they would work well.)

After the last heddle is made, fasten the string around the heddle stick and bring it back over the heddles, pushing the heddles together. Pass it under the original loose tie, fasten it again and bring it back once more over the heddles for the final tie. This keeps the heddles nicely in order. Remove the temporary stick.

Stabilizing the Warp

To keep the warp threads in order at the top loom bar, and to prevent them from slipping when beating down the weft, we insert two extra sticks (e) at the top of the loom in the following manner.

Pick up small groups of threads from the bottom warp threads just below the top loom bar, and bring them up through the top ones to form a cross. (To do this you may have to release the tension of the warp by removing the nails and loosening the lashings at the top of the loom bar.) Insert one stick underneath these threads. Below this stick, pick up the underneath threads and slip the second stick under these. Tie the two sticks and the loom bar securely together.

Mounting the Loom in Tension

Detach the loom bars from the warp winding logs or 2-by-4s, unless you are simply going to use this as your loom frame (which you may do). You are now going to stretch the warp vertically, in tension, by attaching the upper and lower bars to some fixed object. (See heading in this chapter: The Loom Frame and Alternatives.) Although not essential, an intermediate bar (which I call the "intermediate tension bar")—one of the "e" sticks—tied to the upper loom bar, and then lashed to the rigid upper support of the frame (or whatever), makes future tension adjustments easier than if the loom bars themselves are fixed in a rigid position.

However you set the loom up, it should be in a fixed position, so that when you give the heddle stick a yank (which you have to do quite vigorously) the whole loom frame won't come forward—a most annoying occurrence.

Warp Tension

The rope that is lashed around the intermediate tension bar and the fixed upper member of the loom frame should not be tied in a knot, but simply wrapped around with the ends tucked under (leave long ends). This makes it easy to undo and apply or release the tension when necessary.

To apply tension, start at one end and pull each turn of the lashing, taking up the slack from the previous one until you have tightened it all across; then wrap the end around a couple of times and tuck it under to hold it in position. To release the tension simply undo one end of the rope and give the lashing extra length and rewrap the end.

In warp-face weaving (which is what you will be doing on this loom) the tension should not be too great. It should be just enough so that the sheds separate nicely, but at the same time, the warp ends must be allowed to "bend" around the weft. Too tight a warp will mean that the weft cannot be packed down properly. Too loose a warp will mean poor edges. It must be tight enough so that the warp does not rotate when the batten is used to beat in the weft.

How to Operate the Sheds

The first shed is formed by the shed stick, and is called the *stick shed*. It is always present, but to open it for weaving bring the shed stick down to meet the heddle stick at a point about 18 inches above the weaving level. Move them up and down together to separate any sticky warp threads. Insert the batten (sharp edge down) into the shed below the sticks, and turn it on edge (sharp edge back) to hold the shed open, at a point about 1 foot above the weaving level. The space below the batten is the shed through which the weft will pass.

The second shed is formed by removing the batten and pushing the shed stick up and out of the way. With the left hand pull the heddle stick forward with a good tug, and insert the batten into the shed behind it. This is called the *pull shed*. If the warp threads don't separate properly, move the heddle stick up and down on the warp to clear them (although this tends to wear out your warp), or flick the batten across the warp threads above the heddle stick. Turn the batten on edge as before. The heddle stick should be *above* the batten; then it will remain in place and not slide down to interfere with the weaving.

Preparing the Weft

Wind the weft onto the stick shuttle or in the form of a butterfly as described previously.

The Weaving

Start the weaving about 12 inches up from the knots. This will make a 10-inch fringe.

Make the stick shed. Pass your weft through, leaving a tail the same length as the fringe. (If your weft is a different yarn from the warp and would show up in the fringe, lock the tail back in the weaving in the next shed.)

Change to the pull shed. Pass weft back through and pull it up against the edge warp thread. You will notice that the warp threads all bunch up on each other at this edge. To avoid this, hold the weft thread outstretched where it comes out of the previous shed, while you pull the butterfly or shuttle through with the other hand. You must do this with every row of weaving if you want good edges. Adjust the width of the weaving in these first few rows so that the warp nicely covers the weft.

For plain warp-face weaving make these two sheds alternately; with sharp edge of your batten beat down the previous row of weft (a very vigorous beat is required), and pass the shuttle through the shed each time. The beating is always done *after* the shed is changed to make a nice tight weave. The traditional Hopi pickup technique will be described under Project I. Traditional Hopi Belt.

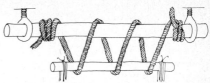

FIGURE 73. The intermediate tension bar properly lashed.

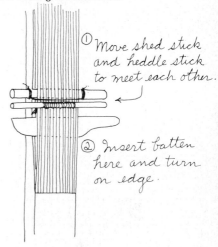

FIGURE 74. Making the stick shed.

① Move shed stick and heddle stick to meet each other.

② Insert batten here and turn on edge.

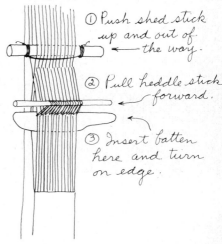

FIGURE 75. Making the pull shed.

① Push shed stick up and out of the way.

② Pull heddle stick forward.

③ Insert batten here and turn on edge.

FIGURE 76. The first two rows of weaving.

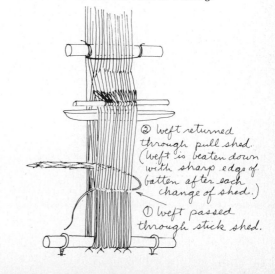

② Weft returned through pull shed. (Weft is beaten down with sharp edge of batten after each change of shed.)

① Weft passed through stick shed.

Keeping the Edges Even

Weaving belts on this loom is very much like weaving on the inkle loom, and many of the same weaving techniques apply. See Chapter III, "The Inkle Loom: Keeping the Edges Even," for notes on how to weave nice tight, straight edges.

Rotating the Warp

When the weaving builds up and you wish to lower the weaving level, rotate the warp around the two loom bars. To do this, release the tension by untying the rope at the top of your loom and loosen the lashings. Now pull the warp down and around the loom bars with your hands, or put the batten in a shed and press down.

Cleaning the Heddles

See this heading in Chapter III, "The Inkle Loom."

Splicing the Weft

See this heading in Chapter II, "Card Weaving."

Mending Broken Warp Threads

See this heading in Chapter III, "The Inkle Loom."

Cutting Off

Weave up to a point that will leave the same fringe allowance as at the start or as far as you can. (The warp will not separate well after a certain point.) The knots in the warp will have traveled around over the top bar. Break off the weft, leaving a tail the same length as the warp ends for fringing. If the weft yarn is different from the warp and you don't want it to show up in the fringe, sew the tail back in the previous shed with a needle.

Loosen the tension; pull the heddle stick out of the heddles and pull the string out of the shed. Remove the shed stick. With scissors cut across the warp threads directly below and above the knots.

Finishing

Trim weft splices and sew in any broken warp threads. Finish with twisted fringe, which is the traditional Hopi way, or a 4-strand braid.

Steam press.

See Chapter VIII, "Finishing Techniques," for directions on how to do all this.

Project I. Traditional Hopi Belt

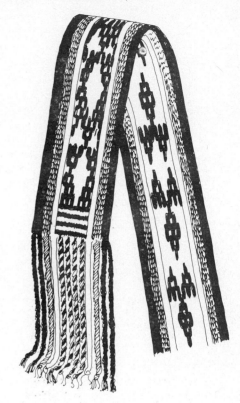

FIGURE 77. Traditional Hopi belt.

(This project can also be woven on the inkle loom.)

The Hopi technique of making a pattern on the belt is similar to the pickup techniques described in Chapter III, "The Inkle Loom." The main difference is that for every thread that is picked up one is dropped, thus making the design come out in the opposite color on the reverse side of the belt. There is no right or wrong side to this type of Hopi belt.

The belts or sashes are usually made in an ample size—often 8 feet long and 4 or 5 inches wide, with elegant long fringes. We will start with a smaller belt and experiment with the different possibilities of patterns and backgrounds. Then you can design a belt as you please.

Materials

Warp—2-,3-, or 4-ply medium-weight wool yarn tightly twisted. (Respun yarn if possible.)

Amount: Approximately 6 ounces.

Suggested colors: Red and black; green for border (traditional Hopi colors); *or* natural black, white, and gray.

Weft—Same as the warp, or cotton yarn the same weight or slightly finer.

Amount: About 40 yards.

Color: Same as the edge warp threads.

Directions

Set up the loom as in the general directions, using 82 threads and following the draft in Figure 78. Notice that in the center area of the draft the black threads (which will be on top of the shed stick), and the red threads (which will be attached to the heddles) alternate. This center section is for the pickup pattern.

FIGURE 78. Draft for Hopi belt.

Weave an inch of plain weave (following the general directions) just to establish your width.

Pickup technique: Make the pull shed, and hold it open with your left hand. This will put the red threads on top and the black underneath.

Row 1. Starting on the right side of the warp, transfer all the upper border threads to your right hand. Pick up the first black thread underneath. Drop the following red thread to the underneath threads. Leave the next black thread below. Transfer the red thread to the right hand. Repeat this all across the pattern area. What you are actually doing is working in pairs. You switch positions of the first black thread and the first red thread. The next pair you leave *as is*. The next pair you switch, and the next pair you leave as is. And so on. Transfer the left-hand upper border threads also. Now insert the batten in this new shed that you have just picked up, beat, and turn on edge. Pass the weft through this shed.

Row 2. Make the stick shed. Weave it in the regular manner.

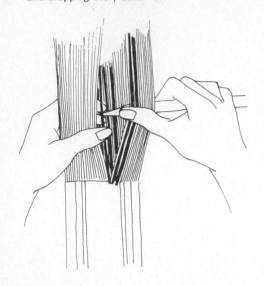

FIGURE 79. Picking up every other black thread and dropping every other red.

Row 3. Make the pull shed and do the picking and dropping as before, but this time pick up the black threads that you left before, and drop the red threads that were not dropped before.

Row 4. Make the stick shed. Weave it in the regular manner. By repeating these 4 rows of weaving you make the pickup pattern in black. To make the pickup pattern in red, simply start on the stick shed (which puts the red threads underneath), pick up the red threads, and drop the black.

All designs are made from these two pickup weaves—one where the black comes to the top and one where the red comes to the top, and the pattern comes out in reverse color underneath.

The design possibilities

1. Make the pickup pattern in black only within a certain shape (like a diamond); leave the background plain weave (striped).

2. Do the same but in red.

3. Make a shape in the black pickup and make the background in the red pickup.

4. Do the same only in reverse colors.

5. Only outline the shape (in either color) on a striped (plain-weave) ground.

6. Outline the shape on a ground of pickup in the opposite color.

Designs 3 and 4 (the authentic Hopi belt weave) are the most complicated to weave. Part of the row of weaving is done in the pick and drop, and the remainder of the row in plain weave. For instance, if the right-hand half of the pattern area is to be black and the other half red, you will be doing the pickup weave for the black on the right half of the row, and the plain weave for the red on the left-hand side of the row. On the return shed you will be doing the plain weave for the black on the right side and the pickup weave for the red on the left side.

Since there won't be as much takeup in the center pattern area (since the threads make long skips and don't have to do so much bending around the weft threads), the border warp threads may begin to be tighter than the center pattern threads. When you first notice this, weave two rows of pattern area for one row of border weaving every once in a while to keep the tension of the warp threads even.

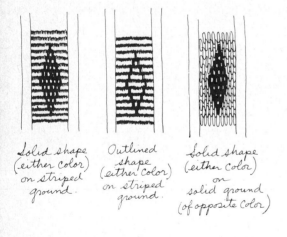

FIGURE 80. Various design possibilities.

Solid shape (either color) on striped ground.

Outlined shape (either color) on striped ground.

Solid shape (either color) on solid ground (of opposite color).

Suggestions for Other Projects

Weave any of the projects and suggested projects in Chapter III, "The Inkle Loom."

Weave the double cloth sash as described in Chapter V, "The Backstrap Loom." The warp must be set up in the figure eight as described there, but may then be mounted vertically. Rather than rotating the warp around the loom bars, the lower end of the weaving must be rolled up as with the backstrap loom. The vertical position of the warp is more convenient than the horizontal warp of the backstrap loom.

THE BACKSTRAP LOOM

FIGURE 81. The backstrap loom and tools.

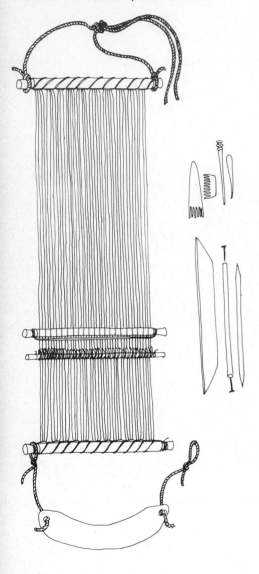

A Description of the Loom

The backstrap loom is one of the oldest and most common looms throughout the world. It consists of two bars around which a continuous warp is wound in a figure eight. One loom bar is attached to a permanent object such as a tree, and the other bar is attached to the weaver by means of a strap around the weaver's back. The weaver sits on the ground in a position that holds the warp in tension, and leans forward or backward to decrease or increase the tension.

A shed stick is permanently placed under every other warp thread, and the alternate threads are strung with string heddles and can be pulled forward with a heddle stick. In this way the two sheds are formed.

A batten (or sword), a smooth flat stick, is inserted in the sheds and turned on edge to hold the shed open, leaving the hands free to insert the weft. The batten is also used to beat the weft into place. Other tools are used to beat in the weft also: these are wooden combs, or just a pointed tool, called a pick, fashioned out of hardwood or occasionally deer horn or llama bone. The weft is usually wound on a crude stick. A stretcher device is used to insure a consistent width to the fabric. As the weaving progresses the fabric is rolled up on the front bar.

In Mexico the words for backstrap weaving are *tejiendo de palos,* weaving with sticks. There are various ways of setting up the backstrap loom. I will describe the traditional Mexican way.

Although some suppliers sell backstrap loom kits, the few sticks of wood and the backstrap are easily assembled at home.

Its Uses

There is no denying the convenience of this loom. It provides a professional weaving tool that can easily be rolled up with the batten, shuttle, and stretcher and put away. It can be set up anywhere, outdoors or in the home, with nothing more than a stationary object at hand to which the one end of the warp can be tied. This is perhaps why it is still used all over the world today.

The use of the weaver's body to provide the warp tension, however, places a limitation on the possible width that can be woven. The weaver cannot, of course, weave wider than the arms can reach; but actually she can't even weave this wide, as the body cannot put sufficient tension on a warp that is too wide. I have seen Indian weavers in Mexico weave about 30 inches wide on the backstrap loom, but I believe that must certainly be the maximum width one can weave efficiently. Usually the weaving is about 15 inches wide or less. For large fabrics, narrow strips must be woven and then sewn together. Whenever you see a blanket or cloth made up of narrow strips like this, the piece was undoubtedly woven on a backstrap loom. Warps may be quite long, if desired, and the excess warp can be rolled up at the far end.

Both warp-face and weft-face fabrics can be woven on this loom, as well as balanced weaves. For weft-face and balanced weaves, the stretcher is an essential tool.

Primitive people usually weave right up to both top and bottom edges so as not to waste their warp and to make a sturdy fabric with four selvedges (see Weaving Four Selvedges in this chapter). This process, which is rather tedious, may be eliminated by allowing an extra foot or 18 inches of warp length and fringing the two ends of the fabric; there will be a certain amount of wasted warp at one end.

The loom is sometimes used with a rigid heddle, but in this book I will only describe the string-heddle-stick arrangement.

What You Will Need to Set Up and Weave on a Backstrap Loom

a. A warping board, or stakes set in the ground.

b. 4 sticks or 3/4-inch dowels a few inches longer than your weaving is wide. (Two of these are loom bars; one is for rolling up the fabric, and one is the shed stick.) They should be grooved around their diameter at both ends at points slightly farther apart than the width of the weaving.)

c. 1 stick or 3/8-inch to 1/2-inch dowel the same length as above for the heddle stick.

d. A ball of medium-fine cotton twine for winding the warp onto the loom bars and making the heddles.

e. A few feet of rope to tie the end of warp to a post or tree.

f. The backstrap.

g. The batten.

h. The shuttle.

i. The stretcher.

j. The comb.

k. Picks.

l. The yarn.

The Backstrap

The backstrap is usually made of a piece of leather about 4 inches wide and about 1 1/2 to 2 feet in length. It should be wide enough so that it doesn't cut into the back, and long enough to extend to the sides of the hips. Each end of the backstrap is attached to ropes long enough to reach the front loom bar, to which it is attached. The length should be adjusted so that the front bar is held right up against the belly. It is usually most comfortable when set just slightly below the natural waistline. Lacking the leather, several layers of cloth sewed together make a nice backstrap.

FIGURE 82. The backstrap.

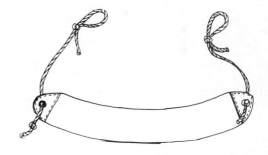

The Batten

The batten for the backstrap loom can be slightly wider than battens for other primitive looms since warp tension on the backstrap loom can be decreased when turning the batten on edge within the shed and then increased again for beating in the weft.

It is made of a piece of hardwood about 3/8 inch thick and 2 inches wide. The ends are cut at an angle so that one edge is shorter than the other. The short edge is whittled or filed down to a fairly sharp edge, while the longer edge is simply squared off. The sharp edge is used to beat in the weft. When the batten is turned to hold the shed open, some weavers bring the sharp edge forward and other weavers do just the opposite. The length should be such that the short edge is just a little wider than the width of the warp.

A hand-carved batten like they make in Mexico is nice to have, but in lieu of this, one may be purchased from a supplier listed in Chapter XIII.

FIGURE 83. The batten.

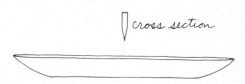

cross section

FIGURE 84. The stretcher and how it is used.

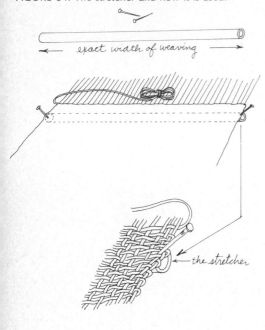

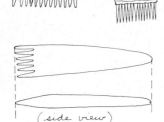

FIGURE 85. Types of combs used with the backstrap loom.

FIGURE 86. Picks made of llama bone (top), deer horn, and wood.

The Butterfly and the Shuttle

For narrow weavings I find the butterfly the most convenient way to package the weft. For wider weavings you will need a shuttle. The shuttle most commonly used with the backstrap loom is the same as described in Chapter IV, ''The Hopi Belt Loom: The Butterfly vs. the Shuttle.''

The Stretcher

A stretcher is nearly always used when weaving on the backstrap loom, to insure an even width to the fabric. This is made out of a hollow stick of reed or bamboo, and must be the *exact* length of the width of the material. It is placed underneath the woven fabric just below the weaving level, and a nail is pierced through the fabric from the top and into the hollow tube on both sides. This keeps the fabric from drawing in as the weaving progresses. It is most essential in weft-face weaving, where improper weft tension would tend to narrow the fabric. An exception to the rule of using a stretcher would be narrow fabrics of warp-face structure, such as belts and sashes.

This tool you will probably have to make yourself, as I don't know of any commercial stretchers made for such narrow fabrics.

The Comb

The wooden combs seen in the Mexican markets are sometimes used to beat in the weft of tightly woven weft-face structures and tapestry weaves. Another type of comb is made by lacing or twining very fine sticks together. A fork similar to the Navajo fork can also be used. If you can't locate one of these wooden combs or forks, an ordinary dime-store comb with coarse teeth will do fine.

Picks

A pointed tool anywhere from 3 to 7 inches long and about 1/2 inch in diameter, tapering down to a fine rounded point, is sometimes used when the weft is to be very firmly packed in place. You can also use it to help separate the shed in warp-face fabrics, by flicking it along the warp threads.

The longer picks are also used for picking up warp threads to form new sheds for brocade and pickup patterns.

You can fashion a pick out of a length of 3/8-inch dowel.

Yarn Specifications

In all cases your warp yarn must be strong and at least two-ply. And it is best that it be smooth rather than fuzzy. This will eliminate exasperating difficulties in the weaving process, which is going to be difficult enough for the beginner. Please read Chapter I, ''The Basics of Weaving: Your Yarns,'' for further information. The specific yarns to use will be listed under each project that follows.

Winding the Warp

In figuring your warp length decide on the finished length of the piece and then add 1 inch per foot for balanced weaves, or 2 inches per foot for warp-face or leno weaves. This will allow for warp takeup. If you are planning to weave right up to the selvedge at both ends—a tedious process—this will be your warp length. If not, allow an extra 18 inches or slightly less to this warp length; fringe can be made from the leftover warp ends.

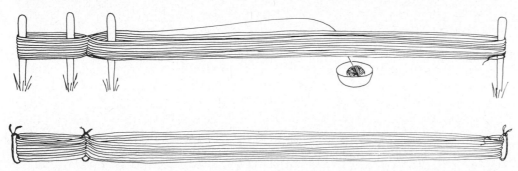

FIGURE 87. Winding the warp.

Wind a continuous warp, using a single ball or spool of the warp thread, in a figure eight on a warping board or onto stakes in the ground. Choose the pegs of the warping board that will make the correct length, or put the stakes in the ground the correct distance apart. Down to the far peg (or stake) and back again makes two warp threads. Wind as many times as necessary to make the correct number of warp threads: number of threads per inch times number of inches wide the fabric is to be. To change color of warp threads, simply tie on a new color to the broken-off end of the first. Make any ties in the warp right at the first stake or peg—and do not tie it *around* the peg. Leave a tail for darning in if you are weaving four selvedges.

Caution: It is very easy for the last threads that are wound to be tighter than the first, because the stakes pull in, or the warping board is flimsy. Be very careful this does not happen; it will make your warp longer on one side, and cause great difficulties in the weaving.

Preserve the cross (or lease) where the figure eight crosses itself by tying a string through both sides of the cross. Tie a string through the loop at both ends of the warp. Remove the warp from the board or stakes.

FIGURE 88. Stretching the warp in tension.

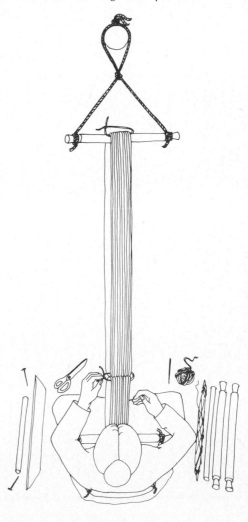

Stretching the Warp in Tension

Place two of the grooved sticks (b) through the loops at each end of the warp. Attach the rope to one end of one of the sticks, lead it around a post or tree, and tie the other end to the same bar. Attach your backstrap to the other bar, put the strap around you, and attach the other end of the backstrap rope to the loom bar. Sit so the warp is in tension. Beside you have all your tools and supplies, as well as a pair of scissors.

Attaching the Warp to the Loom Bars

Now cut the string that was tied through the loop at the end of the warp on your front loom bar, and the string that preserved the cross. Spread out the warp threads in groups of about 1 inch each, with the correct number of warp threads in each group so that the warp is the full width of the planned weaving.

FIGURE 89. Attaching the warp to the loom bars.

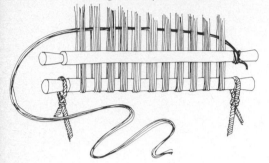
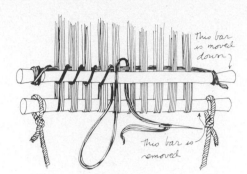
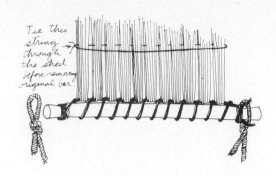

FIGURE 90. Making the heddles.

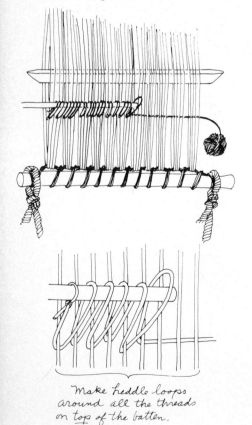

Make heddle loops around all the threads on top of the batten.

Using the ball of twine (d) make a 6-fold strand that is 4 times the length of the width of your weaving.

Take the third grooved stick (b) and hold it above your front bar. Tie one end of the 6-fold strand of twine to the groove on the right side of this new bar, and bring the rest of it through the shed formed by the warp threads around the original bar. Pull it taut and tie a loop around the groove on the left side of this new bar, leaving a long end of the twine free. Thread this free end into a large needle and sew it around this bar and the twine that is under the warp threads at 1-inch intervals. There should be the same number of warp threads per inch in between each turn. Pull this twine through tightly each turn, and fasten its end by tying it around the groove on the right again.

This method of attaching the loom bar to the warp not only allows you to start weaving right at the beginning of the warp (see Weaving Four Selvedges in this chapter), but is a convenient method of spreading the warp and holding it securely to the loom bar even if you do not intend to do this. (To weave 4 selvedges, turn to that heading at this point because things are done in a slightly different order from that which I describe here.) Move this new lashed bar down to the end of the warp.

Tie a string through the shed to preserve it. Detach the original loom bar from the backstrap and remove it from the shed. Turn the loom around and do the same at the other end. The grooved bar you just removed will be your new bar at this second end. (The extra bar will be used eventually when you need to roll the woven fabric up as you weave.)

Making the Heddles

Attach the new lashed bar to your backstrap. Insert the batten into the shed. Attach your backstrap to the new bar and remove the original bar. Turn the batten on edge.

Take the ball of twine (d) and lead the end of it through the shed from right to left, leaving the ball sitting at your right. Tie the end to one end of the heddle stick (c). While holding the heddle stick poised over the warp (see Figure 90), pull the twine out from between the first and second *upper* warp threads (the ones that are on top of the batten) and loop it over the heddle stick. Hold that loop in place with your left thumb until the next loop is made. The length of the heddle (the distance from the warp thread to the heddle stick) should be just slightly less than your batten is wide. Now pull the twine out from between the second and third warp threads and loop it over the heddle stick in the *opposite* direction from the way it was laid before. Repeat this all the way across the warp, attaching each thread that is held up by the batten. You will have to slide the heddles along the stick to make room for the new ones as you make them. Cut the string and tie its end to the heddle stick again.

This clever way of making the heddles (one heddle extending from the top side of the stick and the alternate one from the bottom side) allows you to insert and maneuver a second stick (placed under the heddles right along with the heddle stick) so as to form a shed that lifts only *every other heddled warp thread* (every fourth thread of the warp) when desired. See Project V in this chapter, Figures 109 and 110.

The Shed Stick

Place the shed stick (b) in the shed that is formed on the other side of the cross (under all the warp threads that are *not* heddled). You tied a string through this shed before you removed the first loom bar. Attach this string to each end of the shed stick to prevent it from accidentally falling out of the shed.

How to Operate the Sheds

Now let's practice making the two different sheds before you actually start weaving.

Sit in such a position that when you lean back slightly the warp is in good tension, and when you lean forward slightly it is relaxed. It is most convenient for weaving when the warp is at an angle with the far end raised.

The first shed is formed already by the shed stick. Lower this stick to meet the heddle stick, which should be about 15 inches above the weaving level. With your right hand insert the batten sharp edge down into the space below the heddle stick and turn it on edge (blunt side forward). This opens the shed even wider, leaving a nice space through which to pass the weft. This shed is called the "stick shed." When weaving, the weft will be passed through the shed *below* the batten.

The second shed is formed by removing the batten, pushing the shed stick up and out of the way and pulling the heddles forward (or up) with the left hand. While holding the heddle stick up, insert the batten into the space below and again turn it on its edge. This is called the "pull shed."

This sounds easy, but if your warp threads are close together or sticky, the threads of the pull shed do not separate all that easily. There is a little trick that helps. Before

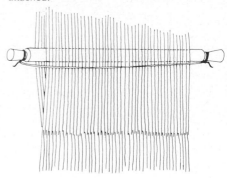

FIGURE 91. The shed stick in place with string attached.

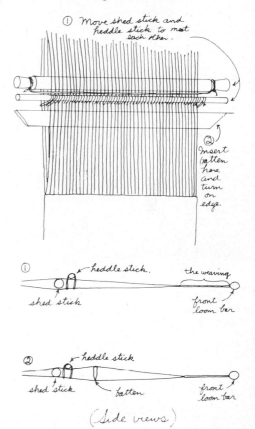

FIGURE 92. Making the stick shed.

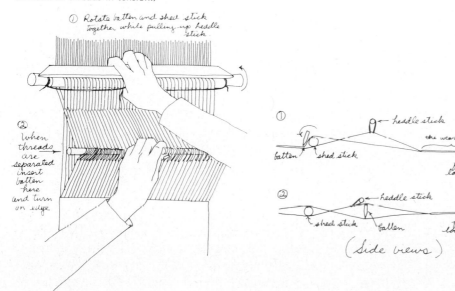

FIGURE 93. Making the pull shed. (Notice how batten and shed stick are rotated to hold *un*heddled threads in tension.)

inserting the batten release the tension on the warp and place the batten right on top of the shed stick. While holding the two together (with right hand) rotate them away from you as you pull the heddle stick up (with left hand). What this does is pulls the threads not attached to the heddles out in a straight line—more or less in tension— while the threads that are attached to the heddles are lifted up at a sharp angle. This separates the threads more distinctly, and you can then insert the batten, turn it on edge, and increase the tension again. For real problem warps, your pick will come in handy for flicking across the sticky threads, or actually running it down vertically to separate them.

Preparing the Weft Yarn

For narrow weavings wind the weft in the form of a butterfly. For weaving 5 inches and wider you will probably find the shuttle more convenient.

The Weaving

If you are not going to weave up to the top selvedge, then you should leave some unwoven warp at the start also, so you can have fringes at both ends. In this case weave the first 6 inches with strips of rags inserted in alternate sheds and packed down with the batten.

Starting after this (or right at the beginning, if you want 4 selvedges) make your first shed and pass the weft through; pull it so that the tail lies an inch or so in from the edge. Change the shed and pack the weft down with the sharp edge of the batten. Pass the weft back through again; this time pull it so that it just pulls up against the edge warp thread but does not pull the warp thread out of alignment. Change the shed and pack this shot into place with the batten. Right at the beginning your warp threads may be spaced very unevenly. Use the wooden comb to pack down the weft also, and this will help bring the warp threads into correct position. After these first two rows of weaving, the way you lay the weft into place is very important. (See Notes on Weft Tension in this chapter.)

Keep changing the sheds, packing in the previous weft, and passing a new weft through the shed, packing it down.

Notes on Warp Tension

Once you get the feel of it, the tension of the warp on your backstrap loom will be perfect all the time. It's not a matter of tightening up the loom bars or beams in a fixed position as it is with other looms. Your body will adjust the tension exactly right for each step in progress. When you are pulling the weft through, up against that edge warp thread, you want the tension to be good so the warp thread puts up some resistance and doesn't allow the weft to pull it out of position. When you are packing in the weft the tension must be strong also—the most for weft-face weaving and the least for warp-face weaving. For weft-face weaving you will lean back as hard as you can and beat down hard with the batten while doing so. Lean forward to decrease the tension when making the sheds.

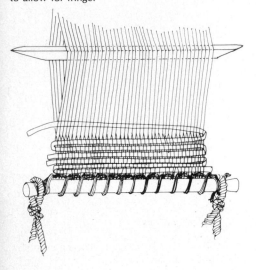

FIGURE 94. Weaving the first few rows with rags to allow for fringe.

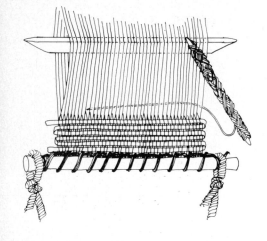

FIGURE 95. Placing the first shot and beating the weft with batten.

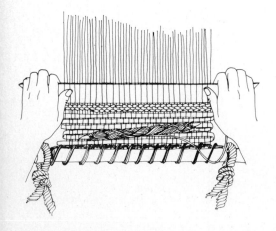

Notes on Weft Tension

You have the same problem of adjusting the tension of the weft in each row of weaving as you do on any loom.

For warp-face weaving the weft is simply pulled straight across and briefly packed in place before the shed is changed.

In balanced weaves the weft should lie in a loose arc before it is beaten into place. This will probably allow enough extra length for it to bend over and under the warp threads. Do not make too big an arc, or the weft will loop in some places after it is packed down. For weft-face weaves the best method is to feed in extra length as needed while you pack the weft into place with the wooden comb. Or, after the weft is laid across the shed in a loose arc, take your pick and press it down to meet the weaving every few inches, starting at the side where weft turns around the warp thread. This will make a series of small arcs that may be beaten down with the batten.

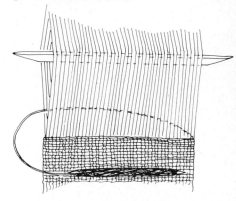

FIGURE 96. Weft lying in a loose arc before being beaten into place (method of allowing extra weft length for balanced weaves).

Beating

The weft can be only minimally beaten into place until after the shed is changed. It is then that the weft gets its real beating—if that is what it needs. The batten does most of the job, and insures a consistent level of the weaving line (the fell). But in some instances the comb is used to advantage—for balanced weaves to help keep the warp spaced correctly, and for weft-face weaves to pack the weft in even more tightly. The comb need not be used in warp-face weaving; a good sharp beat with the batten after the shed is changed will suffice.

In Mexico I have seen a weaver beat with the batten for about one or two inches of weaving, and then, to pack a resisting weft firmly into place to completely cover the warp, the weaver will grasp a group of warp threads in one hand while she packs the weft in with her pick; she does this bit by bit across the entire warp.

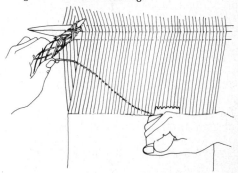

FIGURE 97. Two methods of allowing extra weft length for weft-face weaving.

Keeping the Edges Even

This is one of the most difficult problems on any loom. The weft tension is the primary factor to be considered; it must be exactly right so that after the weft has done all its bending around the warp threads, it will relax into a position that is the exact length to fit between the two edges of the fabric. You can very quickly tell if you are not allowing enough extra length: the weaving will start drawing in at the edges. And conversely, if you are allowing too much, the weaving will start bulging out at the edges, or buckling in the middle.

Pulling the weft thread so that it just barely touches the edge warp thread, but does not move it, will help to make nice even edges.

For balanced weaves and weft-face weaves you must use a stretcher. (See this heading in this chapter.) After you have woven a couple of inches you should apply the stretcher to the fabric, and then move it at least every two inches.

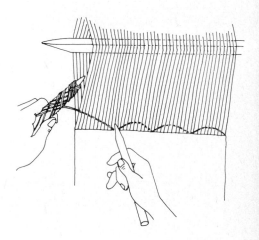

Cleaning the Heddles

See this section in Chapter III, "The Inkle Loom."

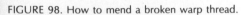

FIGURE 98. How to mend a broken warp thread.

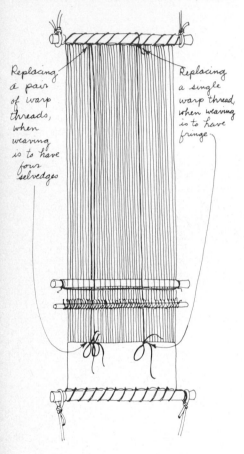

Replacing a pair of warp threads, when weaving is to have four selvedges

Replacing a single warp thread, when weaving is to have fringe

FIGURE 99. Using an extra stick to roll the fabric up.

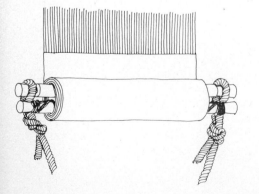

Splicing the Weft

See this section in Chapter VII, "The Treadle Loom." The techniques for joining weft ends are exactly the same.

Mending Broken Warp Threads

For a perfect fabric any knots in the warp should be avoided. You hope no threads will break, but if one does you can simply tie on a new thread of the proper color up at the top loom bar (*if* you are not going to be weaving right up to the selvedge), then bring it down to meet the broken thread at the fell, and tie a bowknot there, making sure the tension is right. The two ends will be woven into the weaving after the fabric is off the loom (see Chapter VIII, "Finishing Techniques: Mending"). If you are going to weave right up to the top selvedge, then the entire warp thread that goes up to the top bar and back down again should be replaced. This will mean tying two knots at the fell, and these can both be woven in later. I prefer this knot-tying technique to using a pin as a cleat as some weaving books recommend; it's much quicker.

Rolling the Fabric Up as the Weaving Progresses

When you have woven so much that the fell is too far from you to weave comfortably, take your backstrap off the loom bar, and place the extra stick or dowel (b) right on top of the front loom bar and roll the two up together to within about two inches of the fell. Reattach your backstrap to *one* of these bars; the other will act as a brake to prevent unrolling.

Weaving Four Selvedges (Optional)

If you are weaving four selvedges, make the heddles and weave a few inches at the first end of the warp before you turn the loom around to attach the second loom bar. Then weave from the second end until it becomes difficult to separate the sheds as you approach the few inches of weaving that you did at the other end, switch to a smaller batten, and follow the directions given under this heading in Chapter VI, "The Navajo Loom." In most Mexican, Central American, and South American weaving, you will discover an area of about three to six inches that is more loosely woven and with the design simplified. This is where the weaver worked with a needle and darned the weft into place.

Cutting Off

When you can no longer weave with ease (or after you have completed the weaving right up to the top selvedge), simply slice through the spiral wrapping with a razor and remove all strings and rags that are not a part of the weaving.

Finishing

If there are any warp ends, finish with any fringe that would be appropriate. Darn in warp and weft ends. Wash, if desired to soften the fabric, and steam press.

See Chapter VIII, "Finishing Techniques," for directions on how to do all these things.

Project I. Quechquemitl (Mexican)*

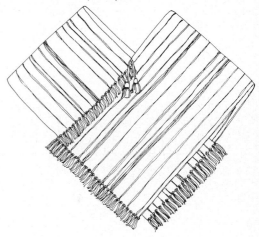

FIGURE 100. A quechquemitl.

(This project can also be woven on the treadle loom.)

This is a unique type of poncho made in Mexico. It is a very ingenious design, simple to make, and fits very well. It is more suitable as a woman's or child's garment than as a man's.

The directions here are for a woman's size in a modified warp-face striped fabric of wool. In Mexico quechquemitls are made of wool, cotton, or sometimes even tie-dyed silk.

Materials

Warp—Medium or medium-fine wool, 2 or more plies, pliable and not scratchy.
Color: Any number of blending colors for adjacent stripes. (See Chapter XI, "Design and Color: Choosing Colors.")
Amount: Approximately 1 to 1 1/2 pounds altogether.
Weft—Same as the warp.
Color: One of the darker warp colors.
Amount: Approximately 1/4 to 1/2 pound.

Directions

The quechquemitl is woven in two identical separate pieces. Each piece is twice as long as it is wide. A single warp is wound that will be enough to weave both pieces.

Wind the warp (see general directions) so that there will be about 12 to 16 warp threads per inch for medium-weight yarn, and 16 to 20 per inch for medium-fine yarn. Multiply the width of the weaving in inches times number of threads per inch; a 15-inch width makes a good size for a woman.

Fringes are very appropriate for the quechquemitl so there is no point in weaving the 4 selvedges.

The length of the warp will be 60 inches for the two pieces, plus an extra 3 feet for takeup, fringing, and waste (8 feet altogether). Change warp colors as you please to make a striped pattern.

FIGURE 101. Sewing the two pieces together to make a quechquemitl.

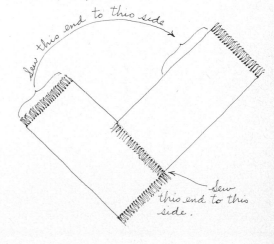

Weave 4 inches at the beginning of the weaving with rags; this will leave warp enough for a fringe. Then weave one length: 30 inches, plus about 3 inches to allow for shrinkage when piece is washed. Measure when not in tension. Then leave an area of unwoven warp for about 8 inches (for fringe at the end of the first piece and the beginning of the second piece). Weave the next piece the same length exactly as the first.

Beat the weft in well with the batten. The weft may be pulled straight across, as it will not need extra length. If you have difficulty with the edges use a stretcher.

Cut off at the top loom bar, leaving 4 inches of warp for fringing, and cut directly through the middle of the 8-inch unwoven area.

Make either whipped fringe or zigzag fringe. The two pieces are then sewn

* A good project for beginners.

together as shown in Figure 101. If you zigzag them together on the sewing machine, it can be done at the same time you are zigzagging the fringe. This makes an almost invisible join. Or hand sew if you are a purist. Add tassels as desired. Wash (optional) and steam press.

Project II. Warp-Face Ikat Stole (West African)

(This project can also be woven on the treadle loom.)

"Ikat" means that the warp or weft (or both) is tie-dyed before being woven. This stole has a tie-dyed warp. A tie-dyed design gives a slightly blurred effect in the weaving, since the threads are not in absolutely perfect alignment after they are woven. It is a very old technique, used in many different countries, for achieving quite intricate designs in a structure of plain weaving. "Ikat" is a Japanese word that is generally accepted as the common term for this technique. It replaces "jaspe," the word originally used in Central and South America.

This particular design comes from the Ivory Coast of West Africa. The original piece was done in indigo-dyed cotton, with single horizontal raised bands of brilliant gold-colored soumak. You will tie-dye only a few sections of the warp, and combine these sections with plain stripes. The stole should be 20 inches wide and 5 feet long, plus a 12-inch fringe on each end, for it to be a luxurious garment.

Materials

Warp—Medium- or medium-fine-weight wool, 2 or more plies. Strong and smooth, but soft; worsted yarn would be just right.
    Amount: Approximately 1 1/2 to 2 pounds.
    Color: Natural white.
Weft—Same as warp.
    Amount: Approximately 1/2 pound.
    Color: Natural white, <u>dyed in same dyebath with tie-dyed warp.</u>

Directions

Wind a warp about 8 feet long. Allow between 16 and 24 warp threads per inch of width, less for medium-weight yarn and more for medium-fine. Wind the warp in 1-inch sections, tying the cross and ends as directed in general instructions, so that each 1-inch section can be removed from the warping stakes or frame *separately* from each other section. Also temporarily tie each section that is to be tie-dyed in 2 or 3 places so the warp threads will stay aligned.

See Chapter X, "Dyeing: Techniques for Special Effects."

Make your design on paper (or use the design shown). Wrap the sections to be tie-dyed with cotton string; wrap very tightly and continuously around areas that are to remain white. Very interesting color blending may be achieved by doing more than one tying and dyeing on the same section, but I suggest you start with one color tie and dye. If desired wrap the sections so that all the fringe will be white.

When all the design sections are tied, dye them with other sections that are to be solid stripes with indigo dye or whatever you like (see Chapter X, "Dyeing"). Two sections dyed one other color, such as orange, may add interest.

Dry the sections and *before* untying all the wrapped areas arrange them in correct order on the loom bars. Untie them carefully so as not to let them get out of alignment; the remaining wet areas will dry out quickly as you attach the warp to the loom bars.

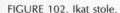

FIGURE 102. Ikat stole.

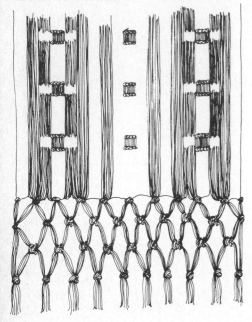

FIGURE 103. Wrapping sections to correspond with the design.

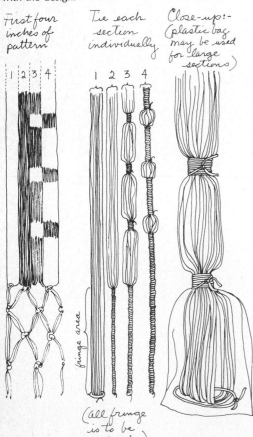

First four inches of pattern

Tie each section individually

Close-up:- (plastic bag may be used for large sections)

1 2 3 4

1 2 3 4

fringe area

(all fringe is to be undyed.)

(If you are doing this project on a treadle loom, of course, the sections will have to be cut and threaded on the loom.)

Continue as in general directions. At appropriate intervals in the tie-dye sections you can weave two rows of soumak in a contrasting color for added interest. See Chapter I, ''The Basics of Weaving: A Definition of Weaving,'' for an illustration of the soumak structure.

Allow 12 to 15 inches for fringe at each end. Cut off and finish with macramé fringe (or any fringe you desire). Wash (optional) and steam press.

Project III. Sash with Warp-Face Stripes and Weft-Face Bands (West African)

(This project can also be woven on the treadle loom.)

This sash is copied from a cloth from Ghana that was woven in narrow stripes of colorful cotton warp, with occasional sections of weft-face weaving. The weaving was about 6 inches wide, and several strips were sewn together to make a piece of cloth a yard wide. We will just weave one width. For the weft to cover the warp completely in the weft-face areas it skips over 6 warp threads at a time. This means that you will set up 2 extra heddle sticks to lift these groups of threads. The interesting possibilities in design are worth this added effort.

Materials
Warp—Medium-fine cotton or wool yarn, 2-ply for strength.
    Amount: Approximately 1/2 pound.
    Color: A variety of bright colors; make one color predominant.
Weft—The same as warp.
    Amount: Approximately 1/4 pound.
    Color: Variety of colors just as in warp.

Directions
Wind the warp about 24 to 30 ends per inch, 6 inches wide and about 8 feet long, changing warp colors about every half inch.

Set the warp on the loom bars and set up the shed stick and heddle stick as in general instructions.

Raise the shed stick and heddle stick up out of the way. Now, using your pick, pick up 6 threads in succession, skip 6, pick up 6, skip 6 all the way across the warp. Insert your batten under the threads you picked up and set it on edge. Now make a heddle stick with heddles for each of these raised threads. Do the same for the opposite groups of 6. This will be the fourth heddle stick.

These last 2 heddle sticks will be raised alternately when you want to weave the weft-face bands. In this case, when inserting the weft you must allow a great deal of extra length before packing it down. You will find that it tends to draw the edges in very easily.

Weave several inches of warp-face stripes and then switch to the weft-face weaving for 2 or 3 inches. By weaving these weft-face bands in various sequences of colors, you can get very interesting changing patterns. Alternating rows of 2 different colors makes vertical bands, which you can switch to make checkerboard patterns; 2 rows of one color and 2 rows of another will make wavy horizontal lines. An extra batten may be helpful in making the sheds. If the shed doesn't open properly

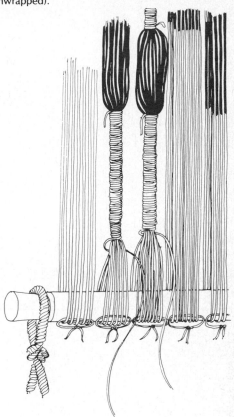

FIGURE 104. Placing the tied and dyed sections on the loom bars (two sections on right have been unwrapped).

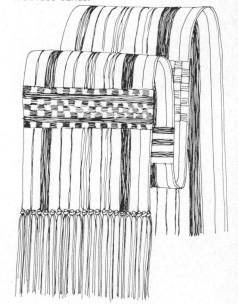

FIGURE 105. Sash with warp-face stripes and weft-face bands.

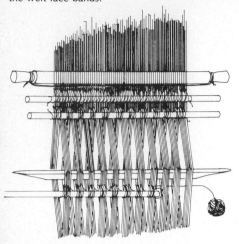

FIGURE 106. Making two extra heddle sticks for the weft-face bands.

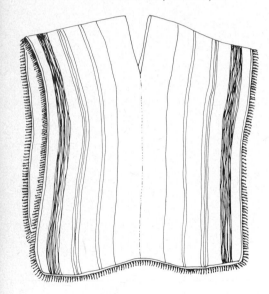

FIGURE 107. Poncho with warp-face stripes.

below the heddle sticks, use the extra batten and insert it immediately below the shed stick or directly under either of the two upper heddle sticks, and open the shed there; it will then open more clearly below the lower heddle stick, and you can insert your regular batten there to hold the shed open for weaving.

Cut off and finish as desired with fringes and/or tassels. Steam press.

Project IV. Poncho with Warp-Face Stripes (Bolivian)

(This project can also be woven on the Navajo loom and the treadle loom.)

The ponchos (which only the men wear) in Bolivia and Peru are always warp-face structures, usually striped, and most often with very intricate pickup designs in some of the stripes. They are woven in 2 pieces—each about 20 inches wide—and in various lengths (a perfectly square poncho is quite common), and the 2 pieces are sewn together, leaving a slit for the neck. The finer ones have about 50 warp ends per inch, the warp being a fine 2-ply handspun yarn from an alpaca fleece. They are woven with 4 selvedges (for durability and economy), and often a decorative woven fringe is sewn on afterward.

We will make a plain striped poncho to begin with, but if you have had some weaving experience with pickup patterns (and are very ambitious) you could plan on a stripe or two with a pickup pattern (see Chapter III, "The Inkle Loom"). It would be nice to weave right up to the top selvedge and then add woven fringe—this would make it really quite authentic; but if you don't think you will have the patience, you had better string the warp up an extra 18 inches long and cut off when the weaving becomes difficult.

In Bolivia they weave these on the ground loom, which is warped exactly like the backstrap, in a figure eight, but held in tension by being tied to four stakes in the ground. This means they can take their weaving into the terraced fields with them when they watch their flocks. In these fields there is often not a single tree to which they could tie a backstrap loom. They can jump up from the ground loom to run after a straying llama more quickly than if they had to undo themselves from the backstrap. The ground loom, however, is a real backbreaker: the warp is stretched out horizontally about a foot off the ground and you have to bend over it.

Actually, I think the most convenient way to weave this type of poncho is to string it up as a backstrap, but then mount it so that it is held in the vertical position (see Chapter VI, "The Navajo Loom: The Loom Frame"). This warp is going to be difficult to separate into the sheds since it is 20 inches wide, and it will be much easier if it is rigidly held in the vertical position. You can yank at the heddle stick much harder. To get the full length for each piece you may have to use the "up and over" technique as described in Chapter VI.

Materials

Warp—Medium-fine *soft* 2- or more ply wool or alpaca yarn. It should be very tightly twisted and smooth if you don't want to have difficulties. A soft plied worsted (like dime-store worsted) that you respin yourself would be perfect.

Amount: Approximately 3 pounds.

Color: A blend of 4 or 5 different colors with 1 predominant; *or* all naturals and perhaps 1 accent color like dark blood red. Make one of the naturals predominant. (By *predominant* I mean at least two-thirds of the yarn will be that color.)

Weft—Preferably the same as the warp; however, it does not *have* to be smooth, strong, or tightly twisted.

Amount: Approximately 3/4 pound.

Color: Same as 1 of the darker warp colors (it will show slightly).

Directions

String your warp up for one side of the poncho (or for the whole poncho if you are using the treadle loom) as in general directions. Allow 24 to 30 warp threads per inch, and make the warp width approximately 20 inches and the length 5 feet (or more for a large man's poncho). Add 10 inches for warp takeup (and shrinkage after washing), and another 18 inches if you are not planning to weave right up to the top selvedge. (If you are weaving this on a treadle loom allow an extra 3 feet altogether, for both pieces, and read the section Planning the Weaving in Chapter VII.)

Arrange the colored stripes as you wish, joining the colors at one peg or stake of the warping device. In Bolivia they leave long ends on these knots, and then when the weaving is finished they untie them and weave them horizontally along the selvedge. They are invisible, but make a rather thickened edge, which is nice.

Weave as in general instructions, setting the loom bars up vertically (as in directions for the Navajo loom) if possible. If necessary, use a stretcher to keep the width even. The weft should be pulled straight across; no extra weft length is necessary for this type of weaving.

Make two identical pieces of weaving in this manner. Sew them together (see Chapter VIII, "Finishing Techniques: Joining"), and then add a woven fringe if desired or the Peruvian rolled edge (added on), also described in the same chapter.

Project V. Huipil with Brocade Design (Mexican)

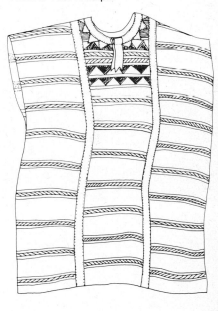

FIGURE 108. A huipil.

(This project can also be woven on the treadle loom.)

Now here is a good project for an intrepid weaver. You have probably seen (or even owned) one of these beautiful garments, the traditional dress of the Mixtec Indian women in Mexico. The yarn is cotton—natural white cotton or, rarely, a dark natural cotton—with a brocade pattern woven in brilliant-colored wool, red predominating. The fabric is woven in three strips, each one with four selvedges. The center strip is more elaborately brocaded in the neck area. Often the center strip is also woven with a warp-face border of heavier-weight cotton in a contrasting color, down each side.

The newer huipils do not have the woven border, but are sewn together with a brilliant satin ribbon sewn over that seam and around the cut-out neck hole. The traditional garments are sewn up the sides only a few inches at the bottom, so the women can get into their money belts (which they wear underneath), or nurse their babies from the side. They are wide enough so that they can be lapped over and secured around the waist with a sash. Sometimes the weave structure is leno instead of tabby.

This project will take you many hours of hard work, so don't think you are making it to save yourself the purchase price (a few dollars in Mexico).

Materials

Warp—A fine cotton (about 20/3).
    Amount: Approximately 2/3 pound.
    Color: Natural white or darker natural.
Weft—Same as warp (same amount and same color) for the structural tabby.
    For the brocade: A fine plied wool (about 4,000 yards per pound).
    Amount: Approximately 1/4 pound.
    Color: Various brilliant colors of your choice.

Directions

Set up the warp about 30 warp ends per inch. Each of the 3 pieces is woven

FIGURE 109. Inserting a twin heddle stick alongside the first.

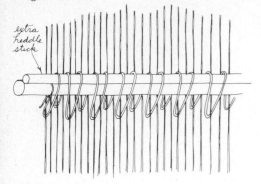

FIGURE 110. Maneuvering the two heddle sticks so that only the front loops lift the warp threads.

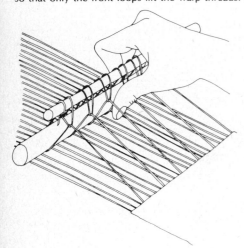

separately. However, if you are not planning on weaving right up to the top selvedge on each piece (a tedious and hardly worthwhile effort on this piece, since the huipil can easily be hemmed), the warp for all 3 pieces should be wound as one. Each piece should measure 14 inches by 7 feet; this means the warp should be 21 feet long plus an extra 3 feet for takeup, shrinkage after washing, and waste. You can roll up the top end of the warp with a second stick to reduce the length while weaving. (A warp for the treadle loom should be the same length.)

You can start weaving the second piece right where you left off on the first, since you will be hemming both cut edges. The 3 pieces will be woven in sequence (the order does not matter) before cutting off. Be careful that each is exactly the same length. The center piece can be more elaborately woven near the neck area if desired, but remember that a round hole will be cut there, so don't waste any effort on brocading within that circle. I will describe a very simple design and you can elaborate on it if you wish.

After setting up the heddle stick, insert an extra stick along with the first, after the heddles are made. This second stick is used to manipulate the heddles to lift only the front ones (which means that you will lift every fourth thread instead of every other thread). (On the 4-harness treadle loom lifting every fourth thread is easily accomplished with a basic twill threading.)

Starting on the first of the 3 strips, weave 3 inches in plain weave with the cotton weft. (I say 3 inches because this could be the distance between brocade stripes. Farther apart would make the pattern rather sparse. Closer together would take much more time to weave because there would be many more stripes of the brocade weaving in the 7-foot length.) The weaving can begin right at the front loom bar— no need to leave an allowance for fringe.

Always use your stretcher. Pack the weft so that there are exactly as many weft threads per inch as there are warp ends (30). Break off your cotton weft and lock a 2-inch tail around the edge warp thread and back in the same shed.

FIGURE 112. The second row of brocade: the weft encompasses the same number of warp ends, moved over one warp thread to the right.

FIGURE 111. Laying in the first row of brocade.

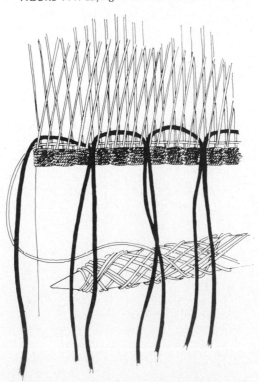

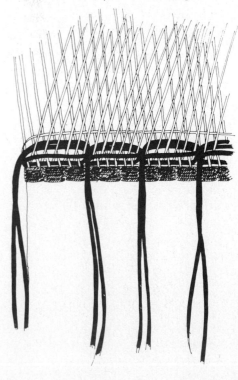

Now take 1 color of your wool yarn and weave 1 shot of this in the stick shed. Your next shed will be 1 thread up and 3 threads down. To make this shed, lift 1 of the heddle sticks up and press the other down. You will see that this lifts only every 4th thread. Insert your batten in this shed and weave it with the same wool weft.

Repeat these 2 rows of weaving (the stick shed alternating with the modified pull shed) for about 1/4 inch. This will make a nice solid band of color. Break off this weft and lock it.

The purpose of this little heddle-stick maneuver is to allow the weft to skip over more than 1 thread at a time, making it possible to beat the weft into a weft-face structure. This would be impossible if the weft went over and under every warp thread.

Now for the brocade pattern. Start the cotton weft again and make 1 shot of this (it doesn't matter which shed). While this shed is still open, place 1-foot lengths of your colored wool yarn in the warp threads as shown in Figure 111.

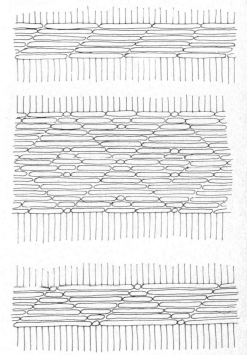

FIGURE 113. Other brocade shapes.

Change the shed and pack these wefts into place; beat hard so they will pack down as much as possible.

In this new shed one end of the colored weft thread crosses over the top of the warp to enter the shed from the same direction as last time, but now *they move over 1 warp thread to the right on each side.* Both ends are passed through the shed, so from now on you are working with a double thread.

Place a shot of the cotton weft in this shed also. Continue weaving in this manner for about 3/4 inch, weaving a shot of cotton weft in each shed and also the colored weft lengths that have crossed over the top of the warp. Moving over 1 warp thread each time will make diagonal edges to the colored wool shapes. You can vary this by switching directions; or make triangles instead of parallelograms. And in the next brocade stripe the diagonals can go in the opposite direction.

You will find that within these bands of brocade you can't leave very large areas of plain weave in between the solid wool shapes, because the tabby structure is very sparse, since the cotton weft cannot be beaten down as close together as usual.

Break off the colored wool wefts and let them just hang out on the underside of the fabric. No further treatment of these ends is necessary. Break off the cotton weft and lock its end.

Now weave another 1/4 inch of the solid color, and after that 3 inches in plain tabby with the cotton weft.

Continue making these colored brocade stripes every 3 inches. This measurement does not have to be exact; the matching-up of the stripes in the final garment is hopeless anyway without making the material pucker in places; it's much better to let the stripes meet haphazardly.

When all 3 strips are woven, cut them off the loom and sew them together. Cut a round neck hole and bind it with satin ribbon. Overlay satin ribbon along the seams. Sew up the sides, leaving armholes, and hem the huipil. (See Figure 114 on the following page.)

And then take a trip to Mexico and wear your huipil around the Oaxaca plaza!

Project VI. Double Cloth Sash (Bolivian)

Here is a challenging project for you. The weaving of it is so interesting and the results are so beautiful that you will probably want to try more than one sash in this technique. On your first try your patterns should be limited to very simple shapes, such as checkerboards and diamonds and triangles. But when you master this technique you will be making beautiful little animals and birds and flowers, just as they do in Bolivia.

FIGURE 114. Sewing the huipil together.

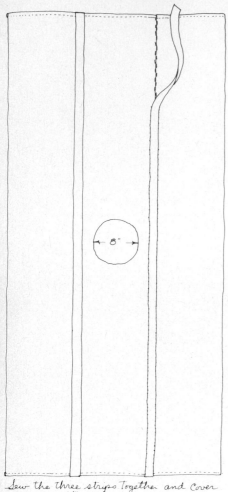

Sew the three strips together and cover seams with ribbon.

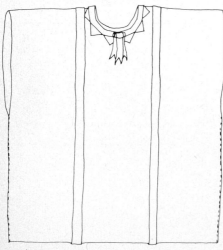

Sew up the sides leaving an armhole of whatever size you desire.

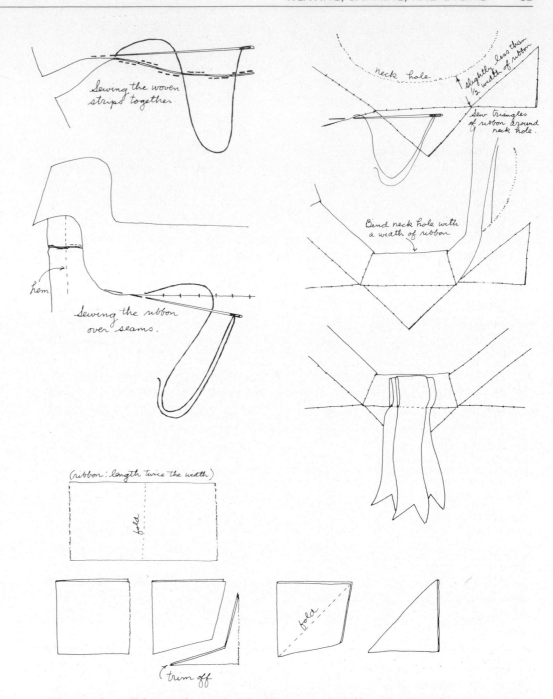

Sewing the woven strips together.

hem

Sewing the ribbon over seams.

(ribbon; length twice the width)

fold

trim off

neck hole

slightly less than ½ width of ribbon

Sew triangles of ribbon around neck hole.

Bind neck hole with a width of ribbon

fold

The results will be similar to the double-weave belt described in Chapter II, "Card Weaving."

What you will be doing is weaving two separate fabrics—one on top and one underneath. Your borders will be plain stripes, and in the center section will be the pattern. You will have two sets of threads in one color (for the warp threads of one fabric). *And* you will have two sets of threads in another color (for the warp threads of the second fabric).

If you just wove this in plain double weave, you would have the top fabric of the first color and the fabric underneath would be the other color. They would be joined only at the edges, where the weft circles around. By manipulating the warp threads, picking up the opposite color from below, and dropping threads from above, you can weave shapes of the second color on a ground of the first. On the underside of the belt, the same pattern comes out in reverse colors.

This weave requires two extra heddle sticks. I suggest you weave a belt such as that in Chapter III, "The Inkle Loom: Project II. Warp Face Belt with Pickup Pattern," to familiarize yourself with the pickup technique before trying this double weave. But, if you are very diligent, perhaps you can weave this with no previous experience; I hope the directions will be clear enough.

Materials

Warp—Medium-fine, strong, smooth, very tightly twisted wool yarn. To avoid difficulties in the weaving, I suggest you respin this yarn yourself. Respun dime-store worsted will be excellent. After you master this technique you may want to use very fine yarn as they do in Bolivia. An excellent yarn for this fine weaving would be Scandinavian 2-ply fine spelsau, respun.

Amount: Approximately 1/2 pound altogether.

Colors: Natural black, natural white (for borders); deep blood red, and pine-needle green (for center pattern area).

Weft—Same as warp (it is not essential to respin this).

Amount: Approximately 60 yards.

Color: Natural black (or same as border color).

Directions

The authentic Bolivian belt is woven right down to the selvedge at one end, and then the last 6 inches of warp at the other end are braided in groups (with uncut ends) and tied together at the end. Then a long tail of braided or woven yarn is attached to this braided end for securing the belt around the waist. You can do this or, if you prefer, allow unwoven warp at each end for a twisted or braided fringe. The Bolivian belts are usually not longer than 3 feet.

Plan your warp length, allowing an extra foot of warp that will be too difficult to weave at the end. I suggest a total warp length of 5 feet, so that it can be fringed at both ends.

Wind your warp in a figure eight as in general instructions for this loom, but *wind 2 balls at the same time.* Wind 2 balls of black for about 7 times; then wind 2 balls of white for about 3 times. This takes care of the border threads on one side.

Repeat this sequence in reverse order for the other border *after* you have wound 1 ball each of the green and red together for about 20 times around. For later sashes you can have a band in the center of this central band that is made up of 2 additional contrasting colors; but for now it would be too confusing.

Attach the warp to the loom bars as in directions above. The warp width should be approximately 2 1/2 inches. (You won't be able to tell exactly how wide the belt will weave until you pull your first or second weft shot through.)

To set up the sheds for this double weave you will need 4 *extra* sticks the same size as the heddle stick.

Before untying the cross, insert one of the sticks on each side of the cross so that you can distinguish the threads better. They will be the lease rods.

Of the threads that are running over the top of the upper lease rod, you will make 2 groups. The first group is made by picking up the alternate threads and inserting the shed stick under them. All the threads of 1 color in the center pattern area will be on top of the shed stick. This will be called shed no. 4. Be sure to tie this stick with a string so it cannot fall out of the shed (see Figure 117).

Pick up the alternate threads from in between each of the previous threads and insert another temporary stick. Now make heddles around these threads (for this belt make the type of heddles described in Chapter IV, "The Hopi Belt Loom"). This will be heddle stick no. 3. Remove the temporary stick.

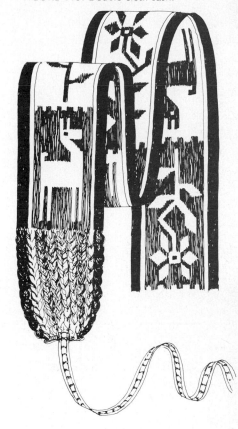

FIGURE 115. Double cloth sash.

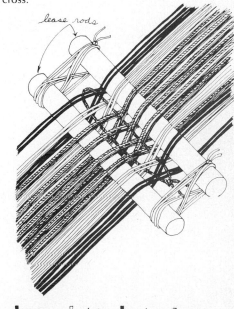

FIGURE 116. Placing a stick on either side of the cross.

lease rods

█ black   ▊ white   █ red   ▨ green

(Number of warp threads reduced for clarity.)

FIGURE 117. Inserting the shed stick no. 4.

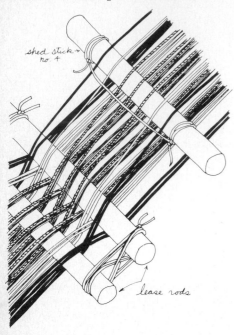

Of the threads that are running over the top of the lower lease rod you will make 2 groups. The first group is made by picking up every other thread (of the same color you picked up for shed stick no. 4). Insert a temporary stick and make heddles around these threads. This will be heddle stick no. 2. Remove the temporary stick.

Pick up the remaining alternate threads from in between the no. 2 threads (make sure they are lined up in order all the way up to the threads of no. 4). Insert a temporary stick under these threads. Make heddles around these threads. This will be heddle stick no. 1. Remove the temporary stick.

The shed stick (no. 4) and these 3 heddle sticks will operate the 4 sheds necessary for the double weave.

If you want to make the belt in the authentic manner, start weaving right at the front loom bar, but I suggest leaving 6 inches of warp for fringe.

Wind the weft in the form of a butterfly; this is more convenient than having the weft on a stick shuttle.

FIGURE 119. Making heddle stick no. 2.

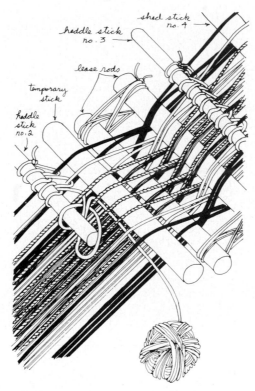

FIGURE 118. Making heddle stick no. 3.

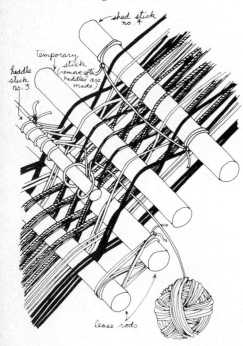

FIGURE 120. Making heddle stick no. 1.

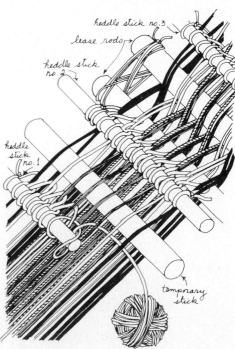

To weave:

1. (First top shed.) Lift heddle no. 3, hold these threads up with both hands. Pick up threads from no. 4 below as desired for the pattern. (To begin with, make the pattern simple: half red and half green, and then switch colors after 1/2 inch of weaving to form a checkerboard pattern.) For every thread you pick up from no. 4, drop one from no. 3 (the one right next to it). These dropped threads are what make the pattern come out on the underneath side in reverse color.

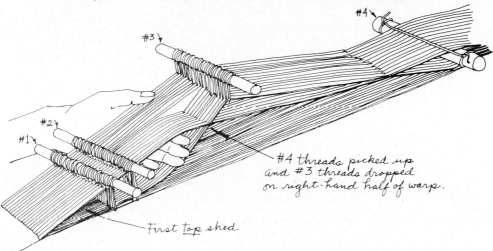

FIGURE 121. Picking up and dropping threads for pattern in first top shed.

Insert batten and beat. The very first shot you won't beat hard because there is no weaving there to beat against. Turn batten on edge and pass the weft through the shed (place shot). *Leave batten in shed.*

2. (First underneath shed.) Lift heddles no. 1 and no. 2 together. (These lifted threads *plus* the threads held by the batten are the upper threads for this shed.) Use a second batten to force this shed open. Move it down to heddle sticks no. 1 and no. 2 and rotate it back and forth until the shed begins to form *below* the heddle sticks. Slip your pick in this shed and then the batten. Now turn the lower batten on edge and then the upper batten on edge. This produces a third shed which can be seen from the side. It is underneath the cross of the two sheds with the battens in them. This is your first underneath shed. Put your fingers in this shed; remove both battens and insert one in this shed and beat. Place shot.

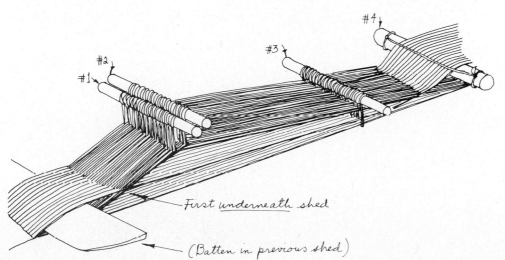

FIGURE 122. The first underneath shed. Threads of #1 and #2 are up as well as those over the batten.

3. (Second top shed.) Lift heddle no. 2, insert batten and turn on edge. Lift heddle no. 1 and hold these threads up with your hands. Pick and drop pattern as you did for first top shed; pick and drop the same colors. Insert batten and beat. Turn batten on edge and place shot. *Leave batten in shed.*

FIGURE 123. Picking up and dropping threads for pattern in second top shed.

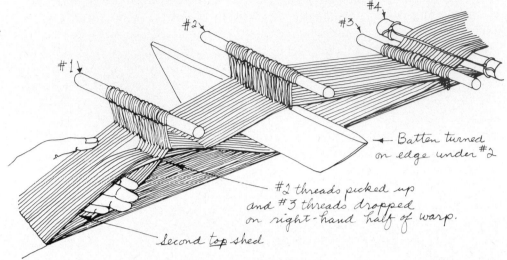

4. (Second underneath shed.) Lift heddles no. 3 and no. 4 together. (These lifted threads plus the threads held up by the batten are the upper threads for this shed.) Use the second batten to force this shed open. Now turn the other batten on edge also. This produces a third shed which can be seen from the side. It is underneath the cross of the two sheds with the battens in them. This is your second underneath shed. Put your fingers in this shed; remove both battens and insert one in this shed and beat. Place shot.

FIGURE 124. The second underneath shed. Threads of #3 and #4 are up as well as those over the batten.

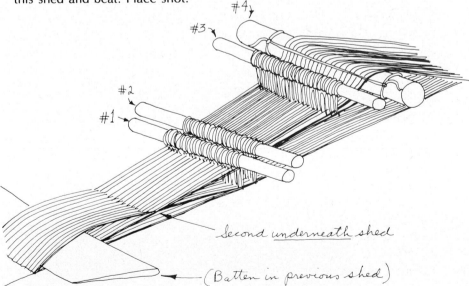

Repeat these four steps.

After you have woven an inch or two you will understand how the pattern is formed by the pickup, and you can vary the design.

When weaving the double cloth belt, I find it most convenient to fix the loom bars in a rigid vertical position, rather than using the backstrap. (See Chapter IV, "The Hopi Belt Loom.")

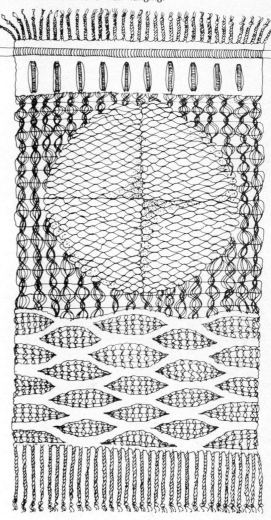

FIGURE 125. Leno wall hanging.

Project VII. Leno Wall Hanging

(This project can also be woven on the treadle loom and the Navajo loom.)

Leno, strictly speaking, is a gauze weave combined with plain weave or another weave. Gauze is a weave structure in which the warp threads are twisted in pairs or groups before the weft is inserted. A fabric made entirely by this technique is called "gauze," but when it is in combination with other weaves it is called "leno."

Lacy, airy fabrics can be made using this technique. If the warp threads are simply twisted in pairs throughout the weaving, a special heddle stick can be made by inserting the batten in between each twisted pair of warp threads, and then making the heddles around the upper thread. Each time this heddle stick is lifted, the warp threads will be twisted.

In many leno projects, however, one uses different combinations of twists and so these are simply done by hand. It sounds like a time-consuming process, and the actual twisting of the warp threads is, but the time taken to do this is compensated for by the fact that the weft threads are held a good distance apart by the twist in the warp, and so the weaving builds up very fast. Also, only every other row of weaving has to be twisted, because in the alternate rows the warp twists by itself back to its original position.

Leno weaving is usually most interesting when of a solid color, with the same yarn for both warp and weft. The structure of the weave shows off to its best advantage when there is not the distraction of various-colored threads.

When you get into tapestry weaving, you can do very interesting things by combining tapestry with gauze weaving in a much more sophisticated form than this project.

Materials

Warp—Medium-weight tightly twisted wool, hair, linen, or cotton yarn.

Amount: Approximately 1/4 pound.

Color: Any natural fiber color.

Weft—Same as the warp.

Amount: Approximately 1/8 pound.

Color: Same as warp.

Decorative weft: A few yards each of four different colors of handspun wool yarn, medium thick and textured. The colors will be best if they are of the same value and intensity (see Chapter XI, "Design and Color: Properties of Color").

Directions

You will need a pickup stick—a flat stick like a batten, but with a pointed end and only 1 inch wide.

Set up the warp 6 or 8 to the inch, 15 inches wide and 4 feet long. This allows an extra 2 feet for fringe at the bottom, and warp that cannot be woven at the top. The finished piece will be only about 2 feet in length.

Position shed stick and make the heddle stick as described in general directions.

Weave the first 8 inches with rags to allow for the bottom fringe. Weave 2 rows in plain weave with the natural weft.

Starting at the right side of the weaving, twist pairs of warp threads for a distance of 3 inches, inserting the pointed end of the pickup stick up to this point to hold the twist. (The twisting of the warp threads takes place with a closed shed.) Then make the pull shed and push the pickup stick along in this shed for a distance of 3 more inches. Alternate 3 inches of twisted warp threads with 3 inches of the plain shed all

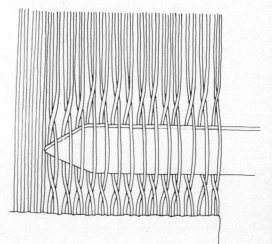

FIGURE 126. Inserting the pickup stick in twisted warp pairs.

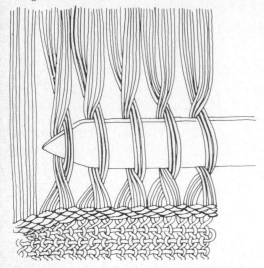

FIGURE 127. Twisting groups of six threads for background of circle.

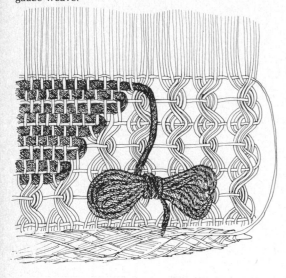

FIGURE 128. Weaving the circle with colored weft after each shot of natural weft; background done in gauze weave.

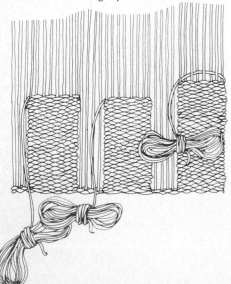

FIGURE 129. Weaving separate 1-inch sections.

the way across the warp. There should be 3 areas of twisted warp pairs and 2 plain areas, the pickup stick retaining the complete shed. Turn the pickup stick on edge and insert the batten. Remove the pickup stick and turn the batten on edge. Insert the weft in this shed, allowing a loose diagonal or slight arc to the weft.

Beat the weft down with the batten. Now weave a plain row in the stick shed. Pack this weft in with a comb; you will see that where you have made the twist the weft builds up much higher. Do one more row of leno weave just like the first row. Now weave 5 shots of plain weave. Pack the weft in with the comb so that the undulating line of the weft is emphasized.

The next gauze areas will be directly over the plain areas this time. Starting at the right again insert the pickup stick in the shed for a distance of 3 inches; then close shed and do the twist for 3 inches, inserting the shed stick along the way. And so forth.

Weave this undulating leno pattern for about 8 inches.

Now weave for about 1 inch or so doing a different gauze structure, twisting *groups* of 6 threads (as in Figure 127) instead of pairs. Do this twisting across the entire warp. This will make the background for the circle.

Now mark a 12-inch circle on the warp threads with a felt-tip pen, or a pencil. (For a pattern, make a circle on a large paper bag or newspaper by attaching a pencil to a string and using it as a compass.)

Do the same gauze pattern (using groups of threads) for the background. Continue the same weft across the circle area, but open a shed for this, so that the circle will be plain weave. After each weft crossing using the natural weft, insert the colored wefts in the shed within the quadrants of the circle (lock the beginning end around a warp thread and put the tail back in the same shed). Depending on the thickness of this colored weft, weave 1 or 2 rows in plain weave between each 2 natural weft shots, so that the weaving level in the circle area will be the same as in the gauze area.

After the circle form is finished—each quadrant a different color—weave the background pattern for another inch or so.

For the next 3 inches try weaving 1 inch of warp at a time (building up only about 1/2 inch at a time). This requires a butterfly of weft for each section. Leave a few warp threads in between each of these 1-inch sections, and later you can wrap these (see Chapter VIII, "Finishing Techniques: Wrapping").

When all the 1-inch sections are woven up to the same level, weave plain weave for about 1/2 inch, insert a nice willow stick or dowel in the next shed, and then weave another 1/2 inch. This stick will be used to hang the weaving.

Now do the wrapping while the weaving is still on the loom and in tension.

Cut off and finish by making 4-strand braid of the warp ends. Steam press.

Suggestions for Other Projects

Weave an entire bedspread of 15-inch wide strips, using the pattern described in Project III. Use medium-weight yarn and the weaving will go quite rapidly. Let the weft-face areas of each strip meet haphazardly.

Any of the projects or suggested projects in the chapter on inkle weaving would be suitable to weave on the backstrap loom. Handbags and pillow covers are good projects also.

Any of the projects in Chapter VII, "The Treadle Loom," that are woven on warp A or B can be woven on the backstrap loom; some will require two extra heddle sticks (the twill weaves and the three-dimensional weave). When making four sheds on a primitive loom an extra batten may be used (see Project III in this chapter).

CHAPTER VI

THE NAVAJO LOOM

FIGURE 130. The Navajo loom and tools.

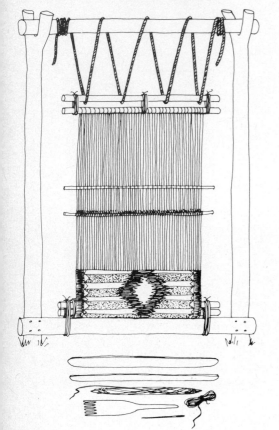

A Description of the Loom

The Navajo loom is the primitive vertical loom used by the Navajo Indians. The warp is wound in a figure eight around two horizontal bars. These two bars are then stretched apart in tension simply by being tied to floor and ceiling or to a specially built frame. A shed rod is placed under every other warp thread, and remains there to form one shed. The other shed is formed by pulling forward a heddle stick to which the alternate warp threads are attached by string loops.

A few tools fashioned out of hardwood are used with the Navajo loom. The batten, a smooth flat stick, is inserted in the sheds and turned on edge to hold the shed open, leaving the hands free to work with the weft. Battens of smaller widths are needed to complete the last few inches of weaving at the top, when it becomes increasingly difficult to open the sheds. A wooden fork is used to pack the weft into place, and occasionally the batten is used to beat the weft; this helps promote an even line in the weaving.

The weft can be wound on a stick shuttle for plain weaving, but is always wound in the form of butterflies for tapestry weaving. For the last few inches of weaving, the weft is threaded through the eye of an umbrella rib or a homemade wire needle to facilitate its passage through the shed, and for the very last fraction of an inch a sacking needle is used.

There are "Navajo looms" on the market today. They consist of a simple frame with dowels for crossbars, and usually a base to keep them from toppling over. In my opinion, if you want to save money, or if you want a large loom, you are better off assembling the loom bars and making the loom frame yourself.

Its Uses

A testament to this loom's efficient design is the fact that it has been used for centuries by the Indians of the Southwest and has survived virtually unchanged to the present day. The only tools the Navajo weaver has to consider permanent possessions are the battens, forks, and needles (and of course the hand spindle and cards for making the yarn). The simple loom is set up on the spot, using logs and saplings.

The design of the loom evolved from the need of a semi-nomadic people to weave large, durable squares of fabric which were used as blankets and clothing. Today its primary use on the reservation is for the weaving of weft-face rugs of great durability and intricate design.

Because of the vertical position of the warp and the extreme tension that can be applied to it, the weft can be beaten into place much more tightly than on the treadle loom. The weaving right up to the top and bottom selvedges—another feature that increases durability—is impossible on a treadle loom. You may have observed that the genuine Navajo rug never has fringed ends, unless they are applied after the rug is woven, as was the case during a short period of Navajo weaving when they used Germantown yarns.

The all-over tapestry design typical of the Navajo rug is a natural development of the weaving technique used on this type of loom. Because of the vertical position of the warp, the weft cannot be "shot" across the entire width of the weaving—as it can on a treadle loom. And so, with very wide fabrics, the weaver works only the area in front of where she is sitting, and then moves to a new area. The weft is inserted by hand and so changes in color are hardly more difficult than plain weaving. In fact, plain areas are even woven in small zigzag sections, which form the well-known "lazy lines" that one finds in authentic Navajo weaving.

The projects that follow employ mostly traditional Navajo techniques—some old and rarely used today—that the contemporary weaver will find interesting. The loom will be useful for many projects besides the traditional four-selvedged rug—which most weavers may not have the patience to complete. For these less time-consuming weavings, the tedious process of weaving right up to the top selvedge may be omitted —a sacrilege, I'm sure, to the Navajo craftsman. You may simply start a few inches up from the bottom selvedge and leave off weaving when it becomes too difficult to separate the warp threads near the top. The woven piece may then be fringed at both ends, just as you would finish a weaving produced on a treadle loom.

Whether you use the traditional selvedge technique or not, the Navajo loom is excellent for rugs, tapestries, rya, leno, or any other weaving where the rapid changing of sheds possible on the treadle loom is not essential. It is most adaptable to weft-face weaving. It is preferable to the backstrap loom for wide fabrics, and better than either the backstrap or the ground loom for tapestry weaving, because you can step back away from it and see the design vertically as you would a painting—a very important consideration when you are creating an organic, free-form tapestry. For tightly woven weft-face fabrics it is superlative. And, finally, it is less tiring to work at than either of these other two primitive looms.

Its most obvious advantage over the treadle loom is the fact that there is little or no cost involved in setting it up and it is easily knocked down (even while weaving is in progress) and portable.

The limitation of the Navajo loom is in the height of the weaving, but this can be overcome by winding a circular warp as is done for the Hopi belt loom, for fairly narrow weavings (and omitting the four selvedges); or by using an "up and over" technique, where the warp, when set up in the loom frame, goes up and over an upper bar and back down the other side.

What You Will Need to Set Up and Weave on a Navajo Loom

a. A loom frame made of poles or 2-by-6s (see The Loom Frame, page 92).

b. 2 poles about 4 inches in diameter (or 2-by-4s) about 1 foot longer than your warp. These are just for a temporary warping frame to wind the warp.

c. 3 smooth round sticks (about 1 to 1 1/4 inches in diameter) about 1 foot longer than the weaving is wide, but they must not be longer than the inside measurement of your loom frame. Dowels or old broom handles are fine for weavings not wider than 36 inches, but for wider weavings a thicker bar is necessary; pitchfork handles are usually thick enough. Two of these bars will be loom bars and the third will be the intermediate tension bar.

d. 2 smooth round sticks (about 1/2 inch in diameter) about 4 inches longer than the width of the weaving. These are the shed stick and the heddle stick.

e. A few yards of heavy cord, for lashing the warping frame together, and lashing the loom bars to the frame.

f. Several yards of medium-fine cord—at least triple-plied. This is for making the heddles, and for attaching the selvedge ends to the loom bars. Cotton is most suitable.

FIGURE 131. Different ways of making a Navajo loom frame.

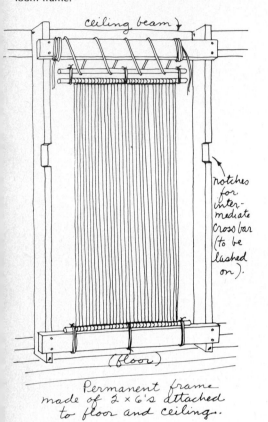

ceiling beam

notches for intermediate cross bar (to be lashed on).

(floor)

Permanent frame made of 2 × 6's attached to floor and ceiling.

g. A few yards of rope about 1/4 inch thick. This is for the final suspension of the loom on the frame.

h. 4 large nails. These are used only in the warping procedure.

i. A metal or wooden rod 3/16 inch in diameter, same length as the shed stick and heddle stick. This will replace the shed stick in the final inches of weaving.

j. An umbrella rib or 2 feet of baling wire. These are to use as large needles.

k. A sacking needle.

l. The batten.

m. The fork.

n. The shuttle.

o. The yarn.

The Loom Frame

If you anticipate doing any amount of weaving on the Navajo loom, it is best to construct a good, sturdy, more or less permanent frame, with vertical poles or 2-by-6s attached to floor and ceiling and crossbars at the top and bottom either fitted into holes or notches in the vertical members, or bolted to them. The vertical members may be posts set in the ground outside (practical in a desert environment, but not too good for most climates). Metal pipes for crossbars are structurally excellent if you're not concerned with aesthetics. But in any case the horizontals must be strong enough to resist bending under extreme tension. Any large frame should have a hole or notch for a bar across the midway point of the verticals, as well as at top and bottom, so the loom may be lowered to this point halfway through the weaving.

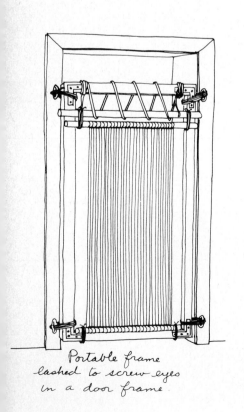

Portable frame lashed to screw eyes in a door frame.

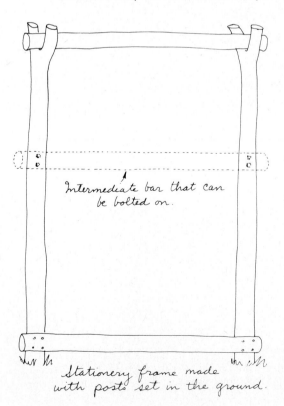

Intermediate bar that can be bolted on.

Stationery frame made with posts set in the ground.

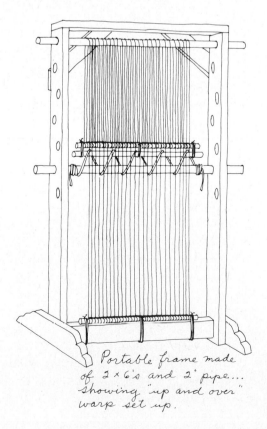

Portable frame made of 2 × 6's and 2" pipe... showing "up and over" warp set up.

If your living arrangements do not allow for this type of structure, you can make a large portable frame (which is what many of the women in Navajo country do today) of finished 2-by-6s, with holes for fitting in 1 1/2- or 2-inch plumber's pipe for the crosspieces. This type of frame must have a good base so the loom won't have any tendency to topple over. Smaller versions of this type of frame may be made with 2-by-4s and pitchfork handles for crosspieces. Or just a perfectly rectangular frame can be used to lash your loom bars to, and then the frame can be secured to screw eyes in a door frame.

The horizontal members of the frame must be placed on the front edge of the vertical members (by shallow notching), or else you will have to allow a foot or 18 inches between frame and sides of the weaving, in order to insert the batten. Your frame should be at least one foot higher than the length of any weaving you might want to make on it. If you wish to omit weaving right up to the top selvedge, you will have to allow an additional eighteen inches for height.

To accommodate very long weaving, the frame can be made in such a way that the warp can go "up and over" a bar and be lashed at the bottom of the loom on the other side, in which case this extra bar must be as strong as the top and bottom members of the loom frame. Since the warp must be able to slide over it (as the weaving level is changed) a 2-inch metal pipe is just about the best solution.

The Batten

The batten, a flat stick that is inserted into the shed and turned on edge to hold the shed open, must be made of hardwood, as it will receive a lot of wear. It should be a few inches longer than the weaving is wide, but certainly never longer than 3 feet. For very wide weaving don't try to make a batten that will span the entire width; it will be extremely awkward trying to insert into the shed. Simply use a convenient length like 24 inches and work at one time only in an area in front of where you are sitting.

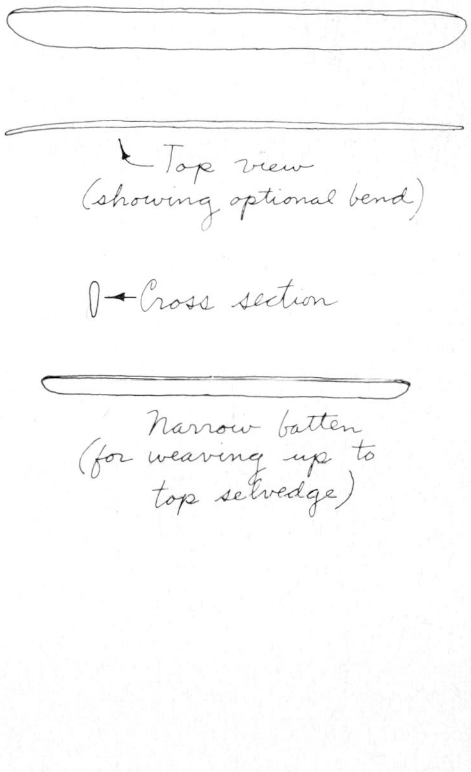

The width of the batten should be about 1 1/2 to 2 inches, and the thickness about 1/4 to 3/8 inch. One or more battens of increasingly narrow widths will be necessary if you intend to weave up to the selvedge at the top. On the first third of a very high weaving you may wish to use a batten of 2- or 3- inch width, as the warp threads can easily be separated this much at first. A set of battens of various widths and lengths, to use for different projects and for different stages of the weaving, is desirable but not absolutely necessary for the beginner. For the projects in this book, 2 battens 36 inches long, one 1 1/2 inches wide and one 3/4 inches wide, will be right for all the projects except Project II, which will require shorter battens—about 20 inches in length.

The two ends of the batten are cut off at an angle, so that one edge is shorter than the other. This short edge is also sharper than the other. The batten is inserted into the shed with the longest edge up and turned on its side so that this same edge is forward. The sharpest edge is used occasionally to beat down the weft.

A slight bend at the left-hand end (when the sharp edge is down) of a long batten will facilitate inserting the batten between the warp threads and help prevent catching on the back threads. But this feature is not essential. The bend can be formed by putting the batten under pressure in the appropriate spots for a few days while the wood is wet or still green.

The batten must be *very* smooth and all edges should be rounded, but no finish is necessary. It soon gets a beautiful patina from the oil in the wool or your hands, and from the constant rubbing.

FIGURE 132. Navajo battens showing top view of the bend.

Top view
(showing optional bend)

Cross section

Narrow batten
(for weaving up to
top selvedge)

A few suppliers have authentic Navajo battens, but other battens and swords are suitable also. They are quite inexpensive.

The Fork

This important tool, sometimes called a comb or beater, is in your hand almost constantly while you are working on the Navajo loom, and so a comfortable and functional shape is essential. See Proper Handling of the Fork and Batten later in the chapter.

The traditional design of the Navajo fork can hardly be improved upon. The tool is usually about 9 or 10 inches long, 2 inches wide, and made of hardwood. The handle is most comfortable if it is rounded. The teeth and body should be thick to withstand breaking but the tips of the teeth must be pointed (as you look down at them) so that they will not catch on the warp threads. The pointed end of the handle has a purpose: it is used for prying threads apart in certain operations of the weaving process, as well as for making arcs to achieve proper weft tension.

A smaller fork is useful when weaving the last few inches, although an ordinary table fork may be used.

Authentic Navajo forks may be purchased through a few suppliers (see Chapter XIII). If you purchase another type of fork or beater it should be about the same length as prescribed, and you may want to round the handle if it is not already round.

FIGURE 133. Two views of the Navajo fork.

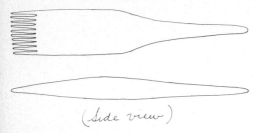

(Side view)

The Butterfly and the Shuttle

See Chapter IV, "The Hopi Belt Loom: The Butterfly vs. the Shuttle." There I describe how to wind your weft around a plain stick. You will use the shuttle when weaving plain or striped fabrics. For tapestry weaving all your weft colors will be wound in butterflies.

Yarn Specifications

All of the projects described for the Navajo loom are weft-face structures. If you weave other types of structures, just remember that your warp must still meet the following specifications.

The warp on a Navajo loom takes an incredible beating, so it is extremely important that it be a tightly and evenly spun yarn, so strong that it is very difficult to break with your bare hands. Wool or hair yarns are best because of their elasticity and the bond they make with the wool weft; cotton will do in a pinch; nylon and linen are not suitable.

You may be able to locate a tightly plied commercial yarn, but lacking this, a good 2-, 3-, or 4-ply commercial woolen or worsted yarn that you respin yourself makes an excellent warp. The amount of warp you will need even for a large project is so little (probably less than a quarter of a pound) that it is no big thing to respin it, even if you only have a hand spindle. See Chapter IX, "Spinning: Respinning Commercial Yarn."

If you decide to spin your warp yarn from scratch (which is hardly worthwhile unless you are an expert spinner, since the warp is usually covered up completely by the weft), a good yarn can be made by blending mohair and wool. (See Chapter IX, "Spinning: Yarn Design and Function.") The length of the mohair fibers gives strength and the wool fiber elasticity. It is best to spin two fine yarns and double-ply them; the plying gives extra strength and greater uniformity.

For weft-face weaving the weight of the warp yarn should be only slightly less than the weft yarn. Wind your warp yarn into a ball.

Although the weft yarn is not subjected to the same wear and tear as the warp yarn, its structure and appearance are all important to the final appearance of the weaving. It is only the weft that forms the surface of the traditional fabrics woven on the Navajo loom.

The weft yarn should be just slightly heavier than the warp—or they could be exactly the same weight. It can be of varying thickness, fuzzy, or whatever you want. Single-ply handspun yarns are probably the most suitable for this type of weaving. See specific projects for further information.

Preparing the Warping Frame

This is a temporary frame that is used just for winding the warp.

Lay the poles or 2-by-4s (b) on the floor or ground parallel to each other and 6 inches farther apart than the planned width of the weaving. Or lay the portable loom frame down on the floor and use it instead of a warping frame.

Using the heavy cord (e), lash 2 of the sticks (c), which are the loom bars, to the poles or 2-by-4s at a distance apart that will be the length of the weaving (18 inches more distance will be needed if you are going to omit weaving up to the top selvedge).

Hammer the four nails part way into the poles or 2-by-4s just inside the lashings; this insures that the loom bars cannot pull toward each other as the warp is wound on.

Mark width of weaving on the loom bars.

Winding the Warp

Tie the end of the ball of warp yarn to one of the loom bars at one of the marks that indicates the width of the weaving. Wind the yarn back and forth between the two bars, *always* going over the top. This forms a figure eight in the center and is called the "cross" or "lease." (If there is not enough room for the ball to pass underneath the bars, raise the poles by putting bricks or books underneath the warping frame.)

1. Spacing the turns: Each turn around the bar makes a pair of warp threads, so the number of turns per inch will be half the number of warp threads per inch that are called for in your project. For instance, if the project calls for 8 warp ends per inch, then you will make a turn every 1/4 inch. If your warp is spaced too far apart, it will take you forever to weave the fabric because the weft will pack down too much. And, if the warp threads are too close together, it may be impossible to cover them completely with the weft. To make sure you have the right spacing for the yarns you are using, make a sample by winding your warp yarn around a book, and weaving with the weft (just darn it over and under the warp threads). If the weft can just barely be packed down to cover the warp, you have the correct spacing.

2. Counting the turns: Count the number of turns on one of the dowels. There should be half as many turns as there are supposed to be warp threads. The number of warp threads should be the number of warp ends per inch multiplied by the number of inches wide the weaving is to be. Add or subtract warp turns as necessary and make a temporary tie around the opposite dowel from the first tie. But do not cut the yarn.

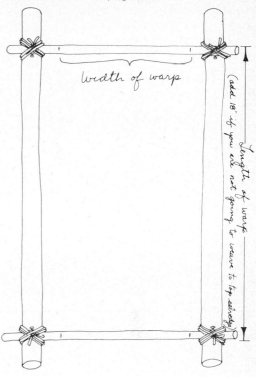

FIGURE 134. The warping frame.

width of warp

(add 18" if you are not going to weave to top selvedge) length of warp

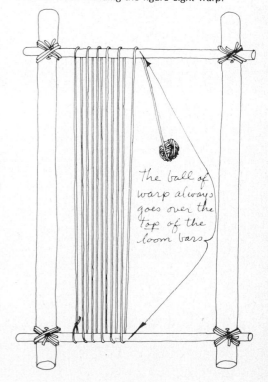

FIGURE 135. Winding the figure eight warp.

the ball of warp always goes over the top of the loom bars.

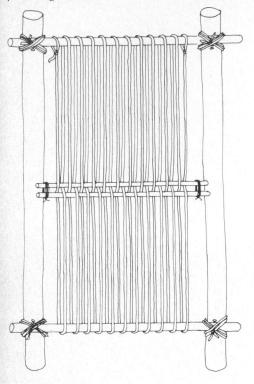

FIGURE 136. Shed stick and heddle stick preserving the cross.

3. Adjusting the tension: The tension should be moderate and consistent with each turn. The tendency is to wind tighter and tighter, so you must consciously counteract this. When you have finished winding, check the tension. If the warp is tighter on one side, correct this by pulling each individual thread to the right tension, by going back all the way to the beginning, taking up the slack in each turn until you reach the original tie, and then retying the thread to the bar.

4. Check for mistakes: As you are winding, if the warp does not go *over* the bar at each turn and form a figure eight in the center, this will have to be corrected. To check this most easily, sight from the side of the frame through the figure eight; any thread that is out of place will be very noticeable. Do this every once in a while as you are winding. When everything is in order, cut the yarn and tie it around the bar.

Preserving the Lease

Insert the two half-inch sticks (d) through the warp threads on either side of the cross. Tie the ends together securely.

Making the Twisted Selvedge

Using the same yarn that will be the weft (or any yarn, if you are not going to be weaving right up to the top and bottom selvedges) take 4 lengths, each about 3 times as long as the width of the weaving. Double-ply 2 pairs of these, and tie the 2 resulting cords together about 3 inches from the end. (Double-plying these lengths may be accomplished most easily by tying the end of 2 pieces to a chair and then simply rolling them together between the palms of your hands. The yarns should be twisted in the direction opposite to the existing twist of the yarn.)

Slip one end under the first warp turn (or through the loop of the beginning tie on the warp), and pull the two ends until the knot reaches the warp turn.

Twist these two cords 1, 2, or 3 times and slip one end under the next warp thread. The number of twists is determined by exactly how far apart the warp threads are to be spaced. You should twist as many times as possible without forcing the warp threads farther apart than they should be. The number of twists between warp turns must, of course, be consistent throughout.

Continue doing this all the way across the warp. Tie a knot similar to the beginning knot and cut off the excess.

Repeat this procedure with 4 more strands of weft yarn at the other end of the warp.

Even if you are not going to weave right up to these twisted selvedges, this edge should be made because it holds the warp threads at the proper spacing.

Binding the Selvedges to the Loom Bars

(Some Navajo weavers remove the warp from the warping frame at this point, but I believe the following method is accepted as the most efficient way even if it is newer.)

Lay the third stick (c) alongside one selvedge and with the sacking needle (k) and the cord (f), bind the stick to the selvedge. Each time the needle must pass around the twisted selvedge between each warp pair. Pull the cord tight each time around. (If you run out of cord simply unthread the needle and tie on another length of cord

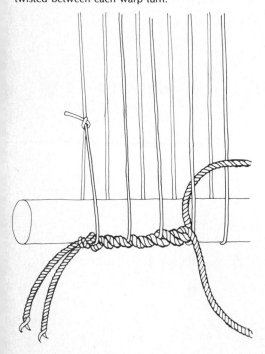

FIGURE 137. Two double-plied weft threads twisted between each warp turn.

and rethread this new length through the needle; this cord will be removed from the finished weaving, so the knot does not matter.)

Tie this new stick loosely to the frame and remove the original stick around which the warp was wound. Use this stick to repeat the procedure at the other selvedge. *Make sure the selvedge is the same width at both ends.*

You now have the warp securely attached to the two loom bars, and the lease is preserved; you may handle the warp quite freely now without worrying about its getting tangled or out of order.

Untie the loom bars from the warping frame and remove the last extra stick (c) from the warp. This will be used as the tension bar in the next step.

Mounting the Loom on the Frame

Using the heavy cord (e), tie one loom bar to the bottom member of the frame at points about one foot apart. Be sure the cord just goes around the loom bar and *not* around the selvedge too.

Tie the other loom bar to the extra stick (now the tension bar) in the same manner, but this time leave a space of about 2 inches between the bars.

Now tie the tension bar to the top bar of the frame with the rope (g). To do this, start at one side and wrap the rope around the top of the frame until it is secure; do not tie a knot. Then wind the rope back and forth, over the upper member of the frame and under the tension bar, supporting this bar at several points across the width of the loom; secure the end by tucking it in under a turn of the rope. Now increase the tension by going back and pulling each loop of the rope tighter at each turn and retying the slack end. Do this two or three more times until the warp is in extreme tension. Make sure the bars are perfectly horizontal.

The Shed Stick

Untie the two half-inch sticks that have served as lease rods, but do not remove them. The upper one will remain in its shed and becomes the shed stick. It is free to move up and down. The lower one remains in place for the next step—making the heddles.

Making the Heddles

Insert your batten in the lower shed along with the lower stick, and turn it on edge; then remove the stick. If your batten is not long enough to cover the full width of the warp, put a string in the shed to preserve it and use the batten at the left side of the warp first, then move it along as necessary. The stick you just removed is now the heddle stick and will be used in the next step.

Lay the fine cord (f) in the opened shed with the end to the left and the ball to the right.

Tie the end of the cord to one end of the heddle stick. Hold the heddle stick parallel to the batten, below it; the right-hand end of the stick should just hover over the left-hand warp threads. Pull the cord out from between the first and second warp threads (the ones held up by the batten) on the left, make a 180-degree twist clockwise in the cord and slip the loop over the end of the heddle stick. Now pull the cord out from between the second and third warp threads, make the twist, and slip it over the end of the heddle stick. Move the heddle stick along and the heddle loops over as they build up on the stick. Do this until heddle loops are made for each upper warp

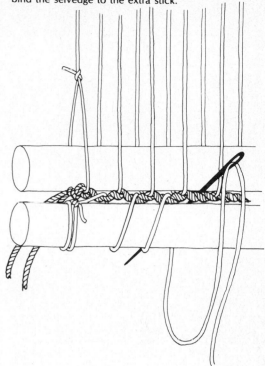

FIGURE 138. With cord threaded through needle, bind the selvedge to the extra stick.

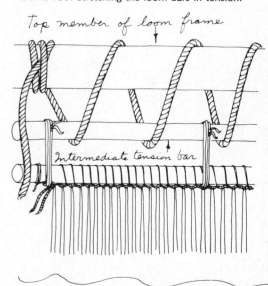

FIGURE 139. Stretching the loom bars in tension.

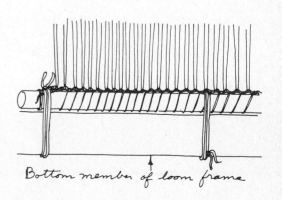

Top member of loom frame

Intermediate tension bar

Bottom member of loom frame

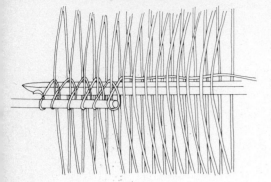

FIGURE 140. Making the heddles.

thread across the entire width of the warp. Cut and tie the cord to the other end of the heddle stick.

The length of each heddle loop from stick to warp thread should be about 1 1/2 inches. The length should be perfectly consistent. If some heddle loops are longer than others simply pull the extra length through and distribute it evenly over the next few heddles. During the weaving this may have to be done occasionally.

Remove the batten after the heddles are made.

For the diamond twill, or other weaves that require more than one heddle stick, the heddles are made for each stick so that *when that stick alone is raised, all the upper threads for that shed are raised.*

How to Operate the Sheds

The first shed is formed by the shed stick. Lower the stick to meet the heddle stick, and move them both to a level about 1 1/2 feet above the lower loom bar. Now with the right hand insert the batten (longest edge up) into the space below and turn it on its side (longest side forward) to hold the shed open. This is called the "stick shed."

The second shed is formed by removing the batten and pushing the shed stick up and out of the way. With the left hand pull the heddle stick forward with a good tug, insert the batten into the space below the heddle stick, and again turn it on its edge. If the warp is wide the heddle stick can be pulled forward bit by bit, starting at the right-hand side, and the batten inserted little by little. This is called the "pull shed."

If the warp threads have a tendency to stick together, a flick of the hand or the fork across the warp will release them *if* the warp is in proper tension.

FIGURE 141. The stick shed.

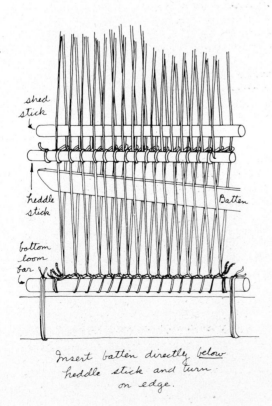

shed stick

heddle stick

Batten

bottom loom bar

Insert batten directly below heddle stick and turn on edge.

FIGURE 142. The pull shed.

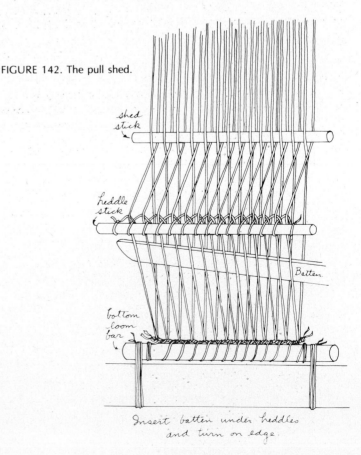

shed stick

heddle stick

Batten

bottom loom bar

Insert batten under heddles and turn on edge.

Preparing the Traditional Side Selvedge (Optional)

On the traditional Navajo rug, the weft threads at the side edges of the weaving are protected by a twisted cord that is woven right into the edge.

To prepare this cord, take 4 strands (each twice as long as the height of the weaving) of the same yarn that was used for the upper and lower twisted selvedge, and double-ply the pairs together. Tie the 2 resulting cords around the bottom bar at one side of the warp and carry them to the top loom bar and tie loosely. Do the same with 4 more strands of yarn on the other warp edge. The method of weaving this edge will be described later.

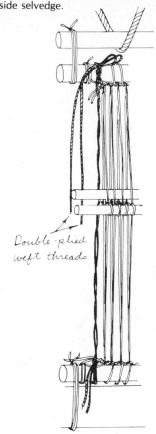

FIGURE 143. A pair of double-plied weft threads for twisted side selvedge.

Preparing the Weft Yarn

For tapestry weaving, make butterflies of all your weft colors. Any weft that is to span a large area, or the width of the warp, should be wound on the shuttles. You will need a shuttle for each color.

The First Rows of Weaving

1. *Traditional beginning:* If you are planning to weave right up to the top selvedge, your first 4 rows of weaving (and the last 4 rows at the top) will be made *without* using the two regular sheds. Instead, raise your shed and heddle stick up out of the way, and insert your batten between the warp threads by going over 2 and under 2 all the way across from the right edge to the left. Turn the batten on edge and insert the weft underneath the batten in this shed, leaving the end of the weft lying just inside the edge warp threads. Pack the thread down with the fork.

Remove the batten and insert it again, this time going over and under the opposite pairs of warp threads. Turn the batten on edge, and return the weft through this shed. This time, the weft yarn, as it turns around the outside warp thread, should just barely touch against the thread but not pull it in. Pack the weft down again with the fork, allowing the weft to feed in and around the warp threads by holding it up as it feeds in. Do not stretch it tight across as you are packing it in.

Repeat these 2 rows of weaving once more. The purpose of these 4 rows of weaving is to cover the warp threads more thoroughly along the selvedge than would be possible using the regular sheds of alternating threads.

2. *Allowing for fringed ends:* If you do not want to take the time to weave up to the top selvedge, you may start and end your weaving a few inches from the twisted selvedge and plan to use these few inches of unwoven warp for fringe. (In this case the twisted selvedge still performs the function of spacing the warp threads, but will be removed when the weaving is complete.)

With the first shed open (see "How to Operate the Sheds") pass a rag strip about 2 inches wide through the shed and pack it down with your fork. In the second shed do the same, and repeat until you have woven with rag strips for about 5 or 6 inches up from the bottom loom bar. This will allow enough length of the warp threads to make a fringe after the weaving is completed.

FIGURE 144. Traditional beginning: the weft passes over and under *pairs* for four rows.

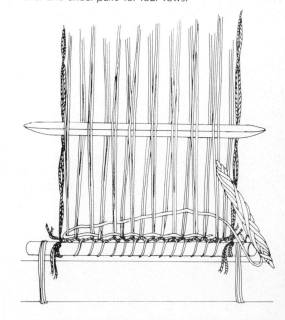

FIGURE 145. To allow for fringed ends, weave 5 or 6 inches with strips of rags.

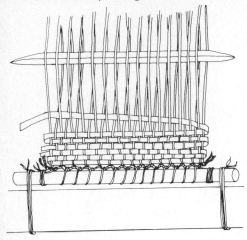

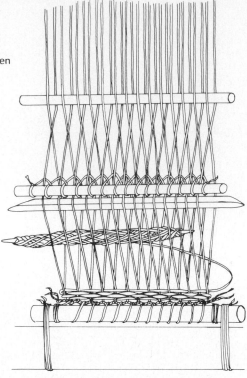

FIGURE 146. Passing the weft through the open shed.

The Weaving

After you have woven the first rows (either in the traditional way or with rags) you are ready to start the main weaving. This consists of opening one shed, passing the weft through, packing it down; then opening the other shed, passing the weft back through, and packing it down. Sounds very simple, doesn't it? Well . . . if these were the only directions to follow, you would soon find yourself in great difficulties. After about an inch or less of weaving you would find that the edges were drawing in drastically, and you couldn't pack the weft down tightly enough to cover the warp. The weaving would start looking pretty dreadful.

And then there is the problem of weaving the pattern—the tapestry technique in which you will be working with several little butterflies of different-colored wefts. I hope you will not be so rash as to start right off with a tapestry project; you should try just plain weaving for a few inches at least. The tapestry technique will be thoroughly discussed under Project IV, Traditional Navajo Rug.

There are many little tricks and techniques to the plain weaving that I must describe in order that your weaving will come out looking good. The weft tension and the way the weft is packed in are probably the most important factors. And you have to know how to handle the fork and batten properly. I will discuss these things immediately after I tell you how to weave those extra threads for the side selvedge —if that is your plan.

Weaving the Side Selvedges (Optional)

If you have prepared the side selvedge threads, you must incorporate them in the weaving from the beginning. The weft passes around 1 thread of the selvedge pair at each side for about 6 rows and then the 2 selvedge threads are given one twist and the weft passes around the other thread for the same number of rows. They are again twisted (in the same direction), and the weft passes around the first thread again for 6 rows. And so forth. As the 2 selvedge threads get too twisted up above, they are untied at the top bar, untwisted, and tied again.

FIGURE 147. Weaving around one selvedge thread for three turns; then switching and weaving around the other for the same number of turns.

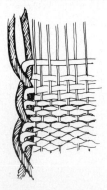

Proper Handling of the Fork and Batten

The batten is either in your hand or in the shed at all times; the fork is in your hand at all times. Since this means handling the two simultaneously (in the same hand) you need to learn the proper grasp for each.

Grasp the fork from the top, with the handle extending out from the thumb and forefinger, and the teeth extending out beyond the little finger. The fork beats down on the weft by a quick repeated rotation of the wrist. The little finger can be slipped under the fork to improve balance while beating.

When you need to grasp the batten (do not set the fork down!), the hand is simply inverted, so that the palm is up, and you use your thumb and first and second fingers to hold the batten; the fourth and fifth fingers are still holding the fork.

Notes on Weft Tension

One of the most common difficulties a beginning weaver has on *any* loom is understanding that the weft needs extra length in order to wind over and under the warp threads. It does not just lie straight across the shed from one side to the other (except in the case of warp-face weaving). Weft-face weaving requires the greatest extra weft length; and so it is very common for the beginning weaver on the Navajo loom (since this loom is used almost exclusively for weft-face weaving) to become very discouraged with the problem of the edges drawing in. If the weft thread is laid straight across and held in that position while it is beaten down with the fork, the fabric *has* to draw in to a narrower width to allow for the undulation of the weft around the warp threads.

For this reason the method of laying in and beating down the weft is *extremely important*. There are two different methods used on the Navajo loom to regulate the weft tension properly.

One way is to hold the weft loosely at a diagonal as you beat it down with the fork. This is just so that the weft is held up in the shed, so that there is no restriction on it whatsoever. I prefer this method because it automatically lets just the right amount of weft feed in.

The other method is to pass the weft across the entire width of the weaving (or the color area, in the case of tapestry weaving), and then, while holding the weft loosely with your hand, "prepack" it at points about 6 inches apart with your finger or the pointed handle end of your fork. This makes little arcs or scallops, which are then packed down thoroughly.

If you make the arcs too high, the weft will protrude in little loops in some places and the weaving width will become wider than was intended. If the arcs are too low the weaving will begin to draw in and the warp will begin to show. You have to find the right height for the arcs by closely watching the weaving and the edge, and make whatever adjustments are necessary.

Notes on Warp Tension

At all times the warp should be stretched as tight as possible. After the first few rows of weaving it may have loosened up. At this point and any other time that it is not in its full tension, you must tighten and retie the top tension rope.

FIGURE 148. How to hold the fork and batten.

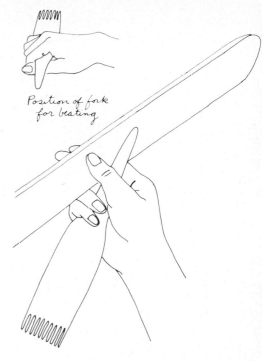

Position of fork for beating

Fork is still held in hand when batten is grasped.

FIGURE 149. Two methods of feeding in the weft so that there will be enough extra length to undulate around the warp threads.

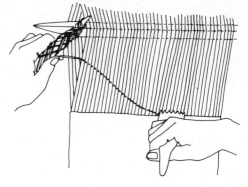

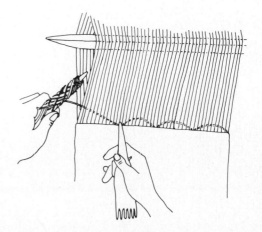

FIGURE 150. Sliding guide string to check on edges.

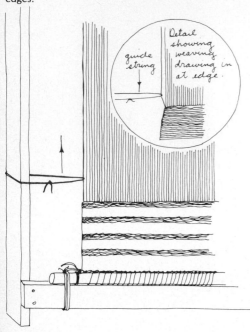

Keeping the Edges Even

The edges can start drawing in before the change is even perceptible to the naked eye. There are two ways to check to see if the weaving width remains constant. One way is simply to measure the width every inch or so. The other way is to have a string looped around the edge warp thread and the side of the frame. It will tell you instantly when the weaving is becoming narrower.

If the edges do start to draw in:

1. Make sure the warp is tightened up as much as possible.

2. Feed weft in more loosely or make bigger arcs (see Notes on Weft Tension).

3. You can put a cord through the weaving 1 inch from the edge and 1 inch down into the weaving and tie this around the vertical support of the loom frame, thus stretching the fabric out to the full width.

FIGURE 152. Splicing weft by laying *broken* ends side by side over a distance of about 2 inches.

FIGURE 151. Cord sewn through fabric and around vertical frame, acting as a stretcher (not to be confused with guide string in Figure 150).

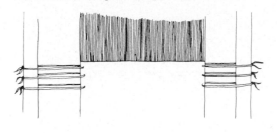

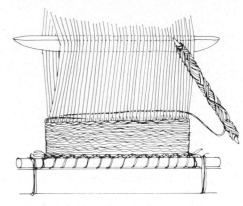

FIGURE 153. Replacing the entire warp thread.

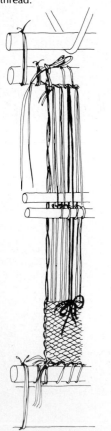

Splicing the Weft

When you run out of yarn on the stick shuttle or butterfly, simply lay a new end alongside the old end, overlapping them for a distance of about 2 inches or more. The yarn should always be broken by hand rather than cut with scissors.

Mending Broken Warp Threads

Let's hope you will not have any warp threads break. But, if this unfortunate incident does occur, here is the best way to treat the problem: *If* you are not going to weave up to the top selvedge, you can tie on a new warp thread up near the top and tie it to the broken one right at the weaving line. If you are going to weave up to the top there should be no knots in the warp. Some weavers do tie a knot, but I feel the best solution is to replace the entire thread, which means from the weaving line up through the twisted selvedge and back down to the weaving line again. Pull the broken thread out and break it off so that you can tie a temporary knot for each thread of the warp pair. These ends will be sewn with a needle into the weaving after the rug is finished (see Chapter VIII, "Finishing Techniques: Mending"). When you tie the knots, make sure the tension is the same as with the other warp threads, and leave the ends long enough so that you can thread them through the eye of a needle and darn them in along the warp line for about 4 or 5 inches.

Cleaning the Heddles

In case the heddles get fuzzed up from the warp threads, see this heading in Chapter III, "The Inkle Loom."

Adjustment of the Warp Spacing

Next to the edges drawing in, the most common difficulty is keeping the warp threads spaced the right distance apart. They tend to get farther and farther apart from each other in certain areas (particularly at a vertical juncture of two color areas in tapestry weaving) and closer and closer together in other areas (particularly in the middle of tapestry shapes).

The tendency for this to happen will be greater if you do not have your warp tightened up as much as possible.

Having the perfect balance between the size and spacing of your warp and weft threads will help prevent this also. The weft should be heavy enough to just *barely* pack down between the warp threads when beaten with the fork. This forces the warp threads to remain properly spaced.

Another preventive measure in tapestry weaving is to weave with a lot of diagonals. When you are weaving diagonal lines you can pull the weft tighter or looser as it turns around the warp threads to adjust their spacing.

If the trouble has already occurred, the only way to remedy it is to take the pointed end of your fork and force the weft threads up for an inch or so in the problem area and then (again with the pointed end of the fork) force the warp threads closer together or farther apart, as need be. Then repack the weft into place.

Keeping the Weaving Level Even

After you have woven a few inches you may notice that your weaving is not perfectly level all the way across. There may be some areas that dip (where the warp threads have gotten spaced a little farther apart) and other areas that seem to build up (where the warp threads are closer together than they should be). You can try adjusting the spacing of the warp threads (as described in the previous paragraph), or just try to beat down the weft harder in those raised areas. But you will probably have to fill in the low areas to make the line perfectly even. It is best never to let it get too uneven.

To fill in the low areas, weave back and forth in that area, turning around a different warp thread each time. It is not necessary to change the shed, using the batten, each time the weft is inserted. In short distances like this it is less time-consuming simply to use the stick shed as it is and pull the alternate threads (for the pull shed) forward with your finger.

Lowering the Loom on the Frame

As the weaving gets too high to work at comfortably, you can change from sitting on the ground to a bench, but eventually (if the weaving is a large one) you will have to untie and loosen the tension rope at the top of the frame. Lower the weaving to the desired height (if necessary use the intermediate bar on the larger frames). The bottom edge of the weaving must be rolled up by placing another bar right alongside the bottom loom bar and rolling the two up together. Tie the two bars to the frame again as shown. The rope at the top must again be tightened up as much as possible.

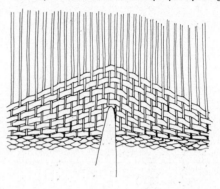
FIGURE 154. Prying up several weft shots to force the warp threads back to their proper spacing.

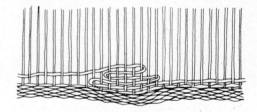
FIGURE 155. To fill in low areas, weave back and forth, each time turning around a different warp thread.

FIGURE 156. To lower weaving level, roll the lower loom bar up with a second bar.

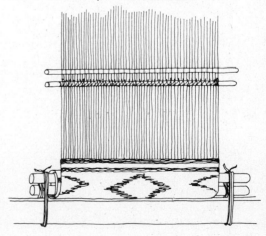

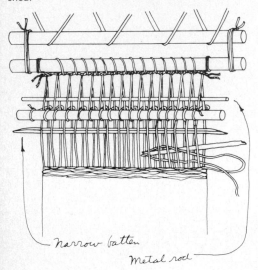

FIGURE 157. Weaving up to the top selvedge (a metal rod is shown replacing regular shed stick), then using a broken stick to push weft through the shed.

narrow batten
metal rod

To Weave Up to the Top Selvedge (Optional)

You will notice that as the weaving progresses and you get closer to the top bar it becomes more and more difficult to separate the warp threads to form the shed. (At this point, if you are not going to weave up to the top selvedge, you can simply cut the weaving down, leaving at least 6 inches of warp for making fringe.)

If you want to weave right up to the top, use the following procedures to continue weaving.

At first:

a. Change the batten to one of narrower width.

b. Use a very thin stick shuttle or smaller butterflies.

Next:

a. Change the shed rod to the metal rod of smaller diameter (i).

b. Use an even narrower batten.

Then:

a. Remove the shed rod, and re-create this shed each time with the smallest batten.

b. Continue using heddle rod as before.

c. Discontinue using butterflies or the stick shuttle, and simply push weft ends through, using a small stick with a broken end. Or use the umbrella rib or the piece of wire (j) bent double and twisted together to make a long needle.

Finally:

a. Remove the heddle stick, by slipping it out of the heddles, and pull the heddle string out of the shed.

b. Weave in 4 rows at the top selvedge, going over 2 and under 2 just as you did in the first 4 rows of weaving.

c. Re-create both sheds with the smallest batten.

d. When each shed is open put in two wefts, one to be packed up to the top selvedge and one to be packed down to meet the main mass of weaving.

e. Thread the weft yarn through the eye of the umbrella rib or the wire needle or the eye of a sacking needle. If the eye of the needle is too small, make a thread eye, and thread the weft through this.

f. If you are using the side selvedge cords do not try to weave them in from now on; they can be woven into place with a needle after the weaving is complete.

The last half inch:

a. These last few rows simply have to be woven with the needle.

b. Use an ordinary table fork to pack in the weft.

c. Continue weaving in the weft with a needle until it is absolutely impossible to force another thread through the warp.

FIGURE 158. A large needle with a thread eye.

Note: Be sure not to draw the weft too tight in these last few inches of weaving; allow it plenty of length so the weaving will not become narrower at this point.

Some Navajo weavers weave 3 or 4 inches at one end of the loom and then turn the loom upside down and weave from the other end to meet the weaving line of the first end. This is a good way to do it, but one word of caution: The first weaving I did on a Navajo loom was about 6 feet high and I thought it would be very smart to weave one half and then turn it upside down and weave the other half—which meant the weaving together with the needle happened in the center of the rug. Well, I did manage to do it but it is definitely easier if that join takes place as close to one of the loom bars as possible, because the warp is much more rigidly held at that point, and the join will be much better.

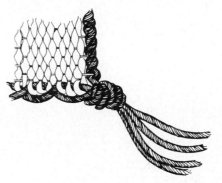

FIGURE 159. The corner tie on a Navajo rug.

Cutting Off

Simply untie the loom from the frame and with a razor slice through the cord that binds the selvedges to the loom bars (or pull this cord out if you wish to save it).

Finishing

Sew in any broken warp ends. Sew in the last few inches of twisted side selvedge if this was used.

Untie the knots of all selvedge threads and retie them in one group at each corner of the weaving. Trim ends to a uniform length.

Make braided fringe or false selvedge if you did not make 4 selvedges.

Steam press or bury in wet sand as the Navajos do.

See Chapter VIII, "Finishing Techniques."

Project I. Tufted Rug (Old Navajo Technique)*

FIGURE 160. Tufted rug.

(This rug can also be woven on the treadle loom.)

This rug is really fun to make and the technique is one of the easiest for the Navajo loom. It's like re-creating a sheepskin with a design in it. You take long tufts of wool from a fleece and lay them in as you weave, leaving the long ends just hanging out. A few rows of tight plain weave between the rows of tufts make the rug strong.

It will be a thick, shaggy rug that looks very much like a real sheepskin—except more pliable and with a design in it if desired. The design possibilities are limitless; since the tufts are laid in one at a time, you can have each tuft any color you want. It is quick to weave and very durable. The technique was used by the Navajos in the old days to make homemade "mattresses." You may make the rug with the traditional four selvedges, or with fringed ends, depending on your reserve of patience.

Materials

Warp—2-, 3-, or 4-ply wool or hair yarn very tightly spun (preferably respun yourself).
Medium weight.
Amount: Approximately 1/4 pound.
Color: Any natural color.

*A good project for beginners.

Weft—For structural plain weave: Same as warp (but it doesn't have to be respun). About 2 pounds: same color.

For tufts: Raw fleece, preferably karakul, mohair, or other long-fibered wool. The tufts must be at least 6 inches long and preferably much longer.

Amount: One whole raw fleece, about 8 to 10 pounds, so you can pick out nice tufts. (The fleece does not have to be washed; the whole rug can be washed after woven. The clumps will be easier to select if the fleece is not washed.)

Color: Different natural colors with one predominating. *Or* dyed colors. (For these you will have to wash the wool and dye it yourself. See Chapter X, "Dyeing.")

Directions

Set up your warp about 8 warp ends per inch, 30 inches wide and 45 inches long. If you are not going to weave up to the top selvedge, allow another 18 inches for warp length.

Do plain weave with structural weft following general directions for about 1 inch.

Now place batten on edge in the next shed. Lay in a tuft of wool behind 2 warp threads, skip 1 warp thread, lay a tuft behind next 2, and so on. The amount of fiber in each tuft should make a clump about 1/4 inch in diameter. I prefer to rearrange the tuft so that half of it has the shorn end alongside the tip of the other half.

After all the tufts are laid in, weave 1 shot of the structural weft in the same shed. Then continue weaving plain weave for about 1/4 to 1/2 inch (depending on how closely you want to lay in the tufts). Place batten on edge in the next shed (this should be the opposite shed from the one used in the previous row of tufting). Lay tufts in this shed in the same manner. Weave one shot of weft in this shed and continue weaving plain for the same distance you did before. Continue this tufting and weaving throughout the rug. Pack the weft and tufts in by really beating hard with your fork, and every once in a while with the batten, to keep the weaving line level.

At the end of the rug weave the same amount of plain weave (about 1 inch) as you did in the beginning.

If you do wash this after it is woven it should be handled as you would raw wool (see Chapter IX, "Spinning: Washing the Raw Wool").

The design: Place the colored tufts according to the design you have in mind or have drawn on paper. The structural weft is woven plain, and is not seen in the finished rug.

Project II. Handbag with Stripes and Tapestry Ovals*

(This project can also be woven on the backstrap loom or the treadle loom.)

The technique used to achieve this design is one of the simplest forms of tapestry weaving—used often by the Spanish colonial weavers in New Mexico. It is a good project for beginners. The size and shape of this handbag is very functional—it holds a lot and things do not fall out of it. It is designed so that it will never pull apart, as some bags tend to do, and if you use good-quality hard-twist yarn it will last for years. If you don't want to take the time, the bag is just as successful without the top and bottom woven selvedges.

*A good project for beginners.

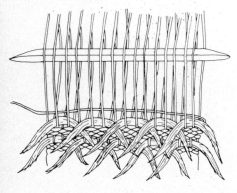
FIGURE 161. Laying in one row of tufts.

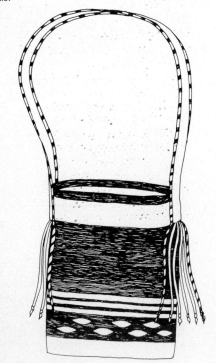
FIGURE 162. Handbag with stripes and tapestry ovals.

FIGURE 163. How the tapestry ovals are made.

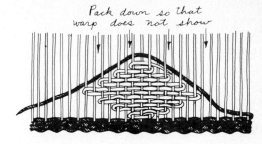

Materials

Warp—Medium-fine 2- or 3-ply wool or hair yarn, tightly spun (Norwegian spelsau yarn would be good). Since such a small amount is needed, you may want to take the time to respin it.

Amount: Approximately 1/8 pound.

Color: Dark natural or any color; the warp will be completely covered.

Weft—Medium-fine or medium-weight single- or multi-plied wool or hair yarn, just slightly heavier than the warp (or if convenient it can be the same yarn as the warp). I suggest Norwegian spelsau, cowhair, or any rather coarse, lustrous fiber, tightly spun. Avoid soft, fuzzy yarns for this project, because with all the rubbing it will get in normal use the yarn will pill badly. The tighter it is spun the longer it will wear—and the more "ethnic" it will look.

Amount: Approximately 3/4 pound plus an extra 1/4 pound for the strap.

Suggested colors: Natural black with small amounts of white for the design.

FIGURE 164. Sewing the top hem and joining the sides.

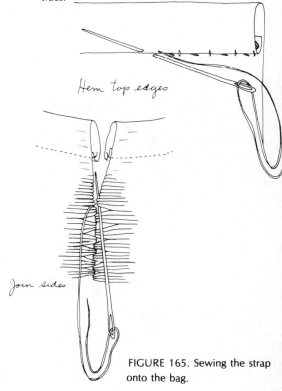

Directions

Set up the warp 10 or 12 to the inch, depending on weight of the yarn. The warp should be set up 9 inches wide and 24 inches long. (Add another 18 inches to warp length if you are not going to weave up to the top selvedge.)

The design: Make up your own design with a combination of plain areas, stripes, and ovals. (Don't have the ovals come near the top if you are going to be weaving the 4 selvedges.)

The ovals are formed by making little tapestry "eyes" or lozenges equidistant from each other, followed by several rows of plain weaving. The weft in these rows of plain weaving will pack in to form wavy lines that follow the contour of the ovals. The next row of ovals is set in the low places formed between the previous ovals. Wind the weft in butterflies for the ovals (one for each), and on a stick shuttle for the plain weaving. Each oval should be about 2 inches wide. You will have to count your warp threads and place the ovals properly.

Pack the weft in as tightly as possible. Leave a long end when you start the oval; this can be sewn in invisibly when the fabric is finished. The top end or tail is *broken* off (not cut) and laid down alongside the oval as shown in the illustration.

If you want the design to be symmetrical on both sides of the bag, after you have woven 12 inches, reverse the design and repeat it as if it were a mirror image.

Finishing: Remove the piece from the loom. Unless it has the 4 selvedge edges, fringe the warp ends with knotted fringe, trim to 1 inch the length, roll edges over to form a hem that covers the fringe completely, and sew with a strong carpet thread or the same thread as the warp. Sew up the sides of the bag. See Chapter VIII, "Finishing Techniques: Joining."

Making the strap: Make a warp-face strap on an inkle loom or Hopi belt loom or by card weaving, and sew it onto the bag securely with the warp thread.

To determine the length of the strap, hold the bag so that the top is at your waistline and measure over the shoulder. Add 4 inches to this measurement so that the strap can be sewn 2 inches down from the top of the bag on each side, and add on whatever you desire for the fringe. (Also allow for warp takeup as described under directions on inkle weaving, backstrap weaving, or any warp-face belt. Probably another 4 inches will take care of this.)

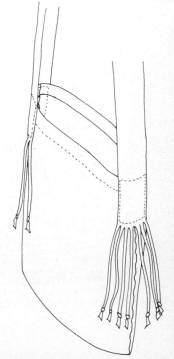

FIGURE 165. Sewing the strap onto the bag.

Project III. Wedge-Woven Rug
(Old Navajo Technique)

(This project can also be woven on a treadle loom; and the wedge-weaving technique can be done on any loom.)

FIGURE 166. Wedge-woven rug.

This rug is made by a technique that was used quite often by the Navajo weavers in the old days to make diagonal-striped designs without using the more time-consuming tapestry weave. It is rarely, if ever, used today, but it makes a very unusual and serene design. The technique is also sometimes referred to as "pulled warp" or "scalloped" because the warp is actually pulled by the weft to an off-vertical alignment and, because of this, the edges of these rugs come out slightly scalloped. This project should not be attempted until you have tried one of the two preceding ones, or unless you have had some experience in weaving. The final weaving up to the top selvedge must be done in the last plain stripe (or you can skip this process and just have fringed ends).

Materials

Warp—Medium-weight 2-, 3-, or 4-ply wool or hair yarn, tightly spun (preferably respun yourself).

  Amount: Approximately 1/4 pound.

  Color: Any natural.

Weft—Medium-weight (slightly heavier than the warp) single-ply wool yarn, preferably handspun with a very tight twist.

  Amount: Approximately 4 pounds (2 pounds of one color for the background stripes and 2 pounds of all other colors together).

  Suggested colors: Earth colors (natural-dyed) with light and dark naturals; or, indigo, cochineal (or madder), and natural black and white.

Directions

Set up the warp about 8 to 10 to the inch (depending on weight of yarn). The warp will be 30 inches wide and 45 inches long; add another 18 inches to the warp length if you are not going to weave up to top selvedge.

Divide the height of the rug into 5 equal areas for the background and 4 equal areas for the stripes; or, 4 equal areas for the background and 3 equal areas for the stripes. (This will require some mathematics on your part.) After the warp is all set up on the loom, mark the warp with a felt-tip pen to indicate these divisions. (Marking the warp thread at each edge will suffice.)

Weave the first background stripe the correct height plus 1/4 inch (to allow for packing down when more weaving is added above this point). Weave the narrow stripe that borders the diagonal stripes.

FIGURE 167. Making the triangle that sets up the diagonal direction of the weft.

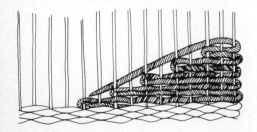

Now start at one edge and build up a small triangle of one of the colors (use all 4 colors for the diagonal stripes). Work back and forth in this small area, using the alternating sheds as usual, but move over 2 more warp threads each time your weft turns to go back through the shed.

After this first triangle is made the weft will follow the angle for all the remaining stripes. Do not make this angle greater than 15 degrees or the rug will be very scalloped and puckered.

Keep laying in one diagonal ("wedge") stripe at a time until you have covered the warp from one side to the other. The final stripes at the other edge of the rug will have to be laid in like the first triangle.

Notice that at the top and bottom of each stripe the weft goes around a different warp thread each time. If you moved over only one warp thread each time, the angle of the stripe would be steep; normally you will skip 2 threads each time; or 3, if you want the angle to be very slight.

Continue weaving horizontal stripes and diagonal stripes. Make the next diagonal area go in the opposite direction; this means you will make that first triangle on the opposite side of the warp.

If you haven't made 4 selvedges, a false selvedge or braided fringe will probably look best.

Steam pressing this rug after it is off the loom will help it lie flat.

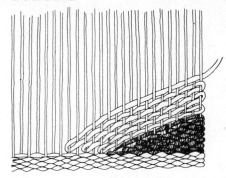

FIGURE 168. Weaving the diagonal weft stripes, one at a time.

Project IV. Traditional Navajo Rug

(This design can be woven on a treadle loom, but you cannot have the four selvedge edges; and if you want it packed as tightly as here, you will have to use a Navajo fork as well as the beater on your loom.)

This rug is woven in the traditional manner of the Navajo tapestry blankets or rugs. Of course, you must realize that we may imitate the technique but to produce one of those beautiful Navajo blankets (which hold a top place in the history of textiles) you may have to get to know what Navajo religion is all about. And I suspect to do that you would have to live the life of a Navajo—and perhaps even have a Navajo grandmother and great-grandmother. But at least you can give it a try.

The design shown here is just a suggestion; you may make up your own design. But for your first rug keep these things in mind: use only verticals, horizontals, and *one* diagonal angle (the weaving of two different angles for your first weaving would be too confusing). Avoid long vertical lines (these are the most difficult to control). Diagonal lines are actually the easiest in this type of weaving, and help immensely in keeping the warp threads spaced evenly throughout the weaving—one of the big problems in working on the Navajo loom.

Be sure to avoid complicated design areas in the last 6 inches of the weaving, where you will be working with an umbrella rib or needle. (I hope. It will be worthwhile trying to weave up to the top selvedge on this rug, since it is 5 feet long and only the last foot or so will be difficult. Then the finished weaving will look like the real thing.) Also make the traditional side selvedge.

This is not an easy project; you will have to plan to spend a good deal of time at it.

FIGURE 169. Traditional Navajo rug.

Materials
Warp—Medium-weight 2-, 3-, or 4-ply wool or hair yarn, tightly spun (preferably respun yourself).
　　Amount: Approximately 1/4 to 1/2 pound.
　　Color: Natural.
Weft—Slightly heavier than warp, single-ply wool, preferably handspun and tightly spun.
　　Amount: Approximately 6 pounds.
　　Suggested colors: Different shades of naturals, from white to black; *or* all naturals with some cochineal or indigo; *or* indigo, cochineal, onion skins, and light and dark naturals (see Chapter X, "Dyeing").

Directions
Set up the warp 8 to 10 threads to the inch, depending on weight of yarn, 3 feet wide and 5 feet long.

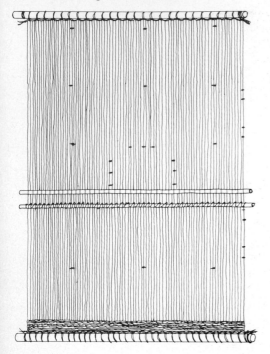

FIGURE 170. The first few inches of plain weave completed, with the warp marked at points to show where design starts and ends.

Mark the centers and divisions of your design on the strung-up warp with a felt-tip pen, so you will know where to begin and end design areas. It is not necessary to mark the entire design on the warp (or have the design drawn on paper, a "cartoon," behind the warp as the traditional European tapestries are done—I really don't believe in that kind of weaving). In fact, it is best *not* to draw your design on the warp. You will not know the exact angle of your diagonals until you start weaving them, and you will want to be free to let them grow at whatever angle is natural, rather than trying to do all kinds of tricks to make them come out exactly like the drawing.

Laying in the pattern colors: One butterfly of weft color is necessary for *each* color area as it appears on the horizontal weaving line. Be sure each color is laid in with the wefts all going in one direction. Loop the broken (not cut) end of the yarn around the warp thread and lay it back in the same shed to start a color. They can be started in either shed. (See below for starting points of diamond shapes.)

Pack the weft in with your fork, feeding in any extra length needed to fit in and around the warp threads.

FIGURE 171. Laying in the tails of butterflies for each color as it appears across the horizontal weaving line.

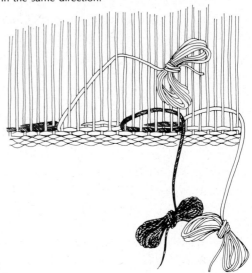

FIGURE 172. Backstepping with all the wefts going in the same direction.

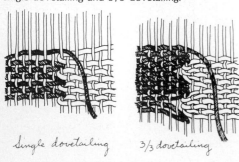

FIGURE 173. Two ways of making vertical joins: single dovetailing and 3/3 dovetailing.

Single dovetailing   3/3 dovetailing

Weaving the design: Change the shed and weave all the butterflies back—each one going in the same direction. (This is very important: *in each row of weaving make sure the weft is woven with each color going in the same direction.*) After each row of weaving all the butterflies should be hanging out the same side of their color area. If you do not follow this rule you will get hopelessly confused.

The other rule is *always backstep.* By "backstepping" I mean if the butterflies are all hanging out the *right* side of the weaving, you start weaving with the color at the *left* edge of the warp, and vice versa. Otherwise, if you are weaving diagonal lines, your weft threads will have to cross over each other.

Be sure to feed in extra weft length and watch the edges of your weaving to make sure they are not drawing in. (See Notes on Weft Tension in this chapter.)

How to make vertical lines: At first you will probably be very confused about which warp thread to turn around. In weaving vertical lines the problem is not too great: just *always* turn around the same warp thread, whether it is from front to back or back to front. In Figure 173 are illustrations of ways to make vertical joins.

The second method has the advantage that the weft threads do not build up.

How to make diagonal lines: The dilemma of deciding which warp thread to turn around in making diagonals is much greater, because sometimes the thread that is to be turned around is in back of the batten and sometimes in front. Look at the four illustrations in Figure 174 of ways to make diagonals, and decide on one; then just keep saying to yourself, "Move over one warp thread each time," or "Move over one warp thread every *other* time," or whatever diagonal method you choose.

Beginning and ending color areas: Starting and ending horizontal lines is no problem; just break off the yarn (never cut with scissors) and lay a short tail back in the same shed.

Starting and ending the point of a diamond, for instance, is not as simple. You can conceivably lock the beginning tail in the next 2 or 3 rows of weaving, but it makes a bulky point. And there is really no way of locking in the end tail at the top of the diamond. The very best solution is to leave a tail long enough to thread into a needle, and when the weaving is completed simply darn in the end in such a way that it will be invisible.

I usually wind the weft around the warp *twice* at the beginning or ending of a point; this makes a sharper point. The problem of which way to wind it around the chosen warp thread is also confusing. It must be wound around in the correct direction so that the butterfly itself is coming out of the correct side of the color area—the same side as all the other butterflies so that in your shed the wefts will all be woven in the *same* direction.

Building up color areas: You can work up one area of color at a time, rather than weaving a row of weft for each color all across the warp. This method is particularly convenient (if not actually necessary) in wide weavings. Of course, the space left to be woven later must be an open-angled space, as you can't weave *underneath* an area. The same method can be used within a solid-color area on a wide rug, making a diagonal join that will be nearly invisible: this is the "lazy line."

Final notes: Weft tension in tapestry weaving involves the same principle as in plain weaving. Either the weft yarn should be held loosely while it is packed in to allow for extra weft length; or an arc should be made of the weft thread before packing it in. To make nice joins of color areas, each weft as it turns around the warp thread to return in the next shed should be pulled against the warp thread *just* enough to make a tight loop and not enough to move the warp from its vertical position.

FIGURE 174. Four ways of making diagonals.

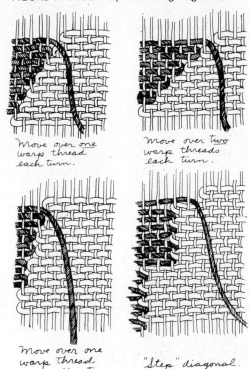

Move over one warp thread each turn.

Move over two warp threads each turn.

Move over one warp thread every other turn.

"Step" diagonal.

FIGURE 175. Starting and ending wefts on the horizontal.

FIGURE 177. Weaving in color areas one at a time, filling in the other areas later. "Lazy lines" made the same way, within a solid color area.

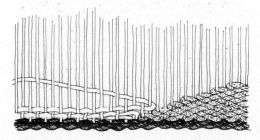

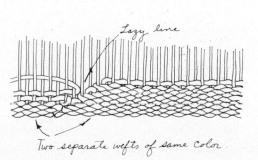

Lazy line

Two separate wefts of same color

FIGURE 176. Starting and ending points; the tails to be darned in later.

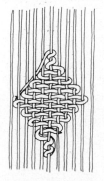

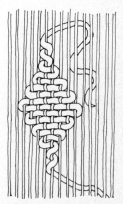

Fine weft with tails woven in.

Thick weft with tails hanging out.

Project V. Diamond Twill Saddle Blanket (Navajo Technique)

(This project can also be woven on a treadle loom—without the four selvedge edges, of course, and the heddles will have to be threaded according to Figure 228 in Chapter VII.)

This weft-face diamond twill weave is very common and popular on the reservation today. It is sometimes referred to as a double weave, because the design comes out in reverse colors on the opposite side. It makes a thicker fabric than the tapestry weave and is therefore very suitable for saddle blankets as well as rugs. This saddle blanket is woven double length so it can be folded over, making a nice thick padding for a saddle. Some authentic Navajo saddle blankets are done in this technique and the second half of the blanket is woven in a different design and different colors, just for variation.

The diamond twill weave necessitates the use of 4 different sheds, operated by 1 shed stick and 3 heddle sticks. The weft is carried from edge to edge in each row of weaving, and 3 different weft colors are used in succession. This project should not be attempted until you have done at least one of the previous projects for the Navajo loom—or unless you are an experienced weaver.

Materials

Warp—Medium-weight 2-, 3-, or 4-ply wool or hair yarn, tightly spun (preferably respun yourself).
> Amount: Approximately 1/2 pound.
> Color: Natural.

Weft—Medium-weight (slightly heavier than the warp) single-ply wool yarn, preferably handspun—tightly twisted.
> Amount: Approximately 6 pounds (2 pounds of each color).
> Suggested colors: Naturals—white, beige, and black; *or* natural black and white with red.

Directions

You will need 2 extra heddle sticks. Follow the general directions for setting up the warp and loom up to The Shed Stick. You do *not* need to preserve the cross, or lease. The warp should be set up 12 threads to the inch (the weft will pack down okay since it goes over and under 2 or 3 threads at a time) and in multiples of 20 threads, plus 1 extra thread to make the design come out symmetrical. In this rug we will make 360 warp threads (20 by 18) plus 1, or 361. This means there will be 18 complete diamond designs across the warp, and the width of the blanket will be approximately 30 inches. Make the warp 60 inches long, so that when it is folded over it makes a perfect square.

Setting the shed stick and making the heddles

In Figure 179, each vertical division represents a warp thread, and a blackened square means that a heddle is made around that warp thread. As you can see from the blackened squares some warp threads are tied to heddles on more than one heddle stick. Heddle stick no. 1 when pulled forward will lift all the threads marked in black in this draft, so the weft, when inserted, will go over 2 threads and under 2 threads (except in the center, where it will go under 3).

FIGURE 178. Diamond twill saddle blanket.

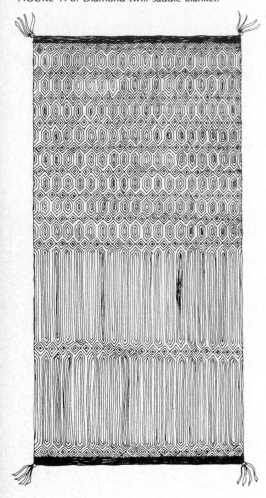

FIGURE 179. Draft for diamond twill.

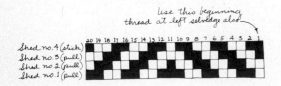

Shed No. 4 (Stick): Starting with this line of the draft, and the right side of the draft and your warp, pick up the threads marked in black. This is done with your batten. After you have picked up the first sequence of 20 threads, repeat that sequence of picking up 18 times, all across the warp. You should have 1 thread left—at the far left-hand edge of your warp—pick it up also.

Now all the threads marked in black in the top line of the draft are lying over the top of your batten. Check the sequence to be absolutely certain it is correct. Turn the batten on edge and insert your shed stick. Also tie a long circle of thread (cotton cord) through this shed, just to preserve the shed if the shed stick accidentally falls out. Remove the batten and push the shed stick up out of the way.

Shed No. 3 (Pull): Now working below the shed stick, with your batten pick up the threads of the warp corresponding to the line of the draft second from the top. Pick up the 1 remaining warp thread on the left side also. Now all the threads marked in black in the line of the draft marked "Shed No. 3 (Pull)" will be lying over the top of your batten. Check the sequence to be absolutely certain it is correct. Turn your batten on edge. Using your heddle stick and heddle cord, make heddles around *each* warp thread held up by the batten, just as in general directions Making the Heddles. When this heddle stick is complete, remove your batten and push the heddle stick up next to the shed stick.

Shed No. 2 (Pull): Using the line of the draft marked "Shed No. 2 (Pull)," make another heddle stick in the same manner as above. Do not pick up last warp thread on the left. Notice you will be picking up the threads exactly opposite to those you did in shed no. 4.

Shed No. 1 (Pull): Using the line of the draft marked "Shed No. 1 (Pull)" make another heddle stick in the same manner as above. Do not pick up last warp thread on the left. Notice you will be picking up exactly the opposite threads to those you did in shed no. 3.

Note: These warp threadings must be accurate or mistakes that cannot be remedied will be occurring throughout the weaving. Check the threads on the batten each time before making the heddles: be *absolutely sure* they are the correct threads. This is the most tedious part of working on this project; the weaving goes very fast.

The weaving

The first and last 1 or 2 inches on a diamond twill rug are most easily woven using the stick shed alternately with pull shed no. 2, and using only 1 of the 3 weft colors.

To weave the diamond twill the sheds are operated in sequence. First pull heddle no. 1 forward, insert the batten and turn it on edge, and place a shot of one of the weft colors. Pack it in, allowing it to feed in and around the warp (this type of weaving does not require quite as much extra weft length as does the plain weave).

Next, pull heddle no. 2 forward, insert batten and place shot (use another weft color this time); pack in the weft. (*Note:* It is less confusing if you start the wefts all from the same direction.)

Next, pull heddle no. 3 forward and weave with the third weft color.

Finally, use the stick shed (no. 4) and this time the weft color will be the first one you used. There are four different sheds, but only three weft colors. The sheds are operated in sequence, and the weft colors are woven in succession. This means that the weft colors appear in different sheds at different times.

If you repeat the sheds 1, 2, 3, and 4 over and over, the diagonal lines continue in the same direction. When you want to reverse the direction of the diagonals to form

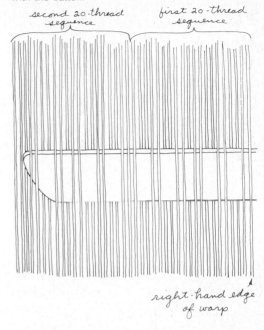

FIGURE 180. Picking up shed no. 4 (stick shed) with the batten.

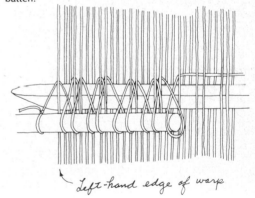

FIGURE 181. Making heddles for shed no. 3 (pull shed) around all the warp threads held up by the batten.

FIGURE 182. Using two battens.

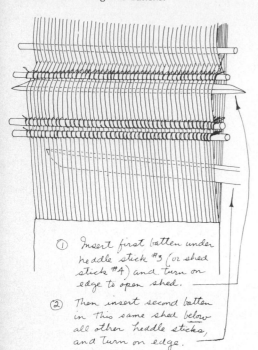

① *Insert first batten under heddle stick #3 (or shed stick #4) and turn on edge to open shed.* —

② *Then insert second batten in this same shed below all other heddle sticks, and turn on edge.* —

FIGURE 183. Two more drafts for diamond twill patterns.

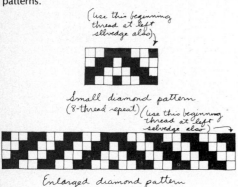

(use this beginning thread at left selvedge also) →

Small diamond pattern
(8-thread repeat) *(use this beginning thread at left selvedge also)* →

Enlarged diamond pattern
(26-thread repeat)

diamonds, reverse the shed sequence—4, 3, 2, and 1, and reverse color sequence also.

Verticals may be made by repeating sheds 2, 3, and 4 (after weaving a diamond ending with shed no. 4); or by repeating 3, 2, and 1 (after weaving a diamond ending with shed no. 1) over and over. The weft colors are woven in the same order.

A second batten will be helpful in forming the sheds below the heddle sticks. When making a shed, insert the second batten directly below the shed stick or upper heddle sticks; turn on edge. This will make it easier to discern the shed *below* the lowest heddle stick—insert your first batten here.

By combining large and small diamonds and verticals you make your overall pattern according to your desire.

Note: Weaving a diamond twill fabric necessitates ''manually'' weaving in the edge warp threads on some rows of weaving. Because of the 3 weft colors used, the return shed for a certain color may be such that the edge warp thread would be missed. In this case you have to see to it that the weft turns around that edge thread on each row of weaving.

Project VI. Double-Face Saddle Blanket (Old Navajo Technique)

(This technique can also be done on the treadle loom, but the warp ends have to be farther apart in order for the weft to be packed in properly.)

Using the Navajo double-face technique, one side of a blanket or rug can be of a tapestry design and the other side an entirely different design—usually stripes. Sometimes considered a great mystery, it is actually a simple but very ingenious technique. Like the diamond twill weave it requires four different sheds operated by a shed stick and three heddle sticks.

For this project I suggest a simple striped or checkerboard design on the front side and a contrasting plain color for the back. If you are very ambitious you may attempt a simple tapestry design on the front and stripes on the back. But do not attempt this unless you are completely familiar with the tapestry technique or you will get hopelessly confused trying to work the double weave at the same time you are handling all the different tapestry colors.

Since this is a saddle blanket, you should try to weave up to the top selvedge; it will be much longer wearing.

Materials

Warp—Fine or medium-fine weight plied wool or hair yarn, tightly spun (respun if possible).

Amount: Approximately 1/4 pound.

Color: Dark natural (the warp may show very slightly in this weave, so a dark warp is best).

Weft—Medium-fine (slightly heavier than the warp) single-ply wool, preferably handspun. This is one of the few instances in Navajo weaving where a soft yarn, rather than a tightly spun yarn, is desirable. A soft yarn will fluff out and cover the warp better.

Amount: Approximately 4 pounds (2 pounds for each side).

Colors: Madder, cochineal, or indigo for the back side and natural black and white for the stripes or checkerboard on the front side.

Directions

You will need two *more* 1/2-inch dowels, just like the shed stick and heddle stick, for this project. Follow the general directions for setting up the warp up to "The Shed Stick." And there is no need to put in the sticks to preserve the lease. The warp should be set up 8 or 10 to the inch—the smaller number unless the warp is quite fine. And set it up 30 inches wide and 30 inches long (add the extra 18 inches to warp length if you won't be weaving up to the selvedge).

Setting the shed stick and making the heddles

In Figure 185, each vertical division represents a warp thread, and the blackened squares indicate that a heddle is made around that warp thread. As you can see from the blackened squares some warp threads are tied to the heddles on more than one heddle stick. When heddle stick no. 1 is pulled forward, 3 warp threads adjacent to each other are lifted, and only 1 warp thread is down.

Shed No. 4 (Stick): Starting with this line of the draft, and the right side of both draft and warp, pick up all the threads marked black—this will be every fourth thread, all across the warp. This is done with your batten. Turn the batten on edge and insert your shed stick. Also tie a long circle of thread (cotton cord) through this shed, just so that if the shed stick accidentally falls out the shed will be preserved. Remove the batten and push the shed stick up out of the way.

Shed No. 3 (Pull): Now, working below the shed stick, with your batten pick up the threads of the warp corresponding to this line of the draft. All the threads marked in black in this line of the draft will be lying over the top of your batten. Turn your batten on edge, and using your heddle stick and heddle cord, make heddles around each warp thread that is held up by the batten—just as in general directions Making the Heddles. When this heddle stick is complete, remove your batten and push the heddle stick up next to the shed stick.

Shed No. 2 (Pull): Do the same for this line of the draft. Make heddles around *each* of the warp threads marked in black—3 up and 1 down—all the way across.

Shed No. 1 (Pull): Do the same for this line of the draft.

Note: These threadings must be accurate or mistakes that cannot be remedied will be occurring throughout the weaving. Check the threads on the batten each time before making the heddles. Be *absolutely sure* they are the correct threads.

The weaving

With the batten inserted in the stick shed (no. 4), weave with the first front color (black).

With batten inserted in pull shed no. 3, weave with second front color (white).
With batten inserted in pull shed no. 2, weave with back color.
With batten inserted in pull shed no. 1, weave with back color.
Repeat this throughout the weaving, packing the weft down as tightly as possible to cover the warp.

By alternating black and white wefts on the front side you will create vertical bars of black and white. If you want a checkerboard pattern, alternate black and white but every 1/2 inch place two shots of black in succession. If you want fine horizontal stripes weave two blacks in succession and then two whites.

Note: Weaving a double-face fabric necessitates manually weaving in the edge warp threads on some rows of the weaving. If the return shed for a certain weft color

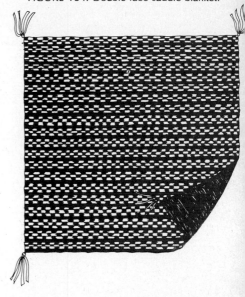

FIGURE 184. Double-face saddle blanket.

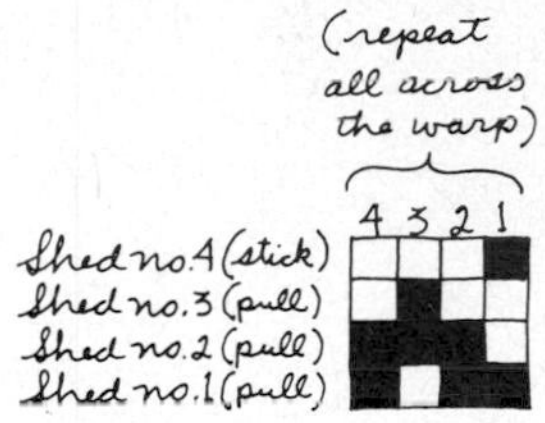

FIGURE 185. Draft for double-face weave.

(repeat all across the warp)

shed no.4 (stick)
shed no.3 (pull)
shed no.2 (pull)
shed no.1 (pull)

FIGURE 186. Picking up shed no. 4 (stick shed) with the batten.

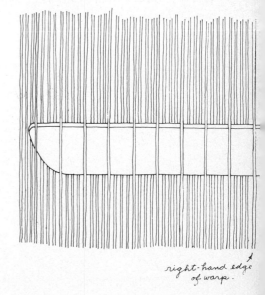

right-hand edge of warp.

FIGURE 187. Making heddles for shed no. 3 (pull shed) around all the warp threads held up by the batten.

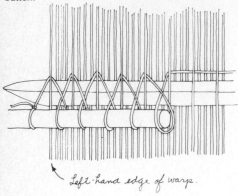

Left-hand edge of warp.

FIGURE 188. Weaving a shot of the back color.

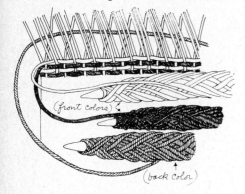

(front colors)

(back color)

is such that the edge warp thread would be missed, see to it that the weft turns around that edge thread on each row of weaving.

Refer to Project V for how to use a second batten to make it easier to form the sheds.

An interesting variation on this double-face technique is to weave one side with mohair yarn and then brush it. This makes one side of the blanket furry, and the other side can have a plain-weave striped or checkerboard pattern. (See Chapter VII, "The Treadle Loom: Project XIX.")

Suggestions for Other Projects

Most of the projects described in Chapter VII, "The Treadle Loom," could be woven on the Navajo loom—especially the tapestry projects and the leno room divider.

The rya technique is well suited to the Navajo loom. (See the rya rug project in the treadle-loom chapter.) It is very similar to the technique for the tufted rug (Project I in this chapter).

Peter Collingwood in *Techniques of Rug Weaving* (page 181) describes another old Navajo technique—the twill tapestry. This is a seldom-seen old technique in which the design follows the twill diagonals. He also describes weft twining which is very suitable for the Navajo loom.

See the treadle loom chapter for other tapestry techniques—such as the kilim.

CHAPTER VII

THE TREADLE LOOM

A Description of the Loom

Supposedly the Chinese are responsible for thinking of using the feet to change sheds in weaving. In Chapter I there are illustrations showing how at first the arrangements for the feet to change sheds were very simple; the warp tension was still maintained by the backstrap method; and the idea of winding the warp onto something (so that many yards of warp could be compactly stored) was in its first stages.

Today's treadle loom is a well-developed machine for storing great lengths of warp, making complicated and quick changes of sheds (allowing very rapid shuttle throwing), and storing the woven fabric. It consists of a sturdy framework that stands on the floor, with a roller for the warp storage at the back of the loom and a cloth roller at the front of the loom to store the finished weaving. The warp passes from the warp roller (or warp beam) up over the back (or slab) beam, and is stretched across a distance of a few feet to the front (or breast) beam, over it and down to the cloth roller (or cloth beam), which is placed underneath, out of the way of the weaver's knees. The warp is held in tension by cranking up the ratchets on both warp and cloth rollers so that the warp is stretched in opposite directions. At the midway point of the tensioned warp are suspended the heddle shafts (or harnesses) for lifting certain groups of warp threads. In front of these, the reed (which is the steel comb that separates the warp threads and maintains their proper spacing) is held in a frame, which is pivoted either from the bottom of the loom or the top, and this frame (called the "beater," or "batten") can be pulled forward to beat the weft into place. Foot treadles work the movement of the harnesses, leaving the hands completely free to pass the shuttle through the weft and do the beating.

There are three basic types of treadle looms used by handweavers today—the counterbalanced loom, the counter marche loom, and the jack loom. We will discuss these in detail shortly.

Its Uses

The multi-harness treadle loom can actually be a menace to beginning weavers—*unless* it is used strictly as a tool to weave some of the basic, simple weaves that one would do on a primitive stick loom, but faster. Too often, all those harnesses and treadles tempt the beginner into fancy threadings and weave structures that she (or he) really doesn't even understand. They just magically appear if she follows the right threading draft in some book and treadles in the proper sequence. This might be all right, but besides this there is an additional temptation for the novice: to use a lot of different colors in the warp and make changes of color in the weft that have no relationship to the weave structure at all. What she ends up with is a fabric that looks like every other beginning weaver's work: a mishmash of various weave structures that change color arbitrarily—something one might find in a cheap upholstery shop. A beginning weaver working on a multi-harness treadle loom is like a student of music trying to compose a symphony for an orchestra before he can make a decent tune on a flute. I'm hoping the advice and instruction in this book will lead you away from this type of weaving, until you understand what you are doing.

The treadle loom should be used with great respect—respect for the power it has to do very complicated things quite quickly. Use its power to do only what you understand, and would attempt on a more primitive loom. Do not let its power dictate what you are going to do. Become its master; don't let it become yours. When you

FIGURE 189. A treadle loom and accessories.

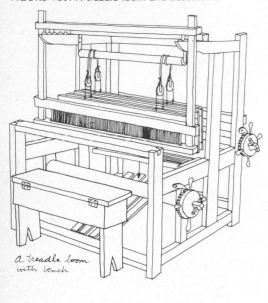

a treadle loom
with bench

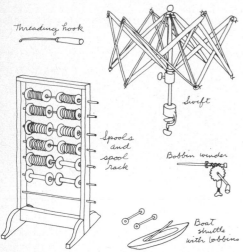

Threading hook

Swift

Spools
and
spool
rack

Bobbin winder

Boat
shuttle
with bobbins

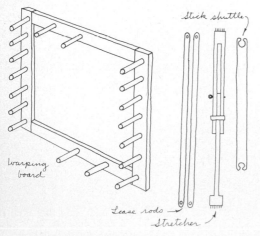

Stick shuttle

warping
board

Lease rods
Stretcher

understand it well, then you can gradually work up to complex weave structures that will have some meaning.

The treadle loom cannot be used to weave fabrics with four selvedges, but you can weave very wide fabrics and very long ones.

Although the treadle loom makes weaving go very fast, it does take up a lot of space. It is not easily disassembled and so it is a real problem that must be faced if you move around much. Also it requires many extra accessories or tools in order to work with it efficiently. However, if you are going to weave a great deal, and especially if you expect to make a living at it, the treadle loom will make it possible to turn out a quantity of weavings in a much shorter time than it would take on the other more primitive looms. To take the greatest advantage of the treadle loom you should wind on long warps and use them for a variety of projects, rather than warping for individual pieces, and cut off the weavings from the loom only as the cloth beam becomes too full.

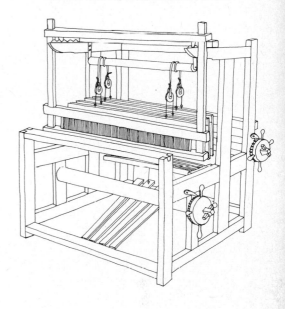

FIGURE 190. A counterbalanced loom.

The Counterbalanced Loom

Some weavers refer to this loom as an "ancient art" or "peasant" loom. Before the Industrial Revolution in Europe it was the type used there and in the colonies by the woman of the family to weave fabric for clothing and household fabrics. It is "counterbalanced" in that its harnesses are hung in *balance* on rollers, pulleys, or horses, and move up and down *counter* to each other; that is, when one harness is pulled down by the treadle, its mate is automatically pulled up. This action is called a "sinking shed," because the treadles pull directly down on the corresponding harnesses. The warp is stretched in a perfectly straight line (allowing the extreme tension necessary for rug weaving) from the back beam to the front beam. The harnesses must be positioned so that the eyes of the heddles are in perfect position for the warp to go through, not interrupting the straightness of the warp line. One harness pulls one set of threads down at exactly the same angle as the opposite harness pulls the other threads up. The greater the distance from the back beam to the breast beam, the greater the tension of the warp can be and still allow for this opening of the shed.

The loom is *supposed* to be good only for balanced treadling—the same number of harnesses down as up. If you want a combination of three down and one up (or vice versa), the shed will not open as perfectly. However, the difficulties in accomplishing this are negligible, and I have always done any kind of treadling on this type of loom.

Frames designed to be used with wire or flat steel heddles are used for the harnesses; or occasionally, simple wooden slats (laths) with string heddles are used.

The beater on this type of loom can be either slung overhead or pivoted from the base of the loom. The latter design is most common unless the loom is large.

The treadles can be hinged either in the front (as shown) or in the back. The heddles can be either string, wire, or steel—and the advantages and disadvantages of each are discussed under the heading The Heddles and Harnesses in this chapter.

For keeping the harnesses balanced and level I think rollers (as pictured in Figure 190) are the best arrangement, but pulleys and horses are common too.

Notice that for the four harnesses to be pulled down by their exact centers it is necessary to have an intermediary between the treadle and the harness. This is the lam, a horizontal stick hinged on the side of the loom underneath the harness. On a two-harness counterbalanced loom, lams are not necessary because the treadles can be positioned almost directly beneath the center points of the harnesses.

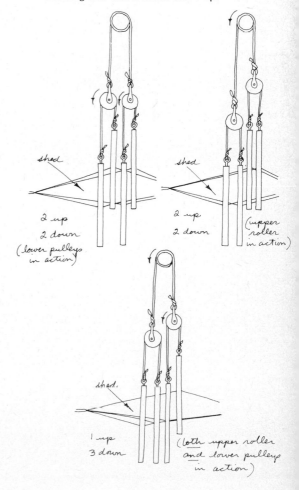

FIGURE 191. Position of the harnesses in balanced treadling and with 3 down and 1 up.

shed

2 up
2 down
(lower pulleys in action)

shed

2 up
2 down
(upper roller in action)

shed

1 up
3 down
(both upper roller and lower pulleys in action)

A well-built counterbalanced loom is a very versatile machine, and (although some weavers might disagree) suitable for all types of weaving with four harnesses. It is simple and quiet (a very desirable feature), and requires a minimum of adjustment and care.

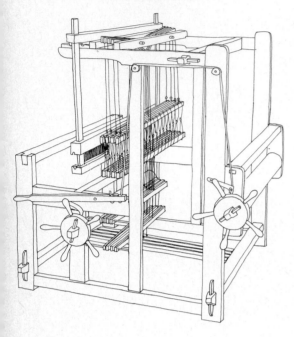

FIGURE 192. A counter marche loom.

The Counter Marche Loom

The counter marche loom is somewhat similar in design to the counterbalanced loom, except instead of pulleys balancing the harnesses in pairs, the treadles pull directly down on individual harnesses, and at the same time raise the remaining harnessess by means of jacks above. Since the harnesses act independently of each other, any combination up and down forms perfect sheds. And, because of the straight alignment of the warp as it is stretched from back beam to breast beam (which are a good distance apart), extreme tension suitable for rug weaving is allowed.

To accomplish the sinking action as well as the rising action, a double set of marches (or lams), the horizontal intermediaries between treadle and harness (or jack), is required. One set is attached directly to the harnesses and pulls them directly down when the corresponding treadles are pressed. A second set of lams below the first set acts counter to the first (hence the name) and pulls down on cords that operate jacks above the harnesses that raise them. Each treadle is tied up to as many lams (either upper or lower) as there are harnesses, so that when the treadle is pressed, whichever harnesses are to be lowered for that shed are pulled down, and all the remaining harnesses are raised.

You can see that the tie-ups for the counter marche loom are more complicated than for the counterbalanced loom. Since it is nearly impossible to get to the tie-up area with a weaving in progress, you are limited to the weave or weaves that can be accomplished with the existing tie-up until you can remove the fabric from the loom and change the tie-up.

The beater on the counter marche loom is usually slung from overhead, since there has to be an overhead structure for the jacks anyway.

Compactness is not a feature of the counter marche loom, and the distance from back to breast beam is greater on most of the counter marche looms than on a counterbalanced and certainly a jack loom, thus making rear-hinged treadles the normal feature and giving greater leverage and ease in operating the harnesses. Most of these looms are designed to be used with string heddles and simple wooden slats (laths) rather than heddle frames with wire or flat steel heddles.

The counter marche loom is designed primarily for multi-harness weaving with the possibility of extreme warp tension. Fortunately some of these looms are designed to be set up with pulleys and horses for a counterbalanced action as an alternative. This means that the loom can be used without the tedious counter marche tie-up when you want to do plain weaves or balanced treadling or want to have more freedom to switch the structure of the weave during progress.

The counter marche loom is well known in Europe, especially Scandinavia, but only recently has become common in the States. Its popularity here now has been made possible mainly through its importation by several fine Scandinavian manufacturers.

The Jack Loom

The jack loom is of more recent design—the American solution to a loom that will form perfect sheds no matter what combination of harnesses is up or down. It was first built at a time when light-weight multi-harness weaving was popular. Each harness has its own independent action: it is raised by a jack beneath the harness that pushes it up when a treadle is pressed (on some the jacks are over the harnesses, and on some simple cords and pulleys operate the individual shafts). The significant thing is that all the remaining harnesses stay in their resting position. Any number of treadles may be pressed, or any number of harnesses can be tied to one treadle to accomplish the same thing.

The action on a jack loom is referred to as "rising shed." To make this rising shed possible, most jack looms are designed so that the warp bends *down* at an angle to go through the eyes of the heddles when the harnesses are at rest. When a certain harness or harnesses are raised, the corresponding upper angle to the shed is formed. This creates even strain on both upper and lower warp threads.

Right away you can see that a warp of extreme tension may not be stretched on this type of loom—making it unsuitable for tight weft-face weaving, especially rugs. Besides this limitation, there is the fact that the rising action of any harness (or harnesses) does not force the opposite action of other harnesses (as happens on the counterbalanced and counter marche looms). For this reason a close-set warp for warp-face weaving may tend to lift *all* the harnesses when one is raised. Some well-built jack looms will minimize this possibility, but it does present a problem for very close-set warp-face weaving.

The loom is, however, superlative for light-weight multi-harness weaving (for which it was designed), because of its perfect shed action and the possibility of a simple (or skeleton) tie-up, which allows the weaver to treadle the various weave structures at will.

The jack loom can be of a very compact design, especially if the jacks that raise the shafts are placed underneath the shafts rather than over them. Then a high center structure to the loom is completely unnecessary, and the loom need only be as high as the top member of the heddle frames. Since there is no overhead structure, the beater (or batten) is naturally pivoted from the base rather than slung overhead. The treadles are hinged from the front, and the depth of the loom from breast to back beam is minimal (another reason that it is not suitable for high-tension warps).

The warp roller can be either the regular type or sectional. The heddles are either wire or steel, but must be set in a rigid four-sided frame that travels up and down in slots on the sides of the loom. Unfortunately, this action on some looms is quite noisy.

This loom has probably been the most common one used in the U.S. for the past few decades. With the popularity of pattern weaving during this period, it was a great improvement over the counterbalanced loom for perfect sheds and for compactness —a desired feature for many modern home weavers. Today, however, with young weavers' change of interest from pattern weaving to rug weaving, tapestry weaving and other hand techniques, I suspect the jack loom is losing its popularity somewhat to the ancient counterbalanced loom and the counter marche loom.

The Table Loom

There is another smaller loom, the table loom, which operates similarly to the treadle loom, except that levers on the side rather than foot treadles operate the harnesses. Thus the loom can sit on a table. The emphasis of this book is on weaves that are hand-controlled, rather than structural weaves requiring multi-harnesses (shafts), and I prefer the use of primitive looms over table looms for small weavings. The table loom can do very complicated weaves for sampling and is used a great deal for teaching purposes.

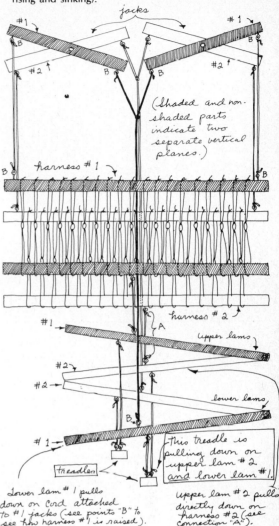

FIGURE 193. The counter marche action (both rising and sinking).

The Treadle Tapestry Loom

There is also a treadle loom built to accommodate a vertical warp for tapestry weaving. Although I do a great deal of tapestry weaving I am so satisfied with the Navajo loom (or my counterbalanced treadle loom) for this purpose that I have never tried this type. Since most professional tapestry weavers throughout the world use a simple vertical framework, on which the warp can be wound in extreme tension, and various types of string heddles operated by the hands, I will risk speculating that the treadle tapestry loom is designed more for the novice. Weavers who do a good amount of tapestry weaving will no doubt do best to acquire a traditional tapestry loom as is used in Europe, a vertical frame with warp and cloth rollers and hand-operated string heddles. Vävstolsfabriken (see Chapter XIII, ''Suppliers'') has one of the best.

Choosing the Right Treadle Loom for You

A good size loom to start with is approximately 45 inches in weaving width. If you are just beginning, do not get a wider loom thinking it will answer all your needs. It is very inefficient weaving narrow items on a large loom; and with a 4-harness 45-inch loom you can weave plain weave double width—meaning you can weave certain items like blankets (not rugs—they're too heavy) 90 inches wide. Most likely, if you become more involved with weaving, you will want two looms. Then you can get a wider one for weaving larger rugs, and larger items of all kinds in weaves other than plain weave.

FIGURE 194. A jack loom.

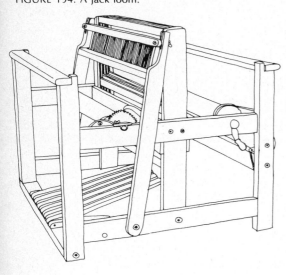

As for the type of loom, if you take my advice you won't get a table loom or treadle tapestry loom, so it's a choice between a counterbalanced, a counter marche, and a jack loom.

The counterbalanced loom, with its setup for extreme warp tension, and the possibility of the simple skeleton tie-up (allowing changes of weave structure during the weaving), is probably the most versatile loom of all. The fact that the sheds do not open perfectly when you treadle 3 down and 1 up (or vice versa) is really a negligible problem. Since the action is counterbalanced (one harness down *forces* its mate up) warps of very close sett can be used. In fact, for all of the treadle-loom projects in this book, the four-harness counterbalanced loom is excellent.

It would seem that the counter marche loom, with its ability to form perfect sheds with any combination of harnesses up and down (just like the jack loom) and yet to handle extreme warp tension, might be the answer. But the great disadvantage to the counter marche loom is the tie-up. In the normal tie-up, each treadle must be tied to *every* harness. This is not only a very laborious job, but the tie-up can't be changed until you have cut off the fabric; you are limited to the weaves that can be done with that tie-up.

There is, however, a tie-up for the four-harness counter marche loom that allows flexibility in changing from one weave structure to another during the weaving; this requires *eight* treadles. Perhaps you can special-order a four-harness loom with eight treadles. (The looms normally come with four or six treadles, with four harnesses; looms with eight treadles are usually eight-harness looms.) Some of the counter marche looms made in Scandinavia today can be set up either as counter marche *or* counterbalanced looms. Then, when you are not weaving the more complicated structural weaves, you can use the counterbalanced setup for simpler weaves and hand techniques. If you can get a four-harness (preferably eight-treadle) counter marche loom like this, it might be the very best loom to buy.

Unless you are strictly interested in fairly light-weight multi-shaft weaves, you should not get a jack loom for your only loom. It is not as versatile as the other two types. It is unsuitable for rug weaving and many tightly packed weft-face weaves, and light-weight jack looms are undesirable for close warp-face weaving. Besides this, the tendency for the beginning weaver to get hung up in complicated pattern weaving is great. The jack loom should be acquired by those weavers who *know* that they need a loom to do light-weight weaves in which the multi-shafts are *essential* to achieve the structures they desire. Many of the projects in this book cannot be done on a jack loom. It will be an excellent loom to have as a *second* loom—particularly for three-dimensional weaving.

Whether your loom should be of hardwood is up to you. The softwood looms are usually less expensive than comparable ones in hardwood, and will show nicks and dents from wear. But as long as the warp roller and the cloth roller are made in such a way that they can resist a tremendous torque (twisting) and the loom is put together with rigid construction, a softwood loom is fine. Many of the beautiful new Scandinavian looms are made of softwood.

In the following pages refer to headings for specific loom features such as warp beams (whether they should be regular or sectional), heddles (whether they should be string, wire, flat steel), reed sizes, and so forth.

Folding looms (ones that have a back beam that folds up close to the heddle shafts, and so can fit through doorways) should be given serious consideration. Some jack looms and counterbalanced looms have this feature. If well designed, these looms work just as well as those that do not fold.

For further information on what loom to buy and where to order, refer to Chapter I, "The Basics of Weaving: Getting Yourself Equipped," and Chapter XIII, "Suppliers: Weaving Equipment."

The Warp Beam

The standard warp beam, sometimes also called a warp roller, is set in sockets, usually in the back vertical members of the loom. The beam can be round or made up of rectangular sections of wood. It is free to turn in the sockets, and on the right end of the beam is set either a ratchet and pawl, or a braking system, and a crank which make it possible to turn the beam in its sockets to a certain position and have it remain in that position under extreme tension, if necessary. (See Ratchet and Pawl and Braking Systems in this chapter.) Either an apron or tapes or ropes form an extension to hold warp beam rods (or apron rod) so that the warp ends may be tied on. The most convenient setup is to have *two* rods (one that fits through a notched hem in an apron, or loops in the tapes; and a second rod that is slipped through the uncut warp ends and then lashed to the first rod).

Regular warp beams of fairly small diameter require special treatment of the warp as it is rolled on (unless only 4 or 5 yards of warp are used), because a warp of any length will build up quite thick on the beam, and with the proper tension it will cut into itself and destroy the evenness of the tension. For this reason the warp must usually be beamed either with a layer of newspaper wound in between each layer of thread or, better, many slats of wood (old Venetian-blind slats are excellent) set in the warp at four points around the diameter every sixth revolution or so.

The tendency for the warp to spread out at the edges on these small-diameter warp beams is another distressing problem, but it can usually be avoided by using the newspapers or slats. Great care must be taken for the warp threads at the edges to form the same diameter as those are in the center. Otherwise the warp threads at the

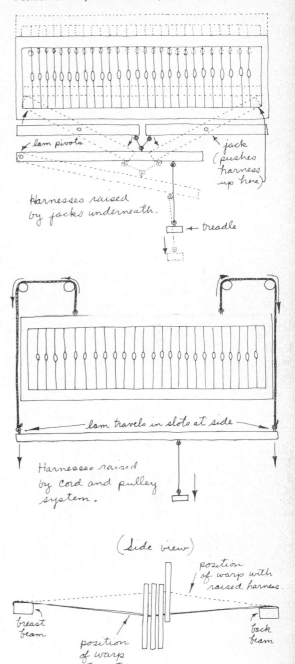

FIGURE 195. Jack or pulley systems, front view. Position of warp and harnesses, side view.

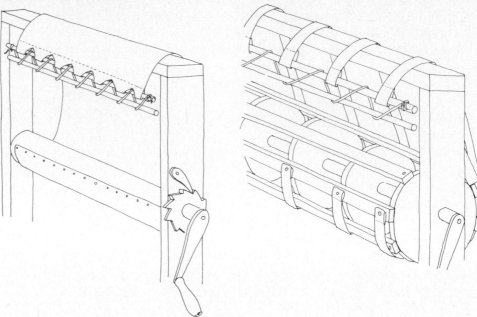

FIGURE 196. Standard warp beams, with apron or tapes and warp beam rods.

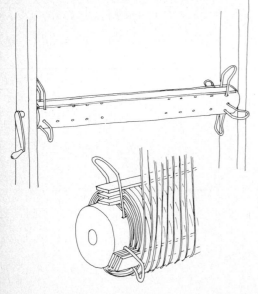

FIGURE 197. Homemade device to keep warp from spreading out during the beaming process.

edges will be shorter in length, causing uneven tension and nearly insurmountable problems in the weaving.

One neat solution to the problem these small-diameter warp beams present, which I have never seen on any commercial loom but which you could easily devise yourself, is shown in Figure 197. At one- or two-inch intervals (to allow for a variety of warp widths) along the warp beam drill holes to accommodate homemade metal rods shaped like a U and bent outward at the closed end of the U. Four of these rods will be necessary for each side of the warp beam. They can be placed in the holes that will be appropriate for the desired width of the warp. As the warp is rolled on, the edge warp threads will be guided exactly into the right width and held there. The U-shaped rods also act as holders for the slats placed every so often along the warp.

The best solution is to have a warp beam that is 2 feet to a yard in circumference. Then all these problems and solutions can be ignored since there is little buildup of the warp threads on top of each other, even with a 25-yard warp. Unfortunately, most looms that you buy—unless they are equipped with a sectional beam—do not have warp rollers of very large diameters. Some sectional beams can be used as a standard beam if desired.

Sectional beams

A sectional warp beam is meant for sectional warping. It is usually at least two feet around, and at four points around the circumference there are set rows of wooden pegs or rounded metal loops at two-inch intervals. The ends of the warp threads required for the two inches of width will be attached to the pegs or metal loops and wound directly from the spools through a tension box, onto that two-inch section of the beam—all at one time. You simply crank the warp beam around the required number of turns to make the desired yardage. After one section is filled, the warp threads of the next two-inch section are wound in the same manner. Sometimes small wooden spacers (made specially for this purpose) can be put in every several turns, if the warp is building up too much, just as the wooden slats were put in on the regular beam.

It is most convenient if the sectional beam has rounded metal loops as guides, rather than wooden pegs, because then an ordinary chained warp (made on a warping board or mill) can be wound onto the sectional beam when this is the more appropriate warping method. Many weavers like to use the sectional method of warping, especially when making plain-colored, fine warps of many threads. But certain warps are not suited to the sectional method (warps of different-colored stripes, for instance), so it is nice to be able to put on the other type of warp also. If the sectional dividers are wooden pegs, the chained warp tends to catch on them, whereas the warp threads glide easily over the rounded metal loops.

You can purchase sectional beam adapters with the rounded metal guides to convert your standard beam into a sectional beam, and this provides a larger diameter to your warp beam as well.

Double warp beams

Some looms are equipped with two warp beams—one regular and one sectional. Then the weaver can choose whichever beam is appropriate. Or they can be used simultaneously when the weave requires two different warp tensions as in combining warp- and weft-face weaves where the warp "takeup" will be different for each weave. The three-dimensional and double weaves in this book require only one warp beam, but it might be nice to have two warp beams to do some experimenting. (How about a pure white handspun silk seersucker bedspread?)

The Cloth Beam

The cloth beam (also sometimes called the cloth roller) is similar to the regular warp beam. It is usually about five inches in diameter. It fits into sockets usually on the front horizontal members of the loom frame (or vertical members set back from the front), and is free to turn in these sockets. The placement of this beam is crucial: it must be placed so that the finished weaving as it rolls over the front beam down to the cloth beam will not interfere with the beater, and at the same time not rub against the

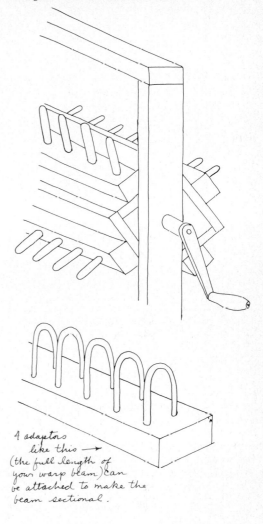

FIGURE 198. A sectional beam; parts to attach to a regular beam to make it sectional.

4 adaptors like this → (the full length of your warp beam) can be attached to make the beam sectional.

FIGURE 199. Cloth beams with apron or tapes for extensions.

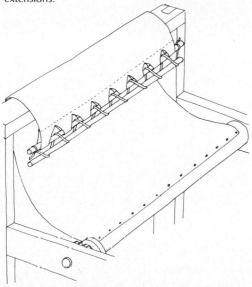
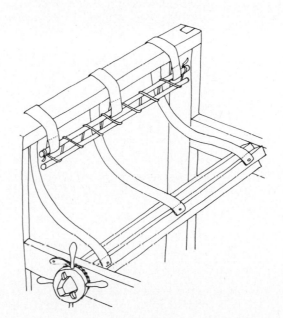

weaver's knees. Sometimes an extra beam is used for the cloth to pass over to keep it out of the way of the knees. In this case that beam can be called the cloth beam, and the beam the cloth is actually rolled onto would be the cloth roller, or the "knee beam" and the cloth beam.

At the right-hand end of the beam is a ratchet and pawl system with a crank for precise adjustment of the warp tension.

Either an apron or tapes or ropes form an extension to the cloth beam so that the warp ends may be tied on. Again, the most convenient setup (I think) is the apron, with two rods—one set in slits in the apron and the other lashed to it. It is around the second rod that the front warp ends are tied.

Ratchet and Pawl and Braking Systems

The ratchet and pawl (or braking system sometimes used on the warp beam) are normally set up so that both beams can be cranked up in a clockwise direction and held there by the pawls, even though there is great tension on the warp. Since there is this torque stress on the joint between the ratchets and the beams themselves, the joint must be made to withstand it. This is one of the most important factors in the arrangement of the ratchets and pawls. They must be secured to the beams in such a way that over the years they will not wear down and the beam will not split. This usually requires the use of metal bands or sleeves on the beam itself, through which screws or bolts are set to attach the ratchet to the beam.

A braking system is sometimes preferable for a sectional beam since this will enable you to set the beam at any position. The beam has such a large circumference that, unless the ratchet has the same and has small teeth, you are limited in the possible adjustments of the positioning of the beam. A ratchet and pawl will be fine if you are not set on having minute adjustments for your warp beam.

For the warp beam the usual arrangement is one pawl with a long lever or cord attached to it so that it can be released without the weaver's getting up from the bench. A simple hand crank is used to turn the beam when rolling on the warp. A similar release lever is used with a braking system.

It is with the cloth beam ratchet that the final tension adjustment is made. So usually this ratchet is accompanied by two or more pawls for minute adjustments. A nice long lever attached to one of the pawls will make it easier to crank up right from your seat.

Some looms, notably the softwood Scandinavian looms, simply have four or five extensions (or handles) on both beams and you turn the beams to the proper positions with these. The several handles are placed so that there are always two in a good position for cranking.

A circular saw blade makes a very adequate ratchet for a homemade loom, but just screwing it into the end of the beam will not suffice. Either a sleeve should be welded onto the blade, with the screws going through that into the side (rather than end) of the beam, or a sleeve and cap of metal should be made to fit over the end of the beam to prevent splitting when under the strain of the torque.

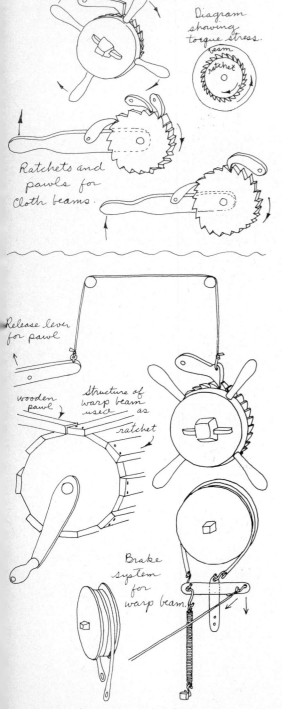

FIGURE 200. Ratchets and pawls for both warp and cloth beams; also braking system that is sometimes used on warp beams. Diagram showing torque stress at the joint of beam and ratchet.

Diagram showing torque stress.

beam
ratchet

Ratchets and pawls for cloth beams.

Release lever for pawl

wooden pawl

Structure of warp beam used as ratchet

Brake system for warp beam.

Warp beam ratchets and pawls, and braking systems

The Heddles and Harnesses

Before discussing this part of the loom we must clear up the terminology. The heddles are the wire, steel, or string devices through which the warp ends are threaded. They are held in a frame (or simply two laths of wood in the case of string heddles). The entire arrangement is called a "heddle shaft" (or simply "shaft") or "harness." "Harness" formerly was used to mean a *set* of shafts, but American usage has deteriorated and here "harness" has come to mean a single shaft, and is the term most commonly used, and the one we use in this book.

As for the heddles, there are several schools of thought as to whether flat steel, wire, or string is best. Some people say that string heddles are easier on the warp; others claim this is absolutely not so. The flat steel heddles are perhaps the least likely to break, but I find the eye too small in some cases, especially if I'm using handspun warp, or if I want to tie onto a dummy warp (see this heading in this chapter); the knots won't go through the eyes if the warp is anything but fine yarn. Most of the contemporary wire heddles are so light-weight that they often break. String heddles are excellent as far as all these problems go, except they have the annoying habit of lapping over each other (and have to be straightened out once in a while so they will be in proper alignment with the warp). They have the advantage of being replaceable—made right on the loom, around the warp thread, if one breaks. In fact, if your flat steel or wire heddles break, this is the only solution unless you have purchased fancy repair heddles.

Most domestic looms come with heddles, and usually you have a choice between wire or flat steel. I would choose the wire because the eyes are bigger, and besides, the flat steel are more expensive. Most of the Scandinavian looms are designed to be used with string heddles, and they usually don't come with the loom. You can make your own string heddles with carpet warp by setting up a jig, and just tying knots all day long. But it's hardly worth it; the string heddles are quite inexpensive.

Two wooden laths, top and bottom, suffice to hold the string heddles in their proper positions. Flat steel and wire heddles usually fit onto specially designed heddle frames. When ordering heddles for the frames of your loom, be sure they are the right length—they come in different lengths, to go with different-size frames. (A heddle frame has a metal band just inside the top and bottom wooden members, onto which the heddles fit; there is a little gadget at each end of the shaft that disengages so you can slip the heddles onto the metal band.) A jack loom has four-sided frames that can slide up and down in slots on the side of the loom and are used with the wire or flat steel heddles.

The harnesses on a counterbalanced or a counter marche loom are positioned so that the heddle eye is exactly in line with the warp thread as it is stretched from back to breast beams. On most jack looms the heddle eye is lower, and the warp, when at rest, should form an angle.

Pulleys, Rollers, Heddle Horses, and Jacks

On the counterbalanced loom, if you have a chance to choose between pulleys, rollers, and heddle horses, choose the rollers. Each side of the heddle shaft then is forced to move up or down level with the other side. Pulleys and horses seem to be the standard setup on some Scandinavian counterbalanced looms.

On the jack loom, two horizontal jacks are pivoted underneath each heddle

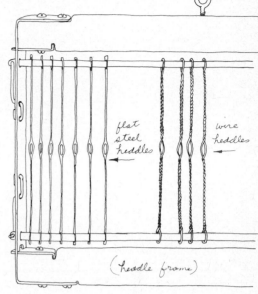

FIGURE 201. Different types of heddles and shafts.

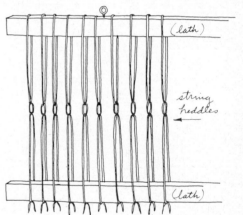

FIGURE 202. Making string heddles on a jig.

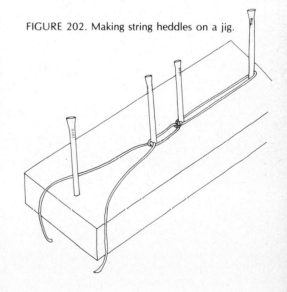

FIGURE 203. Rollers, pulleys, horses, and jacks.

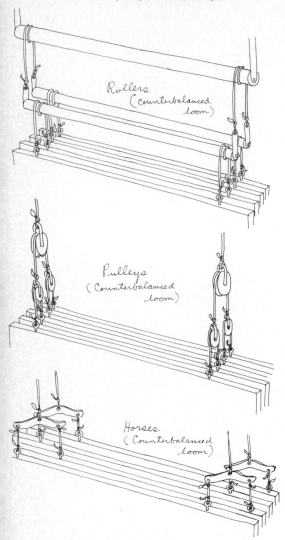

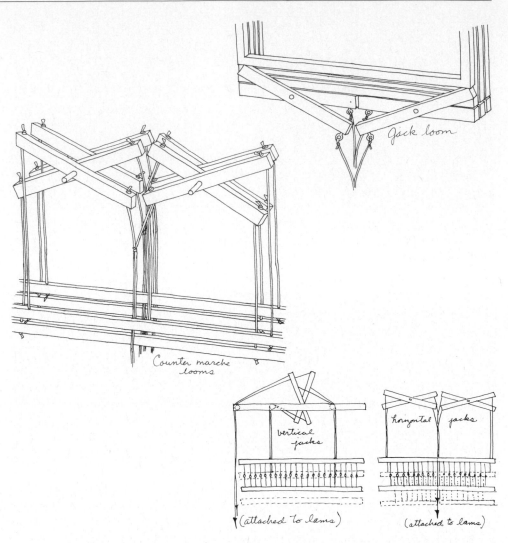

FIGURE 204. Lams for the counterbalanced and jack looms. Double lams for the counter marche loom.

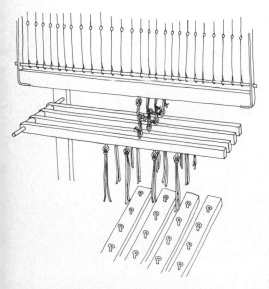

frame, and when their ends are pulled down by treadle and lam, the other ends *push* the frame up. Some jack looms simply have individual pulleys and cords over the frame that run up the side of the loom and lift the frame when a treadle is pressed.

The jacks on the counter marche loom can be of two designs, each positioned above the harnesses. In one design the cord from the treadle and lam travels directly up through the center of the harness and (when the treadle is pressed) pulls down the inner ends of the two horizontal jacks, thus raising the outer ends and pulling the harness up. In the other, the cord from treadle and lam travels up the side of the loom over pulleys to a single vertical jack. When the treadle is pressed, the upper end of this vertical jack is pulled down, thus raising cords attached to two other points on the jack, which in turn lift the harness. Of course, on the counter marche loom, this action works simultaneously with the lowering of the opposite harnesses—which is accomplished by a direct tie-up from treadle to lam to harness.

Lams

The lams are the intermediaries between the treadles and the harnesses. There must be a lam for each harness, so that no matter how much off from center the treadle is, the cord that operates the harness or the jack can be positioned at the appropriate point. The lams, which are simply sticks of wood, are pivoted at the side of the loom and placed horizontally between the treadles and the harnesses.

While one set of lams suffices for the counterbalanced and jack looms, two sets are required on the counter marche. An upper set (just beneath the harnesses) operates the lowering of the harnesses; and a set below these operates the jacks at the top of the loom that will raise the remaining harnesses.

Each lam is tied to its corresponding harness. They are then tied to the treadles in one of two ways: a standard tie-up or a skelton tie-up. For a standard tie-up (see An Explanation of Drafts and Tie-ups in this chapter) on either the counterbalanced or the jack loom, and for any tie-up on the counter marche loom, each lam should have screw eyes and cords (or hooks and chains) on the under side to line up with *each* treadle. For a skeleton tie-up (not possible on the counter marche), only one connection between treadle and lam is necessary, and this can be permanent.

The Treadles

The treadles are the wooden members, pivoted at the base of the loom, that (when pressed down) operate the lams, which in turn operate the harnesses. Since the treadle operates on the principle of the lever, the farther away from the pivot point the pressure is, the more power there will be. For this reason, treadles that are hinged at the back of the loom give greater leverage (or power), since the foot presses down at the very end of the treadle, farthest away from the pivot point. However, a loom with rear-hinged treadles has to be higher and the weaver must sit on a higher bench. Most of the counter marche looms, on which each treadle has to operate all the harnesses (either up or down), and so requires greater leverage, have rear-hinged treadles. Most smaller counterbalanced looms and nearly all jack looms have front-hinged treadles. The loom you select will, no doubt, have treadles hinged at whatever point is best for that loom design.

There should be at least one treadle for each heddle shaft of your loom. These are all that are *necessary*. Some looms, however, have two extra treadles, to which you can tie up the corresponding shafts to make a tabby (or plain) weave.

If you want to be able to tie up your treadles in such a way that each treadle pulls down more than one shaft at a time (the standard tie-up), the treadles should each be supplied with screw eyes and cords (or hooks and chains) at *all* points immediately below each lam. Then the appropriate cords can be tied to each other for the tie-up. If you always use the skeleton tie-up and have no extra treadles for the tabby sheds, only one connection between treadle and lam is necessary—and this can be permanent.

If you want to be able to treadle any combination of harnesses up and down on a four-harness countermarche loom you will have to have eight treadles (see "The Treadle Tie-up" in this chapter).

The Beater (or Batten)

The beater (also called the "batten"), which holds the reed and which is swung forward to beat in the weft, may pivot at the base of the loom or at the top. An overhead beater necessitates a high framework to the loom—a normal feature of the counter marche loom and some large counterbalanced looms. The overhead beater is easier to operate than the underslung one, I think, and much preferable, if properly balanced. It can be made very heavy, and still be easy to operate—a desirable feature for rug making, where hard, heavy beating forms a very tight fabric. An iron strip may be added to the beater for this purpose. The overhead beater can have a counter-

FIGURE 204. continued

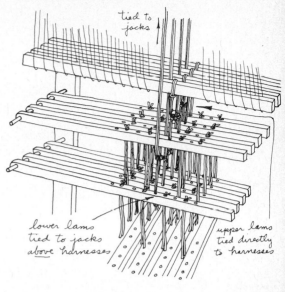

tied to jacks

lower lams tied to jacks above harnesses

upper lams tied directly to harnesses

FIGURE 205. Front-hinged treadles and rear-hinged treadles.

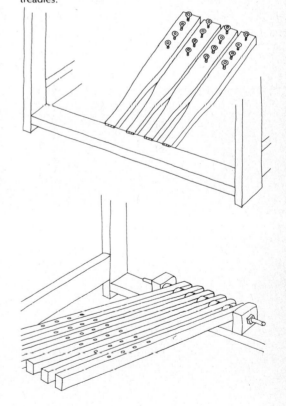

FIGURE 206. Beater pivoted from base of loom and overhead beater.

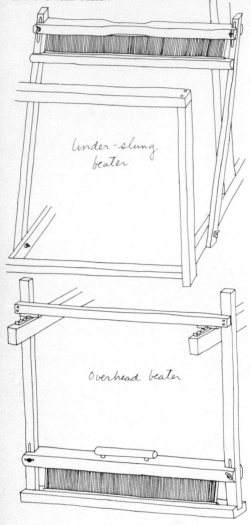

Under-slung beater

Overhead beater

weight at the top so that the beater when at rest hangs back against the heddles, leaving a maximum amount of space for the shed.

Jack looms and small counterbalanced looms usually have underslung beaters.

The top horizontal member of the beater (the "beater cap") is removable so that different-size reeds may be inserted. This piece should be of very smooth hardwood. A softwood piece can get banged up and give you vicious splinters as you grab it.

The lower horizontal member of the beater (the "shuttle race") protrudes and helps support the shuttle as it travels across the lower warp threads of the open shed.

The Reeds

The reed is a steel comb closed on all four sides, through which are threaded ("sleyed") the warp ends to keep them properly spaced. The reed is set into the space made for it in the beater, and acts also as the comb for beating in the weft.

Reeds come in many different lengths, to suit any width loom, and in many different dentages (numbers of dents per inch). The dentage and length are usually engraved or stamped in the metal at one end of the reed. Normally reeds with 12 dents per inch come as the standard accessory with the loom you buy. I recommend coarser reeds. The projects in this book are not done with very fine yarns, and it is generally better to have a reed with fewer and larger dents and double or triple sley it than to have a reed with more and finer dents and skip dents in the sleying. These coarser reeds will also be the best for rug weaving, where the heavy beating will distort the blades of finer reeds.

You should have three reeds, but if you can have only one reed to begin with, get a size 8. Two of the six warps in the following projects have setts of either 8 or 4 epi (ends per inch), and you can conceivably change warp E to 8 epi. You can also sley the 12 epi warps in an 8-dent reed by sleying 1 and then 2 threads alternately. And warp F could be changed to 16 epi and double sleyed. When you can have more reeds, get a 5 and a 6; these will round out nicely the possible warp setts you can get. With the 5 you can weave very coarse rugs with a warp sett of 2 1/2 epi; it can be used for any projects calling for 10 or 15 epi, sleying anywhere from 3 to 6 threads in each dent. With the size 6 reed you can weave rugs with 3 epi, coarse tapestries at 6 epi, homespun warps for tabby weaves, and finer setts such as 12 and 18 by double and triple sleying. You won't be able to have 7, 11, and 13, but 9 can be nicely achieved by using the number 6 reed and sleying 1 thread then 2 threads alternately.

With a variety of reeds you can adjust your warp setts to work with the yarns you have. If you have only one size reed to work with, you *have* to have the right-size yarn.

After you have woven a good deal you will, no doubt, have your favorite-size reeds to use with different yarns for different projects. Reeds may be specially ordered in half sizes also (such as 3 1/2), if desired. Reeds also often come in two different heights. If your loom is a fairly large one of the counterbalanced or counter marche type, it will be good to have the higher reeds. On most small looms and all jack looms, the shed will not open wide enough to warrant the use of any reed other than those of the regular height.

FIGURE 207. A reed.

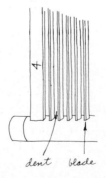

dent   blade

Other Accessories You Will Need for the Treadle Loom

All of the above-mentioned parts usually come with the loom. Following is a list of the other tools ("accessories") that you should have to make weaving on the treadle loom proceed in an efficient manner. These items will be described in detail under their own separate headings.

a. Spools or cones for warping.
b. Spool or cone winder (can be bobbin winder—see below).
c. Creel.
d. Swift.
e. Warping board or mill.
f. Lease rods.
g. Raddle (optional).
h. Tension box (if you wish to do sectional warping and have a sectional beam on your loom), and a counter (optional).
i. Threading hooks.
j. Shuttles, both stick and boat.
k. Bobbins for boat shuttles (optional; you can wind the weft onto paper quills).
l. Bobbin winder.
m. Stretcher.
n. Weaving bench.
o. Hand beater or fork.

See Chapter XIII, "Suppliers: Weaving Equipment," for where to get these accessories.

Spools and Cones for Warping

You may be able to purchase some of your yarns for warping on spools or cones. But usually (unless you are using only the most commonplace warps) you have to wind your own from skeins. Whether to use spools or cones is a matter of preference, but cones require more specialized equipment for winding, and you will have to save up cones from commercial yarns, as I do not know of any source that supplies them.

Cardboard, plastic, or wooden spools usually hold about one-quarter pound of wool; cones will hold more. You will want to order the type that will best fit your winding device. It's nice to have a couple dozen, but one dozen will do.

Spool or Cone Winders

Probably the most economical way to arrange to wind your warp yarns into convenient packages will be to purchase warping spools (rather than cones) and plan on making an adapter for the shaft of your spinning wheel or bobbin winder. By adapter I mean a cardboard sleeve or whatever is necessary to make the diameter of the shaft accommodate the orifice of the spools. If you can spend the money, however, an electric bobbin winder (the type that supports the spools at both ends) is very convenient. With this you can wind either spools or cones, as well as bobbins.

FIGURE 208. Various spools and cones for warping.

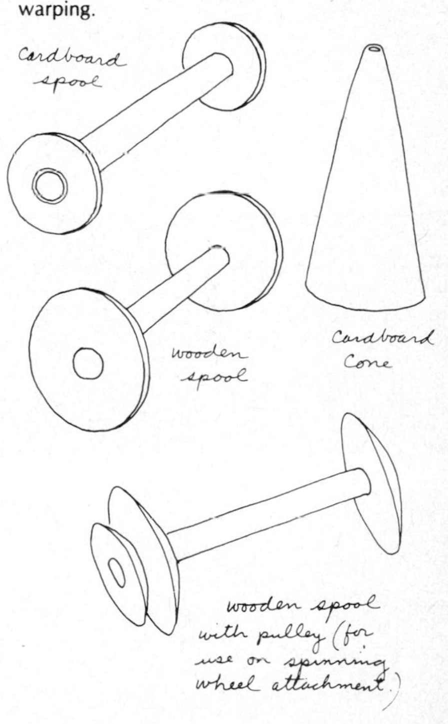

Cardboard spool

wooden spool

Cardboard Cone

wooden spool with pulley (for use on spinning wheel attachment.)

FIGURE 209. Various arrangements for winding spools or cones.

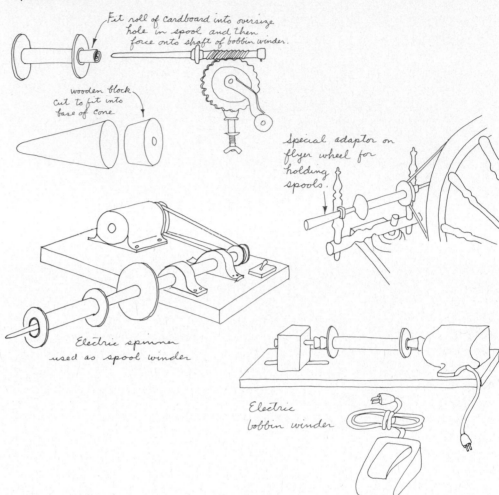

FIGURE 210. Various arrangements for holding cones and spools.

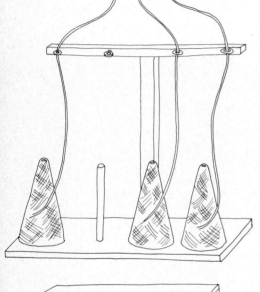

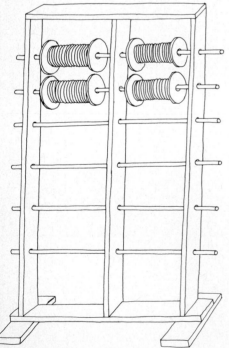

The Creel

No need to spend a lot of money on this accessory. The creel is one weaving tool that is very simply made at home. Just a simple wooden frame that will stand (or hang), with holes drilled into the sides into which will fit metal rods that you can get at any hardware store, will do just fine for a spool rack. A cone stand is even simpler: just dowels or spikes in a board to stabilize the cones, and a "tree" with screw eyes through which the threads are led, to keep them from tangling with each other as they unwind.

The Swift

You will need something to hold the skeins of warp yarn while you are winding your spools and cones from them (and for holding skeins of weft yarn to wind your bobbins or stick shuttles). If you are a spinner, the tool that can be used both to *make* skeins and *unwind* skeins is the adjustable metal swift. If you are not a spinner and don't need a tool to *make* the skeins, your most convenient tool will be either a large umbrella swift or a squirrel cage.

An adjustable skein winder is another tool that could be made by the clever woodworker. Be sure it is adaptable in size so that you can unwind different-size skeins on it.

FIGURE 211. Various types of swifts.

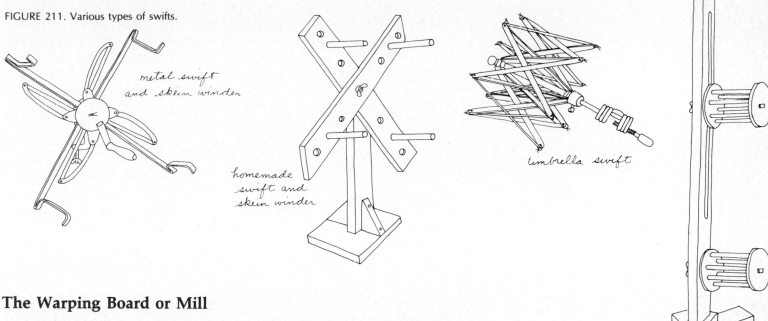

metal swift and skein winder

homemade swift and skein winder

umbrella swift

squirrel cage

The Warping Board or Mill

This will be one of your most important tools, second only to the loom itself. Weaving troubles can be largely avoided by having a well-prepared warp. The tension must be even throughout. If it is greater at the edges or on one side you will have almost insurmountable difficulties in the weaving. So you should have a good strong warping board, or best, a vertical warping mill, on which you will prepare very long and wide warps of even tension. It's nice to have both: a warping board is always best for small warps, such as for belts.

The distance back and forth across the board (or around the mill however many times) from top peg to bottom peg is the length of your warp. You simply choose how many pegs you will go around, or how many times you will turn the warping mill. There must be three pegs in a line at the top or bottom for you to make your cross (or lease) so that the threads will stay in sequence. Most commercial boards or mills have these three pegs at *both* top and bottom for making a cross at both ends of the warp, but the warping method described in this book requires only one cross.

The problem with a warping board is usually that the pegs start drawing in as you wind a warp of any width. This means that the last threads you wind are actually shorter than the first threads, so that one side of the warp will be quite a bit longer than the other side. *You must avoid this.* For this reason a board is useful only for relatively small warps. If you cannot have a mill, you can wind a wide warp in several sections to avoid the problem.

FIGURE 212. Warping board and warping mills, both vertical and horizontal.

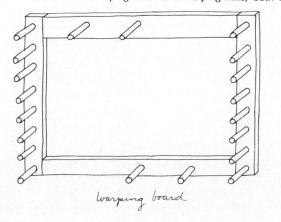

warping board

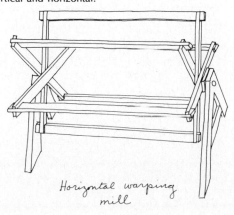

Horizontal warping mill

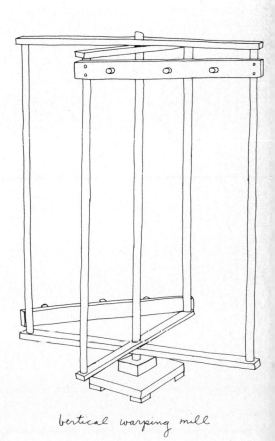

vertical warping mill

The warping mill automatically precludes this particular problem. The mills are usually about 4 yards around, so only 6 turns will make a warp of 24 yards.

The vertical warping mill is used for making a chained warp; the horizontal mill is used for winding the warp onto the mill and from there directly onto the warp beam. This makes the warping process a simple procedure, but you can see that this horizontal mill has its limitations. You can make a warp only as wide as the mill itself; and you can't wind a very long warp without the tension becoming uneven.

I would advise you to get a good vertical mill if at all possible. Or one could be made quite easily. It's simply a matter of having a sturdy frame that will turn smoothly in a base.

A homemade warping board (if it is to be used to wind large warps) must be made with care, so as to prevent the problem of the pegs drawing in. It requires a very strong frame, with a backing or bracing, because a wide warp when wound on the pegs (no matter how strong the pegs are) will actually bend the frame itself, allowing the pegs to shift position.

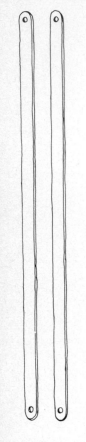

FIGURE 213. Lease rods.

The Lease Rods

Lease rods often come with a new loom. They are a set of two flat sticks used to preserve the lease (or cross) as the warp is put on the loom. They must be of hardwood and completely smooth, since the warp must rub over them as it is wound on. They should be the same length as the heddle shafts, about 3/4 inch wide and 1/4 inch thick. Holes in the ends of each provide a way to tie them together to prevent any warp threads from slipping off.

The Raddle

The raddle (also called a spreader) is used to hold the warp threads in an evenly spread-out position as they are wound onto the warp beam. Some raddles come with an open top and can be fitted into the beater just as the reed is. Others have a removable top piece, or no top at all, and are simply clamped to the breast beam (or the back beam, depending on your warping method). This tool is optional, because a reed can be used as a spreader.

FIGURE 214. Raddles.

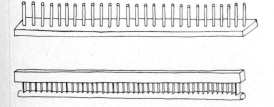

Tension Box and Counter for Sectional Warping

The tension box is necessary for providing even tension to each warp thread as it is wound directly from the spools onto each section of the warp beam in sectional warping. It works very simply: the threads are led over and under a set of large dowels. Combs (or small reeds) at either side of the dowels serve to keep the threads in sequence.

The counter is an optional tool—handy if you're not very good at keeping track of how many times you have turned the warp beam. (Each section must have the same number of turns, or you will end up with some warp sections longer than the others. This is all right except that it is terribly wasteful, because you can weave only up to the end of the shortest section.) This counter can also be used to count yardage as you make skeins from your handspun yarn, or to count yardage as you wind bobbins or warp spools.

Threading Hooks

To thread the warp ends through the eyes of the heddles and the dents of the reed you will want to have a hook that fits through the eye and the dent. You can make something out of a paper clip or use a table knife with a slot cut into it with a hacksaw, or just loop the thread and use your fingers, but a good-looking threading (or sleying) hook with a wooden handle will make the job much easier and more pleasant. These hooks are very inexpensive, some having plastic handles and some wooden. Of course the latter are more pleasing. With the long thin ones reed and heddle can be threaded in one operation, as described in this book. I recommend these. The wide hooks are reed hooks, to be used only for sleying the reed, which can be done in a separate operation if desired.

Better order two or three hooks; they tend to get misplaced.

FIGURE 216. Threading hooks.

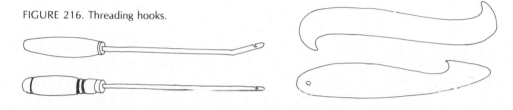

The Shuttles

Sometimes you are provided with shuttles when you buy a new loom. For the treadle loom you will want both types of shuttles: stick shuttles (for heavy yarn) and boat shuttles (for medium and fine yarn). A good starting combination would be two of the largest-size boat shuttles you can locate, two medium-size ones, and at least half a dozen stick shuttles. Boat shuttles are the fastest to weave with, but when you have heavy yarns you have to use stick shuttles, because the bobbins of the boat shuttles do not have the capacity for these yarns. Weavers have different preferences for both stick and boat shuttles. Since the stick shuttles are fairly inexpensive, you might want to try each type to see which you like best. Peter Collingwood praises the ski shuttle; I prefer the rug shuttle with curved ends. For very heavy weft yarns a 30-inch flat shuttle will hold a great deal, and so is handy for rug weaving.

Boat shuttles come in many designs also. Some have rollers (I think these are superfluous), some have double bobbins for weaving with two weft threads at a time, most are fitted with regular bobbins, and some are designed to be used with an open-ended quill. I have come to prefer this latter type. The boat shuttles will be very important. They are tools that you will have in your hands most of the time you're weaving, so don't try to scrimp; get the best you can. You may have to shop around to find the ones you like best. Since most boat shuttles are designed for fine yarns, and the projects in this book are mostly woven with medium yarns, you should order the larger sizes.

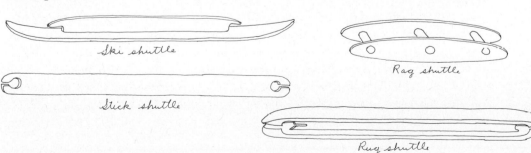

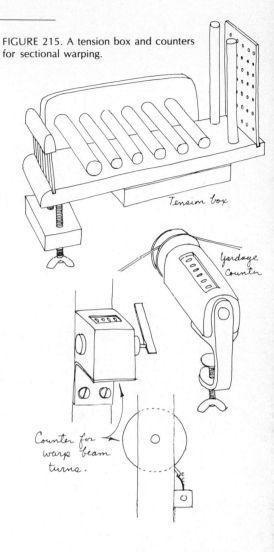

FIGURE 215. A tension box and counters for sectional warping.

FIGURE 217. Various types of shuttles.

FIGURE 218. Various bobbins and quills.

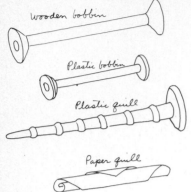
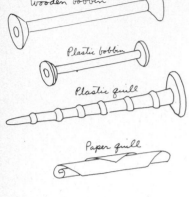

Bobbins and Quills

Figure 218 shows the different types of bobbins for the different types of boat shuttles. Bobbins (usually of wood or plastic) are quite expensive, and its nice to have a least a dozen for each boat shuttle. They are certainly a worthwhile investment, I think. Some weavers make their own paper quills, and wind their weft thread on them (see Winding the Bobbins or Quills in this chapter). This of course saves the expense of bobbins, and you are unlimited in the number you can wind, but I doubt that (even when perfectly wound) they perform as consistently well as plastic or wooden bobbins. If a shuttle and bobbin (or quill) combination keeps catching and giving trouble in unwinding, it slows down the weaving tremendously. Order as many bobbins as you can afford; you never have too many.

FIGURE 219. Various arrangements for winding bobbins.

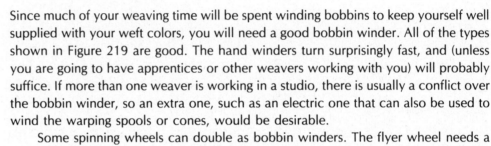

The Bobbin Winder

Since much of your weaving time will be spent winding bobbins to keep yourself well supplied with your weft colors, you will need a good bobbin winder. All of the types shown in Figure 219 are good. The hand winders turn surprisingly fast, and (unless you are going to have apprentices or other weavers working with you) will probably suffice. If more than one weaver is working in a studio, there is usually a conflict over the bobbin winder, so an extra one, such as an electric one that can also be used to wind the warping spools or cones, would be desirable.

Some spinning wheels can double as bobbin winders. The flyer wheel needs a special attachment, and some suppliers have this; the great wheel and some electric spinners with plain shafts are suitable as they are. I used to tape a piece of coat hanger onto the rather thick shaft of my homemade wheel, and believe it or not, this made as good a bobbin winder as I have ever used, until I acquired my electric spinner.

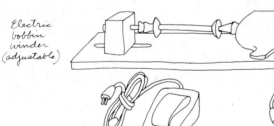

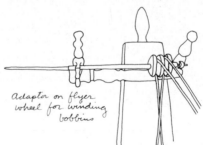

The Stretcher

Some weavers scoff at the use of the stretcher (also called a "temple"). True, it is best to learn to control your weft tension without its use, but, for certain projects (such as double-width fabric), it is almost essential.

Although homemade designs will work, the commercial stretcher is much more convenient and easier on the fabric. It has several sharp little points at the ends that stick into the fabric at the edges, and is made in two separate pieces that join together to make various widths. It should be adjusted so that when it is in its flattened position the base of the prongs comes at the very edges of the warp *as it comes through the reed.* When you stick these prongs into the fabric, less than a quarter inch in from the edge, and slide the holder ring on (to keep the stretcher out flat) it will hold your woven fabric at exactly the right width.

The little prongs on these stretchers break very easily, so be careful where and how you set it down when not in use.

FIGURE 220. Commercial and homemade stretchers.

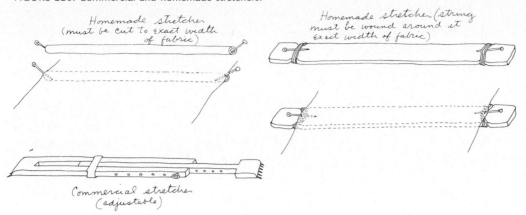

FIGURE 221. Some weaving benches.

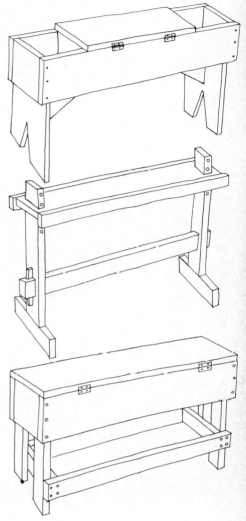

The Weaving Bench

This, also, is not an essential piece of equipment, but sitting in an ordinary chair is very awkward for the weaver, and chairs are usually too low. A nice weaving bench may be purchased or very easily made according to any of the designs in Figure 221. You will find that the type with a cover and two open spaces on the sides will be most convenient. You can put all your bobbins and various other tools such as scissors, measuring tape, etc., in the side compartments, and store less-used items under the seat. The bench should be as high as possible without your knees touching the fabric as it rolls onto the cloth beam. The higher it is the less tiring it will be to throw the shuttle.

The Hand Beater or Fork

For tapestry work where the fell (the weaving line) is not always perfectly horizontal, a hand beater or fork will be needed. The tapestry fork should be light-weight, as you will have it in your hand most of the time, and heavy beating is not necessary. I like the handmade authentic Navajo forks as well as any; but a dime-store plastic comb will do in a pinch.

For rug weaving, you will sometimes want a heavy fork to beat in the weft very tightly. This tool should be heavy; there are even cast-iron forks available to accomplish very tight weaves.

The Yarn

See Chapter I, "The Basics of Weaving: Your Yarn," for a complete discussion of warp and weft yarns. Also see Six Versatile Warps in this chapter. In each project I will specify both warp and weft yarns.

An Explanation of Drafts and Tie-ups

When the beginning weaver opens a book on weaving she is usually confronted with mysterious diagrams marked up with blackened squares, or Xs and Os, or numbers. These diagrams are called *drafts,* and they represent a code by which the weaver can thread the heddles of a multi-harness loom so that certain sequences of threads can be raised and lowered. In plain weave, we do not need this code because we simply

FIGURE 222. Hand beater and forks for tapestry or rug weaving.

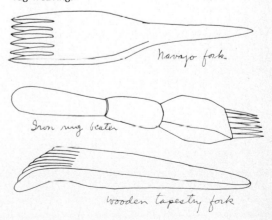

thread the warp alternately through heddles on the first and second harnesses. For the so-called structural weaves where sometimes very complicated sequences of threads are raised and lowered, the weaver needs some kind of simplified directions for threading the heddles, and this is where the draft is indispensable.

Although in this book we are mainly concerned with very simple threadings, you should know how to read a draft when you come upon one. There are many fine weaving books that concentrate on structural weaves, and even if the colonial "over-shot" and other pattern weaves seem to be out of favor now, the imaginative weaver may want to use these structures in some new way.

The most versatile of the threading sequences is probably the basic twill, and it is this threading that we use for all the projects in this chapter.

The threading draft

To understand the draft, imagine you are looking at the harnesses of a two-harness loom from above. They would appear as in Figure 223.

Now draw these two harnesses on graph paper (Figure 224). Every square represents a space where a single heddle could be placed on these harnesses.

To write in the draft for a plain weave, one would mark the graph paper as in Figure 225. Following this draft, the first thread on the right would go through a heddle on the front harness (no. 1); the second thread would go through a heddle on the back harness (no. 2), and so on.

FIGURE 223. Bird's-eye view of two harnesses.

harness #2
harness #1

(front of loom)

FIGURE 224. Blank draft for a two-harness weave.

harness #2
harness #1

FIGURE 225. Threading draft for plain weave.

Threading draft

19 18 17 16 15 14 13 12 11 10 9 8 7 6 5 4 3 2 1

harness #2
harness #1

FIGURE 226. Threading draft for basic twill.

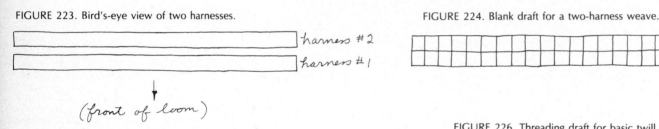
Threading draft

20 19 18 17 16 15 14 13 12 11 10 9 8 7 6 5 4 3 2 1

4
3
2
1

FIGURE 227. Threading draft for basic twill in proper abbreviated form.

Threading draft

4
3
2
1

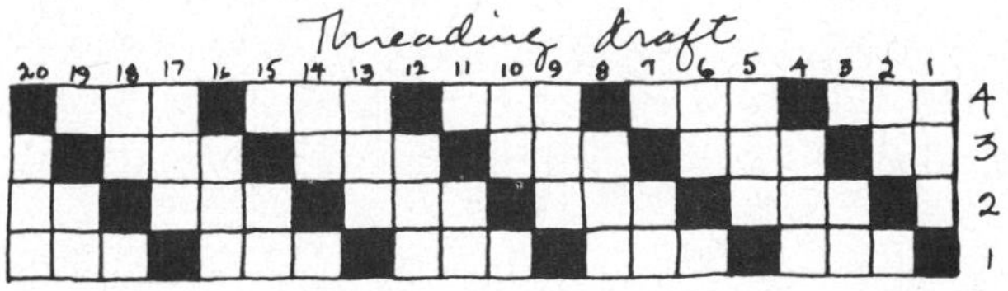

If we use four harnesses and want to draw the draft for a basic twill threading, it would look like Figure 226. Following this draft, the first thread on the right would go through a heddle on the front harness (no. 1). The second thread would go through a heddle on the second harness (no. 2). The third thread would go through a heddle on the third harness (no. 3). The fourth thread would go through a heddle on the last harness (no. 4). The fifth thread would go through the next heddle on the front harness (no. 1), and so on.

Drafts are always written in abbreviated form—just enough to show you the sequence that is to be repeated. So the correct way to make a draft of a twill threading is as shown in Figure 227.

A more complicated threading draft might include many more heddles. The sequence in Figure 228 is for 20 threads.

Sometimes, instead of black squares, a line or a cross is made, and sometimes the number of the harness is written in (see Figure 229).

FIGURE 228. Threading draft for diamond twill.

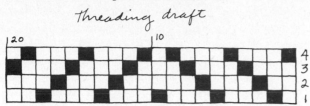

FIGURE 229. Three different forms of a threading draft for basic twill.

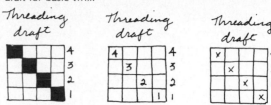

In Swedish drafts the harness toward the back of the loom is considered no. 1 —just the reverse of our system.

The tie-up draft

When using a treadle loom, the harnesses, to be operated, must of course be tied to the treadles. One could tie one treadle to harness no. 1, the next treadle to no. 2, and so forth. This method of tying up the treadles to the harnesses is called the skeleton tie-up, and it is drawn as in Figure 230 (as if you were looking down at your treadles). The tie-up draft is usually drawn right alongside the threading draft so that the spaces correspond. For easy reading, space is left between treadles. The left-hand treadle is considered no. 1. Notice that the treadle on the far left (no. 1) is marked with an X in the lower space; this means harness no. 1 is tied to it. The second space up represents harness no. 2, and so on. Using a skeleton tie-up, your feet simply press the proper treadle (or treadles) for the pattern.

Another tie-up arrangement that is still considered a skeleton tie-up requires 6 treadles. The fifth and sixth treadles are considered the "tabby treadles" and are labeled in the drafts "a" and "b." The other four treadles are called the pattern treadles. To form the tabby sheds harnesses 1 and 3 are tied to "a," and harnesses 2 and 4 are tied to "b." Sometimes weavers prefer to consider the left-hand treadles the tabby treadles, and sometimes even the center two are used for the tabby sheds.

The standard tie-up is a little more sophisticated. As many harnesses are tied to one treadle as are to be pulled down for one shed. For instance, to weave a basic 2/2 twill you lower 2 shafts at a time: 1 and 2, then 2 and 3, then 3 and 4, then 4 and 1, so each treadle is tied to *two* harnesses.

Sometimes the weaver finds it more convenient to tie up the treadles so that the sequence in which they are pressed down can be achieved in a "walking motion." In other words, you would press treadle 1 and then treadle 3, then treadle 2, and then treadle 4. This is particularly convenient on a stand-up loom.

I have discussed only tie-up drafts where the treadles, when operated, pull the harness (or harnesses) down. This type of action is called "sinking shed," and occurs when using a counterbalanced loom. On the jack loom a treadle pressed down means that the corresponding harnesses are raised. This type of action is called "rising shed." A tie-up draft for a rising-shed loom is marked with Os instead of Xs, and exactly the opposite harnesses are tied to the treadles.

FIGURE 231. Skeleton tie-up draft for four harnesses and six treadles (two are tabby treadles).

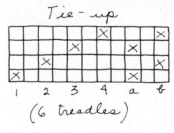

FIGURE 230. Skeleton tie-up draft for four harnesses and four treadles.

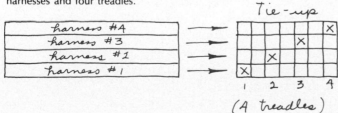

FIGURE 232. Standard tie-up draft for 2/2 twill.

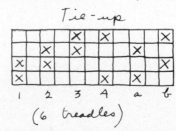

For the counter marche loom the draft would be written as in Figure 234. You have to tie the treadles and lams in such a way that whatever harnesses aren't being lowered are being raised. So this loom has both sinking and rising sheds. The tie-up draft is marked with Xs to show which harnesses are to be lowered and with Os to show which harnesses are to be raised. (See The Treadle Tie-up in this chapter for how to tie up the counter marche loom so that all combinations of harnesses up or down are possible.)

FIGURE 233. Sinking shed tie-up draft and rising shed tie-up draft.

FIGURE 234. 2/2 twill tie-up draft for counter marche loom.

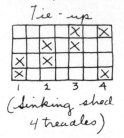

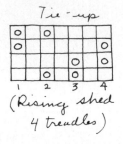

Treadling sequence

The final factor to be considered is the order the treadles are to be pressed. For example, with a standard tie-up, to weave the basic twill with no variations, you treadle 1, 2, 3, 4, and repeat—in other words, you "weave as drawn in." If the draft for the standard tie-up does not include specific treadling directions, it is assumed that the treadles are operated in sequence. If a more complicated sequence of treadling is desired the sequence of treadling is written in (1, 2, 1, 2, 3, 4).

With a skeleton tie-up, you simply press the proper treadles for the pattern. If three harnesses are to be lowered, one foot presses one treadle and the other foot presses two.

The draw-down

So now we have the threading draft, the standard tie-up draft, and the treadling sequence. From this we can actually reconstruct the weave on paper to see what it will look like. Using these three factors, simply draw on graph paper each row of weaving, blacking in squares that are blacked or marked in on the threading draft. If treadle no. 1 is tied to harness 1 and 2, the first row of the draw-down will have blackened squares in the same places where *both* no. 1 and no. 2 have blackened squares. Place your threading draft directly above the line of the draw-down so that you can easily see which spaces to mark. The bottom spaces in the draw-down will represent your first row of weaving, and so on up.

Planning the Weaving

When you are working on the treadle loom, it is most efficient to set up a warp that will serve for many different projects. It usually takes more time to set up the warp than to weave the item, and it is only a little more work to set up a long warp than a short one. This means that, if you weave ten projects on that warp, you have cut your warping time nearly to one-tenth. Farther on in this chapter are several very versatile warps and several projects for each warp.

It is very important that you read Chapter I, "The Basics of Weaving: Your Yarns," before planning your weaving, as well as "Sett and sley," below.

FIGURE 235. Draw-down from the threading draft, tie-up draft, and treadling sequence.

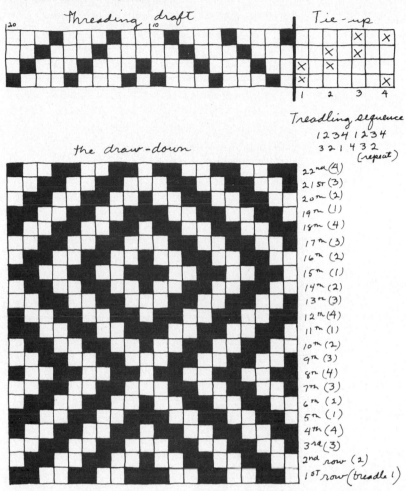

Treadling sequence
1234 1234
321 432
(repeat)

22ⁿᵈ (4)
21ˢᵗ (3)
20ᵗʰ (2)
19ᵗʰ (1)
18ᵗʰ (4)
17ᵗʰ (3)
16ᵗʰ (2)
15ᵗʰ (1)
14ᵗʰ (2)
13ᵗʰ (3)
12ᵗʰ (4)
11ᵗʰ (1)
10ᵗʰ (2)
9ᵗʰ (3)
8ᵗʰ (4)
7ᵗʰ (3)
6ᵗʰ (1)
5ᵗʰ (1)
4ᵗʰ (4)
3ʳᵈ (3)
2ⁿᵈ row (2)
1ˢᵀ row (treadle 1)

FIGURE 236. Normal sleying, triple sleying, and sleying in every other dent.

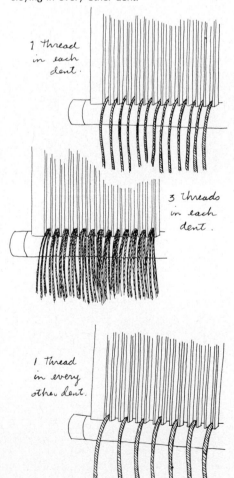

1 thread in each dent.

3 threads in each dent.

1 thread in every other dent.

Sett and sley

These two strange words are used to describe how the warp is spaced and threaded through the reed. *Sett* means how many warp ends there are per inch (*epi* means "ends per inch"). *Sley* means the threading of the ends through the reed. *Single sley* means one thread goes through each dent of the reed; *double sley* means two threads go through each dent; and so forth. *The warp sett can be the most crucial single factor in determining the success of the structure of the fabric.* Having the *correct sley* (single, double, or whatever) for a particular warp sett can facilitate the weaving.

Sley: If you don't have a reed with exactly as many dents as there are ends per inch (epi) you can double sley or skip dents. For very close setts (such as warp-face weaving) it is better to use a reed with only half as many dents (or one-third as many) and double sley or triple sley (you can even sley as many as six ends in one dent), even though you have a reed with exactly as many dents as there are epi. To use a reed that has exactly as many dents means that the spaces are necessarily very narrow because the blades of the reed occupy a great deal of space themselves. You can easily imagine that the threads would have difficulty moving up and down in that restricted space. Two threads will move up and down in a space twice that size much more easily.

If you have fewer warp ends per inch than dents in the reed, you can just thread every other dent, or every third dent, as long as the dent is large enough for the thread to move freely in it. You can even sley two and skip one if, for instance, the reed is 12 and the sett is 8.

Sett: Deciding on the warp sett—how many warp ends there should be per inch to make your weave structure come out as you want it—is a much more difficult problem. There are so many factors involved—the thickness of the yarns, the weave (whether the warp is supposed to show, or the weft, or both), how smooth the yarns are, how stiff or soft they are, how wide the fabric is, and whether it is to be hand beaten or packed in with the loom beater. . . . It would be nice to have a computer to figure out exactly what the warp sett should be.

Here are some very general rules to go by until you become familiar with your yarns and have had some experience with different weaves. The rules are for three different types of fabrics: balanced weaves (where there are to be as many weft threads per inch as there are warp threads), warp-face weaves (where only the warp shows), and weft-face weaves (where only the weft shows). (See Chapter I, "The Basics of Weaving: A Definition of Weaving," for illustrations of this and the following weaves.)

For a *balanced plain weave,* which is properly called "tabby," a good general rule is to leave a space the size of the thread between every two threads. In other words, if you stretched on a ruler as many threads as would fit side by side within an inch of space and then took half this number for your warp sett, it would make a good tabby fabric. For a balanced twill weave the warp threads should be slightly closer together, since the weft goes over and under two warps at a time. About half again as many threads as are required for tabby will be right.

For *warp-face weaving* the number of threads that fit side by side within an inch of space should be doubled, if possible, to make the warp sett. Exactly the same number that fit side by side on the ruler will make a modified warp-face weave.

For *weft-face fabrics* the problem is much more complicated. The warp must be sett as close together as possible so that the weft can just barely be beaten down to cover the warp completely. If it is too close, the weft cannot be beaten down to cover, and if it is set too far apart, the fabric is very loose and takes forever to weave because so many weft threads can be packed in. In general, the number of threads should be about one-half or two-thirds the number that would be used for a balanced plain weave, *if* the warp yarn is the same size as the weft. If the weft is going to be heavier or stiff (stiffness makes it more difficult to pack down to cover the warp), use the lesser warp setting.

A good way to test a warp sett is to wrap a strand of warp around a book several times (to make a two-inch width) at the distance apart that you think is right, and then just "darn" in the weft for an inch or so and pack it down with a comb. You can very quickly see what the final fabric will be like. Just keep in mind that the weft will beat down more easily in a narrow width than on a wide loom, where the beating is done with the reed. So, in weft-face weaves, to allow for this, so as to make sure the warp will be covered, set the warp on your loom slightly farther apart than seems right on your sample or use a warp yarn that is slightly finer.

Planning the warp

1. The first thing to do is figure out exactly what warp sett you should use (how many warp ends per inch). Take the yarns that you have in mind and make the little sample as described in "Sett and sley." This will take only a few minutes and may save you all kinds of trouble in the weaving. You will find out from this sample exactly how far apart the warp threads should be to accomplish the

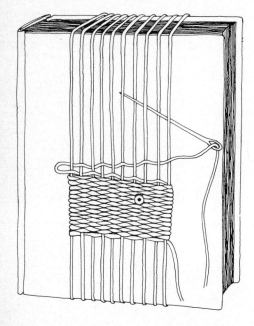

FIGURE 237. Wrapping warp around book and darning in weft to check on warp sett.

weave structure you have in mind. It is good to have at least three different reed sizes; then you can have exactly the right sett for a particular yarn. If your reed is the constant (that is, you only have one reed size), then all you can do to have the right combination of sett and size of yarn is to change the size of the warp yarn. (Recommended warp setts and yarn specifications are given for each of the projects in this chapter but it would be wise to put them through this test.)

2. When you know how many warp ends per inch you need, multiply this by the width (in inches) of your weaving, and you will know how many warp ends there should be altogether. Add about six threads to this, so that you can thread the edge threads double or triple for the selvedge (see Chapter VIII, "Finishing Techniques: Selvedges").

Adjust this total so that it is divisible by eight (this will make the warp winding less confusing, since you will be winding groups of eight threads at a time).

3. Now, to plan on what length your warp should be, add the following lengths together:
   a. Number of feet in *each* project that you plan to weave on this warp.
   b. Allowance for warp takeup (2 inches per yard for weft face; 4 inches per yard for balanced weaves; 6 inches per yard for warp face). These are approximate figures, so allow plenty.
   c. Fringe allowance for both ends of each item (it is very awkward to tie a fringe with less than 4 or 5 inches of warp ends).
   d. One extra yard for tying on and waste at the end of the warp.
Note: The yardage given for the following projects *includes* warp takeup (b) and a fringe allowance (c).

4. Now you know how many threads you need and what length each thread should be. The *total number of yards of yarn needed for the warp* can be figured from this, by multiplying the length (in yards) by the number of warp ends across the total width (no. 2 above). Some suppliers will indicate how many yards of thread there are in a skein (or pound or kilo) of a particular type of yarn. If they do, you can figure exactly how many skeins or pounds or kilos you will need for the entire warp. Then add a little extra so you will have ample. If the yarn you order is sized by the numerical system, you can figure the number of yards in each skein by the method described in Chapter I, "The Basics of Weaving: Your Yarns."

A very approximate estimate of the *weft* yardage you will need is: about four times as much weft as warp for weft-face weaving; about one-third as much for warp-face weaving; and, of course, the same amount for balanced weaves. See Chapter I, "The Basics of Weaving: Your Yarns."

Winding the Warp Yarn onto Spools or Cones

The first step in any warping method is to get all your warp yarn onto spools or cones.

For a chained warp, I find it most convenient to wind the warp from spools or cones onto the warping board or mill from *four* spools at a time. Unless the warp yarn is already on spools or cones, you will wind the skeins of warp yarn in this form, using one spool or cone for each skein of yarn. If your warp is plain colored, it is only essential to have four spools (when these run out you can refill them). But if your warp is made up of a variety of yarns or colors, you will need more spools (so that you can wind some of one color and then leave that spool of color until you need it again).

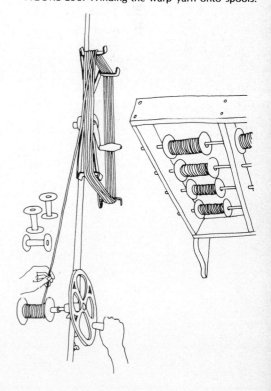

FIGURE 238. Winding the warp yarn onto spools.

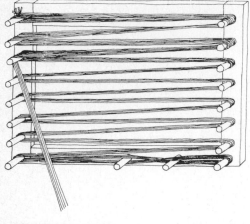

FIGURE 239. Winding the warp onto a board or mill.

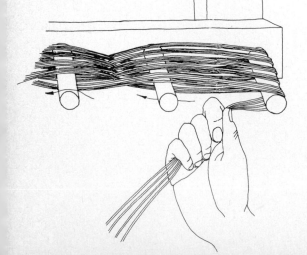

FIGURE 240. Making the cross (or lease) with the group of four threads.

With careful planning of your warp stripes, sometimes twelve spools are enough, but it's handy if you have the right number of spools to wind at least half of the warp.

For sectional warping you have to *have as many spools as there are warp ends within a two-inch warp width.* Since this is the case you may only be able to wind half a skein or less on each spool. You'll have to have more spools for more colors. (Sectional warping is not really appropriate for multi-colored warps.)

To wind the spools or cones, just put them on whatever device you are using to wind them (see The Bobbin Winder in this chapter), and use one hand to guide the thread back and forth so that it winds on evenly. With the cones be careful not to let the thread get too close to the ends or it will spill off and tangle. The final spool should be cylindrical and the cone should be pear-shaped. If you have a good fast winder, hold the thread *very loosely* as it winds on or you can get bad burns; or wear gloves.

Place the spools or cones on the spool or cone rack.

Making a Chained Warp

Below are directions for measuring out the warp threads on a warping board or vertical mill (a chained warp), and for making either an individual cross (or lease) or a group cross. The individual cross is used when the warp is to be threaded through reed and heddles *before* beaming (or if you are tying onto a dummy warp—see this heading below), and the group cross is used when the warp is to be threaded *after* beaming. Problem yarns (sticky, fuzzy, curly, textured, or very close setts) should be beamed first and threaded afterward (see also Beaming a Warp by the Sectional Method, later in this chapter). When practical, it is most efficient to thread the warp first and beam it afterward.

1. Figure which pegs you will carry the warp threads around on your warping board to make the correct length. The three pegs at the bottom must be included so that you can make the cross there. On a warping mill, to determine the correct path to take, simply measure a piece of thread the length you want and tie it to the top peg. Then turn the mill, letting the thread spiral around until it runs out at the bottom three pegs (these lease pegs are usually on a movable member that can be raised). Then follow this thread when winding the warp.

2. Take the threads from four spools and tie them to the top peg.

3. Lead the threads around the proper pegs on the warping board. I like to let the threads pass through the fingers of my left hand as I wind them onto the warping board with my right. If using the mill, hold the group in one hand so that they spiral around the warping mill as you turn the mill with the other. The tension as you wind on the threads should be just *moderate.* It is most important to keep the tension consistent. On a warping board there is the tendency for the threads to be wound tighter as you proceed—mainly because the pegs start to draw in. You must consciously wind with less and less tension to counteract this. If you are winding a warp of many threads on a warping board, it is best to do it in at least two separate sections—removing each section from the board before winding the next.

4. Making the cross:
   a. *Group cross:* When you come to the three pegs at the bottom, lead the threads over one peg, under the next, and around the third. On returning pass the group of threads over and under the opposite pegs. (See Figure 240.)

A key to the color photographs may be found on pages 357-60.

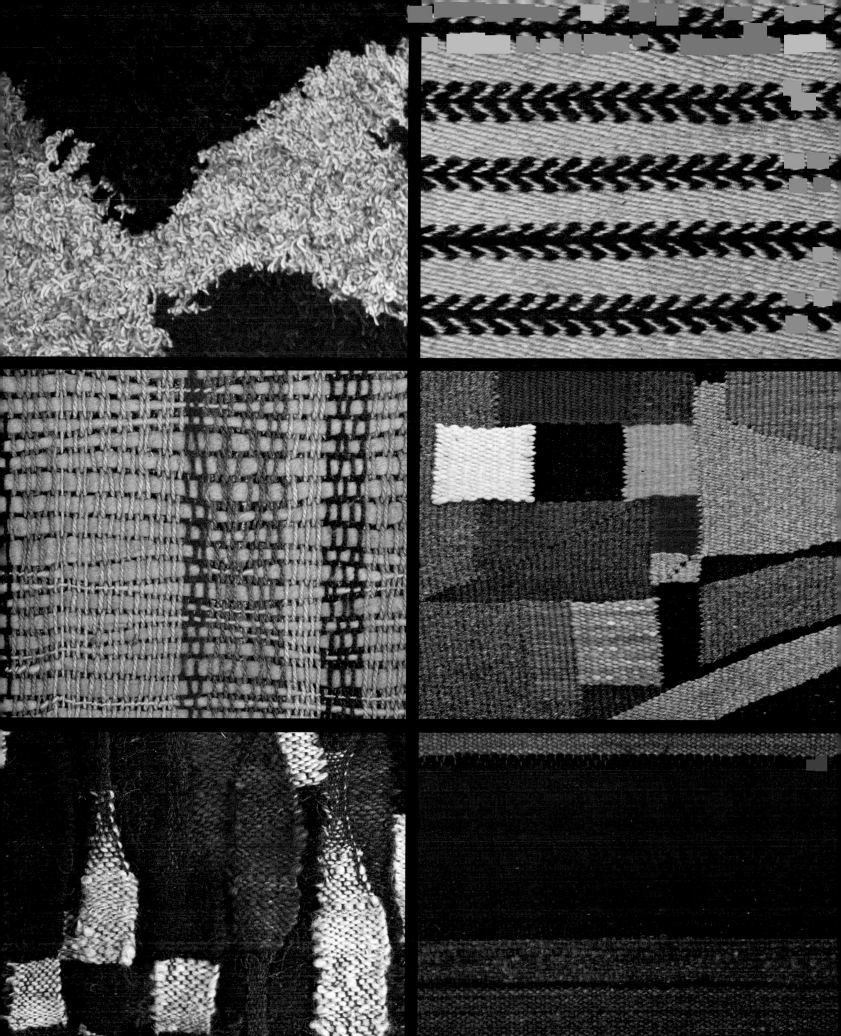

b. *Individual cross:* When you come to the three pegs at the bottom, instead of passing the group together over the pegs, you put the four threads on your fingers (left hand) in sequence in a figure eight and slip them in this position onto the lease pegs. You can't let go of the threads with your right hand, so this has to be done entirely with one hand. To do this most easily, point your forefinger and little finger out like horns and rock them back and forth between the threads as they come from the spools. You have to do this as you approach the lease pegs (see position A in Figure 241) *and* when you return (see position B).

You will probably find this extremely awkward at first, but will soon learn to do it in a flash. When you do become skilled, it is a simpler and faster method than using a warping paddle (a paddle with several holes in it through which the warp ends are threaded), for anything but repeating colors in the warp.

5. Each time you return to the starting point at the top of the board or mill, make a mark on a piece of paper. Wind as many times as necessary to get the total number of threads for the width of your weaving (total threads divided by eight). If you think you have made a mistake in counting, you can count the group crosses and multiply to see how many threads you have already wound. Or take a thread and make a chain around every 8 threads as you wind. (See Figure 21 in Chapter II.) On a warping board it is very easy to miss a peg. If this does happen and you don't notice it right away, there is no way to remedy the situation without taking off all the threads back to that point (a terrible process). *So,* when you make your mark for counting each time you have returned to the top peg, glance down and make absolutely certain you have not made this mistake.

6. When using a warping board, if you need to make color changes in the warp, instead of cutting off and tying on a new thread, simply wrap the first color around the top peg a couple of times and let it sit there until you need it again. There is no problem of exact length at this end; it will be trimmed off eventually anyway. If a spool or cone of yarn runs out in the middle of the route from top to bottom, don't tie a knot and add on there; return to the top or bottom (whichever is closest) and make the knot at either end of the warp.

7. Preserving the lease and making chokes:

When you have completed winding the warp and are sure you have the correct number of threads, tie a cord through the cross in such a way that, when you remove the warp from the board or mill, this cross will be preserved. Also tie cords around the warp close to starting peg and at various points a few yards apart. Then make one good tight tie about three feet from the cross. These are called "chokes."

8. Making the chain:

Now, starting at the *top* of the board or mill (opposite from where the cross is), slip the warp carefully off the first peg and start making a chain. Do not let the warp threads slip off the other pegs. You have to move from side to side of the warping board, holding the warp threads taut at all times. Use your foot to control the unwinding of the mill, or lock it and walk around it.

Make a large loop with the group of warp threads to start with. Put your right hand through that loop and pull a section of the warp beyond that through the loop. Then put your right hand through this new loop and pull a new section of warp through. Continue putting your right hand through the freshly made loop and grasping the warp ahead of it and pulling it through, until you get

FIGURE 241. Making the individual cross. .

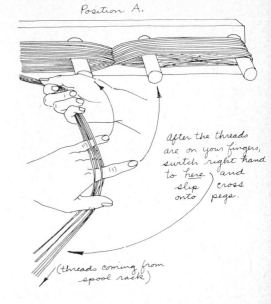

Position A.

after the threads are on your fingers, switch right hand to here, and slip cross onto pegs.

(threads coming from spool rack)

Position B.

(threads coming from spool rack)

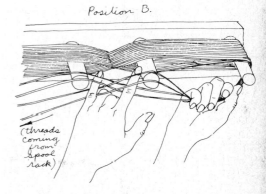

FIGURE 242. Tying a cord through the lease and chokes at various points of the warp to keep it in order.

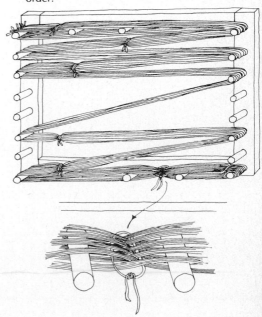

FIGURE 243. Making the chain.

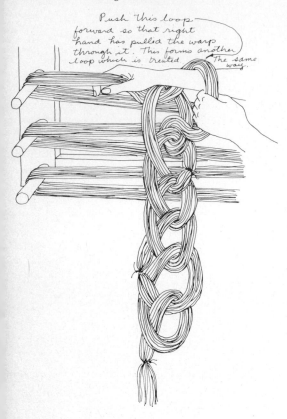

Push this loops forward so that right hand has pulled the warp through it. This forms another loop which is treated the same way.

FIGURE 244. Tape the lease rods with the spread-out warp to the breast beam.

Breast beam

down to the bottom of the warp. Leave a two-foot end with the cross exposed. *Do not lock this end through the last loop.* If you do, the chain will not unwind after you have attached it to the loom.

(If you have done crocheting, you will recognize this chain as simply a giant crochet stitch.)

Now you have your warp in a nice neat bundle. It won't tangle, and you can handle it without worry.

9. Sizing the warp (optional):

If the warp yarn is weak or fuzzy and you anticipate trouble in the weaving, you can size it while it is in the form of the chain, if you wish. Dip it into a hot starch solution (such as laundry starch), press out most of the moisture, and let it drip dry. The starch (or sizing) will help prevent fraying and breaking. This is not a common practice, but is advised if you are using a problem warp, such as handspun. The starch is washed out only after the article is woven and cut off the loom.

10. The use of the lease rods:

Support the lease end of the warp chain on a bench or chair in front of the loom. Take the lease rods and insert one in each side of the cross. Tie a cord through the holes in the rods so the warp threads cannot slip off the ends. Now cut the cord that preserved the cross, and gently spread out the threads over the approximate width of the planned weaving. Tape the lease rods to the breast beam.

Without disturbing the tie a few feet behind the cross, pull the looped ends of the warp through the lease rods so that they are taut and hang down evenly about 2 1/2 feet from the breast beam. (This length should be the distance from the breast beam to about 1 foot beyond the heddles. You'll need this length so that the threads can be looped or tied onto the warp beam rod.)

If you have made the individual cross, cut the loops at the exact end. If you made the group cross, *do not cut the loops.*

Threading a Chained Warp from Front to Back (before Beaming)

You will skip this step if you made the group cross in preparation for beaming prior to threading, and go directly to Spreading a Chained Warp to be Beamed before Threading.

Threading is probably the most tedious and exacting process in the craft of weaving. If you have made the individual cross, you will now sley the reed and thread the heddles, and then wind the warp through them onto the warp beam (beaming).

Position the reed in the center of the beater, and mark the center of the reed (this can be done by tying a white thread around the top). Be sure you are starting the threading at the correct point so that the warp will be exactly centered in the reed. For convenience, lash the beater in an upright position.

Sitting at the front of the loom, thread the reed first, using either a reed hook or a threading hook. Take the threads exactly as they come in sequence from the lease rods.

Double up the threads as planned for the selvedge (see Chapter VIII, "Finishing Techniques: Selvedges"). Put the reed hook through the dent from the back and pull the thread all the way through. Every few inches check to make sure you haven't skipped any dents. Don't wait until you have completed the sleying, because then you will have to take out the threads all the way back to the mistake.

FIGURE 245. Threading from front before beaming.

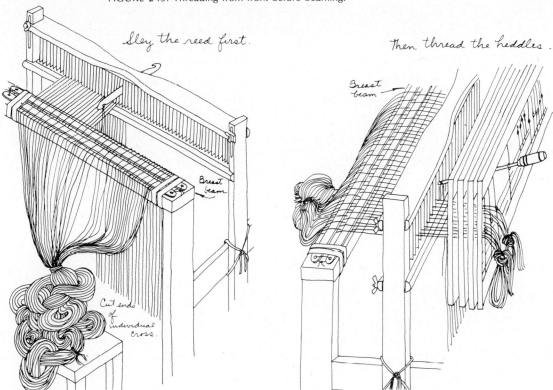

Sley the reed first.

then thread the heddles.

The heddles are threaded next. If you are threading alone, you will probably have to stand at the side of the loom. Push all the heddles to the center of the harnesses and take just one at a time. It is most convenient to thread heddles from right to left as you face them. Take each thread as it comes from the reed and thread it through the heddles, giving the selvedge the special treatment indicated in Chapter VIII, "Finishing Techniques: Selvedges." If you have doubled sleyed through the reed, your lease rods will indicate which thread of the two goes through the first heddle.

All the projects in this chapter are done with a basic twill threading. This means threading the first thread through a heddle on harness no. 1 (the front one), the next thread through a heddle on harness no. 2, the next thread through a heddle on harness no. 3, and the fourth thread through a heddle on harness no. 4, repeating this across the entire warp. This book does not deal with any threadings more complicated than this, except in Chapter VI, "The Navajo Loom," which gives instructions for a diamond twill. (A draft for these weaves on the treadle loom appears in Figure 228.) The basic twill threading will make possible plain weave, twills, basket weaves, double width, double face, and three dimensional.

Every 16 or 20 threads check for mistakes and tie a slip knot in the group of threads when you are sure they are threaded correctly. A simple way to check for mistakes is to hold the threads taut and then lift each harness separately. If there is equal spacing between the threads as they separate in front of the reed, the threading is correct; any mistake will show up. Be *sure* there are no mistakes in the threading. If there are you have to take the whole thing out back to the mistake.

Threading is most easily done by two people.

When all the warp ends are threaded through both reed and heddles, untie the loose knots in the warp threads and gently comb the threads with your fingers until they are all pulled evenly through the reed and heddles.

Tie these ends onto the warp beam rod as shown in Figure 246. *Remove the lease rods*, as these perform no further function.

FIGURE 246. Tying the cut warp ends to the warp beam rod.

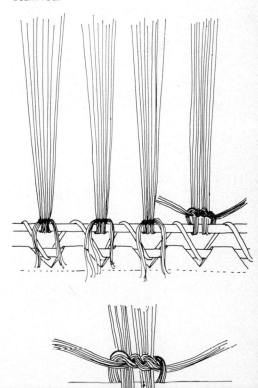

(detail)

FIGURE 247. Rough sleying (instead of using a raddle).

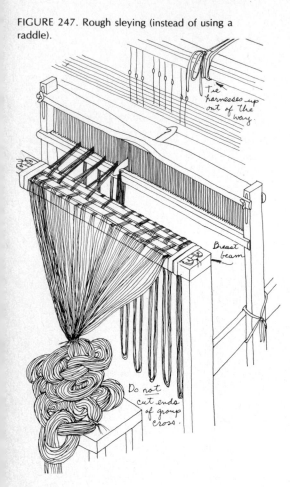

Tie harnesses up out of the way.

Breast beam

Do not cut ends of group cross.

FIGURE 248. Spreading the warp in groups using the raddle.

Tie harnesses up out of the way

Back beam

Spreading a Chained Warp (to Be Beamed before Threading)

(Skip this step if you have already threaded the ends through the reed or heddles or tied onto a dummy warp.) If you intend to beam the warp *before* threading it, you will have wound the group cross. Spread the warp out to the full width of the planned weaving, before rolling it onto the warp roller, by threading the groups of threads through the reed (this is called "rough sleying") or placing the group in a raddle. The heddles must be pushed aside or the harnesses tied up out of the way or removed for this operation, so they do not get in the way of the warp as it is rolled on.

1. Using the reed as a spreader. Make sure the reed is centered in the beater, mark the center of the reed, and start the threading at the proper point so that the warp will be centered in the reed.

Starting at the left, with the groups of 8 threads (2 groups of 4) as they come from the lease rod (taped to breast beam) in sequence, thread the entire group, which forms an uncut loop, as a whole through a dent in the reed. Skip 7 dents, and thread the next group through the next dent. This leaves the exact number of dents for all 8 threads when they are finally threaded through the reed individually (after the beaming process). (This is assuming that the warp is to be threaded [or sleyed] 1 end in each dent. If it is to be double sleyed, then you thread the group through every 4th dent, because the 8 threads would only take 4 dents in the reed. If they are to be sleyed every other dent you would thread the group through every 16th dent.) This will spread the warp out in groups to the full width of the planned weaving, in preparation for rolling it onto the warp beam.

Pull the loops all the way through and slip them onto the warp beam rod, which has been unlashed from the second rod held by the apron or tapes. Spread the loops out evenly on this rod. Lash the rod to the second rod held in the apron or tapes. Crank up the warp beam so that the warp is held taut. At this point you can undo the tie in the warp on the other side of the cross.

2. Using a raddle as a spreader. Remove the reed from the beater. Clamp the raddle to the back beam, and remove the top. Remove the warp beam rod from the apron or tapes. Standing at the back of the loom, slip the warp loops, as they come in sequence from the lease rods, onto the warp beam rod. Space the warp loops as evenly as possible over this bar to the width of the planned weaving. Pull the bar with the loops out taut beyond the raddle. (Untie the first tie in the warp chain if necessary.)

After figuring exactly how many threads should fit in the raddle spaces to spread the warp perfectly evenly over the width, place this number of threads down into the raddle spaces. Replace the top on the raddle. Lash the warp beam rod, with its warp loops in place, to the second bar held in the apron or tapes. Crank up the warp roller so that everything is taut.

Note: When spreading the warp for beaming *previous* to threading *leave the lease rods in the warp.* Undo the tape holding the lease rods to the breast beam. Slide the lease rods forward about 6 inches. Tie a cord from the lease rods to the breast beam; this will act as a brake for the lease rods as they ride along in that position while the warp passes through them. The lease rods are left in for this operation (we don't leave them in when rolling on the warp that has already been threaded) so that after the warp is completely beamed the cross is still there allowing us to thread the ends in proper sequence.

Beaming a Chained Warp (Either before or after Threading)

After the warp is threaded (or just spread) it must be rolled onto the warp beam in tension. This is called "beaming." Although there are ways of beaming a chained warp by yourself (by grabbing short sections of the warp at a time and giving each a good tug after each complete turn of the warp roller, or setting a weight on the warp and letting it slide across a smooth floor), the warp is beamed much more efficiently by two people. (There's got to be *someone* you can recruit for this short operation!) One person cranks the warp beam while a second person holds the warp in two sections. You're supposed to hold it as you would the reins of a spirited horse (I read somewhere, once). But anyway hold it as tightly as you can and still allow the other person to crank the warp beam around.

As you come to them, untie the chokes that were originally tied in the warp chain and unchain it about 15 feet at a time (if the room will allow). Stand way back (the farther back, the more even the tension) and shake occasionally to untangle. If you have already threaded the reed and heddles, the person cranking the warp beam should push the reed gently forward to clear any tangles in the threads and then roll on that distance of warp. Repeat for the entire warp. If the warp is being rolled on in groups and the lease rods are still in place, the person cranking the warp beam must occasionally work out tangles at the lease rods; the person holding the warp should watch for these. A coarse comb is helpful for this, or just use your fingers.

If the warp beam is of large diameter, there will be no further attention needed. But, if the warp beam is small in diameter, you will have to put slats (perhaps old Venetian-blind slats) in at four points around the circumference every sixth turn or so, to prevent the warp threads from cutting down into the roll and changing the tension. Or newspaper that has been folded over twice at the edges and is just about one inch wider than the warp width can be rolled in with the warp to serve the same purpose.

Roll the warp on until the ends are about 6 inches from the breast beam.

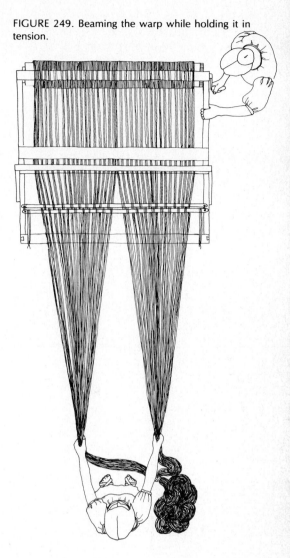

FIGURE 249. Beaming the warp while holding it in tension.

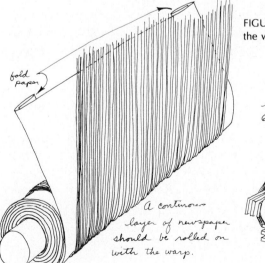

fold paper

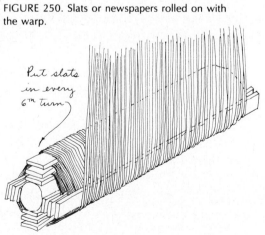

Put slats in every 6ᵗʰ turn

FIGURE 250. Slats or newspapers rolled on with the warp.

a continuous layer of newspaper should be rolled on with the warp.

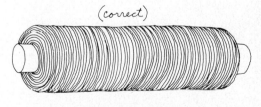

(correct)

FIGURE 251. The final shape of the warp rolled onto the warp beam (correct and incorrect).

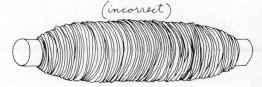

(incorrect)

Important: The most important thing to remember as you are rolling the warp on is that the roll formed on the warp roller should be *perfectly cylindrical*. It must *not* spread out at the edges. This would mean that the diameter would decrease at the edges, and that the warp would be shorter there. The person holding the warp

FIGURE 252. Transferring the lease to the back for threading after beaming.

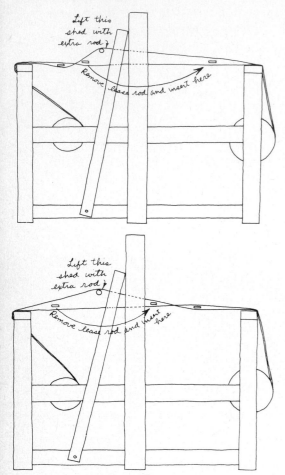

FIGURE 253. Sectional warping: winding on a 2-inch section of warp.

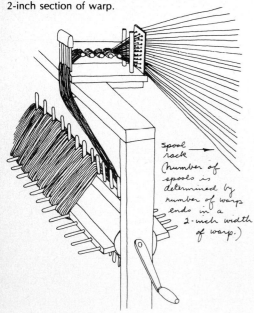

as it is rolled on must watch for drooping threads at the edges; this is an indication that the diameter is decreasing. Pictured in Figure 251 is the correct shape of the finished warp roll, as well as the incorrect shape. You can have some kind of spikes driven into the warp beam (or metal loops inserted in drilled holes—see The Warp Beam in this chapter) to hold the warp threads in this cylindrical form. Finishing nails tacked into the back beam to guide the edge warp threads within these spikes can be used.

If you are beaming prior to threading and have used a reed as a spreader, you will have to transfer the cross to a position behind the reed for threading. To do this, hold the warp taut (you may have to unwind it so it doesn't pull through the reed), lift one lease rod (the one closest to the back of the loom) up high, and insert another stick in the shed that forms behind the reed. Remove the lease rod that you held up. Now lift the second lease rod and insert the first in that shed behind the reed. You now have made the same cross behind the reed, and can tape the lease rods (replace the odd stick with the second lease rod) to the back beam for threading.

If you used a raddle as spreader, remove it and slide the lease rods to the back beam and tape there for threading.

Trim the warp ends off evenly (you can use the breast beam as a gauge). If the threading has already been done, you are ready to tie onto the cloth roller, so skip to that section. If you still have to thread the ends, pull them through the reed (if this was used), let them hang down from the lease rods at the back of the loom, and proceed to the section Threading from Back to Front (after Beaming).

Beaming a Warp by the Sectional Method

(This is an alternate method of measuring out and beaming a warp prior to threading. Skip all previous sections starting with Making a Chained Warp.)

The sectional warping method is most useful for long plain-colored warps of fine threads, close-warp setts, or problem yarn.

Wind a spool or cone of warp yarn for *each* warp end within a 2-inch width or warp. Thread the ends of each spool through a tension box, which is clamped onto the back beam or a table close by, tie the ends to the peg or loop on the beam, and crank the sectional beam around the appropriate number of times to make the right warp length. A counter is handy to keep track of the number of turns you make. As you wind, the group of threads may be guided back and forth within the pegs to insure level buildup. When the required length has been wound on, tape the threads as they come from the tension box to preserve the sequence, cut them and loop them over the peg, and proceed to the next section. The beamed warp should be as perfectly centered on the beam as possible. You can wind the sections in whatever order you wish; the way to wind a striped warp would be to wind all the sections of one color first and then proceed to the sections of the next color.

After all sections have been wound, lift each group of threads up over the back beam and tape in place for threading. You will have to unwind each section by hand from around the beam as many times as is necessary to give you the length needed for threading. (The threads should reach nearly to the breast beam.)

Threading from Back to Front (after Beaming)

If the warp is such that it is best to beam it before threading heddles and reed, then the threading must be done from back to front after the beaming.

Threading from back to front is definitely easier if there are two people—one to

FIGURE 254. Taped ends of finished section secured to pegs while winding the following sections.

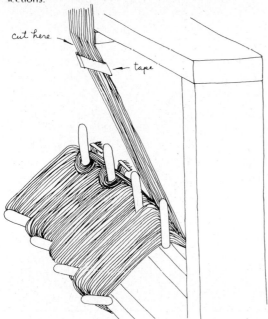

FIGURE 255. Threading the warp ends through the heddles and reed together.

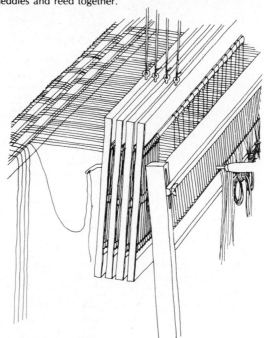

pick up the threads in sequence at the back beam and one to put the threading hook through the reed and heddle simultaneously. Threading the reed and heddle in one operation eliminates the possibility of crossed threads as they come from heddle to reed. If only you are available for threading, it will be best to remove the breast beam and beater. Start at the right and sit up close to the heddles, thread them first, and thread the reed in a separate operation. When threading the reed make sure the threads come in correct sequence from the heddles; it is very easy to get threads crossed. Read Threading a Chained Warp from Front to Back (before Beaming) in this chapter for threading pattern and checking for mistakes. After checking for mistakes, tie a loose knot in the warp ends to secure them.

FIGURE 256. Tying onto a dummy warp.

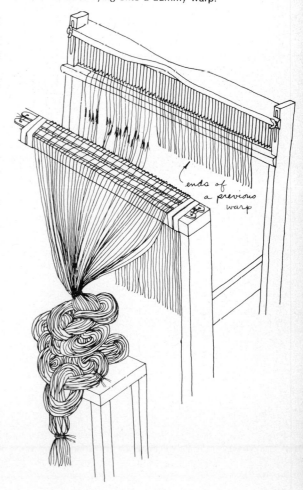

Tying onto a Dummy Warp (Optional)

If you are putting on the loom a new warp that is identical in width, sett, and threading to the previous one, you can simply tie the new ends to the old. This is a little quicker than removing the old warp and threading all over again. Simply tie on your new warp ends to the old instead of threading (from either front or back).

Pull the knotted ends through the reed and heddles gently, and proceed as if you had just threaded the ends. Use a weaver's knot (see Figure 257) to join the new ends to the old.

FIGURE 257. Steps in making the weaver's knot.

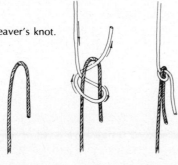

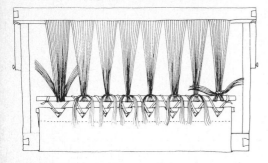

FIGURE 258. Tying onto the cloth beam rod.

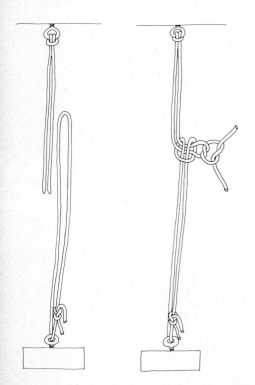

FIGURE 259. Tying the threadles with a switch knot.

Tying onto the Cloth Roller

After the warp has been beamed and threaded it must be attached to the cloth beam. Bring the cloth beam rod up over the breast beam and let it hang down in front (toward the reed) about 6 inches. Start with the center threads of the warp, and pick a group of about 1-inch width. Comb the threads out with your fingers. Tie the group to the extension rod as shown in Figure 258. Using this knot (see detail in Figure 246) you can adjust the tension later without untying the knot, and yet it will hold. Pull the warp very tight when you make the knot. Now make a knot with the next 1-inch group on the other side of center, and work your way out to the edges.

Cautions: (1) The groups of threads must come directly or perpendicularly down to the extension rod. *Do not let them start slanting.* (2) As you work out to the edges, your first ties in the center will have less tension. You can counteract this as you are tying by consciously making less and less tension toward the edges. Or, better, readjust the knots starting at center again so that all the groups will have even tension. Using your hand, press down on the groups to check tension, and readjust. Tie the edge groups just slightly tighter, and with an extra knot, before starting to weave (these edge groups tend to loosen up if you don't do this).

The Treadle Tie-up

Your loom is now "dressed" and ready for weaving, except for the treadle tie-up. To make the "standard" tie-up on the counterbalanced and jack looms refer to An Explanation of Drafts and Tie-ups in this chapter.

For the type of weaving described in this book, the skeleton tie-up is best for both of these looms. This way you simply treadle the combinations with your feet and are free to do any weave structure at any time to make the skeleton tie-up. You will tie up the first treadle on the left to heddle shaft no. 1 (front), the next treadle to no. 2, and so forth: and repeat all across the warp. If your loom has six treadles you can tie two treadles for a tabby weave, if you wish. To do this, take two either on the left or on the right (or the center two) and tie heddle shafts nos. 1 and 3 to one, and heddle shafts nos. 2 and 4 to the other one. By treadling first one and then the other, you will get the tabby weave.

If your loom is supplied with screw eyes and cords, use the switch knot as shown in Figure 259. Some looms have hooks and chains. Actually, if you are doing the skeleton tie-up you can use any knot that will not slip at all (you want the treadles to be absolutely level with each other), since it can be a permanent tie.

There is no such thing as a skeleton tie-up for the counter marche loom. So to make a tie-up on this loom that will enable you to treadle any combination while the weaving is in progress, you will have to have eight treadles (or twice as many treadles as shafts), and you always press two at a time. It is similar to the standard tie-up described below, except that instead of tying a lam for every shaft to one treadle you divide the ties between two treadles. It will always take two treadles to raise or lower *all* the shafts, but this way you can make different combinations (see Figure 260).

If your counter marche loom does not have twice as many treadles as shafts, you will have to make a standard tie-up for each weave, and change the tie-up when you want to change the weave. To make the standard tie-up on this loom, refer to the directions in How to Operate the Sheds (Treadling) and read the numbers as if they referred to shaft numbers. Use two treadles for the tabby treadles (assuming you have six treadles—which you definitely should have on this loom) as described above. After tying the upper lams (which lower the shafts) that correspond to shafts 1 and 3 to the first of these two tabby treadles, tie the lower lams (which raise the shafts) of all the remaining shafts to that same treadle. Do the same for shafts 3 and 4. This tabby tie-up will not have to be changed. With the remaining four treadles, take the first and tie the upper lams of the shafts that are to be lowered for the first shed (2, 3, and 4, for instance, for double width); tie the lower lams that correspond to all the remaining shafts to this same treadle. Do this with the three remaining treadles, tying them to make the next three sheds. *Each treadle should connect with every shaft*—by being tied either to the upper lams or to the lower lams.

Advancing the Warp

Before weaving you will probably have to move the warp forward to give you weaving space. To do this, release the back pawl (or brake) and hold it released until you have cranked up the ratchet and pawl on the cloth beam so that the cloth beam rod is about 3 inches from the breast beam. At this point, let the release pedal (or handle) down, to prevent the warp beam from turning any more, and tighten up the front ratchet and pawl until the warp is in correct tension.

Depending on your loom, the procedure may vary, but what you want is to get the rod (or later on, when weaving, the fell) as close to the breast beam as possible, and yet not have the beater hit it when you start weaving. After you have woven a few rows you may need to tighten the tension once more. This is probably true with balanced weaves, which show up uneven packing of weft the most; but you need not be that particular with weft- or warp-face weaves. Unless this uneven weft packing (due to change in warp tension) becomes a problem, you will need to advance the warp only when the fell gets too close to the reed to pass the shuttle through easily.

A word of caution about unrolling the weaving to look at it: do not unroll it very far or the tension will be badly messed up. You can usually safely get away with unrolling enough to see two or three feet hanging down from the breast beam.

The Warp Tension

Crank up the cloth roller so that the warp is held in the proper tension for the particular weave (see page 154). If your warp is wool, do not leave it standing in tension for several hours. Release it when you are not working at the loom. Constant tension will damage the wool fiber. And for the loom's sake release the tension of any warp if you are leaving it for long periods of time.

If by any chance the warp tension is uneven, you can stuff rags under the warp threads that are loose just as they unroll from the warp beam. If it is *really* bad, you can unroll the warp and chain it as you unroll it. (Don't unroll more than about five yards at a time, because the resulting tangle of threads might be hopeless.) Then wind it back onto the warp beam while someone holds it in tension and combs out the threads to an even tension. Trim the excess and tie onto the cloth beam rod again; weave those five yards and then cut off the weavings. Repeat as many times as necessary until that warp is used up. And then don't ever let it happen again!

Proper warp tension varies according to the weave structure. It is not simply a matter of cranking up the tension as much as possible—which is what many beginning weavers tend to do. Certain weaves require great tension and others less. If you analyze the weave structure and understand which threads are bending around which, then you have a basis for deciding how tight your warp should be.

FIGURE 260. Skeleton tie-up for counterbalanced and jack looms; tie-ups for counter marche loom that allows for treadling all the possible sheds.

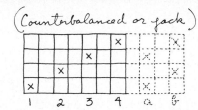

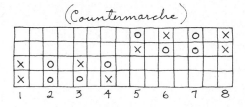

FIGURE 261. Releasing back panel so that the warp can be rolled farther onto the cloth beam.

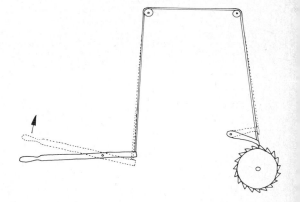

In *weft-face fabrics* it is the weft that does all the bending around the warp threads: the latter remain in a perfectly straight line. So the tighter you can make your warp threads in this case the better the weft will be packed in and around them. Because the jack loom is not designed to operate with extreme warp tension, it is not a suitable loom for weaving weft-face rugs, which are the items that require the greatest warp tension.

In *balanced weaves* (where warp and weft threads are similar in size and spacing) such as tabby and 2/2 twill, warp and weft do an equal amount of bending around each other. In these cases the warp should be moderately tight, and consistent tension is of great importance. If the tension is greater at times during the weaving, then a consistent beating-in of the weft will be to no avail; the weft will automatically pack down more when the warp is tight. Harriet Tidball, certainly one of the great authorities on the subject of handweaving, goes so far as to say that it is impossible to maintain the same tension if an adjustment is not made every four inches; and for this reason, she states, it is not important to have a great distance between the reed and the front beam, so that you can weave several inches without advancing the weaving. This is true for the balanced weaves, where perfectly consistent tension and beating are mandatory, but I believe that this perfection is not essential to weft-face and warp-face fabrics, and the weaving can continue without advancing the warp or changing the tension for a few more inches if the distance between beater and breast beam allow.

The tension of the warp when weaving *warp-face fabrics* must not be too tight or the weft cannot be properly packed down. The warp threads must be loose enough to bend around the weft.

I think if you understand these principles you will be able to decide on the correct tension for your warp.

Winding the Bobbins or Quills

To package your weft yarns for weaving, boat shuttles should be used whenever the yarn size allows. Heavy yarns will have to be wound onto stick shuttles.

In Figure 262 are the proper methods for winding bobbins and quills. The idea is to wind them in such a way that no part of the buildup of yarn on the bobbin or quill will interfere with the thread as it unwinds. If your shuttle and bobbin work and unwind perfectly, you can weave very fast and still your weft tension and edges will be perfect.

In any case, *do not overfill* your bobbins or quills. You may think you are saving time by winding on just that little bit more. But it turns out to be a waste of time, because for the first few rows of weaving the bobbin will not unwind freely. So just fill it very slightly over level. Make sure that when it fits into the shuttle it will turn freely.

Wind as many bobbins as you have at one time so you will have a supply for weaving. If you don't have a boat shuttle for each weft color, wind the extra weft colors onto stick shuttles.

Tangled skeins of yarn lying around your studio will be a dead giveaway that you are a novice. The experienced weaver knows that the little bit of time it takes to tie the skein securely before removing it from the swift will save countless hours of trying to untangle it. Pounds of wool can be wasted this way.

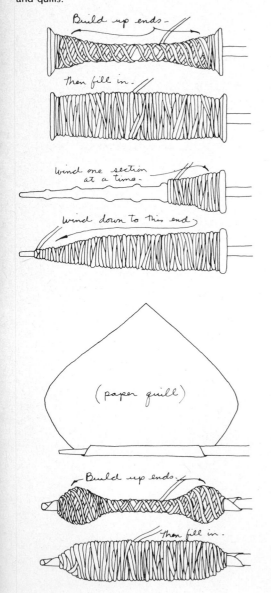

FIGURE 262. Proper winding methods for bobbins and quills.

Build up ends.

then fill in.

Wind one section at a time.

Wind down to this end.

(paper quill)

Build up ends.

then fill in.

Preparing Stick Shuttles

When the weft is too heavy to be wound onto the bobbins of a boat shuttle, use your stick shuttles. Ideally the stick shuttle you use for a particular weaving should be about two inches longer than the width of the warp; this makes it easy to push the shuttle through and grab it with the other hand. With wide weavings, of course, this is impossible, but it's nice to have a shuttle long enough so that it can be pushed through with a minimum of strokes. As with bobbins, do not overfill the stick shuttles because it will just take that much more time to push them through the shed. Wind as many stick shuttles as you have at one time.

FIGURE 263. Winding the weft onto stick shuttles.

How to Operate the Sheds (Treadling)

The sheds on the treadle loom are, of course, operated by pressing the treadles. The shed on a counterbalanced loom is referred to as a *sinking shed,* since when a treadle is pressed the threads on the corresponding harness are *lowered.* The shed on a jack loom is referred to as a *rising shed,* since when a treadle is pressed the threads on the corresponding harness are *raised.* In actuality, then, if the same treadles are pressed on the jack loom as on the counterbalanced loom, the fabric will be woven upside down. This should be borne in mind if you are using a jack loom. With most weave structures in this book it makes no difference. But with a 3/1 twill and the double face, for instance, you should treadle exactly the opposite treadles on the jack loom to make the fabric come out the same side up.

The counter marche loom has both rising and sinking sheds. With the standard tie-up on the counter marche loom, you will only be pressing one treadle at a time (since you will tie up for each weave—see The Treadle Tie-up in this chapter). If you use the more versatile tie-up shown in Figure 260, you will have to figure out yourself which two pedals to press to correspond to the treadling indicated in the following directions.

On the counterbalanced and jack looms, you will be pressing one, two, or three treadles at a time. If the directions call for three treadles pressed down, one foot presses one and the other foot presses two that are next to each other.

Perfect sheds on the counterbalanced loom will not automatically open when three treadles are down or up, but this is no great problem. Simply adjust the pressure on the treadles so that the lower threads of the shed are even.

In warp-face weaves, if the sheds don't open properly and the threads stick together, moving the reed back and forth simultaneously with treadling will help to separate the threads.

If there are any threads out of place in the shed (separate from the upper and lower groups), this means there is a fault in the threading that will have to be corrected. Usually it means a heddle has been missed, or threads are crossed between heddle and reed.

Following are the treadling sequences for making various weaves. Treadle exactly the opposite treadles on a rising-shed loom, or jack loom. On the counter marche loom make the treadle tie-up so that the harnesses that correspond to the numbers below are *lowered.*

Plain weave (tabby)	Treadle	1 & 3
	Treadle	2 & 4
		Repeat

Basket weave (strictly speaking, each shed should have two separate shots of weft)	Treadle Treadle	1 & 2 3 & 4 Repeat	
2/2 twill	Treadle Treadle Treadle Treadle	1 & 2 2 & 3 3 & 4 4 & 1 Repeat	
1/3 twill (with warp predominating on top surface)	Treadle Treadle Treadle Treadle	1 2 3 4 Repeat	
Herringbone twill (if desired, the reversal can take take place after 8 or 12 rows, instead of after 4 rows as described here)	Treadle Treadle Treadle Treadle Treadle Treadle	1 & 2 2 & 3 3 & 4 4 & 1 Reverse to 3 & 4 2 & 3 Repeat from beginning	
Double width (with fold on left side)	Treadle Treadle Treadle Treadle	2, 3, & 4 2 4 1, 2, & 4 Repeat	(Weft from right to left) (Weft from left to right) (Weft from right to left) (Weft from left to right)
Tubular (folds on both sides)	Treadle Treadle Treadle Treadle	2, 3, & 4 2 1, 2, & 4 4 Repeat	(Weft from right to left) (Weft from left to right) (Weft from right to left) (Weft from left to right)
Double-face (one color on one side and another color on the other side)	Treadle Treadle Treadle Treadle	2, 3 & 4 1, 2, & 4 1 3 Repeat	Weave with: Top color Top color Bottom color Bottom color

The Filler

The knots that tie the warp to the extension bar of the cloth beam separate the warp threads into groups. To get the warp threads parallel again, weave a few rows of tabby with strips of rags, sticks, or just plain yarn—the thicker the better.

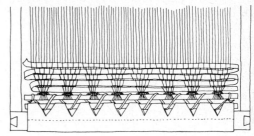

FIGURE 264. Filling the first few inches with rags until the warp threads are parallel.

The Weaving

The process of weaving consists (in simplified terms) of opening the shed, passing the shuttle through the shed, and beating in the weft; opening the next (or alternate) shed, returning the shuttle, and beating the weft down. As these steps are repeated, the fabric slowly grows, and the weaving builds up closer and closer to the reed, until you have to loosen the tension and roll that amount of finished fabric onto the cloth roller, in order to continue weaving.

To start, pull out a long tail of weft from your shuttle (enough to span the width of your warp), open the first shed and pass the shuttle through. The tail of the weft can lie just inside the edge or it can be wrapped around the edge warp thread and laid back in the same shed (see Splicing the Weft for further details of starting). Beat the weft into place with the beater. Change the shed, unwind enough weft from your stick shuttle to span the width of the warp again (if you are using a boat shuttle the weft will automatically feed out as it passes through the shed), and pass the shuttle back through. Beat the weft into place. Before placing another shot read the next three sections, which contain important instructions on how to beat, how to throw the shuttle, and weft tension.

Try to get into a nice rhythmic movement when you are repeating these steps. At first, perhaps, the edges won't be perfect or the beating won't be consistent. But, if you work with smooth flowing motions (and use properly wound bobbins), this will eventually come—more surely than if you stop after each row and adjust the edges with your fingers. Details of exactly how to beat and when, how best to throw the shuttle, and your weft tension are described below.

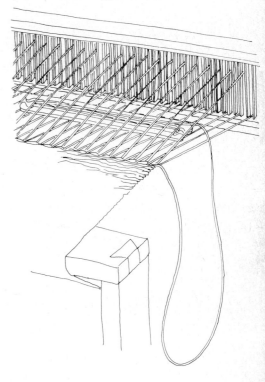

FIGURE 265. Placing the shot.

Beating

Grasp the beater in the exact center, with the hand that is not operating the shuttle, and pull it down toward the fabric. In balanced weaves, where you want exactly as many weft threads per inch as warp ends, the best movement is a pressing stroke. In other weaves, a good quick beat is good. When you want the weft to be beaten in quite firmly, you may want to beat twice or more. On some rugs, you may want to do additional beating with a weighted rug fork.

In beating a balanced weave you may find it difficult to get a consistent-looking weave. You have to concentrate on beating with exactly the same pressure on each shot, or else it will show in the finished product that the weft is closer together in some places than in others. What will cause this most besides an inconsistent beat is inconsistent warp tension. Right after you have advanced the warp, you have to be very careful to beat a little more lightly.

There is some controversy on exactly when you should beat. If the fabric is a weave that requires an arc to be made in the weft (see Notes on Weft Tension in this chapter), it is best to change the shed *before* you beat; this holds that arc of yarn in perfect position while it is being beaten down. If you don't change the shed, it is

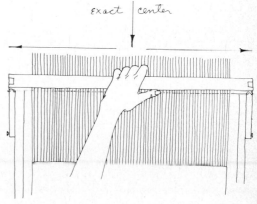

FIGURE 266. Beating: hand should be centered exactly on the beater.

Exact center

possible that the excess length of yarn would form little loops in the fabric. In warp-face weaves drawing the reed over the threads after the shed is changed helps disattach threads that have stuck together. Some books say to beat the weft down *after* you have placed the shot, change the shed, and beat the weft *again*.

In almost all cases I find it most convenient simply to change the shed and beat afterward.

Throwing the Shuttle

In handling the boat shuttle the main thing to remember is that at all times you want to use it in the most efficient manner. This means that you should not change positions or set it down any more than is absolutely necessary.

To throw the shuttle, grasp it as shown in Figure 267. Your finger is used to give it that final thrust across the warp. You want to give it enough of a push so that it will glide all the way to the other side and you won't have to reach down through the warp threads and give it a second push. And yet you should not throw the shuttle with such force that it will shoot out the other side before you have a chance to catch it, or that it will catch on warp threads and break them. You will need some practice to get exactly the right throw.

The hand that catches the shuttle should catch it in the same position (so it will be ready to be thrown back through the shed). The thumb hovers in such a position that it can at any time clamp down on the bobbin and stop the yarn from spinning out.

You can see that it is very important to have the bobbins wound properly, so that the yarn will spin out freely. If it is not able to do just that, it will stop the boat shuttle in midcourse, and a lot of extra handling of shuttle and bobbin will be necessary to release the weft and push the shuttle to the other side of the warp.

When the shuttle is thrown at full speed and caught at the other edge it can be pulled out at that other edge with just the right amount of speed to pull the weft up against the edge warp thread on the other side. If an arc is necessary you can make it at the same time you pull the shuttle away from the warp. The faster you do these, the tighter you will pull the weft around that edge warp thread. By adjusting the speed you gain complete control of just how tightly the weft will turn at the edge, and you can get into a very rapid rhythm and still make perfect edges. (See Keeping the Edges Even in this chapter.)

Pushing the stick shuttles through the shed may seem awkward at first, but soon you will learn to unwind the right amount. When you pull the shuttle through the other side, you should have just enough yarn coming from the shuttle to pull it away from the warp (allowing for the arc, if necessary) and make the weft just pull up against the warp thread at the other side.

Notes on Weft Tension

This brings us to one of the most important factors in creating a successful fabric—the weft tension. The placing of the weft thread in each shed is a procedure that takes skill, believe it or not. You don't just throw the shuttle across, pull it so that the weft thread fits in place, and then beat it down. Beginning weavers will do this and then wonder why the fabric is drawing in at the edges. The fact is that the weft thread must be the *exact* length to allow it to undulate around the warp threads just the right amount so that when the fabric is off the loom, and not in tension, the thread will relax into the perfect length to cover the distance from edge to edge of the fabric.

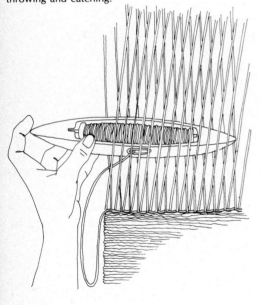

FIGURE 267. Proper grasp of the boat shuttle for throwing and catching.

This sounds like an impossibly delicate procedure—especially since every fabric is different and some weft threads must undulate much more than others, wefts are of different sizes, and some are less pliable than others, etc., etc. Many factors have to be taken into consideration. However, a skilled weaver can tell by experience and feel exactly how much extra length is needed so that the fabric, when off the loom and relaxed, will be of the structure and size that was planned.

Proper Weft Tension for Different Weave Structures

In *warp-face weaving* the weft lies in a perfectly straight line, and the warp threads will do all the bending. This is why in warp-face weaving warp tension is minimal and there is much more "takeup" in the warp (the warp shrinks in length after it is woven) than in any other type of weave.

In *balanced weaves* the warp and weft *both* bend around each other, so only a little bit of extra length is needed for the weft. When the fabric is removed from the loom and the tension relaxed, the warp threads will shrink to bend around the weft.

In *weft-face weaving* it is the warp that lies in a perfectly straight line and the weft does all the bending. So quite a bit more weft length is needed here. The closer together the warp threads are, the more distance the weft has to travel—just as driving on a curvy road adds up to more mileage than if you were on a straight highway. The weft should be pliable enough to make all these "bends." If it is not, the warp will be forced to bend around the stiff weft. (This is a situation I will talk about shortly, so that if you wish to weave with a variety of wefts, all in the same fabric, you will know how to judge proper weft tension.)

Methods of Achieving Proper Weft Tension

Now, as for methods to get the exact extra length, we run into some conflicting theories. I have read a book that describes how to throw the shuttle so that the weft lies loosely at a diagonal across the shed before it is beaten down, and this is supposed to provide the extra length needed. Well, that is fine for all the weaves described in that book—mostly balanced multi-harness weaves. But it would never provide enough extra weft length for a tight weft-face rug, for example.

All right: for *warp-face weaving* we know that the weft is simply pulled straight across the shed and beaten down in that position; no extra weft length is needed.

For *balanced weaves* we need a little extra length in the weft—how much depends on the type of weave (in weaves where the weft skips over groups of warp threads it will of course have to bend less than in weaves where the weft is going over and under each warp thread it comes to). You may have to weave a few rows before you can tell exactly how much extra length is needed. If you are not allowing enough, the fabric will begin to draw in at the edges; if you are allowing too much extra length the fabric will turn out wider than your warp width and will buckle in the middle.

Probably laying in the weft loosely at a diagonal and making sure there is no tension whatsoever on the weft before it is beaten in will be sufficient. If you are using a boat shuttle, it is absolutely essential that the bobbin unwind freely. If this method does not provide sufficient extra weft length, then use a modified version of the method described in the following paragraph.

In *weft-face weaves* much more extra weft length is needed—and this is more difficult. Sometimes as much as several inches extra are necessary. There are two methods for getting this extra length in without having it bunch up and make undesirable little loops. Peter Collingwood (certainly one of the greatest authorities on rug weaving) makes several waves across the width of the warp, pushing the weft up with the right hand and down with the left, while the shed is partially opened; about one wave per foot of width is required. You will have to determine the depth of the waves

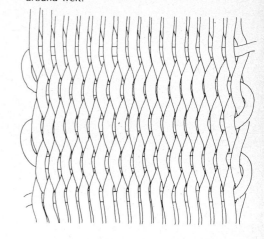

FIGURE 268. Warp-face weaves: warp "bends" around weft.

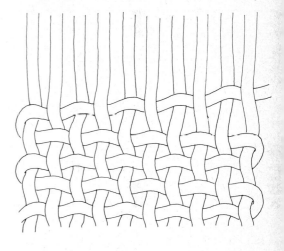

FIGURE 269. Balanced weaves: warp and weft both "bend."

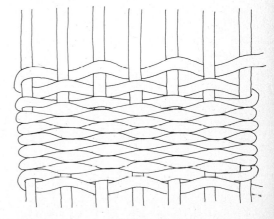

FIGURE 270. Weft-face weaves: weft "bends" around warp.

FIGURE 271. Warp-face weaves: weft is pulled straight across the shed.

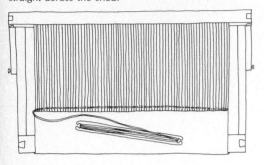

FIGURE 272. Balanced weaves: weft lies in loose arc or diagonal.

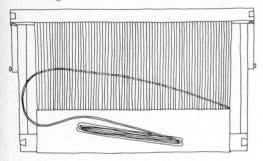

FIGURE 273. Weft-face weaves: weft makes a single arc or several waves.

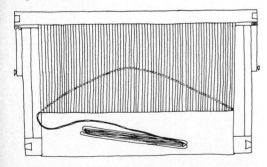

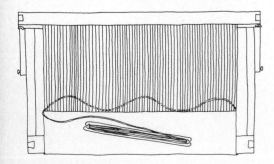

by watching the edges of the weaving as it progresses; if the edges are drawing in, the waves will have to be deeper. Change the shed after making the waves and beat.

The other method, which is the one I learned from the Spanish rug weavers in New Mexico and have always used, is to make a single arc, change the shed, and beat. This can be done in a split second and the results are similar. You can hold the arc in the correct position while changing the shed (this locks the arc in place so there is no possibility of little loops forming) and the weft can be pulled rather tightly at the edges, which is desirable. The fingers of the hand that makes the arc can be spread out so there is no actual point to it. The shuttle remains in the hand that caught it and is pulled down on that side so the weft meets the fell of the weaving. The size of the arc must be adjusted by you so that the edges of the weaving do not draw in, and then that size must be kept consistent throughout the weaving.

I seem to be doing a great deal of talking about warp and weft threads bending around each other, but actually this is an extremely important subject, which baffles beginning weavers more than any other problem.

The weave structure, the yarns, and the spacing or sett of the warp are the major factors in determining how much extra length is needed for each weft shot. And only you, the weaver, can decide in each individual situation what size arc—if any—is needed.

In weaving fabrics where you are using wefts of more than one size and texture, you will need to adjust the weft tension for each type of thread. The finer the thread, the greater extra weft length is needed. So, in order to keep the edges straight and not have any buckling of the fabric, you will make a large arc (or waves) for the fine threads, a medium arc for threads of medium size, and almost no arc at all for the thick threads (or for stiff threads). Sometimes you actually have to pull the weft as tightly as possible across the warp when using thick, stiff yarn, or the material will buckle when taken off the loom. The thick or stiff threads simply cannot bend around each warp thread—and so the warp threads themselves give way to the thick, unpliable weft.

Keeping the Edges Even

There are several factors involved in achieving nice even edges to your weaving. The most important one is to have proper weft tension, discussed in the previous section. If the edges start drawing in the slightest bit, immediately change the size of the arc or waves to allow greater weft length.

Another important factor is the tension of the warp. If the edge warp threads are too loose they will not provide the proper resistance for the weft and a drawing-in of the edges will result.

The third important factor is exactly *how* the weft thread turns around that edge

FIGURE 274. Correct and incorrect positions of edge warp. Thread and weft.

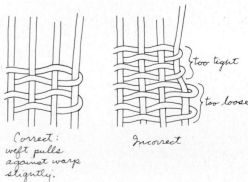

warp thread. It should just barely touch it and pull it in very slightly, but not bend it out of its straight position. The weft should not be allowed to form a loop that extends out beyond the edge.

Beginners sometimes find it helpful to use a stretcher because this holds the warp threads out to their full width. But, when you become a better weaver and know how to adjust the weft tension perfectly, the warp threads should remain in their correct position in most weaving without the use of the stretcher. It is common for the warp threads to draw in about a quarter of an inch on each edge, but there should never be more disparity than this between the width of the warp at the fell and the width of the warp as it passes through the reed. If there is, it will result in excessive wear on the edge warp threads and cause fraying and possibly breaking—or at least a loosening of tension in these threads that will compound the problem. The use of the stretcher will prevent this problem, one which must be absolutely avoided in double-width weaving where the fabric is woven with a fold at one edge.

Try not to get in the habit of adjusting the edge with your fingers after each shot. With proper shuttle throwing and proper warp and weft tension this should not be necessary and slows down the weaving process tremendously.

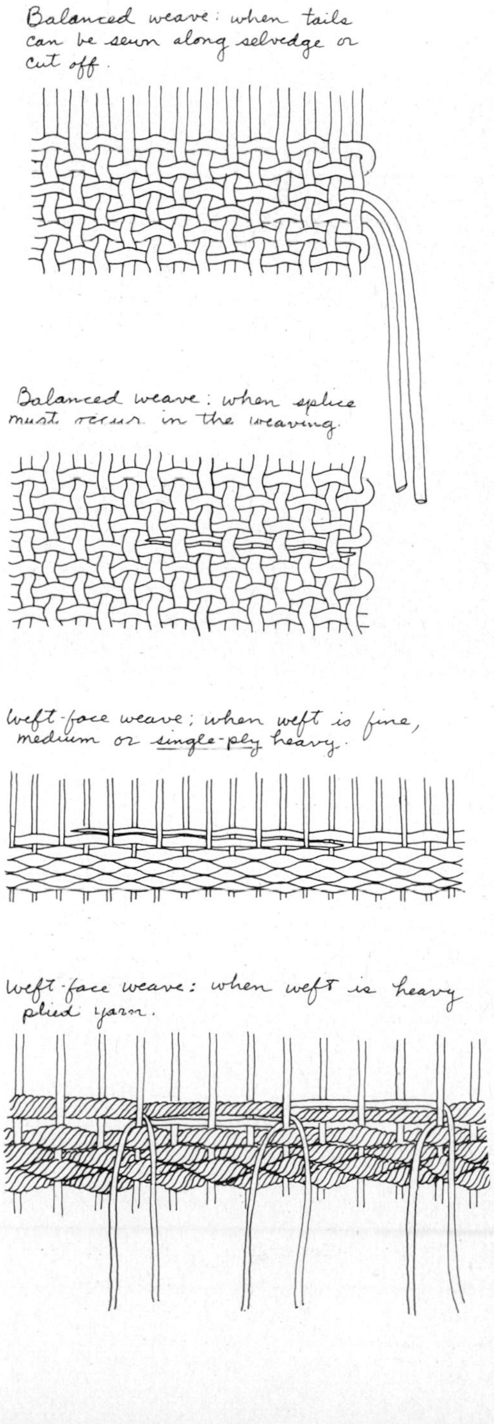

Splicing the Weft

For warp-face weaving the weft should be spliced by overlaying the broken (not cut) ends of the two wefts for a distance of about 3 inches. The ends will be completely hidden by the warp.

For weft-face weaving when using any medium or fine weft yarn, or a *single-ply* heavy yarn, you can use the same system, and the splice will not show. For a heavy plied yarn you will have to unply the yarn and break off each ply at a different place. These ends, which should be left hanging out, can be sewn in after the weaving is completed. (See Chapter VIII, "Finishing Techniques: Mending.")

For balanced weaves a weft splice will be more noticeable. It is best done at the edge of the weaving. If the weft is the same color as the warp, leave the two ends hanging from the selvedge to be woven in later along the selvedge with a needle.

In weft- and warp-face weaving the beginning and ending of weft colors can take place anywhere, just as splicing can. To begin or end a weft in balanced weaves it can simply be turned around the edge warp thread and the end laid in the same shed. Or, let the broken end lie just inside the edge of the weaving.

FIGURE 276. Beginning and ending wefts.

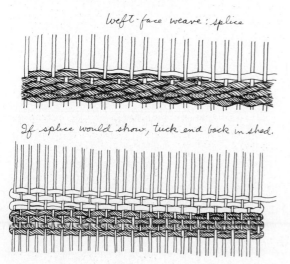

Weft-face weave: splice

If splice would show, tuck end back in shed.

FIGURE 275. Methods of splicing the weft for different types of weave and different types of yarn.

Balanced weave: when tails can be sewn along selvedge or cut off.

Balanced weave: when splice must occur in the weaving.

Weft-face weave: when weft is fine, medium or single-ply heavy.

Weft-face weave: when weft is heavy plied yarn.

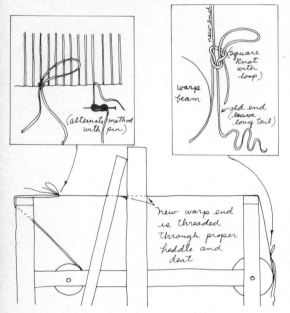

FIGURE 277. Tying at the warp beam and at the fell to replace a broken warp thread.

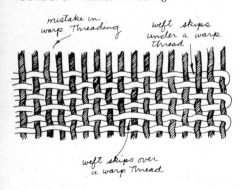

FIGURE 278. Mistakes in weaving.

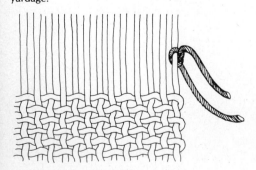

FIGURE 279. Marking the warp to keep track of yardage.

Mending Broken Warp Threads

If for some reason your warp threads break, they can be easily replaced by using a new length of warp that will reach from the warp beam to a foot below the fell. Simply tie the new warp thread to the broken one at the warp beam (leaving the original broken end its full length but pulling it out of the heddle and reed) and bring the new length through the same heddle and dent in the reed. Simply tie it at the fell or wind it around a pin that is secured in the fabric just below the fell (tying is much easier and quicker). Make sure the tension is similar to the tension of the other warp threads.

Continue weaving with this new warp end for a foot or two, or until it is possible to bring the original warp thread forward and tie it in the same way at the fell. Both of these knots can be untied and sewn in with a needle after the weaving is completed. See Chapter VIII, "Finishing Techniques: Mending," for the proper way to sew in the broken warp threads.

If you have undue warp breakage there can be several causes, which should be eliminated. One is crossed threads; sight along the shed when it is open to make sure no threads are crossed as they come from heddle to reed. Violent shuttle throwing will break warp threads. Drawing-in of edges will fray and break them. Using a weak yarn that is really unsuitable for warp could also be a cause.

Mistakes

In throwing the shuttle, it is possible for it to skip over a wrong thread, causing a "mistake" in the weaving. Let's hope you will have noticed this mistake before you have woven more than a row or two, and you will be able to undo the weaving back to that point and correct it. If you have to take out very many rows of weaving, it is easiest to break off the weft from the shuttle and just start pulling the weft end out as you open the sheds in reverse sequence. If the mistake is too far back, you may be able to replace it with another weft thread darned into the weaving after it is off the loom. Or by very clever darning you can make the mistake less visible.

Mistakes caused by wrong treadling sequence may not be noticeable right away, but will show up badly in the final fabric. To avoid this, try to develop the habit of squinting your eyes to get a picture of the whole pattern every once in a while. Sometimes you can darn in an extra weft thread to replace a missing one in the sequence, as in a twill, for instance.

A mistake that keeps repeating is, of course, caused by a mistake in the threading and can only be corrected by taking out the warp ends from heddle and reed up to that mistake and rethreading properly.

Measuring

After every yard of weaving, you can mark the edge, with the warp tension released, by tying another-colored yarn around the edge warp thread. Or, if you are making a long piece of weaving, you can tie little tags with the number of yards written on them. Be sure to allow for shrinkage if you plan to wash the piece. Warp-face weaving especially may shrink considerably in length.

Cutting Off

When you have finished the weaving (or preferably, for efficiency's sake, as many weavings as will roll onto the cloth beam), release the warp-beam ratchet and wind the fabric forward until there is *at least* a foot of warp in front of the reed that will not be used for fringing. Carefully cut with scissors through the warp in as straight a line as possible. If the tension is not released when you do this, the warp threads will snap back through the reed and you will lose your threading. *Immediately* upon finishing the cut, before you even handle the fabric, tie loose knots in the warp ends that dangle from the reed so that an accidental swing of the reed will not wipe out your warp threading.

If you are making fringe, remember that ends less than 4 inches long are *very* hard to tie. You really should have a 5- or 6-inch length to make the tying go fast.

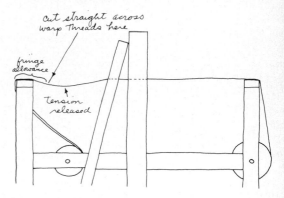

FIGURE 280. Cutting through the warp threads with tension released.

Finishing

The handling of the fabric after it is removed from the loom, as well as decorative and functional additions to the fabric, are discussed in detail in Chapter VIII, "Finishing Techniques." The fabric should be fringed as soon as possible after it is removed from the loom. In fact (for weft-face weaving, the most prone to raveling), I always fringe the cut end before unrolling the fabric from the cloth beam, and then fringe the first end immediately after untying the knots that attached the warp to the cloth beam. This warp end can be left, however, for later fringing as long as you leave the rag filler in.

Besides mending and fringing (which obviously you will do when appropriate), I think steam pressing (which some weavers do *not* do) is very important in making the fabric look its best. Washing the fabric is desirable if it is to be used for clothing. In the projects that follow any special finishing beyond this for each item will be mentioned.

Six Versatile Warps

Here are six different warps, each of which is very versatile and suitable for many different projects. For each of the projects that follow, I will indicate which warp you should use and how many yards of warp you should figure on. Pick out the projects using one warp that interest you, total up the needed yardage, adding one yard for tying on and waste, and make your warp that long. (The given yardage for each project has takeup and fringe allowance included; see Planning the Weaving in this chapter.) If you can stand the suspense, it's best to weave as much as the cloth beam will hold (or at least a few projects) before cutting off. You will waste time and a slight amount of warp with each tying on.

Before ordering your yarn, see Chapter I, "The Basics of Weaving: Your Yarns."

Warp A
Yarn size: Medium fine.
Ply: 2.
Fiber: Wool or hair.
Color: Rich brown or black.
Amount: One pound will make approximately 8 to 10 yards of warp.
Sett: 12 epi.
Width: 10 inches.

Total ends: 128.
Threading: Basic twill.
Selvedge: 3 ends in each of the last 2 dents and heddles at both edges.

Suggestion: Scandinavian yarn.

Warp B

Yarn size: Medium fine.
Ply: 2.
Fiber: Wool or alpaca (preferably not scratchy).
Color: Natural brown or black.
Amount: One pound will make approximately 4 to 5 yards of warp.
Sett: 10 epi.
Width: 24 inches.
Total ends: 248.
Threading: Basic twill.
Selvedge: 3 ends in each of the last 2 dents and heddles at both edges. (When you are weaving a balanced weave, such as twill, the selvedge will look better if you thread each selvedge end through a separate heddle.)

Suggestions: The *softer*-quality wool yarns of some Scandinavian suppliers, Canadian 2/10, *or* alpaca yarn would all be good.

Warp C (rug warp)

Yarn size: Medium heavy, very strong and tightly twisted.
Ply: 4, if possible.
Fiber: Wool, hair, or linen.
Color: Any natural color. (Light naturals are usually nicest for rugs.)
Amount: One pound will make approximately 2 yards of warp.
Sett: 4 epi.
Width: 45 inches.
Total ends: 184.
Threading: Basic twill.
Selvedge: Double sley the last 2 dents and heddles at each edge.

Suggestions: Canadian wool yarn, 4-ply; 2-ply Scandinavian spelsau; 4-ply (or more) linen. See Chapter XIII, "Suppliers," for recommendations for where to get good strong rug warp.

Warp D

Yarn size: Medium weight.
Ply: 2 or more.
Fiber: Soft wool, alpaca, cashmere.
Color: Different colors of your choice for warp stripes. (See Chapter XI, "Design and Color: Choosing Colors.")
Amount: One pound will make approximately 2 yards of warp.
Sett: 8 epi.
Width: 45 inches.
Total ends: 360.
Threading: Basic twill.
Selvedge: Double sley the last 2 dents and heddles at each edge.

Suggestions: Soft Canadian 2/8 wools are excellent for this. Since most of the projects using this warp are wearing apparel, make sure the yarn is not scratchy.

Warp E

Yarn size: Medium fine.
Ply: 2. (If it is single, make sure it is a strong yarn.)
Fiber: Wool.
Color: A very rich dark color, preferably warm (unless you plan to weave with mostly cool colors in the weft).
Amount: One pound will make approximately 2 to 3 yards of warp.
Sett: 10 epi. (If your reed sizes are limited, this warp could be 8 epi.)
Width: 45 inches.
Total ends: 456.
Threading: Basic twill.
Selvedge: Triple sley the last 2 dents and heddles on each side.

Suggestions: Medium-fine 2-ply Scandinavian; single-ply warp from Canada.

Warp F

Yarn size: Medium (or medium-weight average, but use all different sizes).
Ply: 2-, 3-, 4-, and single-ply (if strong).
Fiber: Soft wool, cashmere, alpaca, mohair, and any wool or hair fiber (must be smooth, not textured and not scratchy).
Color: Different colors of your choice. (See Chapter XI, "Design and Color: Choosing Colors." I would suggest several light and brilliant colors, grouping similar colors together in equal-width stripes.)
Amount: One pound will make approximately one yard of warp.
Sett: 15 epi. (You can use 16 if you don't have the proper reed for 15.)
Width: 45 inches.
Total ends: 672.
Threading: Basic twill.
Selvedge: No special treatment.

Suggestions: This is quite a close sett for this weight yarn, so worsted (or smooth) yarn will be best—soft, if possible, because it will be used for garments and blankets. You can use all different yarns to make an interesting striated texture. The coarser the reed the better; use a 5-dent reed if possible and triple sley (see above in this chapter Planning the Warp; Sett and Sley in this chapter). Do not try to use this warp on a jack loom (see The Jack Loom in this chapter).

Project I. Table Scarf (Warp A)*

(This project can also be woven on the backstrap and Navajo looms.)

This is a particularly good starting project for beginning weavers. You can experiment with different weaves and different yarns all in one weaving, and still have it come out looking attractive. If you use yarns and colors that go well together, and have some systematic control of the design, it will be a nice scarf to hang on the wall or use on a table.

* A good project for beginners

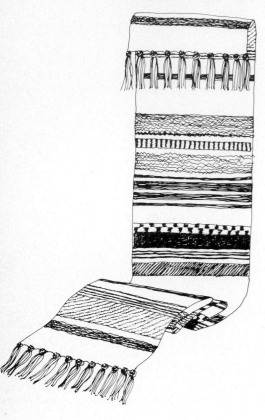

FIGURE 281. A table scarf.

Materials

Warp A (2 1/2 yards).

Weft—Medium-fine and medium-weight yarns, either single or plied; use small amounts of heavy homespun.

Amount: Approximately 1 pound altogether.

Suggested colors: Red, blue, gold, dark natural brown, or black. *Or,* different naturals from white to black (including browns and beiges) with *one* color, such as blood red.

Directions

Wind your yarns on stick or boat shuttles.

Leave 6 inches of warp unwoven for fringe.

Following general instructions, weave different-size bands up to 4 inches wide in different structures (tabby, twill, basket), using your different yarns. When working with the heavier yarns use a 2-down, 2-up combination, such as twill or basket weave; and when using finer yarns weave plain weave. See How to Operate the Sheds (Treadling) in this chapter.

Remember that the more the thread has to undulate over and under the warp threads the more excess weft length is needed (see Notes on Weft Tension in this chapter). For the heavy yarns you will just pull straight across and beat, and for the finer yarns woven in plain weave you will allow a good arc. This will be a good exercise in judging weft tension in different situations to achieve a perfect edge. When using the finer yarns, beat to cover the weft.

If you alternate weft colors, weaving with two shuttles, first one color and then the other, you will get an interesting vertical-stripe pattern that will add interest to the scarf. Whenever you weave with two different weft colors, in order for the edge warp thread to be caught it is necessary to manipulate the weft around the edge warp thread by hand. The treadling alone will not give you a neat edge. (See Chapter VIII, "Finishing Techniques: Selvedges.")

Weave until the fabric measures 6 feet (when tension is released). Allow another 6 inches for fringe at this end.

Finish as in general instructions and make braided or twisted fringe.

Project II. Handbag (Warp A)*

(This project can also be woven on the backstrap and Navajo looms.)

This is a nicely proportioned bag—the most convenient size and shape for a woven bag, I think. If made of good-quality yarn, it will last for years. It will be very quick to weave, so why not figure on making 3 or 4? By the time you get to the third one you'll really be having fun with the designs.

Materials

Warp A (1 yard).

Weft—Single-ply wool or hair about the same weight as warp, or a little heavier. Scandinavian single-ply cowhair yarn is a very good weft yarn for handbags. Your own handspun, of course, would be even nicer; spin it fine and very tight. By spinning your own you can have exactly the right weight—heavy enough so that it takes hard beating of the weft to cover the warp.

FIGURE 282. A handbag.

* A good project for beginners.

Amount: Less than 1 pound.

Suggested colors: Natural black and a small amount of natural white (or vice versa).

Directions

Use boat shuttles for your weft yarns.

Leave 5 inches of warp unwoven for making fringe. Follow general instructions for Table Scarf. This will be a weft-face plain weave. Operate the sheds to make a plain weave and beat so that the weft covers the warp. Figure on weaving the bag 24 to 26 inches in length, with the halfway point dividing the pattern in a mirror image; when the bag is sewn together the stripes will meet at the seam. Weave bands and stripes and checkerboards (alternate black and white weft for 1/4 inch, then 2 black in succession, and continue alternating).

Occasionally switch to a 2-down and 2-up treadling and make a large checkerboard pattern, if desired. You can also make tapestry ovals as in Chapter VI, "The Navajo Loom: Project II."

A word of advice about the design: it will be tempting to change colors often and make all kinds of nice designs. Show some discipline and weave large areas in just black (or white). This will give the areas that are filled with pattern more meaning.

When the weaving measures the desired length, allow another 5 inches of unwoven warp for fringing.

Cut off and make knotted fringe at both ends. Trim this fringe off to 1 inch length. Tuck fringe under and make a rolled hem, sewing with double cotton or linen thread. Using the warp yarn and a large needle, sew up the sides of the bag as shown in Chapter VIII, "Finishing Techniques: Joining."

Now make a warp-face band on the inkle, backstrap, or Hopi belt loom. Use the two colors that you used for the bag, but this time make the opposite color predominant. You can make the strap perfectly plain or with a pattern, but again, if you devise a pattern, use restraint—make it *very* simple. (See Chapter III, "The Inkle loom: Project I.") Make the shoulder strap of such a length that the top of the bag will hang at waist level. Make a 6- or 8-inch fringe on both ends of this strap, using twisted fringe or 4-strand braid. Sew this onto the bag at the sides, covering the seam, so that the fringe begins about 2 inches down from the top edge of the bag. Sew in several spots to secure the strap to the bag so that there is no single point that takes all the strain. You can make a hidden pocket by leaving the bag and strap unsewn at the top edge.

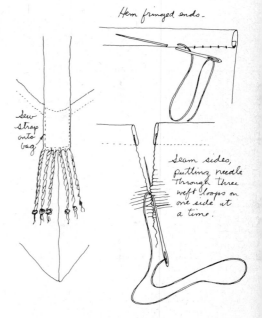

FIGURE 283. Finishing the bag.

Hem fringed ends.

Sew strap onto bag

Seam sides, putting needle through three weft loops on one side at a time.

Project III. Pictorial Tapestry (Warp A)

(This project can also be woven on the backstrap and Navajo looms.)

In this project you will prepare the most simple little drawing—like a child's drawing. Make very plain shapes with an emphasis on verticals. When you weave this "picture" in beautiful colors and yarns, it will be charming—even though you think you are not an artist.

Pictorial tapestries are often woven sideways. The reason for this is that in trees, human figures, buildings, and many other forms many of the lines are verticals, and these are the most difficult (or illogical) to weave in the tapestry technique. So, if you weave your picture sideways, all the vertical lines become horizontals, which are the easiest to weave.

Materials

Warp A (about 2 feet).

FIGURE 284. A tapestry.

Weft—Single-ply wool, tightly twisted if possible. Scandinavian cowhair yarns will be good, or your own handspun. Or, Scandinavian two-ply fine wools will also be suitable.

Amount: 1/2 to 3/4 pound.

Suggested colors: Muted blues, reds, and golds, with all shades of natural from black to white, and any colors that fall within this range.

Directions

Wind your weft colors in the form of butterflies. You will not want fringe on this weaving, since it would protrude from the sides, rather than top and bottom. But you must still allow a few inches of warp to tie or to make a false selvedge. If you plan to tie the warp ends and hem the fabric at the ends, weave about 1 inch of plain weave (see How to Operate the Sheds in this chapter) in one color before starting the "picture." If you are going to make a false selvedge (see Chapter VIII, "Finishing Techniques"), you can start right out laying in the color areas; but first lay a narrow stick (or two rows of heavy yarn) in the shed as a base to start with.

FIGURE 285. Building up areas, leaving "open" shapes to be filled in next.

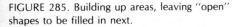

Tack your drawing to the loom for easy reference. You shouldn't try to measure or follow it unconditionally. (The traditional European tapestries are woven by setting up a "cartoon" behind the warp and then making the woven forms correspond exactly to the drawing. I've always felt that results are much more exciting if you let the weaving dictate the shapes to some extent. The drawing will be there so that you will know when to start a new shape or color.)

Before starting to weave, you must thoroughly study Project IV in Chapter VI, "The Navajo Loom." This is the basic tapestry technique. The weave is weft-face plain weave (see How to Operate the Sheds in this chapter). The shapes and changes of color are achieved strictly by weaving the weft of one color area back and forth just within that area, rather than from selvedge to selvedge, and beating it down to cover the warp completely. Project IV in Chapter VI will show you how to start and end color areas, and describes the basic principles of tapestry weaving.

You can build up tapestry weaving in either of two ways. (1) Place one shot of each weft color all across the warp width in one shed (the wefts should all go in the same direction or you will get hopelessly confused). Then change the shed, beat with the beater, and return each weft color; continue weaving in this way so that the fell remains level. Or (2) you can approach each color area separately and weave back and forth in that area, building it up above the level of the other colors. It's sort of like taking a colored crayon and filling in an area with color, and it is much easier to conceive your shapes and designs this way. If you build separate areas, you must use a tapestry fork or comb to beat in the weft.

In this pictorial tapestry you will probably want to use the second method most of the time. Start out laying in your colors and weaving as described in Project IV, Chapter VI. As soon as it is convenient, begin working back and forth in one color area.

There are some limitations to this second method that must be borne in mind. First, areas that join each other with a vertical line cannot actually be joined, since there is no way to interlock the wefts in each row. They can be hand sewn together after the weaving is finished if a slit is undesirable. Second, remember that you can only build up areas where the two sides of the shape are either vertical or slanting in—so that you can fill in the remaining area without having to weave *underneath* the original form. To keep the warp threads evenly spaced, occasionally beat with the beater and reed when the fell is more or less level.

A small arc to allow extra weft length is essential in each shot of weft to prevent gradual drawing-in of the edges. Measure the width of the weaving every 1/2 inch to make sure it is *not* drawing in; if it is, make a higher arc each time.

When the "picture" is woven, weave about an inch in a plain color as you did in the beginning, unless you will be making the false selvedge.

Cut off and finish as in general instructions. Since this is a wall hanging, any threads hanging out on the back side do not need to be sewn in. Hem or make false selvedge.

Project IV. Herringbone Stole (Warp B)*

(This project can also be woven on the backstrap and Navajo looms, but would require two extra heddle sticks.)

This is a classically simple weave that will make a beautiful stole—extremely useful if it is made of soft wool, alpaca, or cashmere. The weaving of it will be good practice in getting an even beat for the balanced structure. It can be "fulled" after it is woven to add to its beauty and usefulness.

Materials
Warp B (about 2 1/2 yards).
Weft—Exactly the same yarn as warp.
   Amount: Approximately 1/2 pound.
   Color: Natural white, or any color that contrasts with the warp.

Directions
See Chapter VIII, "Finishing Techniques: Selvedges," for the best way to treat selvedge threading in a twill or herringbone weave, and change your warp threading if necessary.

Wind your weft onto the bobbins of a boat shuttle.

Leave 1 foot of unwoven warp for a long fringe.

Operate the sheds to make a herringbone weave.

You should beat lightly so that there are exactly the same number of wefts per inch as there are warps per inch. (It will require careful beating to make the fabric consistent.)

Make your weft splices about 6 inches long, as this is a loose weave.

Weave about 5 1/2 feet, measured when not in tension. Allow the same amount for fringe as you did at the beginning.

When the stole is cut off the loom, fringe with macramé, twisted, or braided fringe, and finish according to general instructions. Wash (to soften), or "full" it if the weave is too loose.

* A good project for beginners.

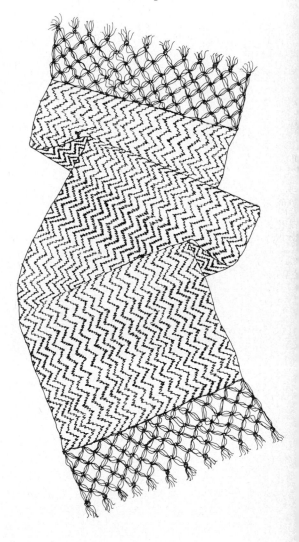

FIGURE 286. A herringbone stole.

FIGURE 287. A handbag with woven-in handles.

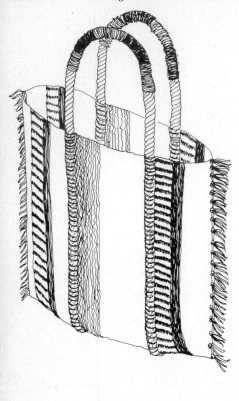

Project V. Handbag with Woven-in Handles (Warp B)

(This project can also be woven on the Navajo loom.)

This makes a small tote bag, and by weaving the handles right into it you avoid the extra work of making and sewing on a strap. Plan on making two or three at least, because it will take one or two before you really get going on your designs. For a larger bag use a wider warp.

Materials

Warp B (2 feet for each bag).

Weft—Medium-fine single- or 2-ply yarn, fine enough so that the weft will pack down to cover the warp, in a plain weave. The Scandinavian 2-ply fine spelsau or regular wool would be good. A tightly spun yarn will be the best weft for this bag. Amount: Approximately 1/2 pound.

Suggested colors: All naturals or a variety of blending colors. Have one of the colors predominant. Use it for more than half of the bag. (See Chapter XI, "Design and Color: Choosing Colors.")

Also, you will need a little over 2 yards of rope; hemp, if you can get it, is the nicest.

A few touches of heavy homespun, woven in single rows, will be nice too.

Directions

Wind the weft onto the bobbins of your medium-size boat shuttle. The heavy homespun, if you are using it, can just be single lengths that measure about 6 inches longer than the warp is wide.

Allow about 5 inches of unwoven warp for knotting the fringes.

Operate the sheds to make plain weave, alternating colors for stripes whenever desired. Beat the weft to cover the warp completely. In weaving this bag, you need not be concerned that the design be symmetrical. As you weave, you can make stripes in any order. You can also make an interesting pattern by weaving 2 down and 2 up with colors alternating each row: this will make large vertical bars, which you can switch to checkerboards by weaving two successive rows in the same color. Beat the weft in as tight as you can. Occasionally lay in 1 row of heavy homespun, locking the ends around the end warp threads and laying the tails back in the same shed.

Weave just slightly less than 4 inches. Now lay the rope in the next shed, with one end extending 8 inches beyond the warp on one side. Change sheds and beat. Continue weaving another 3 1/2 inches. Lay the long end of the rope back in the next shed, leaving a loop the right size for a handle on one side, and the end protruding from the weaving at the other side.

Change sheds, beat, and continue weaving for the same distance as you did before laying the rope in the first time.

Allow another 5 inches for fringe. If you are going to weave another bag, leave 10 inches, then put a stick or rag in a shed, change sheds, and start weaving again.

When the bag is cut from the loom, finish as in general instructions. The warp ends may be tied together very tightly to act as a seam up the sides of the bag. The two ends of the rope handles are tapered and spliced and wrapped with colored yarn (see Chapter VIII, "Finishing Techniques: Wrapping").

FIGURE 288. Weaving the handle into the fabric.

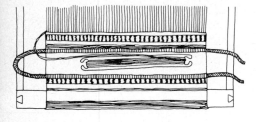

FIGURE 289. Finishing the bag by fringing the sides and wrapping the spliced rope handles.

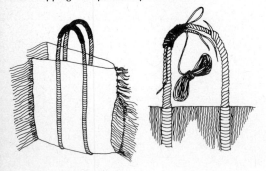

Project VI. Pillows or Cushions, Two Sizes (Warp B)

(Pillows can also be woven on the backstrap or Navajo loom.)

Beautiful pillows can be woven on this warp in two different sizes. You can weave a 1-foot length, fold this in half, and get a 1-foot-square pillow. If you weave a 4-foot length, you can fold that in half and get a 2-foot-square pillow. This is a good way to use up odds and ends of yarn, including bits of homespun. The nicest filler for these pillows is shredded foam, which you can buy in the dime store and make a muslin cover for. If you get into mass production of pillows, you can order ready-made fillers by the gross and save a little time and money.

Materials

Warp B (1 foot 3 inches for small pillows; 4 feet 6 inches for large pillows).
Weft—Medium-weight wool yarn, either single or plied. (It should be heavy enough so that when the weft is packed in tight the warp still shows.) Also a smaller quantity of heavier handspun yarn.
Amount: Approximately 1/2 pound for small pillows. Approximately 2 pounds for large pillows.
Suggested colors: Whatever color combinations you wish. Very subtle variations of all the same color (emphasizing the different textures of the yarn) is very attractive. If you are making pillows for sale, you want to make the pillows vary from each other as much as possible, and the best way to do this is to think of color schemes that can be described in a word or two (a "yellow" pillow, "creamy whites," "magenta and purples," etc.). Too often pillow weavers want to get a little of every color in each pillow—which is fine for a single pillow. But when you have them stacked up for sale it just makes a chaotic mass of pillows that all look more or less the same. If you get into real production, you should make a blue warp for "blue" pillows, a yellow warp for "yellow" pillows, a light natural warp for "natural white" pillows, etc.

Directions

Wind your medium-weight weft onto bobbins for a boat shuttle. Wind the heavy homespun onto stick shuttles.

At the beginning and end of the weaving for each pillow you must weave a 3/4-inch heading in plain weave (see Operating the Sheds in this chapter) with the same yarn as the warp—or any rather fine yarn. This makes a firm binding that will unravel less easily than the heavier yarn used for the pillow itself. If you are weaving several pillows, simply weave this finer texture for 1 1/2 inches in between each pillow, and when you cut the material, cut right down the center of this 1 1/2-inch band.

Operate the sheds to make a plain weave and pack the weft in as tight as possible. Do not use the heavy homespun closer than two inches from the heading that separates the pillows. You can use combinations of 2 down and 2 up for the heavy homespun.

You will have to adjust the tension of your various-sized wefts so that the heavier yarns won't buckle and the lighter-weight yarns won't cause the edges to draw in (see Notes on Weft Tension in this chapter). The lighter-weight the yarn is, the higher an arc you should make. The very heavy homespun should be pulled straight across the warp, held tightly and beaten in. Loosen the tension of the warp often, to check to make sure the fabric lies flat and the edges are even. The homespun yarn will be most attractive if you use it in bands not less than 2 inches wide.

FIGURE 290. Pillows (cushions).

FIGURE 291. Sewing the pillows (cushions).

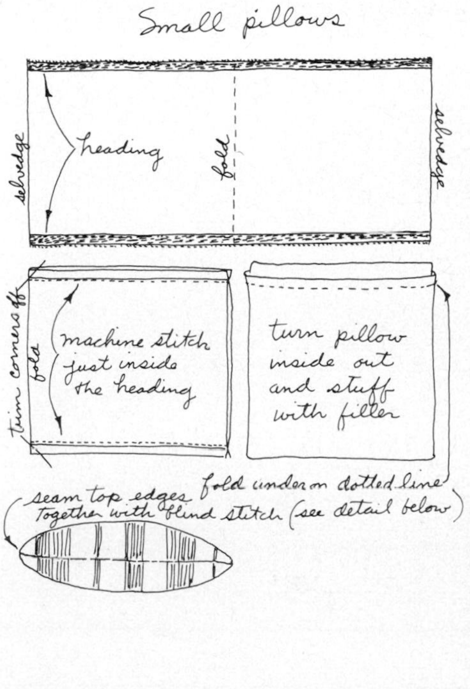

Small pillows

selvedge heading fold selvedge

turn corners fold machine stitch just inside the heading

turn pillow inside out and stuff with filler

seam top edges fold under on dotted line together with blind stitch (see detail below)

FIGURE 291. continued

Big pillows

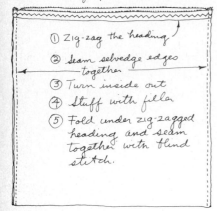

① Zig-zag the heading.

② Seam selvedge edges together.

③ Turn inside out.

④ Stuff with filler.

⑤ Fold under zig-zagged heading and seam together with blind stitch.

The blind stitch

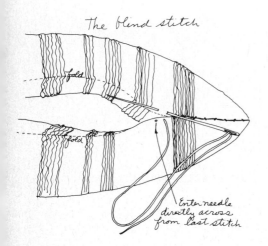

fold

fold

Enter needle directly across from last stitch

FIGURE 292. A twill poncho.

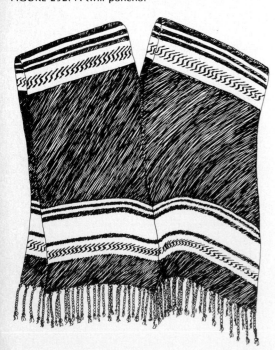

For the small pillows, weave the body of the pillow (not counting the bands described above) 1/2 inch less in length than exactly 1/2 of the measured width of the woven fabric (approximately 1 foot). This should make a perfect square when seamed. You will have to check this out and possibly change the measurement. (To look professional, the pillows should be exactly square, and this requires some exact figuring.)

For the large pillows, weave the body of the pillow (not counting the bands) 1 inch less than twice the measured width of the woven fabric (approximately 4 feet).

A sewing machine is required for stitching up two sides of the pillows. On the small pillows stitch just barely inside the edge bands, trim corners, and turn right side out. Stuff with the filler or form, which is best slightly *larger* than your handwoven material, to make a nice plump pillow, and then hand sew the last seam with a blind stitch. On the larger pillows, zigzag (or plain stitch) along the inner edge of the woven bands to prevent raveling (since these edges will be the ones that are hand sewn together). Stitch up the two selvedge sides, trim corners, turn right side out, stuff with the pillow form, and blind stitch the final seam by hand.

Pillows do not need to be steam pressed.

Project VII. Man's Twill Poncho Woven in Two Pieces (Warp B)

(This poncho can also be woven on backstrap and Navajo looms, but will require 2 extra heddle sticks.)

This is a fairly common pattern for a man's poncho—similar to the way they are woven in Mexico (weft-face and in two pieces). It can be woven in a plain or a twill weave. The latter will make a heavier, more pliable fabric, which I think is desirable. It will be handy to use as a blanket when it is not being worn.

Materials

Warp B (about 4 yards and 1 foot).

Weft—Medium-weight single or plied wool, alpaca, or cashmere. Your own handspun yarn would be very nice for this project. The weft does not have to cover the warp completely.

Amount: About 3 pounds.

Suggested colors: A variety of naturals from white to black, with one of the naturals providing at least two-thirds of the entire poncho. A deep blood red could be used with the naturals also—even as the predominant color.

Directions

Wind the weft onto the bobbins of your larger boat shuttles.

Leave at least 5 inches of warp unwoven for fringe.

Operate the sheds to make a 2/2 twill weave, beating in the weft so that it covers the warp (or nearly so). You don't want to beat too hard and make a very heavy fabric. Make bands and patterns against plain grounds by using two and three colors alternately or in succession. Experiment, but always use a 2-down, 2-up treadling combination. (See Chapter VIII, "Finishing Techniques: Selvedges," for ways of handling edges when using 2 and 3 wefts.)

After weaving 2 feet 9 inches (you will be at the center shoulder), repeat your sequences of stripes and bands in a mirror image, so that the front and back of the poncho will be symmetrical. Then leave at least 10 inches of unwoven warp for the fringe at the end of this first piece and the beginning of the second piece.

Weave the second piece identical to the first. All this will require very accurate measurements which you should record. Leave at least 5 inches at the final end for fringe.

When the fabric is cut from the loom, finish as in general instructions. Fringe the ends with a 4-strand braid or twisted fringe, and join the two strips (matching the bands and stripes) as described in Chapter VIII, "Finishing Techniques: Joining." Leave approximately 15 inches unjoined for the neck slit.

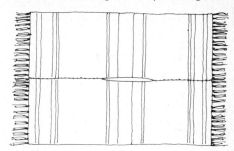

FIGURE 293. Joining the two pieces together.

Project VIII. Kilim (Warp B)

(This project can also be woven on the backstrap and Navajo looms. The real kilims are, of course, woven on primitive looms, normally the horizontal ground loom.)

In the Middle East the tapestry technique takes a special form of its own. The basic principle for achieving the pattern is the same as with the Navajo rug: the weft winds back and forth within its own area of color, and the picture or pattern is built up in this way. The warp is covered completely so that only the color of the weft yarn shows on the final surface of the fabric. The distinctive symmetrical designs with floral, animal, and other symbols, woven individually so that wherever areas join vertically a slit between the two adjacent warp threads is left, and the outlining of small shapes make these pieces of weaving recognizable as from the Middle East. This type of weaving is called the "kilim."

We will attempt to make a simplified version of the kilim. The design should be symmetrical—basically, at least. Each side of center can have slight variations in color and shape (like a flower form on one side and an animal form on the other), but each should be more or less the same size and of the same design importance. Steps and zigzags can be used for borders and for dividing large areas into diamond shapes.

Now, this is going to take a lot of patient work, so you'll have to be feeling very ambitious to do it. It is probably the most difficult tapestry project in this book, so it would be good to try the more simple ones first. In this project you will be working with many more weft colors at one time if the design is at all intricate.

FIGURE 294. A kilim.

Materials

Warp B (about 1 yard and 1 foot).

Weft—Single- or double-ply medium-fine yarn; fine enough to cover the warp completely when beaten into place. The Spelsau or regular wool 2-ply fine yarn of the Scandinavian companies will be excellent. Or your own fine, evenly and tightly spun yarn would, of course, be the nicest.

Amount: Approximately 1 1/2 to 2 pounds.

Colors: Yarns dyed with madder, indigo, natural yellows and greens with natural white and black would be ideal (the same as are used for many of the real kilims), with the madder predominant. But, if this is unavailable, use any blending colors of your choice—mostly soft, muted colors with touches of natural white and black. (See Chapter XI, "Design and Color: Choosing Colors.")

Directions

Wind your weft colors in the form of butterflies.

Leave 6 inches of warp unwoven for fringe.

Thoroughly study Project IV (Traditional Navajo Rug) in Chapter VI for the basic tapestry technique, laying in your weft colors, starting and ending color areas. Operate the sheds for plain weave. You will need a tapestry fork (or an ordinary comb will do) to beat in the weft, since you will be building up areas and shapes above the fell. The weft should be packed down to cover the warp completely.

FIGURE 295. The slit and outlining.

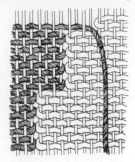

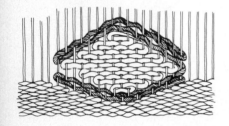

FIGURE 296. A three-dimensional hanging.

Weave each little color area individually, changing the sheds rapidly with your feet, as you push the butterfly back and forth in each shed. Beat the weft in with your fork or comb. If the sides of the shape are vertical, simply go back and forth around the same warp thread at each side of the shape each time. When you fill in the color area adjacent to this, make the weft go around the adjacent warp thread. This leaves the traditional vertical slit. These slits are best not longer than 1/2 inch; if they are longer the warp starts to separate too much.

Watch for drawing-in of the edges of the weaving. If this occurs you will have to allow more weft length (see Notes on Weft Tension in this chapter). This will be your main difficulty in this weaving, so check every 1/4 to 1/2 inch to make *sure* the weaving is not drawing in, and correct the situation immediately if it is. To check, bring the beater down to the fell and see if the weaving is as wide as the warp where it comes through the reed. If it isn't, you know you should be allowing more length to the wefts.

With short lengths of a dark color, you can outline the curved shapes with 2 lines of weaving, changing the shed for each line. The only shapes you can't outline are those that have vertical sides.

Leave another 6 inches of unwoven warp and cut off. Any "tails" from tapestry colors can be sewn in after the weaving is finished.

Project IX. Three-Dimensional Wall Hanging (Warp B)

(This piece can also be woven on the Navajo or backstrap loom, but would require 2 extra heddle sticks.)

This is a very complex weaving and should not be attempted by beginners.

The way this hanging is woven is simply a combination of double-width weaves (two layers of fabric woven independently, one on top of the other, and joined wherever you desire). If you weave one of the double-width projects first (such as Projects XVII, XXI, and XXV) it will help you understand what you are doing.

This makes an interesting relief-like hanging, with flaps protruding from the two-dimensional plane, and once you understand the principle of this type of weaving, you can vary it and make any combination of double layers, tubes, strips hanging free, etc. In this hanging we will combine the double layers with some switching back and forth from weft-face to warp-face weaving, which will make the flaps undulate in width.

Materials

Warp B (about 1 yard and 1 foot).

Weft—Medium-heavy single-ply handspun wool or hair yarn. Since this is double cloth, the plain weave of each layer will only take half of the warp ends (5 per inch), and a fairly heavy yarn will be required, or else the weft will pack down excessively and it will take forever to weave. Some of the Greek goat-hair yarns would be very suitable; they are heavy and stiff enough so that the warp will show slightly and it will weave quickly. Your own tightly spun yarn of medium to heavy weight would also be very appropriate. Irregularities in the yarn will be all the better.

Amount: 2 or 3 pounds.

Suggested colors: Various shades of deep, dark reds; natural beiges, blacks and whites. Choose one of these color groups to be predominant and use it for three-quarters of the weaving. *Or* various shades of grays and gray blues, with small touches of natural white and black, and burnt orange.

Directions

Wind your weft colors in the form of butterflies.

Leave about 6 inches of warp unwoven.

Refer to How to Operate the Sheds (Treadling) in this chapter for the proper treadling for the two layers, the same as double width.

Divide the warp into haphazard widths ranging from 1 to 2 inches wide. Do this by laying in separate weft threads (the butterflies) for each width. The weft threads should all be going in the same direction. For each width there will be 2 wefts—one for the top layer of fabric and one for the lower layer. Each layer can be of a different color if desired. (It is best to have contrasting colors for top and bottom layers in some of the sections, and the same colors in other sections. At any time in either layer you can start weaving with another color.)

Each time a shed is opened, you will weave with all the wefts for that layer— all across the warp. On the bottom layer, each vertical strip should join its neighbor; the weft from adjacent strips should both go around the same warp thread. (This can be done only occasionally, if desired. See following paragraph.) Join the flaps (the upper layer) to the bottom layer at one side by making the weft of the flap go around a warp thread of the bottom layer. For aesthetic reasons it is best to have *all* the flaps join the bottom layer either on their right side or their left side, unless you plan to switch sides partway through the weaving (which is an interesting plan).

You can weave all the wefts for the top layer for at least 4 changes of sheds before weaving the same number of shots in the lower layer. This means that the joins that connect the bottom strips together, and the joins that connect the top strips at one side to the bottom layer, can occur only once every 4 rows. This will prevent the buildup of wefts on one warp thread that would occur if joins were made in each row of weaving.

To make the flaps undulate in width, start pulling the weft tighter and tighter each row until you have the warp threads touching each other, and the weft shows only at the edges of that strip. This will make an additional color, since the warp threads will form the surface of the fabric in these areas. These areas will require fewer shots per inch.

Make color changes in the weft as desired. Little concentrated areas of alternating stripes will be interesting as well as long lengths of one color within one vertical strip —either the background or the flap, or both.

Beating can all be done with the beater, except when you are weaving the warp-face areas; then simply use your fingers to pack in the weft. Allow the proper weft tension for the bottom layer of fabric so that the weaving will not start to narrow.

Remove the weaving from the loom and finish according to general instructions. Make twisted or braided fringe, separating the flaps from the bottom layer of cloth. You may wish to have no fringe at all, in which case you should make a false selvedge on each layer or strip.

This piece is best *not* steam pressed (although a little pressing may be done to help make the flaps protrude) because you want it to be rough and textural.

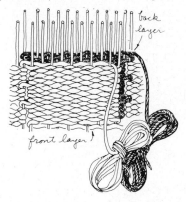

FIGURE 297. Weaving the separate layers with joints every four rows of weaving.

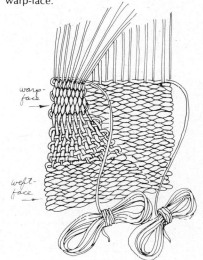

FIGURE 298. Changing from weft-face to warp-face.

FIGURE 299. A handspun karakul rug.

Project X. Plain-Weave Rug of Handspun Karakul (Warp C)*

(This rug can also be woven on the Navajo loom.)

This rug is very easy to weave, and yet it is very handsome. Since it is woven absolutely plain, its beauty depends entirely on its simplicity and the texture and color.

Materials

Warp C (2 yards).

Weft—Handspun karakul, goat or yak hair, or any coarse-fibered wool or hair. The nicest yarn will be your own handspun, spun with no carding, so that the variations in natural color will be most dramatic. See Chapter IX, "Spinning: Yarn Design and Function." The yarn can be of varying thicknesses, with the thickest parts up to 1/2 inch in diameter (if it is a fairly soft fiber), or up to 1/4 inch if it is a stiff fiber, such as goat hair or mohair. The best weight for your weft will be such that it just covers the warp when beaten in very tightly. If your weft is finer than this it will take a long time to weave, and the rug may be too soft and pliable to be functional.

Amount: Approximately 5 pounds.

Suggested color: Any natural color, preferably with variations of color in the fiber itself. For added interest you might use a 6-inch band of contrasting natural color at each end of the weaving.

Directions

Wind your weft yarn onto large stick shuttles.

Leave 6 inches of unwoven warp at the beginning for fringe.

Operate the sheds to make plain weave, packing in the weft very tightly with two hard beats. Use a rug fork for further beating if required. Make a sufficient arc so that the fabric does not narrow. With this heavy-textured yarn, it is important to make good tight edges by pulling the weft right up against the edge warp thread each time.

If it turns out that your weft yarn is too thick to pack down properly, try any one or all of the following: (1) use a stretcher to hold the fabric out to its maximum width; (2) use a heavy (iron if possible) rug fork to beat with; (3) make an ample arc; (4) tighten up warp tension as much as possible. If none of these makes it possible to beat the weft to cover the warp, use a 2-down, 2-up treadling.

Weave the rug approximately 5 feet. Leave another 6 inches of unwoven warp for fringing.

When the rug is cut from the loom, finish as in general instructions. Make 4-strand braid for fringe.

Project XI. A Rug in Giant Fancy Twill (Warp C)

(This rug can also be woven on the Navajo loom, but will require 2 extra heddle sticks.)

Here's a rug you can weave in less than a day. A very striking pattern may be made, using a twill weave and two contrasting colors. The idea for this particular pattern I got from the weavers in San Sebastián, Oaxaca, Mexico. The weft must be very heavy (for this rug—the San Sebastián rugs are much finer), and for the rug to

*A good project for beginners.

be a success it should be of long-fibered, tightly spun yarn. A heavy, soft yarn would get quite scruffy-looking very quickly. Since the twill pattern is the primary design factor, the yarn should be as even and smooth as possible; any texture would detract from the pattern.

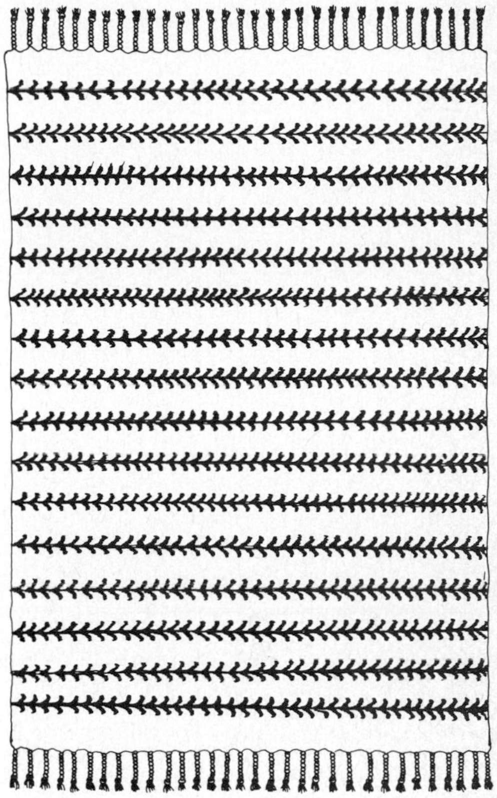

Materials

Warp C (2 yards).

Weft—Heavy, single-ply handspun wool or hair, such as Greek goat-hair yarn. Or heavier yarn if it is soft and pliable. To get exactly the right-size yarn, make a sample as described in this chapter, Planning the Weaving. (This will take only a few minutes.) Try different sizes of heavy yarn, and choose the one that will just pack down nicely with a 2-down, 2-up shed (twill). You definitely want the warp to be covered, but if the yarn is too fine the rug will be flimsy and will take forever to weave. If you spin the yarn yourself, karakul or a mohair-wool combination would be good.

Amount: Approximately 5 pounds.

Suggested colors: Natural black and natural white. About three times as much of one as the other.

Directions

Wind your two weft colors onto separate stick shuttles, the largest ones you have. Leave 6 inches of warp unwoven for fringe.

Weave 2 inches of 2/2 twill—see How to Operate the Sheds (Treadling) in this chapter—with the predominant color. Beat the weft so that it covers the warp completely. Between bands like this 2-inch band will be a pattern band. These two design elements, the plain band and the pattern band, will alternate throughout the whole length of the rug.

The pattern band (assuming white is the predominant color):

Treadle	Weft
1 and 2	Black
3 and 4	White
1 and 2	Black
3 and 4	White
2 and 3	Black
1 and 4	White
3 and 4	Black
1 and 2	White
1 and 4	Black
2 and 3	Black
1 and 4	Black
2 and 3	Black
1 and 4	Black
1 and 2	White
3 and 4	Black
1 and 4	White
2 and 3	Black
3 and 4	White
1 and 2	Black
3 and 4	White
1 and 2	Black

FIGURE 300. A fancy twill rug.

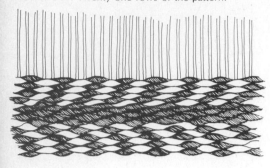

FIGURE 301. Twenty-one rows of the pattern.

FIGURE 302. A rya rug.

You can make all kinds of patterns of your own invention, using 2 wefts and different treadling. Also you can try using 3 consecutive wefts.

This rug will require a heavy beat; you may want to use a weighted rug fork. If the weft beats down very easily, chances are it should be of heavier weight to make a good strong rug.

When working with two weft colors, especially with a twill weave, you will notice that often the edge warp thread is left out. You have to be sure to make the weft encircle this last warp thread. This usually requires manipulation by hand. (See Chapter VIII, "Finishing Techniques: Selvedges," for further explanation.)

Weave approximately 5 feet, ending with the plain 2-inch band. Leave 6 inches for fringe.

When rug is cut from the loom, finish as in general instructions. Fringe with a 4-strand braid, or the Maori edge.

Project XII. Rya Rug (Warp C)*

(This is a fine project for the Navajo loom. Since most of the work involved is knotting, which requires no changes of shed, the vertical primitive loom is almost more convenient for rya rugs than the treadle loom.)

This weave originated in Scandinavia, where warm bedcovers are needed. The old ryas usually had a warp of linen and anywhere from 66 to 304 knots per square inch. They often had pictorial designs framed in a border of decorative flowers. Modern interpretations have come from Scandinavia in free-form, bold painterly designs. Since the knots are tied in individually, each knot can be a different color with no more effort than a single color, so any kind of design is possible. (Of course the design could not be "hard edge"; rather, it necessarily has blurry edges. But very striking, free-flowing designs can be made.)

The knots are often made with more than one strand of yarn, and so within each knot there can be a variety of colors. This gives a great deal of "depth" to the color of the weaving. Besides being a gorgeous-looking object, the rya rug is very functional. Depending on how much yarn is in each knot and how close the knots are to each other, the rug can be loose and shaggy or very firm, so that the yarn of the weft knots stands up vertically. (Beware of concentrating the knots so much that the rug will not lie flat, but will be forced into a curl.)

Materials

Warp C (2 yards).

Weft—Any kind of wool or hair yarn; if it is a fine yarn you will simply use several strands in one knot. (This is a good way to use up odds and ends. But actually so much yarn is needed to make a rya rug that you probably won't have enough odds and ends, and will have to cut up new skeins of yarn.) Handspun yarn will give a very luxurious effect.

Amount: Probably at least 10 pounds.

Suggested colors: Various shades of natural white (to use together in the same knot). Plus several shades of dark brownish black (black, brown, navy, rust, and dark purple will combine to make a very earthy brownish black). Two or three colors, such as gold, orange, and scarlet—to mix and use together. Don't be afraid to mix very violent and brilliant colors together in the same knot. Use the whites or blacks for at least two-thirds of the rug.

*A good project for beginners.

Structural weft: You will need approximately 1 1/2 pounds of the same yarn as the warp to use as weft for the plain weave in between rows of knots.

Directions

Wind the structural weft onto stick shuttles, or the bobbins of a very large boat shuttle.

Cut a good supply of your weft colors in 6-inch (minimum) lengths. This can be done by simply cutting a skein into sections. (Check out this length on the loom before you cut all your yarn, to see if this will be right. This length will make a fairly short pile. The pile is normally trimmed to a nice even level after it is woven.)

Leave 6 inches of warp unwoven.

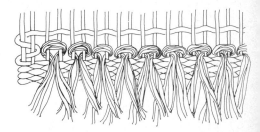

FIGURE 303. The rya knots and structural weft.

Operate the sheds to make a plain weave and use the structural weft for 6 to 10 rows (more if you want a loose pile; and less if you want a very firm pile). Beat well after each shot.

Using a group of cut weft threads that forms a strand from 1/4 to 1/2 inch thick (it's up to you, but keep it consistent), set in a row of rya knots as shown in Figure 303. The shed should be closed for the knotting. In between each row of knots weave 6 to 10 rows of the structural weft (the same number of rows as you did at the beginning), and beat well. By going back and forth around the outer two warp threads at each side for a few rows, you will keep the same amount of buildup as in the knotted area. The rows of knots are staggered so that the knots in one row encircle different pairs of warp threads from the previous row.

Cut the rug from the loom, make a braided fringe or Maori edge. Trim pile with scissors if desired.

Project XIII. Circle Tapestry (Warp C)

(This project can also be woven on the Navajo loom.)

This is a simple but very effective design, the success of which depends mostly on the colors and the preciseness with which the circle is woven.

FIGURE 304. A tapestry.

Materials

Warp C (about 2 yards).

Weft—Medium-weight wool or hair yarn. A smooth-textured commercial yarn will probably be the nicest if you use brilliant colors. A textured handspun yarn would be nice if you choose the white and natural color scheme.

Amount: Approximately 3 pounds.

Suggested colors: Two different types of color schemes are suitable:

1. Very subtle varying shades of natural whites and pure whites, beiges and creams, some naturals toned slightly toward blue or mauve by dyeing with either natural or synthetic dyes (see Chapter X, "Dyeing"). A very few darker naturals, but in general keep to very closely related *light* tones. Use the lighter tones for the circle and the darker tones for the background, but occasionally switch a dark color to the circle and a light color to the background.

2. *Very* brilliant colors all of the same value (see Chapter XI, "Design and Color: Properties of Color"): reds, pinks, oranges, gold; and cool colors—blues, purples, greens. By juxtaposing these colors you will get an op-art effect of vibrating colors. Use the cool ones for the background and the hot ones for the circle (or vice versa) and occasionally put a background color in with the circle and a circle color in with the background.

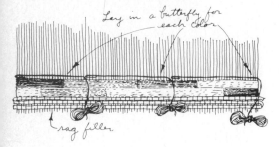

FIGURE 305. Laying in the weft colors.

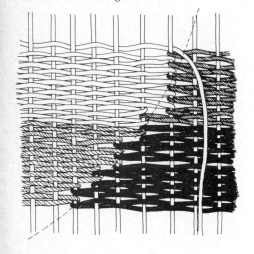

FIGURE 306. Weaving the circle.

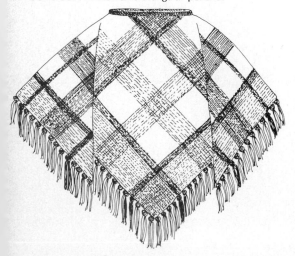

FIGURE 307. A woman's triangular poncho.

Directions

Wind the weft colors in the form of butterflies.

With a felt-tip pen draw a circle centered in the warp. (Tie a string to a pencil; use this as a compass to draw a circle on a piece of newspaper; cut this out and use it as a pattern to draw the circle on the warp.)

Leave 6 inches of unwoven warp for fringe.

Operate the sheds for plain weave, and beat weft to cover the warp completely.

Read directions for tapestry weaving in Project IV (Traditional Navajo Rug), Chapter VI. This design will be woven in 1-inch strips divided vertically at random (like layers of bricks). Lay colors of your background yarns into one shed, with the ends all going in the same direction (see Figure 171).

Change sheds and weave all the butterflies back in this shed. "Backstep" as described in directions for the Navajo rug (see Figure 172). The vertical joins in this rug are best made by the single dovetail rather than the 3/3 dovetail method (see Figure 173). Pack the weft in well with the beater. After you have woven 1 inch in these colors, break off the ends (see Figure 175) and lay in another set of background colors, making the joins of these new sections occur somewhere not too near the previous joins. Keep building up the weaving in these 1-inch horizontal color strips until you come to where the circle should be started.

Be sure you are making big enough arcs in the weft so that the weaving does not start to draw in (see Notes on Weft Tension in this chapter).

When you come to laying in the colors for the circle, the bottom of the circle can be started by laying in a color that spans a distance of 6 inches in the center of the warp. At the bottom of the circle your color joins between background and circle are at a *very* slight angle. In making tapestry circles this is the most difficult part; the tendency is to go at too steep an angle. The weft for the circle will skip over 2 warp threads with each change of shed (perhaps more if your yarn is quite heavy). As the sides of the circle get steeper, you will make the color change between background and circle by moving over 1 warp thread each row; and eventually you will move over 1 warp thread only after several rows of weaving. Make these decreases in how many warp threads you move over consistent.

By the time you are at the more or less vertical sides of the circle you will be weaving vertical joins, and only move over 1 warp thread at the end of each 1-inch band. Eventually you will weave a vertical line (for the side of the circle) that is approximately 6 inches high. Try to follow as exactly as possible the marks on the warp.

When the weaving is cut from the loom, finish according to general instructions. Fringe with braided fringe, or make false selvedge.

Project XIV. Woman's Triangular Poncho (Warp D)

This is an interesting poncho design. Definitely not for men; and some women don't like it because it's not the "ethnic" type, but more like "high fashion." However, made in good yarns and beautiful colors it is a nice piece of clothing. We made hundreds of these ponchos when I had my weaving shop. Some women had a collection of two or three to wear, they liked them so much. They can be woven in a plaid design, or just plain, which reveals the warp stripes.

Materials

Warp D (approximately 1 yard 2 feet).

Weft—Exactly the same yarn as the warp.

Amount: Approximately 3/4 pound.

Suggested colors: For a plaid poncho, exactly the same colors as in the warp. For a striped poncho, any one of the warp colors, or another color that would blend.

Directions

Wind your weft colors onto the bobbins of your medium-size boat shuttles. Leave 6 inches of unwoven warp for fringe.

Operate the sheds for plain weave. Leave a 6-inch tail to the weft that you start with, and make all weft splices by leaving 6 inches hanging out an edge (these tails will later be incorporated in the fringe on all four sides).

Beating the weft in *evenly* will be the most difficult aspect of this project. You want to have exactly 8 weft shots per inch. Advancing the warp often to keep the warp tension even will be important. Uneven beating will show up more in the plain poncho than in a plaid.

For a plaid, weave the weft colors in exactly the same order they appear in the warp. Weave until the poncho measures exactly the same length (with tension released) as it is wide. Leave another 6 inches for fringe at this end.

When the piece is cut from the loom, finish according to general instructions. Make a knotted fringe with the warp ends, incorporating 8 warp ends in each knot. Add fringe on the sides with 1-foot lengths of weft yarn (to match the weft according to the plaid or plain design).

Cut a 14-inch diagonal slit for the neck hole. Do this by folding the poncho diagonally, marking the center and cutting along the fold 7 inches on each side of the center mark. Immediately sew on commercial wool bias tape (or your own home-made gimp) with the sewing machine. Stitch back and forth once at the ends of the slit. Fold tape over and hand sew to cover the raw edges. A sloppy job of making the neck hole can spoil the whole poncho, so be very careful to sew it perfectly. The stitching with the sewing machine will prevent any raveling of the fabric.

Project XV. Long Poncho (Warp D)

This is a light-weight poncho suitable for men or women. The pattern is the same as the traditional Mexican poncho but it is woven all in one piece. The neck hole can be either woven into it, or cut and bound after the weaving is completed. It can be woven with either a plaid design or plain warp stripes. The latter is the most appropriate design, I think.

Materials

Warp D (2 yards).

Weft—Exactly the same yarn as warp.

Amount: Approximately 1 pound.

Suggested colors: One of the colors used in the warp, or (if plaid design is wanted), all the same colors that are in the warp.

Directions

Wind the weft onto the bobbins of your medium-size boat shuttle.

Leave 6 inches of warp unwoven for fringe (at beginning and end).

Read directions for weaving Project XIV. The actual weaving of this poncho will

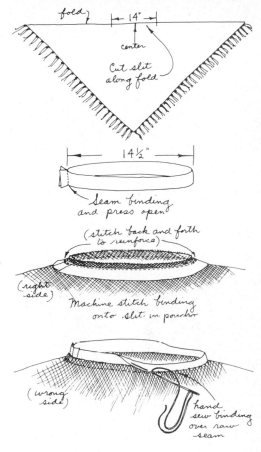

FIGURE 308. Steps in binding the neck hole.

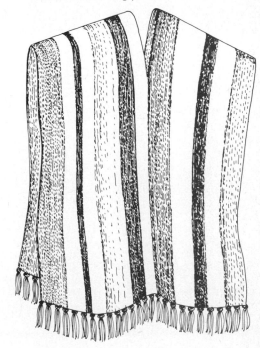

FIGURE 309. A long poncho.

FIGURE 310. Weaving the slit.

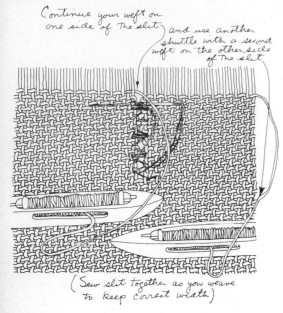

Continue your weft on one side of the slit) and use another shuttle with a second weft on the other side of The slit

(Sew slit together as you weave to keep correct width)

be exactly the same, except for measurements. Weft splices should occur at the edges, with the tails looped around the edge warp thread and laid back in the same shed.

Weave for 2 feet before starting the neck hole. To weave the slit for the neck (15 inches long is a good length) you will need to have 2 shuttles. Weave halfway across the warp with one shuttle and the other half with the other shuttle. The slit will separate right away and you will have to be careful to make the right-size arc with the weft so that the edges remain parallel. It may help to sew the slit together temporarily as it is being woven if you are having difficulty with it. Weaving the neck slit will take a lot more time than weaving the main body of the poncho, and if you prefer, you can weave the whole poncho in one piece and *cut* and bind the slit later (as in Project XIV): this latter method is much faster and advisable if you are mass producing these ponchos.

After weaving the slit, continue weaving with one weft for the same distance on the other side. Leave ample 6 inches for fringe at the other end.

When the poncho is cut from the loom, finish as in general instructions. Fringe with knotted, twisted, or braided fringe, bind the neck slit if desired with commercial wool bias tape or handmade gimp.

Project XVI. Vest (Warp D)

Made from a piece of weaving less than a yard long, this vest makes a nice garment for women and men too (up to a certain size). The width of the material (about 43 inches when off the loom) is the maximum size around the vest can be, so this pattern is not suitable for a large man, but is fine for many people. A full-length vest reaching to the knees makes a nice sleeveless coat.

Materials
Warp D (1 yard).
Weft—The same as the warp.
    Amount: Approximately 1/2 pound.
    Suggested colors: One of the warp colors, or all warp colors for a plaid design.

Directions
    Wind the weft onto the bobbins of your medium-size boat shuttle.
    Leave 6 inches of warp unwoven for fringe at one end.
    (See Project XIV for actual directions for weaving either the plain or plaid pattern.)

FIGURE 311. A vest.

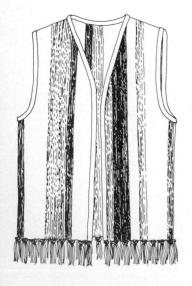

Weave it however long you want the vest to be: from shoulder to hip or from shoulder to knee for a long vest. Weft splices should be made at either edge. Leave only a 1-inch tail: this will be trimmed and covered up by the binding.

When the piece is cut from the loom, finish as in general instructions. Fringe with knotted, braided, or twisted fringe.

If the vest is for a person who is not as big around as the material is wide, then trim off a lengthwise strip as desired (the vest should measure around about 2 inches more than the actual chest measurement). Fold the material so that the selvedge edges meet in the center. Then fold again lengthwise. Cut the armholes about 3 inches in and 9 inches long (depending on size of the person; this is the right size for most adults). Trim a slight slant for the shoulder seam. Trim the front corners of the neck about 3 inches in and 9 inches long. Cut the back of the neck into a fairly deep arc.

With a sewing machine stitch the shoulder seam, steam press the seam open and bind with commercial bias tape (that has been pressed open) or your own handmade gimp. Bind the armholes and neck and front edges with the same. Doing a perfect job of sewing the binding on is very important; the stitching should follow warp threads exactly. (See Chapter VIII, "Finishing Techniques: Sewing.")

FIGURE 312. Cutting and sewing the vest.

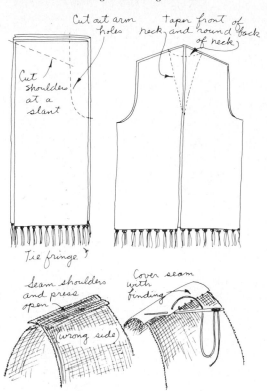

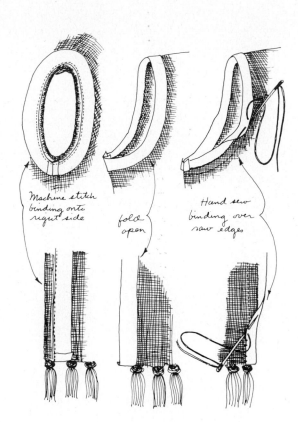

Project XVII. Double-Width Bedspread with Heavy Homespun Weft (Warp D)

This is almost like a thermal weave, and makes a handsome spread that can double as a very warm blanket. It is woven on the loom double width (two layers of fabric with a fold on one side), and is very quick to weave. The finished size will be about 7 by 9 feet; this will fit a double bed and hang down about 15 inches on all sides.

Materials

Warp D (approximately 4 yards).

Weft—The weft must be a very thick, soft, single-ply yarn. The best yarn would be your own handspun wool made from a commercial wool roving. Spin it even and loose about 1/2 inch in diameter.

    Amount: Approximately 5 pounds.

    Suggested colors: Use a single color that will contrast with the warp colors.

Directions

Wind your weft yarn onto large stick shuttles.

Leave 5 inches of unwoven warp so you can tie the warp ends to prevent unraveling.

Weave 3 or 4 rows of both top and bottom layers. See How to Operate the Sheds (Treadling) in this chapter for directions for weaving double width. Beat the weft in firmly. As soon as there is enough weaving, place the stretcher in the fabric to hold the full width. This is very important when you are weaving double-width material.

FIGURE 313. A homespun bedspread.

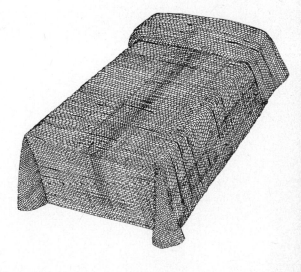

FIGURE 314. The double width weave.

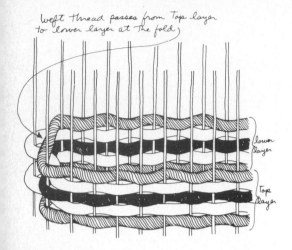

The fabric must not draw in the slightest bit, or the edge where the fold is will start building up badly.

Be very careful that the sheds are opened properly and the shuttle doesn't skip over the wrong threads. If there is a "mistake" it will mean that the two layers of fabric will be joined together at that point, and the weft will have to be cut to release them. You *don't* want to do this.

Make your weft splices at the open edge of the weaving. This edge will eventually be made into a rolled hem, and those weft ends can just be cut off.

Weave a full 3 yards and 1 foot (when tension is released). Leave another 5 inches of unwoven warp for tying warp ends.

When the material is cut from the loom, finish as in general instructions. Mend any broken warp ends and mistakes by darning a new length of warp into the blanket so there will be no splices. The extra selvedge threads at the fold edge should be pulled out. Tie the warp ends so they won't unravel. Make a rolled hem. Decorate with added fringe all around if desired. When you steam press this weaving, do it very lightly so as not to destroy its thick texture.

Project XVIII. Burnoose (Warp E)

The authentic North African burnoose is a simple hooded cape, cut from a single rectangular piece of material: a very simple design and yet an extremely striking garment. Our burnoose is modeled directly on the authentic ones, woven in horizontal stripes with two different-weight yarns—one fairly heavy and textured to add interest.

Materials

Warp E (approximately 3 yards and 1 foot).

Weft—A medium-weight single- or 2-ply yarn (preferably soft, not scratchy); 2/8 Canadian yarn is good. Also small amounts of a heavier handspun yarn.

    Amount: About 3 pounds altogether.

    Suggested colors: Dark reds, deep pine-needle green, and natural brown or black; small amounts of dark, brilliant fuchsia (purplish red).

FIGURE 315. A burnoose.

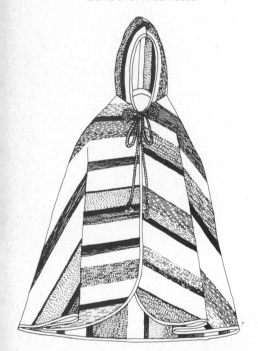

Directions

Wind the medium-weight yarns onto the bobbins of your medium-size boat shuttles. Wind the heavier yarn onto stick shuttles.

Weave a heading of several shots of any scrap yarn just as a base to prevent the actual weft from unraveling (no fringing will be done on this weaving).

Operate the sheds to make a plain weave, making bands of color anywhere from 1/2 inch to 8 inches wide. Beat in weft with a moderately firm beat. Do not cover the warp, however. Use the homespun in bands about 2 inches wide. (You may want to use a 2-down, 2-up combination in treadling if the homespun is very heavy.) The medium-weight weft will require a fairly good-size arc for proper weft tension, while the heavier yarn should be pulled pretty much tight across the warp to avoid a buckling of the fabric when the tension is released. Check to make sure you are getting proper weft tension for the two different yarns by releasing the warp to see if the edges are straight and there is no buckling.

Weft splices can be made by simply overlaying broken weft ends for a distance of 3 or 4 inches.

Weave until the fabric measures (when not in tension) 20 inches longer than twice the width.

When the fabric is cut from the loom, finish as in general instructions.

FIGURE 316. Cutting and sewing the burnoose.

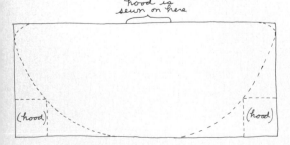

Cut the burnoose in a semicircle.

Cut from the remaining corners 2 squares as large as possible. Seam the squares together on 2 adjacent sides, and press the seam flat. Cover with commercial wool bias tape or your own handmade gimp. Sew the hood onto the center of the straight edge of the semicircular cape. Bind this seam also. Now bind the entire circumference of the cape, including the hood. Make a rope of one of the weft colors, about 5 feet long altogether. Cut in half and sew each half to the neck of the cape by spiraling it several times around like a pinwheel and securing this to the fabric with a needle and heavy thread or warp yarn.

Project XIX. Double-Face Lap Robe with Brushed Mohair (Warp E)

(This project can also be woven on the Navajo loom; it is the same weave as Project VI in Chapter VI, "The Navajo Loom.")

Here is a very unusual lap robe—almost like an animal skin. One side is a heavy, furry fabric of multi-color, and the other side is a flat weave with a pattern in it.

Materials

Warp E (about 2 yards).

Weft—Medium-fine handspun mohair. (If you spin it yourself it should be about the thickness of dime-store worsted knitting yarn.) If you can't spin your own or somewhere obtain handspun yarn, loop mohair, which is available through many different sources, will probably be all right. Also you will need an equal amount of medium-fine single-ply wool (preferably handspun).

Amounts: Approximately 2 pounds of the mohair and 2 pounds of the wool.

Suggested colors: Variegated dyed mohair (see Chapter X, "Dyeing: Techniques for Special Effects"). When the yarn is brushed, the various colors of the dyed yarn all get blended together. The wool yarn should be two contrasting natural colors, like natural brown and natural white.

Directions

Wind the mohair weft and the two different colors of wool weft (which will be used for the underneath surface) onto the bobbins of your large boat shuttles. You will need three boat shuttles and will use all three at the same time. If you don't have three, then wind one of the weft colors onto a stick shuttle.

Leave 6 inches of warp unwoven for fringe.

See How to Operate the Sheds (Treadling) in this chapter for the treadling sequence for double-face weave. Weave the mohair on the top surface, and the two contrasting natural wool colors on the bottom surface. Alternate the two wool colors and you will have a vertical bar pattern. To make a checkerboard pattern, every 1/2 inch weave 2 rows of the same color and then alternate again.

The warp may not be covered completely, but when you brush the mohair it won't show on that side. Pack the wefts in as tightly as possible.

Before advancing the warp each time, brush the mohair surface with a hand card. Refer to Chapter VIII, "Finishing Techniques: Brushing," for further instructions. Be very careful not to brush so hard that you break the warp threads.

Leave another 6 inches of warp unwoven for fringe at this end.

After the throw is cut off the loom, finish as in general instructions and make a 4-strand braid for fringe. Wash, brush some more, mainly to make all the fibers go in the direction you want, and steam press after brushing.

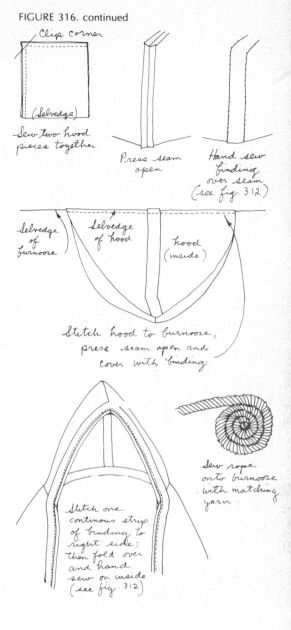

FIGURE 316. continued

Clip corner
(Selvedge)
Sew two hood pieces together

Press seam open

Hand sew binding over seam (see fig. 312)

Selvedge of burnoose   Selvedge of hood   hood (inside)

Stitch hood to burnoose, press seam open and cover with binding.

Sew rope onto burnoose with matching yarn

Stitch one continuous strip of binding to right side; then fold over and hand sew on inside (see fig. 312)

FIGURE 317. A double-face brushed mohair lap robe.

FIGURE 318. A bedspread woven in strips.

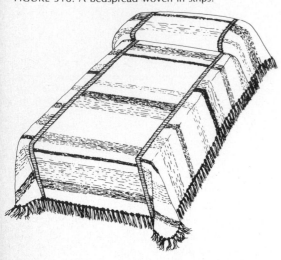

FIGURE 319. Sewing the strips together.

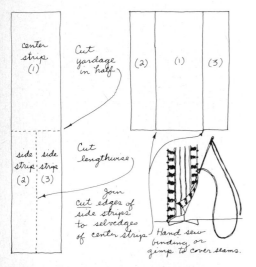

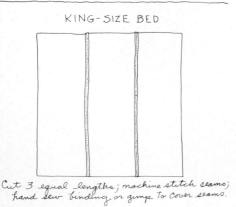

Project XX. Bedspread Woven in Strips (Warp E)

(This bedspread can be woven only on a treadle loom. However, if you wanted to weave narrower strips, you could weave a very beautiful spread with a backstrap loom. Weave bands about 18 inches wide and have lots of them.)

This bedspread is woven in strips (as wide as the warp) of random stripes and bands. The strips are joined together with a decorative gimp covering the join. For twin- and double-bed sizes, weave two strips, each the length that will be needed to hang down at the foot of the bed and to fold over the pillow at the head of the bed. One strip forms the center of the spread and the second strip is cut lengthwise and forms the two sides. (This is nicer than having a seam right down the middle of the bed.) On a double bed the spread will hang down on the sides only about 10 inches, so a skirt will probably be needed to cover the box springs or framework. For a king-size bed, three strips (each 10 1/2 feet long) are sewn together, and this makes a spread about 126 by 126 inches.

It is too difficult to try to match the stripes in each of the separate pieces, but the spread is very effective with the bands of color and stripes meeting at random.

Materials

Warp E (6 yards for twin and double, 10 1/2 yards for king size).

Weft—Various sizes of yarn, medium-fine to medium weight, single or plied, commercial or handspun; and occasional touches of heavy textured homespun.

Amount: Approximately 4 or 5 pounds for single or double; approximately 8 or 9 pounds for king size.

Suggested colors: All natural whites, creams, and very pale beiges, with *tiny* amounts of natural blacks and browns. *Or* reds, blues, greens, and golds. *Or* a color scheme to go with the bedroom.

(The thing to avoid in this large piece of weaving is great variations in value —light and dark. The weaving should be pretty much colors that are of the same value, with only touches of dark colors. If there is a great variety in the values the weaving would be too overpowering, I think.)

See Chapter XI, "Design and Color: Choosing Colors," for more ideas.

Directions

Wind your yarns onto bobbins for boat shuttles. The heavier yarns can be wound onto stick shuttles.

No fringe allowance is necessary, as the spread will be hemmed. If a fringe is desired it will be added on.

Weave the colors in bands varying from 1/2 inch to 8 inches. You can vary the weave from tabby to twill in some bands, if desired. See How to Operate the Sheds (Treadling) in this chapter.

The main problem in weaving this project will be maintaining even width, since you are using so many different weights and types of yarn. Remember: the finer the yarn, the larger the arc. The heaviest yarns will probably need to be pulled straight across the warp. A twill weave using the same weft as a tabby weave requires less of an arc for the correct weft tension.

To check to see if you are getting the correct weft tension, that the edges are not drawing in and the material is not buckling, you must release the warp tension and examine the fabric carefully. If the material is buckling, then you need to pull the weft tighter; if it is narrowing, you need to make a bigger arc (see Notes on Weft Tension in this chapter).

Beat with a moderate beat. The warp should show except where the weft is quite fine.

Weft splices can be made simply by overlapping the broken ends of the wefts.

Try to use the colors in such a way that they will occur regularly all over the spread—so that one strip won't be more one color than another. To do this you should separate out piles of colors for each strip, with the same amount of each color in each pile. Then as you weave be conscious of using each color at certain intervals.

For the twin or double-bed size, weave 6 yards measured when tension is released; for the king size, weave 10 1/2 yards.

When the material is cut from the loom, finish as in general directions. Cut into equal-length strips, and join them (see Chapter VIII, "Finishing Techniques: Joining"). For the twin or double bed, cut one of the pieces right down the center, and join the pieces to the center piece so that the selvedge edges meet and the cut edges will be hemmed. Cover the joins with your own handwoven gimp. You can bind the edges with the same, or make a rolled hem. Add on fringe if desired.

Project XXI. Double-Width Weft-Face Blanket (Warp E)

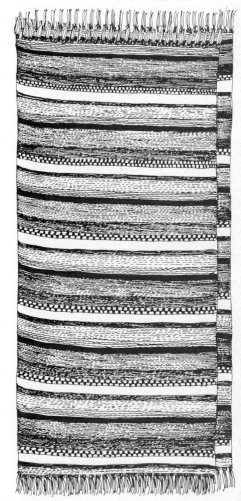

FIGURE 320. A double-width blanket.

This striped weft-face blanket is similar to the ones made in the past century in New Mexico—some of the most beautiful in the area of Chimayo. The Spanish men (for the men wove too, and still do) and women wove these blankets either in two strips, to be joined after removal from the loom, or they wove them on a four-harness loom using the double-width method as we will do here.

The classic designs are repeating (either direct or mirror image) stripes and bands, often with little detailed patterns formed by alternating weft colors. These early Spanish "serapes" were woven with some of the most beautiful handspun yarn (even and fine) I've ever seen—spun on hand spindles and often dyed with natural dyes: indigo, chamizo, onion skin, combined with colors of the natural wool, black, gray, and white. These are among my favorite weavings. Perhaps you can make a blanket that will begin to compare in beauty with them. Ours will be quite a bit coarser than the early serapes. If you get really ambitious you may want to make a fine one sometime. In this case you should have a warp sett of 16 epi, and use a fine handspun yarn.

This blanket will be about 7 feet wide and 9 feet long, so it can be used as a bedspread.

Materials

Warp E (approximately 3 1/2 yards).

Weft—Medium-weight handspun wool. If you spin your own, a combination of half mohair and half wool makes a beautiful glossy yarn that will not pill with use. Or you can very quickly spin yarn for this blanket using a good-quality wool roving sliver, or top. Check the weight of the yarn by making a sample as described in this chapter under Planning the Weaving. It should be heavy enough that it just packs down to cover the weft. If it is too fine, the blanket will be very flimsy and take forever to weave.

Amount: Approximately 8 to 10 pounds.

Suggested colors: If you want to be really authentic, use natural white and natural black or brown wool. Dye some of the white with indigo to get a very deep blue. Also dye small amounts with concentrated onion-skin dye to get a deep burnt orange. Make one of the colors (preferably the indigo) predominant. Use it for about three-fourths of the weaving.

Directions

Wind your weft colors onto the bobbins for large boat shuttles.

Leave 6 inches of warp unwoven for fringe.

Follow the treadling sequence for double-width weaving given under the heading How to Operate the Sheds (Treadling) in this chapter. Definitely use a stretcher, and make sure the weaving does not draw in the slightest bit. The weft should pack down nicely to cover the warp with a good hard beat.

To design your pattern, start weaving with whatever color you feel like, and change colors for bands and stripes as your inspiration dictates. For special interest, use two alternating weft colors to make vertical bars (or checkerboards by weaving alternate colors for 1/4 inch, then two rows of one color, and continue with the alternate colors). Or wavy lines can be made by weaving 2 rows of one color and 2 rows of another, and repeating. Within an 18-inch length of weaving, figure on using the right proportion of colors (the same proportions that you have allowed for the entire blanket).

After weaving 18 inches, repeat the same bands and stripes. Keep repeating this 18-inch pattern six times. This will make a 108-inch length that will suffice for the entire blanket. A much larger pattern may be made by repeating the 18-inch pattern in reverse or mirror image. This will make a symmetrical pattern that will be 36 inches in length. It will take 3 of these symmetrical areas to make the 108-inch length needed. I tend to like the direct repeating method rather than the mirror image, but that is strictly a matter of individual taste. (See Chapter XI, "Design and Color: Repetition," for further discussion.)

Make weft splices by overlapping broken weft ends.

When the blanket is cut from the loom, pull out any doubled-up warp ends that are at the folded edge and finish as in general instructions. A knotted fringe will probably be the most appropriate for this blanket.

Project XXII. Leno Room Divider with Willow Sticks and Found Objects (Warp E)

(This project can be woven on the Navajo loom also.)

This hanging is very simple and quick to weave. It should be hung in the middle of the room or in front of a window to look its best. The leno weave (which is a combination of gauze and regular weave) is described fully in Chapter V, "The Backstrap Loom: Project VII." For this room divider you will combine the leno with tapestry squares and rectangles, and insert sticks and other objects, such as seed pods, in the sheds.

Materials

Warp E (about 2 1/2 yards).

Weft—The same as the warp. Also some homespun of medium to heavy weight.

About 10 willow sticks the width of the warp plus 4 inches. Seed pods or other natural objects suitable for inserting in the sheds.

Amounts: Approximately 1/2 to 3/4 pound of weft (same as warp). Approximately 1 to 2 pounds of homespun.

Suggested colors: The weft yarn that is the same as the warp should be the same color as the warp also. The homespun yarn can be any variety of natural or earthy colors. You can use up a great many odds and ends of homespun here, because each tapestry square or rectangle will take only a few feet of yarn.

FIGURE 321. A room divider.

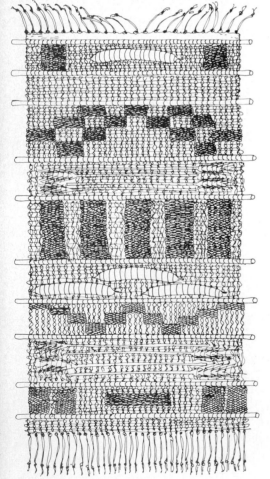

Directions

Wind the weft that is the same as the warp onto the bobbins of your boat shuttles. Wind the homespun yarn into butterflies.

Leave 8 inches or more of warp unwoven for fringe.

Do three or four rows of gauze weave, using the light-weight weft. Twist only single-warp pairs. Set a willow stick in a plain shed, and continue a few more rows of gauze. Make a symmetrical design by weaving squares and rectangles of the heavier weft in plain weave—see How to Operate the Sheds (Treadling) in this chapter—back and forth just within an area like a tapestry weave. (See Chapter VI, "The Navajo Loom: Project IV. Traditional Navajo Rug," for complete instructions on how to do the tapestry weave.) Use a 2-down, 2-up treadling if your homespun is too heavy.

In between these squares and rectangles place seed pods or make a different leno pattern (by twisting groups of threads instead of just pairs). Every so often insert a willow stick.

Make the entire 6 feet of hanging in this way. At the top insert a final willow stick in a shed to act as a hanger, and weave plain weave about 1 inch above that to secure it. Leave 6 inches of unwoven warp for fringe.

When the weaving is removed from the loom, finish as in general instructions and make a 4-strand braided fringe on top and bottom.

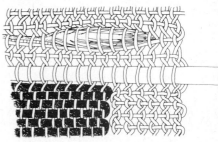

FIGURE 322. Close-up of the structure of the hanging.

Project XXIII. Warp-Face Poncho (Warp F)

(This project can also be woven on the backstrap and Navajo looms; see Chapter V, "The Backstrap Loom: Project IV.")

A warp face weave is one of the most efficient weaves. All the design and most of the material are in the warp, so once the warp is set up it is just a matter of passing the weft through to hold it all together. The number of weft shots per inch are one-fourth or less the number of shots required for a weft-face weave. In a poncho the warp-face weave is probably the most flattering design for the human figure because the stripes are all vertical.

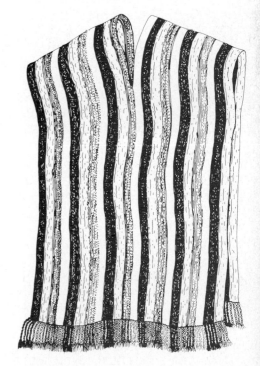

FIGURE 323. A warp-face poncho.

Materials

Warp F (approximately 2 yards).

Weft—A wool or hair yarn that is about the same in size as the warp yarn, single or plied.

Amount: Approximately 1/2 pound.

Suggested color: The color should blend with the warp and be *darker* than the majority of the warp ends.

Directions

Wind the weft yarn onto the bobbins of your medium-size boat shuttle.

Leave 5 or 6 inches of warp unwoven for fringe.

Operate the sheds for plain weave for about 2 feet. If you have difficulty with the shed separating well, move the reed back and forth while you are changing the shed, and make the treadles go up and down several times. Beat the weft in as tightly as possible. The weft can be pulled pretty much straight across; no arc is necessary.

Weave a slit 15 inches long for the neck hole by using two wefts. If the fabric tends to separate too much, sew it together at the slit as you weave it, so that the material will retain its proper width. (See Project XV for illustration of weaving a slit for neck hole.)

Continue weaving the same distance beyond the slit as you did before. Leave 5 or 6 inches for fringe.

When the weaving is cut from the loom, finish as in general directions and fringe with twisted or braided fringe.

Project XXIV. 1/3 Twill Reversible Throw, Brushed (Warp F)

(This project can also be woven on a Navajo loom.)

By using a 1/3 twill structure, you can make one side of this throw predominantly warp stripes and the other side the plain-colored weft. Both sides are brushed to further emphasize the color and make the fabric luxurious. It makes a heavy but very soft and useful throw.

Materials

Warp F (a little over 2 yards).

Weft—Medium-weight single or plied yarn, preferably handspun wool or soft hair.
Your own handspun from a mixture of wool and mohair will be perfect. It should be the same weight as the average weight of the warp threads.
Amount: Approximately 1 1/2 pounds.
Suggested color: A pale color that will blend with the warp (with a pale color, the warp stripes, when brushed, take on a luminescent quality). A very dark brown is also nice as the color for the reverse side; it tends to give the warp stripes a more "hairy" ethnic look.

Directions

Wind your weft onto the bobbins of your medium-size boat shuttle.

Leave six inches of warp unwoven for fringe.

Weave the 1/3 twill as described under How to Operate the Sheds (Treadling) in this chapter. Pack in the weft so that there are about as many wefts per inch as there are warp ends. This will require a moderately hard beat. If you have difficulty making the warp threads separate into a shed, move the reed back and forth as you are changing the shed. See Chapter VIII, "Finishing Techniques: Selvedges," for treatment of the edge warp thread when it is not automatically included in the shed.

Before advancing the warp, brush the fabric with a hand card (the type used for carding wool), or a dog brush. Brush *across* the warp threads to raise the colors of the warp. (See Chapter VIII, "Finishing Techniques: Brushing," for further information on brushing.) As the underneath side of the material rolls around the cloth beam, brush this surface also. This time stroke vertically to raise the nap of the weft.

Weave about 5 or 5 1/2 feet measured with tension released. Leave 6 inches of warp for fringe.

When the throw is cut from the loom, finish as in general instructions, and make knotted fringe. Wash, brush again (the fringe also), and steam press. With the final brushing, make all the warp fibers lie vertical (along the line of the stripes) and the weft fibers horizontal.

Project XXV. Double-Width Mohair Blanket, Brushed and Fulled (Warp F)

This will be a very functional, warm blanket that will measure about 6 by 8 feet after it is fulled (see Chapter VIII, "Finishing Techniques: Fulling"). It should take only about a day to weave after you have the warp all set up.

FIGURE 324. A reversible twill throw.

Materials

Warp F (a little over 3 yards).

Weft—Loosely spun medium-fine to fine single-ply mohair of your own spinning. The yarn should be quite fine and can be unevenly spun. Or use commercial loop mohair or brushed variegated wool.

Amount: 4 or 5 pounds of handspun. Or about 3 pounds of commercial yarn. (Commercial yarn is usually lighter than your own handspun of the same diameter.)

Suggested color: A color (or mixture of colored fibers) that will blend with the warp yarns. For the warp stripes to show up to their best advantage, the weft should not be too dominant, and will be best if it is a pale, muted color. If you mix 2 or 3 closely related colors in the carding, the yarn will have even more interest.

Directions

Wind the weft yarn onto the bobbins of your largest boat shuttle.

Leave six inches of unwoven warp for fringe. Weave double width as directed in How to Operate the Sheds (Treadling) in this chapter. Beat with a moderate beat so there will be about 8 shots per inch.

You must use a stretcher; put it in the fabric as soon as you have a couple of inches of weaving done. Make sure that the weaving does not draw in at all, but maintains its maximum width at all times. You will have to make a generous arc with your weft. Brush the fabric lightly on the top surface before advancing the warp. Brush the other side when it rolls onto the cloth roller. The surface that is inside the fold will have to be brushed after the blanket is off the loom. Weave until the blanket measures 3 yards when not in tension.

When the weaving is cut from the loom, fringe with knotted fringe. Pull out the double threads at the folded edge. Brush the other surface—*carefully*; this loose weave, when not held in tension, will be very easy to tear. After all the brushing is done the blanket should be fulled (slightly), dried, brushed again to untangle fibers, and then steam pressed.

FIGURE 325. A fulled and brushed mohair blanket.

Project XXVI. Basket Weave Throw (Warp F)

See Chapter I, "The Basics of Weaving: A Definition of Weaving," for an illustration of a basket weave. This weave makes possible a very close, thick fabric that is yet very pliable. Using this warp, if it is made up of different sizes and textures of thread, you will get a thick, nubbly fabric. You can use a single color for the weft, or the same variety of colors that are in the warp. If you do the latter, you will get an interesting effect somewhat like a painting in the school of "pointillism." The pointillists were a group of painters working in the late nineteenth century with the impressionists in France. They created color areas in their paintings by juxtaposing tiny dots of various brilliant colors—somewhat like the dots used to print color reproductions today. When you use several different wefts, there will be a problem of starting and ending colors, so I suggest you simply carry over the colors, rather than breaking them off, and plan on making a bound edge around all four sides of the throw.

Materials

Warp F (approximately 2 1/2 yards).

Weft—One of the warp yarns; or the same variety of yarns as in the warp.

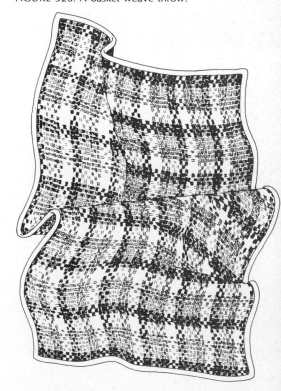

FIGURE 326. A basket weave throw.

Directions

If you are using a single weft color, wind it onto the bobbins of a boat shuttle. If you are using the variety, wind a shuttle or bobbin for as many colors as you have shuttles. It might take as many as 20 or 30 shuttles if you had one for each color, so obviously you will have to choose the first colors you will be using and wind very small amounts of each. Or use butterflies or primitive stick shuttles (see Chapter IV, "The Hopi Belt Loom: The Butterfly vs. the Shuttle").

Leave 6 inches of warp unwoven for fringe, if you are using a single weft color. If you are using the variety, you will have to plan on binding the edges to cover warp "carryovers," and it will be best to bind all four edges. So, in this case, you need not leave a fringe allowance.

Operate the sheds for a basket weave. The weft is shot through each shed *twice*. This means that you will have to lock the weft around the edge warp thread before making the second shot. Beat the weft in well before making the second shot, so the two wefts won't look as if they are just a double weft thread. If you are using the variety of colors, don't break off the wefts; simply carry them over. This will leave many "carryover" loops and these are what will have to be covered by the binding.

Weave 6 feet. Leave another 6 inches for fringe, or not (whichever you did to begin with). Cut off and mend. Make twisted or knotted fringe or zigzag the raw edge on the sewing machine, before binding.

On the throw with the zigzagged edges make the Peruvian Rolled Edge (Added On) (see Chapter VIII, "Finishing Techniques") around all four edges, using any appropriate colors. Make sure the warp you set up for this edge is long enough to go around all four edges; allow for a total warp takeup of about 1 1/2 yards. Or use commercial or handmade gimp.

When you steam press, do it lightly to preserve the texture.

Suggestions for Other Projects

Check through the chapters on other looms; there are many projects that are suitable for the treadle loom.

Try the 2-layer weave (as in Project IX in this chapter) using 2 contrasting warp colors, one threaded through the even-numbered heddle shafts and one through the odd-numbered. Use a very close warp sett—20 epi, for instance—and you can bring either warp color to the top at any time by reversing the treadling so that opposite shafts are raised and lowered. You can make the weave in each layer warp face (by pulling the weft tightly across the shed and beating with your fingers rather than the beater) to reveal the contrasting warp colors; or it can be tabby, with both warp and weft threads matching.

Make pillows of giant twill using heavy homespun yarn for both warp and weft. Make them in natural black and white using a 2/2 treadling and a balanced structure (same number of wefts per inch as warp ends). Some pillows can be all black, some all white, and some with the two colors—with a herringbone pattern for some.

Combine a variety of techniques to make experimental wall hangings, always keeping in mind the limitations discussed in Chapter XI, "Design and Color."

CHAPTER VIII

FINISHING TECHNIQUES

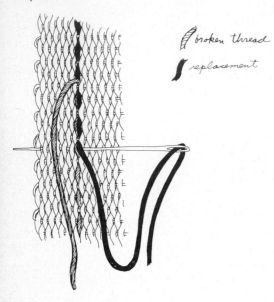

FIGURE 327. Darning in broken warp ends on a warp-face fabric.

broken thread

replacement

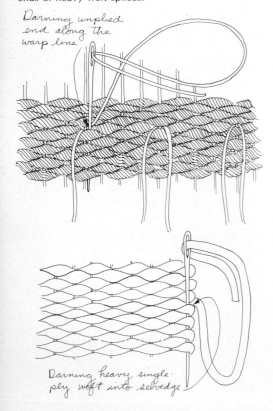

FIGURE 328. Two methods of treating the left-over ends of heavy weft splices.

Darning unplied end along the warp line

Darning heavy single-ply weft into selvedge

The Importance of Finishing

How a piece of weaving is finished determines, in part, its success or failure. A weaving just cut off the the loom can by no means be considered completed. Its durability and beauty depend on what final touches are given to it.

A minimum finishing requires the mending of warp and weft ends that, because of breakage or splicing, are left protruding from the fabric; the securing of warp ends to prevent unraveling of the weft (unless the piece was woven with all four selvedge edges as can only be done on the primitive stick looms); and often washing and pressing.

Following are directions for finishing your weaving properly, as well as some interesting ideas for added decorations.

Mending

With a large-eyed needle sew in any broken warp ends or weft splices as securely and invisibly as possible.

Warp-face fabrics

There will be no problem of weft splicings showing in this type of fabric. If there have been broken warp threads, untie the knot that was made when you repaired the broken thread, and sew one end along the warp line for about four inches, and then hide the end by having it travel along the line of the weft—completely hidden by the warp.

Weft-face fabrics

On many weft-face fabrics, if the weft is a single-ply yarn, the weft splice (if made properly with *broken,* rather than cut, ends) will not show at all and no additional treatment is necessary. If, however, the weft yarn is plied and heavy enough so that a splice would show up in the final weaving, it is treated in the following manner: Unply the end and break off at different points; then sew in these ends down along the warp line.

The treatment of broken warp threads in this type of fabric is simple. Untie the knot you made when you repaired the warp thread, sew *one* end along the same warp line for about 4 inches, and then trim off both protruding ends.

Balanced weaves (or any loose weaves where both warp and weft show)

You have to plan ahead when you are weaving a balanced or other loose weave, when it comes time to make a weft splice. It is best if it can be made at the edge of the fabric with no overlapping. Just start weaving with a new thread and leave both ends hanging out. These ends can then be sewn in along the selvedge line *if* the weft is of the same color as the warp. Or, they can be incorporated in an added-on fringe. Or, they can simply be trimmed off if the fabric is to be sewn or bound. If the ends cannot be dealt with in any of the above ways, the splice will have to be made by overlapping the ends. And the ends should be broken—not cut—in order for this splice to be as unobtrusive as possible, and so no further treatment of the splice is called for after the fabric is removed from the loom.

Warp mendings are more difficult, since you can't control where a warp thread is going to break; it may occur in the middle of the weaving. The only really satisfac-

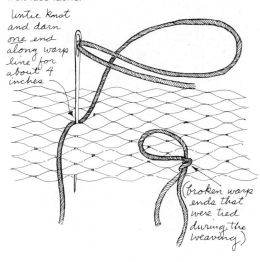

FIGURE 329. Darning in broken warp ends on a weft-face fabric.

untie knot and darn one end along warp line for about 4 inches

(broken warp ends that were tied during the weaving)

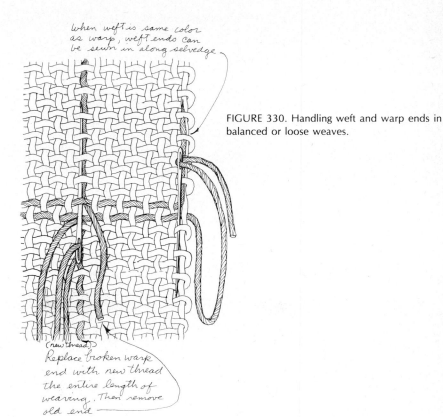

When weft is same color as warp, weft ends can be sewn in along selvedge

FIGURE 330. Handling weft and warp ends in balanced or loose weaves.

(new thread)
Replace broken warp end with new thread the entire length of weaving. Then remove old end

tory way to handle these warp threads is to leave enough of an end (when you tie on the new thread to repair the old) so that it can be sewn all the way to the beginning or end of the piece—completely replacing the original warp.

Whipped Fringe

The simplest fringe ending to prevent weft threads from unraveling when the warp ends are cut is made with a needle and weft thread while the fabric is right on the loom. This is not very durable but is fine for some light-weight fabrics, table mats, and wall hangings when—for some reason—other endings are not desirable.

The needle should pass under a very small group of warp threads and come out in the weaving down two or three weft threads. Draw the needle through, and pass it again under the same group of warp threads—this time keeping it free from the woven part of the fabric. Make sure the previous thread is laid underneath the needle before you draw it through; this makes a nice little loop that can be pulled tight around the warp ends. Continue across the warp. This should be done at the beginning of the fabric also, after you have woven a few inches, because it is much easier to do when the warp is stretched out on the loom. (You'll have to do it upside down at the beginning.)

Zigzagged Fringe

Although many purists scorn the use of a zigzag sewing machine, a very functional ending may be made by simply zigzagging along the edge of the weaving, incorporating 2 or 3 weft threads within the zigzag. If you use thread in a color similar to your yarn color, the stitching will be nearly invisible.

FIGURE 331. Two steps in making a whipped fringe.

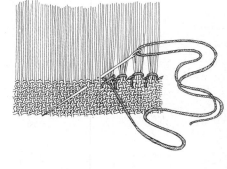

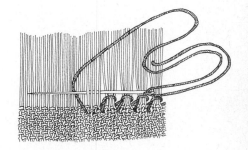

FIGURE 332. Weft threads secured by zigzagging.

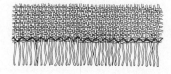

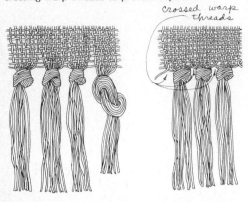

FIGURE 333. Knotted fringe and method of crossing warp threads to prevent separation.

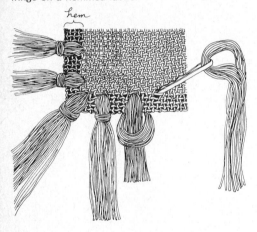

FIGURE 334. Adding on groups of threads for fringe on a hemmed fabric.

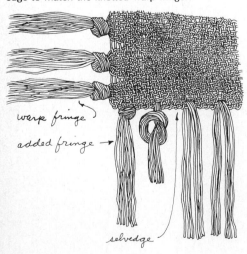

FIGURE 335. Adding on a fringe to the selvedge edge to match the knotted warp fringe.

Knotted Fringe

This is the most common fringe. Besides being decorative, it functions to secure the warp ends so that the weft won't unravel. Knotted fringe is useful for ponchos, blankets, and any weaving where a loose fringe is desirable and the warp ends will not receive much wear. It's not too good for rugs.

Place the material at the edge of a table with a heavy weight on it. Or make the fringe right on the loom immediately after cutting the warp threads and before unrolling the fabric from the cloth roller.

A group of warp threads, covering not more than 1 inch, and preferably less (unless the warp threads are spaced so far apart that it would make a skimpy fringe), is tied in the manner shown in Figure 333. Push the knot up as close as possible to the weaving. For ease in making these knots you will need warp ends at least 5 inches long.

If a separation of warp threads up in the weaving is objectionable, the last thread of one group can cross over and become the first thread of the next group.

The warp ends should be combed out and trimmed after fringing; this is best done on the pressing table. Comb the fringe out, steam press, and then trim.

Added Fringe

On certain pieces such as square ponchos, afghans, and bedspreads a decorative, nonfunctional fringe is desired on all four sides of the weaving (see also Four-Sided Fringe and Woven Fringe). The material can be hemmed in a neat rolled hem and then groups of threads tied on for the fringe. This can produce a heavy tassel-like fringe that is very handsome.

Cut the yarn double the length you want the fringe plus a couple of inches. Poke the group of threads for one tassel through the weaving with a bobby pin and loop it. Press and trim as described under Knotted Fringe.

To make a fringe on the selvedge edge of a fabric to match the warp fringe—or to add extra threads to make a fuller fringe—simply put groups of threads through the material with a bobby pin and tie the groups as in Knotted Fringe.

Twisted Fringe

This is a very beautiful and sturdy fringe, but more time-consuming than just tying knots. It is best suited to warp-face fabrics, where the warp ends are crowded, and it is most attractive if the ends are at least 8 inches long to begin with.

The belt or fabric must be in a fixed position (on a table, for instance, with a heavy weight). Take a small group of threads (six is a good number) and twist—*very tightly*—each individual thread in the same direction as the existing twist of the yarn. Wetting the ends before twisting helps make a good tight twist. It is most quickly done by rolling the yarn against your leg. Twisting each thread individually while holding the already twisted threads—with only two hands to work with—is a bit difficult. A clipboard may be used to hold the individually twisted threads. After all six threads are tightly twisted, hold the ends together and pull them in tension at the same time you twist the group as a whole in the opposite direction. You will see that they automatically hold this twist (the tighter you twist the individual threads to begin with, the tighter the group will hold its twist).

If the warp threads are different colors, you can select the threads of each group to be a common color or whatever you like. You can do this only to a certain extent; of course you can't take a thread too far out of place.

Tie a knot at the end, and trim.

Braided Fringe

A braided fringe is equally beautiful and strong as the twisted fringe—and faster to make. It makes a good ending for belts and especially rugs.

Pictured in Figure 337 are the 3-strand braid (which I presume everyone knows how to do), and the 4-strand braid, which is a bit more complicated, but just as fast when you master the technique. It is well worth learning.

The 4-strand braid is made as follows (2 colors of yarn can be paired up in different ways to get different designs):

1. Consider the 4 strands as 2 pairs (a and b; c and d).

2. Twist the "a and b" pair together once in a clockwise direction. (By "once," I mean just so that they switch positions.) Hold them apart.

3. Now, in the crotch of "a and b," twist "c and d" together in a *counter*-clockwise direction. Hold them apart.

4. In the crotch of "c and d," twist "a and b" together again in a clockwise direction.

5. Keep repeating these twists. This will seem terribly awkward at first, and I couldn't possibly attempt to tell you which fingers should hold which threads at which point. But you will soon figure out a way.

6. Tie a knot, and trim the ends.

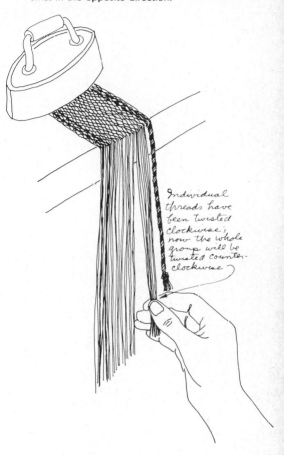

FIGURE 336. Putting an over twist in the individual threads so that the group will hold itself in a tight twist in the opposite direction.

Individual threads have been twisted clockwise; now the whole group will be twisted counter-clockwise

FIGURE 337. Fringe made of three or four strand braid.

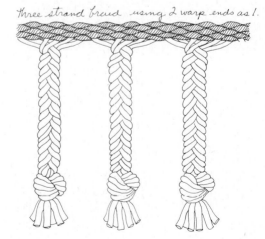

three strand braid using 2 warp ends as 1.

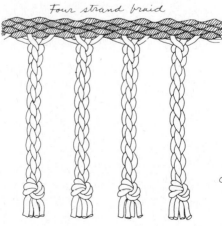

Four strand braid

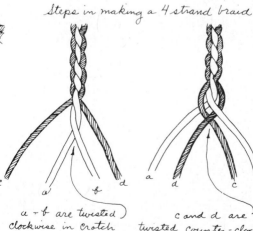

Steps in making a 4 strand braid

a + b are twisted clockwise in crotch of c + d.

c and d are twisted counter-clockwise in crotch of a + b.

FIGURE 338. Macramé fringe made of square knots.

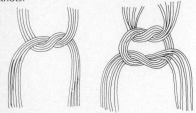

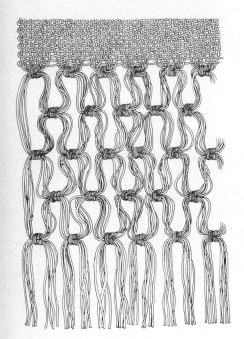

Macramé Fringe

An extravagant lacelike fringe can be made at the ends of stoles or the like, using the macramé technique. After a knot is made of a group of threads, this group is divided in half, and that half along with half of the adjacent group makes the next knot. The knot that is used is the square knot. The warp ends should be at *least* a foot long to start with, and more like 18 inches.

The Maori Edge

Thanks to Peter Collingwood, this neat rug edge, used by the Maoris of New Zealand, has been made known to many contemporary weavers. (At least I never knew about it until I read his *Techniques of Rug Weaving,* and if the credit for this shouldn't go to him . . . well, we have a lot to thank him for anyway.)

This edge serves to protect the weft threads at the beginning and end of the rug (or weaving), as well as to secure the warp ends. Successive warp ends are dropped and new ones added as the edge proceeds from one side of the rug to the other. The warp ends are left hanging out and pointing inward after they have done a couple of twists, and if they are linen, they can be left like this. However, if they are wool, I like either to darn them back into the weaving as in False Selvedge, or to make a 4-strand braided fringe in addition to a double Maori edge.

The edge is made with 4 warp ends at a time, and after certain twists are made, the first of those threads is eliminated and another added (the next warp end in line). The twists are repeated with this group of four (1 new, 3 old).

In Figure 339 are diagrams for making the twists. This illustration shows the original four threads shaded differently so you can follow the movements of each and determine which thread is which at any step along the way. In step 7 a new thread appears, and will be used in step 8. In step 8 the first thread of the original group is eliminated and the remaining 3 plus the new thread make a group exactly as in step 4. Continue repeating step 5 through step 8 all the way across the warp.

This edge leaves the warp ends turned up, toward the fabric. If you repeat the edge from the other side it will turn the ends down away from the weaving, like any ordinary fringe.

FIGURE 339. The Maori edge.

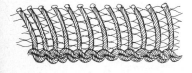

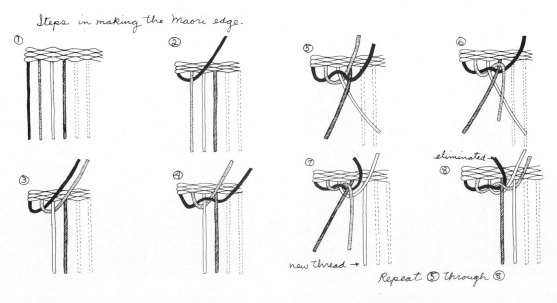

Steps in making the Maori edge.

new thread →

eliminated →

Repeat ⑤ through ⑧

Woven Fringe

Here is an easily and quickly woven tape with fringe protruding all along one edge. It can be sewn onto a finished piece of weaving. They often use it in the highlands of Peru and Bolivia to trim their ponchos (which are made with four selvedge edges). This woven fringe can be made on an inkle loom, a backstrap, or a Hopi belt loom —or even using the card-weaving technique. If you want a continuous tape that will go around the edges of a poncho (15 or 20 feet) you will have to use either the English-type inkle loom, backstrap loom, or card-weaving technique.

The design of the tape itself can be any warp-face design (alternating stripes, checkerboard, or something very fancy like a pickup pattern) or just perfectly plain. *Two* wefts are used: one, used in the regular manner, serves as the structural weft; and the other, which extends out an inch or so from the edge, becomes the fringe. This second weft is placed in *only every other shed,* and returns in the same shed. A common practice of the South Americans is to change the color of this weft every five inches or so to make a multi-colored fringe. It should be very tightly twisted yarn (probably you will have to respin it—see Chapter IX, "Spinning: Respinning Commercial Yarn") so that the loops will twist up on themselves. A tight cord used as a gauge for the length of the fringe can be strung up on the loom bars of an inkle loom, or you can simply use a smooth flat stick and hold it as a gauge each time you place a shot of the fringe weft.

Four-Sided Fringe

To make a piece of weaving that will automatically have weft ends as well as warp ends with which to make fringe, you can simply thread three or four extra warp ends on each side of the warp, spaced out far enough to leave weft ends that can be knotted (or whatever) for a fringe. This technique is only appropriate for balanced weaves where the warp and weft are the same yarns, so that the fringe on all four sides will be the same.

Tab Fringe

This is a technique used often by the ancient Peruvians. It is most suitable for use on the primitive looms, where you weave right to top and bottom selvedges, but can be used on a treadle loom if the warp ends are sewn back in as described under False Selvedge in this chapter. The fringe is achieved by weaving slits in the first and last few inches of weaving. It can be a very interesting addition to certain wall hangings.

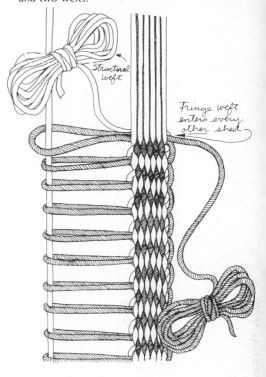

FIGURE 340. Weaving a fringe with a gauge cord and two wefts.

Structural weft

Fringe weft enters every other shed

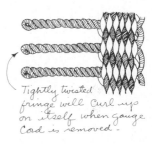

Tightly twisted fringe will curl up on itself when gauge cord is removed.

FIGURE 341. Weaving the weft out a few inches from the sides (using extra warp threads as a gauge to form fringe on sides of the weaving).

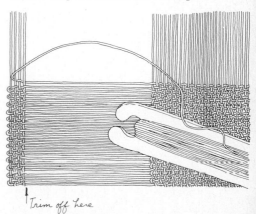

Trim off here

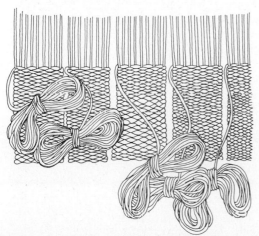

FIGURE 342. The weaving of a tab fringe requires a separate butterfly of weft for each tab.

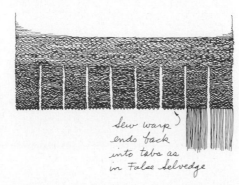

Sew warp ends back into tabs as in False Selvedge

FIGURE 343. A card-woven edge.

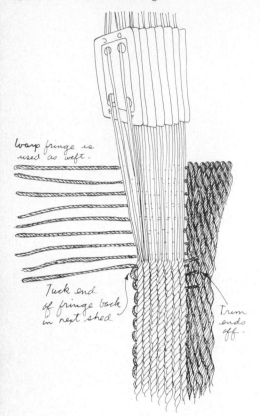

warp fringe is used as weft.

Tuck end of fringe back in next shed

Trim ends off.

FIGURE 344. Bottom and side selvedges on a traditional Navajo rug.

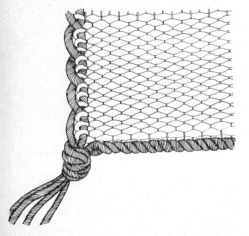

FIGURE 345. Sewing in the warp ends to make the edge look similar to a selvedge edge made on a primitive loom.

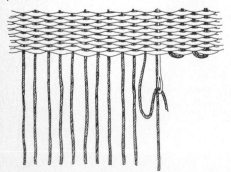

Card-Woven Edge

A warp for a card-woven band can be set up alongside the end of a newly finished rug (or any type of weaving), and the band woven using the warp ends of the rug as weft for the band. A neat—and certainly sturdy!—ending for a rug.

Navajo Selvedges

Directions for making the traditional top and bottom twisted selvedges and the side selvedge of a Navajo rug are given in Chapter VI, "The Navajo Loom."

False Selvedge

This is a perfectly simple technique—but very time-consuming. Just thread each warp end through the eye of a large needle and sew it back into the weaving along the line of the warp thread adjacent to it. If warp ends are very short, push needle into fabric, then thread the eye with the warp end and pull it into the weaving.

Selvedges

There are different ways of making the side selvedges in fabrics, each way suitable for certain types of weaves. Generally, what it amounts to is a crowding of warp threads in the last quarter or half-inch at each edge—and this gives the edge more strength.

The crowding is accomplished by sleying twice or three times as many threads through the last two or three dents of the reed at each edge. *Then,* the threads may be threaded through the heddles in one of three ways: (1) double or tripled sleyed through the heddles (just the same as through the dents of the reed); (2) threaded in the same manner as the body of the weaving; (3) threaded in a tabby weave, regardless of the type of weave used for the fabric.

The first method is usually used in weft-face fabrics, such as rugs, where a thickened corded effect is desired. The second is suitable for blankets, throws, ponchos, etc., where a differentiated selvedge is *not* desirable; the weave *looks* the same, but is just slightly tighter at the edges. The third method is really only suitable for yardage; it forms a selvedge similar to what you see on commercial fabrics.

When weaving certain weaves the edge warp thread or threads are sometimes missed by the weft. This is not the result of anything you are doing wrong, and it will require hand manipulation to make a correct edge. This can also happen when weaving with two or three wefts in succession. What happens is that the edge warp thread is in the same up or down position it was in when the weft *left* the previous shed. This problem can be handled in numerous ways. Sometimes starting the weaving by throwing the shuttle from left to right (or vice versa) is all it takes. You'll have to experiment to see if that will work.

When weaving with more than one color, you can make a nice edge by simply laying one shuttle down and picking the next one up in such a way that the two weft threads cross over each other and are thus locked at the edge. And there are ways of manipulating the threads—sometimes even wrapping one color around the edge warp thread an extra time to make up for the gap left by another color when it missed the edge thread—so that one color alone makes the edge.

In a weave where the edge thread is missed regularly, you might try taking it out of its heddle, and just have it go through the reed. This means that it will float in the middle of the shed, and you can choose whether to put the shuttle over it or under it. It is called a floating selvedge.

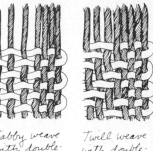
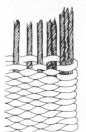

FIGURE 346. Different ways of treating the edge warp threads.

Weft-face weave with triple and double sleyed warp threads at selvedge.

Tabby weave with double-sleyed tabby selvedge.

Twill weave with double-sleyed tabby selvedge.

Rolled Hem

On certain items, a neat rolled hem is the most suitable finishing for edges. The roll can be as large or small as desired.

I find using a good sewing thread (doubled) of an appropriate color and weight is the neatest and most invisible way to hem. The warp ends should first be secured, either by tying a knotted fringe and then trimming close, or by hand whipping or zigzagging on the sewing machine, then trimming the warp ends quite close to the stitching. The edge is then rolled under to hide the knots or stitches and hand sewn with a slip stitch.

The needle enters the fabric in a spot *directly opposite* (this is the whole secret to the invisibility) where the thread comes out of the rolled hem. It just barely catches in the material, then diagonals up underneath the roll, and comes out right at the edge of the roll. When pulled tight the thread is invisible.

FIGURE 347. Sewing a rolled hem so that the thread is invisible.

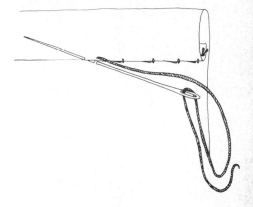

Peruvian Rolled Edge

This is a woven edge that actually rolls around to meet the back surface of the weaving. It is useful mostly for belts and sashes; occurring naturally on belts woven in the double cloth technique—see Chapter V, "The Backstrap Loom: Double Cloth Sash (Bolivian)"—but can be an added attraction on a plain warp-face belt. The edge where the roll is to occur is simply woven with the weft circling around an extra time.

On the left-hand side, the weft enters the warp at the inside edge of the roll (about ten warp threads in) and passes all the way across to the right outer edge. The shed is changed and the weft then passes in the *same direction* (from left to right) but only through the ten warp threads in the section to be rolled. At this point the weft is pulled tight to close the gap made by the weft crossing over the warp threads.

With the shed in the *same* position, the weft passes from right to left, entering the warp (*not* at the edge) at the inside of the roll. It passes all the way across to the left. The shed is changed, and the weft again enters on the inside edge of the roll and passes from right to left. The shed *remains* in this position, and the weft again skips over the warp threads in the rolled section and enters the warp to return to the right-hand edge of the belt, and is pulled tight. Obviously the weft must be hand beaten (no reed can be used), so the technique is most suitable for primitive looms or the inkle loom.

FIGURE 348. A Peruvian rolled edge showing the route of the weft.

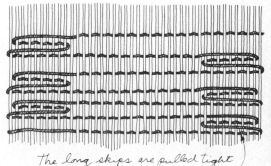

The long skips are pulled tight and the edge rolls around.

Peruvian Rolled Edge (Added On)

An edge similar to the one described above can be added onto a piece of completed weaving. It is actually a warp-face tape that is *woven and sewn on all in the same operation.* Those clever Indians of the Andes use it to bind the side seams and top edges of their coca bags, and sometimes to trim the edges of their ponchos. You will find it useful mainly for edging handbags, pillows, or blankets. It is not the time-consuming process you might think; actually it proceeds very quickly.

A warp of a few threads (enough to make a warp-face tape the width you need

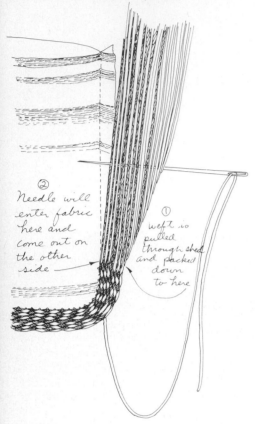

FIGURE 349. The item to which the edge is to be added is held alongside a warp and the weft is threaded through a needle. The edge is woven *and* sewn to the item all in one operation.

② Needle will enter fabric here and come out on the other side ⟶

① weft is pulled through shed and packed down to here

—maybe a half-inch width; the narrower it can be and still do the job of covering the seams or edge, the nicer it looks) is set up on an inkle, backstrap, or Hopi loom, with heddles operating exactly as if you were just going to weave a narrow band.

Now hold the edge of the weaving that you want bound right along parallel to the warp, on the left-hand side of the warp. Thread a large needle with your weft. Pass the needle through the first shed from right to left. Insert the needle into the edge of the material to be bound, and bring it out underneath. Change sheds. Pack down the weft. Now pass the needle through this new shed, again from right to left; then down through the material and out from the underneath side. In this way you are weaving the band and sewing it on with the weft thread all in one operation. Notice that the weft passes through each shed always from right to left.

You can, of course, turn corners when necessary.

Gimp (Narrow Woven Band)

"Gimp" is any narrow flat woven band of trimming that is sewn onto material. Very attractive gimps can be woven on the inkle, backstrap, or Hopi loom—either in warp-face or tabby weave (weft-face is not as practical because of the time involved). Card-woven bands are beautiful but tend to be a bit thick unless made with very fine yarns. Bands about one or one and a half inches wide provide a decorative edging for throws, ponchos, capes, pillows, etc. They are very quickly made and give the item they are added to a very professional, finished look. Just follow the directions for Project I in Chapter II, "Card Weaving," Project I in Chapter III, "The Inkle Loom," and hand sew the gimp to the item.

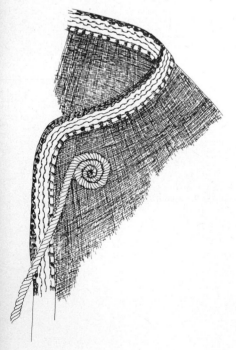

FIGURE 350. Gimp used as edging for a cape.

Peruvian Braid

This is an unusual hand-braiding technique. The look of the final product is my favorite of all bands, belts, or sashes. It cannot be classified as weaving, but I want to show you how to do it . . . so here it is, under "Finishing Techniques." It is time-consuming, but the results are beautiful.

Cut your yarn (a strong, tightly twisted wool yarn, medium fine) half again as long as you want the final belt or sash. Cut several lengths in different colors, but always figure on *pairs* in each color since it takes two threads of the same color to make a line in the braiding. And there should be an *even* number of pairs—so there can be the same number of pairs on each side of center. For your first attempt use only 10 pairs, each about 1 yard long.

Tie these threads to a stick or dowel that is about a foot long (a ruler or thick pencil will do in a pinch). Leave tails long enough so that you can later make a fringe; the braiding will start right at the stick. Tie the threads to the stick in pairs, making several pairs of one color in certain areas for variation in size of the bands. If you want an asymmetrical pattern (my favorite), just tie the threads on in any sequence and let it be a surprise how the pattern comes out. If you want a symmetrical chevron pattern then you have to arrange the colors symmetrically on each side of center.

Beginning these braids is difficult even when you know how to do it, so you will just have to muster up all your courage and patience to get started. But believe me, when you know how to do it, you will agree that it is a worthwhile technique to learn.

Divide the threads into two equal groups on either side of center. The threads are always handled as two separate groups, even though pairs from one side eventually transfer to the other side. (As a beginner, you had better tie the stick rigidly to a chair or other stable object so you won't have any problems with it. Later you can just hold it between your knees or pin the braid to the leg of your pants.)

1. Take the outer pair of threads on the right side and twist it in a clockwise direction, encircling each adjacent pair of threads as you come to them. Make a single twist around the first pair, and another twist around the next pair, and so on until every pair of the right-hand group has been encircled. Always concentrate on keeping the threads in the *two separate groups.*

After you have twisted the first pair around all the other pairs on that half of the band, that first pair will have its ends all tangled among the other ends. Pull these two ends through the others so that they are free and untangled; this sometimes means doing it one thread at a time if they are very long. Do this *every* time an outer pair reaches the center and that's all you will have to do to keep the threads in perfect order.

2. Now start with the outer pair of threads on the left-hand group, and twist it around each pair in succession until you reach the center. This left-hand pair will be twisted *counter*clockwise. Pull the ends through just as you did with the first pair.

3. Both pairs are now at the center. Interlock the four threads as shown in Figure 354. The outer pair that was originally at the right becomes the inner pair of the left-hand group, and vice versa. Hold the two groups in your hands and pull them apart; this serves to tighten up the braiding.

These three steps are the entire braiding process. So now you will start at the right side again and take the new outer pair and twist it around the adjacent pairs. But the twist this time is in the opposite direction from the twist of the first pair—in other words *counter*clockwise. The same with the left-hand group. Each pair on each side is twisted in the opposite direction from the previous row.

This is *one* of the great difficulties in this technique—knowing which way to twist the pairs. But at any point you can tell which way you should twist by doing one of two things. First, when you are starting a new pair from the outside, look at the direction of the twist in the previous row and make it the opposite. Second, at any point down the line of twists if you have forgotten which way you are twisting, just remember that you are making a *two-ply rope* of your pair of threads and keep the rope twisting in the same direction. Pull the braiding apart a little so you can observe the pair you are working with as an entity in itself; it will then be obvious which way you should twist.

The other great difficulty (at times to the point of utter confusion) is keeping the threads equally divided at the center. Sometimes the pair that you have just twisted on the right side is mistaken for an inner pair on the left, and is encircled by that left-hand pair when it gets to the center. The only way to prevent this from happening is always to hold the two groups separately, *and* allow any pairs that have just been twisted to hang down *alone* in the center. This really means making good use of just about every finger you have.

As a beginner at this technique, don't ever stop in the middle of steps 1, 2, and 3. Proceed with the twisting of the outer pairs from *both* sides, interlock them in the center, and separate those two groups well—before you lay your work down. (Forget the telephone or the pot burning on the stove!) Tie the right-hand group and the left-hand group into two separate loose knots if you are leaving your work for some time.

FIGURE 351. A belt made with the Peruvian braid technique.

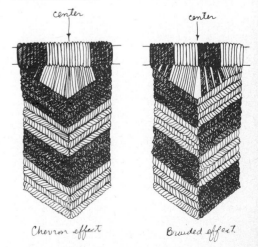

FIGURE 352. Chevron or braided effect, depending on symmetrical or asymmetrical arrangement of treads on the stick.

center   *center*

Chevron effect   *Braided effect*

FIGURE 353. Starting the first row of twists.

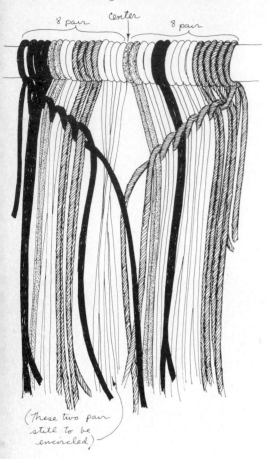

8 pair   center   8 pair

(These two pair
still to be
encircled)

FIGURE 354. Interlocking the center pairs and grouping them with the threads of the opposite side.

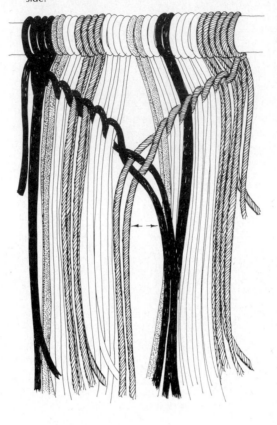

FIGURE 355. Keeping the pair that has done the twist isolated so it won't be mistaken for a pair of the other side.

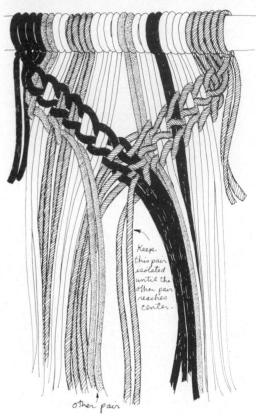

Keep
this pair
isolated
until the
other pair
reaches
center.

other pair

FIGURE 356. Six strand rickrack.

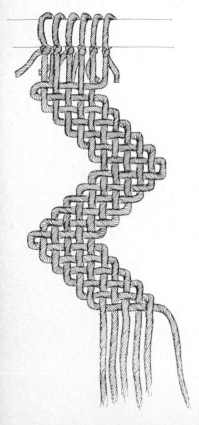

Rickrack

Never did I realize when I was stitching dime-store rickrack onto my first dress in junior-high home-economics class that the little braid I was working with was invented by the ancient Peruvians. Handmade rickrack of beautiful tightly twisted wool or hair (or cotton or linen) is quite different from the dime-store rickrack—and a delightful decoration for vests or skirts, or even tacked onto the edges of a belt or sash.

Four or more threads may be used, and the illustration will have to be self-explanatory.

Rope

Ropes are sometimes desired as belts for handwoven garments, ties for capes, etc., or handles for bags. They are very nice when made from the same yarns as the weaving.

Take two groups of threads (anywhere from two to ten threads to a group), all of the same color, or each group a different color. They have to be about four times as long as you want the final rope to be. Tie ends of each group to some fixed object. Take the free ends of one group, stretch the threads out tight, and twist by rolling between your palms or a palm and a thigh—very tightly in one direction (it doesn't matter which). Lay a weight on this group or secure it in some fashion while doing the same to the other group—twisting in the same direction as the first.

Now take both twisted groups and twist them *together* in the opposite direction, *very, very tightly*. Now, while still holding the ends, double that twisted rope over at the halfway point and let it twist up on itself. Tie both ends of this final rope with a knot to prevent the ends from unraveling. How tightly the final rope is twisted depends on how tightly it was twisted just before it was folded over.

There are inexpensive little wooden gadgets called "rope machines" that I hear are marvelous for making ropes (see Chapter XIII, "Suppliers: Weaving Equipment").

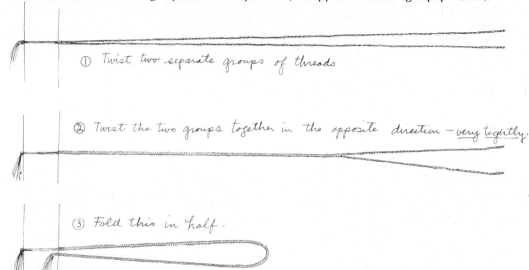

① Twist two separate groups of threads

② Twist the two groups together in the opposite direction — <u>very tightly</u>.

③ Fold this in half.

④ Let it twist up on itself. Tie ends where rope is cut.

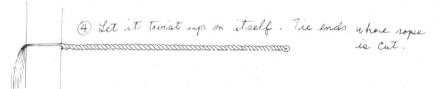

FIGURE 357. Four steps in making a rope of several strands of yarn.

Wrapping

Sometimes you want to wrap colored thread around a group of threads to bind them together, or just for decoration. Beautiful multi-colored bands of wrapping can be made on belt fringes, ropes, etc., or on groups of warp ends on wall hangings. The diagrams in Figure 358 will show you how to lock the ends of the wrappings invisibly.

Tassels

Tassels are another bit of decoration to add to weavings when appropriate. They are nice when locked onto the end of a four-strand braid. The illustrations in Figure 359 will (I hope) be self-explanatory. The preceding wrapping technique can be put to good use in making tassels.

Feathers

Feathers may be added to weavings in many different ways, two of which are described here.

1. Attach feathers to the ends of strands of yarn (warp ends, for instance) by

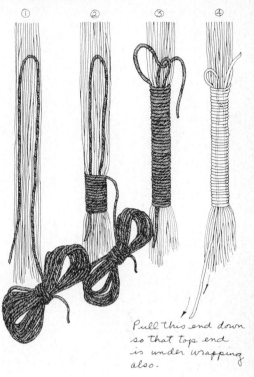

FIGURE 358. Four steps in wrapping to make ends secure and invisible.

Pull this end down so that top end is under wrapping also.

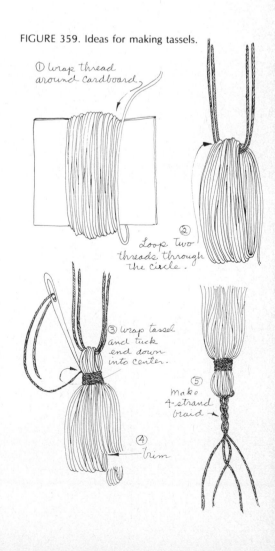

FIGURE 359. Ideas for making tassels.

① Wrap thread around cardboard.

② Loop two threads through the circle.

③ Wrap tassel and tuck end down into center.

④ trim

⑤ make 4-strand braid

FIGURE 360. Feathers attached to warp ends by wrapping technique and feathers sewn onto fabric.

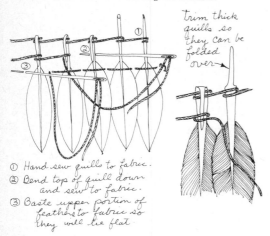

FIGURE 361. Method of sewing on feathers.

trim thick quills so they can be folded over→

① Hand sew quills to fabric.
② Bend top of quill down and sew to fabric.
③ Baste upper portion of feathers to fabric so they will lie flat

FIGURE 362. Beads incorporated in the weaving and added to warp ends.

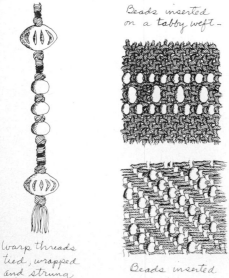

Beads inserted on a tabby weft.

Warp threads tied, wrapped and strung with beads.

Beads inserted on a twill weft.

wrapping the quill and the strand of yarn with appropriate yarn, using the wrapping technique described on page 205.

2. Several layers of feathers, arranged in a design or pattern, can be sewn onto a finished piece of weaving. Use the method illustrated in Figure 361, each layer covering the sewing of the previous layer. The stitching for the final row of feathers could be covered with gimp or rickrack or other trimming. Large feathers with thick quills require the previous trimming of the quill.

Beads

Many interesting things can be done with beads. Figure 362 shows how to incorporate them in the weaving (by threading them on the warp or on the weft); and how to add them to ends of yarn. Obviously beads cannot be threaded on the warp if you are using a treadle loom and reed.

Brushing

Brushing is also sometimes called "napping"—a contradictory word, since this process, when done by hand, is one of the most strenuous processes in weaving. Most manufactured woolens are brushed to raise a nap. In handweaving this is sometimes done on a throw or rug, if you want it to be fuzzy. Weavings of mohair yarn, when brushed, are very luxurious. Brushed wool is nice too, but tends to ball up more than mohair, unless it is shorn evenly after it is brushed—a process that would be very difficult to do well by hand.

Ordinary hand cards (for carding wool) or a dog brush may be used. If you do use your hand cards, do not expect to use them for their regular purpose, because the brushing process will ruin them.

The brushing is best done while the fabric is on the loom, in tension. This means that each section as it is woven, and before it is rolled onto the cloth roller, must be brushed. Brushing the material after it is off the loom can be difficult, as the cards sometimes catch on threads and break them before you realize what is happening. There is less likelihood of this happening when the material is held in a rigid position.

The direction in which the fabric is brushed depends on which threads—the warp or the weft—you want to be raised the most. If the pattern or color that you want to stand out is in the warp, you should brush horizontally *across* the warp. If you wish the weft color to predominate, you should brush vertically, across the weft. Or you can brush both ways. If both sides of the fabric are to be brushed, the under side is done as it passes around the cloth roller.

For a particularly interesting effect with brushing, see Chapter X, "Dyeing: Techniques for Special Effects."

Dampening the fabric facilitates the brushing, but increases the danger of tearing the threads.

Washing

In textile mills, nearly all fabric is washed after it is woven. The washing can take place during the common commercial practice of "fulling" or "felting" (which I will discuss in a moment)—a process that actually thickens and mats the material. In handweaving, washing is a matter of preference. It tends to soften the fabric. For this reason I usually wash any weaving that is to be used for clothing and don't wash rugs or wall hangings, belts, or bags because they are nicer when they are "crisp."

Washing handwoven wool fabrics (or fabrics of other fibers) is a simple process. If wool or hair fibers are involved, you should read the section Washing the Raw Wool in Chapter IX, "Spinning," so you'll know what actually happens to the wool fiber when it is subjected to water, soaps or detergents, heat and agitation.

The fabric should be washed as a good sweater would be: in cold water, with a mild detergent. Detergent will cause less change in the fiber than soap. If your yarns are dyed with fast colors, you can let the fabric soak for 15 minutes; then slosh gently and press the moisture out of the fabric, or spin dry. With dyes that bleed you will have to make the process much shorter—2 minutes at the most. You can check the yarns to see if they will bleed by soaking them in hot water. The synthetic dyes in this book will not bleed.

The fabric should be rinsed a couple of times in cold water, spun dry, and laid out on a towel or hung up to dry on a pole or some such rounded object rather than on a wire or rope clothesline. (If this is impossible, any creases formed by the clothesline will usually come out during steam pressing.) Unless you want the material to fuzz up and thicken (felt) a bit, never put your wool or hair weavings in the dryer—even at cool temperatures.

A word of warning when using an automatic washer: Certain yarns (usually hair) and types of weaves (tight, hard weaves) will crease badly during the spin-dry cycle; and in plain-colored fabrics these creases can show up quite badly, *and* will not come out even with excessive steam pressing. Most textured, heavy, patterned fabrics come out beautifully from the spin-dry cycle. It is desirable to get as much water as you can out of the fabric before setting it out to dry: excessive moisture remaining in the fabric may cause very slow drying and result in stains.

If you use this careful washing process, all your handwoven items can be washed when the time comes, rather than dry-cleaned, if you wish to avoid the expense. However, dry cleaning is still the safest of all cleaning methods for wool fabrics, because it causes no change whatsoever in the wool fiber or the dyes. Some weavers simply send all their finished weavings to the cleaners, but this gets to be much too expensive if you are producing a lot.

Steam pressing, which I will discuss shortly, is usually necessary after washing, to make the fabric look its best.

An Indian woman showed me how she cleans her rugs: she lays the rug out on the snow, sprinkles broomfuls of fresh snow onto it, and then sweeps it clean.

Fulling

Also called "felting," this is a washing process designed purposely to mat or "felt" the material. As I mentioned before, many commercial fabrics receive this treatment. The materials are woven loosely, so that when they are agitated in hot soapy water they mat up, to whatever degree is desired—depending on how long they are subjected to the hot water, soap, and agitation.

Wool flannels are made this way. When touring a textile mill once, I saw huge bolts of material that was eventually to be gray wool flannel for suiting. Just after it was taken off the loom it was similar in texture to cheesecloth—a very skimpy, light, airy fabric. The final appearance—soft and thick—depended entirely on the fulling process; and sometimes the material is brushed and shorn as well.

Handweavers rarely use this process, but sometimes an item such as a scarf or blanket can purposely be woven loose and airy, then put in the washer with hot soapy water and agitated for five minutes or so to make it thicker, softer, and fuzzier.

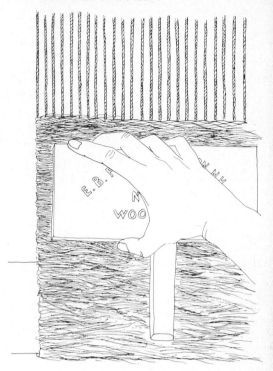

FIGURE 363. Brushing with hand cards while fabric is still on the loom.

Pressing

Steam pressing the finished weaving, whether it has been washed or not, serves to take out any slight bulges that might have occurred in the weaving because of imperfect warp or weft tension, and also makes the yarns "relax."

Steam pressing should be done on a soft padded surface, with a very hot iron, and (*most important*) with a wet cotton cloth, such as an old sheet. *Never* touch an iron directly to the fabric if it is wool or hair—even a steam iron on its lowest setting. The cotton pressing cloth should be rewetted each time it is put on a new area of the fabric to be pressed, and the iron should be passed over it lightly (using the weight of the iron only) until the pressing cloth is completely dry. Heavy pressure on the fabric tends to flatten out the yarn and take away the beauty of the texture. Allow the fabric to dry out (because it will still be slightly damp from all the steam) in a flat position for a half-hour or so.

Comb out fringes and press them *before* trimming.

For large items such as rugs and blankets, a large table temporarily padded with two or three blankets (it won't hurt them) makes a good ironing board. Or better still, you can make a heavily padded table about 2 feet wide and 6 feet long with a sleeve extension on one end.

The Navajos have an interesting way of "pressing" their rugs. They bury them perfectly flat in damp sand and leave them for several hours (or maybe days . . . I'm not sure).

Joining

FIGURE 364. Two methods of joining two fabrics.

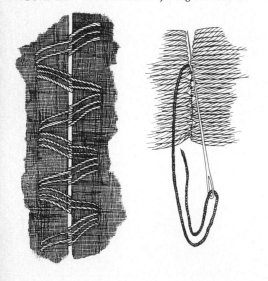
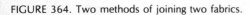

Sometimes you can't weave a fabric as wide as you want all in one piece. For such cases here are two professional-looking ways of joining two pieces of weaving.

Method 1. The two pieces of fabric are laid side by side on a flat surface, making sure ends match (check this often as you sew, because they tend to get out of line). With a large needle and the same thread as the warp, you sew up through a few weft threads on one edge and then up through the same number on the other. This method is mainly useful for weft-face fabrics.

Method 2. Using a large needle and yarn to match the weft (or any color if you want a decorative effect, even changing the color every time the needle runs out), sew from the under side of one piece to the top surface of the other piece at a diagonal. In other words, your needle enters one side from the top (about one-quarter inch in from the edge), comes up *in between* the two fabrics, and enters again from the top side of the second piece (about one-quarter inch in from the edge). This is a nice joining for poncho widths: they use it a lot in South America.

Sewing

People often are afraid to cut into a handwoven fabric for fear it will unravel. And it *is* tricky, for anything but very tightly woven, more or less balanced weaves. Warp- and weft-face fabrics—no matter how tightly woven—unravel very easily, and, of course, so do loosely woven fabrics of any weave. You have probably noticed that authentic "ethnic" garments of handwoven materials are usually designed in such a way that no cutting of the fabric is necessary; only squares and rectangles are put together. If any cutting and seaming is done, the seams are always nicely covered with some tape or handmade binding.

If you are going to cut and seam garments of your handwoven fabric, it is almost essential to have a sewing machine. The stitches of a machine serve to catch all the warp and weft threads, allowing none of them to fray. Probably the safest way to cut into the fabric is to do so only after a line of stitching just inside the cutting line is made. This keeps the fabric not only from fraying, but from getting stretched out of shape. Certainly this method should be used for any very loose fabric woven with very heavy yarns, where only two or three threads make up an inch of fabric. But I find that for most handwoven fabric, if it is handled very carefully after it is cut, and sewn up immediately after cutting, the preliminary stitching is not necessary.

I find commercially woven wool binding indispensable (unless you weave your own gimp) for binding edges and covering seams—for a really professional look. This binding can be found in most sewing centers of department stores or dime stores. It is a folded-over wool bias tape about one inch in width (one-half inch when folded over). Unfortunately Orlon (which you should not use) is replacing wool, and it may be difficult for you to locate pure wool. The wool tape can usually be purchased in white or gray as well as in many different colors. I always buy it in the white or natural and dye it along with the yarn for a specific project.

A sloppy job of sewing will ruin the effect of any garment, no matter how beautiful the material was to start with. Concentrate on sewing in very straight lines and keeping perfect alignment of the stitches and the tape (if you are using it). Basting is not necessary if you feed the tape in with the same tension as the fabric. Feed in plenty of extra length around outside corners. For binding edges, it is best to stitch the tape (or gimp) to the front side of the material, fold it over the edge, and hand sew it on the back side. Always hand sew it over inner seams.

If you can't locate this tape, try making your own (the finished product will be just that much more beautiful), or make the Peruvian Rolled Edge (Added On), described in this chapter.

Instead of cutting and sewing buttonholes, try adding on loops of leather or cord (made of the same yarn as the fabric). Approach the sewing not as a seamstress, but as a craftsman.

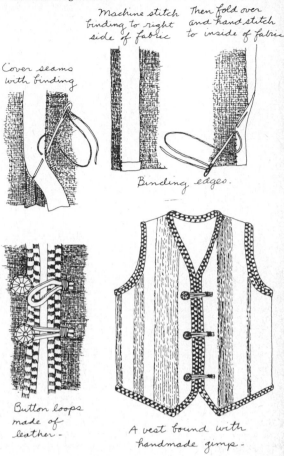

FIGURE 365. A few techniques used in sewing handwoven garments.

Machine stitch binding to right side of fabric

Then fold over and hand stitch to inside of fabric.

Cover seams with binding

Binding edges.

Button loops made of leather.

A vest bound with handmade gimp.

Overdyeing

Once in a while you may finish a piece and find that you don't like the colors at all —they're too garish. You may be able to save it (maybe actually make it terrific) by overdyeing it. By this I mean dyeing the material a light tint that will serve to harmonize the colors. This has to be done carefully—choosing the right color to overdye and doing it lightly enough so the piece won't look like just an amateur job. Nothing is more disturbing than a fabric heavily dyed so that it is all more or less the same color, but in which you can just distinguish the pattern that was originally there.

The overdye job should be so subtle that it just barely tones down the colors. For example: Suppose you made a throw of yellows, oranges, and deep reds. When you chose the colors you thought they would go together, but now that the throw is woven it seems too bright. If you put this in a dye bath of clear pale blue, you will end up with greenish yellow, rust or brownish orange, and maroon. The blue will tone down each of the colors just slightly, to make them more muted and harmonizing.

In general it is best to make the dyebath a clear pale color of the hue *opposite* to the majority of colors in the weaving. Another example would be a fabric of bright blue, bright green, yellow, black and white. If you dyed this a clear light reddish orange (the opposite hue), you would get slate gray, an earthy green, yellow orange, black and light orange or peach. Sounds interesting, doesn't it?

The dyeing of the fabric can be done in a washing machine with very hot water.

If you do it in a pot you will have to stir it constantly to make sure it doesn't come out uneven. Uneven dyeing of yarn before it is woven is one thing; uneven dyeing of fabric is very unattractive. You will have to be careful that the fabric is not subjected too long to the hot water and agitation; remember these cause "felting." For this reason the dyebath should have a fairly concentrated amount of dye, so that to get a pale color you have to leave the fabric in it for only a minute or two. I, of course, use the acid wool dyes described in this book; but, if you have not gotten into dyeing, and just want to do this one overdye job, simply get some Rit or other dime-store dye and follow the directions—except use a large amount and a short dyeing time.

Be sure *not* to pull the fabric from the dyebath and put it in cold rinse water. Either let it cool off first or have the rinse water hot also. It should be spun dry if possible, so as to get all the moisture out, before laying or hanging it out to dry. Steam press and comb and trim fringes (if there are any) afterward.

You could also try tie-dyeing the finished weaving.

Wall Hangings

Wall hangings present a special finishing problem. How to hang them? After years of working with and thinking about this problem I have finally come to the conclusion that the weaver should *not* provide any special device for hanging. But if one is absolutely essential, that device should be a structural part of the design. The textile should be hung with no special rods or bars attached as intermediates. To put it bluntly: the weaving should be just nailed onto the wall. I have rarely seen a rod, slat, or bar permanently attached to the weaving for the purpose of hanging it that I thought was completely artistic.

But, if you disagree with me (and you probably will), here are some suggestions for ways of hanging your weaving.

Perhaps the most successful method would be to design the top end of the weaving in such a way that a beautiful hardwood rod could be slipped into slits or loops. This is better than weaving the rod right into the fabric, because then there is the disadvantage that the weaving could never be cleaned.

For a large tapestry weaving where you would not want the hanging device to show (and which you don't want to nail to the wall directly), you can sew a tube of linen or cotton on the back top edge and slip a sturdy slat through it. The slat can have screw eyes at each end to which wires or cords are attached that would go straight up to the molding. Or the two ends of the slat could rest on only two nails in the wall. Then nothing but the actual weaving shows.

For three-dimensional free-hanging weavings, the problem is more complex, and usually some device for hanging is essential and is best worked right into the woven design.

FIGURE 366. Some ideas for hanging tapestries and wall hangings.

warp threads wrapped to make loops for holding rod.

Slits woven in fabric.

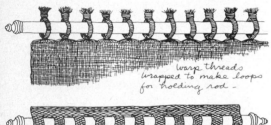

Fabric sewn to back side of hanging; wooden slat inserted and provided with screw eyes.

CHAPTER IX

SPINNING

Why Spin Your Own Yarn?

If you are familiar with handspun yarns you know how much more interesting and beautiful they are than most commercial yarns. Almost anything woven with home-spun is more valuable than the same thing made of commercial yarn. The main reasons weavers, knitters, or anyone doing crocheting and embroidery *don't* use handspun yarn is probably its lack of availability and its cost. Handspun yarn is definitely more costly than commercial yarn—even when it is imported from countries where the spinner is paid virtually nothing for his work. By the time everyone has taken his cut and the craftsman has it in his hands, the price is high.

Some weavers think it would take too much of their time to spin their yarn, or think they don't have the right personality for such "boring" work. But with the right equipment and the right raw materials you can prepare and spin a pound of medium- to heavy-weight yarn in approximately an hour. The cost of the raw materials is very little, and spinning is actually a very soothing activity if one is feeling harassed. It is not the tedious, exacting craft you might think.

For thousands of years people have been spinning fibers on many different kinds of homemade equipment. It is a skill that is easily learned, and you will find—if you try it—that after about the first hour of spinning you will be feeling comfortable with it. You don't need to have a spinning wheel. In fact, if you want to right now, you can take a pencil, a potato, and a few balls of cotton batting and become a spinner. Of course, if you plan to do much spinning you will probably want some equipment that will speed up the process—a good spinning wheel, or maybe even an electric spinner. But we'll discuss that later.

I'll teach you how to spin wool on a drop spindle (or that pencil and potato), and within an hour you can be spinning perfect, fine yarn. It will be very slow, but speed will come with practice. I've found that it is better to learn on a drop spindle than on a spinning wheel. On the latter the tendency is to have difficulty keeping up with the speed of the spindle, and you learn to make thick, lumpy yarn that is overspun. The basic principle with a spinning wheel is the same as with the drop spindle; you just have to learn slightly different techniques.

First, however, you'll need to know something about the raw materials—as well as where to get them and how to prepare them for spinning. Our emphasis will be on wool and hair, but once you have learned to spin wool, you will have no difficulty spinning other fibers.

Some Interesting Facts about Wool

The original sheep long ago actually had a coat of hair with an undercoat of wool, like the husky dog with its fine wool (or down), which is shed in warm weather. Gradually the hair was bred out of the sheep, so that now many sheep have coats that are all wool. The Merino sheep is the most highly bred of the wool-bearing animals and has the finest wool. If you can believe it, as many as *fifty-six thousand* fibers grow from one square inch of hide on this sheep.

The individual wool fiber is a fantastic little object in itself. It is composed of a *cuticle*: an outer layer of tiny gelatin-like scales laid somewhat like shingles from root to tip, thus shedding moisture and dirt away from the animal's body. (The Merino sheep again takes the prize for number of scales per inch—twenty-five thousand!) Inside the cuticle is the *cortex*: this is a cellular structure of protein. The protein forms a coil-like structure that can be stretched and then will return to its original shape. In coarser wools and hair fibers there is an air space at the center of the cortex, called the *medulla,* but in the finest wools this is absent altogether. Each fiber has tiny waves called *crimps;* and the finer the wool the more crimps per inch there are.

The sebaceous glands of the sheep secrete *wool grease,* which is actually a wax (unlike grease, this wax is soluble in water), and sweat glands secrete *suint;* the wool grease and the suint combine to make the *yolk. Lanolin* is the commercial product made from the wool grease. Some breeds have no sebaceous or sweat glands; in general, the coarser the wool or hair the less wool grease there is.

This is what the wool fiber looks like under a very powerful microscope. It is important to understand this structure if you want to know how to handle wool properly when washing and dyeing.

Talk about miracle fibers! Wool is by far the most miraculous. It can absorb up to 30 percent of its own weight in moisture without even feeling wet. When it is wet, it generates heat; thus a wool garment, when wet, will actually keep you warm. It can be stretched as much as 30 percent beyond its normal length and then return to its original form. Besides being extremely elastic, it is wrinkle resistant, water repellent with its grease left in, soil resistant, and probably one of the best insulators (desert dwellers use it to keep heat *out*). For all these reasons it is probably the most functional and healthful of all fibers, for any use.

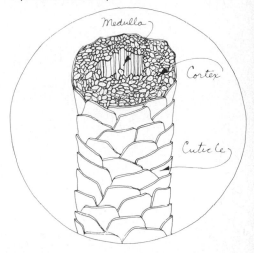

FIGURE 367. A single fiber of wool as seen under a powerful microscope.

Hair Fibers

Hair is slightly different in structure from wool. It has less distinct scales and they do not project from the shaft as is characteristic of the wool scales. Also there is almost no crimp. The medulla is present in hair fibers. The following fibers are classified as hair.

Mohair is the long silky coat of the Angora goat, originally from Angora, Turkey. Mohair is one of the strongest of animal fibers, and any fabric made of it, particularly a pile fabric, is extremely durable. Pure mohair is always white, but often you can get beautiful grays that are only slightly coarser, resulting from cross-breeding.

Angora is the fur of the Angora rabbit. Its fleece is very soft and fuzzy—*and* difficult to spin. It is similar in texture to husky down, which is sometimes used in handknit sweaters.

Alpaca is from the domesticated animal of the same name. This animal lives in the Andes of South America and resembles the llama (a beast of burden *not* raised for its fleece), and both are related to the camel. Alpaca has a crimp like wool and comes in beautiful shades from creamy white to dark blackish brown. Its most distinctive color is a very rich chocolate brown.

Camel's hair is from the two-humped camel, whose protective coat is a nonconductor of heat and cold and naturally water repellent. This animal has two types of fiber, the outer hair and an undercoat of down (or wool). The camel sheds its coat, so shearing is not necessary. It is the down that is used for fine camel's-hair coats. The fiber is always one color—camel color.

Cashmere is the underhair of a goat native to Kashmir in the Himalayas. Its undercoat is a very luxurious fine fiber.

Quivit, a fiber just becoming known, is the extremely fine, long hair of the musk ox, which lives in the arctic regions. This fiber is not now available to hand spinners. So far, its fleece is limited to commercial spinning and the yarn made available only to native people of Alaska, who knit it into gossamer shawls and the like, which are exported and sold in fine shops.

Vicuña, the precious fiber of the Incas, comes from a wild animal that roams in the Andes at altitudes over 13,000 feet. Every year the Incas would round up the wild flocks and shear them. A single animal yielded only one-quarter to one-half pound of yellowish tan hair. The yarn made from this fiber was used in the fabrics made for the Inca, the god-king of the people. The texture resembles raw silk. Today vicuña is considered the most valuable animal fiber in the world, and the animal from which it comes is protected by the governments of South America. Illegal dealing in vicuña carries heavy penalties. The flocks still roam wild and must be rounded up for shearing, because attempts to domesticate the animal have not been successful. Often the animal dies from fright or exposure, so shearing can be considered tantamount to killing.

Karakul is a breed of sheep (probably one of those original versions) whose wool is mixed with hair; its fleece is considered extremely low grade and used commercially mainly for carpets. It is usually dark in color, and when it is white it is never pure; there are always some black hairs in the fleece. Sometimes the hair and the wool are different colors, and this makes a beautiful yarn when spun without carding. The hide of the newborn lamb is what we call "Persian lamb" and it is used for very fine fur coats, and especially for those Russian-style fur hats.

Yak hair is a very coarse long hair coming from the animal of the same name that is native to central Asia. *Goat* hair is simply the fiber from long-haired goats—not Angora. It is a very coarse fiber also. *Human* hair is now available to handspinners. It's the coarsest of all. *Cow*hair and *horse*hair are often spun into yarn; the cowhair is usually pulled from the dead animal or the hide; the horsehair is from the tail and mane fibers.

Breeds of Sheep and Grades of Wool

This gets to be a very complex subject, and believe me, you can feel like a complete idiot when you're talking to the man at the wool warehouse. He usually knows nothing of the problems of the handspinner, and you, of course, will be quite ignorant of the terms used by the industry. Here, then, is a crash course in breeds of sheep and methods of grading the wool fiber.

Sheep were first introduced to this country by Columbus, on his second voyage in 1495. Long before Columbus was born, sheep had been bred and crossbred to make animals that would yield different types of wool, be more suitable for different climates, and still be good for meat. This is still being done.

Here is a list of the more common breeds. Since this information comes from the North Central Wool Marketing Corporation in Minnesota, these are mostly breeds common in the United States. The numbers are used in grading and are explained later.

Fine-Wool Breeds

American, or Delaine-Merino	64s to 80s
Rambouillet	62s to 70s

Crossbreed-Wool Breeds

Corriedale	50s to 60s
Columbia	50s to 60s
Panama	50s to 58s
Romeldale	58s to 60s
Targhee	58s to 60s

Medium-Wool Breeds

Southdown	56s to 60s
Shropshire	48s to 56s

Hampshire	48s to 56s
Suffolk	48s to 56s
Oxford	46s to 50s
Dorset	48s to 56s
Cheviot	48s to 56s

Long-Wool Breeds	
Lincoln	36s to 46s
Cotswold	36s to 40s
Romney	40s to 48s

This list does not include the Australian fine wool Merino, which has a grade up to 90s, nor the Navajo sheep, which is actually a breed. The latter is rarely listed among breeds of sheep because the wool is considered so coarse. Of course, it is perfect for handspinning. Karakul is also omitted—which is the coarsest of all.

And this is what you have to understand in buying raw wool to spin yourself. What is considered the best (or finest) wool in the industry is the worst for your purposes. Actually, in this whole long list of breeds, the only ones that will interest you (for most purposes, anyway) will be those classified as "long-wool." The other grades can be used if you wish to have a very soft wool for certain purposes, but they will be more difficult to spin. In general, the coarser the wool, the longer each fiber is—another desirable characteristic for handspinning.

Those mysterious numbers like "64s to 80s" are used in the *numerical count system* for grading the fineness of wool. What they mean is the number of "hanks" of yarn, each 560 yards long, that can be spun from one pound of wool. So a 64s wool would make 64 hanks of yarn, each 560 yards long. This is 20.7 miles!

Another system of grading is called the *blood system.* It is all based on the Merino and Rambouillet, which are on top and whose wool is considered *fine.* From there the system goes to *half,* which is slightly coarser. Then comes *three-eighths, quarter, low quarter, common,* and *braid.*

The *micron system,* which actually measures the diameter of the fiber in microns, is also used.

Besides this, U.S. wools are divided into four categories: California wools; territory wools (all the western states); Texas wools (the primary source of Rambouillet-type wool); and fleece wools (all the wool grown east of the Mississippi). These last are generally coarser than those from other areas and would be better for handspinning.

Where to Get the Raw Wool

When I first drafted this chapter (five years ago!) I suggested going to your local sheep rancher or the wool warehouse in the city nearest you to pick out good fleeces for spinning. This is the way I got my wool, but it wasn't very good wool for handspinning, although the rancher would boast that it was very fine. Since then I've discovered that interest in handspinning is so great that there are all kinds of good sources of raw fiber —a bit more expensive, to be sure, but you no longer have to struggle away with some fleece that was really meant for industrial carders and spinners. The difference between working with fiber especially grown for handspinners (and there are some ranchers that specialize to this extent) and with an ordinary fine wool from one of the western sheep ranchers will mean that many more weavers will take up spinning, because it is such fun.

The sources for raw fibers to spin are plentiful; the main concern is to get the fibers as cheaply as possible. Some wool and hair are available cleaned and/or carded, at greater expense, of course, but not so much greater if you know the right source. New Zealand and Australia are probably the best and cheapest sources of high-quality wool, cleaned and carded, and ready for handspinning, and Romney raw wool is available from there all carded in the grease for only a little more than you would have to pay the wool warehouse for raw fleeces. The carding process is so time-consuming that it is often more economical to buy the wool already carded. I would think every weaver would want to have the equipment and a supply of exotic fibers to spin at least some special yarns for weaving. This way you can have beautiful yarn for the same price as the very cheapest commercial yarn; and it won't take all that much time. See Chapter XIII, "Suppliers: Fibers for Spinning," for where to order your fibers.

A Note about Raising Your Own Sheep

Raising your own sheep is hardly a worthwhile venture economically, when you consider that one sheep will yield only about five pounds of clean wool each year. And you can't just let the sheep pasture on your land. You have to take *care* of them, which means seeing that they get a good diet, worming them, de-ticking them, etc. —and then having an expert shearing job done. A good wool coat on a sheep can be utterly ruined by a bad shearing job.

Paula Simmons, the well-known spinner, and her husband, who sell their hand-spun yarns and weavings made with this yarn, raise their own sheep. They have carefully bred them to get beautiful colors (she prefers a half Lincoln breed). They have gone into sheep raising in a professional way, and she has written an article, "How to Raise Sheep," for the *Handweaver and Craftsman* magazine (available through The Unicorn; see Chapter XIII, "Suppliers: Books"). This would probably be the best information available for handspinners who want to raise their own sheep. Your county agricultural agent would also have information, but of course it would not be geared to the handspinner.

There is the great advantage in raising your own that you can have very unusual colors in your fleeces, and just the type of wool you like, *and* you'll have occasional lambs to eat. But, unless you plan to do it properly, you should leave the sheep raising to professionals.

Picking a Good Fleece

It is important to get a good fleece whether you are a beginning or experienced spinner. Sometimes beginners start out with wool that someone has found in his barn —maybe a sack that has sat there for two or three years. Their beginning career may soon end in disgust because of the hassles that will arise from trying to spin up a short-fibered, dirty old fleece with grease dried hard.

The industry has all kinds of wonderfully descriptive words for wool that is in bad shape: "frowsy" (dull-appearing), "tender" (breaks easily), "tippy" (with brittle dry tips), "wasty" (short, weak, tangled wool that will be wasted in the spinning), "cotty" (matted), "kempy" (having an occasional thick wiry fiber—kemp—that does not take dye—from undernourished sheep).

There are four classifications for the good or bad condition of the fleece: (1) *choice,* (2) *bright,* (3) *semi,* and (4) *burry and seedy.* You will want to deal only with choice fleeces, which will be those that are cleanest and in best condition.

The grease in the wool will be soft and an aid in spinning *if* the fleece is newly shorn. When a fleece is old this has hardened, and although it can be softened somewhat with heat (or by adding kerosene), spinning an old fleece is nothing like spinning a fleece that is freshly shorn.

You may come across "pulled" wool—that is, pulled from a dead animal; it will have the roots on the fibers. You will not want to work with this.

Also avoid "second cuts" in the fleece. Examine it to see if there are a lot of very short fibers—clumps about one-half inch long. These result when the shearer does not cut close enough to the skin the first time and then goes over that area again with the shears. This happens occasionally to any shearer, but if the shearer is not an expert, it will happen often.

Any fleeces that aren't pure white are referred to as black wool, even if they have only a few black hairs, and in the industry they are not as desirable as white wool. For your purposes, "black" wool is the most desirable. You can often get beautiful grays and beiges and browns and blacks. The beiges and browns are rarer than blacks and grays. If you see a brown sheep in a meadow, it most likely actually has black wool with sun-bleached tips. Beige wool is brown and white fibers growing on one sheep; and gray wool is a mixture of black and white fibers.

Examine the fleece to determine the length of the fiber ("staple"). It should be four inches at least—unstretched—and the longer the better. Even if you find a beautiful section that has four-inch fibers, that particular section may be from the shoulders, and the rest of the fleece may have shorter fibers. Shearers wrap the fleece up so that you see the nicest, longest fibers. Shorter-staple wool will be harder to card and spin into nice yarn.

How Many Fleeces Should You Buy?

A fleece can weigh anywhere from 2 pounds (the Navajo breed) to 25 pounds (Rambouillet). The wool you will be buying will probably weigh somewhere around 8 to 12 pounds per fleece. In many breeds the yolk and dirt account for *more than half* the weight of the fleece. The finer wool breeds generally have much more grease than the coarser wools, and therefore have more weight loss. This loss of weight from raw fleece to cleaned wool is called "shrinkage," and the person you buy the wool from should know the standard shrinkage rate for a particular type of wool. If not, you can roughly figure on losing 50 percent of the weight when it is washed. So, if you are buying washed wool, even though it is more expensive, you are getting twice as much wool for each pound you buy. This is an important fact to remember; often cleaned carded wool doesn't cost much more than twice as much as raw wool.

You'll probably want to buy enough raw wool at the time of shearing to last you a year. See Chapter I, "The Basics of Weaving: Your Yarns," for how much finished yarn you will need for certain projects. Keep two things in mind: (1) Your handspun yarn will not be as light and fluffy as most commercial yarns; handspun yarn will usually weigh more than commercial yarn that *seems* to be about the same size. So add a little poundage to what is suggested. (2) It is easy to overestimate your production capabilities. Don't buy a huge quantity of wool that will sit for more than a year before you get around to using it.

Handling the Fleece

A sheep is sheared in such a way that the fleece comes off in one piece. The edges are folded in and it is rolled up so that the good fluffy fibers from the back and shoulders are on the outside. It is then tied with paper twine. This practice is pretty general in the United States except among the Navajos, who often make no attempt to keep the fleece in one piece. Actually what often happens is that the spinner of the family is right there to pick out the best fibers for her own uses, and the remaining wool is bagged and taken to the trading post for sale.

Untie the fleece and carefully unfold it to spread out like a hide with the tips up. You will then be able to sort the raw wool to suit your purposes. First of all, you will probably want to "skirt" it—that is, remove about three inches all around the edges. These edges consist of the "britch" or "breech" wool from the hindquarters and the "taglocks" (other short and dirty ends). It is hardly worthwhile dealing with these ends, and they can just be thrown away (good for compost), unless you are particularly frugal. Often fleeces that you buy from a spinning-supply house will already have been skirted, and will be sold as such. Even if you are paying a higher price per pound, it may end up the same since you won't have that waste.

FIGURE 368. Divisions showing how wool is sorted commercially, no. 1 being the best grade.

Sorting the Fleece

In Figure 368 is a picture showing how wool is sorted commercially, the no. 1 being the best grade—longest and best-quality fiber. If you plan to use the entire fleece for one batch of yarn you should mix all parts together to make a consistent-textured yarn. If you plan to make several different yarns from the same fleece (which you will probably want to do if it is a "black" fleece), sort out areas of different colors and/or textures. Paula Simmons points out that often very subtle shades occurring only in one small area can be used for some very special yarn. The best wool of the fleece can often just be "teased" (pulled apart with your fingers) before spinning, eliminating the time-consuming carding process, while the shorter fibers must be carded.

Dry Cleaning the Fleece

If you have a good fleece, you may "dry" clean it rather than wash it. The Indians and Spanish settlers in the Southwest rarely washed the raw wool until breeds such as the Rambouillet were introduced that had so much grease that the wool could not be worked without some of it being removed. It is known that in earlier days the housewife usually spun her yarns in the grease, and the Navajos say that the finest yarn is always washed *after* spinning. Of course, this may have had something to do with the fact that hauling and heating water were heavy tasks, which few of us know about today. There are certainly many well-known and expert spinners who do wash their wool before spinning. Using the right washing methods, and restoring the oil to the wool before working it, probably produces just as good a yarn—and is more pleasant.

To dry clean the fleece, it should be laid out, shorn side up, in the sun—on a rock, a bush, a wire rack, or sand. Shake it gently and spread it apart. The sun will soften up the wool grease and this makes it easy to separate the fibers. Having the shorn side up means that those little scales (like shingles) will tend to shed the dirt and organic matter down to the tips of the fibers, where it will fall out. The Navajos sprinkle a little white clay or toasted pulverized gypsum over the fleece to aid in the cleaning.

The commercial process for cleaning out foreign organic matter from the raw wool is called "carbonizing"—a process of steeping the wool in a sulfuric-acid solution. The acid eats away all foreign matter but does not harm the wool fiber. This process is not suitable for home use, and is only a way to clean huge quantities of wool.

Washing the Raw Wool

This is called "scouring" in the industry. There are occasions when you will definitely want to wash the wool before spinning (aside from pure preference): (a) when you want to dye the wool before spinning to make yarn of heather mixtures; (b) when the wool is exceptionally dirty; (c) when the fleece contains so much grease that it will be difficult to spin; (d) if you object to the insecticides that have been used on the fleece. Almost all sheep are put through a dip before shearing time to kill pests that live in the animal's coat. Often the fleece is further sprayed in the warehouse to prevent other pests from taking over during storage. You have to decide for yourself whether you want to be handling these poisons. Ask your sheep rancher or the warehouse what has been used and then make your decision.

Many people think there is some great mystery about washing wool, but when you understand how the wool fiber is constructed and how it is affected by moisture, heat, and chemicals, you will always know how to handle wool, whether it is in the form of fleece, yarn, or fabric. The gelatin scales described previously in this chapter will soften and protrude in hot water. If the wool is agitated excessively at this stage the scales tend to get mashed together and that is what causes wool to mat. Or, if the fibers, in this softened state, are suddenly plunged into cold water, the scales are congealed together permanently, causing similar results. Commercially, wool is sometimes treated with chemicals (chlorine is a common one) to smooth and harden the scales so they won't stick together in hot water. This is called "preshrinking."

So . . . throughout the washing procedure, handle the wool as little as possible, and use water as cool as possible and still do the job. (This latter is not very important —the hot water alone will not harm the fiber.) To promote ease in carding and/or spinning, try to keep the fibers lined up parallel to each other just the way they were in the fleece.

To wash your raw wool, use a sink, washtub, or automatic washer (this is an excellent aid in washing large quantities of wool, but *never* allow the washer to agitate). Fill the vessel with cold to hot water (depending on how much of the wool grease you want to remove) and the washing agent. The hotter the water the more thoroughly the grease will be removed. Then add the wool; never run water directly onto the wool.

As for the washing agent, there are several possibilities. Steer away from real soap, as it contains an alkali. This is not only harmful to the wool fiber (it is used as an aid to felting in the industry) but is hard to rinse out and will affect dyes if any remains in the wool. Many handspinners believe soap is the best washing agent, but actually—according to Werner von Bergen in *Wool Handbook*—in the industry neutral detergent scouring has pretty much replaced the old soap-alkali systems of washing wool, *with improved results.*

Use a mild detergent (any residue of detergent will be an aid to level dyeings), or a commercial organic cleaner such as the Basic H or Amway product. If you want to get really earthy, use yucca root. Clean and crush the root and use one handful to one quart of cold water. Rub the crushed fibers together until a very heavy lather forms. Then add warm water to the solution and strain. Use this strained solution to wash the wool. If you wish to store the yucca root, it should be pounded into shreds and then dried. (The yucca makes an excellent shampoo, also.)

Do one or two soakings for as long as you can afford (overnight is good), and then thoroughly rinse in water of the same temperature as the wool, or colder. Press out as much excess moisture as possible (this is where the automatic washer with its spin-dry cycle comes in handy as the perfect tool).

The wool must then be spread out to dry on a newspaper or towel or sheet. If there is still a lot of moisture in the wool, do not put it out in the sun, because long drying in the sun tends to stain the wool (especially if it has been washed with real soap). If the wool is only damp, a sunny and airy place is very suitable. Fluff and spread the wool as it dries. It will pull apart much more easily when damp, and you may get away with no carding at all.

Oiling the Washed Wool

If you have washed the wool in fairly hot water, most of the grease will have been removed, and to card and spin it you will want to add a slight amount of lubrication. It promotes slippage of the fibers, and therefore a more even yarn can be spun.

The oil can be added to the last rinse water, or it can be sprayed on with a spray bottle when the wool is still slightly damp. Only a very slight amount will do the job. It penetrates and spreads evenly through the fibers best if the wool is wrapped in a newspaper and allowed to stand a day or so in this condition; but you may be too impatient to start working.

Olive oil, mineral oil, and neatsfoot oil are commonly used. Paula Simmons markets her own special mixture of spinning oil, and I believe you can order direct from her. It is also carried in stock by a few other suppliers. (See Chapter XIII, "Suppliers: Spinning Equipment.")

Teasing

FIGURE 369. The teasing process: holding the lock of wool in one hand while gradually separating the fibers in a parallel fashion.

To prepare the wool for spinning, the fibers must be separated and arranged more or less evenly. This is accomplished by pulling apart the locks of wool quite thoroughly with your fingers, a process called "teasing" or "picking." After that the fibers are sometimes separated more completely and evenly by the use of hand cards or a carding machine.

If you are using raw wool it should be slightly warm. This makes the wool grease soft and more fluid, and the fibers will separate more easily. So place the fleece in the sun, by the fire, or near a heater.

Take a lock of warm wool in the left hand with the fibers running up and down (shorn end up). Now, while holding the wool firmly, start separating the fibers with the fingers of your right hand so that the fibers remain parallel with each other but are more spread apart. If the wool has not been washed first, more dirt will fall out at this stage; that's the reason for holding it with the shorn end up.

Some spinners tease each handful as they card or spin, rather than teasing the whole batch of wool first. But, if you want a consistent yarn, it is well to tease the whole batch, mixing evenly the different qualities of fibers as you do so.

Paula Simmons points out that "neps" (bunches of short, tangled fibers) in the wool after it has been carded can be largely prevented by proper oiling and careful teasing.

Some of the wool may be spun after this teasing process. To me this is preferable to spinning the carded wool, since the fibers are naturally lying parallel (making more of a worsted yarn), and the color variations in the wool are more distinct than when all the fibers are thoroughly mixed in the carding process. (When the yarn is to be dyed after spinning, teased wool will often take the dye in a more interesting fashion. Since the dried tips of the wool absorb more dye, and these dried tips tend to stay together when the wool is just teased, an interesting two-tone yarn results.) So, if you are a moderately good spinner, I suggest you spin without carding the parts of the fleece that are nice long fibers. Card only the shorter fibers. Besides saving yourself a tremendous amount of work, you will make a more interesting yarn.

Hand Cards (Carders)

Hand cards are wire brushes that come in pairs. Attached to a wooden back is a piece of leather, heavy cardboard, or sometimes rubber, and set in this are hundreds of short metal teeth. The ordinary-size card is about 4 by 9 inches with about a 4-inch handle, but they do come larger and smaller. They also come with curved backs (it's quite pleasant carding with these) and different-size teeth. Also available now to handspinners are mill sampling cards, which are very sturdily made cards used in the industry (larger than the usual hand cards).

I have always used inexpensive flat-backed cards with teeth set in cardboard: fairly fine teeth (no. 8 wool card) for wool carding, and much coarser teeth (tow card) for carding mohair, karakul, and other coarser fibers.

Almost every spinning- or weaving-supply house carries hand cards of some sort —often imported. Large cards will get the job done faster, but I find working with them too tiring. The normal-size card seems the most efficient.

Always store your cards with the teeth together to prevent them from being crushed—this can easily happen if they are just set down separately. Also, a Spanish woman here in New Mexico told me to put a piece of unwashed wool between the cards when they are not in use. This helps protect the teeth, and the grease will keep the leather and wood in good condition.

To clean out fine dirt and fibers that collect in the teeth, you can press the teeth of one card right into those of another and rub the cards back and forth vigorously. This is rather difficult to do but gets the job done very neatly. Another way is simply to clean the teeth with an ordinary table fork.

When you first use a new set of cards the teeth will be set really tightly, and carding will be difficult until the teeth loosen up a bit. When the cards have seen many hours of use, the teeth become very loose in their setting, and they will not card the wool efficiently. Then it is time to get a new pair; replacing the teeth (unless you own a pair of mill sampling cards) is hardly worthwhile. Efficient carding depends a great deal on the condition of the cards: *don't try to be frugal and use cards with smashed or very loose teeth*—it will be a waste of time.

Some spinners label their cards right and left, and always use them in the appropriate hands; the cards then wear differently. I prefer to use them interchangeably.

How to Card Wool

Step 1. Distributing the wool on the cards

Resting your left hand on your knee, grasp the card as shown. With your right hand take a lock of teased wool (it is best warmed, if the natural wool grease is still in it) and distribute it evenly on the teeth by catching it on the top teeth and drawing your hand toward you. Do this all the way across the card. Put enough wool on so that the teeth just barely show through. If you put on too much wool, the teeth cannot

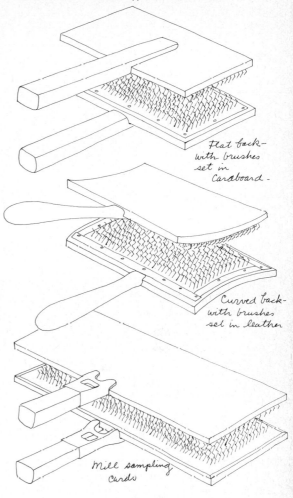

FIGURE 370. Different types of hand cards.

Flat back— with brushes set in cardboard.

Curved back— with brushes set in leather

mill sampling cards

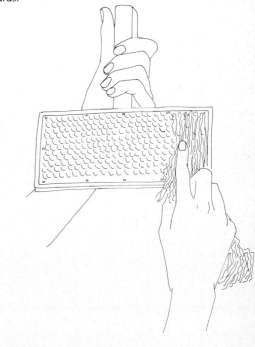

FIGURE 371. Step 1. Distributing the wool on the cards.

FIGURE 372. Step 2. The carding stroke.

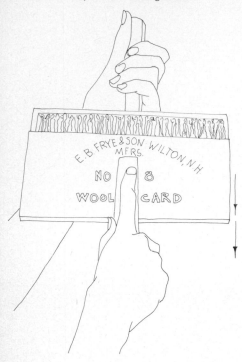

comb through the whole thickness and your wool will not be carded thoroughly. (Left-handed people should use the left hand where I say "right.")

Step 2. The carding stroke

Grasp the other card in the right hand as shown and place it directly over the left card so that all the teeth of the right card touch all the teeth of the left card. Now draw the right card toward you, *lightly* combing the fibers. Do this five or six times. You will see that the wool is distributed evenly on both cards. At this point some of the fibers underneath on both cards are not combed out thoroughly, so you must remove the wool from each card separately and recard it. This occurs is steps 3 and 4.

Step 3. Removing the wool from the right card

Keep hold of the cards with the same grasp. Turn the right card to the position shown in Figure 373. Place its front edge on the back edge of the left card. The teeth on the left card will pick up the wool on the right card as you draw the latter across in the direction of the arrows. The right card should be at an angle to the bottom card. All the wool from the right card should now be lying on the teeth of the left card. It is difficult for beginners to master this operation; think of it this way: the teeth of the bottom card are what are doing the job.

Now card again as in step 2.

Step 4. Removing the wool from the left card

Now all the fibers have been combed thoroughly except for those underneath on the left card. Again keep hold of the cards with the same grasp, but turn the right card so that the teeth are up. Place the front edge of the left card at the back edge of the right card, as shown. Slowly draw the left card backward over the teeth of the right. The teeth of the right card will pick off the wool from the left card, so that all the wool will now lie on the right card.

Card again as in step 2.

Removing the wool from each card can be repeated as many times as you find necessary to get the wool fibers combed thoroughly. Usually you'll want to do it at

FIGURE 373. Step 3. Removing the wool from the right card.

FIGURE 374. Step 4. Removing the wool from the left card.

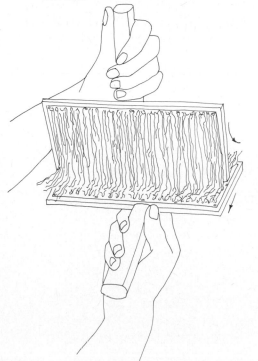

FIGURE 375. Step 5. Removing the wool from both cards.

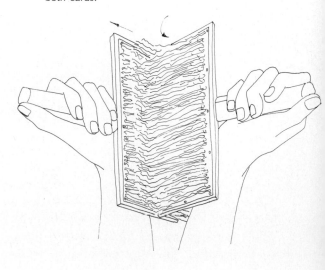

least twice with each card. Repeat steps 2, 3, and 4 until you feel the fibers are thoroughly combed out.

Step 5. Removing the wool from both cards and making the rolag
This is the only point at which your hands change the grasp, and now only the right hand does. Grasp the right card in the same way you are grasping the left card. Now, holding the cards as shown in Figure 375, remove the wool from the right card by running its front edge across the left card from back edge to front. Lift all the wool off the left card, using the teeth of the right card. Or, lift it off with your hands and you can make a roll (rolag) as you take it off. Or you can roll the carded mass on your lap. Or it can be rolled and patted on the wooden back of one card with the back of the other. I usually leave the mass of carded fibers in the form of a batt (the rectangular shape they are in when they first come off the cards) and I notice that most primitive spinners do the same—spinners using hand spindles. I've always found this rectangular mass of fibers as convenient to work with as a rolag—with any type of wheel or electric spinner; it tends to make more of a worsted yarn than the rolags (see The Difference Between Woolen and Worsted).

You may come across people who card differently; there are many different positions and ways to card. But for proper carding the principle is the same: *always* the fibers should be removed from *both* cards in the combing process to insure the complete combing of all fibers. If you learn to card in the position described here—that is, without changing your grasp on the cards—you will be carding faster and more efficiently and with least effort.

Mixing Fibers

Black and white wools can be mixed in the carding process to produce gray yarn. Or mohair can be mixed with wool to make a silkier and stronger yarn. Wool may be dyed before carding and then different colors mixed on the cards to make heather mixtures. Blanket brushings (from brushing a weaving) may be mixed with new fibers to make interesting tweedy yarns. And so on.

To mix two colors (or two different fibers) evenly, distribute one color halfway across the card in step 1 and the other color across the remaining half of the card. In steps 3 and 4 the colors will be laid over their opposites, so that perfect blending will occur.

If you want a variegated yarn, place one color in the center of the card and another color on the sides. The center color will always remain in the same position through steps 3 and 4, so your rolag will come out exactly the same as you laid out the colors on the card.

Carding Machines

It has been said that it takes seventeen people hand carding wool to keep up with one person weaving. In any case, hand carding is definitely a time-consuming process. There are carding machines available at a few of the supply houses. The round type is called a bench or drum carder. The other type I have seen only in the brochure of one well-known manufacturer in Germany, and I have not had the opportunity to try it. The design looks very good, and I have often fantasized, during the many long hours of hand carding I've done, that some such gadget would be awfully nice to have. It consists of a stand with a carding surface and one hand card.

These machines will cut down on your carding time. However, I never thought

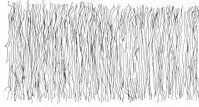
FIGURE 376. Batt on rolag ready for spinning.

Batt

Rolag

FIGURE 377. Method of laying the fibers on the cards for variegated mixtures and for even blending.

Variegated mixtures

Even blending

FIGURE 378. Two different types of carding machines.

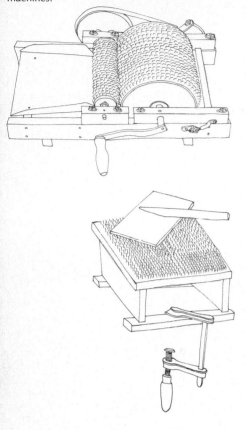

FIGURE 379. Separating the batt into 1-inch strips or into one continuous piece.

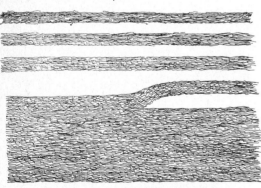

1 inch strips

One continuous piece

that the drum carder did a very thorough job; I had one for a long time, but never did get to like it. I used it mainly for preparing large quantities of wool or hair for rough-textured yarn, and for mixing. However, some spinners really like the machine and say it can do a fine job.

The secret of getting well-combed fibers out of the drum carder is in the preparation of the wool to begin with. The wool should be very well washed, oiled, and teased. The fiber is fed gradually into the roller from the pan, while the drum is turned with a hand crank.

When carding is complete, the wool is removed from the drum in the form of a rectangle. Run a knitting needle or closed scissors along the seam in the leather that holds the brushes, and simply pull apart the fibers rather than cutting them. This rectangle can be removed from the drum using a hand card to pick it off, while the drum is turned in reverse.

This mass of wool, called a "batt," "lap," or "web," is then separated vertically into narrow strips, which are treated as rolags for spinning. Or one long continuous piece can be made by separating widths as shown in Figure 379. The separation doesn't go all the way to the ends, but zigzags back and forth, and the wool can then be stretched out into one long piece.

The care and adjustment of the drum carder are important factors in the production of well-carded fibers. The teeth of the small roller should *barely* touch the metal pan. The teeth of the two rollers must not touch each other, but be less than 1/16 inch apart. The belt must be tight enough to get good traction, and the machine must be oiled frequently.

The Difference Between Woolen and Worsted

There are two different methods of preparing fibers for spinning. One method, called "carding," which has just been described, separates the fibers, but in the final rolag there are short and long fibers and they lie in all different directions. The rolag from carded wool produces *woolen* yarn, which is soft and fuzzy.

There is another process, called "combing," which produces *worsted* yarn. This is a process of combing out all short fibers (noils) and leaving just the long fibers all lying parallel. The yarn resulting from spinning up these fibers is hard and smooth. You need a special tool for this combing process (a deadly-looking comb with a few very long, sharp teeth) and it is a more tedious process than carding. It is doubtful that the results are worth the extra effort for the handspinner. Using very nice raw long-fibered wool, you can make a more or less worsted yarn by simply drafting the *un*carded fibers in such a way that they all lie parallel, or see Flicking below. If you are interested in learning the combing process with the special tools for worsted yarn, refer to Allen Fannin's *Handspinning: Art and Technique.**

Flicking

This is a simple process for fluffing up the raw wool, often used in Australia and New Zealand, instead of carding. You use one card, called a "flicker" (it is smaller than the regular-size card, but very much the same). While holding the *shorn* end of a clump of wool in your left hand, you simply flick the tips of the fibers, using a quick, light stroke. This serves to separate the tips of the fibers (the part that tends to stick together because of weathering). The fibers then remain parallel. This is a good procedure for making a more or less worsted yarn. A dog brush will substitute for a real flicker.

*In England, *Hand Wool Combing and Spinning* by Peter Teal is recommended.

Learning to Spin with the Drop Spindle

To understand the principle of spinning any fiber, pretend for a while that you are a primitive man first discovering how to twist fibers into a continuous thread. To do this, take a lock of wool (or a clump of cotton batting) in your hands and fluff it up by teasing it. Now try to make a length of fine thread by drawing out the fibers and twisting them between your fingers. You can see as you draw the thread out that the twisting gives it strength enough not to pull apart.

Try in this way to make a continuous *even* piece of thread about six or eight inches long. In doing this you will see that where the mass of fibers is thinnest it twists most, so in order to make the yarn even you must draw out the thicker places so that they will spin tightly. You will also see that, if part of the thread is tightly spun, you only have to draw out the remaining fibers and the twist will travel up into these unspun fibers without your doing anything. The drawing-out of the fibers is called "drafting." And this whole process is what spinning is all about. There is nothing more to it except the winding up of the finished thread.

You will discover that it is difficult to spin much more than six inches without having something to secure one end to, and something to wind the finished thread onto. The *drop spindle* was created to handle these problems. The yarn is attached to it and the spindle can hang (or stand) freely and spin. The whorl (the heavy disk near the base) gives it momentum, and the shaft is used to wind on the finished thread.

Now take a *small* drop spindle and some *well-carded* wool. (Or, if you are like me and have to do it *right now* and don't have a drop spindle or the wool, take a full-length pencil with a sharpened end, and stick it through half of a small potato.) Use a package of cotton batting from the dime store for fiber. Follow these instructions step by step. The cotton is more difficult to spin than wool, because the fibers are shorter and finer, so don't be discouraged when the thread breaks. Try to get hold of a good spindle and good wool before you get too discouraged. *Don't try to learn how to spin seriously with any fiber but wool.*

Step 1. Attaching a leader to the spindle
You may sit or stand to spin with the drop spindle; the spindle should be free to drop to the floor. Take a length of any fine yarn (or even thread will do in a pinch) about one and a half times the length of your spindle. This thread is called a "leader." Tie it to the shaft just above the whorl, and make a hitch at the point of the shaft as shown in Figure 381. (If you are a knitter, this hitch is made just the way you would cast on.) Some drop spindles have a notch at the top, but this is not necessary and actually I prefer them without the notch. The spindle should not be released from your right hand for either making these hitches or undoing them. (Left-handed people should use the left hand where I say "right" and spin in a counterclockwise direction.)

Step 2. Joining the wool to the "leader"
For beginning spinners the better the fiber is carded, the easier it will be to spin. The yarn end of the leader should extend about two inches beyond the point of the spindle. Take a rolag or batt of carded wool in your left hand and overlap it about one inch behind the yarn end, holding both between the thumb and forefinger. With your right hand, give the spindle a twirl in a clockwise direction, and let it spin freely in a hanging position. Now your right hand will be free to help draw out the fibers.

At this starting point remember how you worked slowly and carefully with your fingers when you had no spindle and approach this spinning in the same way. Let the twist just begin to catch the yarn and the rolag together before you start drawing out the rolag to the correct thickness. It is important to get the rolag drawn out to the right

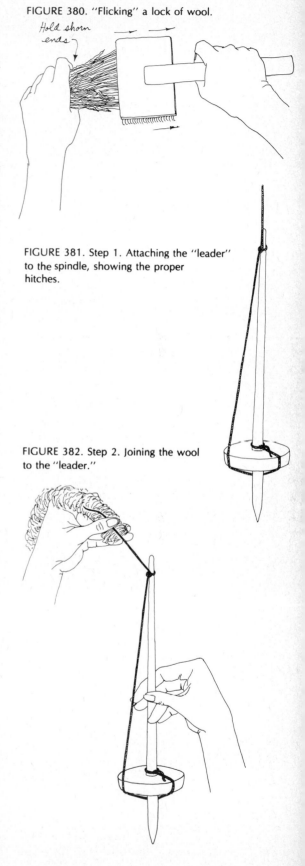

FIGURE 380. "Flicking" a lock of wool.

Hold shorn ends

FIGURE 381. Step 1. Attaching the "leader" to the spindle, showing the proper hitches.

FIGURE 382. Step 2. Joining the wool to the "leader."

thickness before it is twisted too tightly. Until there is a foot or more of yarn spun you will have to give the spindle a short twirl often.

The secret to successful drop spinning is making *fine* yarn. A drop spindle *cannot* be used to spin thick yarn, because the twist of a heavy yarn offers too much resistance to the spinning spindle. So, if you are having trouble keeping the spindle spinning, probably the yarn is too thick for the weight of the spindle. The heavier the yarn the greater twisting power needed. For heavier yarns the Navajo spindle is best; this is forcibly twirled, and does very little spinning from momentum as does the drop spindle.

Step 3. Drawing out the fibers (drafting)

In the spinning process the function of the left hand is to support the rolag and let it feed through the thumb and forefinger with just the right amount of tension to draw it out to the correct thickness at the point where the twist takes effect. The function of the right hand is more complicated: it twirls the spindle when necessary, and the rest of the time the thumb and forefinger are grasping the already spun yarn just an inch or so below the point of twist to provide some resistance for the left hand, which is drawing the fibers out. When you get to be good at it, the distance between the left and right hand can be much greater without the yarn breaking. In fact, an expert spinner rarely takes her right hand away from the spindle.

When the right-hand fingers are closed on the yarn, no twist can go past that point, and it is at this time that both hands pull apart slightly to draw out the unspun fibers that are being fed through the left fingers. When the right fingers are opened, the twist will travel up the yarn and start twisting the drawn-out fibers. Your right fingers will constantly be opening and closing to control the twist, while the spindle goes on spinning from momentum. Study and practice these movements slowly and carefully. The important thing is never to let the twist overtake the fibers of the rolag that have not been sufficiently drawn out. If you do, then you'll simply have to use both hands to untwist them until they can be drawn out to the right thickness.

While you are a beginner, your left-hand fingers should stay close to the point where the twist takes effect. When you get good at it, your left hand will *loosely*

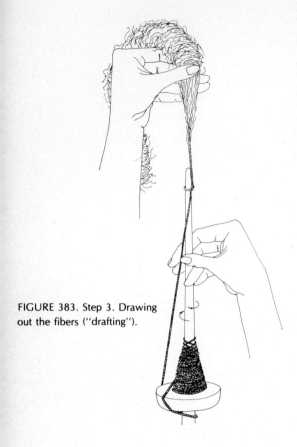

FIGURE 383. Step 3. Drawing out the fibers ("drafting").

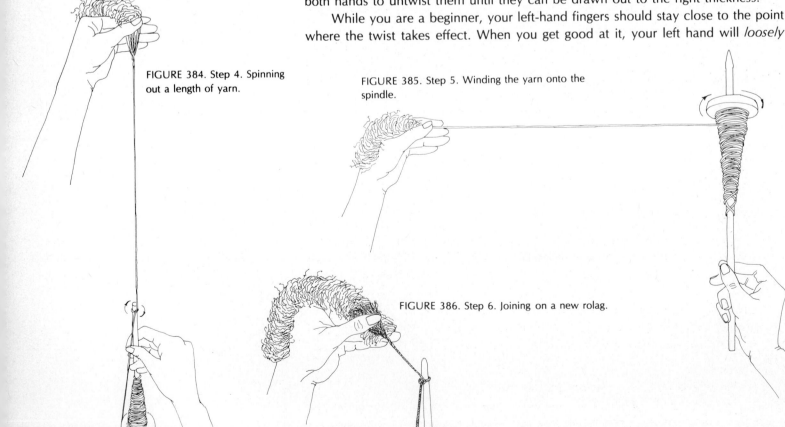

FIGURE 384. Step 4. Spinning out a length of yarn.

FIGURE 385. Step 5. Winding the yarn onto the spindle.

FIGURE 386. Step 6. Joining on a new rolag.

support the rolag and pull it out to the right thickness quite a way beyond the point where the twist is taking effect.

Step 4. Spinning out a length of yarn

Continue in this way to spin out a length of yarn until it is the span of your outstretched arms, letting the spindle drop to a distance where the right hand can just reach it, until the left hand is outstretched over the head or off to the side. As you get very skilled you may work with your two hands farther apart than shown in Figure 384. You will be drawing out the rolag with your left hand and most of the time keeping your right hand down near the spindle, grasping both it and the yarn when resistance is needed, and giving it a twirl whenever necessary. Working this way you will be putting a slight twist in the entire length between your hands, just enough to hold it together; then you will stop the twist by closing your right fingers and draw out this length of loosely twisted thread. *Notice that automatically the thicker areas will draw out and the thinner areas won't.* Keep repeating these motions until the thread is even and twisted enough so that it is strong. Very occasionally both hands will be used to untwist and draw out a thick area in the thread.

How tightly you spin the yarn depends on how the yarn is to be used, but in general fine yarn should be very tightly spun for strength (tight enough so that it will very quickly twist up on itself when given the slack to do so). However, very thin areas where the yarn is overspun (tending to curl up like a corkscrew) will be very weak, so try to avoid this. When the yarn is washed it will even out some and seem less tightly spun.

Step 5. Winding the yarn onto the spindle

While holding the length of yarn taut with the left hand in its position, and while holding the spindle in the right, loosen the upper hitch on the spindle with your right forefinger. (If you let go of the rolag—or even release the taut position of the spun yarn—the yarn will twist up into a tangled mess.) Slip the hitch off the spindle and unwind the lower loop. Now grasp the spindle by the upper part of the shaft with the whorl away from you. Turn the spindle in a clockwise direction and, still holding the yarn taut, let it wind onto the spindle against the whorl, shaping a cone as it winds. Leave a length of yarn that is one and a half times the length of the spindle; this is just about the right amount to make the hitches (the same as described in step 1) and leave a couple of inches to start spinning again.

Holding a full length of the spun yarn out taut is sometimes a real arm stretcher. If you don't like this awkward feeling, wind a few feet of the spun yarn onto your left-hand fingers in a figure eight—by rocking your outstretched fingers back and forth, taking up the yarn as you do so. This gets complicated with the loose rolag dangling in the way, but if you get good at it, it feels much better than just stretching your arm out all the way.

Step 6. Joining on a new rolag

When you run out of one rolag, leave an inch or so of unspun fibers. Join an end of a new rolag on by overlapping its end over the unspun end of the last one. (This splice is most easily made when the excess yarn is wound onto the spindle and only a couple of inches extend from the end.) Just hold the two together with your left hand (*don't* do what every beginning spinner tries to do, twist the two together) while slowly twirling the spindle. When the two groups of fibers begin to twist together, draw them out slightly. Make the splice carefully this way, and then it will be as strong as the rest of the yarn.

Step 7. Removing the yarn from the spindle.

Simply slide the cone of yarn off the spindle when it becomes too large to spin efficiently and then make a skein from this (see Making the Skein in this chapter).

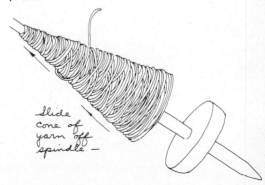

FIGURE 387. Step 7. Removing the yarn from the spindle.

Slide cone of yarn off spindle —

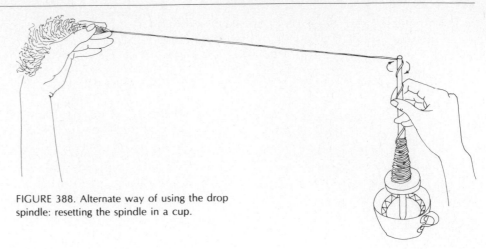

FIGURE 388. Alternate way of using the drop spindle: resetting the spindle in a cup.

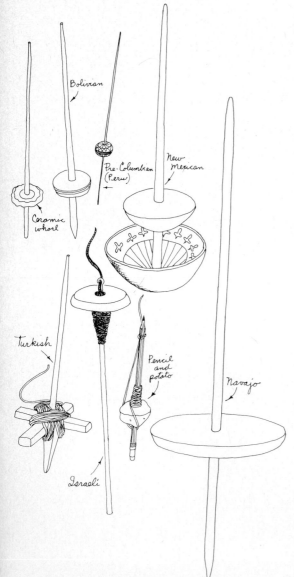

FIGURE 389. Various types of hand spindles.

Note: I find it easiest to handle the drop spindle the way I have just described —and it certainly will be easiest for you as you start learning. But most expert drop-spindle spinners use it in another way also, when they don't *have* to be standing or walking while they spin. They sit down on the ground or floor, cross-legged (or you can sit anywhere, as in a chair), set the spindle in a little cup (most convenient when at hip or waist level), and spin the yarn off to the side rather than over the head. And some spinners give the spindle a fast twirl by rubbing the shaft between the palms of *both* hands. When it is time to wind the yarn onto the spindle they undo the hitches but leave the spindle in the cup, give it a fast twirl, and guide the yarn on so that it will make a cone shape. They often do the little figure-eight trick to hold the yarn taut.

Types of Hand Spindles

There are many types of hand spindles for drop-spindle spinning (as described above) and spinning in a cup or bowl. Some spindles have ceramic whorls to give extra momentum; some have the whorls placed at different points on the shaft; some are very, very slim and light-weight (for spinning very fine cotton); some are quite large and have to be used with the cup because they are heavy. The Turkish type is made so that the crossbars that form the whorl and onto which you wind the yarn can be pulled out, and you end up with a neat ball of yarn, rather than a cone. The type with the whorl at the top is common in the Middle East and is designed this way so it can be rolled on the thigh, somewhat like the Navajo spindle.

The Navajo Spindle

The Navajo spindle is quite a different tool from most hand spindles. It is much longer (about two or three feet long) and has a huge whorl (about four to six inches in diameter) set about a quarter to a third of the way up the shaft. Thick yarns as well as fine yarns may be spun on it, since the spindle is forcibly turned, and its spinning does not depend so much on momentum.

The spinner sits on the ground or in a chair and with her right hand rolls the spindle shaft against her right thigh toward her; the end of the shaft rests on the ground. (Practice spinning the spindle without any yarn on it. Roll it with the palm of your hand as far as you can on your thigh, then return it to its beginning position near your knee by cupping your thumb and forefinger loosely around the shaft; it will continue to spin somewhat. Do this in fast strokes to get the spindle turning as fast as possible.)

The carded wool is usually not made into a rolag, but left in the rectangular shape as it comes off the cards. In starting, to attach the carded wool to the spindle, the spinner moistens the wool and sticks it onto the point of the spindle. You can attach a preliminary length of already spun yarn (a "leader") to the spindle if you prefer, and add onto this.

Proceed to spin by drawing out the carded wool in the same manner described under Learning to Spin with the Drop Spindle (keeping the right hand at the spindle if at all possible). The major difference in technique is this: most Navajo spinners spin the wool twice or more, the first time into roving (a soft continuous coil of fiber about one-quarter to one-half inch in diameter and *very* loosely twisted—just enough to hold together). The roving is removed from the spindle and then spun again; this time it is drawn out evenly and spun more tightly. It is respun as many times as necessary to get the desired yarn. I understand that warp yarn is sometimes spun as many as *five* times.

Some spinners accomplish this process of making roving and then respinning by spinning a couple of arm's lengths into the roving and right then unwinding this length from the spindle and respinning it into the final yarn; winding this (the final yarn) onto the spindle and then attaching a new batt to this end and spinning the roving. The spinner continues in this way until the finished yarn is all spun and wound onto the spindle.

During the spinning and drafting the right hand remains as much as possible at the spindle and provides the resistance needed in drawing out the fibers. You will see a good spinner even out the partially spun fibers by giving the spindle a series of short jerks that actually snap the length of spun yarn as it is held out by the left hand. And occasionally she will use both hands at a problem area—where the yarn was spun before it was drawn out to the right thickness; and she will untwist the yarn and draw out the fibers.

The spinner winds the yarn onto the spindle by positioning the spindle vertically, turning it *counter*clockwise to unwind what yarn has spiraled to the tip of the shaft, and then twirling in the same direction the yarn was spun (clockwise) and winding the yarn on, guiding it so that it makes a nice cone shape that rests against the whorl. This cone can be slipped off the spindle and wound into a skein.

FIGURE 390. Spinning with a Navajo spindle.

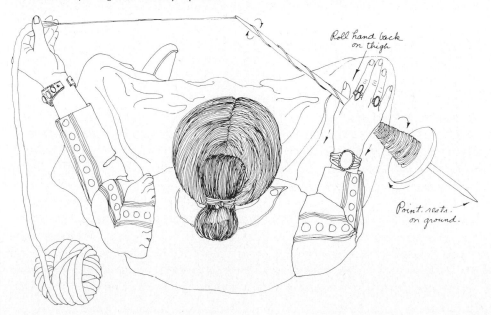

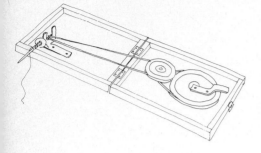

FIGURE 391. The Charkha.

The Charkha

The development of the wheel and a drive belt to turn the spindle is credited to India, and the very simplest form of this tool was called the "charkha." A special model of the wheel was designed by Mahatma Gandhi, and he recommended that everyone spend some time each day spinning cotton.

The charkha is very small and can be disassembled and kept in a carrying case, which is the size of a briefcase (some models fit in a case the size of a book). The tool is only suitable for spinning very fine thread.

A few suppliers stock these wheels. Colonel James A. Ronin of Richardson, Texas, has made a special study of them and has printed directions for their use that may be obtained through the weavers' quarterly *Shuttle, Spindle, and Dyepot,* published by Handweavers Guild of America (see Chapter XIII, "Suppliers: Books").

The High Wheel

The idea of driving a spindle with a wheel (India's invention) was introduced to Europe in the 1600s and resulted in the design of the high wheel (also called the great, wool, bobbing, or walking wheel). Supported on a three-legged base is a large wheel about four feet in diameter, which drives a spindle shaft by means of a drive band, which is led around the wheel and the horizontally held spindle. Every time the wheel turns once, the spindle turns many, many times (actually the speed is directly related to the ratio of the diameter of the wheel and that of the spindle base or pulley). Thus the spinner is provided with a spindle in a fixed position that turns at great speed. Quite an improvement over a hand-operated spindle as far as speed is concerned, anyway. To keep the spindle turning the spinner has only to give a spoke of the wheel a turn every now and then. The spindle is positioned at about waist level and the spinner stands alongside the wheel facing the spindle. Two or three steps backward are required to spin out a good long length of yarn before winding it onto the spindle (thus, the name "walking wheel").

FIGURE 392. The High Wheel.

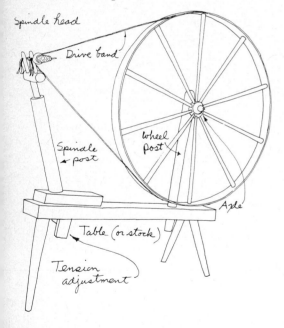

Spindle head
Drive band
Spindle post
Wheel post
Axle
Table (or stock)
Tension adjustment

Early in the nineteenth century, Amos Miner discovered that if a secondary wheel (four or five times the diameter of the spindle pulley) was used as an intermediary between the large wheel and the spindle, the speed could be multiplied even more. He called the device an "accelerating wheel head." It is sometimes called the "Miner's head," and you will find it on some of the old high wheels.

The traditional way of using this wheel requires the perfect preparation of your fiber, because only the left hand is used to draw out the rolags; the right hand is used exclusively for turning the wheel.

To start spinning, a damp corn husk is wound around the spindle and the end of the rolag is split and slipped onto this. That is supposed to be enough to get your thread attached to the spindle. If you prefer, however, you may use a leader. Or what I do, with any plain spindle, is twist one end of the rolag into a thread about eight inches long and simply tie this onto the spindle; this is enough to attach the fiber to the spindle until you can spin more length.

You proceed to spin by drawing out the rolag with the left hand, keeping it drawn out just ahead of the twist. The thread should angle off the spindle; if it is held straight out from the end of the spindle it will just pull off; and if it is at right angles it will wind onto the spindle.

The wheel is turned with the right hand in a clockwise direction. Give it a good turn so that you will be able to step back two or three steps for a length of yarn before the wheel stops or slows down too much. According to the *Home Craft Course in Pennsylvania German Spinning and Dyeing,* by Bernice B. Osburn, you should hold your arm next to your body and step back rather than stretch your arm out. This is, no doubt, to prevent tiring. But many people use the wheel in different ways. I, for instance, use both hands for drafting because I don't prepare the fibers so thoroughly —sometimes only tease them so as to make a worsted-type yarn. And I step back as well as stretch out my arm. Allen Fannin, on the other hand, in *Handspinning: Art and Technique,* describes the arm-stretching technique with no stepping back, the right hand being kept on the wheel, controlling its turning at all times, and the rolag is grasped a few inches back from the point where the twist takes place for fast, even drafting.

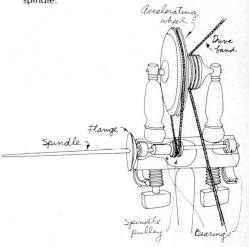

FIGURE 393. The accelerating wheel head ("Miner's head"): it multiplies the speed of the spindle.

To wind the yarn onto the spindle in the same cone shape as with the drop spindle, you must first unwind what yarn is spiraled out to its point. To do this you turn the wheel backward (less than a quarter turn is necessary) until the yarn is unwound to the cone of spun yarn. The wheel is then given a turn forward and the usual system is for the left hand to guide the yarn onto the spindle, winding it back and forth to form the cone. I find this very awkward, and have always used my right hand to guide the yarn while holding the end taut with my left. It means a quick transfer of the right hand from the wheel—after you give it a turn—to the yarn. After the yarn is wound onto the spindle, about four inches of spun yarn should remain coming from the point of the spindle for spinning to continue. Attach a new rolag by the same method as described for the drop spindle.

To wind the yarn off from the spindle to a skein winder, slip the drive belt from the wheel and spindle so the spindle can turn freely. Or, simply slip the cone of yarn off the spindle and wind the skein from it.

When you are first learning to use this wheel the tendency may be to overspin the yarn. First try to spin a medium-weight wool that is just strong enough not to pull apart with a good tug. As you get skilled, you will count *unconsciously* the times the big wheel turns for each length of yarn, by listening to and feeling its rhythm, and use the same rhythm throughout the spinning, thus making a consistent twist in the entire length of yarn. With fine yarn, after you have drawn out and spun a length, several more turns of the wheel are required to provide enough twist to make the yarn strong.

This is a versatile wheel: fine, heavy, or textured yarn may be spun on it. However, there is the disadvantage that you have to be standing for the entire operation. Also, the wheel has to be stopped and reversed before the finished yarn can be wound onto the spindle. It is said that the spinner in the old days walked several miles each day spinning the yarn. These old wheels are very difficult to find and usually require a great deal of restoration. And I find the original spindle frustratingly small anyway.

No contemporary manufacturers of wheels are making this type as far as I know, except the Meisterheims (see Chapter XIII, "Suppliers: Spinning Equipment"), who make a smaller version, called a "Shaker-style wheel," which looks very good.

Restoration and care of the high wheel

Usually the spindle mechanism on these old wheels needs repair or replacement. In the repair or replacing of the spindle the important thing is that the spindle should turn freely and should be set so there is no wobble. If the spindle is off balance, the speed at which it spins will be slowed down tremendously when there is any amount of yarn on it.

The spinning mechanism is simply a metal spindle much like a hand spindle, supported horizontally by two bearings. The bearings of the old wheels were made of oiled leather or corn husks, and when properly adjusted work beautifully. A longer spindle than the original one is desirable, but it can't be too long and still allow the wheel to turn easily. A wooden spindle is fine.

The drive band, a strong cotton cord (plumb line from the hardware store is good), must be spliced and wound with fine thread so there is as little protrusion at the joint as possible. The cord may be rubbed with beeswax to help eliminate slippage. It passes around the large wheel and the spindle pulley, which has grooves of different diameters: the larger diameter gives more power and less speed, and should be used for heavy yarns.

Tension adjustment for the drive band is made by moving the spindle post closer to or farther from the wheel. When you put on a new drive belt, set this distance at its minimum so that when the belt stretches you can adjust the tension. The cord should be just tight enough so that it doesn't slip; if it is tighter than this the wheel will be hard to turn. The post that supports the wheel can be turned in its socket; it should be positioned so that the drive band does not slip off the turning wheel, and then wedges are used to stabilize the post in that position.

To drive the wheel in the opposite direction, instead of pushing the spokes in the opposite direction, the drive band can form a figure eight; this will require a longer drive band. The spindle will then turn in the opposite direction.

Norman Hicks, a contemporary specialist on great wheels, who writes about them often in *Shuttle, Spindle, and Dyepot* (and makes his own out of old bicycle wheels), gives us a recipe for cleaning these old wheels: 1 part turpentine, 1 part boiled linseed oil, 1 part white vinegar; apply with 000 or finer steel wool; wipe dirty mixture off before it dries.

FIGURE 394. The flyer wheel.

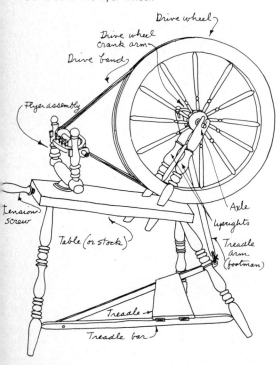

The Flyer Wheel

Wouldn't you know that old Leonardo da Vinci would put his brain to work on tools for this most universal craft? In his time, there was still one disadvantage to both the hand spindle and the wheel-driven spindle: every time you spun a length of yarn, the spindle had to be stopped and the yarn wound onto the shaft before you could spin the next length of yarn. Leonardo designed a system in which the yarn was wound onto a bobbin *simultaneously* with the spinning of it. This was a major breakthrough in spinning techniques, and it is the same principle that is used on industrial spinners today.

The problem of leading the spinning yarn to a bobbin on which it was stored he solved very cleverly by making a *hollow* spindle, with a hole down one side. The spun thread entered the turning spindle at one end, and came out the hole on the side; from there it passed through a hole on one arm of a U-shaped gadget which is called the "flyer." The flyer turned with the spindle and had two arms for reason of balance only. The arms of the flyer were suspended directly over the bobbin, and thus, as the spindle turned and the flyer with it, the thread was wound onto the bobbin. He even designed a device that made the flyer slide from side to side so that the thread wound onto the bobbin evenly. Now, if the bobbin were stationary, the flyer would wind the yarn on much too fast. So he made the bobbin turn also, by a second drive belt, but the bobbin turned at a slightly different speed because its pulley was of a different diameter than that of the spindle shaft.

Leonardo's idea was not used, however, until 1530, when Johann Jürgen actually started making wheels using this device. Jürgen modified the design. Instead of having the flyer slide back and forth to wind the thread evenly onto the bobbin, he simply put a lot of little hooks along the arms of the flyer, and the spinner manually changed the yarn to a different hook to make the thread wind onto a different area of the

FIGURE 395. The original flyer system designed by
Leonardo and the later design by Johann Jürgen.

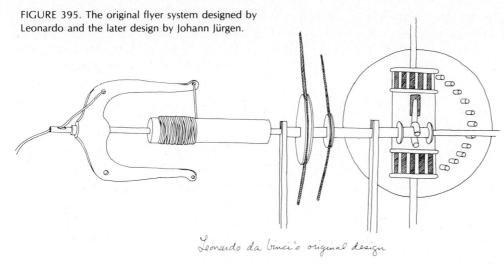

Leonardo da Vinci's original design

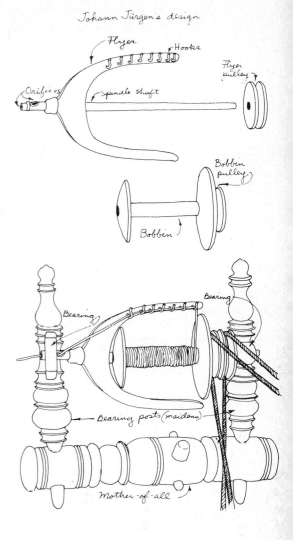

Johann Jürgen's design

bobbin. It is this system that is used today on almost all spinning wheels of the flyer
type.

On most wheels, the diameter of the bobbin pulley is *smaller* than that of the
spindle, which means the bobbin turns slightly faster than the flyer and spindle, thus
pulling the thread onto it. This difference in the rates of the flyer and bobbin is called
"lead." This lead can also be achieved by having the diameter of the bobbin pulley
larger than that of the spindle pulley. In this case the flyer would turn slightly faster
than the bobbin and the yarn would be *wound* onto the bobbin by the flyer.

Further adjustments of this lead are accomplished by slippage of the drive band
on the bobbin pulley. Such adjustments are necessary to accommodate such factors
as tighter-twisted or looser-twisted yarns, increased diameter of the bobbin shaft as
the yarn winds on and fills it up, and increased weight of the bobbin because of the
yarn on it.

The flyer wheel gained immediate popularity in Europe and many different designs were made. The wheels, in general, were much smaller than the wheels of the
original high spinning wheel. And they were all designed so that the spinner sat at the
wheel and treadled to keep the wheel turning.

The most common design, called the "Dutch wheel" because it was first designed in Holland, had the flyer set up ahead of the wheel, often a little higher than
the axle of the wheel, necessitating a diagonal base for the stand. This type, now
usually referred to as the "Saxony wheel," seemed to be the most popular.

The second most common design among flyer wheels was the upright wheel, in
which the flyer mechanism was directly above the wheel. (This wheel is sometimes
referred to as the "castle wheel," which actually was a design peculiar to Ireland. In
it the flyer mechanism was directly *below* the wheel.)

The wheels were designed primarily for spinning the fine threads of flax that were
needed for household linens, and so the wheel is sometimes called the "flax" wheel
(as opposed to the "wool" wheel), or the "low" wheel (as opposed to the "high"
wheel). When flax is spun, the prepared fiber is wrapped around a distaff, which is
supported in its own socket at the front of the wheel.

Besides these two main types of wheels, the Saxony and the upright, there were
many variations in the antique wheels, and there are even more being designed today
—all with the flyer mechanism virtually unchanged except for size. To combat the
problem of not being able to adjust the flyer to pull thick yarn (which requires very
little twist per inch) in fast enough, some manufacturers today make giant flyer mech-
anisms to accommodate the heavy yarns that are in demand today. *Some* of these
are real monstrosities and would make spinning a gross activity instead of the peaceful,

FIGURE 396. Two major types of flyer wheels: the
"Saxony" and the "Upright." (Here the upright is
furnished with a distaff for flax spinning.)

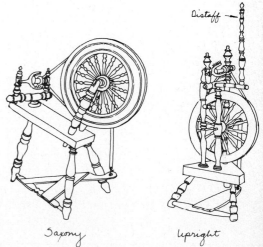

Saxony   *Upright*

soothing occupation it can be. But there are many excellent contemporary designs of the traditional type that are being reproduced mainly in the Scandinavian countries and in Australia and New Zealand.

For spinning medium to fine yarns the flyer-type wheel is a superlative machine. It is not, however, suited to spinning textured, hairy, or heavy yarns.

Adjustment and care of the flyer wheel

If you buy an old flyer wheel and there are parts missing, your best solution is to buy new parts to replace them. There are suppliers who specialize in restoring old wheels and who carry all the different parts of the flyer mechanism. Some suppliers are equipped to make new pieces especially for your wheel. If you are lucky enough to live near one of these suppliers, take your wheel to him for advice. If not, a great deal may be done by mail, and you would do well to consult them. (See Chapter XIII, "Suppliers: Spinning Equipment.")

A new wheel will usually have directions on how to assemble and work it. The parts are all nicely lathed pieces that fit together with no screws or bolts. In assembling the wheel the first consideration will be to get the uprights that support the wheel positioned just right so that the wheel will line up properly with the pulleys of the bobbin and spindle. If necessary, the uprights can be fixed in position by wedges that are slipped in between the base of the upright and the socket it fits into. The spindle supports (called the "maidens") may be adjusted in the same manner.

The drive band on a flyer wheel is a single cord that is looped double and placed so that two strands go around the wheel itself, one loop drives the spindle pulley, and one drives the bobbin pulley. A single drive band works better than two separate ones, because the correct tension adjustment between the two is automatic. The tension of the drive band can be adjusted by turning the tension screw, which moves the mother-of-all closer to or farther from the wheel. The cross in the band should occur below the flyer, and the upper thread of the cross should come from the bobbin pulley because its diameter is smaller and there will be no undue wear on the cord where it crosses itself. (If your wheel has a bobbin pulley of larger diameter—rare—then the upper thread of the cross should come from the spindle pulley.)

If you have to replace the drive band on a wheel, it should be a heavy cord of cotton or linen (plumb line is good) spliced and wound with fine thread so the joint will be as negligible as possible. To determine the right length, measure around the wheel and pulleys when the tension screw is turned so that the mother-of-all (the horizontal member that holds the maidens, which hold the entire flyer assembly) is at its position closest to the wheel. When in this position the band should be just *barely* tight enough to turn the empty bobbin. All further adjustments will be made by turning the tension screw to move the mother-of-all away from the wheel, thus tightening the drive band.

When you are actually spinning a thread, and it is being wound onto the bobbin, the thread can be held back and the bobbin will slip so that the thread is not wound on at all; it just goes on spinning tighter and tighter. When you let up your grip, it will be drawn into the orifice of the spindle and onto the bobbin. You can see that the tighter the belt, the less slippage there will be, and the yarn will be pulled in before it is spun very much. This is the situation you want in order to spin thick yarns, which require few twists per inch. The looser the belt, the more slippage there will be, and the yarn can spin a great deal because it is pulled in so slowly. This is what you want for thin yarns, which require much more twist per inch than thick yarns. Therefore, the thickest yarn you can spin on your wheel will be that which can be spun when there is absolutely no slippage of the bobbin cord, and the bobbin is pulling the yarn in at the fastest rate possible.

In the first few yards of spinning, you will make the necessary adjustments to spin the kind of yarn you want. As the bobbin fills up and gets heavier further adjustments may be necessary to keep the yarn pulling in at the same rate it did at the beginning of the spinning (the fact that the diameter of the yarn on the bobbin has increased and should pull the yarn in faster usually is not enough to compensate for the increased weight).

The important parts to oil are the axle, the joint of the treadle arm and crank arm, the spindle bearings, and the spindle itself. Use light machine oil or vegetable oil. To oil the spindle, the spindle pulley must be unscrewed and the bobbin removed. Rub the oil liberally over the entire spindle shaft.

See The High Wheel in this chapter for a good recipe for cleaning an antique wheel or keeping a contemporary wheel in good condition.

The chair or stool you sit on for spinning should be of such a height that your elbow is at the same height as the spindle.

Spinning technique

Sit facing the wheel with your right foot on the treadle. First of all try treadling the wheel without spinning any yarn and master that. Then use a ball of yarn (already spun) and spin with this until you get the feel of it. Do all this before trying to spin fiber. And I would suggest that you learn how to spin with the drop spindle before ever attempting spinning at this wheel, unless you want to go through a *very* exasperating experience.

Most wheels turn in a clockwise direction. You can tell which way your wheel is designed to turn by checking the curved crank at the back of the hub of the wheel (some wheels have a straight crank and so are made to turn in either direction). The curved crank makes it easier for the wheel to get started in the right direction. It should turn in the same direction as the curve of the crank. Give the wheel a turn with your hand by pushing down on a spoke and practice treadling until you can control the wheel without using your hand. If you always stop the wheel when the crank is just past the top, you can easily start it again without using your hand. This means both hands will be free for spinning.

Now take a length of yarn (a "leader"), about 1 1/2 to 2 feet, and thread it through the orifice at the tip of the spindle. With a hook made of a paper clip, pull the yarn out of the side hole and pass it over the farthest guide wire on either side of the flyer and tie it around the shaft of the bobbin. Now take your carded rolag or teased wool and join it to the existing yarn end coming out of the spindle by overlapping the two about an inch. (This is the same process exactly as in drop-spindle spinning.) Start the wheel and let the yarn and the carded fibers twist together slightly before drawing out the fibers.

You will see that immediately the yarn will be pulled into the hole in the spindle —sometimes before the join is secured. (This is one of the most maddening aspects of this wheel for beginners, and for this reason beginners should leave about a foot of already spun yarn protruding from the spindle to start with.) If the tension of the drive band is loose enough (which it should be), at this point you can hold back on the yarn so that the band around the bobbin pulley slips and the bobbin will not pull the yarn in if you restrain it.

When the join is made, start drawing out the fibers with your left hand as in drop-spindle spinning. Grasp the yarn close to the orifice with the right fingers to keep the twist from traveling to the rolag before the fibers are sufficiently drawn out. When they are drawn out to the right thickness, release the fingers of the right hand and the fibers will be rapidly twisted. Close them again when it is time to draw out the fibers again with the left hand.

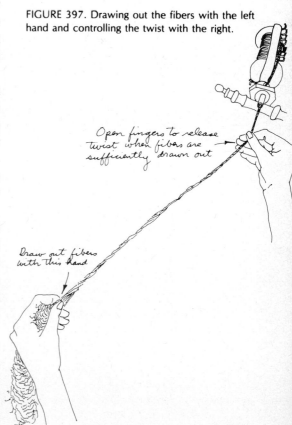

FIGURE 397. Drawing out the fibers with the left hand and controlling the twist with the right.

Open fingers to release twist when fibers are sufficiently drawn out

Draw out fibers with this hand

FIGURE 398. Some homemade wheels.

Spinning wheel with
treadle, and armature as
spindle.

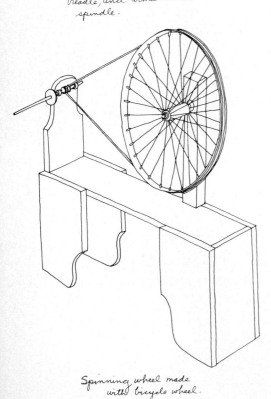

Spinning wheel made
with bicycle wheel.

There are two different techniques that may be used with the flyer wheel. One way is to let the yarn feed into the spindle hole and onto the bobbin as it is spun—at its natural speed without restraining it at all. In this case the hands are working with the wool just a foot or so away from the spindle.

The other way is to pull on the yarn enough so that it doesn't feed into the spindle hole until you have spun out an arm's length (as you do when spinning on the high wheel or drop spindle). Then you let this length feed into the spindle and onto the bobbin. Although this makes the spinning and the winding on two separate operations, it is a slightly faster technique if you are skilled at it, because you are spinning in more sweeping strokes and you can have the wheel turning much faster and still have control. It is actually the speed with which you draw out the fibers with your left hand that provides the tension to keep the yarn from feeding into the spindle. Spinning with this technique also allows you to work with less perfectly prepared fibers.

When you are spinning the first few lengths of yarn, you may need to readjust the tension of the drive band so that the bobbin does not pull the yarn in so fast that it is not spun sufficiently, or pull it in so slowly that it is overspun. Remember, the heavier the yarn, the greater the tension should be; the finer the yarn, the looser the tension should be.

After spinning each rolag, butt, or specific quantity of fiber, change the yarn onto the next guide wire. When all the guides on one side of the flyer have been used, start on the other side (the guides are set so that the second side tends to fill in any low places left by the first winding). After both sides have been used, start again with the first guide, *and at this point* if the thread seems to be spinning tighter than it was when you started, increase the tension of the drive band by turning the tension screw about one-quarter turn.

How often and how much you have to increase the tension (if at all) as you fill the bobbin may vary from this method, but whatever you do, do it consistently, making the same amount of increase in tension at regular intervals.

Continue spinning, adding rolags (see Learning to Spin with the Drop Spindle in this chapter), changing positions on the guide wires, and increasing tension until the bobbin is filled. Slip the drive band off the bobbin pulley or remove the bobbin and put it on a rack (lazy kate) so it can turn freely, and wind the yarn into a skein (see Making the Skein in this chapter). Some spinning wheels come with several bobbins, so you can spin them all before making skeins. The bobbins are also used when plying yarns.

You will soon see with this flyer mechanism that if there are lumps in the yarn, or if it is thick or hairy (like mohair) or overspun in areas, there is a great tendency for these lumps and hairs to get caught on the guide wires, or get blocked at the orifice of the spindle, causing *immediate* and drastic results (overspinning). This is another limitation of the flyer wheel—the fact that it is only good for spinning fairly even, medium- to fine-weight yarns.

However, once you grow accustomed to this wheel and know its idiosyncrasies, and use it for the purpose for which it was designed, it is a joy.

I have described spinning off to the left, with the left hand doing the drafting. This is the way most people use this wheel, because it is the same direction used for most other spinning equipment. Actually (at least according to Elsie Davenport in *Your Handspinning*—and she is certainly an authority), these wheels were designed for spinning off to the right, the fibers being drawn out with the right hand. You will see that the treadle is actually positioned in such a way that if your body is turning to the right as you spin, with your right arm outstretched doing the drafting, your foot aims more directly at the treadle. You may want to use this position if you are doing all your spinning on this wheel. Miss Davenport recommends learning to spin either way, interchangeably.

Homemade Wheels

There is no reason why you cannot make a very good spinning wheel if you are a good craftsman and engineer. Unless you are very ambitious, your best bet for the wheel itself is an old bicycle wheel. The two most important considerations in building your own wheel are that the framework of the wheel be sturdy so that it will not topple over at times, and that the spindle be perfectly balanced (the slightest wobble means the wheel will be very difficult to turn as soon as there is any amount of yarn on it). The first consideration will require only a good stable design. The second consideration is more difficult to achieve.

My husband made me a wheel in my beginning days of spinning and weaving, and he very cleverly made the spindle out of used armature (I'm told that a Volkswagen armature has a longer shaft than most, so it might be even more suitable). Thus the spindle, pulley, and bearing system were all there. This turned out to be an excellent arrangement. The spindle was, of course (because it was an armature shaft), thicker than the type on a high wheel, but this made it very handy for winding cardboard spools for warping. I could also tape on a piece of a hanger so that I could use the wheel for bobbin winding also. This wheel became a constantly used tool.

If you make a wheel with a plain spindle, make the spindle as long as possible to hold a lot of yarn. If it is too long for the wheel to function properly, it can always be cut off.

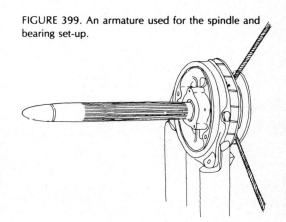

FIGURE 399. An armature used for the spindle and bearing set-up.

If you will be using the wheel for spinning only fine to medium-weight yarns, you may prefer a flyer assembly on your wheel. You can buy these from some suppliers. Make sure you are getting a well-made one (flyers that don't work well are nearly useless, and you would be much better off with a plain spindle).

The bicycle wheel can even be set up with a treadle device, if you wish. My spinning wheel was kind of a bastard type (accidentally so, because my husband and I didn't know *any*thing about wheels at the time): it used the components of a high wheel, but it was built low with a treadle, like the low wheel. A fine design that I have just discovered recently is similar to a Shaker wheel.

If you concentrate on the functional aspect of your wheel rather than the aesthetic, you will probably end up with a fine machine.

Some homemade wheels (like those in Mexico) are turned with a hand crank. The disadvantages to these are that only one hand can be used for drafting and your fiber has to be very well carded. I advise against this type of wheel.

Electric Spinners

My brother-in-law, an amateur inventor and manager of a paper mill, built me an electric spinner that is the answer to a spinner's dream. It will spin any kind of yarn, from the very finest and most even to the very thickest, lumpiest, hairiest yarn. It has foot and manual switches, can go backward and forward at the flick of a foot switch, and has a complete range of speed. The plain spindle is metal, about 12 inches long, and will hold up to a pound of yarn. When the motor is turned off, the spindle turns freely, allowing me to wind off to make the skein. But just the *parts* for this machine cost over $300.

I am now working on the manufacture of a similar electric spinner (with less

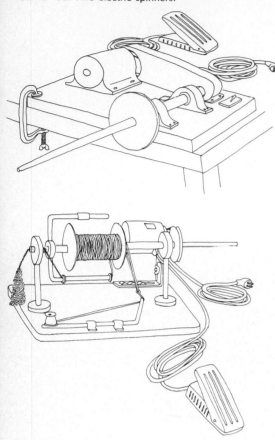

FIGURE 400. Two electric spinners.

expensive parts) that should be on the market by the time this book is in the book-stores. I recommend it with no reservations. (See Chapter XIII, "Suppliers: Spinning Equipment.")

Except for this spinner and one other (see next paragraph), I have never seen a decent electric spinner on the market or privately owned. Everyone is always saying, "Oh, just make one with sewing-machine parts." But they never turn out well; they are flimsy and/or noisy, and some of the electric spinners I have seen (actually manufactured in quantity and put up for sale) would turn anyone away from spinning on the very first try. You simply can't make a good spinner without heavy-duty parts (well machined); you want a machine that is strong and silent if you are going to spend hours sitting at it.

Walter Kircher, an internationally known manufacturer of weaving and spinning equipment, has in his brochure what looks like an excellent electric spinner of the flyer type; the bobbin-winding arrangement seems to be the type I described of Leonardo's —there are no little hooks for the yarn to catch on. This spinner is well worth looking into. It can also double as a bobbin winder. A drawing of it is in Figure 400.

Choosing Your Spinning Equipment

It is difficult to advise you what to get to spin your yarn. If you are a beginning spinner, you are going to take this advice seriously—so it has to be good. If you are already a spinner and have your favorite equipment, maybe you need to broaden your thinking and consider some new ideas; I know that many spinners are familiar with only one tool, and that is the flyer wheel—which definitely has its limitations.

We have five types of spinners to choose from: (1) hand spindles, (2) spinning wheels with a plain spindle, (3) spinning wheels with the flyer assembly, (4) home-made wheels, and (5) electric spinners. Each type has its pros and cons. And in choosing the right equipment there are personal considerations that have to be taken into account: How much spinning do you intend to do? How much money do you want to spend? What type of yarn do you want to spin? Do you travel a great deal? Do you have electricity always available?

1. Hand spindles

If you do not have much money to spend, and do not intend to spin yarn in great quantities—obviously the hand spindles should be your equipment. Even for a spinner who has all the most elaborate equipment, it is nice to have a hand spindle so that you can spin away from home, or while watching TV, or any time that it would be awkward to have a wheel with you. It is also the best tool with which to teach someone how to spin.

If you can have only one, get a fairly large drop spindle—about one foot long with a whorl about two to three inches in diameter. You will be able to spin fine to medium yarn on this. I prefer them without a notch, and my favorites are those perfectly simple ones from Peru and Bolivia. Some of the suppliers listed in Chapter XIII that make small accessories have very nice hand spindles of different sizes and types. One supplier sent me a complimentary spindle; it has a ceramic whorl, and so I was introduced to a spindle with a weighted whorl and liked it very much.

I've never used a Turkish spindle—the kind with crossbars on which the yarn is wound; nor have I tried the type with the spindle shaft *below* the whorl. My only comment is that the standard type is more universally used throughout the world.

The Navajo spindle is suitable for spinning yarn of any size, and it is the only spindle that is designed to spin thick yarns. I prefer the drop spindles for spinning fine to medium yarns, and that is why I do not recommend the Navajo spindle for your *only* spindle. Other people, of course, do rely on it for every type of spinning. If you can, get a Navajo spindle just for spinning the heavier yarns. Authentic Navajo spindles are available. Don't get one that has a huge whorl; it should never be over 6 inches, and 4 or 5 inches is better.

If you can get two drop spindles, get one quite small (10-inch length and very light) for spinning threadlike yarns, and one quite large, for spinning medium yarns. If you can have three spindles, get these two and a Navajo one.

Test the spindle by spinning it on a flat surface—like a top (if you have the opportunity). Some of the more primitive ones are quite crudely made and need to be tested for balance. It should not wobble as it spins.

2. Spinning wheels with a plain spindle

The high wheel fits in this category, of course. I don't think an antique high wheel is the wheel you will want, however, unless you can have other types of equipment and want it mainly because it is so beautiful. The spindles are too small to do all types of yarn—and producing all types of yarn is the main advantage of a plain spindle. I doubt that the design of these old wheels could handle an extra-long spindle that you could put on yourself. These antique wheels are hard to find and there are no contemporary manufacturers making them as far as I know.

A very versatile contemporary wheel with a plain spindle is the one listed in Chapter XIII, "Suppliers: Spinning Equipment." It is called a "Shaker-style" wheel. The wheel is smaller than the old high wheels, and you sit and treadle it. The plain spindle makes possible the spinning of any weight yarn. But I don't know how long the spindle is, and whether it can hold a quantity of yarn. This is a desirable feature on any piece of spinning equipment, because, unless you are spinning fine yarn, you would have to be stopping to remove the yarn on the spindle too often. This wheel would, no doubt, satisfy the requirements of a single piece of equipment (not electric) that will spin any type of yarn.

3. Spinning wheels with the flyer assembly

Unless you will be satisfied with fine to medium-weight yarns that are evenly spun and not too hairy, do not get the flyer wheel for your *only* piece of spinning equipment. If I were going to get a flyer wheel to supplement my electric spinner, I would get the very best and not worry about the expense. Part of the joy of using a flyer wheel is that it is so aesthetically pleasing, and so I would choose a nice wooden one. The Scandinavian countries and Australia and New Zealand are the top flyer-wheel-producing countries. The upright and the Saxony are equally good designs.

I advise against getting an enlarged flyer that is supposed to spin any size yarn —a plain spindle is much better for spinning heavy yarns. The wooden flyer systems, as we know them, are simply not suitable for spinning the heavy, textured yarns so in demand today.

As a beginner, however, you may be satisfied with just spinning the type of yarn the wheel is designed to spin. If that is the case, you couldn't have a better piece of equipment than one of the best contemporary flyer wheels.

4. Homemade wheels

If you are going to make a wheel, you will probably want it to spin any type of yarn, and for that reason you should make a wheel with a plain spindle, and one at which you can sit and treadle. This will be the most useful wheel you could make. You will save $200 or $300 (because that is what a really good spinning wheel costs these days), but it will also be a big job to make.

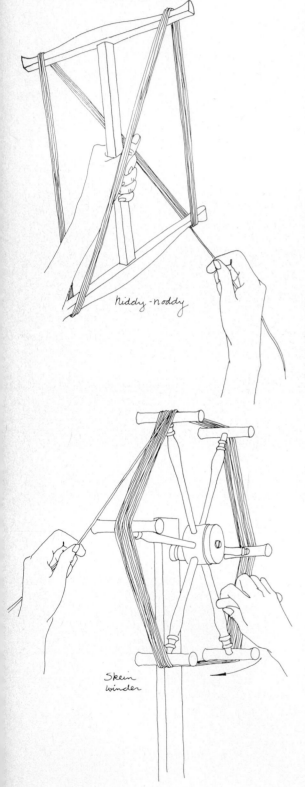

FIGURE 401. Winding the skein.

niddy-noddy

Skein winder

5. Electric spinners

One or the other of the two electric spinners described in this chapter will be your most versatile *single* spinning tool (except for a homemade wheel or, possibly the Shaker wheel). If you are going into spinning to make a living, you will want an electric spinner because with it, it is possible to sit all day spinning. Treadling the whole time is the really tiring part. Most spinners, however, will not be spending so much time at it, and so whether or not the plain spindle is run by a treadle or by electricity is not important.

A good electric spinner will also be a major investment.

Making the Skein

All handspun yarns are easier to handle in the weaving process if they are washed or at least wetted: this evens out any overspun areas and serves to make the yarn "relax." For this reason the yarn is usually wound off the spindle into a skein. (There is a primitive method for accomplishing the same thing by winding the yarn directly from the spindle into a ball, moistening the fingers so that the yarn is dampened as it is wound; after a couple of days of standing the yarn is ready to use.)

Lacking any equipment you can wind the yarn around your thumb and elbow. This does not make a very good skein because it is difficult to keep the tension consistent. Or you can wind the yarn around four legs of a straight chair (turn the chair upside down to do this). Certainly, however, if you are doing any amount of spinning you will want a good niddy-noddy or skein winder (see Chapter I, "The Basics of Weaving: An Explanation of Weaving Methods and Equipment"). And, unless you can have both a skein winder *and* a swift (designed specifically for *un*winding skeins), you had better get an *adjustable* skein winder, so you will have something to use to *un*wind your skein. (Yarns shrink when washed and will not fit onto the same size winder.)

When using the hand spindle, the easiest way to get the yarn off the spindle is simply to slip the cone of yarn off the spindle shaft. The cone can then be put in a large jar or bowl to keep it from traveling all over the floor while the yarn is being wound onto the skein winder. With the high wheel the same can be done, or the drive band can be removed so the spindle can turn freely and the skein can be wound directly from the spindle. With the flyer wheel you can wind your skein directly from the bobbins. Just remove the drive band from the bobbin pulley.

As you wind the skein, one hand will be used to guide the yarn and the other to turn the skein winder. After completing the winding (don't try to wind more than one-quarter pound—less if it is fine yarn), the two ends are crossed over each other and *loosely* wrapped around the skein two or three times and tied. At one or two other points opposite the tie, the skein should be secured by a length of any strong yarn wrapped in a figure eight and tied as shown, again *loosely*. If these ties are made too tight, the wool cannot be washed or dyed properly.

FIGURE 402. Making the proper ties on the skein.

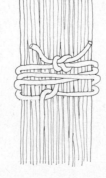

Wrap ends of spun yarn around skein.

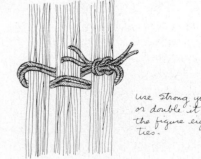

use strong yarn or double it for the figure eight ties.

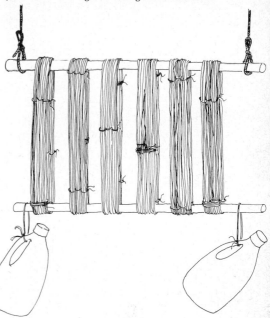

FIGURE 403. "Blocking" the skeins of hand spun yarn after washing or wetting to set the twist.

Washing the Yarn

If the fiber was washed before spinning, only a brief wetting is necessary to set the yarn, unless you are planning to dye it. In that case, or, if the yarn was spun in the grease, the skeins should be thoroughly washed in warm sudsy water, and rinsed—preferably just before dyeing (an exception to this rule is described under Techniques for Special Effects in Chapter X, "Dyeing"). Exactly the same method of washing should be used as is described under the heading Washing the Raw Wool, in this chapter. Oil or lanolin may be put into the final warm rinse water if water-repellent yarn is desired.

If you wish to set the twist of the yarn further, the skein may be dried under tension. This is called "blocking" and is most easily done by looping one end of the skein over a horizontal pole, and putting another pole through the bottom loop of the skein. Weights (such as plastic bottles, with handles, filled with water) can be hung from the bottom pole. This method produces a very professional-looking skein, and you may wish to follow it if you are marketing your handspun yarn. The procedure is absolutely necessary for very tightly twisted yarns in order to weave with them without their curling up on themselves.

Spinning Other Fibers

After you have pretty well mastered the spinning of wool you may try other fibers. In this book, we deal mainly with wool and hair fibers. For flax preparation, refer to Elsie Davenport's *Your Handspinning*.

Long-staple hair is easy to spin because the unspun fibers do not pull apart accidentally while being drawn out by the inexperienced spinner. But, just because the fibers are long, once the twist has taken there is not a chance of drawing out the

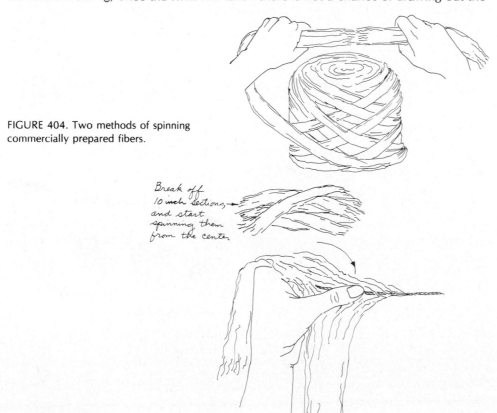

FIGURE 404. Two methods of spinning commercially prepared fibers.

Break off 10 inch sections, and start spinning them from the center

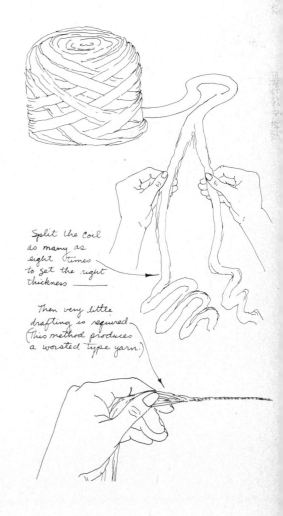

Split the coil as many as eight times to get the right thickness

Then very little drafting is required. (This method produces a worsted type yarn.)

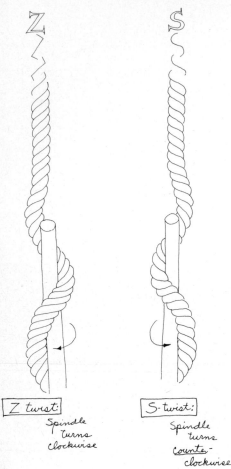

FIGURE 405. "S" and "Z" twists in yarn.

Z twist:
Spindle
turns
clockwise

S-twist:
Spindle
turns
counter-
clockwise

fibers to even out the yarn. For skilled spinners who have complete control of the twist, it is really easy to spin long hair fibers. For beginners the thing to watch carefully is that the fibers are sufficiently drawn out *before* the twist is allowed to overtake them.

Rabbit fur and dog hair may be spun, but they are so soft and fine that it will be difficult unless you combine them with wool fibers. Black poodle hair and white wool make a beautiful combination.

When you are spinning hair yarns, keep in mind that hair will make a stiffer yarn than wool, and for most weaving purposes the yarn should be one-half to one-third the thickness of woolen yarn to be used for the same warp setting. A hair yarn, because it is stiff, will not pack down as well as wool, so it has to be much finer.

There are many types of cleaned and carded fibers available through spinning-supply houses (see Chapter XIII, "Suppliers: Fibers for Spinning"). They come in the form of roving, sliver, or top (continuous coils of carded fibers). I find the easiest way to spin any of these is to break off 8- to 10-inch sections of the continuous roll, spread apart the parallel fibers, and join the center side of this mass to the yarn end that you are spinning. If you want a worsted yarn, it is best to split the coil down its length into several narrow strips. The yarn is spun very quickly from this, and needs only an occasional drafting. You can spin a pound of medium-weight yarn from this roving in about an hour on a good wheel or electric spinner. Many Navajo women use commercially carded or combed fibers for their spinning.

S and Z Twists

These letters are used to describe the direction of the twist in yarns. The S twist results from a spindle or wheel turning in a counterclockwise direction, and the Z twist results from a spindle or wheel turning in a clockwise direction. Most handspun yarns are formed with a Z twist.

Double Plying

FIGURE 406. Double plying with a spinning wheel.

Sometimes it is desirable to double ply your yarn—to make it stronger, more even, or more elastic. To double ply, wind two equal-size balls of single-ply yarn and put each ball into a large jar with a couple inches of water (water makes the yarn cling together). Take the two ends and attach them to the spindle, and spin them together in the *opposite* direction from the original twist. (Plying in the *same* direction gives a highly elastic hard-twist yarn, which is sometimes desired.) Or triple ply them in the same manner, using three strands of single-ply yarn. The water is not essential, so if you have a lazy kate or spools and a spool rack, you may prefer to use these for double plying in place of the balls and jars of water.

If you don't have any equipment but a drop spindle, the technique of hanging it from the ceiling (described in the next section) is probably the quickest way to double ply your threads.

Respinning Commercial Yarns

Some commercial yarn can be greatly improved for certain projects where a tightly twisted yarn is desirable (like warp for a Navajo loom, and for belt projects). The commercial yarn can be respun into a very tight, hard yarn. To do this with a spinning wheel or electric spinner, just put the skein on a skein winder or swift (or put a ball in a jar), attach the end to the spindle shaft, and respin it in the same direction as the existing twist.

To do this with a hand spindle it is helpful to run the yarn through a hook in the ceiling. The yarn is locked on the spindle with the same two hitches used for spinning fibers. Good long lengths of yarn can then be respun by letting the spindle hang nearly to the floor and twirling it between the palms of your hands.

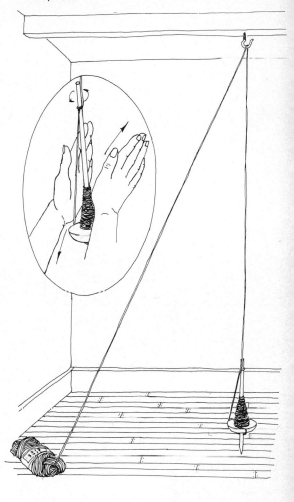

FIGURE 407. Respinning commercial yarn with a hand spindle.

Yarn Design and Function

One of the great advantages to spinning your own yarn is that you can design and spin the exact yarn that you have in mind for the job. It should be mentioned again that your handspun yarns are going to be *denser* than most commercial yarns, and so slightly more poundage of yarn will be needed for any given project. Please refer to Chapter I, "The Basics of Weaving: Your Yarns," for a further discussion of yarn.

Here are a few ideas for making different kinds of yarns:

Salt-and-pepper single-ply yarn (double-ply detracts from the effect of the two colors, I think) can be made by using black and white raw wool (or white mohair and black karakul) and carding all the white together and all the black together. As you are spinning, pick up clumps of either one color or both and spin them. This will make a yarn that has some areas of pure black and some pure white and some twisted black and white—very striking. This also can be done when you are only teasing the yarn and not carding it.

Thick and thin yarn, which is popular for knitting, can easily be made using the wool roving. Simply draw out the fibers alternately thick and thin as you spin.

Fine, tightly twisted yarn from uncarded fibers from a karakul fleece (or other "black" wool) makes a beautiful yarn for bags, pillows, rugs, or tapestries. Take the best fibers from the fleece, with good color variation, and just tease them so that they are still lying parallel to each other. Spin this into a tight, fine worsted-type yarn.

Heavy, textured yarn for rugs and hangings can be spun at the rate of about one pound per hour (including the preparation of the fiber) on a good homemade wheel with plain spindle or one of the electric spinners described in this chapter. This is a beautiful "ethnic"-looking yarn made just by teasing karakul (or other coarse, long fiber) slightly and spinning it into thick, uneven yarn about the weight of five-ply rug yarn. This can be used in its natural colors or dyed. If you dye it, try dyeing without washing first (see Chapter X, "Dyeing: Techniques for Special Effects"). This is probably the most spectacular-looking handspun yarn and the fastest to make; therefore, a good one for selling.

Warp yarn that is extremely strong is made by mixing mohair and wool in the carding process and then spinning a fine even, tightly twisted yarn; then double-ply with a very tight twist and set by wetting and drying in tension. This is the very best warp yarn for a Navajo loom.

Heather yarns for knitting or weaving can be made by dyeing the raw wool before carding or teasing it. Then spin it any way you wish—double-ply for knitting if desired. Blanket brushings (see Chapter VIII, "Finishing Techniques: Brushing") can be used to make heather yarns, but since they are likely to be short broken fibers you should mix them with some long new wool. This latter type of heather mixture is most successful when lightly overdyed.

Variegated mohair for use in brushed rugs or blankets is simply a fine, single-ply mohair, which is dyed in the skein three separate colors (see Chapter X, "Dyeing: Techniques for Special Effects"). When the yarn is woven and then brushed, the effect is spectacular! Similar to the fur of a striped cat . . . but, of course, the colors can be anything.

Single-ply plain yarn for any purpose is most quickly made by using the wool, mohair, karakul, alpaca (or other fibers) already cleaned and carded. These rovings or tops are readily available to handspinners. True, it costs more than the raw wool, but the time you will save is well worth the money—and then you will have real handspun yarn at very little cost and very little expended energy.

Double-ply yarn, particularly good for knitting, can be made very even and tightly twisted by using the flyer wheel. Using commercially carded wool (such as the gray or white Romney wool from New Zealand) in the grease will make excellent waterproof yarn for "fishermen's sweaters." This smooth, strong yarn would also be good for warp-face ponchos.

Natural gray or beige yarn is made by mixing black (or brown) and white fibers in the carding process. Sometimes you can find a fleece that is "gray" or "beige" (in these fleeces some of the hairs are black or brown and some white), but if you can't find a fleece like this you can make your own mixture. See the heading Mixing Fibers in this chapter.

Notes: Any fine, even, handspun yarn can be made even more nearly perfect if any little nubs are removed by running the yarn over a dried corn cob or sandstone. This is a trick the Navajos use. Paula Simmons points out that handspun yarns can be sized (by dipping the warp chain into a hot starch solution) and then they can be used for warp. (See Chapter VII, "The Treadle Loom: Sizing the Warp.")

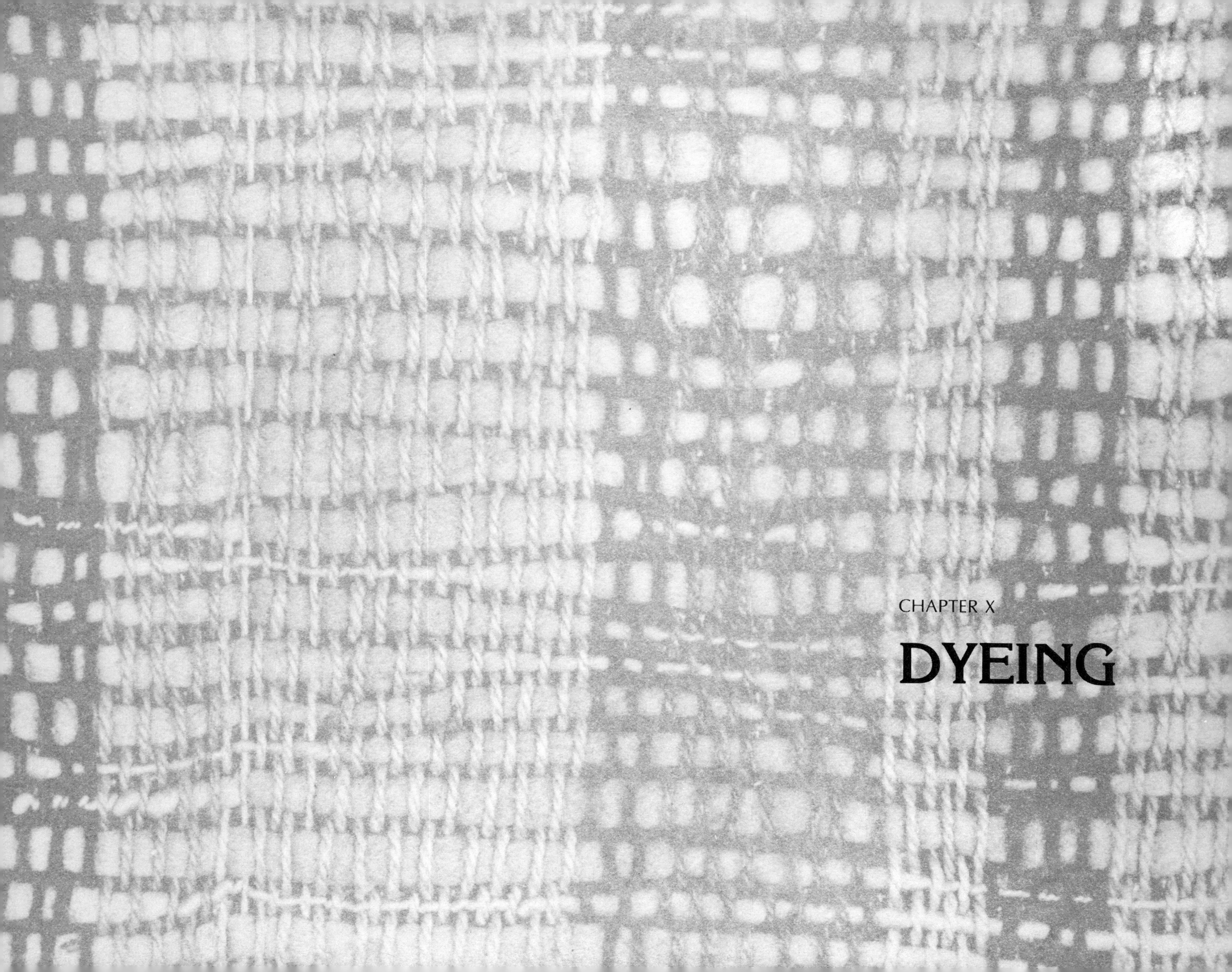

CHAPTER X

DYEING

FIGURE 408. Recipe on page 100 of *Dyes and Dyeing, Nature's Fadeless Colours . . . Over 300 Secret Recipes in Tinctorial Art and Fabrics.* Edited and reprinted verbatim from the rare original by William Jaggard. Stratford on Avon, Shakespeare Press, 1926. (Issue limited to 300 copies.)

To Dye Linnen Thread Blew

For every six pound of thread, take half an Ounce of Allom, five Ounces of Tarter, two quarts of sharp Lye, and as soon as it boils, put in your thread and let it soak therein four Hours, then rince or pass through fresh water.

And afterwards Dye it Blew:

With a Pound of boiled Brownwood, three quarters of an Ounce of Verdigrease Pulverized, one Quart of Sharp Lye, two Ox or Cowes Galls, half an Ounce of Calcined Tartar; half an Ounce of Calcined White Vitriol; put in the thread at twice, so that you may dye it light or deep at pleasure, and then the thread having first lain two Hours in the Woad Lye, must be rinced Clean. If it be put in this Dye, when it is cold, it becomes much brighter and blewer than when it is boiling hot. But the most lasting Dye for thread is performed with Woad: But if you would dye it in the Indigo Copper, you ought to use the same preparation Suds, as this Dye, and the colour will be durable; and lastly, the thread Dyed with Indigo, ought to be rinced through warm Water, in order to give it better lustre.

Why Dye Your Own Yarn?

Well, reading over this recipe should make you glad you are a twentieth-century craftsman and don't have to go through all that to get a little thread with some color in it. Actually, to dye yarn with natural dyes today is not very much more complicated than dyeing with synthetic dyes; the most time-consuming part is gathering and preparing the dyestuffs. There is, however, a certain satisfaction in knowing that the woven tapestry (or whatever) that you have produced is made from nothing more than raw wool from the sheep's back and certain plants—and that you alone have transformed these natural materials into a work of art. We take for granted the multitudinous textiles on the market today, forgetting that little more than a hundred years ago all fabrics were produced by hand methods, and dyed with natural dyes.

But, if tromping through the fields for dye materials sounds too primitive for you, and your creative urges do not allow you this time, you will still want beautiful colored yarns to work with, and these may be had by using the excellent synthetic dyes now available. I predict that, once you have used acid dyes for wool, and get used to having an infinite range of colors available for your creations, you will only occasionally buy commercially dyed yarn.

To put my point across more dramatically and give you evidence of how efficiently you can color wool, let me give you an example. When I directed the spinning, dyeing, and weaving at the Craft House in Arroyo Seco, New Mexico, we dyed all our yarns—never buying anything but natural colors: white, grays, and natural browns and blacks. On "Dyeing Day," which occurred about every six weeks, we set up two tubs of boiling water over two separate outdoor fires. Using Ciba acid dyes, four or five of us prepared, dyed, and rinsed up to 150 pounds of yarn in one eight-hour day. In each large washtub we dyed 5 pounds of one color at a time: so we dyed 30 different colors, and we used about $15 worth of dye and acid. This means the cost was approximately 10¢ per pound. And these dyes are among the very best-known dyes for wool—the same that are used by the foremost textile houses today.

The important thing is that you can get any color you want, as well as groups of related colors to use together. This is something that you simply can't get in commercially dyed yarn. True, some of the better yarn manufacturers today are concentrating on a good variety of color, but compared to what you can do they seem very limited. And some colors (especially of the less-expensive yarns) are actually dead and uninteresting—as well as not fast to light and washing.

Natural Dyes Versus Synthetic Dyes

There are pros and cons to both natural dyeing and synthetic dyeing. You may have heard that natural dyes are better and more beautiful than synthetic dyes. This statement may have had some basis for truth back in the last half of the nineteenth century when synthetic dyes were first introduced. Then the colors were brighter and less fast than the old standby natural dyes. When the weavers had available all these new synthetic colors they sometimes got carried away, and some of the color schemes were very gaudy.

You see, when natural dyes are used, there is an automatic limitation of color and brightness. The weaver simply can't miss coming up with a harmonious color combination. Even the most brilliant natural dyestuffs, when all used together, are still so soft and muted that anything goes with anything else. What is not generally known is that with synthetic dyes you can get exactly the same colors as with vegetable dyes, as well as literally hundreds more. Using these new synthetic colors, however, you have to know something about color design if you want your color schemes to be as beautiful as those achieved with natural dyes.

Perhaps this chart on the pros and cons of natural and synthetic dyeing will be helpful.

The Story of Natural Dyeing

Hundreds and hundreds of years ago man went to great trouble to color his fabrics something other than the colors of the natural fibers themselves. Although many plants yielded dyestuffs that colored fibers various shades of earthy yellows and browns, the more brilliant colors were very hard to come by—and so, of course, were more desirable.

You have probably heard mention of "royal purple." This was *Tyrian purple*. The story goes that it was first discovered, many centuries before the Christian era, by a shepherd whose dog broke a shellfish in his mouth with the result that his mouth turned purple. The Tyrians found that the extracted dyestuff, when heated with sea

NATURAL DYEING

Advantages

Nonpolluting.
Automatically harmonizing colors.
Rare color ideas (subtle colors that you might not normally think of).
Perhaps more challenging because of the element of chance.

Disadvantages

Only a few have good fastness to light and washing.
Costly, either in money or time. (Even if you gather your own dyestuffs, the mordants cost as much as the synthetic dyes or more.)
Some of the mordants are harmful to the wool fiber.

SYNTHETIC DYEING
(Using acid dyes, not all-purpose dyes.)

Advantages

Any color possible.
Quick and simple procedure allows for quantity dyeing.
Inexpensive.
Very fast to light and washing.
Least harmful to the wool fiber.
Methods allows for adjusting the color as you dye.

Disadvantages

Polluting, since these dyes are derived from coal-tar products.

The storage and use of the concentrated acid requires caution.

Knowledge of color design is needed to get subtle and harmonizing colors.

salt and allowed to ripen for a few days, then diluted and kept at a moderate heat for several more days, could be used to dye their threads for weaving. It became a very precious dyestuff and the Tyrians exported it to Rome and other countries. To give you some idea of the work involved in extracting this color, more than 8,500 mollusks were needed to obtain one gram of color. Material dyed with this color was so costly that it was available only to royalty—hence the name.

Sources of good reds, probably the color most desired by man of any era, were very few. *Kermes,* the oldest dye we have on record, was a dyestuff obtained from the bodies of insects found on a particular species of oak (a textile from a neolithic grotto of Adaouste at Bouches du Rhône, dated 1727 B.C., is said to be dyed with this). It is mentioned in the Old Testament simply as "scarlet."

Madder became the most common red dyestuff and was extensively used because of its beautiful rose-red color, its great fastness, and its availability. The plant from which it came, *Rubia tinctorum,* was cultivated for centuries by the Egyptians and East Indians, and later on by the Europeans. There are about thirty-five different species of madder. Its long, thin roots, measuring about one-quarter to one-half inch in diameter, are used for the dye. It takes about three years for the roots to reach their best quality. At this time they are harvested and pounded into a pulp. The strongest pigment is just under the rind, and the fresh root is said to be twice as potent as the dried, but of course it is marketed in the dried form. "Turkey red" was a dye made from madder by a special process, long and tedious. It was especially valuable because it dyed cotton.

The important chemicals in madder are alizarin and purpurin. Now the exact chemical equivalent of alizarin can be synthesized. (I have seen dye packets in Navajo trading posts that are called "Turkey red." I wonder if this is not alizarin, which would mean that the red in some Navajo rugs is actually the same as madder. This, of course, is pure speculation.)

The Spanish conquerors of Mexico found the natives dyeing beautiful reds with a dyestuff called *cochineal,* made from the bodies of *Coccus cacti,* insects that feed on the cactus *Nopala coccinellifera.* The Aztecs collected tribute in the form of this dyestuff from the tribes they conquered. The Spaniards liked this tribute system, continued it, and exported the dye to Europe, where for a time it was used to dye fine fabrics, among them the fabric used to make the British soldiers' jackets. This fabric in turn found its way back to the New World in the eighteenth and nineteenth centuries, where it was unraveled, respun, and rewoven by the Navajos to make their blankets. It is called "bayeta," and Navajo blankets containing this wool are now rare and extremely valuable.

To produce this dyestuff, approximately three months are allowed for the insect to mature on the cactus plant. At that time the female, dye-producing insects are shaken from the plant and killed by immersion in hot water or sun dried or stove dried. The sun-dried dye is called "negra" because of its black color, and is supposed to be the best. The stove-dried dye is called "silver cochineal." In one pound of cochineal dye there are approximately seventy thousand insects, and it takes approximately one acre to yield two hundred pounds. The cactus is native to Mexico, but has also been cultivated in Algeria, Java, the Canary Islands, and parts of Australia. The dye has fairly good fastness to light and washing—not as good as madder. Carminic acid is the coloring principle in cochineal.

One of the most brilliant yellows known by the Romans was *saffron,* collected from the pistils of the autumn crocus. And *safflower* was another important dyestuff in the Old World, especially in India and Indonesia. In a special process the yellow can be rinsed out to make a beautiful reddish dye. According to Seonaid Robertson in *Dyes from Plants,* this is the dyestuff that was originally used to dye the tape that binds legal documents—whence comes the term "red tape." It is still used in the manufacture of rouge and lipstick.

Indigo, that most famous of all dyes, is also the most unusual one (it is insoluble in water) used by the ancients. We know that it has been used for at least four thousand years. Its name is derived from *indicum,* a Latin word meaning "from India." The word "indigo" replaces the old Arab word "Al-nil," which means blue, and which, incidentally, is the ancestor of the modern word "aniline" (one of the first chemicals used in the making of synthetic dyestuffs). I presume Marco Polo must have been responsible for introducing this dye to Europe, where it has been used extensively for centuries. It is still used today, all over the world, perhaps most dramatically in Nigeria, where many villages have an area for great vats that are set in the ground for dyeing cotton yardage for the traditional clothing of the people. Real indigo rubs off from cotton, and the skin of these people usually has a bluish cast to it.

Indigo is a plant, and its leaves contain indigotin, the actual dyestuff, which is insoluble in water. If the dye is insoluble, how can it color fibers? I like to imagine that the process that makes it possible to dye with this insoluble dye was discovered in this manner: The leaves of this plant fell into a stagnant pool of water (some four thousand years ago) and several days later somebody accidentally dropped his loin cloth into this fermenting pool of yellowish-green slime. When he pulled it out, lo and behold, it proceeded to turn blue right in front of his eyes. And to his delight this blue was a permanent color that would never wash out.

The actual chemical process that was taking place was this: fermentation caused oxygen to be removed from the indigotin. In this state it was soluble in water with the help of lime or some other alkali that happened to be present. When the soaked cloth was pulled out of the pool the indigotin was again exposed to the oxygen in the air, and it slowly turned back into its original form—blue and insoluble.

(This is the principle that is involved with the vat dyes of today—among the fastest dyes known for cotton. The dyestuff itself is insoluble in water, but by a chemical process it is made soluble, and in this state it is made to penetrate the fiber. The fiber is then put through another chemical process that returns the dyestuff to its original insoluble form.)

Natural indigo is produced for the market as follows. The leaves are steeped in water until the liquid changes to a yellow-orange slimy substance. It is then beaten, causing it to change in color to green and then blue. The sludge that is formed is made into a paste and this, in turn, into bars. It was in this form that it was marketed in Europe, where the dyers, for a time, thought it was some wondrous mineral. By 1897 indigo was being made from colorless chemicals. Synthetic indigo differs from the natural product only in that it contains no impurities. When you buy indigo today this is what you will get, unless you specify genuine natural indigo. The synthetic product is about four times as potent as the natural.

In the old days it took great skill and constant attention to make an indigo dyebath, or "vat" (so called because wine vats were used). However, this vat could be used for years with only an occasional replenishing. One vat was supposed to have been in continuous use for over ninety years. Bran and madder were used in these old recipes as agents to induce fermentation. Today sodium hydrosulfite is used to remove the oxygen from the indigotin, and the resulting compound, called "indigo white," is dissolved in a solution of water and caustic soda. The process of dyeing is similar to what occurred when the fellow dropped his loin cloth into the pool and pulled it out: a series of dippings and airings, repeated over and over until the desired shade of blue is reached. I read somewhere that in the Middle East sometimes as many as fifty dippings and airings are made to obtain a deep blue black.

Woad is another plant whose leaves contain indigotin, but in much smaller quantities than found in the indigo plant. In this country and in Europe, woad was grown in the sixteenth and seventeenth centuries. Indigo, at one time during this period, was actually outlawed in England to protect the woad industry. (No doubt Mr. Jaggard, who wrote the recipe reprinted on the first page of this chapter, was a victim of that propaganda program.) Woad supposedly makes a faster color, and indigo a brighter color. When indigo became available again through importation, it was generally accepted that woad produced an inferior dyestuff.

Quercitron, logwood, old fustic, and *cutch* (or *catechu)* are four more well-known dyes from the old days. Fustic, grown in Cuba and Jamaica, and quercitron (from the black oak of that name) give strong yellow dyes, and logwood was used for purples and blacks. Cutch yields a brown dye. All four of these dyes are chips of wood of certain trees.

Weld, a plant, is one of the very best yellow dyestuffs. It is native to the Mediterranean area and has been used for thousands of years.

Lichens are another plant source of dyestuffs. For years they have been used, particularly in the British Isles, where the manufacturers of the famous Harris tweeds use handspun yarns dyed with lichens. They yield a variety of colors, from soft beiges and browns to pinks. They are unusual in that they require no mordant in the dyeing process, because of the acid they contain.

With the exception of lichens and some barks and indigo, most natural dyes require a *mordant* to fix the dye. "Mordant" comes from the Latin word *mordere*: to bite. The mordant seems to bite into the fiber, making it possible for the dye to penetrate. What actually happens is this: the mordant and the dye, although each separately is soluble in water, combine on the fiber to make a more or less insoluble chemical compound. Most mordants tend to harm the fiber, however, so they must be used with care. Normally the fiber is treated with the mordant prior to immersion in the dyebath. This allows more accurate control and tends to give clearer colors. The mordant can, however, be used in the dyebath itself, or the fiber can be treated after it is dyed.

In the early days leaves and roots of certain plants were used for mordants, as well as urine, which contains ammonia and uric acid, and lye of wood ashes (potash). Tannin, which occurs in the barks of trees and is concentrated in oak galls (little round formations sometimes found on oak trees), also acts as a mordant, particularly useful in cotton dyeing. Smoking the dyed wool over a fire that is covered with manure and urine-soaked wool is sometimes done by Navajo women to further brighten and fix the colors: the principal chemical released by the smoking wool is ammonia.

Alum has been used for centuries in Europe. Today the most common mordants used for wool dyeing are these metal salts: *alum* (potassium aluminum sulfate; or aluminum ammoniate will work); *chrome* (potassium dichromate); *tin* (stannous chloride); *iron* (ferrous sulfate), also known as "copperas" or "green vitriol"; *blue vitriol* (copper sulfate) also known as "bluestone." *Tannin* is an astringent vegetable compound that occurs in the bark of trees, especially oak, and in large quantities in oak galls; it is used mainly in the dyeing of cotton.

Alum, which damages the fiber least for the brilliance of color it gives, is probably the most often used. Chrome actually softens wool and gives warm, rich colors, and is next in importance, although difficult to use because it is sensitive to light. Iron is hard to use, and damages the fiber; for this reason it is usually added near the end of the dyeing to dull or "sadden" the colors. It is used primarily to get dark colors. Tin, although it produces some of the most brilliant colors, tends to make the yarn brittle, and must be used with care. It is often used in small amounts to "bloom" or brighten already dyed colors, being added toward the end of the dyeing. Blue vitriol is used to make yellows go toward greens. *Cream of tartar* is often used in combination with any of these mordants, and *Glauber's salt* acts as a leveling agent—helps to make the dyeing even.

Obtaining Natural Dyestuffs

I'm going to give you some recipes using some of these famous old dyes that can be purchased from many of the suppliers listed in Chapter XIII, as well as colors you can get from plants that you gather yourself. (If you live in the city, and have no access to vegetation, you can even buy these from some suppliers.) The mordants also are most easily obtained from one of these suppliers, although most of the chemicals you can get at a pharmacy, and chrome at a photography-supply store.

FIGURE 409. Gathering rabbit brush in New Mexico.

Many shops supply natural dyes, but most are very pessimistic about a continuing supply and about the cost—especially of indigo, cochineal and madder, probably the most useful of the natural dyes because of the colors they produce. So in ordering be ready to be told that they are out of stock. As for buying these dyes and the other natural dyes (such as fustic, logwood, and some of the old stand-bys), unless you are just dyeing for special projects, such as wall hangings, or for some very special rug or piece of clothing, you should be prepared to spend quite a bit. Cochineal is too expensive to use except in *very* special pieces; madder will be the least expensive good red. The best thing to do is to gather most of your dyestuffs at the right time of year and do your dyeing then, or dry the stuff for later use, and use the bought dyes only occasionally.

In ordering indigo, note whether it is natural or synthetic (either of these is the type you use for the real indigo vat dyeing, but the synthetic is many times stronger than the natural). What you *don't* want is indigo crystals or indigo extract (that is, if you want to use the authentic dye method described in this book, and if you want the dye to be colorfast).

In ordering cochineal, note whether it is real insect cochineal, or cochineal coloring. The first is what you want and is *very* expensive.

If you are gathering your dyestuffs, you will be looking for roots, berries, barks, flowers, and leaves—and sometimes the whole plant. Any of these parts should be collected for the most part at the peak of maturity. If it is the whole plant that is required, gather it when it is young and vigorous. Pick flowers just when they come into bloom (these are the most delicate of all, and to obtain the most brilliant color from them they must be treated with great care; Seonaid Robertson, a well-known dyer, gathers flower petals directly into a jar of water). Collect leaves just when they are out in full. Berries are best when a little overripe. Bark, if resinous, should be gathered in the spring, otherwise in the fall (you can use bark from recently felled trees), the best color coming from the inner bark. Dig roots in late summer and in the fall. Lichens can be most easily gathered in damp weather because they swell up in the rain.

Very generally, figure on about one peck to half a bushel of fresh plant material per pound of wool to be dyed. The dye is stronger when the plant is fresh (tender green plants should be used immediately), but if desired the material may be dried and used later.

Read Seonaid Robertson for information on a dye-plant garden.

Testing Natural Dyes for Fastness

The dyes in the recipes that follow are all proven to be good natural dyes, you will want to experiment using plants that you have gathered in your area, but which you may not know much about. One of the most important things you will want to consider in using these experimental plants is whether or not they yield a dye that is fast. There is nothing more discouraging than to spend days or weeks spinning or weaving something only to have it fade out into pale, insipid colors, or to have the colors bleed when you wash it.

Test for light fastness by putting a small swatch of the dyed yarn in a sunny window and after a week compare it to the rest of the skein, which has been kept away from light entirely. Dyes from tree barks (which have tannin) will actually darken when exposed to sunlight.

Test for wash fastness by washing a small amount of the dyed yarn in hot water and soap along with some white wool yarn. If the white yarn becomes stained with the color, you will know just how much the color bleeds.

Equipment Needed for Natural Dyeing

Two enamel or stainless-steel pots. (Aluminum, copper, or iron pots will change the color—although these can be purposely used to act as mordants by adding a little soda. Iron pots should be used if you want dark, dull colors.) Figure on pots that will hold 1 gallon of *boiling* liquid for every 4 ounces of yarn to be dyed one color. Thus a 5-gallon pot will be needed to dye a full pound without any spillage. The yarn itself will not add any appreciable volume.

A large spoon or stick for stirring and lifting the yarn.

Rubber gloves for handling the steaming-hot yarn (optional).

Soft water. If your water is not naturally soft, use lake, stream, or rain water (rain or melted snow water will be the best); or soften it by adding acetic acid, vinegar, or a commercial softener like Calgon. *This is very important*; the type of water you use will affect the final colors. As a last resort buy distilled water.

Thermometer (needed only if you are dyeing madder or indigo).

No need to have a lot of fancy equipment for dyeing. I've found that many people are totally discouraged from trying to dye yarns because everything sounds so complicated and exacting. What you have in your kitchen will probably do—except perhaps for the big pots. Scales are not really necessary: the only dyestuffs for which weight is specified are those that you will be ordering from a supply house, and you will know how much you have ordered and divide that amount in half or whatever for the recipe. Many books say to use glass rods for stirring; this is too fussy—use wooden sticks and just be careful about colors staining lighter colors.

For quantities larger than 1 pound, refer to "For Quantity Dyeing" in Equipment Needed for Dyeing with Acid Dyes in this chapter.

General Instructions for Dyeing with Natural Dyes

Use these general directions for dyeing with any natural dye except indigo. Refer to recipes that follow for amounts of dyestuff, kind of mordant, and any special directions. These directions and the recipes that follow are for 1 pound of wool. I think

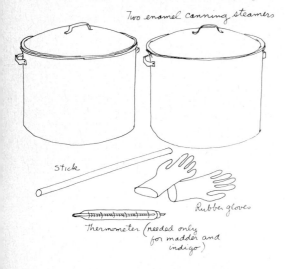

FIGURE 410. Equipment needed for natural dyeing.

Two enamel canning steamers

Stick

Rubber gloves

Thermometer (needed only for madder and indigo)

you will find it most efficient to dye this amount; then you will have a good supply of that color even if you won't be using it all in one project. There is always an element of chance in natural dyeing, so be flexible in your plans. Usually figure on dyeing more than one batch in the same dyebath. The dyebath will still have a lot of color in it for second or third dyeings; sometimes these yield the most beautiful and subtle colors.

One day before dyeing

1. Prepare the wool.

Make the yarn into skeins of not more than 4 ounces per skein. Tie *loosely* in 2 or 3 places with figure-eight tie as described in Chapter IX, "Spinning: Making the Skein." (Commercial skeins for weaving are usually tied properly for dyeing.)

Wash yarn, fleece, or fabric that has any oil or dirt in it. (See Chapter IX, "Spinning: Washing the Raw Wool" or "Washing the Yarn", for proper procedure.) Rinse.

Or soak clean yarn, fleece, or fabric in water at least half an hour. If hot water is used, soaking time can be shortened. Leave it sitting in the sink or pot, or tie it up in plastic bags until ready to use. (Moisture is absorbed by the wool fiber very slowly: if you put a dry skein of yarn into the mordanting bath or dyebath, the chemicals will penetrate unevenly.) Fiber that is to be mordanted the next day can soak overnight.

2. Mordant the wool.

When the recipe calls for alum, tin, or blue vitriol, it is best to mordant prior to dyeing. Because of its sensitivity to light, chrome is best used to mordant immediately before dyeing. Iron is best added to the dyebath toward the end of the dyeing so as not to harm the fiber unnecessarily. Because tin and iron can be damaging to the fiber, it is best not to use them unless absolutely necessary to obtain a certain color.

To mordant 1 pound of wool with alum:

4 ounces alum (potassium aluminum sulfate)—slightly less than 1/2 cup

1 ounce cream of tartar (about 2 tablespoons)

4 gallons soft water

1 pound clean, wetted wool

Dissolve the alum and tartar in boiling water (about 2 cupfuls). Add to the 4 gallons of water. Enter the wetted wool, and heat *gradually,* stirring often. Simmer gently about 1 hour. Poke and stir occasionally. Cool and let stand in liquid, or squeeze out excess moisture and store in towel, or dry for future use. Do *not* rinse.

To mordant 1 pound of wool with tin:

1/2 ounce tin (stannous chloride), or 1 rounded tablespoon

1/2 ounce cream of tartar . . . (or 1 tablespoon)

4 gallons soft water

1 pound clean, wetted wool

Same procedure as with alum, but *wash and rinse* wool immediately afterward; use immediately, store in damp towel, or dry for future use.

(To brighten, or "bloom," colors mordanted with other chemicals, tin can be added toward the end of the dyeing, just as iron is added to dull, or "sadden," the

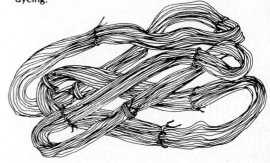

FIGURE 411. Skeins of yarn properly tied for dyeing.

colors. The dyed wool should be washed *thoroughly* after using either of these mordants.)

To mordant 1 pound of wool with blue vitriol:

1 ounce blue vitriol (slightly less than 3 tablespoons)

4 gallons soft water

1 pound clean, wetted wool

Same procedure as with alum.

FIGURE 412. Chopping the plant material to be soaked overnight.

3. Chop and soak the plant material.

Chopping, crushing (to release any acids in the plant), soaking, and boiling are usually necessary to extract the dye from the vegetable matter. In general the coarser the material the longer it should soak and boil. Tough barks should soak overnight. Robert and Christine Thresh in *Introduction to Natural Dyeing* tell that they accidentally discovered that aging plant material by soaking in water for two months or more seemed to improve the intensity of the color. Fermenting often improves the color from berries. Cover material with soft water and let soak overnight.

On dyeing day

1. Prepare dye liquor.

Bring dyestuff and water it has soaked in to a boil and simmer for 1 hour. Rough material such as wood chips should be boiled longer, and flower blossom less. (To get the *clearest* colors from flower blossoms they are sometimes best simply added to the dyebath *with* the wool, because long boiling dulls the color.)

Strain the liquid into a container and tie the remaining loose material in a piece of cheesecloth (unless it will be too much to fit into the dyepot). Add these to a pot of warm water to make 4 gallons of liquid.

2. Mordant with chrome (if this is called for in recipe).

Chrome mordanting must be done just prior to dyeing, since this chemical is sensitive to light, and everything possible must be done to keep the mordanted wool away from light.

To mordant 1 pound of wool with chrome:

1/2 ounce chrome (potassium dichromate), or slightly less then 2 teaspoons

4 gallons soft water

1 pound clean, wetted wool

Proceed as in mordanting with alum. A ceramic plate should be put on top of the wool in the mordanting bath to make sure it keeps under water. A lid must be used on the pot also. Keep the wool in the pot until you are ready to transfer it quickly to the dyebath.

3. Dye the wool.

Add mordanted wool to the dyebath (wet any pre-mordanted and dried wool) and bring slowly to a boil. Simmer gently for 1 hour, stirring occasionally. About 1 1/2 to 2 tablespoons of cream of tartar may be added to the dyebath to improve the color. Tin may be added near the end to brighten the color, or iron to darken it. Whenever you add these chemicals, you must first remove the yarn from the dyebath.

Allowing the yarn to remain in the dyebath to cool—overnight sometimes—will make the color faster, but usually darkens and dulls it.

4. Wash, rinse, and dry.

Wash the wool with mild soap or detergent. Rinse well, and dry in an airy place, preferably not in sunlight.

5. Dye a second batch of yarn.

There will still be some color left in the dyebath. If you wish to produce some interesting pale, subtle shades, dye another pound of wool in this, using the same procedure.

Or the dye liquor may be saved in tightly covered jars. It will keep a long time in the refrigerator.

Recipes for Natural Dyes

Beet root

(To extract the dye: Boil beets whole, being careful not to break the skin. Then remove the skins and cut up beets and cover with a solution of half water and half vinegar. Let this stand for 2 days. Add this solution, beets and all, to the dyebath with a handful of salt. Boil only 10 minutes with the yarn. This dye has only fair fastness to light and washing, but because of its availability I have included it here. As with many vegetable dyestuffs the brilliant color of the beet is not retained and only a gold color results.)

Gold   3 pounds beet roots (very fresh)
          Alum mordant

Birch bark

(Also try oak, maple, walnut, hemlock, and apple, from fresh prunings. Black oak is where quercitron—one of the best yellow dyes—comes from. Use the inner bark; no mordant necessary.)

Light brown   1/2 bushel bark, white birch
                No mordant

Bracken (common fern)

(Gather when fern is still curled, and use immediately if possible.)

Yellow green   3 gallons ferns
               Alum mordant
Warm yellow green   3 gallons ferns
               Chrome mordant

Cochineal

(No preliminary soaking of cochineal is necessary. Add the powder directly to the dyebath, and heat with the wool *very gradually*. Not as fast as madder, so the dyed fiber should not be exposed to sunlight.)

Rose   4 ounces cochineal
          Alum mordant
          (Add tin near end to brighten, if desired.)
Purplish red   4 ounces cochineal
            Chrome mordant
            (Color may be blued by adding a little ammonia or sodium carbonate.)
Scarlet   4 ounces cochineal
          Tin mordant

NOTES

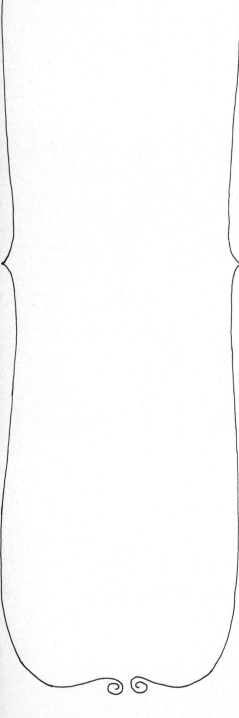

Coffee beans
Dark yellow tan   3/4 pound ground coffee
                    Chrome mordant

Coreopsis
(Also try dahlias and zinnias.)
Burnt orange   3 gallons coreopsis heads
                 Chrome mordant

Elderberries
(Add 1 tablespoon salt when boiling the berries to extract the dye.)
Lilac blue   2 gallons berries
             Alum mordant
Violet   2 gallons berries
           Chrome mordant

Elderberry leaves
(Also try peach, pear, plum, poplar, rhododendron, and birch.)
Brass   1/2 bushel elderberry leaves
          Chrome mordant
Beige   1/2 bushel elderberry leaves
          Alum mordant

Fustic
(If fustic extract is used, no preliminary soaking of fustic extract is necessary. Boil only 30 minutes; longer boiling makes fustic turn brown.)
Gold   1/2 ounce fustic extract (or 4 ounces chips)
         Chrome mordant
Yellow tan   1/2 ounce fustic extract (or 4 ounces chips)
               Alum mordant (After completing this dyeing, add yarn immediately to another boiling water bath to which have been added 1/6 ounce chrome and 1/6 ounce acetic acid, or 1/2 cup vinegar. Boil this 10 minutes.)

Goldenrod
Gold   3 gallons goldenrod flowers
         Chrome mordant

Indigo
Because of their complexity, directions for this recipe appear at the end of this section, on page 258.

Lily-of-the-valley
(Only fair fastness to light.)
Greenish yellow   3 gallons new leaves
                    Chrome mordant

Logwood
(Boil soaked logwood chips only 1/2 hour to extract the dye.)
Purplish gray   4 ounces logwood chips
                  Alum mordant

Black (or near black)   8 ounces logwood chips
1/2 ounce fustic
Chrome mordant
(Add 1 ounce acetic acid or 1 quart vinegar to
dyebath.) For best results use naturally dark wool.

Madder
(Avoid boiling this dyestuff. High temperatures tend to yellow the color. After soaking madder overnight, do not boil. Bring to a temperature of only 140 degrees and hold it there for 15 minutes. Then add the wool. Instead of boiling the wool in the dyebath, keep it at approximately 190 degrees. This is the only dyestuff that does best in *hard* water. Deep wells usually yield hard water. If only soft water is available add a little slaked lime to the water if possible.)

Red   1/2 pound madder
          Alum mordant
Rust red   1/2 pound madder
          Chrome mordant

Wash with mild *soap,* and rinse. Soap brings out the brilliance of the color.

Marigolds
Dark gold   3 gallons flower heads
          Chrome mordant
Brass   3 gallons flower heads
          Alum mordant

Onion skins
(Use yellow onions, or red-skinned onions for a deeper color.)
Burnt orange   3 gallons yellow onion skins
          Alum mordant
Brass   3 gallons yellow onion skins
          Chrome mordant

Prickly pear cactus fruit
(This dye is extracted strictly by fermentation; no boiling and no mordants are necessary. The color is quite poor in fastness to light, but because it makes such a beautiful color it is worth trying.)
Purplish pink   4 pounds prickly pear cactus fruit (peeled)
              1 pound wool
Mash the cactus, add water and wool to make 4 gallons. Let ferment in a warm place for 10 days or 2 weeks. Stir occasionally. For a deeper color, repeat the process, using fresh batch of fruit.

Red clay water
(The Navajos sometimes use this. Simply dip up water that collects in puddles in red-earth area.)
Beige   4 gallons red clay water
          Alum mordant
Simmer for four hours.

Rabbit brush
Yellow   3 gallons flower heads
          Alum mordant

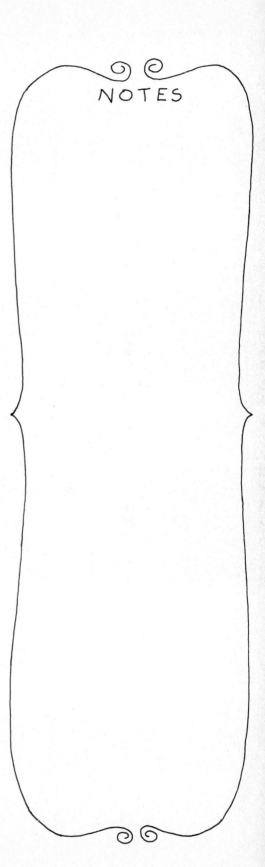

NOTES

Saffron

(Overnight soaking not required. Boil saffron gently for 1/2 hour only before adding to dyebath.)

Yellow   1/4 pound saffron
          Alum mordant

Sassafras

Rose brown   3/4 pound sassafras
              Chrome mordant
Brown   3/4 pound sassafras
              Alum mordant
              (After completing this dyeing, add immediately to another boiling-water bath to which 1/6 ounce chrome and 1/6 ounce acetic acid [or 1/2 cup vinegar] have been added. Boil this 10 minutes.)

Tea leaves

(Boil tea only 15 minutes before adding to dyebath.)

Rose tan   1/2 pound black tea
              Alum mordant
Light brown   1/2 pound black tea
              Chrome mordant

Walnut hulls

(Also try butternut, hickory, and pecan. These dyestuffs require no mordant, but a richer color may be obtained if you use alum. After soaking hulls overnight in water, boil 2 hours.)

Dark brown   6 quarts green walnut hulls
                No mordant necessary
Golden brown   6 quarts green walnut hulls
                Alum mordant

Weld

Lemon yellow   1/2 bushel weld (whole plant)
                Alum mordant
Gold   1/2 bushel weld
        Chrome mordant
Bright orange yellow   1/2 bushel weld
                        Tin mordant
Olive   1/2 bushel weld
         Alum mordant (iron added the last 15 minutes)

Indigo

Indigo blue is dyed by a unique process. (See The Story of Natural Dyeing in this chapter.) Indigo itself is insoluble in water. In order to dye with it we must first make it soluble. This is achieved by the addition of sodium hydrosulfite and sodium hydroxide (caustic soda). The former chemical removes the oxygen from the dyestuff, and in this form it is soluble in a solution of caustic soda and water. In this dissolved state it becomes a clear yellow. The fiber is dyed in this solution and then "aired." When the dye solution in the fibers is exposed to the oxygen in the air, it turns back to its original blue color, which again is insoluble. As the yarn is aired you can see it turn

FIGURE 413. Making the indigo stock solution.

① Add caustic soda (which has been mixed with water) to the indigo—

Caustic soda and water

Powdered indigo

② Add hot water (about 120°) to make 1 gallon.

③ Sprinkle in the sodium hydrosulphite

blue. This process of dyeing and airing is repeated until the desired depth of blue is reached. If the dyebath is more concentrated, more vivid blues are possible.

The method described here is called the hydrosulfite vat. In *Your Yarn Dyeing,* Elsie Davenport mentions a simple method of dyeing with "indigo extract" and sulfuric acid, but cautions the craftsman not to use it because it has such poor fastness. Indigo dyed by the method described here is extremely fast to light and washing, although it does have a tendency to "rub" off, especially in cotton.

Since this is a fairly complicated procedure you will probably want to dye as many skeins as possible with the dyebath. Depending on how many dippings each skein gets, you will be able to dye quite a bit more than one pound of wool with this recipe. Plan, also, to overdye skeins of yellow to get greens; and skeins of reds to get purples. Indigo over walnut-hull-dyed wool makes a good black. You can also dye some skeins blue with the intention of overdyeing them later, although it is better to do the reverse so you will have more control over the exact color.

Make an indigo stock solution:
4 1/4 ounces natural indigo (or 1 ounce synthetic)
3 ounces sodium hydroxide (caustic soda)
2 3/4 ounces sodium hydrosulfite

Put the indigo in a jar. In another jar mix the sodium hydroxide (caustic soda) with enough water to dissolve it. *Use caustic soda with caution—it burns.* Add this to the powdered indigo and mix well. Add this and hot water (about 120 to 130 degrees, but definitely not over 140) to fill a gallon jar. Stir very gently. Avoid air bubbles, because at this point we don't want any oxygen mixing with the indigo. Sprinkle in the hydrosulfite. Let stand for 30 minutes.

The liquid should now be a clear yellow green. Test this by dipping into the liquid a piece of clear glass. As you pull it out the liquid on the glass should be yellow green, and should turn to blue in about one-half minute. At this point, if there are white specks on the glass, they need to be dissolved by the addition of a very small amount of caustic soda. If there are blue specks, this means the indigo still contains oxygen and needs a little more sodium hydrosulfite.

This solution may be kept in a tightly covered jar for future use.

Make a sodium hydrosulfite solution:
1/2 ounce sodium hydrosulfite
1 quart water

Mix and keep in a tightly covered jar. This will be used to add to the dyebath as needed. Each time the yarn is returned to the dyebath it brings oxygen along with it. Small additions of this solution will remove that oxygen and keep the dyebath the clear yellow green it should be.

Prepare the dyebath: Heat 3 1/2 gallons water to 120 degrees and keep at this temperature throughout the dyeing. Add 1/2 cup sodium hydrosulfite solution. Stir well, but gently. Let stand 10 minutes. Add 2 to 2 1/2 quarts of the clear yellow-green indigo stock solution. Stir gently . . . remember, no air bubbles. Let stand for 20 minutes. The dye liquor is now ready.

Dip and air the wool: Add the wool, submerge, and stir gently. Let stand for 20 to 30 minutes, stirring regularly. Lift yarn from the dyebath and air for 30 minutes, spreading the yarn regularly so that all parts get exposed to air. This is the process that returns the oxygen to the indigo and changes it back to blue.

Repeat: Repeat this process until the desired shade is achieved. Add a small amount of the sodium hydrosulfite solution immediately after lifting yarn out, to keep the dyebath yellow. (After each addition the dyebath must stand for at least 15

FIGURE 414. The indigo vat.

the dyebath (indigo stock solution and 120° water) ready for first dipping

Indigo stock solution (surplus)

Sodium hydrosulphite solution (for replenishing the dyebath after dippings)

minutes before entering the yarn again.) More indigo stock solution may be added if vivid color is desired.

Final airing: The yarn should be aired finally for a couple of days.

Rinse: After the final airing, rinse several times, using a small amount of acid (or large amount of vinegar) in the first rinse, to neutralize the caustic soda, since this alkali will damage the wool.

Wash: Wash well with mild soap or detergent and rinse. Indigo tends to rub off some, but becomes a clearer and lovelier blue as time goes by.

Lichens

I have had no experience with lichen dyeing, so the information here is strictly from what I have read. For more information about lichen dyeing, see *Lichens for Vegetable Dyeing* by Eileen M. Bolton (available in both U.S. and England). Lichens contain acids, so no mordant is required; however, you can use one. Supposedly there are few lichens in the United States that yield dye colors, and those that do are found mainly by the sea or at high altitudes. You will simply have to test what you have gathered; some will produce a color, and some will not. Some lichens will produce purplish and reddish colors with fermentation. Seonaid Robertson tells of a way to test for this that she learned from Marie Aitken of Ontario. Put a drop of chlorine (in bleach) on the inner part of the lichen; if it turns red, this means that a purplish or reddish color can be achieved by fermenting the lichen.

Either the fresh plant may be used or the dried. In either case the skin should be broken into as much as possible to release the acids, so chop the fresh plant thoroughly or crumble the dry plant into pieces as fine as possible. In general the lichens are kept in the dyebath along with the wool, and long simmering is required. *Slow* heating and cooling are required.

Boiling Method
1 pound dried lichens
1 pound wetted wool
1/4 cup vinegar

Simmer lichens in soft water to which vinegar has been added. Let cool overnight. Add wool to this, reheat slowly, and simmer for 1 hour or longer. Let stand to cool. Rinse. Shake out pieces of lichen and dry.

Fermenting Method
1 pound dry lichens
5 quarts ammonia
2 1/2 gallons soft water
1 pound wetted wool

Crumble the lichens into a 4-gallon container with a top. Add the ammonia and soft water. Let this stand in a sunny spot or warm place between 55 and 75 degrees, stirring twice a day, for 10 days or 2 weeks. Add the wetted wool to this fermenting mixture and simmer for an hour or so.

Note: Seonaid Robertson points out that some lichens take 50 to 100 years to reach the size of your hand, so test out the lichen with the boiling method and the fermenting method before you do wholesale gathering.

Navajo mordant

Ashes of juniper:
Gather juniper branches from trees that have a reddish appearance. Set fire to a handful and hold over a skillet to catch the ashes. Burn only the green needles. To

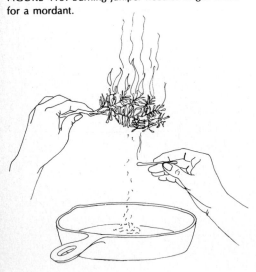

FIGURE 415. Burning juniper needles to get ashes for a mordant.

1 cup of hot juniper ashes add 2 cups boiling water, stir throughly, and strain. Use this as the mordant. (From Nonabeh G. Bryan's *Navajo Native Dyes,* compiled by Stella Young.)

Additional Natural Dyestuffs

Reds, pinks, brazilwood	Rose hips, mountain mahogany root, sorrel, ladies bedstraw (roots), bloodroot (roots), pokeberries
Yellows, oranges, golds	Snakeweed, barberry (the tips, bark, and roots), leaves of peach, pear, poplar, plum, rhododendron, and birch; turmeric, osage orange, chamiso
Yellow greens	Wild holly root, dock, sagebrush, nettles, lamb's-quarters
Blues, purples, grays	Blueberries (canned if necessary), whortleberries, yellow iris root, juniper berries, wild holly berries, dandelion root, young shoots of blackberry, dock root, juniper mistletoe
Browns	Juniper root, chokecherries, ground lichens, scarlet bugler, walnut root, wild plum root, waterlily root, sumac berries or leaves

Mixing Natural Dye Colors

One of the most exciting things to do with natural dyes is mix colors so that you get every color of the rainbow. In most cases mixing colors requires two separate dyeings unless the dyestuffs require the same method and mordant.

Indigo and madder are the most useful colors to use for mixing because with them you can get bright purples, oranges, and greens. To get green, dye indigo over yellow; for oranges, madder over yellow; for black, indigo over walnut hulls; for purple, indigo over madder (or cochineal gives an even brighter purple). These combinations would give you a complete range of colors in very fast natural dyes.

In any combination with indigo, do the indigo last, as you will then have more control of the exact color you want.

To dye a color with the intention of overdyeing it later is called "bottoming," and the overdyeing is called "top-dyeing."

To even out skeins that have streaks, or to bring two skeins dyed with the same dye but in different dye lots to the same color, simmer the dyed fiber in a bath with 1 cup of Glauber's salts to each gallon of water.

The Story of Synthetic Dyeing

Until the middle of the nineteenth century all dyes were derived from animal, vegetable, or mineral sources—and very complicated and sometimes laborious methods and formulas were worked out to get the brightest and most lasting colors from these limited sources. In 1856 William H. Perkin discovered the first artificial dyestuff at the Royal College of Chemistry in London. It was purplish in color, and he called it "mauve." This mauve coloring matter dyed silk directly. By 1859 other chemists had discovered other colors—all synthesized from aniline, which is derived from coal tar. Thus England claims to be the discoverer of aniline dyes.

The Badische Anilin und Soda Fabrik began dye manufacture at Ludwigshafen a few years later and for some sixty years Germany led the world in the chemistry and technology of dyes. The yarn mill in Germantown, Pennsylvania, used these aniline

NOTES

dyes, and the Navajos even used Germantown yarns for a short period toward the end of the nineteenth century. These early coal-tar dyes were quite fugitive (faded quickly) and so there was a great prejudice against them. Later, azo compounds (also derived from coal tar) were developed, and extremely fast colors became available.

Synthetic dyes can be described as synthetic, organic compounds formerly derived entirely from coal tar, and originally called "aniline dyes" because they were specifically derived from aniline, one of the coal-tar products. Coal tar is a dispersion of carbon in oil. The oil consists of a mixture of hundreds of compounds, and many more are formed in the further process of distillation of the coal tar. They are called hydrocarbons. Aniline is made from some of these by a synthetic process; it occurs in fairly small amounts and was used mainly in the middle to late 1800s. Later other chemicals were used in place of aniline. Many of these components are now obtained from petroleum and other sources as well as from coal tar. The occurrence of skin cancer as an occupational disease among workers in coal-tar plants has been traced to some of these polynuclear hydrocarbons. Anyone working with synthetic dyes should be aware of this.

There are several different types of synthetic dyes; they are applied in many different ways to different materials (not necessarily fiber or fabric). Some dyes are mainly good for cotton, others mainly good for cellulose, and so on. The all-purpose dyes that you buy in the dime store consist of a combination of these many different dyes, so they will dye any material. Only a small amount of dye in the packet will actually dye wool, and so these dyes are wasteful and expensive.

All the best wool dyes are used with an acid dye liquor; and they are called *acid dyes.* The acid dyes possess a direct affinity for wool, silk, nylon, some acrylics, and jute. It is these dyes that I recommend for your synthetic dyeing. Sulfuric acid is most commonly used with these dyes, but acetic acid may be used. It has the advantage of being less dangerous for the home dyer to use and store. But, if you handle sulfuric acid properly, you will have no trouble. Vinegar will work in a pinch (if you are out of acid), but its cost compared to sulfuric acid is prohibitive for quantity dyeing. (Vinegar contains less than 10 percent acetic acid.)

Ordering Acid Dyes

Acid dyes for wool are available from chemical and dye companies, two of which are listed in Chapter XIII, "Suppliers: Dyes." These are Ciba and Allied Chemical. Allied Chemical will sell in one-pound quantities, and Ciba has distributors (also listed in Chapter XIII) that will sell one-pound quantities. I have always ordered from Keystone Ingham Corporation, and the dyes listed here are Ciba dyes from this company that just happen to be the colors I use (they originally sent me sample packets when I asked for those colors that would have good fastness to both light and washing).

The average cost of these dyes is approximately $8 per pound (including a charge for repackaging, since normally they are sold in barrels). Certain dyes are much less and others more. The Rhodamine is not even included in averaging of the prices because it is so expensive; it is three times the average price of the other dyes—but it is a 400 percent concentrate. If you order different colors be sure to specify that they must have good fastness and good leveling qualities (the quality of dyeing evenly).

Ciba Acid Dyes from Keystone Ingham Corporation

Color	Name
+ Intracid Rhodamine B 400%	(Shocking pink)
*Intracid Scarlet Moo Conc	(Pure red)

+ Intracid Fast Orange G Conc   (Pumpkin orange)
*Cibalan Yellow GRL   (Soft yellow)
+ Cibalan Brilliant Yellow 2GL Ex.   (Brilliant lemon yellow)
Intracid Green V Ex. Conc   (Emerald green)
+ Intracid Pure Blue L   (Peacock blue)
*Intracid Fast Blue CB   (Royal blue)
Intracid Violet 4 BNS Ex. Conc   (Bright purple)
+ *Cibalan Brown 2 GL   (Cocoa brown)

To economize: Order these four basic colors.* This group will give you all colors except brilliants. Or: Order these five basic colors.+ This group will give you all colors including the brilliants.

To further economize: Order these dyes with 1 or 2 other people. These dyes may *seem* to be expensive but in actuality are much cheaper than all-purpose dime-store dyes: 1 ounce will dye from 3 to 5 pounds of wool.

Equipment Needed for Dyeing with Acid Dyes

Sulfuric acid (commercial strength). This may be purchased or ordered through any pharmacy. One quart will last a long time unless you get into production dyeing.

Dyepot: enamel or stainless steel. Allow 1 gallon (of boiling water) capacity for every 4 ounces of wool to be dyed one color. Large canning steamers are fine for the purpose.

Plastic or enamel bucket or pan (to receive the dripping hot wool from the dyebath).

Wooden stick for stirring the yarn and lifting it out of the dyebath. (Cut-off broom handles do fine.)

Rubber gloves for easy handling of the steaming-hot yarn.

Glass jar to mix the water and acid solution.

Electric, gas, or wood stove—or an outdoor fire. (Because of the bad fumes from the boiling acid bath, it is best to have the setup outdoors, or at least in a well-ventilated room. And acid will scar your good stove.)

An old automatic washer. This is very handy for rinsing and spin-drying the dyed yarn. Don't use your good one: the acid will eventually ruin it.

For Quantity Dyeing:

2 outdoor fires with cement blocks to hold the dyepots.

3 large galvanized washtubs. (The acid will quickly dissolve away the galvanizing, but the tubs will last quite a while.) One of the tubs will be for wetting and rinsing the yarns.

2 or 3 long (3 feet) strong sticks (broom-handle diameter minimum) for stirring and lifting the yarn.

Rubber gloves.

2 stainless-steel teaspoons (the type you use to stir coffee).

2 glass jars.

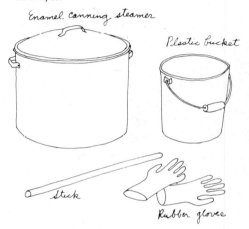

FIGURE 416. Equipment needed for dyeing with acid dyes.

Enamel canning steamer

Plastic bucket

Stick

Rubber gloves

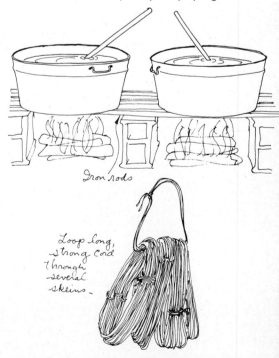

FIGURE 417. Set-up for quantity dyeing.

Iron rods

Loop long, strong cord through several skeins.

Fence or clothesline for drying the skeins.

Hose or easy source of water.

Patch of ground that you don't care about. (It will have fire burns and spilled acid and dye water.)

Two ambitious people. (It takes two people to lift 5 pounds of wool wet from the dyebath.)

Wood for the fires.

Dyes and acid.

Skeins of yarn tied *loosely* together (not more than 2 1/2 pounds tied in one group) with very strong string (see Preparing the Wool to Be Dyed), so that you can lift the wet yarn from the dyebath by inserting the stick under this string, and two people can hold the dripping yarn over the dyebath until most of the dye liquor has dripped off. These dripping-hot dyed skeins are hung on the fence or clothesline until cooled down enough to rinse. The rinsed yarn is just drip-dried.

Lots of large plastic bags to hold the wetted skeins until ready for the dyepot.

General Instructions for Dyeing with Acid Dyes

Preparing the wool to be dyed

Tie the skeins of yarn *loosely* in a figure eight in a least two places (see Making the Skein in Chapter IX, "Spinning). Wet skeins or raw wool thoroughly and store in plastic bags until ready to use (at least a half-hour, unless you use hot water for soaking). If the yarn or raw wool has any dirt or oil in it, wash thoroughly, except if dyeing intentionally unwashed wool (see Techniques for Special Effects).

If you are dyeing several skeins one color, loop four feet of strong string (doubled over) through the skeins (that have already been properly tied) and tie in a secure knot. Use this string to lift the yarn out of the dyebath. Use cotton or linen; the dye won't take on the string, so you will be able to spot it in the dyebath when you are ready to remove the yarn.

Dye method

My method of dyeing with these acid dyes is fast, simple, and quite unorthodox. Some may raise their eyebrows in horror at what seems to be a haphazard procedure, but I assure you the final results are excellent, and the time required for the process is cut to one-quarter. Usually recipes for these dyes require weighing and measuring all ingredients, using thermometers, and starting with a lukewarm fresh dyebath for each color. I dye the same way I cook—rarely use a recipe and rarely measure. I know the basic principles and I'm good at judging amounts. And this is the way I would like you to get started dyeing.

If you are the methodical type, by all means keep notes on amounts and mixtures if you wish, but make them your own discoveries. By being more experimental you will get to know the dyes and you will be able to think of a color in your head and know pretty well just which dyes and amounts to use to get that color.

So put on your old clothes (because the acid can eat holes in them), fill the dyepot with water, and put it on the fire to heat. Now get all your dyes out on a newspaper (they are really potent and one speck of powder when it comes in contact with moisture will stain badly) and open up the cans. The pot of water you have on the stove (or fire) heating up is going to be *the* dyebath for all the colors you're going to

FIGURE 418. Planning the order in which you will dye the colors.

dye. That's the great thing about these dyes: the water comes out nearly clear and all the color is in the yarn. (The official word for this is "exhaust.")

The dyeing principle with these acid dyes is *heat* and *acid*. Neither one alone is sufficient, but together they make the dye penetrate the fiber—*quickly* and *permanently*. (The official word for this is "strike.")

Now write down a list of the colors you want to dye. (I always dye several pounds of wool and several colors when I dye. It's just too inefficient to get out all that equipment and set it up just to dye a few skeins.) Then reorganize the list so that your lightest, clearest, and brightest colors come first, while the dyebath is completely clear, and each color that follows is related to the previous color, ending with the darkest, most muted colors.

Two colors that require absolutely clear water if you want the full brilliance of the color are Intracid Rhodamine and Cibalan Brilliant Yellow. If you want to dye both, start with the brilliant yellow and simmer the wool until the water is completely clear, because with the rhodamine there is always a bit of pink left in the dyebath. Both the rhodamine and the green are hard to exhaust. Choose your next color to utilize whatever is still left in the dyebath. For instance, red, orange, magenta, or purple are all related to pink. Dye the colors in this manner, always choosing the next color to be dyed according to the tiny bit of color that's left in the dyebath.

First color

1. Put the dye in the water. Stir it up. It doesn't matter how cold or hot the water is at this point. The dye will dissolve nicely (except for the yellows and the brown, which have to be mixed into a paste with water first). Don't be timid; you can always overdye if you don't like the color. See Mixing Acid Dye Colors in this chapter for amounts. Some colors (Cibalan Yellow, Cibalan Brilliant Yellow, and Cibalan Brown) require mixing in paste form first and then adding the paste to the dyebath.

2. Put wetted yarn in dyebath. Poke it down and stir. The dye will penetrate the fiber somewhat, but the full brilliance of color will not come until you've added the acid and boiled it.

3. Mix acid. Put about a cup of cold water into a glass jar. Pour into this a small amount of sulfuric acid. By small I mean about 1 tablespoon per gallon of water that you have in the dyepot. Try to avoid using measuring utensils. *Never add water to acid. Always add the acid to water.* (What happens if you add water to acid is that the small amount of water that first hits the acid heats up so quickly that it explodes.)

4. Add acid solution to dyebath. When the dyebath is steaming, lift the yarn completely out of the water and pour in the acid and water mixture (slowly and carefully—you don't want it to splash) and stir. Let the yarn down into the water and immediately poke and stir to get all the yarn under water as soon as possible. *Now* the dye is going to "strike": both heat and acid are present.

5. Stir and bring to boil. Keep stirring and poking and turning the yarn so that all parts move through all parts of the dyebath. If part of the yarn is allowed to rest on the bottom of the pot for long, the dye will take more quickly in that portion since it is hotter there. This constant stirring and poking right after the acid is added are the most important things for obtaining even (level) dyeings. Keep in mind, however, that agitation is bad for the wool, so handle it gently and only enough to do the job. (*Note:* Most instructions tell you to put the acid in when the water is still cool to get level dyeings, but that means you have to stand there stirring for sometimes half an hour while the dyebath heats up. Don't put the acid in until the water is quite hot, and have a good hot fire under the pot.)

You will see, after a minute or two, that the water will begin to clear. The nearer the water is to the boiling point, the sooner it will become clear. It should be poked and turned constantly until it does boil.

6. *Simmer until water clears.* When the water is simmering, the dye should exhaust quite quickly, over a period of 10 to 15 minutes. As the water begins to clear you can cover the pot and stir only every couple of minutes. If, after 20 minutes, the boiling water is not almost completely clear, this means you should add more acid. Add about half the amount that you did in the beginning, lifting the yarn out of the water first. After you get really good at dyeing, you can simply push the yarn to one side in the dye pot, add the acid and immediately stir the yarn to mix.

7. *Remove yarn and cool.* After about 20 minutes of simmering (rapid boiling is not good for the wool), when the water is clear (or nearly clear: intracid rhodamine and intracid green will leave traces in the water), the dyeing process is complete. With a stick lift the yarn from the water and hold over the dyepot for several seconds to let the dye liquor drip back into the pot (to save the boiling hot water and acid). Then put the yarn into a plastic or enamel bucket or pan to let it cool. (If you are dyeing outside you can dispense with the bucket and simply hang the yarn on a line or fence to cool.) It is very important to cool it before rinsing in cold water as the tiny gelatin scales on each fiber will congeal, causing the wool to be matted and ruined.

8. *Rinse.* After the wool is completely cooled, rinse it well in cold water. It is important to get all the acid out of the wool, so add a little baking soda to the rinse water to help neutralize the acid. The soda too has to be rinsed out thoroughly. If you are dyeing small amounts, it's nice to wash the wool in warm water and detergent or soap, but with large amounts of yarn this is impractical.

9. *Dry.* Press out moisture. Hang loosely in an airy place; sun won't hurt it. If you're dyeing huge quantities you don't have to get all the moisture out—just let the skeins drip dry, spreading the yarn in a different position occasionally. An automatic washer with a spin-dry cycle comes in very handy for this step.

It's easiest to straighten out the skein—since it will be slightly tangled—before it is completely dry. If the yarn is tightly spun you may want to block it. (See Chapter IX, "Spinning: Washing the Yarn.")

Following colors

If experienced dyers, reading these last few paragraphs, have been shaking their heads in disapproval, they will be totally aghast at the next few paragraphs, because this is where we *really* depart from the standard rules. Instead of throwing out this dyebath and starting all over again, we use this same boiling water with acid already in it. A tricky situation, since, as you remember, we now have the two ingredients present that make the dye "strike"—heat and acid. These next few steps can be done immediately upon removing the first batch of yarn from the dyebath and putting it to cool.

1. *Put dye in water.* Put the dye for the new color into the boiling water. Remember that if there is any color left in the water it will affect very slightly the new color, so it should be a related one.

2. Put wetted yarn in dyebath. As soon as that yarn hits the dye liquor, the color is going to start penetrating the fibers, so *immediately* poke and stir with your wooden stick to get all parts of the yarn submerged and moving in the water. Stir and lift and turn from the bottom of the pot so that the yarn won't sit at the bottom. (Don't panic, though. You'll spill boiling-hot acid liquor all over the stove or fire.)

3. Proceed as in directions for first color, from step 5 on.

Dye all the following colors in this manner. Every second or third color you will probably need to add to the pot a little more hot water (always keep the optimum water level so that the yarn is not crowded) and a little more acid. As long as the dyebath is exhausting well after it has come to a boil, don't add more acid. When, after 10 or 15 minutes of boiling, the water is not getting quite clear, that means you need more acid.

Troubles?

1. Dye does not dissolve in the dyebath. Cibalan Yellow GRL, Cibalan Brilliant Yellow 2 GL Ex. and Cibalan Brown 2 GL have to be mixed with a little water into a paste form before being added to the dyebath. Sometimes, if there is an excess of acid in the water, the Brilliant Yellow will form little lumps in the dyebath. These can be rinsed out after the dyeing.

2. Water not clear at end of dyeing. Some colors take a very long time to exhaust. Boil 20 minutes. If, by then, the water is not quite clear, add more acid and simmer another 10 minutes.

3. Color not right. If the color is not as bright, or deep, as you had wished, lift the yarn from the water completely, add more dye, stir, and return the yarn to the water. Stir, poke, lift, and turn yarn *immediately* to prevent the new dye from striking unevenly. If the color needs to be more yellowish, or greenish, or whatever, add more of that color, using the same method. *Never* add the dye to the dyebath while the yarn is in the water. If the color is too dark for what you wanted, there is no way you can lighten it. Either use it as it is, or add the proper dye to make it another dark color that you can use, and try again at the original color. This is one reason it's good to be dyeing several colors on the same day.

4. Uneven dyeing. Are the skeins tied loosely? If not, they will have to be dried and retied and dyed again a darker shade of the same color: this will usually hide the light areas that were tied too tightly.

Were the skeins well wetted before entering the dyebath? This is a very important part of even dyeing.

Is there at least 1 gallon of water for every 4 ounces of wool? If not, add more hot water, a little more dye and boil longer.

If these conditions were correct, then it may mean there was too much acid in the dyebath, thus making the dye take too fast. Or, more likely, you didn't stir it well enough as the dyebath was exhausting. As long as there is color in the water, you have to stir. If there is a lot of color in the water you should stir constantly. As the water begins to clear you can stir more occasionally.

If the skeins are dyeing unevenly for one reason or another, this can usually be corrected by simply boiling them longer. Detergent or Glauber's salt is supposed to aid in level dyeing, but I have never had to use either. If the skeins are very uneven, add a little more dye of the same color, boil until water is clear, then another 10 or 15 minutes.

Note: Pale, light colors are the hardest to dye evenly. Sometimes they can only be dyed successfully by the method I described for the first color. In other words, the yarn is well saturated with the dye liquor before the acid is added and the dyebath brought to a boil with constant stirring. Sometimes extremely pale colors can be achieved by simply dunking the yarn in a stronger dyebath and removing it after a few stirs.

Mixing Acid Dye Colors

For a more thorough understanding of the principles involved in mixing colors, please read Chapter XI, "Design and Color."

Following are suggestions for combinations of colors on different natural yarns —white, light gray, and dark gray. This chart will also tell you how to get all the colors from the primaries. These are just a *few* of the more successful combinations.

CODE

Rh	Intracid Rhodamine B 400%
Sc	Intracid Scarlet Moo Conc.
Or	Intracid Fast Orange G Conc.
Yl	Cibalan Yellow GRL
Br.Yl	Cibalan Brilliant Yellow 2GL Ex.
Gr	Intracid Green V Ex. Conc.
P.Bl	Intracid Pure Blue L
F.Bl	Intracid Fast Blue CB
Vi	Intracid Violet 4 BNS Ex. Conc.
Br	Cibalan Brown 2GL

lv—level spoonful; rd—rounded spoonful; hp—heaping spoonful. (The spoon is a stainless-steel teaspoon—the kind you would use to stir coffee or tea.)

	Natural color of wool, 1 pound		
Dye and amount	White	Light Gray	Dark Gray
Rh (1 lv)	Shocking pink	Old rose	
Rh (1 lv) & Sc (1 lv)	Brilliant pinkish red		
Rh (1 lv) & Or (1 lv)	Red		
Rh (1 lv) & Vi (1 lv)	Magenta		
Rh (1 lv) & P.Bl (1 lv)	Intense purple		Dark purple
Sc (1 hp)	True red		
Sc (1 rd) & Or (1 rd)	Deep blood red		Dark maroon
Sc (1 lv) & Yl (1 hp)	Orange	Brilliant rust	
Sc (1 rd) & F.Bl (1 lv)	Purple	Muted purple	Dark purple
Or (1 hp)	Pumpkin orange	Brilliant rust	Rich brown
Or (1 lv) & Br.Yl (1 hp)	Brilliant egg-yolk yellow	Rich gold	Intense brown
Or (1 hp) & GR (1/2 lv)	Intense autumn gold		
Or (1 hp) & P.Bl (1 lv)	Rich light brown		
Or (1 hp) & Br (1 lv)	Rust		Dark brown
Yl (1 hp)	Ripe yellow	Golden beige	Dark brown
Yl (2 or 3 hp)	Burnt sienna		
Yl (1 hp) & Rh (1/4 lv)		Copper	

NOTES

Yl (1 hp) & Gr (1 lv)	Avocado	Heather avocado	
Yl (1 hp) & Gr (1 hp)	Pine-needle green		
Yl (1 hp) & F.Bl (1 lv)	Green		Dark green
Yl (1 hp) & Gr. (1/2 lv)	Brass	Dark brass	
Yl (1/4) & Br (1/8)	Cream	Beige	
Br.Yl (1 hp)	Clear lemon yellow	Acid green	Dark yellow green
Br.Yl (1 hp) & Gr (1/4)	Chartreuse		
Br.Yl (1 hp) & P.Bl (1 rd)	Green	Hunter green	Dark green
Gr (1 hp)	Emerald green	Deep heather green	Dark green
Gr (1 hp) & Br.Yl (1 hp)	Brilliant kelly green		Dark green
Gr (1 lv) & P.Bl (1 lv)	Brilliant aqua-marine		
P.Bl (1 hp)	Peacock blue		
F.Bl (1 hp)	Royal blue	Cadet blue	Navy blue
F.Bl (1 rd) & Vi (1 rd)	Deep midnight blue		
F.Bl (2 hp) & Br (2 hp)	Black	Black	Black
F.Bl (1/2 lv)		Slate blue	Steel gray
Vi (1 hp)	Purple		Dark purple
Vi (1 lv)	Lavender		
Br (1 hp)	Cocoa brown	Heather brown	Seal brown
Br (1/2 lv)		Cocoa beige	
Br (2 hp) & Yl (1 hp)	Dark brown		Blackish brown

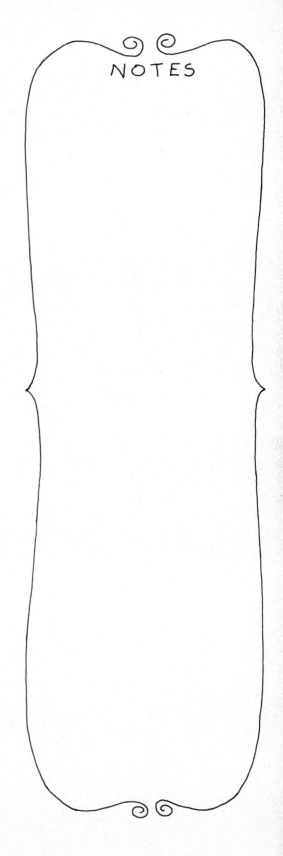

NOTES

Pale Shades: Beautiful pale shades may be achieved with any of these colors or combinations, but using 1/4 level spoonful of dye or more, depending on how deep you want the color. The yellows (or mixtures of yellows, oranges, and browns) yielding creams and buffs, and the blues (or mixtures of blues, purples, and browns) yielding pale blues, pearly grays, etc., are the most successful. These pale shades dyed over naturally light gray wool are very beautiful. See under Troubles? above for method of dyeing pale shades.

Dark, intense colors: Use more dye—up to 3 times the basic amount.

Earth colors: I class any of the warm colors, starting with red orange when muted, all the way down to avocado green, as earth colors. Cibalan Yellow GRL is probably the most useful dye to use in mixing any of these colors. If your selection of dyes includes only Brilliant Yellow, tone it down to approximate the riper yellow by combining it with a small amount each of orange and brown. Just experiment with combinations of reds, oranges, yellows, and greens (or yellow and blue combined), always toning them toward earth color by using yellow and brown.

I like to mute colors by using their opposites, whenever possible, rather than just adding brown. The resulting color has more life. Brown is useful too, but mainly to darken. One of the reasons some commercial yarns have such "dead" colors is that it is standard practice to add a graying agent to their brilliant colors to tone them down, instead of using other brilliant colors on the opposite side of the color wheel.

Closely related colors: Some of the most beautiful color combinations are those that are closely related; for instance, a whole group of brilliant pinks and oranges, or several shades of yellows and golds, or cool greens with blues. These are fun to dye because within that limitation you can try to get the greatest variety of color (pale lunar-moth green as opposed to dark pine-needle green and so on). Just start dumping different combinations and amounts of dye in the dyepot and see how much variety you can get—always staying within the range of two (or, at the most, three) adjacent colors. No matter what results, at least they are bound to harmonize.

Designing Your Colors as You Dye

Using natural dyes, you will have to take the colors you get—and they will all blend very nicely anyway. In synthetic dyeing, you can design the colors as you dye.

In Chapter XI, "Design and Color," I will discuss ways of achieving harmonious and exciting color combinations, in case you don't already have a flair for this. But here, in the dyeing section, I want to urge you to go about this dyeing with a flexible attitude. Don't just decide that you are going to make a rug (for example) and it's going to have red, and brown, and yellow in it, and then dye some red yarn, some yellow yarn, and some brown yarn.

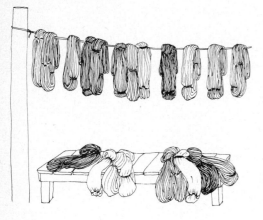

FIGURE 419. Grouping the dyed skeins to judge the color combinations.

Of course, you may start out with the idea that it will have these three colors in it. So perhaps first you will dye the yellow. With the actual color in front of you, you can tell better what you should dye next, whether it should be an orange red, a pure red, or a purplish red—and how much red there should be in relation to the amount of yellow. After the red is dyed, you have *two* colors to work with. After you see these two colors together in actuality, it may strike you that they are very hot and overwhelming together, and that at least the brown that you're going to dye should be a cool brown, and maybe there should be lots of it. Or perhaps you shouldn't have had that much yellow to begin with. There's still time to redye it a different color.

Keep laying the colored yarns together on the floor (or the fence) and judge how your color combination is coming along before you dye the next color. You may decide that a more exciting color combination would result if you dyed an entirely different third or fourth color than you had originally planned.

An artist doesn't arbitrarily decide on all the colors exactly that he is going to use in his painting. He mixes the colors as he goes along, and as the colors get applied to the canvas he can tell what he needs to make the color combination even more beautiful, or to correct a bad combination. This is the way you should dye your yarn for a project—just like an artist, always willing to change your plans or adjust to get something that is better. Only after you see the actual colors in front of you can you best decide.

And, when all the colors are dyed, think carefully if the combination could be improved in any way. Be ready to dye one more time if necessary to make the whole group more pleasing. You are working with a lot of costly material in this yarn. The final product can be a success or failure, depending on the color and the design.

You can wait to rinse the yarns until you are sure that all the colors are right, and then rinse them all together.

Techniques for Special Effects

Tie-dyeing yarn: A skein of yarn may be dyed in a variegated pattern by tying the skein tightly in certain sections so that when it is put in the dyebath the dye cannot penetrate. Use cotton string and wind it tightly around the skein continuously for the whole section that you want to remain the original color. After the yarn is dyed, untie it and retie in a different section and dye it another color. You can leave the dyed area *untied* as well as some of the original undyed areas, thus producing two different colors in the second dyebath. And so on.

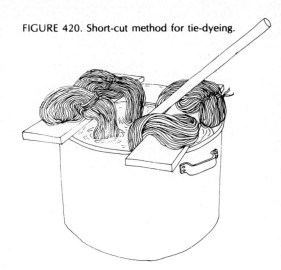

FIGURE 420. Short-cut method for tie-dyeing.

A short-cut method for tie-dyeing that I use is to put part of the skein into the dyepot and let the other part hang over the edge of the pot (have it supported in some way so the heat or fire does no damage). After that is dyed, turn the skein around so that a new section hangs in the dye liquor.

Actually some of these yarns, when woven or knitted, are quite hideous, unless a deliberate design is planned, so I would experiment in a small way, if I were you. The only occasion that I have used tie-dyed yarn successfully, without a deliberate, measured plan, was with handspun mohair, which was brushed with hand cards (see Chapter VIII, "Finishing Techniques: Brushing") after it was woven. The result was a sort of striped fur, like a tabby cat, only in a fantastic color combination.

Ikat: This is a tie-dye method with deliberate planning. Usually it is the warp that is tie-dyed. The warp is first wound, then tie-dyed. When it is strung up on the loom, of course, the color areas do not coincide perfectly, so a sort of blurred effect is attained. This technique is used in Guatemala a great deal—*both* warp and weft being tie-dyed. In Chapter V, "The Backstrap Loom," there is a project using this technique.

Dyeing unwashed handspun yarn: This is a technique that my friend and tapestry weaver Joan Sihvonen Loveless discovered. It works best with synthetic dyes. Take a skein of handspun yarn (that has only been teased, not carded, before it was spun —and, of course, of unwashed fibers) and dump it *unwashed and unwetted* into the boiling dyebath. What happens is that the dye takes more quickly in the ungreasy parts (the most in the weathered tips) so they are dyed a deeper color, and by the time the grease and dirt in the other parts are dissolved, much of the dye has exhausted so these parts are dyed a lighter shade. The effect is a heather yarn, which looks as if you had dyed two or three different shades of fleeces separately, then carded them together and spun them. The results are even more spectacular if you are using two different acid dyes in the same dyebath. One color strikes at a slightly different temperature than the other, and by the time the grease is dissolved the other color strikes, so the yarn can be composed of fibers of totally opposite colors, if desired. This makes a gorgeous yarn when the right colors are used.

Redyeing Commercial Yarns

If you happen to have some commercial yarn in colors that you don't like, you can redye them very successfully. The technique is exactly the same as with undyed yarn. Be sure it is thoroughly wetted first. Don't be surprised if the original color bleeds into the dyebath—and remains there; many of the commercial yarns are not dyed with fast colors. Of course, you have to take into account the color of the yarn to begin with. For example, a yellow skein dyed red will come out orange.

CHAPTER XI

DESIGN AND COLOR

What Is Good Design?

Have you ever wondered what makes one design really great, and another just mediocre? That's something artists and designers spend their lives thinking about. Many artists, critics, and philosophers have worked out some pretty good theories. Wouldn't it be nice if we could only learn the rules and just apply them? Guaranteed success! It's one thing to be able to *appreciate* a work of art, but quite another to *create* it.

A more specific aspect of the same problem that I have pondered for years is: Why is it that when we see examples of weaving done by "primitive" people alongside weaving done by "contemporary craftsmen," the primitive pieces usually stand out as far more exciting and beautiful than what we do?

Is it because they use mostly handmade natural materials? Is it because they are craftsmen who work many more hours, days, and years at their craft than we? Or because they work with traditional, proven designs and techniques that their people have used for centuries? Is it because their weavings have a real purpose to them— either a practical daily purpose or a religious purpose? Or because their lives are closer to nature and they are simply revealing their harmony with the universe in their work? Or because they are necessarily very disciplined people? Is it because their thoughts are unfettered with the conscious effort to make something "beautiful"—and so the beauty that exists within them and everywhere is free to come alive in their work? Is it because they are not concerned with time and so their work is very fine and intricate and we are awed at the work and effort that went into the piece?

A few weavers in advanced countries have somehow found the secret, for there certainly are some good weavings around that have been created by people of our culture. But why can't many more of us make beautiful things when thousands of folk artists in more primitive countries can?

I feel inadequate talking about these philosophical aspects of art and design. Nor can I tell you how to make a good design. And I'm not going to suggest specific ideas. What we can do is talk about a few basic, more or less accepted principles of design and color that may help you in your work.

Uniformity vs. Variation

Consider these two weavings: (1) a large, pure white weaving made of thread so fine that the texture of the weave is hardly discernible; (2) a large weaving, with areas woven by different techniques, with different yarns, different colors, different sizes, different shapes, and with some areas set close together and other areas far apart. The first weaving would be an example of uniformity (simplicity, order), and the second an example of variation (complexity or chaos).

In good design we try to achieve the perfect balance between uniformity and variation: enough uniformity to satisfy the mind's desire for order, and enough variation to challenge interest. The mind cannot handle too much variation. It wants to be able to comprehend, and if too many factors are forced upon it, the full comprehension of the variations is impossible, and only chaos is felt.

Actually, the white weaving, woven so fine, is not perfectly uniform. For one thing, it has boundaries . . . edges. For another, as soon as it is not held out flat it folds into many complex forms, and perhaps that is enough variation in itself.

In great works of art there is always some kind of underlying order. Johann

FIGURE 421. Examples of uniformity and variation.

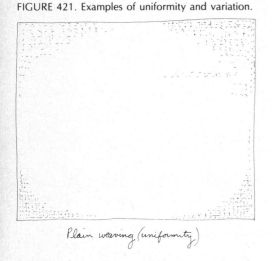

Plain weaving (uniformity)

Tapestry in different colors yarns, and techniques (variation)

Sebastian Bach, the great composer, used variation to the utmost, but in his complexities there is always a pattern or scheme that satisfies the desire for order. During the first few times of listening to one of his compositions, perhaps the order is not discernible, but after a while it is comprehended. At the same time, the music is so complex that it never becomes boring; there is always some new relationship of the notes not appreciated before.

But it would be a mistake for you to push variation too far until you are completely sure of what you are doing. Start out with order and proceed to variation, rather than vice versa.

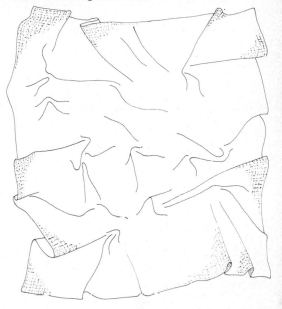

FIGURE 422. Variation is provided when a plain (uniform) weaving lies in folds.

Limitation

One way to achieve both uniformity and variation is to set artificial limitations.

In a design, there are several different elements: shape, size, color, structure, texture, direction, placement. One can put a limitation on any or all of these elements. Let's take a striped blanket and examine its limitations of design. By virtue of its being striped, there is a complete limitation on shape—all the shapes are long rectangles (or stripes); there is no other shape. If the stripes are all the same size there is a complete limitation on size. If the weave structure is the same throughout—plain weave, weft face, for instance—then there is limitation on structure. If the same yarn was used throughout, there is a limitation on texture. If the stripes are just two colors alternating, there is a severe (although not complete) limitation on color. The stripes are all going in the same direction, so there is a complete limitation on direction.

So you can see that a striped blanket, of two-colored even stripes, is a severely limited design, and yet consider the interest it gives—especially if it lies in folds. By eliminating the limitation on size of stripes alone (which would actually change their shape also, because the stripes could vary from lines to rectangles), one could get a fairly complex design.

A good way to "make up" a design is arbitrarily to set severe limitations on some or all of the elements—shape, size, color, texture, etc.—and then (always staying within the limitations) work as wildly as possible. For example, suppose you were going to make a wall hanging. You could decide to set the following limitations:

Complete limitation on structure (make it all weft-face plain weave).

Complete limitation on type of texture (use all the same yarn).

Complete limitation on shape (use all squares).

Complete limitation on direction (the sides of the squares would have to be vertical and horizontal).

Severe limitation on color (use only yellows).

No limitation on size (the squares can be any size).

No limitation on placement (the squares can be any place).

When you first think about this it might sound rather dull—just an arrangement of yellow squares of different sizes. But imagine what you could do with those squares. You could have huge ones and tiny ones. They could be all bunched together in some places and there could be big spacious squares in other places. You could make little areas of startling checkerboards. The colors could range from pale cream through brilliant lemon yellow and deep egg-yolk yellow, all the way to dark ochre and blackish yellow.

FIGURE 423. Sequence of stripes—repeated in order, and then in reverse order.

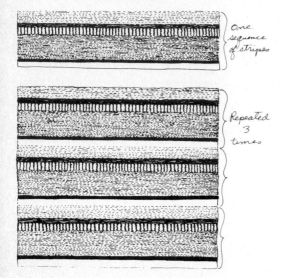

One sequence of stripes

Repeated 3 times

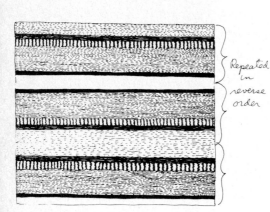

Repeated in reverse order

Repetition

Repetition is simply another aspect of uniformity. It is a design trick that, of course, lends itself perfectly to weaving. By repeating the same design (figure, stripe, or groups of figures or stripes) over and over, one achieves a certain uniformity. One can vary the repetition by making mirror images of the figures or stripes. In other words, instead of repeating a sequence in the same order, repeat it backward, thus making an overall symmetrical pattern.

Scale and Interest

I've noticed that in much primitive art the object encompasses large general forms (or a feeling of vastness that could be likened to sky, ocean, space), and also fascinating minute detail (that is, like looking into a blossom). One certainly doesn't question the aesthetics of nature, and in nature there do exist these two themes: the macrocosm and the microcosm—the extreme contrast of scale and interest. Much contemporary art lacks this (I think) in its obsession with bold, simple forms.

In weaving one has the perfect opportunity to utilize this exciting contrast, because the final object—though perhaps large—is made up of tiny stitches of threads that can be emphasized by variations in color or texture if one desires.

"Push and Pull"

I'm borrowing the words of the famous painter and teacher Hans Hofmann. He used these words to describe a nonstatic interrelation of forms and colors. To achieve variation, or contrast, one can use two or more elements opposing each other. This sets up a tension between the two: one is not at rest in space because the other affects it in some way. It's most interesting when there is a little give and take between the two elements. One element shouldn't do all the pushing, and the other all the pulling; each should do a little of both.

For instance, a concave form tends to be a receding form, or "pulling" form, as opposed to a convex form, which asserts itself or "pushes." Certain colors do the same: cool muted colors tend to recede, and brilliant, hot colors tend to assert themselves. Well, if we make the concave (or receding) form of a color that asserts itself, and the convex (or assertive) form of a receding color, we can balance the "push and pull" between the two. This is exciting because there is a movement back and forth between the two. A vitality is created.

This is a pretty advanced concept in designing that you may not feel at ease with at first, but the more you work at your craft, the more you will crave this very "push and pull" in your shapes and colors.

Backgrounds

One very basic way to understand about this "push and pull" is to consider backgrounds. We often talk about backgrounds in a rug design, for instance, though for some artists and designers "background" is a naughty word—there is no such thing. But in certain weavings, like some old Navajo pieces, one could say there is a "background"—a predominant color that is the ground for the design elements. In analyzing these weavings we find that although this ground prevails throughout the

FIGURE 424. Exaggerated examples of backgrounds that do and don't become an important part of the composition.

weaving, it never recedes from the figures. It is dynamic because it works on this "push and pull" theory; the background form asserts itself by virtue of its shape and color.

So, in designing figures on a "background," consider and feel the shape that is made by the background—or its outline—as much as you consider the shape of the figures. Try to make the background assert itself (by color or form) as much as it recedes, and the whole design will hang together better and have more life. Avoid thinking of it as a background, and consider it as a form in itself. Study some pictures of old Navajo weavings and you will see what I mean. (Mary Hunt Kahlenberg and Anthony Berlant in *The Navajo Blanket* have presented reproductions of some of the most beautiful old Navajo weavings, and their book will be instructive about this very point.)

FIGURE 425. Different ways of achieving balance.

Balance

A well-balanced design is pleasing, but a design that is off balance can be very disturbing. A design can be balanced on the vertical axis or the vertical *and* horizontal axes. (It would never have to be balanced on the horizontal axis only.) It can be balanced by perfect symmetry (exactly the same on one side of the axis as the other), *or* it can be balanced by interest, weight, and direction.

The human body in its standing position with arms hanging and head straight is an example of perfect symmetry on the vertical axis: it is the same on one side of the vertical line as the other (on the exterior, anyway). As soon as the body changes position—moves a leg forward or an arm out, twists the head—it is no longer symmetrical, but (if it doesn't topple over) it is balanced. There is as much weight on one side of the vertical axis as on the other. Since we see things vertically most of the time, it is not important for an art object to be balanced on the horizontal axis, unless it is lying flat on the floor.

The principle of the "balanced" body is the same one you use in making a balanced design on the vertical axis. There should be as much "weight" on one side as on the other. This can, of course, be interpreted in many ways. The "weight" could be simply large "assertive" background space, or it could be a line pointing in a certain direction to counteract weight in the opposite direction.

Whether you balance your designs by perfect symmetry or by interest is simply a matter of taste.

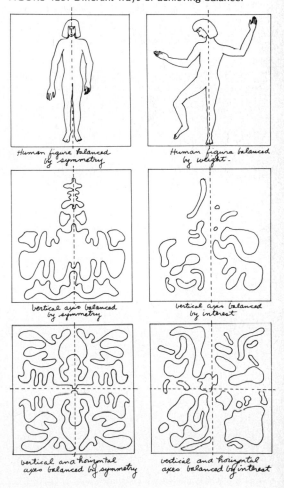

Human figure balanced by symmetry

Human figure balanced by weight.

vertical axis balanced by symmetry

vertical axis balanced by interest

vertical and horizontal axes balanced by symmetry

vertical and horizontal axes balanced by interest

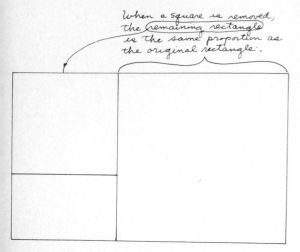

FIGURE 426. The golden section.

When a square is removed, the remaining rectangle is the same proportion as the original rectangle.

Proportion

In weaving, the size and shape of the piece are usually decided by its function, but for certain hangings or rugs, pleasing proportions are important to the overall design. As long as the proportions are related to the design, almost any proportions can be good. But, if you are at a loss as to what dimensions to make the weaving, one proportion guaranteed to please is the "golden section" (I think the Greeks invented it). This is a rectangle so shaped that if one end of it (a perfect square) is cut away there will be left a rectangle of the same proportions as the original. That rectangle, in turn, can be divided so that a perfect square is on one side and a smaller rectangle of the same proportions as the first . . . and so on. In the "golden section," one side is approximately 1.6 times longer than the other.

The Medium

"Do not overextend the medium." This is a common rule in design class. An artist friend of mine used to amuse himself with the idea of making a sculpture of a bicycle out of adobe. This would be the perfect example of overextending the medium. Another sculptor and teacher made the statement that a stone sculpture, to be of good design, should be capable of being rolled down a hill and yet remain intact. Perhaps that's a bit rash; this would exclude some of the Greek statues that did roll down hills, and did lose heads and arms, wouldn't it?

And then there is the famous teacup that is lined with mink, and created a sensation in the exhibition of Dada art several decades ago.

It seems to me that one can use the medium in its most logical way, or one can spoof it (like making a woven sculpture of a car), as long as the medium itself is used in such a way that we are *conscious* of it. Weavings are sometimes made in such a way as almost to deny that they are weavings. For example, an artist (not a weaver) designs a pictorial or abstract design for a tapestry, and then it is woven into a piece of fabric by skilled weavers in a workshop. This is common practice in Europe. Sometimes the tapestries are so fine and the pictorial forms so skillfully done that it actually looks as if they were paintings on cloth. Well, it certainly would have been much easier to paint them. Why weave at all if the medium itself is not an important part of the design?

I feel that anything woven should be obvious about being woven. This does not mean that it can't be fine and intricate, but the forms and designs should be *logical* outgrowths of the medium itself. An excellent illustration of what I'm talking about is the difference between some nineteenth-century tapestries of European origin and the ancient textiles of Peru. Both are woven by extremely skilled weavers, and the materials are so fine and the fabric so intricately woven that they are almost a mystery. But the one (the European tapestries) art form is a *denial* of the medium, and the other (the Peruvian textile) is a *celebration* of it.

The Materials

Choosing the right materials for a certain project is a very important part of designing. So often I see a weaving that is a failure only because the materials themselves were a failure, or at least not suitable for that particular item. Have you ever seen one of those beautiful little Bolivian coca bags? They are about four to seven inches square, woven in intricate patterns—sometimes with little horses or other animals in the design. The thread is handspun alpaca, spun so fine that you have to look at it through a magnifying glass to determine whether it is single- or double-plied. (It *is* double-plied.) If you can imagine the weave of that coca bag being duplicated in shiny, coarse mercerized cotton or rayon rug yarn, you get the idea of how important your materials are.

Yarns can be of good or bad design just as weavings can, and if you start out with a bad yarn you have an insurmountable problem. In general, yarns that retain their form and individuality even after they are woven are the most beautiful to use in weaving; and these are simple, tightly spun yarns of natural materials.

If you are going to use designs that depend on color, the differentiation of colors is shown off to best advantage, I think, on a matt surface. For example, a plain yellow mercerized (slightly shiny) cotton belt would look fine, but as soon as you use other colors with it, the design will not show up as well; there will be a conflict between the shininess of the thread and the changes of color. This is one of the reasons I favor wool for weavings. Wool is probably the most matt-surfaced fiber. Cotton is naturally matt, but the common practice of mercerizing makes it shiny—and this is the cotton yarn that is usually made available to handweavers.

Types of yarns for specific uses are more thoroughly discussed in Chapter I, "The Basics of Weaving: Your Yarns."

Craftsmanship

The excellence of your craftsmanship is extremely important, and should be considered a factor in good design. As a child, when I was to perform in a piano recital, and I was trying to decide what to play, my mother told me that it would be better to pick a simple piece (one within my capabilities) and play it perfectly than to pick a more difficult (and impressive) piece and risk a mediocre performance. I've never forgotten that advice, and it can well be applied to weaving. Often one comes across a weaving that is quite ambitious but obviously beyond the capabilities of the weaver. A simple weaving in which one can see the work of a craftsman who has mastered a technique, in my mind, is much preferable.

This doesn't mean that you shouldn't push yourself to new horizons, but do it only when you feel completely secure in the steps that bring you to that point.

Originality

And that brings us to that magic word—"originality." Everyone wants to be original. It seems to have really become a raging fashion sometime in the mid-twentieth century —when individual expression became so important. When the renaissance in weaving came, slightly later, somebody must have made an "original, expressive piece"— some long, gangly, hairy hanging sculpture in the weaving medium; and ever since then "creative" weavers have been trying to produce these "original" pieces. They are as common in weaving today as table mats were before this craze—a dime a dozen—great shapeless monstrosities (as though a Himalayan tiger had torn an Abominable Snowman to shreds and left him hanging on a tree). Can you imagine coming across one of these in your grandmother's attic? I'd rather find a table mat any day.

If you will even consider taking my advice after this tirade of prejudice, it is this: Don't push being original. A really original piece of weaving comes from extensive work in the medium—a slow development of a new technique or new design that you can claim as your own. You don't have to *try* to be original; it will happen naturally, if, as you work in the medium, you try to understand its potentials.

Inspiration

If you need inspiration, go to the library and get out some books on old weaving—African, Peruvian, Navajo, Middle Eastern, Mexican, etc. Check out books on painting, with color reproductions, to get ideas for color. Breughel has always been one of my favorite sources of inspiration for color. Go to exhibitions of weaving. An exhibition of the Spanish colonial weaving of New Mexico is what inspired my first attempts.

Then, of course, nature itself will be your greatest inspiration. If you are not used to singling out patterns in nature, you may have to train yourself to do this. Sometimes you can find in magazines pictures taken by photographers who have made a profession of photographing the designs and patterns in nature. They will give you ideas for colors and designs in your weaving.

A long time ago I saw a colored photo of a hornets' nest. It was a structure of more or less spherical shape, made up of little sections of different-colored mud. You could just imagine the little hornets going out and getting sand or dirt and coming back and spitting it out to form the shell-like wall in one section of the nest. The mud changed color arbitrarily: either the same hornet or a different one got the sand or dirt from a different area. The whole thing was in shades of beige and pinkish tan—all slightly different—and the shape of each section was just a bit different from the others, although the same size approximately. The size of each section probably represented what the hornet could carry in one trip (limitations at work here). I can never forget the beauty of it, and I often remind myself of the way it was made when I am designing a weaving.

Designing as You Weave

The way the hornets went about building their home is a good way for you to go about weaving. Have an idea of what you want the finished product to look like, but then weave it in an organic way—just letting it grow bit by bit, sometimes even letting arbitrary things (like running out of your butterfly of yarn) be the deciding factor in the size and shape of your areas.

We know the Navajos never make drawings of their patterns and set them up behind their looms. They decide in their minds what colors they will use, and the general idea of how the stripes, diamonds, zigzags, or other shapes will be formed, but as they weave, they let the yarns and the structure of the weave decide on the exact angles. And they are always ready to insert a new little design if they get the inspiration. It's much easier to decide on a color change or exciting new pattern *as you weave* than to decide on paper beforehand and then stick to that shape or color (no matter what) while you are weaving. Your weaving will have a presence about it—as if the particular result was meant to be.

The Importance of Color

You could weave a wall hanging with certain yarns, using a certain technique and design, in certain colors. The identical wall hanging could be woven, different only in colors. One wall hanging could be a masterpiece, and the other a monstrosity. There are all the intermediate possibilities, of course, but what I'm trying to point out is that the colors of yarns you choose for your weaving will be the most important single factor in determining the success or failure of your work. Don't spend hours and hours at the loom if you are not quite confident that the color combination you are using is really good. The importance of color cannot be overemphasized.

This does not mean that each color you weave with has to be one of your favorite colors—the most beautiful color you can imagine. I'm talking about color *combinations*—using colors together in such a way that each makes the other actually more exciting—using one color beside another so that you see something in that other color that you wouldn't have seen if it stood by itself. In the hornets' nest that I just described, for instance, any one of those colors by itself was quite uninspiring—just a muted beige—but the fact that some were pinkish beige, some yellowish beige, some just grayish, was what made the whole color scheme so effective.

This all sounds terribly subtle, and you may ask, "Well, how do I know when I've got a good color combination?" Until you have worked with color a great deal you may feel inadequate in making comparative decisions about color groups. So here I would like to discuss a few ways by which you can systematically work out color combinations for your weaving that at least will be safe—if not positively exciting. As you work with these theories, you will become more aggressive in knowing what you want, and more confident in making unusual and pleasing color combinations.

But now we have to discuss color itself—its properties—so that we will have terms with which to describe the color.

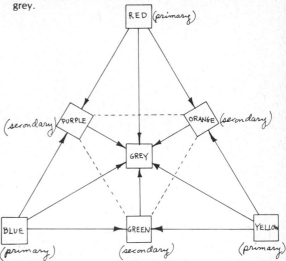

FIGURE 427. A triangle showing the primary colors and how they mix to make secondary colors and grey.

Properties of Color

There are many theories of color that have been worked out by scientists and artists, and, surprisingly, they don't all agree. Some theories have four or five primaries (including green!). Physicists consider red, blue, and green the primaries—no yellow at all. One theory works on the basis of beams of colored light, the mixtures of which give white light. It is called "additive mixture" because by this theory all the rays add up to white light. (The rainbow is simply a breaking down of all the different-colored rays of white light; the light rays are bent as they go through the raindrops and the longer rays are separated from the shorter rays.)

Another theory of mixing colors is called the "subtractive mixture" and it works on the principle of each primary blocking out (or subtracting) the other colored rays. So the combination of all the primaries (which subtracts all light rays) produces no light at all—or black. It is this theory that is applicable to the mixing of dyes and paints.

For our purposes we will use a little of one theory and a little of another. We will use the theory of three primary colors, red, yellow, and blue (the only primaries that work when mixing dyes). Long ago it was discovered by dyers and painters that these three primaries cannot be produced by mixtures of any other colors, but, when mixed together, produce all (or most) of the other colors. (I say "most" because, with the chemical structure of dyes today, many extremely brilliant colors, which are not just combinations of any of these primaries, are available—e.g., shocking pink.)

Our three *primaries*—red, yellow, and blue—can be mixed to form what we call the *secondary* colors: red and yellow make orange; yellow and blue make green; blue and red make purple. *Tertiary* colors are in between any two of these six primary and secondary colors: red orange, orange yellow, yellow green, green blue, blue purple, and purple red. Beyond these is, of course, an infinite range of colors. The three primaries when mixed together will make a completely neutral color—a grayish black.

I find it easier to describe how these colors mix together to form other colors by arranging them in a triangle rather than the usual color circle.

The triangle with gray in the center demonstrates how *only* the primaries can be mixed to form other bright colors. Notice that purple and green will *not* mix to make a bright clear blue. They will make only a grayish blue. And orange and green will certainly not make yellow—they will make only a grayish yellow; purple and orange will make a grayish red. Mixing colors exactly opposite each other will give you gray —like orange and blue, red and green, yellow and purple.

So far we have talked about only one aspect of color, its name—whether it is red or yellow or yellow orange or whatever. We have not mentioned how light or dark it is or how saturated it is.

Albert Munsell, an American color theorist, worked out what is probably the most useful system for describing colors. He proposed that colors have three distinct properties:

Hue, the actual color by name—red, green, etc.

Intensity, the amount of color as compared to gray—the saturation of hue. (Later this word was changed to "chroma," but I prefer to use "intensity" because it describes what it means.)

Value, the lightness or darkness of a color. Different colors of the same "value" would appear the identical shade of gray in a black-and-white photo.

Using these terms we can describe color quite accurately, and we become more conscious of those three properties in any color.

Instead of thinking of yellow as one color, we know that it can be an extremely different "color" depending on its exact hue, intensity, and value. For example, we call a lemon "yellow" and we call butter "yellow," but they are really quite different colors. The lemon yellow is very slightly more greenish, and butter yellow is definitely of lower intensity. They are both approximately of the same value. To distinguish this you can squint your eyes and pretend you are a camera with black-and-white film: would one appear lighter or darker in the photo? In this case of the lemon and the butter, I would say no.

So, when you say "red," it means little until you say whether it is a pure red, or bluish or orangish; whether it is extremely bright or muted; and whether it is very dark or very light. If it were very light, we would call it pink.

In working with and talking about colors we can describe them sometimes more succinctly by saying "lemon yellow," "pumpkin orange," "grassy green," "violet"— because we know exactly what hue, intensity, and value are involved, since we have seen these objects. But, in order to understand the color and how it will work with other colors, we must learn to be very conscious of its three properties . . . hue, intensity, and value.

A Project to Help Understand Hue, Intensity, and Value

If you are unused to thinking of color in these terms, I suggest you do the following project with a set of dime-store watercolor paints. You can use ordinary white typing paper. (These dime-store sets have the primary and secondary colors, and each hue is very true: the red is a true red; the orange is a true orange, and so forth.)

1. A Study in Intensity

Take one of the colors—red, for instance—and paint a little square of red, as bright as you can get it. Now in five more squares paint colors that gradually get grayer and grayer until, in the sixth square, you have pure gray. Each square must be of a value that would appear identical to the other squares in a black-and-white photo. To do this you can just add a little black to the red. Try to make each square an *even*

FIGURE 428. A study in intensity.

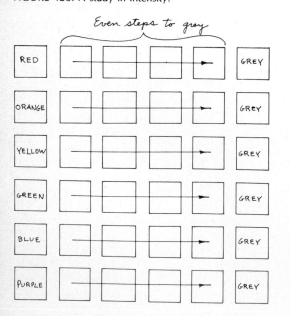

step toward gray. Squint your eyes to check on the value to make sure it remains the same in all the squares.

Do the same thing, making six squares of color (the first square will be the brightest possible and the last square will be pure gray) for *each* color in your paint box—but not black and brown. In doing this you will observe that all the colors are not of the same value. The gray that is in the same line with yellow, for example, will be much lighter than the gray that is in line with your purples. (At least it should be; if it isn't, then your values are wrong.)

2. *A Study in Value*

Now take each color (except brown and black) in your paint box and make a vertical set of squares. Start with the bright pure color in one square and in squares above it make the color lighter and lighter, by diluting with water, until it is pure white. Paint the squares below the color darker and darker until you reach black. Try to keep the color as brilliant as possible but still make it darker. In doing this you will notice that, if the steps are even ones from white to black, there will be fewer squares above the yellow than there are below, because yellow is closer in value to white than it is to black. When you are painting the purple squares there will be only a few steps to black and several to white.

3. *A Study in Hue*

Now take each pure color and, starting with red, make squares of graduated *hue* (24 squares altogether). You can make these squares in a circle, so you can see exactly what colors are opposite each other. There will be *three* steps between each primary and secondary color.

Choosing Colors

The theory of good color design is similar to the theory of good design. "Limitation" is again the key word.

If you weave something with just one solid color, you really have the psychological effect of only that color to be concerned with. For example, a bright orange rug will have quite a different effect on the observer (or user) from a pale grayish blue.

But, as soon as you add even one more color to the first one, you have the colors affecting each other in many ways. To the human eye the color will appear a certain way *relative* to the second color. Take a deep red—rather dark—and put it next to a light gray. That gray will automatically appear to be greenish gray (because the opposition of hues is brought out in adjacent colors, and green is the exact opposite of red). The red will appear to be quite intense because it is in contrast or opposition to a completely neutral tone. And the light gray will appear much lighter in value than it would if it were next to white, for instance. The two colors accentuate the opposites.

In good color combinations, ones that are pleasing or exciting, you are given the chance to *savor* these oppositions rather than being hit across the face with them. If we take Nature as an example, we notice that she never blasts us with all the possible colors all at once. Her color schemes, if you analyze even the most brilliant ones, are always greatly limited.

I'm going to describe a few schemes for limiting these oppositions in color to the point where the mind can comprehend and enjoy them.

There are three things we can limit in color—hue, intensity, and value. We can limit them singly or together and to whatever degree we wish.

Let's take a black-and-white color combination for an example. We find that this is completely limited in hue and intensity, and partially limited in value (there are no

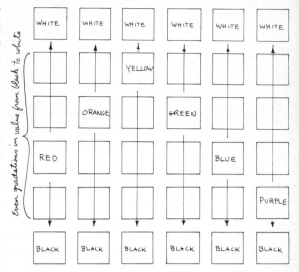

FIGURE 429. A study in value.

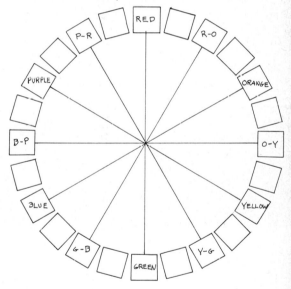

FIGURE 430. A study in hue.

grays, only black and white). Another example of the complete limitation of two color properties, and the partial limitation of the third, would be bright red, bright green, and bright blue. There would be a partial limitation on hue (only three hues are used), and a complete limitation on value (the three colors could be of exactly the same value; if bright yellow had been used it would have been lighter in value than the rest; but red, green, and blue can all be the same value and retain full intensity). There would be a limitation on intensity—that is, each color, although bright, is of exactly the same intensity; one is no brighter than the other. In both of these color schemes —the black and white, and the red, green, and blue—the viewer feels a certain homogeneous quality.

Sometime just sit down with a pencil and paper and figure out several different color schemes by limiting (to a fairly heavy degree) any or all of these properties of color—hue, intensity, and value. If you have a hard time envisioning the colors in your mind, use your set of paints. Here are three examples of ways to get unusual, harmonious color schemes.

1. Choose two opposite hues: orange and blue. (This is a fairly severe limitation of hue.) No limitation on value (colors can range all the way from very dark to very light).

   Partial limitation on intensity: a complete range of intensity, but only a very small *quantity* of the very intense tones.

   Result: Blues all the way from the palest sky blue to dark navy blue. Oranges all the way from the palest peach through brilliant orange to blackish orange (very dark brown). The blue and orange would never vary in hue: the blue could never be a greenish or purplish blue, and the orange could never be a yellowish or reddish orange. The majority of the weaving would be muted, with occasional spots of brilliant color.

2. Choose three adjacent hues: for example, blue, purple, red. Never go past the blue to greenish blue or past the red to orangish red. No limitation on value (colors can range all the way from very dark to very light)—except in this case let's make most of the colors very light, and use dark or brilliant tones in small amounts.

   Severe limitation on intensity. Never use a color of full brilliance except in extremely tiny amounts.

   Result: Muted blues, violets, wisteria, and pinks from the very palest shades to medium shades. Dramatic accentuations of intense magentas, red, purple, blue in very tiny amounts.

3. Use the three primaries and the three secondary colors: Red, orange, yellow, green, blue, and purple. Use no variations of those hues. Use *equal* amounts of each. Completely limit the values to a medium-dark tone (so that a black-and-white photo would reveal only a medium-dark gray).

   Limit the intensity of each color so that it matches the intensity of the yellow. In this case the yellow cannot be very intense because it has to be dark.

   Result: Yellow ochre, rust, brick red, muted purple, cadet blue, and hunter green. To make any of these lighter or darker in value than the others would spoil the effect.

Notes: Sometimes a dramatic effect can be achieved by using a very large quantity of one color and only smaller quantities of all the other colors.

If you use only limited hues and limited intensities you nearly always need accentuations of light and dark. Very often beginners have nice homogeneous and muted colors, but there is no life in them because they are too uniform. Using the complete range of value from dark to light can counteract this.

Light pale colors in a monochromatic (single-hue) color group have the effect of giving luminescence to the scheme.

Besides making theoretical color schemes, pick out some painting or weaving or whatever you like, and analyze the color scheme. Figure out just what limitations are at work. All this will help you become more conscious of the minute differences in colors, and make it possible for you to come up with good and unusual colors in your weaving.

CHAPTER XII

MAKING A LIVING AT IT

The Mercenary Aspects

You may, at first, think you are going into spinning, dyeing, and weaving (or any one of these) only because of a personal creative interest. But at some time it may become realistic to accept offers of remuneration for your work—if only to help you pay for your materials, supplies, and equipment, so that you can support your craft; for it can be an expensive hobby. And, if your work is good, these offers will surely come.

Or you may intend from the very beginning to make a small profit from a part-time involvement. This could very easily, possibly from a desire on your part, grow into a full-time business of producing, wholesaling, and retailing—a business involving many employees. I have often seen (in fact, it happened to me) a creative craftsman get so involved in the business end of a very successful production and marketing operation that there is little time left to devote to the completely creative and experimental work that one started out doing. Of course, there is the great advantage that in producing a quantity of work, working with other weavers, and sharing ideas (very important), the design and technical aspects of your work progress in leaps and bounds. Nevertheless, one can get bogged down in the business end of it.

In this chapter I would like to pass on a few things I've learned about making a living weaving, spinning, and dyeing, so you'll know what you are getting into.

One-of-a-Kind or Art Weaving

A piece of art weaving—whether functional or decorative—should bring more money than production work. The point of differentiation between the two types of weaving is rather vague, but by "art weaving" I mean weaving that reflects a personal creativity, has a unique design, and is produced by techniques that would prohibit mass production. This work will take a great deal of energy, creative effort, and talent to produce. In fact, it is so demanding that one could not possibly work at it eight hours a day, five days a week, over a long period of time. Unfortunately, sometimes the work involved turns out to be a waste, and the weaving is unsuccessful, ugly, and undesirable. For the above reasons, in calculating the selling price, you have to give yourself a very high hourly wage, in order to make any kind of a living selling works like this exclusively.

In general, you have to have made a name for yourself to get paid anywhere near what you should for the creative effort you put into an art weaving, and the object has to be quite desirable. So, even though the buyer will expect a much higher price on this piece than on production work, you are not necessarily going to make more money. For the first few years you will be a "struggling artist." In fact, you will be worse off, because people simply do not expect to pay as much for a weaving as they do for a painting, sculpture, or drawing.

But an advantage is that you have a great deal of freedom doing this kind of work. You need very little equipment to create a work of art, your time is your own, and you will be spending much of your working time using your brain rather than your "brawn." You will learn to know the special reward of struggle and success. And I'm not talking now about the monetary angle, but about the struggle of trying to express something through the medium of mere textile fibers, if only to reveal the simple beauty of the fibers themselves—and succeeding.

This type of work is best sold through galleries, or by entering exhibitions, or just privately to collectors (who will seek you out when you get known).

Production Work

I classify as production work weaving done in the same technique and on the same warp, with different colors and slightly different designs. For example, you can set up a warp and do twenty handbags, all similar in style, technique, and materials, but each can have a different design and different colors. You can do the same thing with rugs, pillows, stoles, ponchos. Even wall hangings, for that matter. These items are creations of your own and beautiful, yet they require less time to weave than single, unique items. By setting up a long warp and doing many similar items, you can cut down tremendously on the average time spent on each item. (And you have to keep in mind that any weaving that *could* have been done this way would have to be considered production work, even if you set the warp up just for one item and wove nothing else like it.)

In many ways this is a good way to develop your design sense. By the time you've woven ten or fifteen bags or pillows in a similar technique you gain an easy confidence in making design decisions; and as the weaving starts having a sureness about it, the designs begin to relate better to the technique. So you are producing good designs and yet using your time very efficiently.

Production weaving is not as exhausting as "art weaving," because you can work into a nice physical rhythm that doesn't have to be interrupted every ten minutes or so for a critical aesthetic decision. Even so, there are very few people who can work at just this for a full eight-hour day on a regular basis.

Fortunately, there is a compensating factor that occurs automatically. When you get into this type of work, selling will be a more time-consuming problem, simply because of quantity. You will probably need to have several different shops selling your work, unless you have your own retail outlet. It will take time to find good, reliable consignment shops or places that will buy outright, and to deal with them on a regular basis. This means you can work full time at your craft and yet not actually be throwing the shuttle all day long.

Keep in mind that, if you get into large production, your margin of profit on each piece is much less, because you now will have the expense of work space (you can't very well carry on this business in your living room), more equipment, and perhaps employees. So, even though you are selling more, you are not necessarily netting any more money.

Probably your work will be a little bit of both "production" and "art" weaving.

Efficiency

By efficient use of your time you can cut the time of producing a weaving in about half—or, conversely speaking, make twice as much per hour for your time.

First of all, let me point out that if you train yourself to work fast it begins to come naturally. Once you've learned to use your body movements and your brain in a fast, sure, rhythmical way, it is actually an effort to work slowly and inefficiently. But we must differentiate between frantic rushing (for haste does make waste) and complete concentration on efficient movements.

Next, be your own efficiency expert. Analyze the steps and processes you go through in your weaving or spinning or dyeing to see if any could be speeded up or eliminated—without any loss of quality. For example, if you are going to dye your warp yarn, don't order it in the form of spools or cones, so you will have to make skeins of it before dyeing. Or, if you are planning to dye wool, since you have to get out all your equipment and dyes and set up for it, plan on spending the whole day and get enough wool dyed to last you several weeks. Set up long warps, and cut off the weaving only when the cloth beam is too full to continue weaving. Each cutting off and tying on takes a little time. If you have washing and pressing to do, save up your weavings and do several items at once. And the same with sewing. Of course, now I'm talking about real production, where you are turning out many items of weaving a day.

All this talk about time and efficiency may seem a bit crass, and you may wonder, "What's the purpose of all this rush if I'm in this thing for the pleasure it gives?" But, don't be fooled—actually it's not *rushing;* it's making efficient use of your movements and time, and this is an art in itself. As in mountain climbing: if you stumble or miss a step the rhythm you have worked out between your breathing and climbing is disturbed and you become exhausted quickly.

The True Cost of Production

When I had my shop, with several weavers producing right there on the spot, and all of our productions were on display with price tags, one question was often asked by people who wandered in: "How long does it take to weave one of these?" Suspecting that they were thinking that the price was terribly high and that we were probably making a "killing," I would (once in a while) take a demonic pleasure in answering, "Oh . . . about an hour." From the price tag on the item they deduced that we were indeed making a killing—$45 an hour—and they left, outraged.

Well, the fact is the item *did* take only one hour to *weave*—after the yarn had been ordered and paid for, picked up at the post office, duty paid on it, unwrapped, prepared for dyeing, dyed, designed, wound into a warp, threaded on the loom—*then* it took an hour to "weave." After that it was removed from the loom, mended, fringed, washed, pressed, sewed, labeled, displayed, and with luck sold, with a sales slip and package. All this taking place in a building that had to be rented, heated, lighted, equipped, repaired, supplied, cleaned, insured; and books had to be kept and workers paid.

All these hidden costs of production and overhead have to be taken into consideration. To keep the price of your weavings reasonable and yet make a little money, at every one of these steps you have to be conscious of expenditures. We've already talked about efficiency in time. Besides this you have to cut costs wherever possible, allow no waste, no careless breakage or losses. Try to get all your materials at wholesale prices (do not sacrifice quality), and use all scrap ends for tapestries, belts, rya rugs. Get into fast production spinning to keep yarn costs down. Dyeing your own yarn can be a great saving—not that colored yarn is more expensive than natural, but to get good, unusual colors you have to order yarn from companies that have higher-priced goods.

To cut overhead costs, combine as many activities as possible—production and sales—in the same space and with the same employees. Don't let expensive looms stand idle; get an apprentice to produce something. Or, to avoid overhead costs almost completely, use your own home for your work space and you may be able to deduct up to one-half of all your home expenses (utilities, rent, insurance, mortgages, repairs, etc.) as business expenses.

Pricing Your Goods

All this previous talk brings us right down to: "What do I charge for this weaving?" First, we'll talk about *wholesale* price. The wholesale price is what *you* have to get for your weaving (or spinning) in order for you to be paid fairly for having produced it and made it available to wholesale buyers.

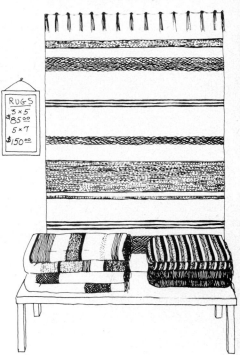

FIGURE 431. Pricing your goods.

1. Figure the time it took you to go through all the steps in weaving to produce that piece. (If you made several similar pieces on the same warp, figure the total time and divide by the number of pieces.)

2. Now add about 25 percent of this for time spent ordering materials and supplies, correspondence, designing, dealing with wholesalers, bookwork.

3. Add the number of hours (nos. 1 plus 2) and multiply this by what you think is a fair hourly wage. In deciding on a fair hourly wage just remember that you're not too special—there are lots of weavers and spinners producing for very reasonable prices. If you are a beginner, take one-third or one-fourth of this wage, because you will be working at about one-fourth the efficiency of an expert weaver. This is your learning period and you can't expect to make the hourly wage of an expert. For the first few years of weaving I'm sure I averaged less than $1 an hour for the time I put in.

4. Figure the actual cost of raw materials used in that piece of weaving. If you have spun and dyed the wool yourself, either add the time it took or figure on the cost of the yarn at a good retail price.

5. Add overhead. Figure what it costs you on a monthly average to maintain your work space and equipment, and then divide this by the number of hours per month you work. (Figure in utilities, rent, average monthly repairs, additional new equipment, and so on.) This will give you an *hourly* "overhead" cost. Multiply this cost by the number of hours computed in 1 and 2. (Here I should mention that if you've built yourself a fancy studio or have a lot of costly equipment, and you don't use it full time, you can't charge people for equipment sitting idle. You'd have to assume in your figuring that you work at least 150 hours a month.)

6. Add vehicle expenses, if you have to have a vehicle for running around to do some of your work.

7. Add no. 3 through no. 6 and you should come up with a wholesale figure that is about right.

The retail price is usually *double* the wholesale price. Compare your computed retail price with prices you have seen on other handwoven items on the market, and adjust for the success (or failure) of your piece.

The Relationship of Design, Function, and Price

One of the facts you have to get used to in the weaving business (or any craft, for that matter) is that people have preconceived ideas of what things should cost.

For instance: it is simply accepted that a wall hanging should cost more than a handbag. One could make a handbag that took many, many hours to weave and that was superior aesthetically and more unusual (an "art weaving," in other words) than a wall hanging that took only a few hours to weave—and yet the hanging will probably sell for two or three times what the bag could possibly sell for. One little glimmer of hope is that just recently people seem to be forgetting the old boundaries and are appreciating (and willing to pay for) beautiful things, whether they are classified as "art" or functional objects.

In general, however, to sell your weaving for the best price, consider the design and function of the piece in relation to the time you put into it and the sale price. The pricing of the "art" handbag and the wall hanging is one example. Another example might be a beautiful 45-inch square of weaving. Now, you could sell this simply as yardage, or you could call it a baby blanket, or you could make it into a woman's poncho. To make it into something other than just the yardage would take very little extra time, but it might double the price. And the woman's poncho would command the highest price because women expect to pay outrageous prices for their clothing. Likewise, a tapestry rug that could take many long hours of work would no doubt have to sell for less than the same piece if it were simply called a wall hanging.

You may be idealistic and want to refuse to consider these things. But if you are out to make a living you may have to "play the game."

Selling Directly to Private Buyers

You may be able to sell all your weavings directly to private buyers who know you or your work. This would probably be the ideal way for the work to pass from the craftman's studio to the owner or collector—no middlemen and expenses, so the craftsman gets the most for his work and the buyer pays the least. If you are just starting and have few weavings, or if you are a well-known weaver of very special items and your production is not large, this will work.

The buyer, if he bought the piece in a retail shop or gallery, would be paying the retail price—double the wholesale price. Since he has sought you out, he might be entitled to some discount, but certainly not the wholesale price. You have to spend a good amount of your time dealing with him as a buyer, and you have to count the time spent with other people coming to buy, taking your time, and then ending up not buying anything. Perhaps a splitting of that 100 percent markup would be fair, which means you would give him a 25 percent discount from the retail price.

If you are selling at retail outlets in the vicinity at the same time you are selling out of your home or studio, the outlets may insist that you do not undersell them. *If* they are selling well for you, it is wise not to antagonize them. The buyer will still be willing to pay the price (full retail). He has had the opportunity of talking with you and seeing your studio, and can say that he purchased his little prize from the craftsman himself.

Selling at Craft Fairs

A way of promoting and marketing your craft that has become very widespread is to rent a booth or space at a craft fair. There are many very good fairs all over the country that draw hundreds of thousands of visitors over a period of a few days or weeks. This means that, unless you are into large production, you can probably attend a few fairs a year and sell most of what you produce. You can sell your goods for less than retail price (making it desirable for the buyers to attend the fairs) and still come out ahead yourself. I would suggest a pricing similar to what I suggested for private buyers—25 percent off the retail price. Although you will be selling quantity amounts in a short period and you might think you could sell wholesale, remember, you still have the expense of booth rental, travel, survival expenses away from home, etc.

The items that sell best at fairs are moderate- to low-cost items. Very expensive art goods do not do so well. (At least that is my experience.)

These fairs are fun but very exhausting. And a word of caution: There are often professional "rip-off" artists around, so keep a sharp eye on your goods if you don't want to come away from the fair with more goods stolen than sold.

The fairs are usually announced in newspapers, craft magazines, and on posters.

FIGURE 432. Selling at craft fairs.

Selling Through Shops or Galleries on Consignment

This is probably the most common way for the craftsman who is not well known, but who produces a quantity of work, to sell his goods. Shops are hungry for work. Beginning craftsmen often feel lucky to have a shop "accept" their work, but you should realize that it's not costing the shop anything, and they *need* your work to fill up their shop. Most craftsmen will agree that the consignment system is not very desirable, however, because about half or more of the shops or galleries—even though you know the shopkeepers, and they appear to be (or even are) good people—just can't seem to pay their bills. And always their rent and insurance and taxes and other bills come before you.

Once in a while, though, you come across a shop that is a steady and reliable outlet. If you keep them well supplied (and this is the secret to good monthly sales at *any* shop or gallery) they will send you a nice check every month. Three or four outlets like this can make you a living. So it's worth a try. Start out with just a few things in a shop near you (so you can check up on them regularly), or with even fewer things in a shop farther away—and take the risk. It will soon prove itself one way or the other.

The usual commission charged by a shop that takes your goods on consignment is 33 1/3 percent of the *retail* price (which, as we said before, should be double the wholesale price). Some shops in high-rent areas (where sales *should* be excellent) can, and have to, take more—sometimes 40 percent or even 50 percent. This is *not* a good deal for you unless the shop is very reliable and sales *are* excellent. Any shop (unless it is endowed with private funds or has volunteer workers) that takes *less* than one-third will probably fail in a few months, even though they should be commended for their altruistic effort.

You might think that in this case the retail price could be less, since the shop only takes a third—which means you are getting more than your standard wholesale price. But, believe me, the hassle of checking up on your payments and the tying up of the goods—sometimes for months—with delayed payments, is just barely compensated for by the fact that you get this little extra money.

Be sure you get proper receipts for everything you leave at a shop and a payment agreement, as well as the assurance that you will be notified if any item leaves the shop for any reason (special displays, exhibitions, etc.). Sometimes things can disappear that way.

Often a shop or gallery cannot afford insurance. You should understand whether you are leaving your things at your own risk or whether the shop will take the responsibility in case of damage or theft. If it does not take this responsibility, you have to decide whether it's worth the risk. In all the years I've had things out on consignment, there has never been occasion where I've lost anything from theft or damage.

If a consignment place asks for an exclusive (this means the guarantee that you will not sell elsewhere in that town or city) consider first whether it can promise you the business you need from that area—and whether or not the proprietors are prompt payers.

Selling Wholesale

Very few good shops and galleries can afford to buy outright, even though they can get the items at half price. They can never seem to get ahead enough to invest in what would amount to thousands of dollars' worth of goods. If you do find an outlet that will buy your goods outright, be sure you give the 50 percent off, because such shops can't possibly afford to have their money tied up if they don't at least double the price in the final sale.

You won't find a place like this unless you're lucky, or unless the items you have for sale are so desirable and reasonably priced that they move fast. Then the shop-keepers will risk the investment, because they know they will get the money back very soon.

If the shop is reliable, you can give a thirty-day payment period. This is fairly customary and makes it much more possible for a shop to buy outright. The first time you deal with one on this basis do not sell a large quantity—there is always the possibility they will never pay. Some will ask if there is a discount for cash payment; in my opinion, you can't afford to give them this. Your wholesale price is already at rock bottom. What you can do to encourage prompt payment is to add a 10 percent service charge if they are later than thirty days. This should be understood at the time of delivery.

Outright purchasers do often insist on exclusives. If they are buying enough from you on a regular basis, you should be happy to grant this request.

It is customary to give the buyer an invoice. This mysterious-sounding business term is simply a list of the articles that are being purchased, their prices, and the terms of payment. The invoice should accompany the goods on delivery.

Selling Through an Agent

This is not a very common way for a craftsman to market his goods, unless he's involved in a huge production. An agent acts as a salesman of your goods to retail outlets. He does your wholesale selling for you, but in return he usually takes 15 percent or more of the wholesale price—and normally asks for an exclusive for a large area of several states. All future orders go through him, so once he has established a buyer for you he gets his percentage on everything you sell to that buyer.

Entering Exhibitions

I have mentioned that making a name for yourself helps sell your work. Well, one way to get well known in the craft business is to enter all the exhibitions you can—especially juried shows. And there are lots of them. A jury's decision (when the shows are juried) certainly can't make or break you as an artist or craftsman; and you shouldn't take the decisions to heart, whether they reject your work or give you first prize.

The good thing about these shows is that other craftsmen see your work; visitors tend to respect the juries' decisions and feel very confident when they buy from a museum or juried exhibition; the works are usually fairly well displayed and get good exposure; the promoters normally take less than the standard commission, and make no profit on the sale; and it's a good way to get an objective view of your work, seeing it in an exhibition hall with many other works.

Being included in many exhibitions can make your work familiar to the interested public and make your name known. It can lead to invitational exhibitions and one-man shows.

There is a certain amount of effort involved in entering the more important exhibitions now because of the red tape they require. You have to send slides and entry blanks weeks or months ahead, which means the work is tied up for that long before the exhibition ever opens.

The announcements for entering exhibitions are listed in craft magazines, but once you have entered a certain show one year you are automatically on its mailing list and you will be sent entry forms for the next.

One-Man Shows

Some craftsmen try to have as many exhibitions and one-man shows to their credit as possible. It makes their "biographies" look impressive. It does not necessarily mean they are very good artists. One-man shows can, however, have a good effect on the craftsman himself—despite these self-aggrandizing aspects. He is encouraged into a good period of production, and (if he can remain free from the desire to make his displays pretentious and impressive) he tends to try to produce his best and most personal work. Besides all this he gets to see his work under the most favorable circumstances, which should allow him some satisfaction, and, one hopes, the right atmosphere for useful self-criticism.

If you think you are prepared to have a one-man show, and haven't already been approached by one of the shops or galleries in which you sell, you can take them some slides or samples of your work and perhaps be scheduled for a show. Often shows combine two or more craftsmen to make an interesting exhibition.

Sales are usually quite good if your prices are reasonable. Don't make the mistake of overpricing your works. It's more important to get the pieces into homes where they will be appreciated and seen. When and if you become famous you can demand high prices. Use the same rules for pricing as before.

FIGURE 433. Running your own retail-wholesale shop.

Running Your Own Retail-Wholesale Shop

If you are ambitious enough to make this craft a full-time business and are ready to work regular hours at it, one of the best ways to assure sales is to have your studio in a business location and make it open to the public. If you enjoy display, a little bookwork, and people, this is still another way to be making money at your craft and yet not be sitting at the loom all day long. You will be amazed at the increases in your sales. There is nothing the buyer likes better than to be able to visit the craftsman's studio and talk with him personally. Many laymen need this confidence when they are spending their money on something out of the ordinary.

It is also an excellent way to establish wholesale contacts. Shop owners from other states may happen into your studio-shop and order from you, and become regular buyers in the future.

There are many advantages to this arrangement of studio and shop together. For one thing, I found by having regular hours I produced much more. Besides this you are combining the overhead of a studio and a shop, so you're actually getting one of them more or less free, and any retail sales you make are at a very good profit. Any days that no one comes in the shop, you are still making good use of your time at your loom. It is definitely an efficient combination.

Of course, you may find it difficult to work with people watching you and asking questions. At first it bothered me, but eventually I could do even creative tapestry work in public.

I have a few suggestions that may help make your shop a success.

If you will be depending on the "drop-in" trade, do try to have regular hours—simple for the public to comprehend, like: "Open 12 to 6 every day except Sunday"; or "Open Tuesday thru Saturday 9–5"; or "Open weekends only, Fri., Sat., Sun., 10–6." Something they can remember without copying it down. And the important thing is to stick to those hours. If customers come and find you closed when they expect you to be open they will soon be discouraged. You will get the reputation of never being open, and of running an erratic and not very dependable business. Your image is important.

Your marked retail prices should be double your wholesale prices—the same prices the items would be in any other shop. If you are also wholesaling to other shops in the vicinity, they won't like it at all if you undersell them. And there is really no advantage to you; those shops will be selling certain things for you to a different clientele—one that might never come to your shop. The bulk of the buyers will probably come directly to you anyway; you won't have to entice them with discounts. They will come because they want to buy from *you.* If you choose, you can give private discounts, but your regular sales should be at a standard retail price.

As for wholesaling out of your shop, my advice is to make wholesale commitments *only* when you have an excess of goods and only to keep the money coming in during off seasons. Your margin of profit is so much less wholesaling that you would make a mistake to deplete your own stock. Also do not make the mistake of committing yourself at Christmas or other good seasons to huge wholesale orders that will be a terrible strain to fill and perhaps mean that you would have to empty your own shop space just at the best time of year.

Insist that wholesale buyers prove they are in the retail business by showing you their tax numbers or business cards (see Taxes, Bookkeeping, and Other Red Tape in this chapter). Sometimes people try to buy six of one thing just to get the wholesale price for their Christmas presents. Also have a standard minimum quantity that they must purchase in order to get the discount.

Two of the most important factors to consider in keeping sales high are good display and plentiful selection. Do not allow your shop to get empty, rundown, and untidy. Your window display will draw the customers in; be sure it is well lighted and changed often enough so that it doesn't collect dust. Customers like to feel that they are buying from a successful business.

I've always felt that an orderly, systematic way of displaying goods is best for sales. Except for an occasional artistic grouping of objects, as in your window display, it is better to group similar objects together in a nice stack or on the same shelf or rack or whatever. Then the customer can see all the variations of a particular item that are available in the shop. For instance, if you have several handbags for sale and they are all in one place, the buyer can make a selection much more easily than if you had to point out all the different handbags in the shop—some hanging on this wall and some on that shelf, another displayed with a poncho, and another in a glass case. A group of similar items attracts interest more than scattered single items. The shop will have a much less cluttered appearance, and the overall artistic impact will be much more dramatic.

Price tags on all objects are definitely helpful. Many customers are shy and don't want to bother you by asking the price, or they just assume the price will be too high for them anyway.

If you want to display and sell other items in your shop, like other crafts, you will save yourself much bookwork if you choose things that are good sellers and buy them outright. You'll have to start small, no doubt, but eventually you will make more money this way. I found that handling things on consignment took much too much of my time—signing things in and out, and sending checks to the craftsmen each month.

Selling weaving equipment and yarns can be another very good way to pick up extra money. In the first place you can get all your equipment and yarns at wholesale prices, and by the time you've sold the extra you are in effect getting all your supplies free—a big help in production weaving. If you spin and dye your own wool, people will be begging you to sell it to them. Make them pay a good price unless you want to make this your exclusive business. The demand could get so great that you would be spending all your time spinning and dyeing and never have a supply of yarns for yourself to weave.

I will discuss employees, books, and taxes under separate headings because there is a lot to be said about how to approach these problems without "losing your shirt."

Apprentices

To work at the loom (or spinning wheel) eight hours a day, five days a week (which you would probably have to do if you actually hope to make a living at this), is nearly impossible. It is very hard, tedious work. It is good to have breaks doing other related things—like selling and teaching.

Whether you have a shop or not, by taking on an apprentice you can pass your knowledge on to someone else anxious to learn the trade, and there need be no money exchange. The apprentice can help you with your production (at first the more tedious aspects, to be sure, but these are necessary to learn), or help you run your shop. It is a fine way to trade your knowledge and experience for a little work.

A few words of advice about taking on apprentices. A two- or three-month learning period is reasonable with no money exchange. To go to a school to learn weaving, a person would have to pay a good deal. Granted, he would get to keep what he wove, but he would have to pay for the materials as well as the tuition. Not many beginners can afford this, so you are providing them with free instruction, and they are compensating you by working for you for no pay.

Start with only one apprentice. It is important that he commit himself to a certain number of hours daily or weekly. It is very frustrating to provide a project and equipment and then have that equipment sit idle for days on end. I always asked for a commitment of at least twenty hours a week.

Take a second or third apprentice only if you think you can keep him busy with instructive work.

Since apprentices are going to be providing a service for you, you have an obligation to them—to make their time with you worthwhile and teach them all the steps, from ordering supplies through creating the design, to the final finishing of the woven item. Do not give them only routine dirty work.

Having an apprentice for two or three months does not mean you're going to be getting a lot of work out of someone for nothing. The time you spend with him will just barely be compensated for by the help he gives you. It is really just another way to be working at your craft without throwing that shuttle all day long.

Employees

After a few months you may want to take on the apprentice as a regular employee. The legal aspects of this are a headache. The law now says that anyone having even *one* employee is classified as an "employer" and must withhold income tax, social security (and pay half of the social security himself), and send quarterly reports of these accounts. If you have more than one employee you may have to get into workmen's compensation, unemployment insurance, etc. The government will constantly be sending you new instructions and forms to fill out. It drove me out of my mind *and* out of business actually. Well, more about these taxes and red tape later. Right now let me say: if possible do not have any "employees." There are some ways of getting around this.

Instead of having "employees" over whom you can exercise control to direct them in the details and methods of their work, you may save yourself a substantial amount of book work and money by having your work done on a "contract" basis by independent contractors. If they contract to do the work (weave rugs or pillows, etc., by the piece) and you are willing to give up control over their work except as to the final product, they will probably qualify as "independent contractors" and you will avoid withholding taxes, social security payments, workmen's compensation, etc. Often weavers will prefer to work in their own homes anyway and you can provide them with equipment and materials with the understanding that they will be paid a certain contract price when the project is completed. The safest course is for you to check with a lawyer concerning applicable federal, state, and local laws, any of which may have changed from the time of this writing to the time you read this. It's just a warning not to become an "employer" without knowing what you're getting into and what the available alternatives are.

The same problem of equipment being tied up by an apprentice who doesn't put in enough hours of work applies to your workers. Do not hire a weaver who will not commit himself to a certain amount of production each week or month that will be reasonable for the amount of equipment involved.

Now for figuring out the right price for piecework. Assuming that you are a pretty expert weaver by the time you have weavers working for you, you should be able to figure out reasonable piecework prices. Weave the items yourself, working fast and efficiently, and time yourself. Allow a good hourly wage for this time, and let this be the price that will be paid to any weaver, slow or fast, beginner or expert, for that particular item. The beginner or slow weaver will not be making as much for his time, but he shouldn't be. Fast weavers and diligent workers will be able to make a good living.

Workshops and Classes

Many weavers, spinners, and dyers conduct workshops or have regular classes to make extra money. It is particularly easy to set up workshops in spinning and dyeing. Weaving requires a little more effort because of the equipment involved. These workshops can usually be conducted in shops, museums, and craft guilds (many cities have guilds you can join for the purpose of getting together with other craftsmen in your field) rather than your own home, in case you prefer. Once you have prepared for a workshop and done it once, it is easy to do again. If you are really an expert, you should get a nice fee, plus expenses if you have to travel.

For dyeing workshops you can offer instructions free for those who are willing to work. There is a lot of muscle work involved in dyeing quantities of yarn, and there are usually more than enough people wanting to see the process in exchange for helping. I used to offer to teach someone to spin free if they would spin five pounds of wool for me.

FIGURE 434. Handspun yarn for sale.

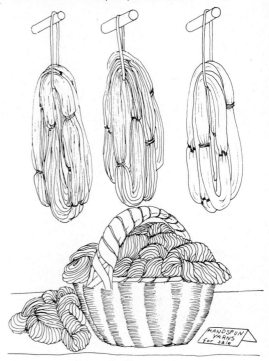

Holding classes in your studio is another way to make extra money. This, however, usually requires extra equipment and space and means you have a regular commitment each week. If you enjoy teaching this can be very remunerative, but it cuts into your own creative time tremendously. On the other hand sometimes getting involved in teaching simply serves to stimulate your own creative urges, and you actually get as much accomplished yourself as you would if you weren't teaching.

You won't have difficulty getting students if you offer good classes—there are so many people now wanting to learn spinning, dyeing, and weaving.

Selling Handspun or Hand-dyed Yarn

There is such a demand for beautiful yarns now that a craftsman can make a living just spinning and dyeing yarn. But you have to be very smart and efficient in order to keep the price reasonable and still make money. To spin a medium or fine even yarn you will have to charge a good fat price, but there seem to be people willing to pay this for very special projects. You can probably make more money for your time by spinning cruder and heavier yarns (from nice fleeces that do not need carding) on one of the good electric spinners I have described. See Chapter IX, "Spinning: Yarn Design and Function," for some ideas. Your best way of marketing handspun wool is direct to the weaver through craft-magazine ads.

By dyeing the wool you can add another $1 or more per pound to the price of the yarn. It is possible for four people to dye 150 pounds of yarn in one day (see Chapter X, "Dyeing: General Instructions for Dyeing with Acid Dyes") using only a few dollars' worth of dye. If you are a good color artist you can make colors that are far more interesting and desirable than the commercially dyed yarns. Weavers are always looking for really unusual colors.

Taxes, Bookkeeping, and Other Red Tape

For most craftsmen this is the worst part of having one's own business. I won't expound on my social and political thoughts, but it does seem to me sad that our society has developed to the point where we can't freely trade or sell our goods without being expert accountants, tax collectors, and unpaid bookkeepers for the government.

As I pointed out while we were talking about employees, there are ways that you can get around doing some of this bookkeeping, by contracting with independent contract workers instead of hiring employees. You are not cutting the government out of what it says is its due. But *you* are not responsible; the worker is.

Here are some of the things you will have to know about your obligations to the state and federal governments if you are selling your work—either wholesale or retail—to anyone; or if you have employees. (At least at this time of writing. Goodness knows, it may get worse.)

The Internal Revenue Service (income tax) requires that a self-employed person report his income on Schedule C (the self-employment form). On this form you are required to state your business activity, the name, and the location. You compute your gross income from sales or services, and any expenses incurred that relate to the business, and from these figures you compute your net profit (or loss). You must have books (simple account books showing sales and expenses—you don't have to take a course in accounting) and receipts for all your expenses to back up this Schedule C report. You don't have to send in these receipts, but keep them in case of an audit. If you are in large production you will have to do an inventory of goods on hand at the end of the tax year, and the value of this inventory (or cost to you) is *added* to your gross income. If at all possible avoid the necessity of an inventory; if you are a small-production or art weaver, you can just say "not applicable."

You are required to pay a social security tax (which at the time of this writing is over 10 percent) on your net income, as well as income tax. (You remember, if you have worked for a regular employer, that he deducts this from your pay check as well as the withholding tax; he has to pay half of the social security and he withholds the other half from your check.) When you are self-employed you pay the entire 10 percent plus.

The other thing you are supposed to do if you are self-employed is make estimated quarterly reports and pay your tax quarterly.

Your *state income tax* is usually simply a percentage of your federal tax, and there are no special forms to be filled out as a self-employed person—just the regular state income-tax forms.

So much for income tax: this you are required to do even if you don't have a store or any employees, but are just producing and selling your work to *anyone*.

Almost every state has some form of sales tax. It is a certain percentage collected on every dollar spent by the buyer. The customer or retail buyer is expected to pay this and the seller is required to have a license to make retail sales and collect this tax. He must send in all the collected taxes each month to the state. So if you are legitimately selling your goods *retail* (not for resale), you must apply for this retail license and collect these taxes.

If you do not have your own retail shop, you will probably be selling wholesale or on consignment or through museums, and you will *not* be responsible for this tax. In fact, be sure *not* to apply for a license because, if you do, the government expects a monthly report (penalty if not sent in) and any wholesale transaction must be backed up by the wholesale purchaser's retail license number—or else the state will charge *you* the tax on the transaction.

Withholding, unemployment insurance, and workmen's compensation will be things you'll have to know about if you are classified as an "employer." Different states have different laws concerning these items, but this is more or less what will be involved.

You must have on file your employee's social security number and a statement of his exemption claims. Each week you must figure what should be withheld from his pay check for his income tax and social security. Quarterly you send in a report of all these deductions for each employee, pay what has been withheld from his pay check, *and* pay half of his social security tax yourself.

Usually the unemployment insurance and workmen's compensation or insurance must be paid quarterly also.

What it all means is that every three months, just when you thought your business was making a profit, you have to come up with several hundred dollars and send it off to the government, along with incredibly tedious reports (which are always changing and requiring further study of the instructions).

You can always hire a bookkeeper to do all this for you and simply figure on paying the price, but I always considered it a real argument for not getting into too large a business.

One further little government requisition in your particular business will be complying with the Wool Products Labeling Act of 1939. Your articles of wool or hair are supposed to be labeled. Virgin wool means wool converted into yarns or fiber for the first time. Reprocessed wool is that made from samples or scraps . . . mill ends (never used, however). Reused wool means exactly what it says. Your products must be labeled according to what they are, and all hair products can be considered the same as wool.

Conclusions

All these words of advice will be starters for you. You will undoubtedly find your own best way of making money doing what you like most. Probably the old saying "Don't put all your eggs in one basket" is a good one to follow. Combining your creative work with some smart business schemes, plus keeping in contact and sharing ideas with other craftsmen through magazines (there is now one devoted entirely to sales opportunities), exhibitions, guilds, will keep you on your toes, and will probably mean that you can pursue your work and actually make a living at it.

CHAPTER XIII

SUPPLIERS

General Information

The first thing to be noted in this chapter is that the information (compiled in 1975) may, in some cases, be outdated by the time this book reaches you. I chose to give you rather detailed information about what these suppliers carried (knowing full well that their stock might have been changed or most likely expanded; or their addresses might have changed or they might be out of business)—rather than just list their names and addresses. This way you will at least get an idea of whether they might have the item you are looking for. So please be tolerant. (And, dear supplier: please also be tolerant of errors or possible omissions. It was an incredibly tedious and complex job to get all this information down in a fashion organized enough to be useful to the craftsman.)

The second thing that must be mentioned is this. Although many of these suppliers are really very helpful (usually they are craftsmen themselves), they are flooded with letters asking for brochures and samples. The amount of work that goes into preparing these brochures and sample cards is considerable and they must charge for them. When you come across an ad in a crafts magazine you will usually find they say, "Send $— for samples." Although many suppliers asked me to mention exact charges, I decided not to. I felt it would be much less complicated if you first contacted them by sending a *large-size business envelope, self-addressed and stamped,* asking how much to send for samples and brochures. If you send the envelope, you will get an immediate response and be told the correct, up-to-date amount. Even when the samples cost $3 or $5 they are worth it—you'll see.

The third noteworthy point is that many fine new sources will not be included, because new shops and suppliers are cropping up every day now. Be sure to check in crafts magazines such as *Shuttle, Spindle, and Dyepot* for suppliers; this will keep you informed on new equipment and new yarn and fiber sources. The Handweavers Guild of America (see this chapter, Books) now has a very complete and up-to-date directory.

Supply stores are so numerous now that you will probably have one or two near you, which you should definitely check into. And remember that the foreign sources are well worth investigating. Don't let the lack of speedy delivery turn you away. Overseas mail usually takes two months for packages and five days for airmail letters.

Yarns

AYOTTES' DESIGNERY
Center Sandwich, N.H. 03227

500 different yarns available at their weaving shop or through the mail. $4 membership entitles you to their samples indefinitely. Minimum: $15 purchase per year.

BARTLETTYARNS, INC.
Harmony, Maine 04942

2-, 3-, and 4-ply woolen yarns in naturals, colors, and heathers; fisherman's bulky (very softly spun 4-ply whites and naturals). Very reasonable prices. Wholesale prices for 10 pounds and over.

HYSLOP BATHGATE & CO.
Galashiels, Scotland

Extremely fine botany yarn; woolen yarns; loop mohair; some single-ply; mostly 2-ply; 2-ply worsted; nice single-ply gray tapestry wool; 2-ply white and gray coarse carpet yarn. Special offerings at very low costs. Very good prices.

THE BEGINNINGS
3449 Mission Ave.
Carmichael, Calif. 95608

Agents for CUM; Canadian, Scottish, and some American yarns; handspun yarns from Greece and Mexico.

BERGA/ULLMAN, INC.
P.O. Box 918
North Adams, Mass. 01247

Weaving and knitting yarns; linens, cottons. Sold through dealers only. Write them for dealers' names and samples.

BERNAL WOOLEN MILLS
851 Hamilton Ave.
Menlo Park, Calif. 94025

Very soft medium- and heavy-weight single and plied woolen yarns in natural white and gray and a few basic colors.

BEV'S YARN SHOP
11 West 17th St. (10th floor)
New York, N.Y. 10011

Complete line of Berga/Ullman wools, linens, and cottons; Tahki "Donegals" and Greek yarn; also nice natural white yarns in heavy loose plies.

CHRISTINE BLAKE
2310 West State St.
Boise, Idaho 83702

Agent for CUM and Oregon Worsted; novelty yarns, mill ends. Discounts for professional weavers.

DICK BLICK
Dept. 11
Box 1267
Galesburg, Ill. 61401

Variety of wool, cotton, linen, and synthetic-blend yarns in skeins, balls, and cones.

BRIGGS AND LITTLE WOOLEN MILLS LTD.
York Mills, Harvey Station
New Brunswick
Canada

1-, 2-, 3-, 4-, and 6-ply woolen yarns in nice naturals, colors, and some heathers. Single- ply warp yarn. Reasonable prices. Good medium-weight 3-ply warp yarn.

CHARLES Y. BUTTERWORTH
Box 3603
Philadelphia, Pa. 19125

Synthetic and novelty yarns.

BY REE WEAVING STUDIO
62 Rolling Meadows
Madison, Conn. 06443

Imported yarns.

CAMBRIAN FACTORY LTD.
Llanwrtyd Wells
Breconshire, Wales

Very fine single-ply wool yarns. Some nice colors, including heathers.

CAMBRIDGE WOOLS LTD.
16–22 Anzac Ave. (P.O. Box 2572)
Auckland 1, New Zealand

Vegetable-type colors in medium-weight 2- and 3-ply yarns; lamb's wool 2-ply medium-weight in brilliants and pastels; 2-ply naturals. Reasonable prices with postage paid.

J. & H. CLASGENS
New Richmond, Ohio 45157

Weaving yarns at low prices. Production weavers should write them for large orders.

COLORADO FLEECE CO.
Gerrie Gordon
516 W. Ute
Grand Junction, Colo. 81501

Mill-end yarns; very cheap.

WILLIAM CONDON & SONS LTD.
P.O. Box 129 (65 Queen St.)
Charlottetown, Prince Edward Island
Canada C1A 7K3

Good-quality wool yarns in 5 different weights from 1-ply fine to 5-ply rug. Naturals and dyed colors. Reasonable prices.

CONLIN YARNS
Woolen Spun Yarns
P.O. Box 11812
Philadelphia, Pa. 19128

Matching yarns for weaving and knitting. Beautiful Australian wool in muted heathery tones. Very fine single-ply for weaving and very soft 4-ply for knitting in matching colors.

CONTESSA YARNS
P.O. Box 37
Lebanon, Conn. 06249

Silk, wool, rayon, linen combinations. Mainly fine yarns and novelty yarns; also synthetics.

CRAFTSMAN'S MARK LTD.
Trefnant, Denbigh LL16 5UD
Wales

Beautiful single- and 2-ply natural wool yarns that look much like homespun—fine and rug weight; also linen carpet warp. Approximately 5% discount on large orders. Reasonable prices.

CRAFT YARNS OF RHODE ISLAND, INC.
Harrisville, R.I. 01830

Large assortment of colors and textures in weaving yarns—wool, rayon, jute. Handled by many dealers.

CREATIVE HANDWEAVERS
P.O. Box 26480
Los Angeles, Calif. 90026

Excellent source for beautiful handspun ethnic yarns—wool, cotton, alpaca, goat hair, camel's hair, human hair (from India), artificial silk, jute, munj (palm rope). Very reasonable prices.

CUM TEXTILE INDUSTRIES LTD.
Roemersgade 5
1362 Copenhagen K.
Denmark

$5 will get you their sample book; then order from agent (now sells only through agency affiliation). All types of beautiful Scandinavian wool, linen, and cotton yarns —excellent color range.

CUSTOM HANDWEAVERS
Allied Arts Guild
Arbor Rd. at Creek Dr.
Menlo Park, Calif. 94025

Excellent variety of beautiful yarns from all over the world; many handspun as well as the best of foreign commercially spun yarns; mill ends. (Special note: natural color 2-ply Navajo-type rug warp, and handspun Navajo wool.) Beads, buttons, and rings.

THE DARBY RAM
5056 Lee Highway
Arlington, Va. 22207

Agents for Berga/Ullman, Tahki, Texere, Maypole, and others.

DAVIDSON'S OLD MILL YARNS
P.O. Box 115
Eaton Rapids, Mich. 48827

CUM agent. Really good natural white yarns in all sizes and plies, from very fine to giant 2-ply roving; some excellent warp yarns; wool yarns in lovely colors; also alpaca, cashmere, goat. Excellent prices, and unit prices decrease as you buy more.

DEDE M
Box 486
Hampton, N.H. 03842

Knitting and weaving yarns, some nice naturals, mill ends, brushed mohair; Tahki "Donegals."

EAGER WEAVERS
183 Jefferson Rd.
Rochester, N.Y. 14623

Agents for Craft Yarns, Lily Mills, Tahki, Maypole, Colonial, Filature
Lemieux; Lopi, alpaca, novelties, and selection of mill ends.

EARTH GUILD/GRATEFUL UNION MAIL
ORDER SERVICE
15 Tudor St.
Cambridge, Mass 02139
(Retail store at 149 Putnam Ave.)

Agents for CUM and Fawcett; also Lily Mills; Australian wool; goat
hair from Crete; Finnish yarns; 4-ply rug yarns; mohair loop.

EARTHWARES
Weaving Supplies
103 N. Pleasant St.
Amherst, Mass. 01002

Agents for CUM yarns, Lily Mills; large supply of wool and synthetic
mill ends; rug wool, novelty yarns, alpaca, Lopi, Mexican, etc.
Beads.

LINDA ERWIN
570 Lamplighter Rd.
Horsham, Pa. 19044

Handspun yarns in heavy and medium weight; beautiful, dyed in
either vegetable or synthetic colors. Very reasonable prices.

ESSAYONS STUDIO
8725 Big Bend
St. Louis, Mo. 63119

Complete line of weaving yarns.

EUGENE FIBRE
1157 High St.
Eugene, Ore. 97401

Excellent yarns—Canadian, English, Greek, Swedish, Afghanistan;
camel's and horsehair, etc. But *no mail order.*

FANCY THREADS
843 North Cleveland-Massillon Rd.
Akron, Ohio 44313

Agents for CUM, Paternayan, Stanley; primitives from Mexico and
India; precut wool for rya rugs.

FREDERICK J. FAWCETT, INC.
129 South St.
Boston, Mass. 02111

Imported linen yarns—large selection of sizes, finishes, and colors;
also worsted yarn in 56 colors.

FEHRENBACHER FARM
Rte. 2, Box 233
Milton-Freewater, Ore. 97862

Handspun white and dark wool, and mohair.

THE FIBER STUDIO
P.O. Box 356
Sudbury, Mass. 01776

Good cheap rug wools; nice natural yarns and some dyed; also
good natural 2-ply warp.

FILATURE LEMIEUX, INC.
St.-Ephrem
Beauce, Quebec
Canada

Nice weaving and knitting yarns—single-ply up to 4-ply, medium
and fine weights, naturals and colors. Reasonable prices.

FOLKLORICO
P.O. Box 625
(522 Ramona St.)
Palo Alto, Calif. 94302

Beautiful Icelandic wools in naturals, fine and heavy single-ply and
medium-fine 2-ply; Mexican wool and Angora mixture. Wholesale
also.

FORT CRAILO YARNS CO.
2 Green St.
Rensselaer, N.Y. 12144

Some nice medium- to very light-weight wool yarns, good single-ply
wool; also cotton. Reasonable prices.

FREED COMPANY
P.O. Box 394
Albuquerque, N.M. 87103

Very nice single-ply mohair yarn—very cheap on cones of 4–5
pounds. Beads.

GORDON'S NATURALS
P.O. Box 506
Roseburg, Ore. 97470

Handspun yarns from Greece, Ecuador, Tennessee, Mexico in naturals; also commercial yarns in naturals—good yarns for dyeing yourself; good wool warp yarn. Reasonable prices.

A. K. GRAUPNER
Corner House
Valley Rd.
Bradford BD1 4AA
England

Deals in all kinds of yarns—mainly animal fibers. He does not prepare a full sample sheet, so you will have to tell him of your special interest.

GREAT NORTHERN WOOLS
Prickly Mountain
Warren, Vt. 05674

These people raise their own sheep and hand spin 1- and 2-ply yarns in natural colors—some lanolin left in. Also beautiful creamy white wool yarn in 1, 2, or 3 plies—the result of Vermont sheep growers pooling their fleeces and having a Vermont mill spin it; 40% discount for 25 pounds or more.

GREENMONT YARNS & LOOMS
Greenmont Center
West Rd.
Bennington, Vt. 05201

Berga/Ullman wools and linens; Craftsman's Mark Yarns (from Welsh mountain sheep); Tahki; from Scotland—homespun, wool bouclé, mill ends of fine yarns; from Greece—homespun and goat hair; natural fisherman's yarns; Vermont handspun (Shelburne Spinners); linen and cotton warp yarns.

GREENTREE RANCH WOOLS
COUNTRYSIDE HANDWEAVERS
163 N. Carter Lake Rd.
Loveland, Colo. 80537

Agent for CUM; goat-hair yarn; Wollspinnerei; Japanese silk; Berber yarns in 12 different types and colors; jute; and many others.

HANDCRAFT WOOLS
Box 378
Steetsville, Ontario
Canada

Good selection of weaving yarns . . . 2/12 worsted 60s count Merino wool with special warp twist and ply. "Primitive" and mohair.

THE HANDWEAVER
460 First St. East
Sonoma, Calif. 95476

CUM yarns; mohair; Mexican handspun; Greek handspun; Ecuador —natural handspun on drop spindles; Angora; linens; Folklorica.

HARRISVILLE DESIGNS
Harrisville, N.H. 03450

Beautiful weaving yarns, spun at their mill; reasonable prices. 1-, 2-, and 3-ply dyed; medium-weight single-ply alpaca, cashmere, camel's hair. Wholesale—$100 minimum initial order, 10% to 15% off.

THE HIDDEN VILLAGE
215 Yale Ave.
Claremont, Calif. 91711

Agents for CUM, Bernat, Craft Yarns, D.M.C (brilliant cotton floss, crochet, etc., tapestry wool), Fawcett, Paternayan. Cordage (heavy stuff); handspun karakul, goat; Peruvian handspun; Ungernaturwol (unwashed). They keep a good stock of untreated yarns for dyers. Feathers, beads, and hardware.

HUNGRY HILL HOMESPUN
John and Sally White
Rte. 3, Box 22
Scio, Ore. 97374

Very nice handspun yarns, single- and 2-ply, naturals and vegetable dyed. Good prices.

T. M. HUNTER LTD.
Sutherland Wool Mills
Brora
Scotland KW9 6NA

Very nice single-ply fine cheviot. Good for weaving suitings—nice also for very fine belt weaving. Good prices.

HUSFLIDEN OF BERGEN
5001 Bergen, Norway

Beautiful 1- and 2-ply medium and fine weaving yarns; spelsau wool. Excellent color selection and naturals. Good prices. Also cotton and linens.

INTERTWINE
101 Trolley Sq.
Salt Lake City, Utah 84102

CUM; silk; Greek wool; giant Mexican; Turkish cotton; fancy alpaca; horsehair yarn with synthetic binder; camel-goat mixture.

IRONSTONE WAREHOUSE
P.O. Box 196
Uxbridge, Mass. 01569

Natural brown and black wool yarns, spun at their mill; brushed mohair; mill ends.

JACKSON'S RUGCRAFT LTD.
Croft Mill
Hebden Bridge, Yorkshire
England HX7 8AP

6-ply rug wool, 2-ply medium, 4-ply knitting— in variety of colors. Specialize in rug making, backings, etc.

S. JONES
Rte. 2, Box 123-D
Monroe, Ore. 97456

Very nice single-ply handspun yarn—medium- to heavy-weight. All hand carded and handspun; naturals, white, and natural-dyed colors. Reasonable prices for domestic handspun.

J. T. L. CRAFTS
777 Williams Dr.
Crown Point, Ind. 46307

CUM, Lily Mills; mill ends and many other yarns.

MARGARET KILGORE
Navajo Trails Shopping Center
P.O. Box 37
Tuba City, Ariz. 86045

Authentic handspun Navajo wool.

WALTER KIRCHER
Handwebgeräte
3550 Marburg/Lahn
Postfach 1408
West Germany

Beautiful natural-colored yarns— some handspun—from medium-fine to giant rug yarns; also a nice medium-fine two-ply; cotton rug warp.

STAVROS KOUYOUMOUTZAKIS
Workshop Spun Wool
166 Kalokerinon Ave.
Iraklion, Crete
Greece

Beautiful natural-colored wool and goat hair yarns— heavy and fine, single- and double-ply; also dyed colors; also Australian white. Incredibly cheap —prices include shipping by sea mail. Probably one of the *very best yarn sources* for ethnic yarns for the price.

ROBERT LAIDLAW & SONS LTD.
Seafield Mills, Keith
Scotland, AB5 3HR

Fine single-ply wool in nice colors and heathers. Good prices.

LA LANA WOOLS
Box 2461
Taos, N.M. 87571

Beautiful handspun wool yarn in naturals and vegetable-dyed colors Reasonably priced.

LENOS HANDCRAFTS LTD.
1602 Spruce St.
Philadelphia, Pa. 19103

Handspun Greek wools; CUM yarns; Craft Yarns; Mexican handspun Angora and wool bouclé; alpaca; cashmere; Welsh yarns; Scottish linens; cottons; silks; mill ends; novelties; domestic handspun.

ROXANNE LEWIS
5630 Wisconsin Ave. North
New Hope, Minn. 55428

Very lovely, handspun, soft medium-fine 2- or more ply natural wool yarn for knitting and weaving. Will do custom orders.

LILY MILLS
P.O. Box 88
Shelby, N.C. 28150

Fine to medium-fine wool, cotton, linen, jute, synthetic, and novelty yarns. Reasonable prices.

LIVING DESIGNS
313 South Murphy Ave.
Sunnyvale, Calif. 94086

Concentrates on Navajo weaving supplies. Very nice single-ply commercial wool yarn in 3 weights; some authentic handspun. Good warp yarn for the Navajo loom. Very beautiful colors and naturals.

LOOM & WHEEL
221 Forest Ave.
Palo Alto, Calif. 94301

They stock a variety of weaving yarns.

LOOMS & LESSONS
6014 Osage Ave.
Downers Grove, Ill. 60515

CUM yarns; also specials; inexpensive natural wool yarns for dyepots; novelty yarns; cotton; linens; Donegal tweed; Icelandic; Greek; Lily Mills; Mexican mohair-wool blend. Primarily walk-in trade.

LOOMS 'N YARNS
A Division of Spangle Supply Co.
Box 460
Berea, Ohio 44017

Cotton, linen, and wool yarns from Borgs of Lund, Sweden. Beautiful yarns.

MAGNOLIA WEAVING
2635 Twenty-ninth Ave. West
Seattle, Wash. 98199

Agents for CUM, Paternayan, Fawcett, Craft Yarns, Lily Mills, Oregon Worsted Co., American Thread Butterworth, Bernat.

MA GOODNESS
Box 142
Mauricetown, N.J. 08329

Susie Graut spins single- and double-ply bulky yarns in all types of fibers. Will spin to order (3–6 weeks.) any fiber, any size.

THE MANNINGS
R.F.D. 2
East Berlin, Pa. 17316

Mannings' rug wool comes in over 300 colors— 2-, 3-, 4-, and 6-ply. Very cheap. White plied wool in various weights for dyeing; Mexican handspun; CUM; Fawcett; Maypole Willamette; Folklorico; Lopi; Columbian Handspun in colors. Goat hair, camel's, mohair, jute, Lily Mills cottons, many different yarns.

MAYATEX
P.O. Box 4452
El Paso, Texas 79914

Very heavy Mexican homespun; natural and dyed colors; mohair; hard-twist wool (good for warp). Very low prices.

EL MERCADO IMPORTING CO.
9002 Eighth N.E.
Seattle, Wash. 98115

All natural homespun and Torzal from Argentina and Mexico; also 30% mohair–40% wool– 30% polyester single-ply colored yarn (quite nice). Reasonable prices; discounts on large orders.

MEXISKEINS
P.O. Box 1624
Missoula, Mont. 59801

Heavy- and medium-weight Mexican handspun yarns—naturals and dyed colors; also 2-ply wool warp. About 30% off for wholesale orders over 25 pounds.

THE MULTIPLE FABRIC CO. LTD.
Dudley Hill
Bradford, England BD4 9PD

Magnificent hard tight-twist worsted yarns—camel's, white wool, gray hair, black mohair, white mohair, horsehair.

NATURALCRAFT
2199 Bancroft Way
Berkeley, Calif. 94707

Excellent variety of ethnic handspun and commercial yarns from all over the world; also linens, cottons, jute, cords, and twines. Huge selection of beads and feathers. Just about anything you could want.

NEEDLES and KNOTS
20956 Mack Ave.
Grosse Pointe Woods, Mich. 48236

Agent for CUM yarns; also a variety of cottons, linens, and novelty yarns.

NEWFOUNDLAND WEAVERY
P.O. Box 354, Station K
Toronto, Ontario M4P 2G7
Canada
        or
170 Duckworth St.
St. John's, Newfoundland
Canada

Lopi Icelandic; loop mohair; Greek handspun— naturals and colors; 1-, 2-, and 4-ply wools—colors and nice heathers; heavy ethnic yarns—camel's hair, goat, jute, cotton.

NORSK KUNSTVEVGARN A/S
P. Hoelfeldt Lund
Arnevik, 4897 Grimstad
Norway

Absolutely beautiful Norwegian spelsau wool (the original type of sheep in Norway—long and lustrous fiber). Single- and 2-ply in naturals and lovely colors; fine and heavy weights. Very good prices.

NORTHWEST HANDCRAFT HOUSE LTD.
110 West Esplanade
North Vancouver, British Columbia
Canada

Fabulous selection of Greek, Icelandic, German, CUM, Swedish, British, and Canadian yarns. Also jute, sisal, linen, cotton, raffia; horsehair; natural hair (tightly spun—excellent for warp).

OAXACA LOOM EXPORTS
1243 Seward Way
Stockton, Calif. 95257

Mexican handspuns, all different weights, naturals, inexpensive.

1111 IMPORTS
P.O. Box 1745
Laguna Beach, Calif. 92652

Heavy handspun alpaca in many different natural shades—beautiful grays, creams, cocoa, and jet black.

OWL AND OLIVE WEAVERS
704 Twenty-ninth St. South
Birmingham, Ala. 35233

Presently distributors for CUM, Folklorica, Fawcett, Lily Mills, Condon, Craft Yarns, Mexiskein. Hope to produce own low-cost Yarns in natural fibers, and mill ends from rug industry.

PATERNAYAN BROS, INC.
312 East 95th St.
New York, N.Y. 10028

Weaving and embroidery yarns in large assortment of beautiful colors. Sell through dealers only—they will refer you to nearest dealer.

THE PENDLETON SHOP
Box 233 (407 Jordan Rd.)
Sedona, Ariz. 86366

Authentic handspun Navajo yarn, some vegetable dyed; reasonably priced.

PHALICE'S THREAD WEB
W. 1301 Fourteenth Ave.
Spokane, Wash. 99204

Agent for CUM yarns; also many hand spun yarns at various times.

LA PIÑATA YARNS 'N GIFTS
7102 N. 35th Ave.
Phoenix, Ariz. 85021

Berga/Ullman, Condon, Craft Yarns, Creative Handweavers, Folklorico, Lily Mills, Oregon Worsted, Stanley Berroco, Tahki; also mill ends.

POTOMAC YARN PRODUCTS CO.
P.O. Box 2367
Chapel Hill, N.C. 27514

1/2-pound skeins of fine to medium-weight plied yarns in variety of colors (some tweed). Very, very cheap.

RAMMAGEROIN h.f.
Hafnarstraeti 19
P.O. Box 751
Reykjavik, Iceland

This is the source of the beautiful Icelandic Lopi yarn. A very soft 100% sheep wool yarn in 6 natural colors—single-ply medium-weight. Very reasonable prices. 10% discount on 100 skeins or more.

RAYE'S ECLECTIC CRAFT YARNS
8157 Commercial St.
La Mesa, Calif. 92041

Wholesale only, minimum order $25. All kinds of very unusual yarns, especially giant yarns; 8-ply goat yarn (some call it plaited); 4-ply alpaca; some very good wool tightly spun; mill ends. All kinds of incredible hardware, beads, etc. Good prices.

THE RIVER FARM
Rte. 1, Box 169A
Timberville, Va. 22853

Priscilla Blosser-Rainey, spinner, will spin wool (or cotton, linen, alpaca, goat—even your dog hair) into any kind of yarn—fine or heavy; plied or single. Very nice yarns.

ROBIN & RUSS, HANDWEAVERS
533 North Adams St.
McMinnville, Ore. 97128

Agents for Lily Mills. Good selection of cotton, linen, jute, and wool yarns; commercial and exotic handspuns.

THE RUG HUT
6 University Ave.
Los Gatos, Calif. 95030

CUM yarns; Scottish wool bouclé; Craft rug yarns; Oregon Worsted; cotton warp; mill ends—100% wool; Folklorico; Lopi.

SCHOOL PRODUCTS CO., INC.
1201 Broadway
New York, N.Y. 10001

Complete line of CUM yarns; mill-end wool rug yarn (cheap); discounts for large orders.

L. J. SERKIN CO.
1 Elliot St.
Brattleboro, Vt. 05301

CUM yarns. Also extensive selection (but no mail order) of Irish, Mexican, Greek, Icelandic, and domestic yarns, and mill ends.

SHEEP'S KIN
12 S. 15th St. (upstairs)
San Jose, Calif. 95112

Beautiful fine rya yarn from Finland.

THE SHEEP VILLAGE
2005 Bridgeway
Sausalito, Calif. 94965

Agents for CUM and Lily Mills; brushed mohair; linen and cotton rug warp; handspun yarns from Colombia, Afghanistan, Haiti (cotton); Persian handspun (these are really beautiful).

SHUTTLECRAFT
P.O. Box 6041
Providence, R.I. 02904

Extremely fine yarns. Most notable is mohair (not loop)—2,450 yards per pound; good prices.

PAULA SIMMONS
Suquamish, Wash. 98392

Well-known spinner provides superior handspun yarns . . . medium-weight single-ply (92¢/oz.—same price for 18 years). She and her husband grow and shear their sheep; specialize in beautiful natural colors. Spun to order.

SKANDIA FIBERS
Rte. 1 "Woodland"
Eagle River, Wis. 54521

Single-ply (looks like Swedish cow hair yarn) in brilliant colors (no naturals).

SOME PLACE
2990 Adeline St.
Berkeley, Calif. 94703

Mill ends—cheap. Handspun 2-ply, light-weight and medium-weight; 2-ply heavy rug yarn, natural; cottons, linens, nylon, sisal.

THE SOURCE
P.O. Box 28182
(18 Peachtree Place N.E.)
Atlanta, Ga. 30328

Agents for CUM, Lily Mills, Berga/Ullman, Tahki; wool rug yarns (good prices); handspun yarns from Mexico, Greece, Australia, Iceland, Denmark, Germany, Ireland. Wool, cotton, and linens.

SPIDER WEB
803 South Ft. Harrison
Clearwater, Fla. 33516

Agents for Tahki, Berga/Ullman, Golden Fleece, Folklorico, Paternayan, Reynols, Brunswic, Unger. Also novelty, and very heavy camel, wool, and hair yarns at good prices. Dacron and wool fine twist for warp (very fine).

SPIN IT—WEAVE IT STUDIO
840 Leland Place
El Cajon, Calif. 92020

All kinds of beautiful yarns, foreign handspun, hair yarns, etc. From Greece, Sweden, Peru, Iran, England, Ireland, Mexico, Turkey, Crete, Haiti.

THE SPINNING WHEEL
130 Church St.
San Francisco, Calif. 94114

Agents for Berga/Ullman; complete selection of all types of yarns, including handspuns, mill ends, etc. Also beautiful brushed wool yarn in variegated colors.

THE SPINSTER
34 Hamilton Ave.
Sloatsburg, N.Y. 10974

This lady spins yarns in many different sizes and fibers; also dyes the yarns with natural dyes.

STANLEY WOOLEN CO.
140 Mendon St.
Uxbridge, Mass. 01569

Manufacturers of wool yarns, mostly loop and novelty, some with a little viscose; quite nice brushed wool yarns. Brushed mohair also. Good prices.

STRAW INTO GOLD
P.O. Box 2904
Oakland, Calif. 94618

Excellent selection of white and natural yarns for dyeing; Australian lamb's wool; Welsh wool (good naturals); Greek; Norwegian; Persian handspun, wool-camel blend; owner's handspun—she will custom spin anything for you. Reasonable prices. Beads.

MEG SWANSEN
Box 57
Trumansburg, N.Y. 14884

In partnership with Elizabeth Zimmermann. Very beautiful imported yarns primarily for knitting. Canadian, Finnish, and Shetland.

TAHKI IMPORTS LTD.
Dept. S
336 West End Ave.
New York, N.Y. 10023

Greek handspun—naturals and colors; Colombian handspun; Irish Donegal tweeds and solids in two weights.

TEXERE YARNS
9 Peckover St.
Bradford, Yorkshire
BD1 5BD
England

Good selection of fine yarns (warp also); natural medium-coarse yarns (Berber); loop mohair; many special offerings; cotton, silk. Very inexpensive—worth keeping in contact with.

TEXTILE CRAFTS
Box 3216
Los Angeles, Calif. 90028

Agents for Lily Mills, Craft Yarns, CUM, Paternayan, American Thread, Betty Soderburg (handspun); other beautiful yarns—good selection.

LES TEXTILES DU GRAND MOULIN, INC.
Saint-Pascal, Kamouraska
Québec, Canada

93% wool with 7% nylon yarns in natural white and grays. Excellent rug warp. Good prices.

THE THREADMILL
111 E. University Dr.
Tempe, Ariz. 85281

Agents for Berga/Ullman.

TRADITIONAL HANDCRAFTS
John and Gloria Teeter
571 Randolph St.
Northville, Mich. 48167

Fawcett linen; cotton warp yarn. Also they can supply handspun yarns— available on order (both natural and natural dyed).

TRAIT TEX INDUSTRY
Division of Colonial Woolen Mills, Inc.
6501 Barberton Ave.
Cleveland, Ohio 44102

Some good commercial yarns—wool, Shetland, cashmere—medium to fine; good warp; reasonable prices.

THE UNIQUE
Creative Craft and Art
21 1/2 Bijou
Colorado Springs, Colo. 80901

Good selection of the best foreign yarns—Norwegian spelsau wool in different weights and plies; Scottish cheviot. Excellent color selection.

VILLAGE WOOLS
401 Romero N.W.
Albuquerque, N.M. 87104

Ecuadorian yarns; also synthetics as well as wools; are in the process of getting a complete selection of very good weaving wools. Reasonable prices; discounts to professional weavers and regular customers.

WARP WOOF & POTPOURRI
514 North Lake Ave.
Pasadena, Calif. 91101

Good variety of yarns—some thick homespuns; novelty, linens, and ropes.

LINDA WATSON STUDIO
13502 Edwards
Westminster, Calif. 92683

Handspun yarns—very heavy weight in natural and natural dyed colors— wool, alpaca, camel's, goat, cotton, and human hair; expects to spin finer yarns also in the future.

THE WEAVERS' SHOP
King St.
Wilton, Salisbury SP2 OAY
Wiltshire, England

2-ply medium-fine wool yarn as used in Wilton Royal Carpet Factory; also thrums (long ends of unsorted yarn)—good for rya or tapestry; thrums are classed as waste yarn and incur little or no duty.

THE WEAVER'S STORE
273 Auburn St.
Newton, Mass. 01266

Very interesting variety of wool, hair, cotton, synthetic yarns; good prices; discounts to craftspeople for quantity purchases.

THE WEAVER'S TRADE
530 Miller Ave.
Mill Valley, Calif. 94941

Canadian yarn, Colombian, Scandinavian; Irish, Icelandic, Mexican; exotic fibers; heavy homespun; mill ends (cheap); linens, cottons, cords, twines; handspun Turkish cotton—everything.

THE WEAVER'S TRADE
450 Duane St.
Glen Ellyn, Ill. 60137

Handles Mexiskein, Tahki (worsted and Donegal), Golden Fleece, Folklorico and Viking, Maypole, Stanley, Cooper-Kenworthy, Ironstone, Pakistani (Tahki), Henry's Attic, Alicia, Lily Mills, Hampshire, Craft Yarns, Eaton Rapids—all beautiful yarns.

WILDE YARNS FOR HANDWEAVING
John Wilde & Bro., Inc.
3705 Main St.
Philadelphia, Pa. 19127

All natural wools custom spun—2-, 4-, and 6-ply . . . all rather coarse and hairy (very nice); 4-ply wool rug yarn in 21 colors. Responsible prices and discounts for quantity orders.

THE WOOL MERCHANT
731 Canyon Rd.
Santa Fe, N.M. 87501

Excellent source of all kinds of reasonably priced natural-colored fine and heavy, single and plied yarns—good for dyeing; some excellent warp yarns; owner dyes yarns with chemical acid dyes, so beautiful colors are available also. Here's a lady who is trying to make good weaving yarns available to craftsmen at very low prices. (Colors not available by mail order.)

THE WOOL WORKS
1625 E. Irving Place
Milwaukee, Wis. 53202

Canadian wool yarns; Scottish; CUM; Colombian handspun wool; cotton, jute, and other interesting fibers.

WORLD ON A STRING
P.O. Box 405
June Lake, Calif. 93529

Agents for Folklorico, CUM, Bernal; novelty yarns; brushed variegated wool (beautiful); 2-ply goat hair—naturals.

MARGARET AND KENNY WRIGHT
3079 Nestall Rd.
Laguna Beach, Calif. 92651

Very handsome heavy-weight handspun yarn in 4 naturals and 12 dyed colors. Custom colors available with swatch.

THE YARN BOX
P.O. Box 1428
451 Southwest Dr.
Jonesboro, Ark. 72401

Good source of very cheap medium-fine wool yarns—muted color selection; also synthetics. Minimum order 10 pounds.

THE YARN CORNER
9633 A Metcalf
Metcalf South Shopping Center
Overland Park, Kan. 66212

Agents for Berga/Ullman, Craft Yarns, Creative Handweavers, Mexiskein, Lily Mills, Stanley Berreco.

YARN DEPOT
545 Sutter St.
San Francisco, Calif. 94102

Tremendous variety of all kinds of yarns from all over the world— commercial and handspun; agents for many domestic companies. For bimonthly yarn samples, specials, and closeouts send self-addressed stamped envelopes (6 for one year's worth of samples).

YARN PRIMITIVES
P.O. Box 1013
Weston, Conn. 06880

Mostly Greek yarns; very nice coarse and hairy handspun wools in beautiful naturals and colors.

ELIZABETH ZIMMERMANN LTD.
Babcock, Wis. 54413

In partnership with Meg Swansen. Very beautiful imported yarns primarily for knitting. Canadian, Finnish, and Shetland.

Weaving Equipment

ANDERS LERVAD & SON A/S
Askov
DK-6600 Vejen
Denmark

Three generations of loom builders. A variety of counter marche looms— light-weight airy construction of beechwood. Some available with double warp beams and fly shuttle arrangements. Very nice rigid heddle table loom. Other accessories.

GUNNAR ANDERSSONS
Vavskedsverkstad
S-79200 Mora
Sweden

Manufacturers of pine and hardwood counterbalanced looms up to 160 centimeters weaving width. The large looms have overhead beaters. These are heavy-duty well-built looms at reasonable prices. Up to 10 harnesses. Also a folding loom 90 cm. Table looms, tapestry looms, floor and table ribbon looms (for belts), reeds, ribbon reeds (rigid heddle), many sizes and kinds of boat shuttles, stretchers, string and steel heddles, skein winders and swifts, bobbin winders, flossa knives, flossa rods and rya rods, warping reels, nice wooden pulleys, spool racks, etc. Very nice equipment.

AYOTTES' DESIGNERY
Center Sandwich, N.H. 03227

Complete line of Nilus Leclerc weaving equipment; most items in stock.

THE BEGINNINGS
3449 Mission Ave.
Carmichael, Calif. 95608

Construct their own weaving equipment. A 26-inch 4-harness jack loom, compact design. (Looks good for small loom—nice design.) Hansen inkle loom—also good design. Warping board and warping reel.

BEKA LOOMS
Beka, Inc.
2232 Draper Ave.
St. Paul, Minn. 55113

Rigid-heddle-frame loom (20-inch); backstrap loom with rigid heddle (16-inch); inkle loom; warping board; weaving seat and stick shuttles. Hardwood construction. They "ship on receiving orders."

BERGA/ULLMAN
P.O. Box 918
North Adams, Mass. 01247

Distributors for Gunnar Anderssons (see under this name). Also manufacture their own looms and major weaving accessories— incorporating those changes that they felt important.

BEV'S YARN SHOP
11 West 17th St. (10th floor)
New York, N.Y. 10011

Berga/Ullman looms and accessories. Also a counterbalanced loom; both in 40-inch and 45-inch widths. Beka inkle, backstrap and rigid-heddle looms.

BEXELL & SON
2470 Dixie Highway
Pontiac, Mich. 48055

Manufacturers of the Cranbrook Weaving Loom with counter marche harness systems. Also warping reels, skein winders, spool racks, reeds, and other accessories.

BITTERROOT LOOMS
Rte. 2, Box 87
Stevensville, Mont. 59870

15-inch table loom.

CHRISTINE BLAKE
2310 West State St.
Boise, Idaho 83702

Distributors for Nilus Leclerc and Beka. Cards for card weaving; inkle looms.

DICK BLICK
P.O. Box 1267
Galesburg, Ill. 61401

Complete weaving equipment. Distributor for Leclerc, Herald, Artcraft, and Schacht. Every kind of weaving accessory, including electric bobbin winder, warping paddle, cards for card weaving.

BY REE WEAVING STUDIO
62 Rolling Meadows
Madison, Conn. 06443

Distributors for Nilus Leclerc and Purrington.

COLONIAL TEXTILES
82 Plants Dam Rd.
East Lyme, Conn. 06333

Table looms, shuttles, swifts, etc.

COLUMBINE MACHINE SHOP
1835 South Acoma St.
Denver, Colo. 80223

Yardage counter for yarn; hand and electric bobbin winders; metal temples (stretchers).

THE CRAFTOOL CO.
1421 W. 240th St.
Harbor City, Calif. 90710

Manufacture their own equipment: theCraftool Dryad Loom—floor looms, table looms, tapestry looms (look good), inkle looms. Many accessories, including a very aesthetic spool rack, string heddles, celluloid cards for card weaving, bone beater (or pick) like those they use in South America.

CRYSTAL RIVER LOOM COMPANY
Box 261
Carbondale, Colo. 81623

Very good-looking jack-type loom, folding, hard maple. 40-inch and 50-inch widths; 4 and 8 harnesses.

CUSTOM HANDWEAVERS
Allied Arts Guild
Arbor Rd. and Creek Dr.
Menlo Park, Calif. 94025

Distributors for Nilus Leclerc.

THE DARBY RAM
5056 Lee Highway
Arlington, Va. 22207

Distributors for Norwood, Harrisville, Pioneer, Purrington, and Beka. Handmade wooden tools to order.

DORSET LOOMS
F. C. Wood
Woodin Road, R.F.D. 1, Box 1076
Waterford, N.Y. 12188

Manufacturers of a portable, saw-horse jack-type 10-inch loom, 4 harnesses.

EAGER WEAVERS
183 Jefferson Rd.
Rochester, N.Y. 14623

Distributors for Leclerc, Trade, Dorset, Schacht, Harrisville, and Herald.

EARTH GUILD/GRATEFUL UNION
MAIL ORDER SERVICE
15 Tudor St.
Cambridge, Mass. 02139
(retail store at 149 Putnam Ave.)

Distributors for Toijalan Kaidetehdas. Huge warping mills and all kinds of weaving accessories. Inkle looms.

EARTHWARES
Weaving Supplies
103 N. Pleasant St.
Amherst, Mass. 01002

Distributors for Nilus Leclerc, Tools of the Trade, Beka. Also inkle looms.

EDGERTON'S HANDCRAFTS
210 West Town St.
Norwichtown, Conn. 06360

Distributors for Nilus Leclerc.

ESSAYONS STUDIO
8725 Big Bend
St. Louis, Mo. 63119

Complete line of weaving equipment.

EUGENE FIBRE
1157 High St.
Eugene, Ore. 97401

Finnish boat shuttles, bobbin winders, handmade sley hooks, wooden combs. (No mail order.)

FAMILY LOOMS
P.O. Box 724
Tempe, Ariz. 85281

Manufacturers of table looms with floor stands, tapestry looms, frame looms, English-type inkle looms, warping boards, comb beaters, shuttles, weaving needles, etc. Hardwoods, mostly maple.

FANCY THREADS
843 North Cleveland–Massilon Rd.
Akron, Ohio 44313

Distributors for Nilus Leclerc, Herald, Beka; functional hardware, bag handles, etc.

FREDERICK J. FAWCETT, INC.
129 South St.
Boston, Mass. 02111

Distributors for Nilus Leclerc.

E. B. FRYE & SON, INC.
Wilton, N.H. 03086

Inkle looms.

GALLAGHER SPINNING & WEAVING TOOLS
318 Pacheco Ave.
Santa Cruz, Calif. 95060

Manufacturers of table looms, stands, all kinds of nice shuttles (large boat shuttle), raddles, reed holders (to hold reed while sleying), warping boards, clamp warping boards, tapestry needles (wood), weaving picks (with carved bird), assorted wooden combs, Navajo beaters, battens, swords, sley hooks, spool racks, and umbrella swifts. Hardwood.

E. E. GILMORE
1032 North Broadway
Stockton, Calif. 95205

Manufacturers of 32- to 40-inch jack-type floor looms—very well built. Will pass through doorways. Nice weaving bench and other high-quality accessories. Inkle loom. (36-month waiting period on floor looms.)

GORDON'S NATURALS
P.O. Box 506
Roseburg, Ore. 97470

Distributors for Nilus Leclerc. Also Salish looms, card-weaving looms and cards, rigid heddles, Navajo combs and battens with traditional bent tip, shuttles, wooden weaving needles, many tapestry combs, shed sticks, etc.

GREENMONT YARNS & LOOMS
Greenmont Center
West Rd.
Bennington, Vt. 05201

Varpa (Finnish) counter marche looms available in widths up to 73 inches, also tapestry looms. Also distributors for Anders Lervad & Sons, Schacht, and Gallagher. Two-sided inkle looms; rigid-heddle looms; tapestry frame looms; all other accessories.

GREAT NORTHERN WOOLS
Prickly Mountain
Warren, Vt. 05674

They sell (but don't give maker's name) a beautifully designed floor loom, counterbalanced, but can be converted to rising-shed jack— or extra lams available for counter marche setup. Cherry. Very refined loom, well worth looking into. 40-inch width. Also nice-looking table loom up to 12 harnesses. Maple. Other weaving accessories, including wool baskets, firkins (round wooden boxes) and other very special nice wooden things pertaining to sheep.

GREENTREE RANCH WOOLS and
COUNTRYSIDE HANDWEAVERS
163 N. Carter Lake Rd.
Loveland, Colo. 80537

Distributors for Nilus Leclerc and Walter Kircher. Also Navajo looms; Countryside jack looms. All kinds of accesories, including yardage counters, electric bobbin winders, spools (for warping).

HALCYON I
1121 California St.
Denver, Colo. 80202

Distributors for Nilus Leclerc and Loomcraft.

J. L. HAMMETT CO.
48 Canal St.
Boston, Mass. 02114

Manufacturer of counterbalanced loom of maple, large warp beam, good crank up to 4 harness, 32- and 45-inch weaving widths. Also Marcoux 45—revolutionary folding jack loom (45-inch metal and maple 4-harness). Large warping reel, spool rack, table looms, shuttles, bobbins. Good equipment at very good prices.

THE HANDWEAVER
460 First St. East
Sonoma, Calif. 95476

Distributors for Nilus Leclerc and J. L. Hammett. Also Swedish floor looms; various tapestry looms; every kind of accessory.

HARRIS LOOMS LTD.
North Grove Rd.
Hawkhurst, England

Manufacturers of very ruggedly built floor looms, both counterbalanced and counter marche; multi-harness, 42 inches maximum width; double-warp beams if desired. Also table looms, vertical rug looms, tapestry frames, and other well-built weaving equipment.

HARRISVILLE DESIGNS
Harrisville, N.H. 03450

Manufacturers of small jack-type loom, folding, maple, 22 to 36 inches. Kit to assemble yourself about $50 cheaper and less costly to mail. Also reeds, heddles, shuttles, bobbins, bobbin winders, warping boards.

HEMSLÖJDEN
Box 433
501 07 Boras 1
Sweden

The Ulla Cyrus loom, counter marche with overhead beater. Well-designed strong loom. Many other handicrafts.

HERALD LOOMS
118 Lee St.
Lodi, Ohio 44254

Manufacturers of multi-harness jack loom with patented all-metal scissor-like harness lifting action. 45 inches maximum width. Option of double warp beams. Kiln-dried mountain ash. Horizontal warping reel that attaches to loom. Other accessories.

HIDDEN VILLAGE
215 Yale Ave.
Claremont, Calif. 94711

Distributors for Herald, Schacht, Gallagher, Strona inkle, Tissanova hand loom. Also backstrap looms, cards for card weaving; all manner of weaving accessories including tapestry beater (iron and rare woods), wood needles, swords.

INTERTWINE
101 Trolley Sq.
Salt Lake City, Utah 84102

Kliot tapestry loom, inkle loom. Plastic weaving cards, shuttles, swords, sley hooks, etc.

J. T. L. CRAFTS
777 Williams Dr.
Crown Point, Ind. 46307

Manufacturers of select hardwood accessories—shuttles, raddles, benches, etc. Also distributors for Nilus Leclerc.

MARGARET KILGORE
Navajo Trails Shopping Center
P.O. Box 37
Tuba City, Ariz. 86045

Navajo handmade battens, forks, sacking needles.

WALTER KIRCHER
Handwebgeräte
3550 Marburg/Lahn
Postfach 1408
West Germany

Manufacturer of very nice table, frame, tapestry, and rigid-heddle looms; also good folding floor loom— simple (1-meter weaving width). Many accessories.

RANDALL KRITKAUSKY &
CAROLYN SCHMIDT
Rte. 547, Box 199
Harford, Pa. 18823

Antique counterbalanced looms for low prices. Large 4-poster and smaller types; sometimes looms in exotic woods. Well worth looking into. Will deliver looms in the East for only $15: Guaranteed antique and functional. Also other antique weaving equipment.

LECLERC CO.

(See NILUS LECLERC)

LENOS HANDCRAFTS LTD.
1602 Spruce St.
Philadelphia, Pa. 19103

Distributors for Nilus Leclerc; inkle looms, tapestry looms.

LILLSTINA, INC.
P.O. Box 1373
Binghamton, N.Y. 13902

American distributors of loom made in Sweden— fast delivery. Collapsible, 4-harness counterbalanced loom, many clever features. Maximum weaving width 46 inches. Also accessories, including vertical warping mills. Good prices.

LILY MILLS
P.O. Box 88
Shelby, N.C. 28150

Distributors for Nilus Leclerc. Two-sided inkle looms, Artcraft table looms; tapestry looms; cards for card weaving; accessories.

LIVING DESIGNS
313 South Murphy Ave.
Sunnyvale, Calif. 94086

Excellent source for all Navajo weaving tools—authentic. Even willow sticks and umbrella ribs. Navajo looms; tool pouches of leather; sheepskin to sit on!

LOOM & WHEEL
221 Forest Ave.
Palo Alto, Calif. 94301

Distributors for Loomcraft, Motte, Schacht, Gallagher. They rent and repair looms.

LOOMCRAFT
P.O. Box 65
Littleton, Colo. 80120

Well-built jack loom in maple, cherry, or walnut, hand-rubbed; 4-, 6-, or 8- harness—40- or 45-inch. By easy removal of warp beam loom can pass through doorway.

THE LOOMERY
3237 Eastlake Ave. East
Seattle, Wash. 98102

The Nesika kit-built loom—jack type. Also Pioneer loom, ski shuttles, stick shuttles.

THE LOOM FACTORY
Marcola, Ore. 97454

Manufacturers of 45-inch counterbalanced, folding, maple, 4-harness, 6-treadle loom; same loom kit for $50 less; also 60-inch loom kit. Inkle loom and belt kit. (Inexpensive.)

LOOMS & LESSONS
6014 Osage Ave.
Downers Grove, Ill. 60515

Distributors for Nilus Leclerc, Sachacht, Aircraft, Heritage, Beka, Lily Mills. Also handcrafted maple jack-type 24- to 42-inch 4- to 8-harness loom—"well engineered." Navajo looms, rigid heddles, inkles, tapestry; some used looms; repair service. Accessories. (Primarily walk-in or phone.)

LOOMS 'N YARNS
A DIVISION OF SPANGLE SUPPLY CO.
Box 460
Berea, Ohio 44017

Distributors of Swedish-built looms (Glimakra), counterbalanced, overhead beater in widths up to 64 inches. Also available very large heavy-duty rug looms with rugged ratchet construction. Good prices.

LORELLYN LOOMS
By Lorellyn Weavers
Box 56
Chicago Park, Calif. 95712

Manufacturers of 21 3/4- and 31-inch 4-harness counterbalanced loom— designed to be used with a chair.

MACOMBER AD-A-HARNESS LOOMS
570 Lincoln Ave.
Saugus, Mass. 01906

Manufacturers of well-built looms designed primarily for multi-harness weaving, jack type—up to 12 harnesses may be added. 56 inches maximum width.

MAGNOLIA WEAVING
2635 Twenty-ninth Ave. West
Seattle, Wash. 98199

Distributors for Nilus Leclerc, Herald Looms, J. L. Hammett Co., Bergerman Looms. Good selection of all kinds of weaving equipment.

MAILES LOOMS
4620 Glen Haven Rd.
Soquel, Calif. 95073

Manufacturers of fly-shuttle looms and accessories; vertical-frame loom.

THE MANNINGS
R.F.D. 2
East Berlin, Pa. 17316

Distributors for Nilus Leclerc, Gallagher, and Dorset. Complete accessories, most models in stock.

MORGAN INKLE LOOM FACTORY
Railroad Engine House
Guilford, Conn. 06437

Manufacturer of double-sided inkle loom and small frame-type table loom.

MOTTE LOOMS
5748 Old San Jose Rd.
Santa Cruz, Calif. 95065

Manufacturers of jack looms in 32- , 40- and 45-inch weaving width—4, 6, 8 harnesses, folding type; also hand looms with 4 harnesses (frame with 4 heddle rods); inkle loom.

NATURALCRAFT
2199 Bancroft Way
Berkeley, Calif. 94707

Inkle looms, swifts, cards for card weaving— 3 different styles; Navajo and drop spindle, shuttles, etc., at reasonable prices.

NEEDLES AND KNOTS
20956 Mack Ave.
Grosse Pointe Woods, Mich. 48236

Distributors for Harrisville Looms; Bexell Cranbrook looms, made to order in widths of 36 inches and more, with multiple harnesses and treadles and overhead beater. Frame looms, inkle looms, rigid-heddle looms; umbrella swifts, shuttles, tapestry beaters, etc.

NEWCOMB LOOM CO.
P.O. Box 3204
Davenport, Iowa 52808

Manufacturers of fly-shuttle looms and other looms especially adapted for structural weaves.

NILUS LECLERC
L'Islet, Quebec
Canada
or
LECLERC CORP. (U.S. distributions office)
Highway 9 North
P.O. Box 491
Plattsburg, N.Y. 12901
    or
LECLERC WEST DIST.
P.O. Box 7012
Landscape Station
Berkeley, Calif. 94707
(for Calif., Ore., and Wash.)

Manufacturers of very complete line of all weaving equipment. Leclerc Corp. can give you list of dealers closest to you. Counterbalanced looms up to 100-inch weaving width (operated by 2 people); jack looms up to 60-inch weaving width up to 12 harnesses; 3 types tapestry looms; folding looms; fly-shuttle attachments; table looms; rigid-heddle loom; backstrap; English-type inkle loom—doubles as warping board; custom looms to order; sectional warp beams; tension boxes, combs, and counters; large warping mills and warping boards; bobbin racks and creels for both spools and cones; bobbin winders including electric; metal skein winders—adjustable; reeds; heddles and frames; stretchers; hooks; plastic and wooden spools; all kinds of shuttles and bobbins; every kind of loom part. Reasonable prices.

NORDICWEAVE BACKSTRAP LOOMS
3241 Elliot Ave. South
Minneapolis, Minn. 55407

Rigid-heddle backstrap kit with instructions—inexpensive.

NORTHWEST HANDCRAFT HOUSE
110 West Esplanade
North Vancouver, British Columbia
Canada V7M 1A2

Distributors for Nilus Leclerc. Inkle loom that weaves up to 12 inches wide. Cards for card weaving. Rope-making machine.

NORTHWEST LOOMS
Rte. 4, Box 4872
Bainbridge Island, Wash. 98110

Manufacturers of the Pioneer loom (10- to 15-inch table loom with open reed and heddle system so you can change threading). Up to 12 harnesses.

NORWOOD LOOM CO.
Box 272
Baldwin, Mich. 49304

Manufacturers of jack-type loom solidly built of cherry—unique folding design. 4 harnesses, 42-inch weaving width. Accessories including cardboard warping spools.

ORIENTAL RUG CO.
Dept. 9580
Lima, Ohio 45801

Manufacturers of small counterbalanced loom, loom parts, and accessories.

OWL & OLIVE WEAVERS
704 Twenty-ninth St. South
Birmingham, Ala. 35233

Distributors for Nilus Leclerc, Tools of the Trade, Schacht, Harrisville. Also manufacturers of a counter marche loom designed by Tom Turnbull.

THE PENDLETON SHOP
407 Jordan Rd.
Sedona, Ariz. 86366

Manufacturer of Pendleton floor looms —jack type, folding; up to 46-inch 8- harness, 12-treadle; also mini-model folding looms up to 30-inch weaving width. Table looms, good warping frames and horizontal warping reels, spool rack, shuttles, cards for card weaving; electric bobbin winders, large umbrella swifts. Also specialize in Navajo equipment: Navajo loom (good), combs, battens.

LA PIÑATA YARNS 'N GIFTS
7102 N. 35th Ave.
Phoenix, Ariz. 85021

Distributors for Pioneer Looms and Family Looms; accessories.

PIONEER LOOM

(See NORTHWEST LOOMS)

PUTNEY MOUNTAIN LOOMS
Marks Greenberg
R.F.D. 3
Putney, Vt. 05346

Manufacturer of clean-cut, simple jack-type looms in various hardwoods; folding. Up to 60-inch weaving width, up to 8 harnesses. Heddles, reeds, bobbins. Sectional warp beams available.

ROBIN AND RUSS HANDWEAVERS
533 N. Adams St.
McMinnville, Ore. 97128

Distributors for Norwood Looms, Nilus Leclerc, Herald, Macomber, Oregon Trail Loom: rigid X-frame jack loom with patented "Roller Jack" mechanism. One of the most complete weaving-supply places —everything right down to adapters for bobbin winders, labels, cardboard spools, counters, scissors, reostats, etc.

ROLAND ROSE
Fuchs Inkle Loom
1010 N.W. 8th St.
Andrews, Texas 79714

Manufacturer of patented inkle loom, convertible for left-handed weaver. Good price (economy price for no finish).

THE RUG HUT
6 University Ave.
Los Gatos, Calif. 95030

Distributors for Motte looms, inkle looms, some accessories—yarn winders, tapestry beaters, cards for card weaving.

SANJO LOOMS
Box 24, Star Rte.
Greenleaf, Ore. 97445

Manufacturer of very good-looking, simple hardwood jack-type loom (4 or 8 harnesses), 38 to 48 inches, oak or walnut. Beautiful bench; raddles, warping boards, boat shuttles; 12-inch table loom.

SCHACHT SPINDLE CO.
1708 Walnut St.
Boulder, Colo. 80302

Manufacturer of very good inkle loom, table loom, tapestry loom— well built at very reasonable prices. Also make beautiful shuttles, beaters, etc. Hardwoods. This is an exceptionally good source.

SCHOOL PRODUCTS CO., INC.
1201 Broadway
New York, N.Y. 10001

Distributors for Nilus Leclerc; also Swedish looms, counterbalanced and counter marche, with overhead beaters; Schact Spindle Co.; Artcraft Looms; English-type inkle; all accessories, including ball winder.

SERENDIPITY SHOP
1547 Ellinwood
Des Plaines, Ill. 60016

Small looms including backstrap and inkle; shuttles, tapestry beaters, cards for card weaving.

SHEEP'S KIN
12 S. 15th St. (upstairs)
San Jose, Calif. 95112

Cards for card weaving, shuttles, sley hooks.

THE SHEEP VILLAGE
2005 Bridgeway
Sausalito, Calif. 94965

Kliot tapestry loom; rigid-heddle loom inkle loom. Cards for card weaving, shuttles, reed hooks.

THE SHOP
Highway 49
P.O. Box 133
Amador City, Calif. 95601

Distributors for Nilus Leclerc. (No mail order.)

SOME PLACE
2990 Adelaide St.
Berkeley, Calif. 94703

Manufacturer of Navajo loom (quite good design—you sit on base to stabilize); Aubusson-type tapestry loom and other small tapestry table looms; inkle loom; tapestry combs and Navajo fork; Navajo battens with bent end; plastic cards for card weaving.

THE SOURCE
P.O. Box 28182
(18 Peachtree Place N.E.)
Atlanta, Ga. 30328

Distributors for Nilus Leclerc; cards for card weaving.

SPIDER WEB
803 South Ft. Harrison
Clearwater, Fla. 33516

Distributors for Nilus Leclerc. Also ski shuttles, walnut Navajo fork.

SPIN IT—WEAVE IT STUDIO
840 Leland Place
El Cajon, Calif. 92020

Distributors for Nilus Leclerc, Loomcraft; backstrap loom, rigid-heddle loom, frame looms, inkle loom (including English type doubling as warping board), cards for card weaving. Electric bobbin winders, wooden weaving forks, sley hooks, shuttles, ball winders, etc.

SPINNERS' AND WEAVERS' SUPPLIES
Box 56
Woollahra
New South Wales 2025
Australia

Distributors for Nilus Leclerc, Troijalan, and Vävstolsfabriken Glimakra; also access to looms from other companies (Scandinavia, England, and elsewhere); loom kit with directions for 32-inch floor loom; English-style inkle; cards for card weaving; many types of small table looms. All accessories, including iron rug beater, warping pegs to clamp on table, weavers' scissors.

THE SPINNING WHEEL
130 Church St.
San Francisco, Calif. 94114

Distributors for Harris Looms —table model in stock; other looms, including inkle, backstrap. All accessories, including leather backstrap, battens, ball winder.

STRAW INTO GOLD
P.O. Box 2904
Oakland, Calif. 94618

Table looms; reeds (much cheaper than other domestic ones); shuttles, including ski shuttles; cards for card weaving.

TAWAQUIVA WOODSHOP
1836 Candelaria N.W.
Albuquerque, N.M. 87107

Manufacturer of floor looms and weaving tools.

TEXTILE CRAFTS
Box 3216
Los Angeles, Calif. 90028

Distributors for Nilus Leclerc and Schacht Spindle Co. Card-weaving kit; rope machine.

THOUGHT PRODUCTS, INC.
R.F.D. 2
Somerset, Pa. 15501

Manufacturer of "The Barbara IV Weaving Loom": jack-type, counterbalanced, 2-harness Goblin tapestry—all in one integrated system. 36-, 48-, and 60-inch weaving widths.

THE THREADBEARER, SOUTH
P.O. Box 1844
Winter Park, Fla. 32789

Manufacturers of the Heirloom (small tapestry frame loom).

THE THREADMILL
111 E. University Dr.
Tempe, Ariz. 85281

Distributors for Herald, Family, Berga/Ullman, and Beka looms.

TOIJALAN KAIDETEHDAS (TOIKA)
37800 Toijala
Finland

Manufacturers of very nice birch counter marche looms up to 185-centimeter weaving width (about 6 feet) and 12 shafts; tapestry looms; table looms; loom parts. Reeds, stretchers, all kinds of shuttles, bobbin winders, bobbin makers for spinning wheels, warping mills, spool racks, skein winders, string heddles, metal heddles, heddle frames, reed hooks, skein stands, spools, raddles. (English catalog.)

TOOLS OF THE TRADE
R.F.D.
Fair Haven, Vt. 05743

Manufacturers of hardwood jack-type floor looms, folding, up to 8-harness 45-inch weaving width. "Designed to be sturdy and heavyweight to allow rug weaving." Also table looms, benches, warping boards, reeds, heddles, tie-up chains, aprons, sectional warp beams. Well-built equipment.

TRADITIONAL HANDCRAFTS
John and Gloria Teeter
571 Randolph St.
Northville, Mich. 48167

Distributors for Harrisville Designs, and Pioneer Loom. Also inkle looms, tapestry looms, rope machines, shuttles, (including ski type), tapestry beaters.

TURNBULL LOOMS
P.O. Box 4296
Mobile, Ala. 36604

Manufacturers of jack-type loom, multi-harness, folding, mahogany — well built and good looking. Plans for home-built loom. Kit of parts for jack loom (not including wood). Also warping equipment.

THE UNIQUE
Creative Craft and Art
21 1/2 E. Bijou
Colorado Springs, Colo. 80902

Distributors of Swedish counter marche and counterbalanced looms (probably Vävstolsfabriken Glimakra); exceptionally rugged rug loom; tapestry looms and ribbon looms—all excellent equipment, good prices. Distributors also for Nilus Leclerc.

VÄVSTOLSFABRIKEN GLIMAKRA AB
S-280 64 Glimakra
Sweden

Manufacturers of beautiful pine counterbalanced (convertible to counter marche) looms, overhead beaters, up to 160-centimeter weaving width (over 5 feet); excellent tapestry looms, ribbon looms; huge warping mills, skein winders, spool racks, reeds, bobbin winders, baskets, every kind of shuttle, heddles, raddles, pulleys—all kinds of superior equipment (heavy-duty).

VILLAGE WOOLS
401 Romero N.W.
Albuquerque, N.M. 87104

Tawaquiva Looms exclusive. Good selection hardwood rug shuttles; heddles; reeds; hand beaters, including Navajo type; good inkle loom.

WARP & WEFT
Belle Meade
P.O. Box 50504
Nashville, Tenn. 37205

Distributors for Nilus Leclerc.

WARP WOOF & POTPOURRI
514 North Lake Ave.
Pasadena, Calif. 91101

Distributors for Nilus Leclerc. Also Swedish tapestry loom, inkle loom, backstrap, table looms, cards for card weaving.

THE WEAVER'S STORE
273 Auburn St.
Newton, Mass. 01266

Distributors for Nilus Leclerc; also the Barbara IV (see Thought Products); inkle loom. All accessories, including ball winders and ski shuttles, rigid heddles.

THE WEAVER'S TRADE
530 Miller Ave.
Mill Valley, Calif. 94941

Distributors for J. L. Hammett. Also tapestry, inkle, and frame looms. Some accessories.

THE WEAVER'S TRADE
450 Duane St.
Glen Ellyn, Ill. 60137

Distributors for Nilus Leclerc, Schacht, Beka, and Some Place.

THE WHITAKER REED CO.
P.O. Box 172
Worcester, Mass. 01602

Reeds of all sizes. Will make to order any reed you want. Also stainless-steel reeds.

THE YARN BARN, INC.
(BERGMAN LOOMS)
Route 4, Box 660
Poulsbo, Wash. 98370

Manufacturers of the Bergman loom for 40 years, counter marche from 25 to 45 inches, up to 12 harnesses. Inkle loom and all types of accessories.

THE YARN CORNER
9633 A Metcalf
Metcalf South Shopping Center
Overland Park, Kan. 66212

Distributors for Nilus Leclerc and Herald Looms.

Spinning Equipment

ALBION HILLS FARM SCHOOL
R.R. #3 Caledon East
Ontario, Canada

Upright spinning wheels and colonial saddle wheels (by Mr. Blackburn); drop spindles, niddy-noddies, carders.

GUNNAR ANDERSSONS
Vävskedsverkstad
S 79200 Mora, Sweden

Two spinning wheels: one Finnish (similar to, if not the Toika wheel); one larger, first quality, that they make.

ASHFORD HANDICRAFTS LTD.
P.O. Box 12, Rakaia
Canterbury, New Zealand

Simple, well-built Saxony-type spinning wheel in kit form—very inexpensive and considerable discounts for 5 or more, and 10 or more.

BAILLIE & WATTS LTD.
P.O. Box 1512
Auckland, New Zealand

"Sleeping Beauty"—reproduction of genuine British Isles cottage wheel; "Thumbelina"—based on the style of wheel used in Latvia (upright); carding machine—"best value in rotary carders."

THE BEGINNINGS
3449 Mission Ave.
Carmichael, Calif. 95608

Saxony wheels from Scandinavia, hand and bench carders, drop spindles.

CHRISTINE BLAKE
2310 West State St.
Boise, Idaho 83702

Spinning wheels, drop spindles, carding machines, niddy-noddies, hand cards, lazy kates.

DICK BLICK
Dept. 11
Box 1267
Galesburg, Ill. 61401

Mill sampling cards (large hand cards used in the industry). Yarn winders.

RACHEL BROWN
Electric Spinner
Arroyo Seco, N.M. 87514

Heavy-duty electric spinner with plain spindle shift. Will spin any kind of wool. Spindle holds up to 1 pound of wool.

CAMBRIDGE WOOLS LTD.
16-22 Anzac Ave.
Auckland 1, New Zealand

The Ashford spinning wheel; hand cards

CLEMES & CLEMES SPINNING WHEELS
665 San Pablo Ave.
Pinole, Calif. 94564

Four kinds of spinning wheels—castle, Finnish, Scottish, electric spinner with flyer (looks good); Turkish, Navajo, and many other hand spindles; carding machines—two types; hand cards (made by them; vulcanized rubber, curved or flat); umbrella swifts; niddy-noddies; lazy kates. Also spinning-wheel repair. Good prices.

COLONIAL TEXTILES
82 Plants Dam Rd.
East Lyme, Conn. 06333

Spinning wheels, drop spindles, parts, reels, umbrella swifts. Spinning kit with directions and 1 pound assorted wool.

COLUMBINE MACHINE SHOP
1835 South Acoma St.
Denver, Colo. 80223

The Columbine Spinning Wheel—all-metal construction, 7-inch-long aluminum bobbin holds large quantity of yarn.

THE CRAFTOOL CO., INC.
1421 W. 240th St.
Harbor City, Calif. 90710

Make spinning wheel patterned after a Scandinavian wheel, complete with three bobbins, pair of carders, spindle, two pounds fleece, and instructions.

CRAFTPLANS
Rogers, Minn. 55374

Plans for 3 different spinning wheels to make yourself.

CREATIVE HANDWEAVERS
P.O. Box 26480
Los Angeles, Calif. 90026

The charka (Indian spinning wheel modeled after the one Gandhi used).

CUSTOM HANDWEAVERS
Allied Arts Guild
Arbor Rd. and Creek Dr.
Menlo Park, Calif. 94025

Ashford wheels, cards, spindles.

THE DARBY RAM
5056 Lee Highway
Arlington, Va. 22207

Haldane wheel, Walter Kircher wheel, and a wheel from New Zealand. Drop spindles.

EARTH GUILD/GRATEFUL
UNION MAIL ORDER SERVICE
15 Tudor St.
Cambridge, Mass. 02139
(Retail store at 149 Putnam Ave.)

Toika traditional Finnish flax wheel; flyers, drive shafts, spool pins (for converting spinning wheels into bobbin winders), distaffs. Toika cards (curved back). Drop spindles. Good prices.

EARTHWARES
Weaving Supplies
103 N. Pleasant St.
Amherst, Mass. 01002

Polish and Finnish spinning wheels.

EDGERTON'S HANDCRAFTS
210 West Town St.
Norwichtown, Conn. 06360

Haltec spinning wheel.

ESSAYONS STUDIO
8725 Big Bend
St. Louis, Mo. 63119

Spinning equipment.

EUGENE FIBRE
1157 High St.
Eugene, Ore. 97401

Finnish spinning wheels, hand cards, swifts. (No mail order.)

FAMILY LOOMS
P.O. Box 724
Tempe, Ariz. 85281

They make a chair-type spinning wheel; Navajo and drop spindles.

FANCY THREADS
843 North Cleveland-Massillon Rd.
Akron, Ohio 44313

Ashford wheels.

FIBER TO FINISH
South Rd.
New Hartford, Conn. 06057

Walter Kircher wheel; drop spindles, hand cards, niddy-noddies. Starter kits of drop spindle and New Zealand wool and instructions. (Here's a lady spinner who is anxious to help.)

THE FREEDOM WHEEL
Kent Klippenstein
Rte. 3, Box 476 A
Loveland, Colo. 80537

Very long spindle, turned by kick wheel. Can spin any weight yarn; unconventional design well worth looking into.

FREED COMPANY
P.O. Box 394
Albuquerque, N.M. 87103

Wool cards (inexpensive, post-paid).

CURTIS FRICKE
Rte. 1, Box 143
Granite Falls, Wash. 98252

Manufacturer of carding machine (metal frame). Hand cards, heavy-duty.

E. B. FRYE & SON
Wilton, N.H. 03086

Cards in different sizes. They make no. 8 wool cards and a tow card, as well as extra-large ones.

GALLAGHER SPINNING & WEAVING TOOLS
318 Pacheco Ave.
Santa Cruz, Calif. 95060

Makers of many types of hand spindles, including Navajo and Turkish; also niddy-noddies.

GORDON'S NATURALS
P.O. Box 506
Roseburg, Ore. 97470

Leclerc spinning wheel; beginning spinner sets with wool, cards, and hand spindles. Tropical hardwood spindles—beautiful. Small cotton spindles from Africa; Turkish and Navajo hand cards; New Zealand flickers; niddy-noddies; ball winders; Jen-Til (a specially formulated wool washing aid—ecological).

GREAT LAKES WOOL GROWERS COOP.
901 Sentry Dr.
Waukesha, Wis. 53186

Spinning wheel in cherry, oak, or maple.

GREAT NORTHERN WOOLS
Prickly Mountain
Warren, Vt. 05674

Can locate antique wheels for you.

GREENMONT YARNS & LOOMS
Greenmont Center
West Rd.
Bennington, Vt. 05201

Ashford wheel kit; Finnish wheel; hand spindles; carders; niddy-noddies.

GREENTREE RANCH WOOL
COUNTRYSIDE HANDWEAVERS
163 N. Carter Lake Rd.
Loveland, Colo. 80537

Penguin quill wheel; Columbine wheel; Leclerc wheel; Kircher wheel; electric spindle (not for serious spinning); Turkish spindle; hand cards.

HANDCRAFT WOOLS
Box 378
Steetsville, Ontario
Canada

Small Saxony-type wheel; contemporary wheel for spinning large, bulky yarns with Indian head, or with spindle head; large flyer heads, also plain spindle head for attachment to spinning wheel or treadle sewing machine. Hand cards, hand spindles; lazy kates.

THE HANDWEAVER
460 First St. East
Sonoma, Calif. 95476

Greentree wheel; traditional colonial wheel; many types of hand spindles; hand cards; Paula Simmons spinning oil.

HARRISVILLE DESIGNS
Harrisville, N.H. 03450

Handspinning kits—drop spindle; 1 pound fleece, carded; instructions.

HIDDEN VILLAGE
215 Yale Ave.
Claremont, Calif. 94711

Carding machine (rental or sale); hand cards, New Zealand flicker. Haldane wheels, castle and Saxony types from Scotland; American- and Swedish-made spinning wheels; Navajo, Turkish, and silk spindles; cotton spindles, porcelain drop spindles; charka wheel.

HUSFLIDEN OF BERGEN
5001 Bergen, Norway

Spinning wheels.

INDIAN VALLEY SPINNERS
Rte. 2, Box 17
Bradfordsville, Ky. 40009

Maker of a flyer wheel, large enough for thick and textured yarns, black walnut. Scottish tension to control draw-in and amount of twist. Bobbin has a capacity of about 2 pounds wool (greasy). The spinner head sold separately to mount on old treadle sewing machine. Lazy kates and extra bobbins.

INTERTWINE
101 Trolley Sq.
Salt Lake City, Utah 84102

Drop and Navajo spindles, reasonable.

J. T. L. CRAFTS
777 Williams Dr.
Crown Point, Ind. 46307

Makers of hardwood drop spindles.

MARGARET KILGORE
Navajo Trails Shopping Center
P.O. Box 37
Tuba City, Ariz. 86045

Handmade Navajo spindles. Hand cards.

WALTER KIRCHER
3550 Marburg/Lahn
Postfach 1408
West Germany

Makes upright wheel that looks very well built— large flyer; electric spinner with flyer mechanism (looks good); hand spindles; hand cards; hand card and carding stand to clamp on table—an interesting variation on the carding machine.

MYRON W. KLEIN
7207 Edgecreek Lane
Springfield, Va. 22152

Makes a hand spindle with a ceramic whorl. He sent me a sample and I find it works beautifully keeps spinning much longer than the ordinary drop spindle; nicely shaped shaft and very well balanced. Very cheap.

LECLERC CO.

(See NILUS LECLERC)

LENOS HANDCRAFTS LTD.
1602 Spruce St.
Philadelphia, Pa. 19103

Hand spindles, hand cards, niddy-noddies, ball winders.

LIVING DESIGNS
313 South Murphy Ave.
Sunnyvale, Calif. 94086

Dedicated to Navajo techniques— spindles, hand cards.

LOOM & WHEEL
221 Forest Ave.
Palo Alto, Calif. 94301

Ashford spinning wheel; I. Nagy wheel; Shetland wheel: castle and Saxony types from Scotland. Rent and repair wheels.

LOOMS & LESSONS
6014 Osage Ave.
Downers Grove, Ill. 60515

Spinning wheels and hand spindles. (Primarily walk-in or phone business.)

MAGNOLIA WEAVING
2635 Twenty-ninth Ave. West
Seattle, Wash. 98199

Leclerc and Penguin Quill spinning wheels; hand spindles. Carding machines and hand cards; niddy-noddies, ball winders, spinning oil.

THE MANNINGS
R.F.D. 2
East Berlin, Pa. 17316

Swedish spinning wheel; antique Saxony-type wheels as well as walking (wool, great) wheel with accelerated drive head or direct; spare parts, including flyers. Hand spindles, hand cards, Swedish skein winders.

THE MEISTERHEIMS
R.R. 5, Box 210
Dowagiac, Mich. 49047

Makers of very nice Shaker-style wool wheel (like the old-type wool wheel with plain spindle, but just the right size for sitting while spinning). Oiled walnut or cherry. One-year wait. Spinning heads for wool wheels, flyers for flax wheels. Distaffs, bobbin caddy to hold four bobbins. Will make parts in wood to match your wheel. Hand spindles (including Turkish type). Spinning-wheel repair. Everything handmade in hardwood of your choice. Even notepaper with spinning and weaving designs. Hand cards.

I. NAGY
P.O. Box 9637
Wellington
New Zealand

Maker of an upright wheel, supposedly excellently designed—"for the connoisseur spinner."

NATURALCRAFT
2199 Bancroft Way
Berkeley, Calif. 94707

Navajo and drop spindles; hand cards.

NEEDLES AND KNOTS
20956 Mack Ave.
Grosse Pointe Woods, Mich. 48236

Penguin Quill wheel. Also Saxony-type wheel, drop spindles, hand cards.

NILUS LECLERC
L'Islet, Quebec
Canada

Makers of reasonably priced Saxony-type wheel—can spin heavy yarns also. Niddy-noddies, hand cards.

NORTHWEST HANDCRAFT HOUSE
110 West Esplanade
North Vancouver, British Columbia
Canada V7M 1A2

Cottage Indian spinner (design based on one used by Indian spinners —huge flyer). Can purchase flyer separately. Very inexpensive.

OWL & OLIVE WEAVERS
704 Twenty-ninth St. South
Birmingham, Ala. 35233

Spinning wheels; hand spindles—drop and Navajo.

THE PENDLETON SHOP
Box 233 (407 Jordan Rd.)
Sedona, Ariz. 86366

Spinning wheels, hand spindles, hand carders. Good place for Navajo equipment.

LA PIÑATA YARNS 'N GIFTS
7102 N. 35th Ave.
Phoenix, Ariz. 85021

Spinning wheels, spindles, wool cards.

ROBIN AND RUSS, HANDWEAVERS
533 N. Adams St.
McMinnville, Ore. 97128

Several different spinning wheels and kits: Ashford, Finnish, Kircher, Columbine, and an "outstanding castle wheel" from Clemes. Hand spindles—many different kinds. Several hand cards and two bench carders. Motors, rheostats, electric spinners, etc.

THE RUG HUT
6 University Ave.
Los Gatos, Calif. 95030

Hand spindles; hand cards—curved or flat backs.

SANJO LOOMS
Box 24, Star Rte.
Greenleaf, Ore. 97445

Spinning wheel by Paul Pirtle. Very large spinning head with 1-inch orifice. Simple design. Oak or mahogany.

SCHACHT SPINDLE CO.
1708 Walnut St.
Boulder, Colo. 80302

Very good source of all sizes hardwood hand spindles. Very inexpensive

SCHOOL PRODUCTS CO., INC.
1201 Broadway
New York, N.Y. 10001

Leclerc wheel. Also traditional wheel in natural wood. Mill sampling cards (used in the industry).

SERENDIPITY SHOP
1547 Ellinwood
Des Plaines, Ill. 60016

Ashford spinning-wheel kit; Penguin Quill wheel; a Saxony wheel; niddy-noddies; hand spindles; hand cards.

SHEEP'S KIN
12 S. 15th St. (upstairs)
San Jose, Calif. 95112

Drop spindles.

THE SHEEP VILLAGE
2005 Bridgeway
Sausalito, Calif. 94965

The I. Nagy wheel ("a wheel superior to any other"); Ashford spinning-wheel kits; many hand spindles, including Turkish type; hand cards.

THE SHOP
Highway 49
P.O Box 133
Amador City, Calif. 95601

Spinning equipment. (No mail order.)

PAULA SIMMONS
Suqaumish, Wash. 98392

Spinning oil.

SOME PLACE
2990 Adeline St.
Berkeley, Calif. 94703

Kliot-designed wheel (it will take any hand spindle—you add the bicycle wheel; good cheap way to get yourself a spinning wheel). Hand spindles. Hand cards: vulcanized type and very small ones—2 by 4 inches.

SPIDER WEB
803 South Ft. Harrison
Clearwater, Fla. 33516

Hand spindle, Turkish type.

SPINCRAFT
Box 332
Richardson, Texas 75080

Beginners' spinning kits; hand cards; hand spindles.

SPIN IT—WEAVE IT STUDIO
840 Leland Place
El Cajon, Calif. 92020

Ashford spinning-wheel kit. Bulk head spinner that can be attached to the Ashford for spinning very thick yarns. Spinning wheel of alder wood, designed after colonial spinner. Bulk spinner—a nice clean design of black walnut with very large flyer. Hand spindles, including Turkish type; niddy-noddies; hand carders and bench carders (metal).

SPINNERS' AND WEAVERS' SUPPLIES
Box 56
Woollahra
New South Wales 2025
Australia

Many different wheels: "Pipy," modeled after an old Irish design, "one of the best wheels being made today"; small upright type (with suitcase!); "Little Peggy," evolved from the Shetland design, very compact; "Sprite," upright also. Ashford spinning-wheel kit. Carding machines, niddy-noddies, hand cards, lazy kates, hand spindles and instructions. Also the I. Nagy wheel.

THE SPINNING WHEEL
130 Church St.
San Francisco, Calif. 94114

Ashford kit; castle wheel; Scottish double-tension wheel; Indian spinning wheel—head can be purchased separately. Hand spindles; many different hand cards, and both metal and wooden carding machines. Niddy-noddies; spinning oil.

THE SPINSTER
34 Hamilton Ave.
Sloatsburg, N.Y. 10974

"Gossip" wheel, upright; hand spindle; hand cards; niddy-noddies; *Spinster Pack*—an introduction to handspinning.

STRAW INTO GOLD
P.O. Box 2904
Oakland, Calif. 94618

Complete spinning wheels and accessories —and a very helpful lady (her brochures pack in about as much information as some books). Finnish wheel; heavy-duty wheel; New Zealand wheels; Indian spinner head; Gandhi spinner (charka)—with instructions (this is for cotton, fine wool, or silk); all kinds of hand spindles, including ones from Bolivia for $1! Carding machines; many different kinds and styles of hand cards; New Zealand flicker; niddy-noddies; lazy kates; yarn winders; distaffs; umbrella swifts; spinning oil—just about everything.

TEXTILE CRAFTS
Box 3216
Los Angeles, Calif. 90028

Penguin Quill wheel.

TRADITIONAL HANDCRAFTS
John and Gloria Teeter
571 Randolph St.
Northville, Mich. 48167

American-made wheel, Finnish wheel, flyers and bobbin assembly, drop spindles, hand cards, ball winders, niddy-noddies, umbrella swifts.

VILLAGE WOOLS
401 Romero N.W.
Albuquerque, N.M. 87104

Hand spindles; hand cards.

WARP WOOF & POTPOURRI
514 North Lake Ave.
Pasadena, Calif. 91101

Castle-type wheel in oak, walnut, rosewood, or eucalyptus. Also Indian spinner (large flyer); hand cards; hand spindles.

THE WEAVER'S TRADE
530 Miller Ave.
Mill Valley, Calif. 94941

"Pipy" ("New Zealand's finest," it says); also New Zealand upright wheel; Indian Valley spinner; Ashford kit; hand spindles, including Sudanese (roll the whorl down leg); hand cards.

WILDERNESS WEAVERS
Wilderness Rd.
Branscomb, Calif. 95417

(This is a cooperative.) They sell a sturdy mahogany and copper spinning head—fit easily onto a treadle-sewing-machine base; large spindle eye and huge bobbin; bolts for attaching; leather drive belt and instructions. Learn-to-spin kit with drop spindle, wool, and instructions.

WOOL 'N' SHOP
101 Twenty-seventh Ave. S.E.
Minneapolis, Minn. 55414

Ashford kit; a Saxony wheel. Rents wheel with option to buy. Hand cards, ball winders, and other spinning equipment.

THE WOOL WORKS
1625 E. Irving Place
Milwaukee, Wis. 53202

Ashford kit; a Saxony wheel of walnut, cherry, or maple. Navajo and drop spindles; hand cards.

WORLD ON A STRING
P.O. Box 405
June Lake, Calif. 93529

Hand spindles and hand cards.

MARGARET & KENNY WRIGHT
3079 Nestall Rd.
Laguna Beach, Calif. 92651

Makers of the Wright spinning wheel. Weighted wheel; 7/8-inch orifice for spinning large or small yarn. Large bobbin holds over a pound of wool; side or front orifice. Also hand spindles, niddy-noddies, brass needles.

Fibers for Spinning

ANGORA DIABLO
805 La Gonda Way
Danville, Calif. 94526

Raw mohair—kid and adult. Minimum order 5 pounds. Wholesale to tradespeople, 20% reduction in price for over 40 pounds.

ASHFORD HANDICRAFTS LTD.
P.O. Box 12, Rakaia
Canterbury, New Zealand

New Zealand Romney fleeces: white or natural colors. 5-inch staple, clean as possible. Good price includes postage costs.

THE BEGINNINGS
3449 Mission Ave.
Carmichael, Calif. 95608

Fleeces.

CHRISTINE BLAKE
2310 West State St.
Boise, Idaho 83702

Rovings.

BRIGGS AND LITTLE WOOLEN MILLS LTD.
York Mills, Harvey Station
New Brunswick
Canada

Carded wool (loose form).

CAMBRIDGE WOOLS LTD.
16–22 Anzac Ave.
Auckland 1, New Zealand

White, black, gray Romney wool—raw greasy, greasy carded, scoured, or scoured and carded. Very low price includes postage.

CLEMES & CLEMES SPINNING WHEELS
665 San Pablo Ave.
Piñole, Calif. 94564

Raw New Zealand wool in white and black; can also clean carded or combed wool; flax; nylon; polyester. China silk. From time to time other fibers are available.

COLONIAL TEXTILES
82 Plants Dam Rd.
East Lyme, Conn. 06333

Raw Corriedale fleece. Wool and alpaca roving; flax, silk, Angora, cashmere.

COLORADO FLEECE CO.
Gerrie Gordon
516 W. Ute
Grand Junction, Colo. 81501

Good source of raw fleeces: Suffolk, Columbia, Corriedale—all different natural colors; karakul; Montedale; mohair. Occasionally top.

WILLIAM CONDON & SONS LTD.
P.O. Box 129 (65 Queen St.)
Charlottetown, Prince Edward Island
Canada C1A 7K3

Greasy or scoured white wool.

CRAFTSMAN'S MARK LTD.
Trefnant, Denbigh LL16 5UD
Wales

Roving in good naturals, and wool matchings (fleeces). They will specially pick wool to suit your needs. This is very nice wool.

CREATIVE HANDWEAVERS
P.O. Box 26480
Los Angeles, Calif. 90026

All kinds of fleeces. Also tops of alpaca, goat, karakul, camel, yak, mixtures—very beautiful.

CUSTOM HANDWEAVERS
Allied Arts Guild
Arbor Rd. at Creek Dr.
Menlo Park, Calif. 94025

Raw fleeces.

THE DARBY RAM
5056 Lee Highway
Arlington, Va. 22207

Domestic and New Zealand combed top. Flax in roving and ginned cotton. Raffia, sisal, sea grass.

EARTH GUILD/GRATEFUL UNION MAIL
ORDER SERVICE
15 Tudor St.
Cambridge, Mass. 02139
(Retail store at 149 Putnam Ave.)

Skirted fleeces; combed wool, alpaca, linen, mohair, etc., "as cheap as possible." Also "lag"—a lower grade than top and cheaper.

EARTHWARES
Weaving Supplies
103 N. Pleasant St.
Amherst, Mass. 01002

Camel, goat, and sheep fleeces.

EDGERTON'S HANDCRAFTS
210 West Town St.
Norwichtown, Conn. 06360

Raw fleeces.

ESSAYONS STUDIO
8725 Big Bend
St. Louis, Mo. 63119

Raw fleeces.

EUGENE FIBRE
1157 High St.
Eugene, Ore. 97401

Many types of fibers for spinning, but no mail order.

FANCY THREADS
843 North Cleveland-Massillon Rd.
Akron, Ohio 44313

Rovings.

FREDERICK J. FAWCETT, INC.
129 South St.
Boston, Mass, 02111

Flax line fiber for spinning.

FEHRENBACHER FARM
Rte. 2, Box 233
Milton-Freewater, Ore. 97862

Fleeces—white and dark, raw, carded, greasy, etc.; also mohair.

THE FIBER STUDIO
P.O. Box 356
Sudbury, Mass. 01776

Wool, alpaca, cashmere, camel *wool,* mohair, Angora—cleaned and carded.

FIBER TO FINISH
South Rd.
New Hartford, Conn. 06057

Skirted fleeces of different breeds; New Zealand fleeces, alpaca, camel's hair, karakul, mohair, domestic and New Zealand roving, other fibers on request.

FILATURE LEMIEUX, INC.
St.-Ephrem
Beauce, Quebec
Canada

Carded wool in naturals and same colors as the yarns they manufacture. 5-pound bales only.

C. D. FITZ HARDING-BAILEY
15 Dutton St.
Bankstown NSW 2200
Australia

Fleece wools (the wools are stud wools, and not the usual commercial grades—the best available there); mohair, silk, cotton, and Angora.

THE FREED CO.
415 Central N.W.
P.O. Box 394
Albuquerque, N.M. 87103

Merino fleece in the grease. Very low price for 10 pounds delivered.

GORDON'S NATURALS
P.O. Box 506
Roseburg, Ore. 97470

Raw fleeces including New Zealand; also combed or carded; alpaca, mohair, Samoyed dog, cotton, camel down, cashmere.

A. K. GRAUPNER
Corner House
Valley Rd.
Bradford BD1 4AA
England

Mainly animal fibers. Write him with a specific need in mind and he will no doubt be able to fill your request.

GREAT LAKES WOOL GROWERS COOP.
901 Sentry Dr.
Waukesha, Wis. 53186

Raw fleeces. Medium and coarse wool tops.

GREAT NORTHERN WOOLS
Prickly Mountain
Warren, Vt. 05674

Delinda and Duncan Syme are dedicated to breeding good sheep (especially dark) for handspinners. Everything from karakul to Merino; many fleeces are good enough to spin directly with no carding. Reasonable prices. Also mohair.

GREENTREE RANCH WOOLS
COUNTRYSIDE HANDWEAVERS
163 N. Carter Lake Rd.
Loveland, Colo. 80537

Fleeces (white and naturals). Also combed alpaca, fine Australian, and wool-mohair blend. Linen. Bargain bags of assorted fiber (some dyed)—good for practice.

HANDCRAFT WOOLS
Box 378
Steetsville, Ontario
Canada

Flax of all kinds. Wool in fleece or combed, including New Zealand. Combed alpaca, cashmere, camel's hair, mohair, Angora, goat hair.

HARRISVILLE DESIGNS
Harrisville, N.H. 03450

Carded fleeces of wool, alpaca, cashmere, camel's hair, mohair-wool blend, dyed wool. These are carded at their mill—good prices.

THE HIDDEN VILLAGE
Textile Handcraft Supplies
215 Yale Ave.
Claremont, Calif. 91711

Alpaca—fleece and roving; camel, cashmere fleece; flax line fiber; wool—raw, roving, including long-staple New Zealand; dyed and blends; yak; cotton.

HUNGRY HILL HOMESPUN
John and Sally White
Rte. 3, Box 22
Scio, Ore. 97374

They sell well-skirted fleeces grown on their farm; Romney-Suffolk and Corriedale.

INTERTWINE
101 Trolley Sq.
Salt Lake City, Utah 84102

Camel tops; mohair tops; yak fleece; karakul fleece; cotton—cleaned.

S. JONES
Rte. 2, Box 123-D
Monroe, Ore. 97456

Hand-carded wool in natural colors and dyed . . . from owner's own flock of sheep or local farmers.

JONES SHEEP FARM
R.R. 2
Peabody, Kan. 66866

Booklet on their herds of sheep with pictures and information. Their black sheep breeding stock guaranteed to produce wool 6 inches long.

STAVROS KOUYOUMOUTZAKIS
Workshop Spun Wools
166 Kalokerinou
Iraklion, Crete, Greece

Coarse Cretan wools and goat hair, some washed. Very inexpensive, postage paid. Also Australian washed white and white top. Wholesale for shops.

LENOS HANDCRAFTS LTD.
1602 Spruce St.
Philadelphia, Pa. 19103

Carded black or white fleece or scoured white fleece; wool top.

LIVING DESIGNS
313 South Murphy Ave.
Sunnyvale, Calif. 94086

Wool in the grease, high quality in all natural colors; card sliver—cleaned and carded ready for spinning.

LOOM & WHEEL
221 Forest Ave.
Palo Alto, Calif. 94301

Spinning fibers.

THE MANNINGS
R.F.D. 2
East Berlin, Pa. 17316

Flax; all colors alpaca; all colors mohair; wool roving; camel's-hair fleece; yak (wild goat) top; raw wool—black or brown (not always available); white fleeces.

NATURALCRAFT
2199 Bancroft Way
Berkeley, Calif. 94707

Cotton roving.

NEEDLES AND KNOTS
20956 Mack Ave.
Grosse Pointe Woods, Mich. 48236

Spinning fibers.

NEWFOUNDLAND WEAVERY
P.O. Box 354, Station K
Toronto, Ontario M4P 2G7
Canada
        or
170 Duckworth St.
St. John's, Newfoundland
Canada

Fleeces; wool roving in all colors and naturals; jute, hemp, sisal.

NORTHWEST HANDCRAFT HOUSE
110 West Esplanade
North Vancouver, British Columbia
Canada V7M 1A2

New Zealand raw wool; same—greasy carded; silk; camel's hair (soft fawn color); raw flax rovings; ramie; raw manilla, raffia, cane, raw sisal.

1111 IMPORTS
P.O. Box 1745
Laguna Beach, Calif. 92652

Alpaca tops—beautiful colors, great variety. Some in stock; others take approximately 6 weeks for delivery.

OWL AND OLIVE WEAVERS 704 Twenty-ninth St. South Birmingham, Ala. 35233	Fleeces.
THE PENDLETON SHOP Box 233 (407 Jordan Rd.) Sedona, Ariz. 86366	Roving in white, gray, brown, black, and red.
LA PIÑATA YARNS 'N GIFTS 7102 N. 35th Ave. Phoenix, Ariz. 85021	Raw wool; ginned cotton.
RAYE'S ECLECTIC CRAFT YARNS 8157 Commercial St. La Mesa, Calif. 92041	Beautiful wool tops.
THE RIVER FARM Rte. 1, Box 169 A Timberville, Va. 22853	Very good fleeces, well skirted. Specializes in dark but carries some Corriedale and cheviot. Owner raises sheep, spins, and teaches.
ROBIN & RUSS, HANDWEAVERS 533 North Adams St. McMinnville, Ore. 97128	Fleeces including Romney; colored carded wool, mohair, ramie, linen sliver, Angora rabbit, silk tops, etc.
THE RUG HUT 6 University Ave. Los Gatos, Calif. 95030	Raw fleeces.
SAN ANGELO WOOL PROCESSING CO. P.O. Box 1769 San Angelo, Texas 76901	This is a company that prepares wool and hair fibers for textile mills; they have wool top, alpaca, mohair, and kid mohair for about as low cost as anywhere. You have to buy a whole ball, which is about 20 or 25 pounds.
SCHOOL PRODUCTS CO., INC. 1201 Broadway New York, N.Y. 10001	Raw fleeces.
SERENDIPITY SHOP 1547 Ellinwood Des Plaines, Ill. 60016	All types of fibers—raw and combed.
SHEEP'S KIN 12 S. 15th St. (upstairs) San Jose, Calif. 95112	Fleeces, mohair, camel's hair, gray carded New Zealand wool.
THE SHEEP VILLAGE 2005 Bridgeway Sausalito, Calif. 94965	Fleeces—good quality, including New Zealand; carded greasy wool; wool top; mohair and alpaca top; silk; many exotic fibers, including camel's, yak, and human hair. Cotton, linen, jute.
SOME PLACE 2990 Adeline St. Berkeley, Calif. 94703	Fleeces in the grease or scoured: karakul, mohair, Merino.
SORIA STUDIO Spelsau 1454 Helvik, Norway	Spelsau wool—raw or carded.
THE SOURCE P.O. Box 28182 (18 Peachtree Place N.E.) Atlanta, Ga. 30328	Fibers for spinning.

SPIDER WEB
803 South Ft. Harrison
Clearwater, Fla. 33516

Beautiful gray and black alpaca; raw sheep's wool.

SPINCRAFT
Box 332
Richardson, Texas 75080

Flax.

SPIN IT—WEAVE IT STUDIO
840 Leland Place
El Cajon, Calif. 92020

Domestic fleece, alpaca, cotton, flax, camel, yak, cashmere, mohair, wild goat.

SPINNERS' AND WEAVERS' SUPPLIES
Box 56
Woollahra
New South Wales 2025
Australia

Greasy fleece wools in all naturals; alpaca, cashmere, karakul, camel, silk, mohair, flax, hemp, sisal. Many types of combed fibers. Reasonable.

THE SPINNING WHEEL
130 Church St.
San Francisco, Calif. 94114

Complete selection of fibers, raw and combed.

THE SPINSTER
34 Hamilton Ave.
Sloatsburg, N.Y. 10974

Raw fleece, wool roving, mohair top, cotton, alpaca (raw), silk, opossum, camel's hair (very soft), Angora, buffalo.

STRAW INTO GOLD
P.O. Box 2904
Oakland, Calif. 94618

Many different New Zealand fleeces and rovings; British raw wool (very long and coarse); Icelandic fleece—this has down in it that makes Lopi; mohair; karakul; Angora; fox; cashmere; camel down and hair; alpaca; goat hair; silk; flax; very thin wool roving (no drafting necessary); sisal; hemp; ramie. Also seeds for flax and cotton. Tries to keep prices as low as possible.

J. STRUBIN TEXTILES
P.O. Box 4008
Basel, Switzerland

Animal fibers, wool, mohair, camel, silk.

TEXTILE CRAFTS
Box 3216
Los Angeles, Calif. 90028

Silk from China. Possible discount for designer-craftsmen who use large quantities.

TRADITIONAL HANDCRAFTS
John and Gloria Teeter
571 Randolph St.
Northville, Mich. 48167

A complete selection of fibers—alpaca, Angora, camel down, cashmere without hairs (dark and light), cotton, Samoyed dog, silk top (good price), fine wool top and medium wool top. All types of fleeces in grease from Merino to cheviot. Spinning oil and Arctic syntex (for washing wool).

TRAIT TEX INDUSTRY
Division of Colonial Woolen Mills, Inc.
6501 Barberton Ave.
Cleveland, Ohio 44102

This is a mill that produces yarns and sells combed fibers to handspinners. Wool, natural or dyed; New Zealand wool; mohair; alpaca—all combed. Good prices, and discounts. Spinning oil.

VILLAGE WOOLS
401 Romero N.W.
Albuquerque, N.M. 87104

Fleeces—Suffolk-Hampshire cross (homegrown), also mohair; other types of wool, including Navajo in brown and black. Alpaca, flax. Aiming at having a complete supply of fibers at very reasonable prices; discounts to professional weavers.

WARP WOOF & POTPOURRI
514 North Lake Ave.
Pasadena, Calif. 91101

White wool, greasy and washed; brown greasy; wool top; flax.

GARY H. WATSON
15 Birdwood Rd.
Lower Hutt
Wellington, New Zealand

Romney crossbred fleeces—very long staple. Raw and carded greasy in white and naturals. Price slightly higher for carded. Dark colors more expensive. Also washed white. Postage included in price. Reduction in price for orders 6 pounds and over.

THE WEAVER'S TRADE
530 Miller Ave.
Mill Valley, Calif. 94941

All types of fibers; raw fleeces as well as combed.

THE WEAVER'S TRADE
450 Duane St.
Glen Ellyn, Ill. 60137

Wool and hair rovings.

WILDE YARNS FOR HANDWEAVING
John Wilde & Bro., Inc.
3705 Main St.
Philadelphia, Pa. 19127

Carded wool in very nice natural colors.

WILSONS' HOLIDAY FARM
Rte. 2
West Center Rd.
Waupun, Wis. 53963

Their only product is Columbia wool. Sell carefully skirted fleeces (2 to 4 pounds of the undesirable parts removed) for very good price.

WOOL 'N' SHOP
101 Twenty-seventh Ave. S.E.
Minneapolis, Minn. 55414

A farmers' co-op, marketing raw wool for the farmers to the mills, dealing in about 20 million pounds of wool per year. Natural white grease wools and dark naturals. Wool top and other exotic fibers: mohair, camel, yak, alpaca, goat; ginned cotton.

THE WOOL WORKS
1625 E. Irving Place
Milwaukee, Wis. 53202

Raw fleece, raw camel and alpaca. Also wool, camel, and alpaca tops.

WORLD ON A STRING
P.O. Box 405
June Lake, Calif. 93529

Raw New Zealand fleece, wool top, camel's hair, goat, flax, silk; cotton roving.

Dyes

ALLIED CHEMICAL
Colors Dept.
P.O. Box 419
Hawthorne, N.J. 07507
        or
237 Hymus Blvd.
Pointe Clair 730, Quebec
Canada
        or
1111 Main St. (Suite 105)
Moncton, New Brunswick
Canada
        or
100 North Queen St.
Toronto 540, Ontario
Canada
        or
2695 Granville St.
Vancouver, British Columbia
Canada

Acid dyes—same type of dyes as Ciba produces, but will have different names. They will sell in 1 pound amounts.

COLONIAL TEXTILES
82 Plants Dam Rd.
East Lyme, Conn. 06333

Many different herb dyes, including leaves and flower tops. Also madder and indigo color in crystals (not real indigo).

CUSTOM HANDWEAVERS
Allied Arts Guild
Arbor Rd. at Creek Dr.
Menlo Park, Calif. 94025

Vegetable dyes, including lichens; mordants.

THE DARBY RAM
5056 Lee Highway
Arlington, Va. 22207

Natural dyes, including indigo, madder, logwood, some lichens; mordants.

DOMINION HERB DIST., INC.
136 Oneida Drive
Pointe Claire, Quebec
Canada

Good cheap source of about 60 different natural dyes: madder, cochineal insect, cochineal coloring, indigo and indigo color in crystals, juniper berries, bracken, etc.

EARTH GUILD/GRATEFUL UNION
  MAIL ORDER SERVICE
15 Tudor St.
Cambridge, Mass. 02139
(Retail store at 149 Putnam Ave.)

Natural dyes; mordants; gram and ounce scale for weighing dyes and mordants.

FIBER TO FINISH
South Rd.
New Hartford, Conn. 06057

Natural dyes (all the standard ones); mordants; starter kits.

C. D. FITZ HARDING-BAILEY
15 Dutton St.
Bankstown
New South Wales 2200
Australia

Natural dyes—the real thing; he has 3 kinds of cochineal, including "fine ruby," which is rare.

GORDON'S NATURALS
P.O. Box 506
Roseburg, Ore. 97470

Many different dyes, including lichens; mordants; seeds for all kinds of dye plants; publishes pamphlet on dyeing.

HANDCRAFT WOOLS
Box 378
Steetsville, Ontario
Canada

A few Ciba acid dyes by the ounce.

THE HANDWEAVER
460 First St. East
Sonoma, Calif. 95476

A few of the most desirable and basic natural dyes: madder, indigo, logwood, cochineal, fustic, birchbark, brazilwood, osage orange, etc.

THE HIDDEN VILLAGE
Textile Handcraft Supplies
215 Yale Ave.
Claremont, Calif. 91711

Natural dyes and mordants.

KEYSTONE ANILINE AND CHEMICAL CO.
321 North Loomis
Chicago, Ill. 60607

Distributors of Ciba dyes. (This is the main office; they will either fill your order or direct you to a subsidiary office near you.)

LENOS HANDCRAFTS LTD.
1602 Spruce St.
Philadelphia, Pa. 19103

Natural dyes and mordants.

NATURE'S HERB CO.
281 Ellis St.
San Francisco, Calif. 94102

This is an herb store—sells some natural dyes: madder, cochineal, etc.

NORTHWEST HANDCRAFT HOUSE
110 West Esplanade
North Vancouver, British Columbia
Canada V7M 1A2

All kinds of natural dyes: indigo, madder, cochineal, etc.; mordants. Also some Ciba dyes.

OWL AND OLIVE WEAVERS
704 Twenty-ninth St. South
Birmingham, Ala. 35233

Natural dyes and mordants.

LA PIÑATA YARNS 'N GIFTS
7102 N. 35th Ave.
Phoenix, Ariz. 85021

Gordon's Natural Dye Paks.

PYLAN PRODUCTS CO., INC.
95–10 218th St.
Queens Village, N.Y. 11429

Distributors of Ciba dyes in small quantities.

SERENDIPITY SHOP
1547 Ellinwood
Des Plaines, Ill. 60016

Natural dyes (small selection, but good); mordants; scale for dyes.

SHEEP'S KIN
12 S. 15th St. (upstairs)
San Jose, Calif. 95112

Natural dyes, including whole-bug cochineal; mordants.

THE SHEEP VILLAGE
2005 Bridgeway
Sausalito, Calif. 94965

Natural dyes, including cochineal, madder, indigo (natural and synthesized), logwood, etc. (Reasonable.) Mordants.

SHERMAN'S
P.O. Box 10116
Alameda, N.M. 87114

Some natural dyes—cochineal, indigo; extremely cheap mordants. (Only serves New Mexico residents.)

SPIN IT—WEAVE IT STUDIO
840 Leland Place
El Cajon, Calif. 92020

Mordants.

THE SPINNING WHEEL
130 Church St.
San Francisco, Calif. 94114

All the most important natural dyes; mordants.

THE SPINSTER
34 Hamilton Ave.
Sloatsburg, N.Y. 10974

Natural dyes, including indigo, madder, cochineal, logwood; mordants.

STRAW INTO GOLD
P.O. Box 2904
Oakland, Calif. 94618

Natural dyes and mordants; scales. Proprietor tries to get the real thing—indigo, real cochineal (not just cochineal coloring), madder; weld, grown in Oregon. Also seeds for natural dye plants. Bulk discounts for 5 pounds or more.

THE TREADMILL
111 E. University Dr.
Tempe, Ariz. 85281

Natural dyes and mordants.

TRADITIONAL HANDCRAFTS
John and Gloria Teeter
571 Randolph St.
Northville, Mich. 48167

Large selection of natural dyes put up in 4-ounce packages: whole-bug cochineal, indigo, lots of berries, leaves, chips. Also mordants.

THE WEAVER'S TRADE
530 Miller Ave.
Mill Valley, Calif. 94941

Natural dyes and mordants—standard selection.

WIDE WORLD OF HERBS LTD.
11 St. Catherine St. East
Montreal, Quebec
Canada H2X 1K3

Good cheap source of about 60 different natural dyes: madder, cochineal insect, cochineal coloring, indigo and indigo color in crystals, juniper berries, bracken, etc.

THE WOOL WORKS
1625 E. Irving Place
Milwaukee, Wis. 53202

Natural dyes including cochineal. madder, indigo extract (not real indigo); mordants.

WORLD ON A STRING
P.O. Box 405
June Lake, Calif. 93529

Natural dyes, including cochineal, indigo; mordants. Some Ciba dyes that can be used with vinegar.

Books

AYOTTES' DESIGNERY
Center Sandwich, N.H. 03227

Some books on all three subjects.

CHRISTINE BLAKE
2310 West State St.
Boise, Idaho 83702

Books on all three subjects.

DICK BLICK
P.O. Box 1267
Galesburg, Ill. 61401

Small but good selection of books on all three subjects.

BOOK BARN
Books for Craftsmen
P.O. Box 256
Avon, Conn. 06001

Excellent selection of books, including the Shuttle Craft Guild Monographs.

CLEMES & CLEMES SPINNING WHEELS
665 San Pablo Ave.
Piñole, Calif. 94564

Books on spinning and dyeing.

COLONIAL TEXTILES
82 Plants Dam Rd.
East Lyme, Conn. 06333

Small but good selection of books mainly on spinning and dyeing.

THE CRAFTOOL CO.
1421 W. 240th St.
Harbor City, Calif. 90710

Dryad books on weaving as well as other selections.

CUSTOM HANDWEAVERS
Allied Arts Guild
Arbor Rd. and Creek Dr.
Menlo Park, Calif. 94025

Full selection on all three subjects.

EAGER WEAVERS
183 Jefferson Rd.
Rochester, N.Y. 14623

CUM book *Scandinavian Handweaving and Rya.*

EARTH GUILD/GRATEFUL UNION
MAIL ORDER SERVICE
15 Tudor St.
Cambridge, Mass. 02139
(Retail store at 149 Putnam Ave.)

They try to keep a good selection on all three subjects.

EARTHWARES
Weaving Supplies
103 N. Pleasant St.
Amherst, Mass. 01002

Good selection of books on all three subjects.

EDGERTON'S HANDCRAFTS
210 West Town St.
Norwichtown, Conn. 06360

Books on weaving and spinning.

FANCY THREADS
843 North Cleveland-Massillon Rd.
Akron, Ohio 44313

Books on all three subjects.

GORDON'S NATURALS
P.O. Box 506
Roseburg, Ore. 97470

Good selection of books on spinning and dyeing.

GREENMONT YARNS & LOOMS
Greenmont Center
West Rd.
Bennington, Vt. 05201

A few *good* books.

GREENTREE RANCH WOOLS
COUNTRYSIDE HANDWEAVERS
163 N. Carter Lake Rd.
Loveland, Colo. 80537

Books on weaving and spinning.

HANDCRAFT WOOLS
Box 378
Steetsville, Ontario
Canada

Small selection of books on all three subjects.

THE HANDWEAVER
460 First St. East
Sonoma, Calif. 95476

Good selection of books on all three subjects.

HANDWEAVERS GUILD OF
AMERICA, INC.
998 Farmington Ave.
West Hartford, Conn. 06107

Publisher of *Shuttle, Spindle, and Dyepot,* a quarterly. (You should subscribe to this if you want all the up-to-date information on weaving, spinning, and dyeing, as well as supplies.)

THE HIDDEN VILLAGE
215 Yale Ave.
Claremont, Calif. 91711

Good selection of books on all three subjects.

INTERTWINE
101 Trolley Sq.
Salt Lake City, Utah 84102

Some books on all three subjects.

J. T. L. CRAFTS
777 Williams Dr.
Crown Point, Ind. 46307

Books on weaving and spinning.

LECLERC CO.

(See NILUS LECLERC)

LENOS HANDCRAFTS LTD.
1602 Spruce St.
Philadelphia, Pa. 19103

Large selection of books on all three subjects.

LIVING DESIGNS
313 South Murphy Ave.
Sunnyvale, Calif. 94086

All the classic books about Navajo weaving; also Navajo-related subjects.

LOOM & WHEEL
221 Forest Ave.
Palo Alto, Calif. 94301

Selection of books for beginning and advanced weavers and spinners.

MAGNOLIA WEAVING
2635 Twenty-ninth Ave. West
Seattle, Wash. 98199

Good selection of books on all three subjects.

THE MANNINGS
R.F.D. 2
East Berlin, Pa. 17316

Quite complete selection of books on weaving, dyeing, and spinning.

NILUS LECLERC
L'Islet, Quebec
Canada

Small selection of books, many by Robert Leclerc on weaving.

NORTHWEST HANDCRAFT HOUSE LTD.
110 West Esplanade
North Vancouver, British Columbia
Canada

Books on all three subjects as well as on design.

OWL AND OLIVE WEAVERS
704 Twenty-ninth St. South
Birmingham, Ala. 35233

Books on all three subjects.

LA PIÑATA YARNS 'N GIFTS
7102 N. 35th Ave.
Phoenix, Ariz. 95021

Books on all three subjects.

ROBIN & RUSS, HANDWEAVERS
533 North Adams St.
McMinnville, Ore. 97128

Complete selection of books.

THE RUG HUT
6 University Ave.
Los Gatos, Calif. 95030

Small but good selection of books on all three subjects.

SCHOOL PRODUCTS CO., INC.
1201 Broadway
New York, N.Y. 10001

Good selection of books on all three subjects

SELECT BOOKS
Textile Craft Center
218 Seventeenth St. (P.O. Box 626)
Pacific Grove, Calif. 93950

Formerly Craft and Hobby Book Service (see The Unicorn), Rose Perl director. She no longer does a mail-order business, but Select Books does. They publish the Elsie Davenport books (*Your Yarn Dyeing,* etc.) and a few others.

SERENDIPITY SHOP   Small but good selection of books on all three subjects.
1547 Ellinwood
Des Plaines, Ill. 60016

SHEEP'S KIN   Stocks a few books on these subjects.
12 S. 15th St. (upstairs)
San Jose, Calif. 95112

THE SHEEP VILLAGE   A small selection of books on all three subjects.
2005 Bridgeway
Sausalito, Calif. 94965

SOME PLACE   Small selection of books, 12 of which are "Some Place"
2990 Adeline St.   publications.
Berkeley, Calif. 94703

THE SOURCE   Van Nostrand Reinhold arts and crafts books on all three subjects.
P.O. Box 28182
(18 Peachtree Place N.E.)
Atlanta, Ga. 30328

SPIDER WEB   Some books on these subjects.
803 South Ft. Harrison
Clearwater, Fla. 33516

SPINCRAFT   Books on spinning.
Box 332
Richardson, Texas 75080

SPIN IT—WEAVE IT STUDIO   Small selection of books.
840 Leland Place
El Cajo, Calif. 92020

THE SPINSTER   *Spinning and Dyeing the Natural Way.*
34 Hamilton Ave.
Sloatsburg, N.Y. 10974

STRAW INTO GOLD   Obviously trying to stock the best books on all three subjects.
P.O. Box 2904
Oakland, Calif. 94618

TRADITIONAL HANDCRAFTS   Some of the best basic books on spinning, dyeing, and weaving.
John and Gloria Teeter
571 Randolph St.
Northville, Mich. 48167

THE UNICORN   The most complete selection of books on weaving, dyeing, and
CRAFT AND HOBBY BOOK SERVICE   spinning—anywhere. They will locate books for you if they don't
Box 645   have them.
Rockville, Md. 20851

WATSON-GUPTILL PUBLICATIONS   Publishers of some excellent books on weaving and dyeing.
2160 Patterson St.
Cincinnati, Ohio 45214

THE WEAVER'S TRADE   Small selection of books on all three subjects.
530 Miller Ave.
Mill Valley, Calif. 94941

WOOL 'N' SHOP   Small selection of books.
101 Twenty-seventh Ave. S.E.
Minneapolis, Minn. 55414

THE WOOL WORKS   Small selection of books.
1625 E. Irving Place
Milwaukee, Wis. 53202

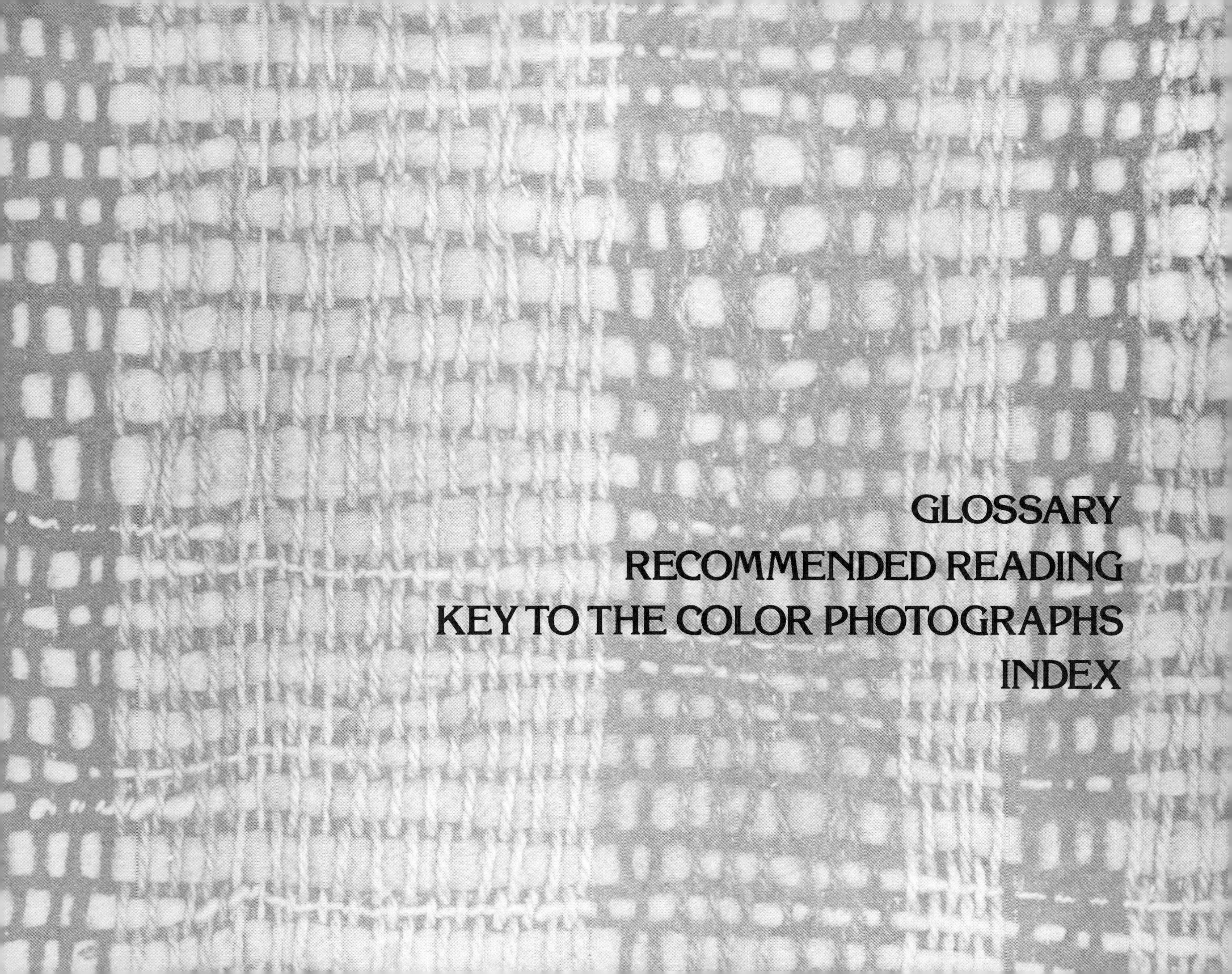

GLOSSARY

RECOMMENDED READING

KEY TO THE COLOR PHOTOGRAPHS

INDEX

Accelerating wheel head: On the high wheel, the extra pulley used to increase the speed at which the spindle spins, invented by Amos Miner in 1830. See also **Miner's head.**

Acetic acid: Acid used in dyeing, contained in vinegar in very small amounts.

Acid dyes: Synthetic dyes that combine with the fiber in an acid dyebath.

Additive mixture: A color theory based on adding light rays together to get colors, the total of which equals white light; as opposed to subtractive mixture.

Alizarin: The aniline dye that is the chemical equivalent of madder.

Alpaca: South American animal raised for its fleece.

Alum: Short for potassium aluminum sulfate, a mordant.

Aniline dyes: The first synthetic dyes, so named because produced from aniline, a coal-tar product.

Angora: The short, silky hairs of the Angora rabbit.

Angora goat: Goat from which comes mohair.

Apron: Cloth extension on the warp and cloth beams of a loom.

Apron rod: The rod in the apron to which warp ends are tied.

Back beam: The upper horizontal beam at the back of a treadle loom.

Backstrap loom: Primitive stick loom with strap around weaver's body to hold warp in tension.

Balanced weave: Weave structure in which warp and weft are similar in size and spacing.

Ball winder: Device for winding balls of yarn.

Basket weave: A balanced weave structure in which warp and weft threads are paired or grouped.

Batt: The mass of carded fibers from a carding machine; also called "matt," "lap," or "web."

Batten: Flat stick with one sharpened edge that holds sheds open on primitive looms and is used to beat weft. Also, same as beater on treadle loom.

Bayeta: Cochineal-dyed yarn from imported fabric unraveled and respun by Navajos; or a blanket made from this yarn.

Beaming: Winding the warp onto the warp beam.

Beater: Pivoted frame that holds the reed on a treadle loom. Also, a fork or comb for hand beating.

Beating: Packing in the weft.

Belt shuttle: A short stick shuttle with one sharpened edge for beating.

Bench carder: See **Drum carder.**

Bias: The line on a piece of fabric that is diagonal to the warp and weft.

Black wool: In the industry, any wool that is not 100 percent white.

Blade: The vertical divider in a reed.

Bleed: To lose color into water during immersion of a dyed fiber.

Blind stitch: A stitch in sewing in which two folded edges are joined together without the stitch showing.

Blocking: Placing fabric or yarn in a stretched-out position while it is being dried or pressed.

Blooming: In natural dyeing, term used to mean brightening of colors by the use of additional mordants in the dyebath toward the end of the dyeing. The developing of the blue color in indigo dyeing when the dipped fiber is exposed to the air.

Bluestone: Old term for copper sulfate, a mordant.

Blue vitriol: Common term for copper sulfate, a mordant.

Boat shuttle: A shuttle shaped like a boat that holds a spindle and bobbin of weft yarn.

Bobbin: The small spool used in a boat shuttle; or the larger wooden spool onto which the yarn is wound on a flyer-type spinning wheel.

Bobbing wheel: See **High wheel.**

Bobbin pulley: The grooved circumference of one end of the bobbin on a flyer wheel.

Bobbin winder: Tool used to wind bobbins; can be hand or electric.

Bottoming: In natural dyeing, the dyeing of a first color with the intention of top-dyeing a second color.

Braid: The lowest quality of wool in the blood system of grading.

Braiding: Same as plaiting.

Brake: The release-and-hold band on the warp beam of a treadle loom.

Breast beam: The upper horizontal beam at the front of the treadle loom over which the woven fabric passes.

Breech wool: The short dirty fibers that come from the hindquarters of the sheep.

Bright: The second-to-top classification in the grading of the condition of wool fleece.

Britch wool: Same as breech wool.

Brocade: A weave structure in which there are two wefts—a structural one and a decorative one that floats back and forth over warp threads in the area of the pattern only.

Brushing: Raising a fuzzy surface or nap on a fabric by brushing with fine wire brushes or hand cards; also called "napping."

Burnoose: A North African garment that is a cape cut from a single rectangle of fabric; the corners left from cutting a semicircle for the cape provide the pieces for the hood.

Burry and seedy: The lowest classification in the grading of the condition of wool fleece.

Butterfly: A small skein of yarn made by winding a figure eight on the fingers of one hand; also called a "finger hank."

California wools: One of four categories in the geographical classification of U.S. wools.

Camel's hair: The fiber from the fleece of the two-humped camel; usually means the fine down or wool from the undercoat, but can mean also the coarser hairs.

Carbonizing: Commercial cleaning of raw wool by steeping in sulfuric-acid solution to dissolve all foreign organic matter.

Carding: The process of combing out fibers with hand cards or carding machine in preparation for spinning.

Carding machine: A machine consisting of two wire brush surfaces through which fibers are pulled to separate them in preparation for spinning; see also **Drum carder** and **Bench carder.**

Cards: See **Hand cards.** Also the set of cards for card weaving.

Card weaving: A unique process of weaving in which individual warp threads are threaded through holes in a set of cards, which are turned to form the different sheds. (Also called "tablet weaving.")

Carpet warp: A smooth plied cotton thread of good strength that is commonly used for warp by handweavers.

Cartoon: A full-scale drawing of a proposed tapestry that is mounted behind the vertical warp on a tapestry loom as a guide for weaving the design.

Cashmere: The soft down from the undercoat of the Kashmir goat.

Castle beam: The beam across the top of the treadle loom from which harnesses are hung.

Castle wheel: An upright wheel of Irish design in which the wheel is directly over the spindle.

Catechu: East Indian tree the wood chips from which make a brown dye; also called "cutch."

Caustic soda: Common name for sodium hydroxide.

Centimeter: One-hundredth of a meter.

Chained warp: A warp that has been wound on a board, frame, or mill and removed in the form of a chain for easy handling.

Charkha: The East Indian word for spinning wheel; or, more specifically, the small Gandhi-designed wheel for spinning cotton.

Cheviot: A medium-wool breed of sheep, approximately 48s to 56s in the numerical count system.

Choice: The highest classification in the grading of the condition of wool fleece.

Chroma: Term used by color theorist Albert Munsell to describe saturation of color; see also **Intensity.**

Chrome: Short for potassium dichromate, a mordant.

Ciba dyes: Synthetic dyes made by the Ciba Chemical Co.

Cloth beam: The roller beam at the lower front of a treadle loom, onto which finished weaving is wound.

Cloth beam rod: The rod attached to the apron or other extension of the cloth beam to which the warp ends are tied.

Cloth roller: Same as cloth beam; or, can mean knee beam.

Coal tar: A dispersion of carbon in oil, formerly the only source of compounds used to make synthetic dyes.

Cochineal: The reddish dye made from the bodies of the insects *Coccus cacti,* which feed on the cactus *Nopale coccinellifera,* native to Mexico.

Columbia: Crossbreed sheep yielding wool approximately 50s to 60s in the numerical count system.

Comb: Tool usually made of wood for hand beating the weft on primitive or tapestry looms.

Combing: The process of removing short fibers and combing all long fibers parallel in the preparation of wool or hair for worsted spinning.

Common: The second-to-lowest quality of wool in the blood system of grading.

Cone: The conical-shaped spool on which yarn is wound.

Cone holder: A rack for holding cones of yarn for unwinding.

Cone winder: A tool for winding cones of yarn.

Controlled weave: A weave in which the weaver makes variations in the weave structure by hand techniques such as tapestry, pickup, brocade; as opposed to structural weaves.

Copperas: Old name for ferrous sulfate (iron), a mordant.

Copper sulfate: A metallic salt used as a mordant in natural dyeing, commonly called "blue vitriol," and also known as "bluestone."

Corduroy: A weave structure in which the weft floats over groups of warp threads and is then cut to form a pile surface to the fabric.

Corriedale: A crossbreed sheep yielding wool approximately 50s to 60s in the numerical count system.

Cortex: The protein cellular core of a wool fiber.

Cotswold: A long-wool breed of sheep, approximately 36s to 40s in the numerical count system.

Cotty wool: Term used in the industry to mean matted fibers in a wool fleece.

Counter: A tool to count off yards of thread passing through it; used primarily for sectional warping.

Counterbalanced loom: A treadle loom that has its heddle shafts (harnesses) balanced in pairs over pulleys, rollers, or horses.

Counter marche loom: A treadle loom that has a double set of marches (lams) to lower some shafts and at the same time raise the remaining shafts.

Count system: See **Numerical count system.**

Cowhair: Fiber from the coat of a cow, usually pulled rather than shorn.

Cream of tartar: Potassium bitartrate, a household chemical used as a mordant in natural dyeing.

Creel: A rack on which spools or cones can be set for unwinding.

Crimp: The serrations in a wool fiber.

Crocheting: A single-thread textile craft in which one produces the fabric by making a chain of loops.

Cross: The cross formed by winding warp threads in a figure eight to keep them in sequence; same as lease.

Crossbreed wool: Second-to-top classification of four categories of grades of wool.

Cutch: Same as catechu.

Cuticle: The outer layer of scales on a wool fiber.

Damask: A weave structure in which a pattern is formed by alternating warp and weft face satin.

Darn: The handweaving of a cross thread into a group of parallel threads, using a needle.

Delaine-Merino: Variety of Merino.

Denim: A fine twill weave in cotton in which the warp is usually a color and the weft white.

Dent: The space between the blades in a reed.

Dentage: The number of dents per inch.

Diamond twill: A point twill in which the treadling is reversed at intervals so as to form diamonds.

Dorset: Medium-wool breed of sheep; approximately 48s to 56s in the numerical count system.

Double cloth: A weave structure in which two separate layers of fabric are formed; the layers can be joined at certain points or can intersect each other to appear on the reverse surface of the fabric. Same as double weave.

Double-face: A weave structure in which the warp or weft threads that show on one surface are the opposite from those that show on the other surface.

Double ply: Two single threads twisted together.

Double sley: Thread two warp ends through the same dent.

Double warp beam: Two separate warp beams at the back of a treadle loom; usually one is sectional. The beams may be used singly or in combination for certain weaves requiring different warp tensions.

Double weave: See **Double cloth.**

Double width: Double cloth joined at one side in a fold.

Dovetailing: A vertical join in tapestry weaving in which two adjoining weft colors turn around the same warp thread, alternating single or multiple threads.

Down: The soft undercoat of a hair-bearing animal such as a husky dog or Kashmir goat.

Down shed: On the inkle loom, the shed that is made by pushing the unheddled warp threads down; as opposed to the up shed.

Draft: The graph or code drawn on paper to show the threading sequence through the different heddles on the different shafts; or the code to show which shafts are to be tied to which treadles.

Drafting: Drawing out fibers to the right thickness for spinning.

Draw-down: The pattern of a weave drawn on paper by following the threading draft, the tie-up draft, and the treadling sequence.

Drawing in: Same as threading.

Dressing the loom: Preparing the loom with the warp, so that it is ready for weaving.

Drop spindle: A hand spindle consisting of a light-weight shaft and whorl that is spun while hanging from the twisting yarn.

Drum carder: A machine for carding wool or other fibers; consists of a drum with wire brushes that turns with a hand crank against a fixed set of brushes. Also called "bench carder."

Dry-cleaning wool: Cleaning a fleece without subjecting it to water, by spreading the fleece out, shorn side up, and shaking out the dirt and organic matter.

Dummy warp: Warp threadings kept on the loom so that new warp ends may be tied to them, thus eliminating the threading process.

Dutch wheel: Same as Saxony wheel.

Dyebath: The water and dye mixture in which yarn, fabric, or fiber is submerged for dyeing.

Dye liquor: Same as dyebath; or a concentrated solution of dye and water.

Dyestuff: Material yielding dye.

End: A single warp thread.

English inkle: A large inkle loom, which stands on the floor and which accommodates long warps.

English worsted: Yarn spun of the longest and glossiest fibers of the fleece; as opposed to French worsted.

Epi: Abbreviation for "ends per inch."

Exhaust: To deplete the color in the dyebath as the dye enters the fibers.

False selvedge: The ends of a woven fabric where the warp threads have been sewn back into the weaving so that they are invisible.

Fast: Describing dyes that do not fade in water or light; the opposite of fugitive.

Fell: Top line of the weaving, where the warp threads cross in the most recent change of shed.

Felting: Same as fulling, but done to a degree that actually makes the fibers join together as in felt.

Ferrous sulfate: The metallic salt used as a mordant in natural dyeing, commonly called "iron."

Filler: A thick weft or rag used to "fill in"; primarily used at the beginning of a weaving where the warp ends have been tied in groups to the cloth beam rod.

Fine: Top grade of wool in the blood system of grading. Merino and Rambouillet are the only breeds that fit in this category.

Finger hank: Same as butterfly.

Flax: The vegetable fiber used to make linen thread.

Flax wheel: Same as flyer wheel, as opposed to wool wheel.

Fleece: The shorn coat of a wool- or hair-bearing animal.

Fleece wools: One of four categories in the geographical classification of U.S. wools; obtained from sheep grown east of the Mississippi.

Flicker: The single hand card that is used in "flicking."

Flicking: The process of combing out briskly the ends of a lock of raw wool in preparation for spinning.

Float: A warp or weft thread that "floats" over the top of several threads at a time.

Floor loom: Same as treadle loom.

Flyer: The U-shaped device on the spindle mechanism of certain spinning wheels which flies around the bobbin and winds the yarn onto it simultaneously with the spinning of it.

Flyer wheel: A spinning wheel with a flyer mechanism; also called "flax wheel" or "low wheel."

Fly shuttle: The metal-tipped shuttle that is automatically thrown back and forth after each beat of the batten on the fly shuttle loom.

Fork: The hand beater shaped like a fork and usually made of wood, used to pack in the weft in tapestry or rug weaving, or when weaving on a primitive stick loom.

Four-harness: Describing a loom that has four harnesses or shafts.

Frame loom: Any hand loom that consists of a four-sided frame on which the warp threads are wound and held in tension.

French worsted: Yarn made from the longest and finest fibers of the wool fleece all combed parallel to each other; as opposed to **English worsted.**

Frowzy wool: Term used in the industry to describe dull-appearing wool.

Fugitive: Describing dyes that fade in light and/or water; the opposite of "fast."

Fulling: A commercial process that subjects woven fabric to hot soapy water and agitation, for the purpose of matting and shrinking it.

Fustic: Wood chips of a large tree of the same name growing in tropical America used for a yellow dye.

Fustic extract: A concentrated dyestuff made from fustic ships.

Gauze: A weave structure in which the warp threads are twisted in pairs or groups before the insertion of the weft.

Gimp: A narrow woven band used to bind edges or seams.

Glauber's salt: A crystalline sodium sulfate used in dyeing.

Goat hair: The fibers from the fleece of any goat but the Angora, whose fleece yields mohair.

Golden section: A rectangle in which the lesser of the two dimensions is to the greater as the greater is to the sum of both dimensions.

Gram: A metric unit of weight: one-thousandth of a kilo; approximately .035 ounce. 100 grams equal approximately 3.5 ounces.

Grease, in the: Term used to describe spinning or weaving with raw wool or yarn that has not been washed, so that the wool grease remains in the fiber.

Great wheel: Same as high wheel.

Ground loom: The horizontal loom that holds the warp in tension with stakes driven into the ground.

Guides: The pegs or metal loops that divide the sectional warp beam into two-inch sections.

Half: Second-to-top category in the blood system of grading wool.

Hampshire: A medium-wool breed of sheep; approximately 48s to 56s in the numerical count system.

Hand cards: The pair of wire brushes set onto wooden backs and with which fibers are combed out in preparation for spinning. See also **Wool cards** and **Tow cards.**

Hand spindle: Any spindle for spinning that is rotated by hand rather than by wheel or other power.

Handspinning: The guiding by hand of fibers onto a spindle, which can be turned by hand, wheel, or other power.

Handspun: The yarn or thread that has been made by handspinning methods.

Handwoven: Woven by hand on a loom.

Harness: Originally a set of heddle shafts and their roller or pulley system; now, in U.S., means a single heddle shaft.

Heading: First few rows of weaving before the actual fabric is started; serves to equalize the spacing of the warp threads where they are tied to the cloth beam rod, and at the same time keep wefts from unraveling.

Heather mixture: Describes yarns made with various-colored fibers mixed together.

Heddle: The string, wire, flat steel (or other material) that encircles a warp thread, so that it can be pulled up separately from other warp threads.

Heddle, rigid: See **Rigid heddle.**

Heddle frame: The four-sided frame that holds the heddles on the treadle loom.

Heddle horses: On a counterbalanced loom, the levers, pivoted from the center, from the ends of which are hung the heddle shafts, so that when one shaft is lowered, the other is pulled up; performing the same functions as rollers or pulleys.

Heddle jig: The form or pattern around which strings are tied to make string heddles.

Heddle rod: Same as heddle stick.

Heddle shaft: The heddle frame with its heddles. See also **Harness.**

Heddle stick: The stick around which heddle loops are made on primitive stick looms, and which serves as a grasp.

Herringbone: A twill weave that reverses treadling sequence every so often, so that the diagonals run in opposite directions.

High wheel: The first spinning wheel designed in Europe, consisting of a base with a large wheel turned by hand, which drives a horizontal spindle by means of a drive band; designed for spinning while standing up; as opposed to the low wheel. Also called "walking wheel," "great wheel," and "bobbing wheel."

Homespun: Yarn that resembles handspun yarn, but which has not necessarily been spun by hand; usually a slightly unevenly spun single-ply yarn.

Hopi belt loom: A narrow stick loom on which a warp is wound in a continuous circle; the loom can be mounted vertically, or on a portable frame, or set up as a backstrap loom. The traditional loom used by the Hopi men to weave belts and ceremonial sashes, also used by other Indian weavers of the Southwest.

Hopsacking: Bagging or material made of coarse tabby weave.

Horsehair: Usually the mane or tail hairs of a horse, but can also mean the fibers of its coat.

Hue: Color theorist Albert Munsell's term to describe the property of color that we call red, orange, yellow, etc.

Huipil: A Mexican Indian garment similar to a poncho, but sewn part way up the sides; usually made of cotton and worn by women.

Hydrocarbons: Compounds containing only hydrogen and carbon; can be formed by the distillation of coal tar; aniline and other compounds are made from these and are used in making synthetic dyes.

Ikat: A weaving technique using tie-dyed warp and/or weft yarns; the resulting design when woven gives a blurred effect because of the slight displacement of each thread during the warping and/or weaving procedure.

Indigo: An ancient blue dye processed from the plant of the same name; in its natural state insoluble in water; one of the fastest blue dyes known.

Indigo extract: An extract of indigo dye, which can be used without making the indigo vat, but rather with sulfuric acid; results in a fugitive color.

Indigotin: The actual dyestuff in indigo.

Indigo vat: The process in which indigo is made soluble so that it can penetrate the fiber.

Indigo white: Term used to describe the indigo at a certain state of the indigo vat when white specks appear.

Inkle loom: Small portable loom consisting of a framework with numerous pegs around which the warp is wound; used mainly for belts and bands of warp-face structure.

Intensity: Color theorist Albert Munsell's original term meaning saturation of color; later changed to "chroma."

Iron: Short for ferrous sulfate, a mordant.

Jack: A lever, one end of which raises a heddle shaft by pushing or pulling when the other end is pulled down by a treadle.

Jack loom: A treadle loom with jacks for raising the heddle shafts.

Jaspe: Same as ikat.

Jute: A coarse fiber obtained from an East Indian plant.

Karakul: A Middle Eastern breed of sheep with very coarse, hairy fleece.

Kemp: A coarse fiber that occasionaly grows on sheep; it resembles vegetable fiber and tends to resist dye; the result of malnourishment of the animal.

Kempy wool: Term used by the industry to mean wool that has kemp in it.

Kermes: The ancient red dye made from the bodies of insects found on the evergreen oak of the same name.

Kilim: A Middle Eastern tapestry weave in which open slits are formed at the vertical joins of color areas; the rug, blanket, or fabric made in this technique.

Kilo: A metric measure of weight equivalent to 1,000 grams; approximately 2.2 pounds.

Knee beam: A beam occasionally included on a treadle loom; it is positioned in front of and slightly higher than the cloth beam and serves to keep the woven fabric away from the weaver's knees.

Knitting: A single-thread textile craft that forms an elastic fabric by looping the thread within previous loops held in position on a needle.

Lams: The horizontal bars on a treadle loom that provide the intermediary action between the treadles and heddle shafts.

Lanolin: The commercial product consisting of the natural wool grease from the fleece of a sheep with suint and any foreign substances removed.

Lap: Same as batt.

Lath: A narrow slat of wood, two of which serve as the frame for string heddles on a treadle loom.

Lazy kate: A rack on which bobbins of spun yarn can be put for unwinding.

Lazy line: In Navajo weaving, the diagonal join of two weft threads of the same color, formed because the weaver is too "lazy" to stretch her arms to pass the weft from edge to edge of a wide color area.

Lead: The difference in speed of the rotating spindle and bobbin on a flyer wheel, resulting in the yarn's being wound onto the bobbin.

Leader: A short length of yarn tied to a spindle to which the first fibers for spinning can be joined.

Lease: Same as cross.

Lease rods: A pair of slender sticks that are inserted on each side of the lease to preserve it when the warp threads are spread out to the width of the planned weaving.

Leno: A weave structure in which gauze weave is combined with another weave.

Level: The word used to describe the even penetration of dye into material.

Lichens: Leafy funguslike growth on trees or rocks, some varieties of which are useful as dyes; they contain acids so no mordant is required.

Lincoln: A long-wool breed of sheep; approximately 36s to 46s in the numerical count system.

Linen: The thread made from flax fibers.

Llama: A domesticated South American animal, similar to the alpaca, but raised mainly as a beast of burden; its coat yields a rather coarse fiber, which the natives use in making ropes and coarse sacking.

Logwood: Dyestuff consisting of the wood chips of a West Indian and Central American tree, yielding a purplish-gray color.

Long wool: A category of sheep breeds in which the fleeces have long, rather coarse fibers; excellent for handspinning.

Loom: Any tool for holding a warp in tension for the insertion of a weft to form a woven fabric.

Loom bar: One of the two bars of a primitive stick loom around which a continuous warp is wound, and which is held rigid to provide tension for the warp.

Loom frame: Any frame upon which a stick loom is stretched.

Loop mohair: Yarn made of loops of mohair usually bound together with a fine two-ply thread.

Low quarter: Third-to-lowest category in the blood system of grading wool.

Low wheel: Same as flyer wheel; as opposed to high wheel.

Macramé: Textile craft in which fabric or forms are made by knotting the threads together in various types of knots.

Madder: An ancient and very fast red dyestuff from the roots of the plant of the same name.

Maidens: The vertical members that hold the flyer assembly on a flyer wheel.

Maori edge: A technique for securing the leftover warp ends of a woven fabric, used by the Maoris of New Zealand.

Marche: English, Scotch, and Scandinavian term for lam.

Matt: Same as batt.

Mauve: The name given to the first synthetic dye, a purplish color, discovered by William H. Perkin in 1856 at the Royal College of Chemistry in London.

Medium wool: One of four categories of breeds of sheep, the fleeces of which have medium-coarse fibers.

Medulla: The central core of air present in coarse wool fibers and hair fibers.

Mercerized cotton: Cotton fiber that has been treated under tension with caustic alkali, resulting in a shiny surface and greater strength.

Merino: A breed of sheep developed in Spain and yielding the very finest wool of any sheep.

Meter: A unit of length in the metric system, equal to 39.37 inches.

Mill sampling cards: Hand cards used in the wool industry.

Miner's head: On the high wheel, the extra pulley used to increase the speed at which the spindle spins; named for Amos Miner, who invented it in 1830.

Mohair: The long, silky fiber from the coat of the Angora goat.

Mordant: Chemicals, usually acids or metallic salts, which combine with dyes on fibers to make more or less insoluble compounds.

Mother-of-all: The horizontal member into which the maidens are set on a flyer wheel.

Musk ox: Animal of the arctic regions of North America from which comes the extremely fine fiber called quivit.

Nap: Surface of a fabric formed by fibers standing at an angle to the plane of the fabric.

Napping: See **Brushing.**

Natural dyes: Dyes from natural sources (animal, vegetable, or mineral) as opposed to synthetic dyes.

Naturals: Colors of fibers that are in their natural undyed state.

Navajo loom: A stick loom suspended in a rigid vertical frame, used by the Navajo Indians.

Navajo rug: The weft-face rug or blanket, usually of tapestry design, woven by Navajos on a Navajo loom, and characterized by selvedge on all four sides.

Navajo selvedge: The characteristic twisted cord edge formed around the continuous warp at the top and bottom edges of the weaving.

Navajo sheep: A breed of sheep raised mainly on the reservation; has coarse-fibered fleece with little wool grease.

Navajo spindle: The hand spindle used by Navajos and Hopis for handspinning wool, characterized by its large size, which necessitates rolling the shaft on the thigh to make it spin.

Nep: A bunch of tangled fibers that sometimes form in the carding process.

Niddy-noddy: A two-ended T frame, with top and bottom Ts at right angles to each other, on which yarn is wound from a spinning wheel or spindle to make a skein.

Noils: The short fibers that are removed from the long fibers in the combing of wool for worsted spinning.

Numerical count system: A system of grading the fineness of wool fibers according to numbers, which represent the number of hanks of yarn, each 560 yards long, that can be spun from one pound of wool. Numbers range from 30s to 80s, which is the very finest Merino.

Oak galls: Small round formations found on oak trees caused by depositions of insects; contain concentrated amount of tannin, which acts as a mordant in natural dyeing.

Overshot: A weave structure in which the weft shoots over several warp threads at a time to make decorative color areas.

Oxford: Medium-wool breed of sheep; 46s to 50s in the numerical count system.

Panama: Crossbreed sheep yielding wool approximately 50s to 58s in the numerical count system.

Paper quill: Piece of paper rolled onto a bobbin winder shaft and around which yarn can be wound to use in a boat shuttle.

Pawl: The lever that fits into the teeth of a ratchet to stop the ratchet from turning backward.

Pick: A sharp-pointed stick for picking up warp threads. Also, a single shot of weft—term used most often in industrial weaving.

Picking: Same as teasing.

Pick-up: A technique of picking up by hand certain warp threads other than those lifted by the heddles, to form patterns in weaving.

Pile: The surface of a fabric formed by threads protruding more or less perpendicularly from the fabric.

Pill: The formation of little balls of fiber on a fabric.

Plaid: A design formed by bands of weft colors crossing bands of warp colors.

Plain weave: The simplest type of weave, in which the weft alternates going over and under the warp threads.

Plaiting: Intertwining threads that hang parallel.

Ply: A single strand of yarn often twisted with others to form two-ply, three-ply, or other yarn.

Point twill: A twill weave in which the threading sequence is reversed at intervals so that the diagonals meet to form points.

Potassium aluminum sulfate: The metallic salt more commonly known as "alum," which is used as a mordant in natural dyeing.

Potassium dichromate: The metallic salt more commonly known as "chrome," which is used as a mordant in natural dyeing.

Primary color: A pure color that cannot be produced by mixing other colors together. In dyeing and painting, red, yellow, and blue are considered primaries.

Primitive loom: A hand loom made of sticks or bars and usually requiring the hand manipulation of heddles.

Pulled warp: Same as wedge weaving.

Pulled wool: Wool fleece that has been pulled by the roots from a dead sheep.

Pulley: Small wheel over which pass the cords that support the heddle shafts so that the shafts can be pulled up or down. See also **Bobbin pulley** and **Spindle pulley.**

Pull shed: The shed on a primitive loom that is formed by pulling the heddle stick up or forward.

Quarter: One of the grades of wool in the blood system of grading.

Quechquemitl: A Mexican Indian garment somewhat like a poncho, but made of two rectangular pieces; one end of each piece is sewn to the side of the other piece, leaving an unsewn area between the joints that can be slipped over the head.

Quill: A bobbin with one pointed end off which the yarn unwinds.

Quivit: The long, very fine fiber of the musk ox.

Raddle: A comblike tool that is clamped onto the treadle loom during the beaming process to keep the warp threads evenly spaced.

Rag shuttle: A large stick shuttle consisting of two pointed side pieces joined together by two bars around which rags or heavy weft threads are wound.

Rambouillet: A fine-wool breed of sheep, one step down

from the Merino, approximately 62s to 70s in the numerical count system.

Ramie: A heat-resistant vegetable fiber, very white and silky.

Ratchet: A circular gearlike device, used with a pawl, on the cloth and warp beams of treadle looms to allow them to turn in only one direction.

Raw wool: Wool that has been shorn from the sheep, not carded or spun.

Reed: The comblike device on a loom through which warp threads are threaded to keep them properly spaced during the weaving, and which acts as a comb for beating in the weft.

Reed hook: A flat hook for drawing warp threads through the reed.

Rep: A ribbed texture formed in either warp- or weft-face fabric in which the invisible threads are larger than the visible threads.

Repair heddle: A heddle constructed so that it can be added to the heddle shaft in between other heddles to replace a broken one and enclose the warp thread.

Reprocessed wool: Yarn or fabric made of shredded samples or scraps from mills.

Reused wool: Yarn or fabric made of fiber shredded from a used fabric.

Rickrack: A narrow band made by braiding; the direction of the braiding reverses regularly to form zigzags.

Rigid heddle: A combination reed and heddle with eyes in every other tooth for the threading of alternate warp threads; by pushing the rigid heddle down or up one forms alternate sheds.

Rising shed: The shed formed when a treadle is pressed and the corresponding heddle shafts are raised; as opposed to sinking shed.

Rolag: The roll of carded wool that is the result of rolling a mass of fibers when they come off the hand cards.

Rolled hem: A type of hem in sewing where the fabric is rolled under and sewn in that position with a slip stitch.

Rollers: The cylindrical bars on a counterbalanced loom from which the heddle shafts are hung, and which provide the pulley action for the shafts.

Romeldale: A crossbreed sheep yielding wool approximately 58s to 60s in the numerical count system.

Romney: A long-wool breed of sheep; 40s to 48s in the numerical count system.

Rope machine: A wooden device that twists yarns into a rope.

Rough sleying: Sleying groups of threads rather than single threads when using the reed as a spreader.

Roving: The continuous rope of loosely twisted fibers prepared for spinning.

Royal purple: See **Tyrian purple.**

Rug beater: A hand beater, usually made of heavy-weight material such as iron.

Rug fork: Same as rug beater.

Rug shuttle: A large stick shuttle that will hold a good quantity of heavy-weight yarn for rug weaving.

Rya: A Scandinavian weave structure in which short lengths of yarn are tied around pairs of warp threads to form a pile fabric, these being secured by a structural weft.

Sacking needle: A very large needle designed specifically for sewing sack tops together.

Sadden: To dull and darken colors in natural dyeing, usually by adding iron mordant to the dyebath.

Safflower: An important Old World dyestuff made from the plant of the same name; the yellow can be rinsed from it in a special process.

Saffron: Dyestuff collected from the pistils of the autumn crocus.

Sassafras: An aromatic root bark that yields a pinkish-beige color in natural dyeing.

Satin: One of the basic weave structures, in which the weft floats over the top of groups of warp threads, forming a very smooth weft-face surface on the top side of the fabric.

Saxony wheel: A spinning wheel design in which the flyer, bobbin, and spindle are positioned slightly higher than the axle of the wheel, requiring a diagonal base.

Scalloped: Same as wedge weave.

Scouring: Washing dirt, yolk, and any foreign matter out of a fleece.

Secondary colors: The colors (orange, green, and purple) that are produced by mixing primary colors.

Second cuts: Short fibers in a fleece that are the result of shearing the fibers twice in the same area.

Sectional beam: A warp beam, usually at least two feet in circumference, on which the warp is wound in sections.

Sectional warping: A warping method in which sections of warp two inches wide are wound onto the warp beam one at a time.

Seersucker: A weave structure in which alternate groups of warp threads are of less tension than the rest; this forms puckers in the warp.

Selvedge: The woven edge of a fabric.

Semi: The second classification in the grading of the condition of wool fleece.

Serape: Mexican blanket, usually of weft-face stripes and tapestry design.

Sett: Number of warp ends per inch.

Shaft: Same as heddle shaft.

Shed: The space, made by raising certain warp threads and lowering others, through which the weft passes.

Shed rod: Same as shed stick.

Shed stick: The stick that permanently separates alternate warp threads on the primitive looms.

Sheep dip: A solution applied (usually before shearing) to the fleece of the sheep to kill pests.

Shot: The single passage of a weft thread through the shed.

Shrinkage: Loss of weight in fleece due to the removal of the yolk and foreign matter.

Shropshire: A medium-wool breed of sheep, approximately 48s to 56s in the numerical count system.

Shuttle: Any contrivance on which yarn is packaged in order to facilitate its passage through a shed.

Shuttle race: The lower horizontal member of the beater on a treadle loom, which supports the reed and on which the lower warp threads of the shed rest.

Silk: A filament from the cocoon of the silkworm; thread or fabric made from same.

Singles: Thread that is a single ply.

Sinking shed: The shed formed when a treadle is pressed and the corresponding heddle shafts are lowered; as opposed to rising shed.

Sizing: A starchy solution into which yarn can be dipped to protect it during the weaving process.

Skein: A continuous length of yarn wound into a circle or other form.

Skein reel: Same as skein winder.

Skein winder: A tool for winding skeins of yarn.

Skeleton tie-up: The tie-up in which each treadle is tied to only one shaft (or harness). If there are two extra treadles on the loom, each of these can be tied to two shafts to form a tabby shed, and the tie-up is still considered "skeleton."

Skirt: Remove the short, dirty fibers from around the edges of a fleece.

Ski shuttle: A stick shuttle shaped like a ski, with two turned-up ends and a cleat in the center on which the yarn is wound.

Slab beam: Same as back beam.

Sley: To thread the reed.

Sleying hook: Same as reed hook.

Slip stitch: A sewing stitch that is more or less invisible and used mainly for hemming.

Sliver: Industrial term for wool carded and ready for spinning woolen yarn.

Slot and hole: Same as rigid heddle.

Snitch knot: A knot to join two ropes together, used in the tie-up.

Sodium hydrosulfite: Chemical used to remove the oxygen from the indigotin in making the indigo vat.

Sodium hydroxide: Chemical used to dissolve the indigo white in the process of making the indigo vat; commonly called caustic soda.

Soumak: A weave structure in which the weft winds around warp threads instead of passing over and under them.

Southdown: A medium-wool breed of sheep; approximately 56s to 60s in the numerical count system.

Spelsau: A Norwegian breed of sheep yielding long, lustrous, fairly coarse wool.

Spindle: The long, pointed shaft on a spinning wheel; or the hand tool used for spinning. See also **Hand spindle**.

Spindle pulley: On a spinning wheel the grooved circumference at the base of the spindle around which the drive band passes.

Spindle whorl: The disk or sphere on a hand spindle that provides the weight for momentum needed to keep the spindle spinning.

Spinning oil: Oil (usually vegetable, mineral, or neatsfoot) used to ease the slippage of fibers in carding and spinning.

Spinning wheel: A wheel-driven spindle for spinning yarn.

Splicing: Joining wefts by overlapping.

Spool rack: Rack for holding spools of yarn for unwinding. See also **Creel.**

Spools: See **Warping spools.**

Sprang: A braiding or plaiting technique in which the ends of the threads are held in a fixed position and progressive twists are held in place by temporary rods.

Spreader: Same as raddle.

Square knot: A knot used to join two ends in which the looped ends interlock with each other.

Squirrel cage: A swift that is a vertical stand with two free-turning and adjustable cylindrical cages around which the skein is placed.

Standard tie-up: The tie-up in which each treadle is tied to all the shafts that must be raised or lowered for each particular shed.

Stannous chloride: The metallic salt (commonly known as tin) that is used as a mordant in natural dyeing.

Staple: The length of unstretched wool fiber.

Stick loom: A primitive loom on which the warp is simply wound around two sticks, and the sheds are formed by a shed stick and heddle stick.

Stick shed: The shed formed by the shed stick.

Stick shuttle: A flat stick around which weft yarn is wound.

Stretcher: A tool used to hold the fabric out to its full width during the weaving process; same as temple.

Strike: The penetration of dye into the fiber.

Structural weave: A weave in which the pattern or texture is formed by the weft's passing through a variety of sheds from edge to edge of the weaving; as opposed to controlled weaves.

Structural weft: A weft that forms the structure of the fabric as opposed to an additional decorative weft.

S twist: Term used to describe the twist in yarn spun on a spindle that spins counterclockwise.

Subtractive mixture: A color theory based on subtracting light rays from white light, the total subtraction of which leaves no light, black; as opposed to additive mixture.

Suffolk: A medium-wool breed of sheep; approximately 48s to 56s in the numerical count system.

Suint: The secretion from the sweat glands of the sheep that combines with the wool grease to form the yolk.

Sulfuric acid: A very corrosive acid used to make the acid dyebath in synthetic dyeing when using acid dyes.

Swift: A tool for holding different-size skeins of yarn for unwinding.

Sword: The vertical side members of the beater on a treadle loom; or same as a batten for stick looms.

Synthetic dyes: Synthetic organic compounds formally derived entirely from coal tar, and originally called "aniline" dyes because they were specifically derived from aniline.

Tabby: A balanced plain weave; or can refer to a plain-weave shed.

Table loom: A miniature version of the treadle loom but with hand levers for operating the shafts rather than treadles.

Tablet weaving: Same as card weaving.

Taglocks: The short dirty ends in a fleece.

Takeup: The extra length that is "taken up" by the undulation of the yarn over and under threads.

Tannin: An astringent vegetable compound that occurs in

bark of trees, especially oak, and in large quantities in oak galls; used as a mordant in natural dyeing, especially for cotton.

Tapestry: A weft-face weave structure in which the pattern is formed by different-colored wefts woven back and forth just in their color area.

Tapestry bobbin: A bobbin with one pointed end for inserting wefts in tapestry weaving.

Tapestry fork: A fork-shaped beater used in tapestry weaving.

Tapestry frame: A four-sided frame on which a warp is stretched for tapestry weaving; string heddles are operated by hand.

Tapestry loom: Any loom designed specifically for weaving tapestry; can be treadle operated.

Tapestry yarn: Usually a medium-fine two-ply long- and lustrous-fibered yarn.

Targhee: A crossbreed sheep yielding wool approximately 58s to 60s in the numerical count system.

Tease: To pull apart fibers by hand in preparation for carding or spinning; same as pick.

Temple: Same as stretcher.

Tender wool: Term used in the industry to describe wool that breaks easily.

Tension box: A box through which warp threads can pass over dowels to provide even tension for each thread; used in sectional warping.

Territory wool: One of the four categories in the geographic classification of wool in the U.S.; it includes the western states.

Tertiary colors: Colors made by mixing secondary and primary colors.

Texas wools: One of the four categories in the geographic classification of wool in the U.S.; primary source of Rambouillet.

Thread count: Same as yarn count.

Threading: Drawing the warp threads through eyes of heddles and dents of reed.

Threading hook: Hook used for threading the warp through the heddles and reed.

Three-eighths: Third category in the blood system of grading wool.

Tie-dye: A dyeing technique in which fabric, yarn, or fiber is tied tightly in certain areas so that dye cannot penetrate.

Tie-up: The arrangement of ties made between treadles and heddle shafts. See also **Skeleton tie-up** and **Standard tie-up**.

Tin: Short for stannous chloride, a mordant.

Tippy wool: Term used in the industry to describe brittle, dry tips in wool fleece.

Top: A continuous coil of combed fibers in the commercial preparation of wool or hair for spinning.

Top-dyeing: Dyeing a color over already-dyed wool.

Tow cards: Hand cards for preparing flax, hemp, or jute for spinning; distinguished from wool cards by the heavier wire brushes; good for carding coarse wools and hairs.

Tubular weaving: Weaving two layers of fabric at a time, with a fold at both edges; the weft follows a circular route as it alternates from upper to lower layer.

Tufting: Term used for a Navajo technique in which tufts of wool or hair are laid in behind two warp threads with ends protruding.

Turkey red: A dye derived from madder by a complicated process; the brightest and most lasting color from madder especially for cotton dyeing.

Turkish spindle: A hand spindle used in Turkey, which has two removable bars for the whorl.

Treadle loom: A loom that uses treadles to operate the heddle shafts.

Treadles: The pivoted levers at the base of the loom, which operate the heddle shafts.

Twill: A weave structure characterized by diagonal lines formed by the shed sequence moving over one warp thread after each shot of weft.

Twined warp: Warps twisting around weft threads, as in gauze and card weaving.

Twined weft: A double weft strand that is twisted around the warp threads; a technique of weaving used since the very beginning of weaving history.

Twining: The twisting of warp or weft threads in the process of weaving.

Tyrian purple: A pre-Christian dyestuff obtained from a shellfish of the Mediterranean and exported by Tyre to other countries; also called "royal purple."

Umbrella rib: One of the metal ribs of an umbrella that has an eye; used by Navajo weavers as a large needle for inserting the weft toward the end of the weaving.

Umbrella swift: A swift made of ribs that unfold somewhat like an umbrella to accommodate different-size skeins of yarn.

Upright wheel: A spinning wheel of the flyer type in which the wheel and spindle are in vertical alignment.

Up shed: The shed on an inkle loom formed by pushing unheddled warp threads up; as opposed to the down shed.

Value: Term used by color theorist Albert Munsell to describe the property of light and dark in colors.

Variegated yarn: Yarn that varies in color.

Vat dyes: Dyes that are applied to fiber by the vat method. See also **Indigo vat**.

Vegetable dyes: Dyes from plant sources.

Vicuña: The very fine, silky fiber from the fleece of the vicuña, a native South American animal that lives at very high altitudes in the Andes.

Virgin wool: Wool fiber converted into yarn or fabric for the first time.

Walking wheel: Same as high wheel, so called because the spinner steps back and forth as he or she spins.

Warp: The group of parallel threads that are held in tension during the weaving process.

Warp beam: The horizontal roller at the back of the treadle loom on which the warp is wound.

Warp beam rod: The rod at the end of the apron or other extension on the warp beam to which the warp ends are attached.

Warp-face: Describing any flat-weave structure in which the warp threads form the surface of the fabric and the weft is more or less invisible; as opposed to weft-face.

Warping board: A board or frame with pegs on which a warp is wound to measure out the length.

Warping frame: Same as warping board; or the temporary construction of horizontal bars sometimes used in warping for primitive looms.

Warping mill, horizontal: The framework drum that turns on a horizontal axis, on which a warp is wound in preparation for winding directly onto the warp beam.

Warping mill, vertical: The framework drum that turns on a vertical axis, on which a warp is wound in preparation for making a chained warp.

Warping paddle: A small hand paddle with numerous holes for threading warp threads to keep them in sequence as they are wound onto a frame or mill and for making the cross.

Warping reel: Same as warping mill.

Warping spools: The large cardboard, wooden, or plastic spools onto which skeins of warp yarn can be wound in preparation for winding a warp onto a warping board or onto a sectional warp beam.

Warp roller: Same as warp beam.

Warp-weighted loom: A loom in which warp tension is achieved by hanging heavy weights on the ends of vertically hung warp threads.

Wasty wool: Term used in the industry to describe short, weak, tangled wool that will be wasted in the spinning.

Weaver's knot: A knot used by weavers to join two ends with a minimum-size knot so that it can easily pass through the heddles and reed.

Web: The woven fabric. Or same as batt.

Wedge weaving: A Navajo weaving technique in which diagonal patterns are formed by weaving the weft in on a diagonal; this weft "pulls" the warp out of its vertical alignment and makes the edge "scallop," so it is also called "pulled warp" or "scalloped" weaving.

Weft: The independent thread woven across the warp threads in such a way as to join them together to make a fabric; also called "filling", or "woof."

Weft-face: Describing any flat-weave structure in which the weft threads form the surface of the fabric and the warp is more or less invisible; as opposed to warp-face.

Weld: A dye plant that yields one of the best and fastest yellows.

Whipped fringe: A hand-sewn edge that prevents weft threads from unraveling.

Whorl: See **Spindle whorl.**

Winding the warp: Measuring out all the warp threads to a certain length by winding them around pegs or bars a certain distance apart.

Woad: A dye plant that contains indigotin, but in smaller amounts than the indigo plant.

Woof: Same as weft, but the word is more or less obsolete.

Wool cards: Hand cards with rather fine teeth for carding wool.

Woolen: Yarn made from rolags of carded wool; or wool fibers that lie in all different directions.

Wool grease: The fatty substance, actually a wax, that is secreted from the sebaceous glands of the sheep, and from which the commercial product lanolin is made.

Wool wheel: Same as high wheel; as opposed to flax wheel.

Worsted: Yarn made from the longest fibers of the fleece that have all been combed parallel to each other.

Yak hair: Fiber from the coat of a wild ox of the same name from the Tibetan highlands.

Yardage: Fabric by the yard.

Yarn count: The size of thread as given in numbers, based on the size thread that can be spun a certain length out of a pound of fiber; same as thread count.

Yolk: The combination of wool grease and suint in a fleece.

Yucca root: Root of a plant growing in the warmer regions of the U.S.; has saponific (sudsing) qualities; good for washing wool and hair.

Z twist: Term used to describe the twist in yarn spun on a spindle that spins clockwise.

RECOMMENDED READING

There are so many good books on these subjects I will only mention those that I think will be most useful to you. I've put asterisks beside the books that I consider exceptional—every serious weaver should at least have a look at these, and it would be nice if you could own them so they would be on hand for reference; they are full of ideas and information. Be sure to subscribe to *Shuttle, Spindle, and Dyepot*, put out by the Handweavers Guild of America (see Chapter XIII, Suppliers: Books), and get on the Unicorn's mailing list to receive their catalogs and reviews of all the books on these subjects (see The Unicorn Craft and Hobby Book Service in the Books section of Chapter XIII).

Adrosko, Rita J. *Natural Dyes and Home Dyeing*. New York, 1971.

*Albers, Anni. *On Weaving*. Middletown, Conn., 1965.

*Amsden, Charles Avery. *Navaho Weaving, Its Technic and History*. Santa Ana, Calif., 1934.

*Atwater, Mary Meigs. *Byways in Handweaving*. New York, 1954.

Bennett, Noel. *The Weaver's Pathway*. Flagstaff, Ariz., 1974.

Bennett, Noel, and Tiana Bighorse. *Working with the Wool*. Flagstaff, Ariz., 1971.

Bergen, Werner von. *Wool Handbook*. 2 volumes. New York, 1963, 1970.

Beutlich, Tadek. *The Technique of Woven Tapestry*. New York, 1967.

*Black, Mary. *New Key to Weaving*. New York, 1957.

Bolton, Eileen. *Lichens for Vegetable Dyeing*. Newton Centre Mass., 1960.

Bowen, Godfrey. *Wool Away: The Art and Technique of Shearing*. New York, 1974.

Bress, Helene. *Inkle Weaving*. New York, 1975.

Brooklyn Botanic Garden. *Dye Plants and Dyeing: A Handbook*. Brooklyn, N.Y., 1964.

Bryan, Nonabeh G. *Navajo Native Dyes*. Compiled by Stella Young. Chilocco, Okla., 1940.

Burnham, Dorothy K. *Cut My Cote*. Toronto, Ontario, 1973.

Channing, Marion L. *The Magic of Spinning*. New Bedford, Mass., 1966.

Channing, Marion L. *The Textile Tools of Colonial Homes*. New Bedford, Mass., 1969.

*Collingwood, Peter. *The Techniques of Rug Weaving*. New York, 1969.

Constantine, Mildred, and Jack Lenor Larsen. *Beyond Craft*. New York, 1972.

Cordry, Donald and Dorothy. *Mexican Indian Costumes*. Austin, Texas, 1968.

Crockett, Candace. *Card Weaving*. New York, 1973.

Davenport, Elsie G. *Your Handspinning*. Big Sur, Calif., 1964.

Davenport, Elsie G. *Your Yarn Dyeing*. London, 1955.

*Emery, Irene. *The Primary Structure of Fabrics*. Washington, D.C., 1966.

Fannin, Allen. *Handspinning: Art and Technique*. New York, 1970.

Grae, Ida. *Nature's Colors: Dyes from Plants*. New York, 1974.

*Harcourt, Raoul d'. *Textiles of Ancient Peru and Their Techniques*. Seattle, Wash., 1962.

Holland, Nina. *Inkle Loom Weaving*. New York, 1973.

Hollister, U. S. *The Navajo and His Blanket*. Denver, Colo., 1903.

James, George Wharton. *Indian Blankets and Their Makers*. Glorieta, N.M., 1927, 1974.

Kahlenberg, Mary Hunt, and Anthony Berlant. *The Navajo Blanket*. New York, 1972.

Kent, Kate P. *West African Cloth*. Denver, Colo., 1971.

Kluger, Marilyn. *The Joy of Spinning*. New York, 1971.

Lesch, Alma. *Vegetable Dyeing*. New York, 1970.

Osburn, Bernice B. *Homecraft Course in Pennsylvania German Spinning and Dyeing*. Plymouth Meeting, Pa., 1945.

Pendleton, Mary. *Navajo and Hopi Weaving Techniques*. New York, 1974.

Reichard, Gladys A. *Navajo Weaver and Shepherd*. New York, 1936.

Reichard, Gladys A. *Weaving a Navajo Blanket*. (Unabridged and unaltered re-publication of *Navajo Weaver and Shepherd*.) New York, 1974.

*Robertson, Seonaid M. *Dyes from Plants*. New York, 1973.

Simmons, Paula. *Articles from Warp and Weft, on Spinning, Weaving, and Sheep*. Reprints. Suquamish, Wash., n.d.

Simmons, Paula. *Spinning and Weaving Articles* (from Handweaver and Craftsman). Reprints. Suquamish, Wash., n.d.

Specht, Sally, and Sandra Rawlings. *Creating with Card Weaving*. New York, 1973.

Taber, Barbara, and Marilyn Anderson. *Backstrap Weaving*. New York, 1975.

Thurston, Violetta. *The Use of Vegetable Dyes*. Leicester, England, 1968.

*Tidball, Harriet. *The Shuttle Craft Guild Monographs*. Distributed by Craft and Hobby Book Service, Big Sur, Calif., 1963–69.

Tidball, Harriet. *The Weaver's Book*. New York, 1961.

Zielinski, S. A. *Encyclopedia of Handweaving*. New York, 1959.

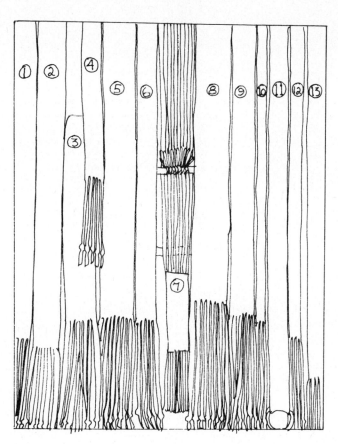

BELTS IN SEVEN DIFFERENT TECHNIQUES DESCRIBED IN THIS BOOK

1. Warp-face belt (Project I, Chapter III, "The Inkle Loom"). (Courtesy of Clay and Fiber, Taos, N.M.) Commercial wool yarn. Woven by Peg Templeton.
2. Double cloth sash (Project VI, Chapter V, "The Backstrap Loom"). Commercial wool yarn, respun. Woven by Brooke Tuthill.
3. Diagonal weave belt (Project II, Chapter II, "Card Weaving"). Natural grey, white, and dyed red commercial wool yarn (contributed by The Wool Merchant), respun. Woven by author.
4. Peruvian braid (Chapter VIII, "Finishing Techniques"). Handspun, Ciba-dyed, New Zealand Romney wool. Spun, dyed, and braided by author and Louise Gelenter.
5. Card woven belt (Project I, Chapter II, "Card Weaving"). Canadian wool yarn, Ciba-dyed, respun. Woven by Madelyn Johannes.
6. Warp-face belt with pickup pattern (Chapter III, "The Inkle Loom: Suggestions for Other Projects"). (Courtesy of Clay and Fiber, Taos, N.M.) Commercial wool yarn. Woven by Peg Templeton.
7. Warp-face belt with pickup pattern in progress on Hopi belt loom. (Chapter III, "The Inkle Loom: Suggestions for Other Projects"). Commercial wool yarn, respun. Woven by author.
8. Traditional Hopi belt (Project I, Chapter IV, "The Hopi Belt Loom"). Commercial yarn, respun. Woven by Rockwell Driver.
9. Peruvian braid (Chapter VIII, "Finishing Techniques"). Norwegian cow hair and wool yarn in natural black and white; and handspun karakul, Ciba-dyed. Braided by author. (From the collection of Luria Wright.)
10. Card-woven belt (Project I, Chapter II, "Card Weaving"). (Courtesy of Clay and Fiber, Taos, N.M.) Commercial wool yarn. Woven by Peg Templeton.
11. Warp-face belt (Project I, Chapter III, "The Inkle Loom.") (Courtesy of Clay and Fiber, Taos, N.M.) Commercial wool yarn. Woven by Joanna Cattonar.
12. Peruvian braid (Chapter VIII, "Finishing Techniques"). Commercial wool yarn, respun. Braided by Louise Gelenter.
13. Warp-face belt (Project I, Chapter III, "The Inkle Loom"). Commercial wool yarn, respun. Woven by author.

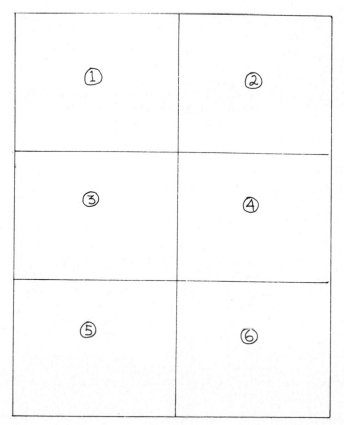

DETAILS OF WEAVING PROJECTS IN CHAPTER V, "THE BACKSTRAP LOOM," AND CHAPTER VI, "THE NAVAJO LOOM."

1. Detail from handbag (Project II, Chapter VI). The stripes and ovals are described in the instructions for this project. The birds are made by the tapestry technique described in Project IV in the same chapter. Commercial wool yarn in natural grey and white was used. Woven by author.
2. Detail from double-face saddle blanket (Project VI, Chapter VI). The brushed technique is described in Chapter VII, Project XIX. Natural black and white Romney wool, handspun by La Lana Wools was used. Mohair (contributed by Straw into Gold) spun and dyed with Ciba acid dyes by author. Woven by Kristina Wilson.
3. Detail from wedge-woven rug (Project III, Chapter VI). Natural black Romney and natural-dyed New Zealand wool, spun and dyed by La Lana Wools, was used. The red is cochineal (contributed by Straw into Gold), the blue is indigo, and the beige is Indian paint brush. Woven by author.
4. Detail from warp-face ikat stole (Project II, Chapter V). Commercial yarn tie-dyed with Ciba acid dyes was used. Dyed and woven by author.
5. Detail of tufted rug (Project I, Chapter VI). Unspun karakul fiber dyed with Ciba acid dyes was used. Woven by Joan Loveless.
6. Detail from diamond twill saddle blanket (Project V, Chapter VI). White and madder-dyed New Zealand wool (contributed by La Lana Wools) was used. Black karakul handspun by author. Woven by Kristina Wilson.

KEY TO THE COLOR PHOTOGRAPHS

DETAILS OF WEAVING PROJECTS IN CHAPTER VII, "THE TREADLE LOOM"

1.   Detail from rya rug (Project XII). Mexican handspun wool dyed with Ciba acid dyes was used. Woven by Joan Loveless.

2.   Detail from fancy twill rug (Project XI). Handspun New Zealand Romney wool dyed with Indian paint brush (contributed by La Lana Wools) was used; black karakul wool handspun by author. Woven by Kristina Wilson.

3.   Detail from double-width bedspread (Project XVII). Warp: Canadian wool yarn; weft: handspun wool. Both dyed with Ciba acid dyes. Spun, dyed, and woven by author.

4.   Detail from tapestry (Project III). This is identical in technique to Project III but is abstract rather than pictorial. Canadian wool yarn and handspun wool, all dyed with Ciba acid dyes, were used. Spun, dyed, and woven by author. (From the collection of Jane Lipman.)

5.   Detail from three-dimensional wall hanging (Project IX). Handspun karakul wool, natural black-and-white, and Ciba-dyed orange were used. Spun, dyed, and woven by author. (From the collection of Frank Stout.)

6.   Detail from burnoose (Project XVII). Canadian wool yarn and handspun karakul, all dyed with Ciba acid dyes, were used. Woven by Noël Ferris. This burnoose is also pictured on the cover. (From the collection of Alicia Cahue.)

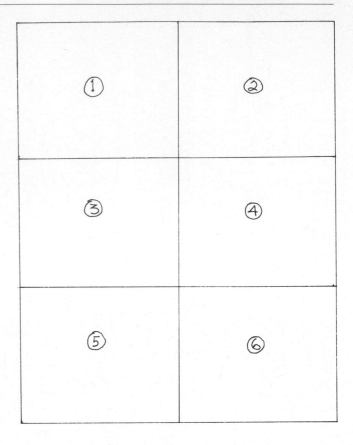

EXAMPLES OF FINISHING TECHNIQUES

NOTE: Instructions for making these items and many more may be found in Chapter VIII, "Finishing Techniques."

1.   Twisted fringe
2.   Braided fringe
3.   Pheasant feather wrapped with yarn, ending in four-strand braid
4.   Peacock feather with beads
5.   Pheasant feathers wrapped with yarn, ending in four-strand braid
6.   Feathers sewn on fabric and covered with rickrack
7.   Joining technique
8.   Rope
9.   Macramé fringe
10.   Group tassel
11.   Single tassel
12.   Brushed mohair (detail from blanket shown on cover, from the collection of Tupper Concho)
13.   Woven fringe, from an authentic Bolivian poncho
14.   Gimp
15.   Added fringe
16.   Peruvian rolled edge, added on

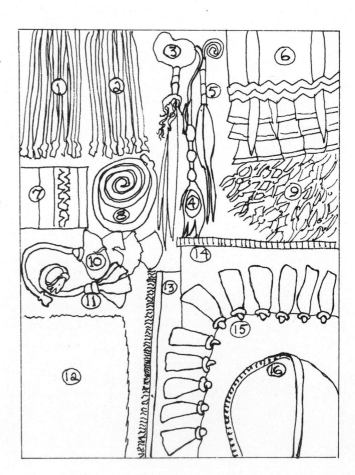

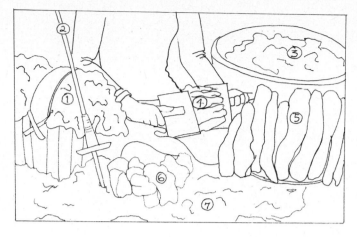

MIXING DYED WOOL COLORS FOR SPINNING "HEATHER" YARNS

1. Basket of raw wool dyed with various acid dye colors.
2. Navajo spindle (courtesy of Living Designs).
3. Another basket of raw wool dyed with various acid dye colors.
4. Three different colors of wool carded together with hand cards.
5. Rolags ready for spinning, made by carding two or three different colors together.
6. Skeins of heather yarn spun from the rolags.
7. Brown sheep's hide used as a seat (courtesy of Living Designs).

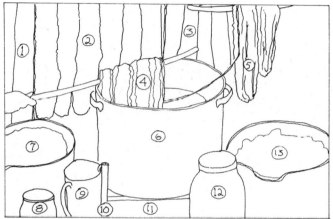

THE INDIGO DYE VAT, SHOWING THE "BLOOMING" OF THE COLOR AS IT IS EXPOSED TO AIR

(This scene was photographed at La Lana Wools' outdoor dyeing area.)

1. Skeins dyed in a previous indigo vat.
2. Skeins dyed in this vat 30 minutes before picture was taken.
3. Skeins "bottomed" with chamizo and dyed in the indigo vat.
4. Skeins lifted from the vat 1 second before picture was taken; notice they are still yellow.
5. Skeins lifted from the vat 10 seconds before picture was taken; notice tops of skeins are already quite blue, and lower parts are still yellowish.
6. The indigo vat.
7. Bucket of water with wetted skeins "bottomed" with brazilwood and chamizo. These skeins, when dyed in the indigo vat, will be purple and green respectively.
8. Jar of sodium hydrosulphite solution.
9. Plastic pitcher for pouring new mixtures into the vat.
10. Thermometer to test temperature of vat, which should be kept at about 120°.
11. Gas burner.
12. Gallon jar of indigo stock solution.
13. Bucket of water with wetted skeins of white wool.

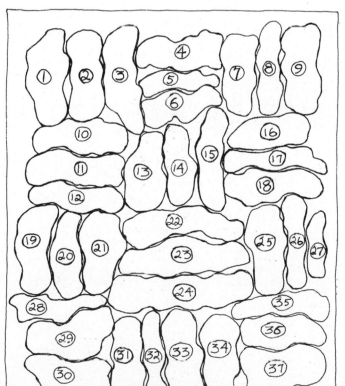

YARNS SPUN FROM NATURAL COLORED FIBERS

NOTE: Many of the fibers were not carded before spinning in order to preserve the variations in color. Names of suppliers who contributed the fibers appear in parentheses.

1. Sheep: half Lincoln, uncarded (Living Designs)
2. Samoyed dog (Nancy Waight of The Weaving Center, Santa Fe)
3. Jute (Straw into Gold)
4. Sheep: British Swaledale, uncarded (Straw into Gold)
5. Sheep: karakul, uncarded
6. Sheep: Columbia, black and white carded together
7. Sheep: breed uncertain, machine carded (La Lana Wools)
8. Pima cotton (Straw into Gold)
9. Sheep: karakul, uncarded
10. Sheep: karakul, uncarded
11. Sheep: half Lincoln, uncarded (Living Designs)
12. Sheep: New Zealand Romney, machine carded in the grease (La Lana Wools)
13. Sheep: Shetland from Scotland, uncarded (La Lana Wools)
14. Cashmere (Mongolian) (Straw into Gold)
15. Yak (The Handweaver)
16. Tussah (undomesticated) silk (Straw into Gold)
17. Sheep: New Mexican crossbreed
18. Goat hair (Straw into Gold)
19. Sheep: karakul, uncarded

20. Angora rabbit (The Handweaver)
21. Sheep: half Lincoln, uncarded (Living Designs)
22. Belgian flax (Straw into Gold)
23. Human hair (The Handweaver)
24. Sheep: Columbia
25. Dog down: Collie and black Samoyed carded together (Nancy Waight of the Weaving Center, Santa Fe)
26. Silk (Straw into Gold)
27. Alpaca, uncarded (Sandy Wright of the Weaving Center, Santa Fe)
28. Alpaca, carded (Sandy Wright of the Weaving Center, Santa Fe)
29. Sheep: New Zealand Romney, unscoured (La Lana Wools)
30. Sheep: probably Romney, uncarded (La Lana Wools)
31. Sheep: half Lincoln, uncarded (Living Designs)
32. Ginned cotton (Straw into Gold)
33. Sheep: Navajo, uncarded (La Lana Wools)
34. Camel down (Straw into Gold)
35. Cashmere (Straw into Gold)
36. Sheep: New Zealand Romney, machine carded (La Lana Wools)
37. Sheep: half Lincoln, uncarded (Living Designs)

HANDSPUN WOOL DYED WITH NATURAL DYES

NOTE: All of these skeins were handspun and dyed by La Lana Wools. The fiber used was New Zealand Romney, machine carded. Unless otherwise indicated, the mordant used was alum and the wool was white to begin with. The indigo was synthetic indigo, which is identical to natural indigo but absolutely free of impurities. A strong indigo stock solution was used, and only one dipping was necessary. Names of suppliers who contributed the dyes appear in parentheses.

1. Walnut hulls (no mordant)
2. Cochineal (chrome) (Straw into Gold)
3. Dried braken (Wide World of Herbs)
4. Red onion skins (chrome)
5. Cochineal over indigo (Straw into Gold)
6. Purple cabbage
7. Logwood (chrome) (Straw into Gold)
8. Birchbark (Wide World of Herbs)
9. Madder (Straw into Gold)
10. Walnut hulls (no mordant; grey wool)
11. Fresh peach leaves (chrome)
12. Lichens (no mordant)
13. Cochineal (chrome) (Straw into Gold)
14. Logwood and fustic (chrome; grey wool)
15. Osage orange (The Handweaver)
16. Cochineal (straw into Gold)
17. Yellow onion skins
18. Indigo over fresh chamizo (grey wool)
19. Madder afterbath (Straw into Gold)
20. Dried Indian paint brush
21. Indigo (grey wool)
22. Fresh marigolds (chrome)
23. American saffron (Nature's Herbs)
24. Logwood (Straw into Gold)
25. Indigo over fresh goldenrod
26. Yellow onion skins (grey wool)
27. Fresh marigolds

28. Dried marigolds (Nature's Herbs)
29. Indigo
30. Fresh Indian paint brush
31. Birch bark (no mordant) (Wide World of Herbs)
32. Brazilwood
33. Canyaigre
34. Cochineal (tin added to dyebath, wool pre-mordanted with alum)
35. Dried braken (grey wool) (Wide World of Herbs)
36. Dried marigolds (chrome) (Nature's Herbs)
37. Madder (Straw into Gold)
38. Fustic and Logwood
39. Logwood afterbath (chrome)
40. Indigo over fresh goldenrod
41. Cochineal (Straw into Gold) over osage orange (The Handweaver)
42. Red onion skin (chrome; grey wool)
43. Madder afterbath (Straw into Gold)
44. Dried goldenrod (Nature's Herbs)
45. Brazilwood afterbath
46. Indigo
47. Osage orange (chrome) (The Handweaver)
48. Fresh peach leaves
49. Brazilwood

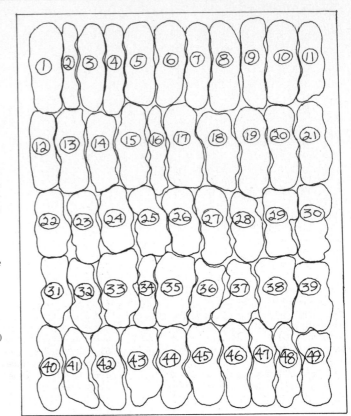

PUFFS OF WOOL DYED WITH CIBA ACID DYES

NOTE: The color samples here mainly show the many colors possible just using one or two pure dyes in varying amounts. It's hard to say just what dyes were used in the exhaust baths that produced the very pale muted colors. Often these exhaust baths with a touch of pure color make the most beautiful shades.

Full name of Ciba acid dye colors:
Rhodamine = Intracid rhodamine B 400%
Scarlet = Intracid scarlet moo conc.
Orange = Intracid fast orange G conc.
Yellow = Cibalan yellow GRL
Brilliant yellow = Cibalan brilliant yellow 2 GL ex.
Green = Intracid green V ex. conc.
Fast blue = Intracid fast blue CB
Pure blue = Intracid pure blue L
Violet = Intracid violet 4 BNS ex. conc.
Brown = Cibalan brown 2GL

1. Rhodamine
2. Rhodamine and scarlet
3. Rhodamine and orange
4. Scarlet (over grey wool)
5. Scarlet
6. Rhodamine, scarlet, orange
7. Scarlet
8. Reddish exhaust bath
9. Exhaust bath with touch of scarlet
10. Rhodamine and brilliant yellow
11. Orange and scarlet
12. Blueish exhaust bath with touches of scarlet and orange
13. Orangish exhaust bath
14. Brown
15. Orange and scarlet
16. Orange
17. Orange (over dark grey wool)
18. Brownish exhaust bath
19. Orange (over grey wool)
20. Brownish exhaust bath
21. Yellowish exhaust bath (over grey wool)
22. Yellow (over dark grey)
23. Brilliant yellow and orange
24. Orange and green
25. Yellow
26. Brilliant yellow
27. Yellow
28. Brilliant yellow (over grey wool)

29. Exhaust bath with brilliant yellow
30. Exhaust bath
31. Yellow and green
32. Green and yellow
33. Brilliant yellow and green
34. Green and brilliant yellow
35. Green and brilliant yellow
36. Green and yellow
37. Green (over grey wool)
38. Greenish exhaust bath
39. Exhaust bath
40. Green
41. Green and pure blue
42. Green-blueish exhaust bath (over grey wool)
43. Pure blue
44. Exhaust bath
45. Blueish exhaust bath
46. Fast blue
47. Fast blue
48. Fast blue and brown
49. Fast blue
50. Fast blue and violet
51. Violet
52. Violet and rhodamine
53. Violet and rhodamine
54. Rhodamine and violet
55. Exhaust bath with rhodamine and violet
56. Violet and scarlet

A Note About the Author

Rachel Brown was born in Buffalo, New York, and educated at Radcliffe College, the Art Students League, and Cooper Union. She began to weave in 1959 and has taught weaving at Colorado Rocky Mountain School and been director of the Craft House in Arroyo Seco, New Mexico. Her own weavings have been exhibited in museums and have won numerous prizes in Southwestern exhibitions during the last 18 years. Rachel Brown has three grown children—all of them artist-silversmiths. She lives in Taos, New Mexico.

A Note About the Type

The text of this book was set in a film version of Optima, a typeface designed by Hermann Zapf from 1952-55 and issued in 1958. In designing Optima, Zapf created a truly new type form—a cross between the classic roman and a sans-serif face. So delicate are the stresses and balances in Optima that it rivals sans-serif faces in clarity and freshness and old-style faces in variety and interest.

The book was composed by Compucomp Corporation, Hoboken, New Jersey. It was printed by Hampshire Press, Melville, New York, and bound by American Book-Stratford Press, Saddlebrook, New Jersey. Color lithography by Creative Lithographers, New York.

Typography and binding design by Christine Aulicino.